ISBN 978-1-5283-0109-1
PIBN 10920951

FB &c Ltd, Dalton House, 60 Windsor Avenue, London, SW19 2RR.
Company number 08720141. Registered in England and Wales.

U. S. DEPARTMENT OF AGRICULTURE.

THIRD ANNUAL REPORT

OF THE

BUREAU OF ANIMAL INDUSTRY

FOR

THE YEAR 1886.

WASHINGTON:
GOVERNMENT PRINTING OFFICE.
1887.

Resolved by the Senate and House of Representatives of the United States of America in Congress assembled, That there be printed thirty-five thousand copies of the Third Annual Report of the Bureau of Animal Industry for the year eighteen hundred and eighty-six, of which ten thousand copies shall be for the use of the members of the Senate, and twenty thousand copies for the use of the members of the House of Representatives, and five thousand copies for the use of the Department of Agriculture; the illustrations to be executed under the supervision of the Public Printer, in accordance with the directions of the Joint Committee on Printing, the work to be subject to the approval of the Commissioner of Agriculture.

TABLE OF CONTENTS.

LIST OF ILLUSTRATIONS.

LETTER OF TRANSMITTAL.

SIR: I have the honor to submit herewith the Third Annual Report of the Bureau of Animal Industry, containing an account of the work during the past year for the suppression of the disease known as contagious pleuro-pneumonia or lung plague of cattle, and also of the investigations of this and other diseases of our domestic animals, and in regard to the present condition of the animal industry of the United States.

Since writing my Annual Report for 1885, the outbreak of pleuro-pneumonia which began in Harrison County, Kentucky, in 1884, and which was allowed to continue there until March of this year, has been entirely suppressed. This would not have been possible except for the act of the legislature authorizing the condemnation of the affected animals and providing compensation for them, and the cordial co-operation of the State Board of Health with the representative of this Bureau. All of the exposed animals were slaughtered and deeply buried, the stables and yards disinfected, and the locality kept under supervision until all danger of a re-appearance of the disease was past. Dr. W. H. Wray deserves much credit for the professional skill and business capacity shown by him in the management of this outbreak, which for many reasons was unusually difficult to control.

The most important event of the year was the discovery of pleuro-pneumonia among the cattle kept in the distillery stables of Chicago, and later among the cows pasturing on the commons of that city and some of the surrounding towns. The disease had existed there for a considerable time, and for this reason its origin could not be definitely ascertained. There can be little doubt, however, that it is a continuation of the outbreak of 1884, at which time herds were affected at Elmhurst, Saint Charles, and Geneva, either place being sufficiently near to account for the extension to Chicago. As a considerable number of cattle were exposed at Geneva, where a strict quarantine could not be maintained at the time, it seems most probable that the contagion was carried by cattle going from there to Chicago. The existence of such a dangerous plague in this great commercial center, and so near to the Union Stock Yards, through which cattle are passing to all parts of the country, is a menace to the cattle industry of the most serious character. Fortunately the managers of the Union Stock Yards have adopted stringent regulations which prevent the admission of any animals from Cook County, and, consequently, the traffic through these yards has been protected since the presence of the plague was discovered.

While the existence of the disease in the distillery stables has attracted much attention because of the number of animals affected and exposed, it does not deserve the attention there that it does among the cows of the owners of small herds about the city. In the distilleries the cattle can be easily quarantined and guarded, and as all are intended for slaughter within a comparatively short time there is neither the difficulty nor the expense which would be encountered in disposing of the same number of animals in any other situation. The exposed animals outside of the distilleries are, therefore, of much greater interest to the country, and immediate measures are needed to crush out the contagion which is being propagated among them. This Department has not sufficient authority or funds to accomplish this, but it was hoped that with the co-operation of the State Live Stock Commission this end might be speedily reached. Unfortunately the State Commission appear disinclined to take rigorous action in reference to the city cows, and also differ with us as to the measures which it is necessary to enforce.

Maryland was the first State to accept the rules and regulations of this Department for co-operation, and owing to the well-known prevalence of the disease there, work was begun almost immediately. The inspectors have examined 1,221 different lots of cattle during the year, containing 11,722 individual animals. Of these 219 lots were found infected, and 652 animals were reported as affected with pleuro-pneumonia. The appropriation for slaughtering sick animals did not become available until July 1, 1886. For the six months ending December 31, 1886, the Department purchased and slaughtered in this State 336 animals affected with contagious pleuro-pneumonia.

From the information at hand we judge that the prevalence of this disease has not been materially modified in the other infected States since previous reports were made.

The investigations of swine diseases during the current year have yielded very important results. It has been shown that there are really two diseases of swine, both of which are widely distributed and both communicable, which have not heretofore been distinguished from each other. Although these two diseases may co-exist at the same time and in the same herd, they are often found separate, and have very different characters. This discovery was foreshadowed in the two previous reports of the Bureau, in one of which the bacterium causing swine-plague was described as a micrococcus and in the other as a bacterium. Our subsequent investigations have demonstrated that each of these germs produces a distinct disease, and in order to distinguish between them we call the micrococcus disease swine-plague, and the bacterium disease hog-cholera.

The investigations of the year abundantly confirm the important discovery, announced in the report for 1885, that the pathogenic germs produce, during their multiplication in culture tubes, a chemical substance which may be used to produce immunity from that particular contagion. This discovery opens a most promising field for investigation, and it indicates that in the future we shall be able to prevent the contagious diseases of both animals and people by the administration of harmless chemical compounds. It will require a long series of investigations, however, to learn how to separate these chemical compounds from the other substances in the culture liquids, to determine their chemical composition and the best methods of producing them artificially.

The experiments which have been made to bring out the characters of the germs of these diseases and the most active disinfectants for their destruction, are of great interest and value from a practical point of view, and when completed will give accurate information of the means that can be employed in combating them.

For the careful and accurate manner in which the experiments referred to above have been carried out, I am indebted to Dr. Theobald Smith, director of the laboratory, and to Dr. F. L. Kilborne, director of the experiment station, both of whom have shown the most commendable activity and interest in the work, and whose intelligence and zeal have enabled us to satisfactorily decide some of the most difficult questions which modern science has been called upon to elucidate.

In addition to the report of the Chief of the Bureau, this volume contains a very important report by Col. H. M. Taylor, agent of the Bureau of Animal Industry, on "The condition of the range cattle industry;" a valuable report by Edward W. Perry "On the cattle trade and allied industries of Michigan, Wisconsin, and Tennessee;" and a most interesting report by Mr. A. S. Mercer on "The cattle industry of California." These papers, in connection with George W. Rust's excellent monograph on "Calf raising on the plains;" and the letter of the Commissioner of Agriculture on the "Dressed meat traffic," make a notable contribution to our knowledge of the great cattle industry of the United States.

The "Investigation of the 'Loco' plant and its effect on animals," by Dr. M. Stalker, and also the investigation of "Staggers" among horses, by Dr. William H. Harbaugh, will be of much interest in the localities where these troubles abound.

To the above has been appended copies of the laws bearing upon animal diseases which have been passed by the legislatures of the several States since the publication of the last report. A knowledge of these laws has become indispensable to those engaged in shipping stock from one State to another. The details of the cattle inspections conclude the volume and are given in full.

Respectfully submitted.

D. E. SALMON,
Chief of the Bureau of Animal Industry.

Hon. NORMAN J. COLMAN,
Commissioner of Agriculture.

THIRD ANNUAL REPORT OF THE BUREAU OF ANIMAL INDUSTRY.

REPORT OF THE CHIEF OF THE BUREAU.

SIR: As the investigation and suppression of contagious pleuro-pneumonia or lung plague of cattle is made by the law establishing the Bureau the most prominent and important part of its work, I shall, as heretofore, devote the first section of my report to this subject.

PROGRESS OF PLEURO-PNEUMONIA AND ACTION TAKEN IN REGARD TO IT.

KENTUCKY.

At the time my last annual report was submitted the outbreak of pleuro-pneumonia in Kentucky, which began in 1884, was still in progress. A portion of the history of this outbreak is recorded in the reports of the Bureau of Animal Industry for 1884 and 1885. When first discovered the plague was confined to one herd. There was an attempt to maintain quarantine by the force of public opinion in the absence of any specific statutes, but, as was to be expected, it was not successful. The danger of the extension of the contagion was such that, on June 15, 1885, the infected premises were declared in quarantine by authority of the State board of health. At that time an additional herd was found infected and included in the regulations, a copy of which will be found on page 35 of the Report of the Bureau of Animal Industry for 1885. By request of the board, an inspector of the Bureau was stationed at Cynthiana to watch the results of this quarantine. November 16, 1885, he reported that the disease had been found at 6 places in Cynthiana, at 3 places in the Indian Creek neighborhood, 3½ miles east of Cynthiana, and at one place near the Pendleton County line, 13 miles north of Cynthiana.

Early in March, 1886, the legislature of Kentucky enacted a law authorizing the State board of health to slaughter the infected cattle, and appropriated money to compensate the owners. The slaughter began on March 15, and on March 27 I received official notification that all exposed animals had been slaughtered. I give below a copy of a letter from the secretary of the board to the Chief of the Bureau of Animal Industry, which shows his estimate of the value of the services rendered by this Department in suppressing the malady:

BOWLING GREEN, KY., *March* 27, 1886.

SIR: I have the honor to inform you, as Dr. Wray has done in detail, that in the execution of the recently enacted law in relation to contagious and infectious diseases of cattle this board has exterminated contagious pleuro-pneumonia in this State by the slaughter of all animals which have been exposed to that disease and rigidly quarantined all infected premises.

In consequence of the foregoing facts, we hope to have the influence of your Department in securing the removal of the restrictions now imposed against Kentucky cattle by most of the Western States.

I desire also to call your attention to the inclosed resolution in regard to Dr. Wray, and to add that there is every reason to believe that but for the timely and efficient aid rendered me by your Department during the last year the disease would have made such headway, and the sum of money required for its extirpation would have been so large, that our legislature could not have been induced to extirpate the disease. I inclose a copy of our law and quarantine blanks.

Respectfully, yours,

J. N. MCCORMACK,
Secretary.

Dr. D. E. SALMON,
Chief of the Bureau of Animal Industry, Washington, D. C.

Resolved, That the thanks of the State board of health of Kentucky be, and are hereby, tendered to Dr. W. H. Wray for the faithful, efficient, and intelligent manner in which he has discharged his important duties in the management of the outbreak of contagious pleuro-pneumonia in Harrison County.

A true extract from the proceedings of the board.

J. N. MCCORMACK, *Secretary.*

Dr. Wray furnished the following statement, showing the number of infected herds and animals in the vicinity of Cynthiana, and the results of the disease at each place:

Previous to August 4, 1885, four animals in the Frisbie & Lake herd had died and 14 sick ones had been slaughtered. From and after August 4 the extent of the disease and the disposition of the animals is seen in the following table:

Owner of herd.	Increase since August 4, 1885.	Number that died.	Number killed that were sick.	Number killed that were exposed.	Number sold to butcher.	Number in herd.
Frisbie & Lake	17	1	38	65		87
W. T. Handy	3	1	9	7	5	10
Mrs. Roberts			1			1
Mr. Woolwinder					1	1
Irving Cox	1		2	1	11	13
J. S. Withers		1	1			2
M. Bridwell	1		1	4		4
George Edsall					2	2
T. J. Megibben			1	3		4
W. S. Morland			1			1
D. N. Brannock			*3	*14		17
Jos. Stephens			1			1
O. Slade			1			1
I. N. Slade				1		1
P. Barhart					1	1
J. W. Lang					1	1
J. D. Feeback			1			1
M. Rule					1	1
T. J. Moffitt			1			1
A. Fitzwater				2		2
A. W. Lydick				1		1
Mr. Kaufman				1		1
J. Cronin			1	2		3
Mrs. Stewart				1		1
D. Shea				3		3
James Brenan				1		1
I. T. Martin				1		1
W. E. Slade	1			2		1
James Doyle				1		1
Mr. Sullivan				2		2
W. S. Wall		1				1
T. Robertson			1			1
F. Reynolds				2		2
Total August 4, 1885	23	4	63	114	22	180
Total increase						23
Grand total						203

* Killed by mob.

Dr. Wray remained at Cynthiana until June 22, or about three months after the last affected animal was slaughtered, and no case of this disease was discovered during that time. I have recently had reliable reports from that vicinity, and I am satisfied that no case of pleuro-pneumonia has occurred since the slaughter of the infected cattle in March.

This outbreak in Kentucky by itself indicates the great superiority of a method which secures the prompt extirpation of the contagion over any temporizing measures, the effect of which is to preserve instead of to destroy it. As soon as pleuro-pneumonia was known to exist in this State the other States of the Union quarantined against Kentucky cattle, and the enormous commerce in these animals was prostrated. The local quarantine measures were looked upon by the authorities of other States as an insufficient guarantee of the safety of cattle from Kentucky, and therefore no bovine animals were allowed admittance from there except under rigid and burdensome restrictions. These restrictions, maintained for nearly two years, are estimated to have caused a loss to the cattle-breeders of the State of from $10,000,000 to $12,000,000; a loss which would have been entirely prevented if there had been authority for this Department to cause the prompt destruction of the infected herds when the plague was first discovered.

ILLINOIS.

In September, 1886, pleuro-pneumonia was found by the State veterinarian to exist among cattle in the city of Chicago and vicinity. It was first discovered on the farm of John Carne, at Ridgeland, near Austin, a station on the Chicago and Northwestern Railroad, 6 or 7 miles from Chicago. The diseased animal was killed September 12, and the *post mortem* examination showed conclusively that it was affected with lung-plague. This cow had been on the premises a long time, but she had recently been exposed to an ailing cow that Mr. Carne had taken for trial with the intention of purchasing. This sick cow was brought on the place by Silas Palmer, a cow dealer, who had pastured her for some time previous on the Harvey farm, near Humboldt Park. It was represented to Mr. Carne that the cow was suffering from bad treatment and would soon recover. After doctoring it for two or three weeks with no success the dealer was notified that it was not wanted, and he removed it.

In an attempt to trace the contagion the Harvey farm was visited by the State veterinarian September 15 and 16, and he found there 250 head of cattle, among which were 8 affected with pleuro-pneumonia. These animals were at once quarantined. An investigation of the history of the disease at this farm led to the conclusion that it had been introduced by a herd of 38 cows brought there to pasture by a milkman named Quinn, who had recently removed his animals from the Phœnix Distillery stables. This led to an examination of the cattle in the distillery stables, and to the discovery that many of them were affected with pleuro-pneumonia.

The Phœnix stables were quarantined September 19. They contained 1,185 animals, of which 297 were Western steers and bulls which had been placed there by Nelson Morris to fatten September 15. The remainder of the animals were milch cows, belonging to a number of different owners. The stables of the Chicago and Empire Distilleries were quarantined the same day. They contained respectively 496 and 207 animals. The Shufeldt stables contained 985 animals, and were quarantined September 20.

A further examination of the cattle of Mr. Carne September 18 showed that another one was sick, and this, together with two exposed ones, was slaughtered. The day before, September 17, two sucking calves were found affected at the Harvey farm and were slaughtered.

September 20 two sick cows were killed at the Phœnix and found affected with pleuro-pneumonia. September 22 the Chief of the Bureau of Animal Industry, in company with the State veterinarian and members of the State Live-Stock Commission, made an investigation at the Phœnix and Shufeldt stables, to satisfy himself as to the nature of the disease. The examination was made on one animal that had died and two that were killed at the former stable, and upon one that was killed and one found dead at the latter. All were undoubtedly affected with contagious pleuro-pneumonia.

The milkmen at first denied the existence of any disease among their cattle, but when the evidence became too strong to be longer contested it was admitted that they had recognized the presence of a lung disease in 1884. They at first attributed it to chemicals used in the mash by the distillers, also to feeding the slop too hot, but they finally concluded it was contagious pleuro-pneumonia, and were practicing inoculation to lessen the mortality.

The progress of the plague after quarantine may be seen from the following notes made from day to day by the veterinarians. A part of these were kindly furnished by Dr. Casewell, State veterinarian, and the remainder were collected by Dr. Trumbower, Inspector of the Bureau of Animal Industry. It is to be borne in mind that the mortality was probably lessened by the practice of inoculation:

September 23: 1 slaughtered and 1 found dead at the Phœnix; 1 slaughtered and 1 found dead at the Shufeldt.

September 24: 2 slaughtered at the Chicago.

September 25: 1 slaughtered and 1 found dead at the Phœnix.

September 27: 1 slaughtered at the Chicago and 2 found dead at the Phœnix.

September 30: 1 dead at the Shufeldt.

October 2: 2 dead at the Phœnix.

October 3: 1 dead at the Phœnix.

October 4: 1 dead at the Chicago and 2 dead at the Phœnix.

October 5: 3 dead and 1 slaughtered at the Phœnix; 1 dead at the Chicago; 1 dead at the Empire.

October 6: 1 dead at the Phœnix; 1 dead at the Chicago.

October 8: 1 slaughtered at the Chicago.

October 10: 1 slaughtered and 1 dead at the Chicago; 1 dead at the Phœnix.

October 11: 1 dead at the Phœnix.

October 12: 1 dead at the Shufeldt.

October 13: 2 dead at the Chicago; 1 dead at the Shufeldt.

October 16: 1 cow and 1 steer dead at the Phœnix (this was the first steer that died of pleuro-pneumonia out of the lot placed in these stables September 15); 1 dead at the Shufeldt; 10 cows were taken at the Shufeldt and slaughtered at the abattoir; lungs found healthy.

October 17: 1 slaughtered and 1 dead at the Chicago; 1 cow and 2 bulls from the Phœnix slaughtered, lungs healthy.

October 18: 1 cow at the Shufeldt slaughtered, affected; 4 slaughtered from the Phœnix, lungs healthy; 7 slaughtered from the Chicago, lungs healthy.

October 19: 2 cows and 1 steer dead at the Phœnix; 1 dead at the Chicago; killed 14 cows from the Phœnix, lungs healthy.

October 20: 1 cow and 2 steers dead at the Phœnix, only 1 of the latter affected with lung-plague; 2 healthy cows from the Phœnix slaughtered; 1 dead at the Chicago.

October 21: 2 dead at the Shufeldt; 1 dead at the Chicago; 3 dead at the Phœnix; slaughtered 2 healthy cows from the Phœnix.

October 22: 2 steers dead at the Phœnix; 1 dead at the Shufeldt; slaughtered 5 affected animals at the Shufeldt.

October 23: 1 dead at the Chicago; 1 dead at the Shufeldt.

October 24: 2 dead at the Chicago and 1 affected animal slaughtered.

October 25: Slaughtered 11 at the Chicago, all healthy; 1 cow and 2 steers dead at the Phœnix; slaughtered 16 cows from the Phœnix, all healthy.

October 26: 1 steer and 1 cow dead at the Phœnix; slaughtered 24 cows from the Phœnix, 3 affected; 1 dead at the Shufeldt.

October 27: Slaughtered 14 cows and 2 calves from the Phœnix, lungs healthy; 1 cow and 1 bull dead at the Phœnix.

October 28: killed 2 cows at the Shufeldt, 1 affected with pleuro-pneumonia and 1 with chronic indigestion.

October 29: 1 dead at the Shufeldt.

October 30: 1 affected killed and 1 died from choking at the Shufeldt; 1 affected steer killed and 3 steers dead at the Phœnix.

October 31: 1 dead at the Shufeldt; 1 dead at the Phœnix.

November 1: Slaughtered 3 at the Shufeldt, lungs healthy; 1 dead at the same place; slaughtered 14 cows from the Phœnix, 5 of which were affected.

November 2: 1 dead at the Phœnix.

November 3: Slaughtered 18 cows from the Phœnix, 5 affected; 1 steer and 2 cows dead at the Phœnix.

November 4: 1 cow dead at the Shufeldt; killed 1 cow, lungs healthy; killed 5 at the Chicago, lungs healthy; 1 steer dead at the Phœnix.

November 5: 2 cows and 1 steer dead at the Phœnix; 1 cow dead at the Shufeldt.

November 6: 1 steer dead at the Phœnix.

November 7: 1 steer dead at the Phœnix; 1 cow dead at the Shufeldt.

November 8: 1 slaughtered at the Shufeldt, affected; 1 steer dead at the Phœnix.

November 9: Slaughtered 14 from the Shufeldt, 9 affected.

November 10: 1 steer and 1 bull dead at the Phœnix; slaughtered 19 from the Shufeldt, 2 affected.

November 11: 2 steers dead at the Phœnix.

November 12: 1 cow dead at the Phœnix.

November 13: 1 cow dead at the Shufeldt; visited Harvey farm and found 3 new cases.

November 14: 2 steers dead at the Phœnix; 1 cow dead at the Shufeldt; examined 45 cows, 2 affected.

November 15: Slaughtered 2 cows from the Phœnix, both affected; also 11 from the Shufeldt, 4 affected.

November 16: 2 cows dead at the Shufeldt; 2 cows dead at the Phœnix.

November 17: 1 steer dead at the Phœnix; 1 cow killed at the Chicago, affected.

November 18: 1 cow condemned at the Phœnix.

November 19: Killed 6 cows from Phœnix, 2 affected; 1 steer dead at same place.

November 21: 1 cow dead at the Shufeldt.

November 22: 1 steer dead at the Phœnix; 1 cow dead at the Shufeldt.

November 24: 1 cow slaughtered from the Shufeldt, lungs healthy.

November 25: Slaughtered 1 diseased cow at Ridgeland.

November 26: 3 cows dead at the Shufeldt, 1 of which died from choking.

November 27: 1 cow dead at the Shufeldt; 1 cow dead at the Chicago; slaughtered 12 cows from the Phœnix, 1 of which was affected.

November 30: 1 cow and 1 steer dead at the Phœnix; slaughtered 5 affected steers and bulls at same place.

On November 28 slaughtering was begun on a larger scale, in order to empty the distillery stables as soon as possible. The figures given below, which show the proportion of slaughtered animals that were more or less affected with pleuro-pneumonia, are of great interest, because they demonstrate the advisability of slaughtering all animals once exposed to the contagion. Many of the affected cattle presented no symptoms of the disease before slaughter, but the condition of their lungs was such as to make it very certain that they were capable of disseminating the contagion for an indefinite period. The record is as follows:

Date.	Number slaughtered.	Number affected.	Date.	Number slaughtered.	Number affected.
November 28	237	85	December 8	166	86
29	183	106	9	205	100
30	143	72	10	85	23
December 1	179	59	14	231	69
2	137	83	15	51	21
3	185	56	16	48	24
6	223	120			
7	198	126	Total	2,271	1,031

Of the 297 steers and bulls which were put in the Phœnix stables September 15 by Mr. Morris, 37 affected with pleuro-pneumonia died or were killed for examination previous to the 28th of November. Three others died of Texas fever and 1 cripple was killed up to the same date. November 29 and 30 and December 1, 244 of the remainder were slaughtered, of which 182 were found affected.

One of the Inspectors of the Bureau of Animal Industry was stationed at the rendering company's platform from October 19 to November 30, to make *post mortem* examination of all cows coming there from the city of Chicago. During that time he examined 19 cows, of which 6 had died of lung-plague.

The following table shows the number of cattle placed in quarantine in Chicago and vicinity from October 13 to December 30, all being in private herds and stables, and the greater part of which were quarantined because of exposure to affected cattle on the various commons about the city:

Date.	Number of herds.	Number of cattle.	Number affected.	Remarks.
October 13	1	66	Several	Two have since died.
15	10	77	12	
16	10	41	1	
18	40	104	3	
19	30	67	3	
20	*6	6	....	Quarantined for exposure.
21	*10	36	15	
22	*17	17	....	Do.
23	2	38	....	Do.
25	*2	3	....	Do.
26	2	2	1	One died November 2.
27	15	34	8	
28	15	20	1	
29	15	30	2	
30	*18	18	1	
November 1	*11	11	1	
2	*8	8	1	Recovered.
3	*18	18	1	
4	9	33	1	Do.
5	7	11	....	Quarantined for exposure.
6	1	66	....	Do.
10	1	1	....	Do.
19	17	48	....	Do.
20	9	20	....	Do.
23	16	53	....	Do.
24	22	80	....	Do.
26	18	49	....	Do.
27	11	108	....	Do.
30	1	2	....	Do.
December 27	19	55	....	Do.
28	20	62	....	Do.
30	19	31	....	Do.
31	11	41	....	Do.
Total	401	1,240	51	

*Stables.

The above is a brief *résumé* of the work that has been accomplished in Chicago by co-operation between the State Live-Stock Commission and the Bureau of Animal Industry since the discovery of the recent outbreak of pleuro-pneumonia. As there was great apprehension that cattle would be removed from the distillery stables and disseminate the disease in Illinois and other States, a guard of deputy sheriffs was placed at each stable and at the Harvey farm. Two were on duty at each place during the day and four at night. Besides these, two men were employed to count the cattle daily, in order that any decrease in number would be at once discovered. Six veterinary inspectors were also ordered to Chicago to inspect the city and learn to what extent the contagion had progressed outside of the distillery stables.

The following rules and regulations for co-operation were certified to the governor of Illinois and accepted by him:

Rules and regulations for co-operation between the U. S. Department of Agriculture and the authorities of the several States and Territories for the suppression and extirpation of contagious pleuro-pneumonia of cattle.

Recent acts of Congress make it the duty of the Commissioner of Agriculture to prepare rules and regulations for the suppression and extirpation of the contagious pleuro-pneumonia of cattle, and authorize expenditures for investigation, disinfection, quarantine, and for the purchase of diseased animals for slaughter. The following are the sections bearing upon this subject:

"SEC. 3. That it shall be the duty of the Commissioner of Agriculture to prepare such rules and regulations as he may deem necessary for the speedy and effectual suppression and extirpation of said diseases, and to certify such rules and regulations to the executive authority of each State and Territory, and invite said authorities to co-operate in the execution and enforcement of this act. Whenever the plans and methods of the Commissioner of Agriculture shall be accepted by any State or Territory in which pleuro-pneumonia or other contagious, infectious, or communicable disease is declared to exist, or such State or Territory shall have adopted plans and methods for the suppression and extirpation of said diseases, and such plans and methods shall be accepted by the Commissioner of Agriculture, and whenever the governor of a State or other properly constituted authorities signify their readiness to co-operate for the extinction of any contagious, infectious, or communicable disease in conformity with the provisions of this act, the Commissioner of Agriculture is hereby authorized to expend so much of the money appropriated by this act as may be necessary in such investigations, and in such disinfection and quarantine measures as may be necessary to prevent the spread of the disease from one State or Territory into another.' (Approved May 29, 1884.)

BUREAU OF ANIMAL INDUSTRY.

"For carrying out the provisions of the act of May 29, 1884, establishing the Bureau of Animal Industry, $100,000; and the Commissioner of Agriculture is hereby authorized to use any part of this sum he may deem necessary or expedient, and in such manner as he may think best, to prevent the spread of pleuro-pneumonia, and for this purpose to employ as many persons as he may deem necessary, and to expend any part of this sum in the purchase and destruction of diseased animals whenever in his judgment it is essential to prevent the spread of pleuro-pneumonia from one State into another." (Approved June 30, 1886.)

In accordance with these laws I hereby certify the following rules and regulations for co-operation between the Department of Agriculture and the authorities of the several States and Territories, which I deem necessary to insure results commensurate with the money expended:

INSPECTION.

1. The necessary Inspectors will be furnished by the Bureau of Animal Industry of the Department of Agriculture.

2. The properly constituted Inspectors of the Bureau of Animal Industry which are assigned to the respective States are to be authorized by proper State authorities to make inspections of cattle under the laws of the State; they are to receive such protection and assistance as would be given to State officers engaged in similar work, and shall be permitted to examine quarantined herds whenever so directed by the Commissioner of Agriculture or the Chief of the Bureau of Animal Industry.

3. All reports of inspections will be made to the Bureau of Animal Industry, and a copy of these will then be made and forwarded to the proper State authorities. When, however, any Inspector discovers a herd infected with contagious pleuro-pneumonia, he will at once report the same to the proper State authority as well as to the Bureau of Animal Industry.

4. The Inspectors, while always subject to orders from the Department of Agriculture, will cordially co-operate with State authorities, and will follow instructions received from them.

QUARANTINE.

5. When contagious pleuro-pneumonia is discovered in any herd, the owner or person in charge is to be at once notified by the Inspector, and the quarantine regulations of the State in which the herd is located are to be enforced from that time.

The affected animals will be isolated, when possible, from the remainder of the herd until they can be properly appraised and slaughtered.

8. Quarantine restrictions once imposed are not to be removed by the State authorities without due notice to the proper officers of the Department of Agriculture.

9. The period of quarantine will be at least ninety days, dating from the removal of the last diseased animal from the herd. During this period no animal will be allowed to enter the herd or to leave it, and all animals in the herd will be carefully isolated from other cattle.

When possible, all infected herds are to be held in quarantine and not allowed to leave the infected premises except for slaughter. In this case fresh animals may be added to the herd at the owner's risk, but are to be considered as infected animals and subjected to the same quarantine regulations as the other members of the herd.

SLAUGHTER AND COMPENSATION.

10. All animals affected with contagious pleuro-pneumonia are to be slaughtered as soon after their discovery as the necessary arrangements can be made.

11. When diseased animals are reported to the State authorities, they shall promptly take such steps as they desire to confirm the diagnosis. The animals found diseased are then to be appraised according to the provisions of the State law, and the proper officer of the Bureau of Animal Industry (who will be designated by the Commissioner of Agriculture) notified of the appraisement. If this representative of the Bureau of Animal Industry confirms the diagnosis and approves the appraisement, the Department of Agriculture will purchase the diseased animals of the owner and pay such a proportion of the appraised value as is provided for compensation in such cases by the laws of the State in which the animals are located when they are condemned and slaughtered by State authority.

DISINFECTION.

12. All necessary disinfection will be conducted by the employés of the Bureau of Animal Industry.

INOCULATION.

13. Inoculation is not recommended by the Department of Agriculture, and it is believed that its adoption with animals that are to be afterwards sold to go into other herds would counteract the good results which would otherwise follow from the slaughter of the diseased animals. It will not be practiced in this State.

The co-operation of governors, of State live stock commissions, and of other officers who may be in charge of the branch of the service provided for the control of the contagious diseases of animals in the States where pleuro-pneumonia exists, is earnestly requested under these rules and regulations, which have been framed with a view of securing uniform and efficient action throughout the whole infected district. It is hoped that with a vigorous enforcement of such regulations the disease may be prevented from extending beyond its present limits, and may be in time entirely eradicated.

NORMAN J. COLMAN,
Commissioner of Agriculture.

WASHINGTON, D. C., *August* 2, 1886.

By virtue of the authority imposed upon me as governor of the State of Illinois I hereby accept the above rules and regulations, and the proper officers of this State will co-operate with the United States Department of Agriculture for their enforcement.

RICHARD J. OGLESBY.

SPRINGFIELD, ILL., *September* 27, 1886.

The Department has not purchased diseased animals for slaughter in Illinois, because the law of that State makes it the duty of the live-stock commissioners to slaughter such animals at once without compensation. With this law on the statute-books of the State, and with no apparent reason why it should not be enforced, it was not "essential to prevent the spread of pleuro-pneumonia from one State into another" that any part of the appropriation should be used in Illinois to purchase diseased animals for slaughter. This conclusion was confirmed by the desirability of adopting only such measures as conform with the statutes of the States in which the work is being done, so long as our only authority to enforce regulations within the States must be obtained from State legislation.

PROGRESS OF CO-OPERATION WITH OTHER INFECTED STATES.

Co-operation with the other infected States has not progressed as satisfactorily as was anticipated. In the latter part of July a conference was held in Philadelphia, at which were present the Chief of the Bureau of Animal Industry, and representatives of the States of New Jersey, Pennsylvania, Delaware, and Maryland. In formulating the rules and regulations for co-operation as much consideration was given for the views expressed at that conference as was consistent with the object that was to be accomplished. It was understood at the time that the four States there represented would co-operate with this Department under any reasonable rules and regulations.

Rules and regulations were issued on August 2, and sent to the governors of the interested States for their acceptance. With the exception of the following rules, which were omitted or changed in the case of Illinois, they were identical with those given above as accepted by that State:

6. To insure a perfect and satisfactory quarantine, a chain fastened with a numbered lock will be placed around the horns, or with hornless animals around the neck, and a record will be kept showing the number of the lock placed upon each animal in the herd.

7. The locks and chains will be furnished by the Department of Agriculture, but they will become the property of the State in which they are used, in order that any one tampering with them can be proceeded against legally for injuring or embezzling the property of the State.

8. Quarantine restrictions once imposed are not to be removed by the State authorities without the consent of the proper officers of the Department of Agriculture.

INOCULATION.

13. Inoculation is not recommended by the Department of Agriculture, and it is believed that its adoption with animals that are to be afterwards sold to go into other herds would counteract the good results which would otherwise follow from the slaughter of the diseased animals. It may, however, be practiced by State authorities under the following rules:

14. No herds but those in which pleuro-pneumonia has appeared are to be inoculated.

15. Inoculated herds are to be quarantined with lock and chain on each animal; the quarantine restrictions are to remain in force so long as any inoculated cattle survive, and these animals are to leave the premises only for immediate slaughter.

16. Fresh animals are to be taken into inoculated herds only at the risk of the owner, and shall be subject to the same rules as the other cattle of the inoculated herd.

17. The Chief of the Bureau of Animal Industry is to be promptly notified by the State authorities of each herd inoculated, of the final disposition of each member of the herd, of the *post mortem* appearances, and of any other facts in the history of the herd which may prove of value.

The State of New York was not represented at the conference, as the State veterinarian, Prof. James Law, was then attending to some business in the Western States. After returning, however, he gave it as his opinion that, with the large number of infected herds known to exist on Long Island and in the city of New York and vicinity, it would be unwise to attempt to control the plague with the present small appropriation.

The governor of New Jersey has not accepted the rules, and it appears that the obstacles to co-operation were Rules 8 and 15. The objection to Rule 8 was removed by an offer from this Department to change the reading from "without the consent of the proper officers of the Department of Agriculture" to "without due notice to the proper officers of the Department of Agriculture." This concession was also made to the State of Illinois, but the experience of the last four months leads me to the opinion that it would be wiser for the Department to adhere to the original reading. State authorities often have very different ideas from those entertained by the officers of this Department as to the time when it is safe to remove quarantine restrictions. They consequently object to restrictions which they cannot remove at will. On the other hand, if the National Government appropriates money to pay the expense of this work, there certainly should be some guarantee that the proper regulations are enforced.

The objection to Rule 15 still stands in the way of co-operation with New Jersey. The State authorities have adopted the practice of inoculation, and release the inoculated herds from quarantine after a short period of isolation. After carefully considering the question and all the scientific evidence bearing upon it, I am of the opinion that it is useless to attempt to eradicate pleuro-pneumonia in States where inoculation is practiced and where inoculated animals are afterwards allowed to mingle with the cattle of other herds. The money expended for the purchase of diseased animals for slaughter under such conditions is consequently largely wasted.

The State authorities of New Jersey, however, have been assisted by employing one or more veterinarians nearly the whole time, whose duty it has been to investigate reported outbreaks of disease and give such aid as was needed in inspection and in enforcing the State quarantine regulations. Thirty-one infected herds have been reported from this State, containing 530 animals, of which 42 were diseased.

The governor of Pennsylvania has also failed to accept these rules and regulations. His reasons for not acting on them are unknown to me. The governor's agent in charge of the pleuro-pneumonia work raised some objections to Rule 15, but admitted that its enforcement would make no great difference to the State. Inoculation is practiced by the Pennsylvania authorities also, but with the small number of outbreaks reported it would certainly be advisable to slaughter all diseased and exposed animals and thus rid the State of the plague at once.

Virginia is the only remaining State infected with pleuro-pneumonia where the authorities have not accepted the rules and regulations. The attention of the governor has been called to the desirability of eradicating the disease from the State, but up to the present time he has taken no action.

The governors of Delaware and Maryland have accepted the rules and regulations as issued, without modification of any kind. No cases of pleuro-pneumonia have been reported from Delaware since such acceptance.

Co-operation with authorities of the State of Maryland has been more satisfactory than with those of any other State. The local laws are good, and the work has been very largely in the hands of the Inspectors of this Department. The number of infected herds reported from this State is 196, containing 2,277 animals, of which 705 were diseased. Dr. Wray, the Inspector who has been in charge of the work in Maryland since September 20, reported under date of December 7 that since the former date 122 herds, containing 1,354 animals, had been put in quarantine, and that 92 herds, containing 1,089 animals, were still held under such restrictions. Since July 1 this Department has purchased and slaughtered in Maryland 308 diseased cattle, for which $7,069 was paid, being an average of about $23 per head.

In Maryland the quarantine has been made very efficient by placing a chain, fastened with a numbered lock, around the horns, or, with hornless cattle, around the neck of every exposed animal. This has prevented the substitution of one animal for another, and it has also led to the prompt detection of any quarantined cattle which have been allowed to stray beyond the boundaries of the infected premises. The sick animals have been promptly slaughtered, and it is believed that the good effects of this work are already seen in the decreased number of new herds infected. In a number of cases where infected herds have been of unusual danger to surrounding cattle this Department has purchased and destroyed the sick animals, and the State has then condemned and slaughtered the remainder of the herd, thus entirely eradicating the disease at once. Unfortunately the State appropriation has not been large enough to do this in as many cases as seemed desirable.

No recent investigations have been made in Pennsylvania. The governor's agent, Mr. T. J. Edge, reports that during the year ending November 30, 1886, 128 diseased animals were condemned and slaughtered.

LESIONS FOUND IN AMERICAN PLEURO-PNEUMONIA.

Many persons who have not had an opportunity for the *post-mortem* examination of animals affected with pleuro-pneumonia, have expressed doubts regarding the nature of the disease in this country, some considering it to be tuberculosis, while others have gone so far as to speak of it as blood poisoning with abscesses of the lungs. To make it clear that the disease in America is identical with the pleuro-pneumonia of Europe, and that the lung lesions are neither the result of tubercles nor abscesses, plates X, XI, and XII have been prepared from actual specimens of lungs encountered in the outbreaks previously referred to. Plate X is a drawing of a lung from a steer belonging to Mr. Nels Morris that died in the Phoenix distillery stables at Chicago. The lung was photographed and the photograph colored in Chicago, and the plate was made by Dr. Marx, the Department artist, from this colored photograph. Plates XI and XII were made direct from fresh specimens removed from the carcasses of cows slaughtered in Baltimore. Plate XI shows an early stage of a very acute attack, in which the lesions consist of distension of the inter-lobular connective tissue with lymph, infarction of a portion of the lobules, and pleuritis, with a great abundance of false membranes. Plates X and XII show more advanced cases in which the lung is completely hepatized, different lobules showing different stages of inflammation, the spaces of the inter-lobular connective tissue being filled with lymph and the pleura greatly thickened. These lungs presented no appearance whatever of tubercles or abscesses, which is true of nearly all lungs we have examined in acute attacks of this disease.

INVESTIGATIONS OF SWINE DISEASES.

In view of the results of investigations which have shown the existence of two distinct infectious diseases in swine, perhaps of equal virulence and distribution, a change in the nomenclature becomes necessary in order to avoid any confusion in the future. Since these two diseases have been considered as one in the past, and the names swine-plague and hog-cholera have been applied indiscriminately, we prefer to retain both names, with a more restricted meaning, using the name *hog-cholera* for the disease described in the last report as swine-plague, which is produced by a motile bacterium, and applying the name swine-plague to the other disease, the chief seat of which is in the lungs. This change is the more desirable since recent investigations have shown that the latter disease exists in Germany, where it is called swine-plague (*Schweineseuche*).

INVESTIGATIONS OF HOG-CHOLERA.

Some additional biological facts concerning the bacterium which produces the disease.—In the second annual report of the Bureau and the Annual Report of the Department for 1885, the bacterium of hog cholera was quite minutely described, so that no one acquainted with bacteriological investigations would find it difficult to recognize it when found. The descriptions of size, shape, and mode of staining referred to cover-glass preparations made from the blood and the internal organs directly. These characters change somewhat when the bacterium is cultivated in artificial media. Thus the bacteria grown upon potato vary slightly in size and appearance from those obtained from meat infusions and from nutrient gelatine. On the other hand, their appearance is the same whether the spleen of mice, rabbits, guinea-pigs, or swine be subjected to microscopic examination.

The microbe was characterized as a motile bacterium 1.2 to 1.5 micromillimeters long and .6 micromillimeter broad, growing readily in neutralized and even slightly acid meat infusions, milk, on potato, and gelatine which is not liquefied. During the past year the bacterium has been studied very carefully, with a view to determine the best means of preventing its multiplication, and thus preventing the spread of the disease itself. The conclusions arrived at are given in full below, but will be summarized from a practical point of view in the chapter on prevention.

Growth of the bacterium in simple hay infusion.—This was prepared by allowing finely cut hay to soak in water for three or four days, filtering off the amber liquid and sterilizing. Two tubes were inoculated with a drop from cultures in meat-infusion peptone at different times. In both the following features were observed: There was a slight turbidity within two days, which did not deepen perceptibly. The bacteria were somewhat larger than in more nutritive liquids. In the shorter forms there could be seen at each extremity more refrangent spherical masses, while the central portions of the rod seemed empty. Longer rods contained three or four of these bodies. When stained they appeared darker than the rest of the rod. They were consequently not spores, but very probably masses of protoplasm, which had contracted into these globules, and which indicated a degeneration of the bacteria. There were also forms present which were beaded, club-shaped, and distorted.

Though the acid hay infusion is not a suitable medium, yet the bacterium of hog-cholera evidently multiplies in it to some extent, and we may infer that in any organic infusions, such as are formed about pens among the food of swine, the bacterium may multiply under the influence of a hot sun and be afterward taken into the system with the food and water.

Multiplication of the bacterium in water.—The hardiness of this microbe is well illustrated by its capacity for multiplication in ordinary drinking water. To determine this the following experiment was made:

September 8: A culture tube containing very clear Potomac drinking water,* which had been sterilized several weeks previous by a temperature above 110°C., was inoculated from a pure culture of the bacterium. By mixing a given quantity of this water immediately after inoculation with gelatine, and making a plate culture of the same, it was found that the water contained about 26,240 bacteria in 1^{cc}. The water was kept in the laboratory, in which the temperature corresponded closely with that prevailing out-doors. It was examined from time to time on gelatine plates, and the number calculated for 1^{cc}. The following figures give the results obtained:

September 8: 26,240 in 1^{cc} (immediately after inoculation).
September 9: 201,600 in 1^{cc}.
September 10: 1,296,000 in 1^{cc}.
September 11: Too numerous on plate to be counted.
September 13: 2,608,200 in 1^{cc}.
September 15: 1,519,560 in 1^{cc}.
September 17: 1,306,308 in 1^{cc}.
September 29: 83,700 in 1^{cc}.
October 12: 19,125 in 1^{cc}.
October 21: 10,880 in 1^{cc}.
November 18: 225 in 1^{cc}.
December 6: A few bacteria still present, as determined by liquid cultures.
January 4: Seventeen in 1^{cc}.
January 11: No growth on plates.

That the bacterium can be kept alive in clear river water for four months and perhaps longer is a fact very significant in itself. When we consider, moreover, that the added bacteria multiplied so that each individual was represented by ten at the end of five days, the hardiness of the bacterium is very evident. The danger from infected streams into which feces from sick animals find their way is thus proved beyond a doubt.

The effect of simple drying on the bacterium of hog-cholera.—The resistance of this microbe to various agencies, physical and chemical, is likewise of considerable importance in determining the manner of infection, the spread of epidemics, and the possible means within reach of destroying the virus. In order to test its vitality when deprived of moisture the following experiments were carried out:

January 19, 1886: A number of cover-glasses were heated in the Bunsen flame and then placed on a flamed glass plate under a flamed funnel. The mouth of the funnel was plugged with cotton wool to allow desiccation while excluding aerial organisms. When cool a drop from a pure liquid culture of the bacterium was placed on each cover with a pipette, and the whole left in the laboratory at a temperature of 65° to 80° F. The culture used had been prepared January 7 from the fifth spleen culture, hence was twelve days old.

January 21: Two tubes of nutritive liquid inoculated by dropping a cover-glass into each. Both turbid next day, containing the bacterium of hog-cholera only.

January 25: Two tubes inoculated in the same way. Same result next day.

January 28: Two additional tubes receive each a cover-glass. They were still clear on the following day.

January 29: Two tubes inoculated.

January 30: One tube. These five tubes remained permanently clear. In one, inoculated January 29, a fungus had developed from the cover-glass in the bottom of the liquid. This, however, remained clear.

---

* When drawn this water did not contain more than 100 to 200 bacteria to the cubic centimeter.

This series placed the death-point of the bacterium between the seventh and the ninth day.

A second series of covers received each one drop from a culture obtained from a mouse which had died from the effect of inoculation. The culture in beef infusion peptone was ten days old. Treated in the same manner as in the preceding experiment, the bacteria were found to resist drying for ten days, when the stock of cover-glasses was exhausted.

To determine whether bacteria in the body of the diseased animal possess a greater power of resistance than those in cultures the following experiments were made: Some bits of the spleen of a pig which was found crowded with the specific bacteria of hog-cholera were dried on sterile cover-glasses as above described, and then dropped into tubes containing beef infusion. Cover-glasses which had been dried for from eight to sixteen days were able to develop pure cultures of the bacterium in the tubes. The stock of covers being exhausted, another series was tried in the same way. The blood of spleen tissue was permitted to dry undisturbed until the seventh day, when the first tube was inoculated. Cover-glasses dropped into cultures on the seventeenth, nineteenth, twentieth, twenty-first, twenty-fourth, and twenty-sixth days left the cultures sterile. Those dropped in on the eighteenth and twenty-second days produced pure cultures of the bacterium. These experiments indicate a greater resistance of the bacterium in spleen tissue, which may live twenty-two days in a dry atmosphere at a temperature of 70° to 80° F.

On May 8 five cover-glasses upon which bits of spleen tissue, known to contain the bacterium of hog-cholera, had been dried under a plugged funnel since March 20, were dropped into tubes of beef infusion. On the following day all tubes were turbid. In one of them *bacillus subtilis* was present. All the others were pure cultures, as determined by microscopical examination. Two of these were tested furthermore on gelatine plates with the same results. This indicates that in the varying temperature of a room desiccation of small bits of tissue (not so large as a pin's head) failed to destroy the bacterium in forty-nine days. In the experiments with dried cultures those ten and eleven days old were chosen, so that if any resistant spore state did form in liquids it would be present. It is highly probable, however, that if cultures but a few days old had been chosen the bacteria would have resisted drying much longer. These experiments give the following results:

A liquid culture eleven days old resisted drying for nine days; another, ten days old, at least ten days. Bacteria in tissue may resist destruction after drying for from twenty-two to forty-nine days.

The method of drying the bacteria on cover-glasses and introducing the latter into liquid does not inform us whether most bacteria die within the same time or whether some resist much longer than others. Hence the following expedient was resorted to, which Koch had introduced in the study of disinfectants: Silk threads sterilized by boiling several times in distilled water were dried and steeped in a beef infusion peptone culture about one week old. The culture containing the threads was allowed to dry in the incubator for one day, then placed in a sterilized bottle plugged with cotton. Each day, beginning with the second, one or two threads were placed in a layer of nutritive gelatine on a glass plate so that the thread was completely covered by the gelatine. Characteristic colonies of the bacterium appeared around the thread within two days, though the plates were usually kept under observation five days. For twenty-one days isolated colonies and groups of colonies appeared in moderate abundance on the threads, when the stock of the latter was exhausted.

In another similar series the threads were laid upon a sterile plate and a twenty-four hours' liquid culture poured upon them and allowed to dry uncovered in the incubator for one day. These threads, still undisturbed on the plate, were placed in the laboratory, covered with a bell glass. On the fifteenth day the testing began, a single thread being placed in the gelatine layer each day for sixteen days. Colonies of the bacterium developed in large numbers until the twenty-second day, when they diminished in number. On the twenty-seventh and twenty-eighth days no colonies appeared. On the three following days a few appeared, when the series was closed.

The bacterium of hog-cholera may therefore remain alive, during continuous desiccation, for from ten days to nearly two months. The variation in the results obtained is no doubt due to the different vitality of the cultures used. The gelatine-plate method is not so delicate a test as the method of liquid cultures, as it would be difficult to tell when the last bacterium died, a single colony under the thread escaping observation very easily. A single bacterium would invariably reveal its presence in a liquid after a time by multiplication. For the same reason the latter method needs greater care; the liquid cultures must be examined microscopically, and if there be any doubt still remaining they must be tested on gelatine; for a single foreign microbe gaining access to the culture tube might introduce an error into the results, which is easily avoided on the gelatine plate by observing the characters of the colonies.

It had been determined by a large number of experiments that cultures of the bacterium of hog-cholera can be sterilized—in other words, that the bacterium itself may be destroyed—by an exposure to 58° C. for from 15 to 20 minutes. To determine whether dried blood or spleen tissue containing the bacterium was more resistant the following experiment was tried:

Spleen pulp from a case of hog-cholera was rubbed upon sterile cover-glasses and allowed to dry under a plugged funnel for 24 hours at a temperature of 65° to 75° F. Four tubes of beef infusion, after a cover-glass had been dropped into each, were exposed to a temperature of 58° C. for 15, 20, 29, and 41 minutes, respectively. These remained permanently sterile, while a fifth tube, which had been inoculated in the same way but not heated, contained on the following day a pure culture of the hog-cholera bacterium. It should be added that each cover-glass contained a considerable number of germs, according to microscopic examination of different parts of the spleen.

The bacterium within the body of the diseased animal cannot therefore be regarded more resistant than when cultivated in liquids.

Effect of boiling water.—Culture tubes containing about 10cc of meat infusion were placed in boiling water until at the boiling-point. They were then removed, and a sterile cover-glass, upon which a bit of spleen tissue had been drying for five days under a plugged funnel, was dropped into each tube. These were immediately placed in ice water. A preliminary experiment had shown that the temperature in these tubes fell below 40° C. in less than a minute. The spleen had been previously found to contain the bacteria in large numbers. Of four tubes treated in this way two became turbid with the specific bacterium; the others remained sterile.

In a subsequent experiment, four tubes were inoculated near the boiling temperature and one as a check. This latter developed into a pure culture of the bacterium; the heated tubes remained permanently clear. An almost momentary exposure of the dried bacteria to boiling water is sufficient, therefore, to destroy their vitality.

Resistance to various chemical substances or disinfectants.—In the following experiments on the effect of various agents on the vitality of the bacterium of hog-cholera the methods used by Koch were not adopted, because liquids are far more sensitive to bacteria than solid media. A single colony upon gelatine, the descendants of a single germ, may escape the eye, but the same microbe in a nutrient liquid would cloud it within a few days. There is, to be sure, for this very reason, greater danger in the use of liquid media, since the introduction of a single foreign microbe might lead to the same conclusions as the introduction of a dozen or a hundred, while a few bacteria accidently caught on the gelatine would lead to no errors of interpretation. The results obtained by the method given below were so uniform, the absence of contamination was so constant, that we can recommend it in all similar determinations.

The disinfectant solution was diluted with sterile distilled water in a test-tube or watch-glass previously sterilized by heat. A few drops from a pure culture of the hog-cholera bacterium were mixed with 4cc or 5cc of this dilution, and a minute portion transferred at given intervals, by means of a platinum loop, to culture tubes containing beef broth. These tubes were then placed in a temperature of 95° to 100° F., where they remained from one to four days. Tubes which remained clear at the end of this period were sterile, as shown by numerous tubes which were watched for several weeks.

The experiments given below refer to the active vegetative state of the bacterium in nutrient liquids, as experiments had failed to reveal any other more resistant state. The cultures were, as a rule, but one or two days old. Previous experiments having shown that older cultures are less resistant to heat than recent ones, it was assumed that the vitality is gradually reduced as the culture grows older.

All the tubes about which there seemed the slightest suspicion of impurity were examined microscopically and often on gelatine plates. In all cases the last of a series of inoculated tubes which became turbid was carefully examined. This served as a check upon tubes exposed for a shorter period of time to the action of the disinfectant. The percentage of the solution used indicates the ratio by weight in grams of chemically pure substances to grams of distilled water.

Mercuric chloride was found destructive to the bacterium when diluted in the proportion of 1 : 75000 (.001 1-3 per cent.).

Several drops of a culture were mixed with about 1^{cc} of a .1 per cent. solution, and tubes inoculated from this at the end of 2, 4, 6, 8, and 10 minutes. Tubes remain sterile. To show that the antiseptic effect of the liquid transferred with the platinum loop was *nil*, one of these tubes was inoculated again from another culture. This tube was turbid on the following day.

Five tubes treated in the same way with .05 per cent. solution. All remain sterile.

Five tubes inoculated from a culture exposed for the same periods of time to a .01 per cent. solution. All remain clear.

Five tubes treated as before, using a .005 per cent. solution. Permanently clear.

Five tubes treated as before, using a .002 per cent. solution. All tubes clear excepting the one inoculated after 6 minutes' exposure.

Five tubes inoculated at the end of 5, 10, 15, 20, 25, and 30 minutes after exposure to a .0001 per cent. (1 : 100000). Tubes inoculated after 5 and 10 minutes turbid next day. On the second day all but the one inoculated after 30 minutes turbid and containing pure cultures of the bacterium.

The limit of disinfection for this period of time must therefore lie between 1 : 50000 and 1: 100000; hence 5 tubes were inoculated as above, using a solution of 1 : 75000, at the end of 7, 10, 15, 20, 25, and 30 minutes. All tubes remained clear.

Carbolic acid destroys the bacterium in solutions containing from 1 to 1¼ per cent. of the acid by weight.

Five tubes inoculated after treating the bacteria from a liquid culture with a 1 per cent. solution for 5, 10, 15, 20, and 25 minutes. All turbid on the following day. The two last tubes were also examined on gelatine plates and the cultures found pure.

With a 2 per cent. solution, five tubes inoculated after 10, 15, 20, 25, and 30 minutes remained sterile. The same result with a 1½ per cent. solution. With a 1¼ per cent., tubes inoculated at the end of 7, 10, 15, 20, 25, and 30 minutes remained clear, excepting the first, which contained *bacillus subtilis*.

Passing to a ½ per cent. solution, tubes inoculated at the same intervals became turbid with the bacterium sown. With a ¾ per cent. solution the result was the same.

Passing back to a 1 per cent. solution, tubes inoculated at the same intervals remained sterile.

There seems to be an incompatibility between the first and last series. If we examine the others, however, we must conclude that the limit of disinfection lies between 1 and 1¼ per cent.

Iodine water was prepared by shaking up some iodine in distilled water, which assumed an amber tint. This solution destroyed the bacterium in 15 minutes, as the following experiment shows:

Six tubes were inoculated with bacteria after they had been exposed to the action of the iodine water for 7, 10, 15, 20, 26, and 31 minutes. On the following day the first tube became turbid; on the second the 10-minute tube was turbid and found to be a pure culture of the bacterium sown. The other tubes remained sterile. One of them, inoculated later, showed its capacity for sustaining growth by becoming promptly turbid.

Permanganate of potash.—A series of experiments with this substance, conducted in the manner described above, showed that the bacterium is killed by 15 minutes' exposure to .02 per cent. solution tion (1:5000).

In order to obtain this result a 5 per cent. solution was tried first. Tubes inoculated after an exposure of the virus for 7, 10, 15, 20, 25, and 31 minutes remained permanently clear. One of these tubes, subsequently inoculated with the unaffected virus, was turbid next day. Two and a half per cent., 1 per cent., ½ per cent., ¼ per cent., 1/10 per cent., and 1/20 per cent. solutions were tried in the same way. The six tubes used for each solution remained sterile. Finally a 1/50 per cent. (1 : 5000) was used. Tubes were inoculated after an exposure of the virus for 2, 4, 6, 10, 15, 20, 25, and 30 minutes. On the following day the four first tubes were turbid; the fifth and seventh remained sterile; the sixth and eighth contained a fine bacillus. These two tubes, as was found later, belonged to a lot which, through some carelessness, had not been properly sterilized, and the majority became turbid before use.

Mercuric iodide was found to destroy the bacterium in solution of 1 : 1000000 in 10 minutes.

Two grams of potassium iodide and 1 gram of mercuric iodide were dissolved in 100^{cc} of distilled water, making a 1 per cent. solution of the disinfectant in a 2 per cent. solution of potassium iodide.

This solution, diluted with sterile distilled water so as to make .1 per cent., killed the bacterium of hog-cholera taken from liquid cultures in less than 5 minutes; .01 per cent. (1 : 10000), .002 per cent. (2 : 100000), .001 per cent. (1 : 100000), and .0005 per cent. (5 : 1000000) destroyed the germ within 2 minutes.

When the solution was diluted so as to make .0002 per cent. (2 : 1000000) and .0001 per cent. (1 : 1000000) it was found that with both solutions tubes inoculated with the bacterium after a exposure of 2 and 5 minutes were opalescent, the bacterium introduced having multiplied, while the remaining tubes (10 to 30 minutes) were sterile. These two solutions, therefore, were still powerful enough to kill the germ in 10 minutes. The dilution had been carried so far as to make them practically equivalent in disinfectant power.

Sulphate of copper.—This disinfectant, which seems to be more effective than most other metallic salts, was tried in solutions containing 2 per cent., ½ per cent., 1/10 per cent. Both the 2 per cent. and ½ per cent. solutions destroyed the germ within 5 minutes. Tubes inoculated with the bacterium after an exposure to the 1/10 per cent. solution for 5, 10, and 15 minutes became turbid; those inoculated after an exposure of 20, 25, and 30 minutes remained clear.

The disinfectant power for short periods of time may be said to lie between ½ and 1/10 per cent. In this, as in other tests, one or two drops of the culture were added to 5^{cc} of the disinfectant. A slight flocculent precipitate formed each time.

Of *hydrochloric acid* a .2 per cent. solution of the acid, made by adding 4.2^{cc} of chemically pure acid (containing about 40 per cent. HCl) to 95.8^{cc} of water, destroyed the germ in less than 5 minutes.

Chloride of zinc.—A 10 per cent. solution of this salt failed to destroy the vitality of the bacterium in 10 minutes; 20^{cc} of Squibbs' chloride of zinc, containing 50 per cent. of the salt, were added to 80^{cc} of sterile distilled water to make a 10 per cent. solution. A drop from a culture five days old was mixed with 5^{cc} of this solution, from which mixture tubes were inoculated at the end of 5, 10, 15, 25, and 30 minutes. The two first tubes became clouded.

Sulphuric acid.—A .05 per cent. solution (1: 2000) was fatal to the bacterium of hog-cholera in less than 10 minutes.

Without going into detail, it is sufficient to say that the results were reached as indicated above. Tubes containing sterile beef broth were inoculated at the end of 5, 10, 15, 20, 25, and 30 minutes with bacteria exposed to ½ per cent. and ¼ per cent. No development. Those inoculated with 1/10 per cent. became clouded, each being a pure culture of the bacterium inoculated. When 1/20 per cent. was tried, only the 5-minute tube became clouded. The solution (by weight) was made from sulphuric acid containing 96 per cent. of the acid (specific gravity 1.838).

It must be remembered that the foregoing tests were made upon bacteria in an active vegetative state. It is probable that in the dried condition it would have taken solutions of the same strength somewhat longer time to dcstroy their vitality. To briefly summarize the results, placing the least effective substance first, we obtain the following table:

Chloride of zinc in a 10 per cent. solution destroyed the bacterium in liquid cultures in 10 to 15 minutes.
Carbolic acid, 1 to 1⅛ per cent. (1 : 100), in 5 minutes.
Iodine water in 15 minutes.
Hydrochloric acid, ⅕ per cent. (1 : 500), in less than 5 minutes. (Only a .2 per cent. solution of this acid tried.)
Sulphate of copper, $\frac{1}{10}$ per cent. (1 : 1000), in 15 to 20 minutes.
Sulphuric acid, $\frac{1}{20}$ per cent. (1 : 2000), in less than 10 minutes.
Permanganate of potash, $\frac{1}{50}$ per cent. (1 : 5000), in 15 minutes.
Mercuric chloride, $\frac{1}{750}$ per cent. (1 : 75000), less than 5 minutes.
Mercuric iodide in $\frac{1}{10000}$ per cent. (1 : 1000000), in 10 minutes.

The above table would no doubt be somewhat changed by mixing virus embedded in large quantities of organic matter with the disinfectant solutions. It gives, however, a good working basis for experiments on a large scale, and it throws out at once the use of chloride of zinc and perhaps carbolic acid.

In order to determine how much stronger solutions than those above given would be required to destroy the dried bacteria, the following experiment was carried out:

Spleen pulp containing large numbers of bacteria was rubbed on sterile cover-glasses so as to make a thin film, and allowed to dry for 2 days under a plugged funnel. A solution of mercuric chloride, 1 : 50000, was poured upon the cover-glasses, and one was removed after 1½, 2, 3, 5, 7, 10, 15, 17, and 20 minutes, washed in about 100cc of sterile water, and dropped into tubes containing beef infusion. After remaining in the incubator for a day it was found that the virus exposed to the disinfectant for 1½, 2, 7, 10 and 20 minutes had been destroyed, the tubes remaining permanently clear. The others contained pure cultures of the hog-cholera bacterium.

The bacterium may be thus killed by solutions of mercuric chloride, which do not destroy spores. Koch found that anthrax spores may remain in solutions of 1: 50000 for over 60 minutes without losing their capacity for germinating. That all of the germs were not destroyed in the above experiment does not weaken the conclusion. They were undoubtedly incrusted with blood and cellular elements, so that the disinfectant could not exert its full power directly upon them. Koch, on the other hand, used spores from cultures only. The experiment demonstrates the absence of any resistant spore state in the tissues of the animal, but points out the necessity of considerably increasing the strength of disinfectant solutions in endeavoring to destroy the bacteria in nature, inasmuch as we have to deal with other things besides the germs themselves, which neutralize much of the disinfecting power.

Is there any resistant spore state in the life history of the bacterium of hog-cholera.

Stained in dilute solutions of aniline colors the bacterium from the tissues of animals which have succumbed to the disease stains in such a way as to leave the impression that it contains an endospore. A narrow band of stained substance bounds an oval pale body, which is but slightly tinged. It appears that a rather resistant envelope prevents the coloring matter from passing readily and quickly into the interior of the bacterium.

If a drop from a recent liquid culture be suspended from the lower surface of a cover-glass and examined in a glass cell with a homogeneous immersion objective and small diaphragm, the following appearances are worthy of record: The bacteria in the center of the drop of culture fluid are in very active motion and quite small. If the periphery of the drop be examined there will be found a dense layer of bacteria caught there by the slow desiccation and consequent contraction of the drop. These, some of which are still moving slowly, are larger than the forms in the center of the drop. As the drying proceeds and the film of water becomes thin the bacteria appear to be made up of a distinct dark border surrounding an almost transparent body. In most forms there is a slightly thicker border at the ends than at the sides of the short rod-like bodies. When stained slightly this border takes the stain well, while the body of the rod remains pale. The fact that the structural and color pictures correspond is strong evidence that the microbe possesses a rather dense membrane, which in optical section is seen as a narrow dark border.

The form and size of the bacteria under consideration depend upon the culture medium and upon the age of the culture. The appearance which they present in the animal tissues is very closely simulated in liquid media, more especially beef infusion with peptone. When grown on gelatine or potato the appearance just described cannot as a rule be made out, as the bacteria are apt to be smaller.

The foregoing facts incline us to believe that we have no true spore state to deal with in this microbe, but perhaps a membrane, which is more or less resistant, according to circumstances, and which is more resistant in the animal tissues than in cultures.

Microscopical characters, however, are now and then misleading, unless we interpret them by physiological experiments. Judging from what has hitherto been considered properties of bacterial spores, the microbe of hog-cholera cannot lay any claim to the production of true endogenous spores. Their absence is determined by results of experiments recorded in the preceding pages: 1. The thermal death-point of the bacterium at 58° C. An exposure to this temperature for 15 to 20 minutes destroys not only the vitality of cultures of all ages, but also the dried germ in the tissues of the infected animal. A momentary exposure to boiling water is equally efficacious. 2. The bacteria are destroyed by disinfectants in solutions which are incapable of destroying spores. 3. They are killed by simple drying far more quickly than are spores; at the same time their resistance to drying is much greater than might be expected under the circumstances. In the experiments recorded some dried bacteria in spleen pulp were killed in less than a month; others resisted forty-nine days. We may put the limit, which is very much less for dried cultures, between one and two months. It is this continued vitality in the dried state that suggests the existence of a membrane which is more resistant than that possessed by the great majority of bacteria in their vegetative state. This difference between bacteria in the vegetative and the spore state is illustrated by the anthrax bacillus. In cultures the bacilli are killed by drying in five or six days; the spores, under the same condition, retain their virulence for years.

All the facts brought out by the study of this bacterium lead to the conclusion that a distinct spore state, so called, does not appear either within the animal body or in nature. *

* There is no reason why the bacterium in the body of animals may not be in an arthro-sporous state, according to the classification of de Bary. The name is of little account as long as we define the properties belonging to a given state.

Observations on the pathogenic properties of the bacterium of hog-cholera.

In addition to the foregoing experiments on the general biological characters of the bacterium of hog-cholera, a few additional observations were made upon its pathogenic activity, with a view to determine more precisely the mode of infection.

Growth in vacuo.—It seemed desirable to learn the extent to which the bacterium was capable of multiplying with a minimum supply of oxygen. The following simple experiment was tried:

An elongated glass bulb of about 15[cc] capacity, terminating in a narrow tube about 10[cm] long, and containing about 5[cc] of beef-infusion peptone, was inoculated from a pure culture. The air was then exhausted by an air-pump for fifteen minutes, while the bulb was kept immersed in a water bath at a temperature of 38° C. It was finally sealed in the flame and placed in the incubator. The results of three separate experiments were practically the same. In the bulbs the culture liquid was turbid on the following day. This turbidity increased but slightly, and within three or four days growth had evidently ceased. Four other microbes, two of which were found in the exudates of hog cholera *bacillus luteus* described in the Second Annual Report of the Bureau, a micrococcus, *bacillus subtilis*, and a microbe producing septicæmia in rabbits, were treated in the same way. None of the tubes became turbid. When, after three or four days, the bulbs were opened and filtered and air allowed to enter, the liquids became turbid within twenty-four hours, the characteristic pigment of the *bacillus luteus* appearing a few days later.

The bacterium of hog-cholera has therefore the power of multiplying in what is practically a vacuum, but this power is limited. The other microbes failed to show any signs of growth whatever. They were purely aerobic. The bacterium of hog-cholera may therefore be regarded as holding a place midway between those microbes which seem to thrive better without air—anaerobic—and those that fail to grow without it.

That no spores were found in these bulbs may be inferred from the following experiment: One of the tubes kept sealed for a month was opened and a number of culture tubes inoculated therefrom. They were then exposed to a temperature of 58° C. for 15, 20, 25, and 30 minutes. All remained sterile. One, inoculated without being subsequently heated, was turbid with the specific bacterium next day, indicating that it was still alive in the bulb when the latter was opened.

MODES OF INFECTION.

(*a*) *By way of the digestive tract.*—In at least 90 per cent. of swine a very severe form of hog-cholera may be induced by feeding to them the viscera of animals which have died of the disease. The lesions produced are exceedingly severe. The mucous membrane of the large intestine is extensively ulcerated or completely necrosed. In animals which have contracted the disease in the ordinary way in infected pens the ulceration of the large intestine, at times very severe, usually stops abruptly at the ileo-cæcal valve. When this is slit up, the mucosa belonging to the small intestine up to the free border of the valve is in the great majority of cases normal, while the mucosa of that surface of the valve facing the cæcum may be extensively ulcerated. In many animals fed with infectious matter the ulceration involves the entire ileum. This is well illustrated by the following cases:

January 8, 1886.—Pig No. 165 was fed with the viscera of two pigs which had died of hog-cholera. It was found dead January 26, after manifesting no marked symptoms of disease except a tendency to lie quietly in its pen. On examination the subcutaneous fat was found diffusely reddened. There was a slight peritonitis, indicated by a considerable quantity of straw-colored effusion and some fibrinous stringy deposits. There were also a few local excrescences on the small intestine, due to the irritation of *echinorhynchi*. Spleen somewhat enlarged; on its surface a few bright red punctiform elevations. Right heart distended with a clot. Local hepatizations in lungs, probably caused by lung worms, which were very numerous. Stomach but slightly reddened. A number of ulcers in the duodenum, the mucosa of which was reddened. The mucosa of the ileum for 1½ feet from valve was completely necrosed, the walls thickened, and the serosa of this portion dotted with ecchymoses. Beyond this portion, near the jejunum, there were scattered ulcerations on a deeply congested membrane for 6 or 7 feet. The entire length of the large intestine was covered with dirty yellowish ulcerations varying in diameter from a pin's head to nearly an inch. The mucosa itself was very deeply congested in the cæcum and colon only and the walls much thickened. Ascarides and *echinorhynchi* numerous in small intestines. The liver attached to diaphragm in several places by whitish exudate.

A tube of meat infusion with peptone inoculated from the spleen of this animal was found to be a pure culture of the motile bacterium of hog-cholera. Line cultures on gelatine plates confirmed the microscopic examination. A tube of nutritive gelatine inoculated from the spleen at the same time contained in each needle track, several days later, from 10 to 15 colonies of the same bacterium. Two cover-glass preparations revealed no bacteria. This fact, combined with the small number of colonies in the tube culture, gave evidence of the small number of germs in the spleen tissue. Inoculations on mice and guinea-pigs gave substantially the same results as those obtained last year.

No. 159 was fed with the viscera of No. 165 on January 28. February 5, its eyes were sore and nearly closed; it was quite weak. It died on the following day, only eight days after infection. The skin on abdomen was reddened in patches; the subcutaneous tissue diffusely. The superficial inguinals, as well as the glands in the abdomen, were deeply congested, the cortex more especially. Those of the thorax were nearly pale. The spleen was dotted with a few punctiform elevations. Beneath the epicardium and endocardium of both auricles and the endocardium of the left ventricle were extensive patches of extravasated blood. Kidneys enlarged and congested throughout. The lesions of the ileum, cæcum, and colon in this animal were quite as extensive as those of the case just described; there were no ulcers in the rectum, however. Those of the colon had black centers, pointing to a recent origin from blood extravasations on the surface of the mucous membrane.

In the spleen of this case the characteristic bacteria of hog-cholera were exceedingly numerous, as determined by cover-glass preparations. Two liquid cultures proved pure when tested on gelatine plates. In the needle tracks of a tube culture in gelatine innumerable colonies appeared in a few days. Inoculations from subsequent cultures proved equally positive.

Pig No. 156 was fed with the viscera of No. 159 February 18, and, after manifesting the usual symptoms of hog-cholera, died February 25, seven days after feeding. Among the marked lesions produced by the disease was a complete necrosis of the upper two-thirds of the colon, with scattered ulcers along the lower third. About an eighth of a foot of the lower portion of the small intestine, beginning at the valve, was necrosed, without manifesting distinct ulceration, for which the period of disease was evidently too brief. In the spleen there were numerous small grayish spots, probably centers of necrosis, as they showed no longer cell structure when crushed on a slide and stained. The fundus of the stomach was also deeply congested.

The spleen, to which organ the microscopic examination was limited, contained the characteristic oval bacteria, as shown by cover-glass preparations. Three liquid cultures made from the same organ were found to be pure cultures of the same microbe when tested by line cultures. A tube culture in gelatine developed in each needle track numerous non-liquefying colonies.

In these animals the mode of introduction of the virus determined the seat of the severest lesions. It is probable that the food passes quite rapidly through the small intestine; that in the stomach the action of the bacteria is more or less limited, because they have not sufficient time to multiply, and probably because hindered by the acid condition of the organ, though they will multiply with considerable vigor in slightly acid infusions. The prolonged stay of th[illegible] in the large intestine permits multiplication, and the first and severest lesions to appear here. When these have become very extensive, so as to paralyze the action of the large intestine, the ileum becomes involved in a similar manner, possibly by a partial stoppage of the infectious matter in this portion of the intestine. This view is supported by the evidence of the above and other *post mortem* examinations in which the disease was produced by feeding.

This mode of infection by feeding viscera was used to keep up the disease at the experimental station, as simple infection in pens could not always be relied upon in furnishing cases for investigation. These few cases might therefore be supplemented by many others to show the ease with which infection may take place in this way.

In general two types of disease appear. In one the lesions are limited quite exclusively to the alimentary tract, involving the stomach, the large intestine, and often the ileum, less frequently the jejunum. There may be complete necrosis of the mucosa in the colon and ileum, with intense reddening of the fundus of the stomach. The internal organs are but slightly affected. There are few or no hemorrhages, and the bacterium is very scarce in the spleen and other organs, so that its presence is only determinable by culture.

In the other type the extensive local lesions are replaced by hemorrhagic lesions of the internal organs, involving the spleen, kidneys, lymphatic glands, lungs, and serous membranes generally. Besides these, the mucous membrane of the stomach and intestines may be congested, and extensive hemorrhages into the submucous tissue, often into the lumen of the digestive tube, take place. These lesions have been described somewhat in detail in the last report. The spleen and blood are found to contain a large number of the hog-cholera bacteria.

Both types of the disease produced by feeding lead to a speedy termination by death in from six days to two weeks. The difference above given may perhaps be referred to a difference in the virulence of the bacteria. In the type first described the bacteria may be less adapted to a parasitic life. Their poisonous effects are exerted locally in destroying the mucous membrane. In the second type the bacteria are capable of entering the blood, to be distributed to all the organs where the hemorrhagic lesions are caused by their growth.

(*b*) *Feeding pure cultures of the Bacterium of hog-cholera.*—In the preceding report (p. 207) two very severe cases of hog-cholera are reported as having been produced by the feeding of pure liquid cultures. These positive results are not always obtained, as some of the following experiments indicate:

Pigs Nos. 155 and 156 were fed February 8, 1886, with 200^{cc} of a beef-infusion peptone culture derived from a mouse which had succumbed to inoculation. The animals remained well. Pig No. 155 was fed February 1 with 100^{cc} of liquid cultures of the bacterium of hog-cholera without manifesting any symptoms of disease.

The rapidly fatal effect from the ingestion of the viscera of swine containing the specific bacterium may be harmonized with the negative results above recorded when we consider the different condition of the bacterium in the liquid cultures and in the infectious viscera. In the latter case the bacteria are enveloped by connective and cellular tissue, which protect them from the destructive effect of gastric digestion, so that they are carried into the intestine where the pathological lesions are first manifested. In culture fluids the bacteria are in the most vulnerable state, and are easily accessible to the action of the gastric juice, which very probably does not permit any to pass alive into the duodenum.

That the condition of the stomach is a very important factor in the production of the disease when the virus has entered it seems a very reasonable assumption. If the virus reaches the empty stomach coated with an alkaline mucus it is more likely to multiply and reach the duodenum than when the stomach is filled with food which is being actively digested. In order to test this assumption the following experiment was tried:

December 18.—Three pigs were fed each with 300^{cc} of beef infusion in which the bacterium of hog-cholera had been multiplying for three days at a temperature of 90° to 95° F. The beef infusion had been neutralized, and sterilized in two flasks, and the cultures, when examined before the experiments, were found to contain the motile bacterium only.

The pigs were prepared for the feeding as follows: No. 848 received no food for over twenty-four hours. A 2 per cent. solution of sodium carbonate in beef infusion was then given to increase the alkalinity of the stomach. Of this about 1 liter was consumed. It was then fed with 300^{cc} of culture liquid mixed with beef-broth to make 1 liter. No. 850 was starved in the same way, but received no alkali before consuming the culture. No. 842 was not deprived of food before eating the culture.

The result confirmed our anticipations. No. 848 showed signs of disease in two days. On the third it was unable to rise, and died on the same day. The *post mortem* examination showed a considerable congestion of the mucous membrane of the duodenum and jejunum, as well as of the large intestine. The fundus of stomach affected in the same way. The liver was gorged with blood, as well as the portal system. There were no marked lesions of the other viscera. That the hog-cholera bacterium had also entered the blood was shown by two pure cultures in beef infusion obtained from the spleen. A gelatine culture from the liver contained about 6 or 7 colonies.

No. 850 was a more typical case, and demonstrated the severe local effects of the bacterium much better, since the animal lived longer. It ate fairly well until the fourth day, when its appetite gave way and diarrhea set in. From this time it grew weak and thin, being scarcely able to walk. It died on the tenth day after feeding. The lesions of the alimentary tract were exceedingly grave. Beginning with the stomach, the mucous membrane was dotted with closely set elevated masses as large as split peas, and larger patches of a whitish viscid substance, made up entirely of cellular elements (diphtheritic?). When removed, a raw depressed surface was exposed. The membrane itself was pale. Besides a general injection of the ileum, Peyer's patches were more deeply congested, and the uppermost covered with a thin yellowish film, not removable, and most likely dead epithelium. In the cæcum and colon the mucosa was superficially necrosed, and converted into a continuous layer of a dirty whitish mass about 1^{mm} thick. The walls of the intestine were greatly thickened and very friable.

Microscopic sections showed an extensive cellular infiltration of the submucous connective tissue which had separated the masses of fat cells, concealed the connective tissue fibers, and caused a great thickening of the entire layer. The mucosa itself was greatly altered. The surface was necrossed and converted into an amorphous mass. In some places the necrosis involved the entire depth of the crypts of Lieberkühn, a series of striæ indicating their former existence. Those whose epithelium still remained were plugged with a cylindrical mass, filled with broken-down nuclei. The bacteria had exerted their poisonous effects from the surface of the mucosa towards the depths, destroying the surface epithelium and glandular structures and involving secondarily the submucous layer. Near the rectum this continuous mass of dead tissue was replaced by isolated ulcers embedded in an intensely reddened mucosa. Plate II, taken from another case, illustrates well the superficial death of the mucosa. The ileo-cæcal valve was much swollen, but the necrosis did not extend into the ileum, although there were a few ulcers near the valve, and the epithelium had a pale, lusterless aspect, as if dead. The liver was filled with blood, which readily clotted as it flowed from the cut surface. Spleen congested and but slightly enlarged. Lungs hypostatic. The lymphatic glands in general not much affected. Two liquid cultures from the blood were turbid next day, and contained the hog-cholera bacterium only. In a gelatine tube culture from the liver about a dozen colonies developed in each needle track.

No. 842, which was fed with the same quantity of culture liquid but was not deprived of food previously, was somewhat ill on the following day. It recovered, however, and continued apparently well for several weeks. It began thereupon to grow thin and weak. On January 26 it was no longer able to rise, and was therefore killed for examination, in order to conclude the experiment. On opening the abdominal cavity it was at once perceived that the animal had been suffering from a very intense disease of the large intestine, a portion of which was firmly attached to the bladder. When dissected out and slit open, the mucous membrane of the cæcum and colon was found replaced by a brownish friable layer of necrosed tissue. The wall of the intestine was infiltrated to such an extent that it was nearly $\frac{1}{4}$ inch thick, and so degenerated that the forceps easily tore through it. The thickness of the walls prevented the intestine from collapsing after it was opened. Its only contents was a brownish liquid mass. The glands of the meso-colon were very large, some like horse-chestnuts. On section the entire tissue was very pale, almost white. The spleen was somewhat enlarged; the malpighian corpuscles unusually large and prominent on section. Lungs and heart normal; kidneys deeply reddened throughout on section.

This case is very interesting in completing the information gained by this feeding experiment. No. 348, which had been fed with sodium carbonate besides being deprived of food, died three days after the ingestion of the culture. No. 350, which was simply starved, died ten days thereafter, while No. 342, which ate the culture without being previously starved, was dying on the thirty-fourth day.

These results show how easily infection may occur by way of the digestive system, provided the destructive action of gastric digestion be prevented, as was done by starving and by the use of an alkaline carbonate.

They also indicate how purely local this destructive action may be. Gelatine cultures from these animals showed that the internal organs contained but very few bacteria. So few were they in fact that the microscope alone could not have demonstrated their presence, as they could not be found on cover-glass preparations.

Other successful experiments by feeding pure cultures will be given in connection with a description of the bacterium from different parts of the country.

(c) *Subcutaneous inoculation with pure cultures.*—The least successful method of producing the disease is the subcutaneous inoculation of pure cultures. In the report for 1885 at least three out of four inoculations produced a rapidly fatal form of the disease. In the numerous experiments to be described later, in which pigs were inoculated with cultures to determine whether any future protection was thereby granted, only five died from the inoculation. In these experiments two subcutaneous injections were practiced, a small quantity being followed by a larger quantity of culture liquid. The deaths occurred from the first injection when this was made comparatively large; the second dose, which was usually quite large, was borne without any ill effects.

These successful inoculations, reported *in extenso* in another section, are briefly as follows: No. 239, inoculated April 27 with $\frac{1}{2}^{cc}$ culture liquid, died May 2, only six days after inoculation. Hemorrhagic condition of vital organs. Though seven others were treated in the same way none took sick. It may be that in this individual the needle entered a superficial vein, and in this way introduced the virus directly into the blood.

Nos. 204 and 212, inoculated April 12 with $1\frac{1}{2}^{cc}$ culture liquid, died eleven and seven days after inoculation, respectively. In the former the mucosa of large intestine was entirely necrosed. In the latter ulceration was just beginning.

Nos. 208 and 209, inoculated at the same time with 1^{cc} of the same culture, died fifteen and six days after inoculation respectively. Numerous extensive ulcers in the large intestine of 208. In 209 general congestion and extravasation along digestive tract and in internal organs. With each pair two others had been inoculated without any untoward results.

The local swelling at the point of inoculation is usually proportionate to the quantity of culture fluid injected. The following cases show how large quantities may be borne without inducing the disease:

Nos. 116 and 154 were inoculated February 8 by the subcutaneous injection of $3\frac{1}{2}^{cc}$ of the second culture from the spleen of No. 165 in beef-infusion peptone, one-half being injected into each thigh. A very large swelling appeared at the seat of inoculation in No. 154, causing considerable lameness. March 4 this animal was killed, although evidently not diseased. The inoculation tumor was over 1 inch long and ½ inch thick; firm, yellowish-white, developed in the loose connective, and only loosely attached to skin and subjacent mucular tissue. There was considerable serum in the abdominal cavity, and the spleen was somewhat enlarged. In the fatty tissue lining the dorsal wall of the abdominal cavity numerous worms were found (*Sclerostoma pinguicola*), occupying tunneled spaces in the fibro-adipose mass. No indications of hog-cholera. No. 116 was not affected.

No. 181 was inoculated February 13 with 7^{cc} of the second liquid culture from the spleen of pig No. 159. Within a few days the animal became lame, but this passed away. At the seat of inoculation large tumors had developed, no doubt causing the stiffness of the hind limbs. This animal was killed March 4. At each point of inoculation were found firm fibrous masses, from 2 to 3 square inches in extent and nearly an inch thick. No suppuration. There were no lesions pointing directly to hog-cholera. There was, however, a considerable quantity of pale serum in the abdominal cavity. Spleen enlarged; cortex of kidneys dull, thickened; lymphatic glands of large intestine somewhat prominent, but pale.

These animals may have suffered from the absorption of ptomaines from the place of inoculation, but dissemination of the bacteria through the internal organs evidently did not take place to any extent.

The failure to produce the disease in even a small proportion of animals by the injection of liquid cultures raised the question whether the cultivation in itself did not attenuate the bacteria. Consequently two experiments were made by inoculating with blood directly. Numerous gelatine cultures of heart's blood had demonstrated the very small number of bacteria compared with the number present in the spleen.

September 10.—A pig dying with the disease was killed, the heart carefully exposed, and the blood drawn with a disinfected hypodermic syringe. Nos. 329 and 333 received subcutaneously 5^{cc} each, one half in each thigh. No. 329 in a few days lost its appetite, became weak and stupid. Found dead October 5. Slight local swelling at the points of inoculation; superficial inguinals greatly enlarged; hypostatic congestion of lungs; complete necrosis of mucous membrane in cæcum; large scattered ulcers in colon, showing as whitish patches on serous surface and encircled by a crown of enlarged blood vessels; bacteria in spleen.

No. 333, slightly ill for a time; fully recovered. Died December 2 with no other lesions than engorgement of liver. No signs of former ulceration.

A second experiment was made in the same way:

October 13.—Nos. 324 and 325 inoculated as in the preceding experiment, 10^{cc} of blood being used for each animal. No. 324 was found dead November 1, after being off feed for a time. Deeply reddened skin over caudal half of abdomen; extremely large and serously infiltrated superficial lymphatics; on section, hemorrhagic points. At point of inoculation the connective tissue is infiltrated; 50^{cc} to 75^{cc} clear amber serum in abdominal cavity; papillæ of kidneys deeply reddened; slight congestion, but no ulceration in large intestine; lymphatics in general moderately tumefied and congested.

No. 325 found dead October 29. Reddening of skin as in 324; extravasation in connective tissue; spleen greatly enlarged, purplish; lymphatics of thorax and abdomen purplish, enlarged; petechiæ on section of kidney and in pelvis, also over entire surface of epicardium; lung tissue mottled both on surface and on section with purple spots, due to blood extravasation into alveoli, so that it scarcely floats. Mucous and serous surface of small intestine dotted with petechiæ; small hemorrhages on the surface of the mucous membrane and into the submucous tissue of the cæcum and upper colon. Ulceration beginning.

These results are more positive than those obtained with cultures, and on first thought we may be inclined to attribute them to a greater virulence of the germs in the injected blood. This view needs further confirmation, however. The injected blood coagulating in the connective tissue contains in it the bacteria, which are not only protected from the aggression of cellular elements, but have actually a store of nourishment upon which they may live and multiply. No such advantages are presented to bacteria suspended in liquids which are readily absorbed, leaving them to the mercy of the tissues surrounding them. The local reaction in the above animals was very insignificant compared with that produced by liquid cultures. In order to come to any conclusion, it would be desirable to add a few bacteria from cultures to fresh blood, and observe the relative virulence in the way indicated above.

Taking the foregoing results into consideration, the alimentary canal must be considered as the most vulnerable point for the entrance of the bacterium of hog-cholera. It is probably the chief, if not the only, entrance of the virus when the infection takes place among herds. The occasional occurrence of lung lesions as extensive hepatization in advanced cases of hog-cholera suggested to Klein the name of pneumo-enteritis. In the many cases carefully examined at the experimental station the lung lesion did not appear to surpass in severity those of the internal viscera and the lymphatic system. In the great majority of animals lung-worms were usually found associated with localized atelectasis. The collapsed portions had a red flesh color. Many cases of chronic hog-cholera, associated with extensive ulceration of the large intestine, had normal lungs. On the other hand, cases of a very acute hemorrhagic type, produced by feeding infectious material or by subcutaneous inoculation, presented throughout the lung tissue small hemorrhagic foci involving several contiguous lobules. On section they were of a dark-red color, and indicated extravasation into the alveoli, which were filled up with coagulated blood. These foci are very likely caused by plugs of bacteria growing in the capillaries, producing necrosis of their walls and consequent extravasation. Taking into consideration the condition of the remaining viscera in such cases, it is highly probable that the foci are not primary, but secondary in character. They are not growths of the bacteria introduced by the inspired air, but carried there by the circulation, the original place of entrance being the alimentary tract. These centers of growth may gradually spread and involve the entire lung substance, giving rise to that extensive hepatization occasionally found. That infection may arise through the air in some cases, especially in summer, when the bacteria are dried and carried away as dust, is not necessarily excluded. The greater activity of the virus in the warm seasons cannot be entirely due to its dissemination in this manner, since drying destroys the bacteria of this disease in from one to two months, and it may reduce their pathogenic power in a much briefer time. The greater diffusion and mortality must be attributed to more favorable opportunities for the bacteria to multiply outside the animal body in streams and in the soil on animal and vegetable substances. In this connection it might be well to record the following experiment:

Two pigs placed in an air-tight box were subjected to the spray of an atomizer containing 10^{cc} of a liquid culture of the hog-cholera bacterium diluted with 40^{cc} of distilled water. The spray was directed upon the faces of the animals, which they could not avoid, owing to the small size of the box. They were removed at the end of thirty minutes and placed in a disinfected pen. After a few days they seemed somewhat dull, but both recovered. Several months after one of them died of hog-cholera on being fed with infectious material. It is highly probable that the bacteria were carried into the lungs at the time.

In view of the fact that another bacterium has been recently found associated with severe lung lesions, and is probably the cause, it becomes necessary to re-examine diseases of the lungs, whether associated with true hog-cholera or occurring independently. The subject is fully discussed further on.

Cycles of virulence.—The variation in the severity and extent of epidemics of infectious diseases has been a subject for observation and comment by all who have studied them more carefully. It is characteristic of infectious diseases attacking man as well as those to which animals are subject.

The change in virulence is indicated both by the number of animals affected in a given time and by the suddenness with which they are struck down after infection. The record of cases of hog-cholera kept at the experimental station for more than a year is very instructive, in showing clearly how the virus of a specific disease may become very much attenuated, then suddenly regain its virulence, sweep away a large number of animals very rapidly, then again lose its virulence until it has scarcely any effect upon the animal system. This change in virulence is indicated in various ways. When attenuated the virus produces a chronic disease, characterized by local ulcerations of the mucous membrane in the large intestine. The affected animal lives for four or more weeks. This is the way in which the disease manifests itself most commonly. When the virulence is great the disease is rapid, the lesions hemorrhagic in character, involving nearly all the vital organs. These are found to contain the specific bacterium in large quantities. Subcutaneous inoculations of cultures derived from such cases will in general produce a disease as severe and as rapidly fatal. When the pigs are fed with the viscera from these same cases even more severe local and general lesions are the result. From such a height of virulence there is a gradual descent. Animals which have become infected in the natural way are attacked by a milder and more protracted disease. Inoculations of cultures become less successful or fail altogether. Even when fed with the viscera of animals which have died of the disease, pigs will after a time become affected with a slow chronic malady. In these milder forms of the disease comparatively few bacteria penetrate into the vital organs to multiply there. Cover-glass preparations of spleen pulp do not show a single microbe in many fields, while the same preparation from hemorrhagic cases may show from 50 to 100 in every field of a $\frac{1}{18}$ homogeneous objective. Nor does the quantity of virus introduced materially change the result. When the disease is at its highest point of virulence cases of natural infection are frequently as severe as those fed with large quantities of virus. On the other hand, when animals are fed with cultures of more or less attenuated virus, the local destruction of tissue in the intestines may be very grave and cause speedy death, but the internal organs remain more or less intact.

This change in virulence has not been observed in experiments upon mice, rabbits, and guinea-pigs. The same peculiar lesions have appeared throughout a period of fourteen months. The duration of the disease may vary, but this depends upon the quantity of virus introduced into the system. The lesions in the protracted cases due to the inoculation of very small quantities are if anything more pronounced.

What agencies are at work in bringing about this variation in virulence is a problem still to be solved. There is no clew to an explanation, and we simply record the facts as observed. There seems to be a sufficient reason for regarding the increase of virulence as due to climatic and meteorological conditions affecting the bacterium outside of the body, for our own observations show that the successive passage of the virus through the body of pigs by feeding diminishes its virulence and may finally destroy it.

The relation of the virulent and attenuated bacteria to the animal organism is expressed by the statement that the former are capable of living and multiplying in the blood vascular system of the infected pig, while the latter are unable to do so. Their destructive action is limited to the intestinal tract. There may be two properties by whose change a virulent bacterium becomes attenuated, and *vice versa*—the capacity of living with a limited supply of oxygen, and the power of forming a poison or ptomaine which is more or less destructive to cellular life. Either or both of these properties, when augmented or diminished, may bring about the differences which are observed between malignant and mild types of the disease.

EXPERIMENTS UPON OTHER ANIMALS WITH THE HOG-CHOLERA BACTERIUM.

Mice infected by feeding.—It was desirable to determine how far the bacterium of hog-cholera was infectious to other animals besides pigs when introduced with the food into the alimentary canal. Mice, being susceptible to inoculation, might contract the disease about the pens, and being eaten by pigs would quite naturally become a source of infection. To determine this point bread and spleen were thoroughly mixed by mincing them together. Two mice ate of this mixture, and one was found stupid, scarcely able to move about on the following day. The same material was fed a second time. Both were ill on the next day. They crouched, somewhat sprawling, with head down, staring coat, and eyes partly closed. On taking them out of the jar they were unable to move; when pushed forward they moved a few steps. These symptoms passed away on the third day. Five days after the first feeding one was found dead. The other was fed again six days after the first feeding. It was found dead two days after the last feeding. The first feeding had therefore taken effect. The liver showed the formation of islets of coagulation necrosis and was crowded with the bacteria of hog-cholera. The very peculiar condition of these animals on the second and third day after feeding can only be explained by assuming the active multiplication of the bacteria in the intestinal canal and the formation of a ptomaine, which, on being absorbed, produced a systemic effect. The invasion of the internal organs themselves from the alimentary canal manifested itself later by the death of the animals and the presence of the ingested bacteria in the spleen and liver.

Two additional mice were fed in the same way. One escaped. The other failed to show any symptoms referable to the ptomaine, though fed four times. It remained well for over two weeks, when it began to breath laboriously and became very weak. It was killed with chloroform twenty-five days after the first feeding. The spleen was found enormously enlarged, but there were no bacteria on one cover-glass preparation. One lobe of each lung was solid, whitish, crumbling, evidently the result of coagulation necrosis. This mass was crowded with what appeared under the microscope as bacteria of hog-cholera. No cultures were made. This animal, therefore, judging from the enlarged spleen and the necrosed lungs, was also the victim of hog-cholera. Another mouse fed in the same way was dying four days after, but found drowned in the drinking cup next morning, thus preventing microscopic examination of the organs.

To determine whether these animals could be infected with pure cultures, a mouse was fed with bread which had been saturated with about $\frac{1}{2}$cc of a liquid culture and dried for an hour in the incubator. The feeding was repeated on four successive days. Seven days after the first feeding the animal was plainly ill, and it died on the following day. This would indicate that the first or second feeding had taken effect. The spleen was enlarged, the vessels of the mesentery very prominent and filled with blood. The bacteria were very abundant in the spleen, moderately so in liver and kidney. A second mouse fed with cultures was found drowned on the eighth day.

Two mice, kept in separate jars, were fed with a mass consisting of bread and gelatine culture thoroughly mixed. The gelatine culture had been prepared by passing a glass rod dipped in a liquid culture over the surface of a layer of gelatine. The gelatine after five days was covered with a thin opaque layer, consisting of confluent colonies. Both mice ate the dose. One was found dead next day in a crouching posture; the poison had evidently killed it in a very short time. The other did not appear disturbed by the absorption of the ptomaine, but it died from general infection on the sixth day. The spleen was considerably enlarged. Both spleen and liver contained large numbers of hog-cholera bacteria.

These few experiments show the possibility of an infection of mice through the food, and of the transportation of the disease through the agency of these animals. They show incidentally the effect on the system of the absorption of the ptomaine produced by bacteria in the alimentary canal.

Feeding was also tried on pigeons by saturating the feed with the culture liquid and allowing it to dry. No marked effect was produced. The feces were unusually liquid and abnormal in appearance for some time.

Guinea-pigs very susceptible to hog-cholera.—In order to determine the effect of very small doses on guinea-pigs, two animals, Nos. 3 and 4, which had been kept for more than a month under observation, were inoculated by injecting under the skin of the inner aspect of the thigh about $\frac{1}{1000}$cc of a culture in meat infusion with 1 per cent. peptone, prepared from the spleen of a pig on the day previous. To obtain such a small dose the culture liquid was diluted with sterile salt solution, and about $\frac{1}{4}$cc of this injected. On the third day both were unusually quiet and rested together; respiration seemed more labored; the animals moved unwillingly when disturbed. No. 3 was found dead on the morning of the eighth day, and No. 4 died at noon on the same day.

On examination the skin of No. 3 was found discolored at the place of inoculation. The surface of the muscular tissue at this point was dotted with ecchymoses, interspersed with whitish areas which corresponded to altered muscular tissue. This was whitish, friable, evidently dead. Such masses could be found to a depth of 1cm in the muscles of the thighs. This alteration seemed to follow along the planes of the intermuscular septa. A patch about 1cm in diameter on the muscular wall of the abdomen contiguous with the place of inoculation was similarly affected. In the abdomen the vessels of the intestine were injected, spleen full of blood, mottled dark red and grayish, friable. Lungs somewhat congested. The stomach contained a small mass of food embedded in considerable viscid translucent mucus; the cæcum and large intestine were filled with a yellowish soft food mass.

The bacteria of hog-cholera were present in large numbers in the liver and spleen. There were fewer in the kidneys and lungs; very few in blood from the heart. A tube culture in gelatine from the spleen developed numberless colonies in each of three needle tracks, growing precisely like cultures from the spleen of swine. A liquid culture from the blood showed the motile bacterium on the following day, and line cultures made therefrom revealed the same growth on plates as that from swine.

Guinea-pig No. 4 presented the same local as well as general lesions. The spleen was dark in spots and very friable. Vessels of the mesentery injected. The bacteria were as abundant in the organs as in No. 3. Cultures made as described for No. 3 proved identical with the latter.

These animals are as a rule more refractory than rabbits with reference to the virus of *rouget*, rabbit-septicæma, and a new pathogenic microbe described in a subsequent section of this report.

Microscopic examination of tissues of infected animals.—In sections of tissues from cases of hog-cholera, cut after being imbedded in pure paraffine, the bacteria stain very well in aniline water methyl-violet. The sections may be treated afterward with a $\frac{1}{2}$ per cent. solution acetic acid without removing the stain. Treated in this way and examined with a $\frac{1}{12}$ or $\frac{1}{18}$ homogeneous immersion the bacteria appear in plugs or clumps, never isolated. In the spleen such colonies are seen in the spleen pulp near the trabeculæ; in the kidney the plugs are rare even in the most hemorrhagic cases. In sections of the wall of the large intestine of a recent case in which there was much extravasation, the submucous tissue was infiltrated with red blood corpuscles, which had forced their way between the bundles of areolar tissue and among the fat cells. Occasionally masses of corpuscles were seen beneath the serosa. In a number of sections carefully examined no bacteria could be detected.

When we take into consideration the coagulation necrosis produced by this bacterium when injected beneath the skin in mice, pigeons, rabbits, and guinea-pigs, and its tendency to grow in plugs or colonies, the hemorrhagic effect is easily explained. The growth in the smaller blood vessels coming in contact with the walls destroys them and gives rise to extravasation. In the intestinal mucosa the extravasation may lead to a cutting off of the food supply and consequent necrosis and ulceration.

The liver of a mouse which had succumbed to hog-cholera, interspersed with whitish specks and patches of necrosed tissue, was examined in the same way. The section contained unstained areas corresponding to the patches of coagulation necrosis seen with the naked eye. These unstained areas are dotted with stained, shriveled nuclei and surrounded by a zone of leucocytes. The bacteria are found in small clumps both within and on the periphery of the unstained areas. They are also present in the capillaries of the surrounding tissues. In the larger vessels they are present, but scattered.

In the muscular wall of the abdomen of a guinea-pig invaded from the seat of inoculation on the thigh the bacteria had penetrated in immense numbers through the connective tissue surrounding the individual fibers and produced extensive extravasation, thereby forcing the bundles of fibers apart.

THE BACTERIUM OF HOG-CHOLERA IN OTHER OUTBREAKS.

In an outbreak of hog-cholera at Ivy City, D. C., several miles from the Experimental Station, the same lesions were found, coupled with the presence of the previously described bacterium, as shown by the following notes:

Pig No. 261.—Brought to the station a few hours after death. Considerable reddening of the skin of the limbs and over the pubic regions. Extravasations into the subcutaneous adipose tissue; considerable deeply stained serum in abdominal cavity; spleen very much enlarged and gorged with blood. Lymphatic glands in thorax and abdomen all deeply congested. Hemorrhagic foci in lungs. Mucous membrane of cæcum and upper colon almost black, the remainder deeply congested. Numerous small ulcers scattered over the mucosa of cæcum and colon. Besides these, there were, about 6 inches from the valve, two ulcers nearly 1¼ inches across, so deep as to produce an inflammatory adhesion between the serous surface of the intestinal wall and adjacent organs. The mucosa of the fundus of the stomach deeply congested; numerous small ulcers near pyloric region. The small intestine unaffected, if we except a few petechiæ. Both kidneys much swollen; glomeruli gorged with blood; also the pelvis and bladder. In the spleen the bactera of hog-cholera were very abundant, as shown by cover-glass preparations. Two liquid cultures therefrom were pure, as determined microscopically and on gelatine plates.

This case is interesting from two points of view. It demonstrates the identity of cause of two virtually independent centers of the disease. It also suggests a double infection; the first causing the few deep ulcers and probably only a very slight general infection; the second invading the entire body, producing rupture of the blood vessels by a necrosis of the vascular walls.

Another outbreak near the city of Washington presented the same features. The spleen of the animals which succumbed contained the bacteria of hog-cholera only.

The Bacterium of Hog-cholera in Nebraska Outbreaks.

Early in March of the present year (1886) Dr. W. H. Rose was sent to the West to collect material for the study of hog-cholera, in order that a comparison with the disease as it exists in the East might be made. Is the disease identical with that described in the Second Annual Report? If the cause can be proved the same, the diseases must necessarily be regarded as identical.

It was thought best to use the spleen, which has nearly always furnished pure cultures of the specific bacterium, and which, in the great majority of the cases, contains the bacteria in such numbers that they may be easily detected in cover-glass preparations. The spleen was removed from the body of pigs killed for that purpose and placed in a bottle plugged with cotton wool, which had been sterilized at 150° C. Spleen pulp was rubbed upon slides, dried, and sent with the bottles.

Ten animals were examined in all, about three from Kansas and the rest from three different places in Nebraska. From the notes sent there seemed to be little doubt that the lesions resembled those described in the preceding report very closely. As to the spleens, none of them arrived at the laboratory in good condition. Some of them were partially decomposed; others were covered with fungi and zoogloea of micrococci. Cover-glass preparations revealed a variety of forms, most of them large bacilli, some spore-bearing. In only one case did a bacterium resembling the microbe of hog-cholera appear amongst a number of other forms. We shall return to this case later on.

Of the slide preparations the dried films were searched in vain for the presence of the bacteria, indicating plainly the external origin of the putrefactive forms. Plate cultures were made in a few cases without any promising results. Mice were inoculated with bits from a number of the spleens by introducing them beneath the skin of the back. A few mice died, probably of malignant œdema, and the rest remained well.

In only one case was the result unexpectedly successful. This came from Tecumseh, Nebr., the spleen in which the bacterium seemed present in cover-glass preparations. Plate cultures and line cultures directly from spleen pulp were equally unsatisfactory, owing to the variety of germs present.

Two mice, Nos. 69 and 70, inoculated with bits of spleen tissue, furnished a key to the problem. Both were inoculated March 23; one died March 30, the other April 1. In No. 69 there was a very large quantity of serum in the subcutaneous tissue of the skin about the abdomen and in the abdominal cavity. The liver, especially along its border, was dotted with small patches of coagulation necrosis. A cover-glass preparation of spleen and liver negative. The culture from the effusion contained several forms of bacteria, as might have been expected. A liquid culture of the blood seemed a pure culture of a *motile oval bacterium*, resembling closely the bacterium of hog-cholera. In No. 70 the lesions were more nearly identical with those observed after inoculating mice with the bacterium found in the East. The lymphatics of the knee fold and the spleen were very much enlarged; the liver contained small patches of coagulation necrosis; lungs and kidneys congested. Bacteria, not to be distinguished from those of hog-cholera, were found abundantly in spleen, liver, and heart's blood; in small number in lungs and kidney. The liquid culture was identical with that from No. 69. A tube culture in gelatine and line cultures from the liquid cultures failed to grow for reasons discovered later on.

In order to determine whether the bacterium obtained from these mice was pathogenic or not, four mice were inoculated April 6, Nos. 75 and 76, from the culture of No. 69, 77, and 78 from the culture of mouse 70, each receiving from 5 to 10 drops of the culture liquid. April 12 all four mice were found dead. In No. 76 there were signs of commencing necrosis in the liver. There were no marked lesions observed excepting a variable enlargement of the glands in the knee fold. In the liver and spleen of every animal the oval bacteria, with pale center, were present in large numbers. As these had succumbed in less than six days, the most characteristic lesions, great enlargement of the spleen and coagulation necrosis in the liver, were absent. These changes were invariably produced with the hog-cholera bacterium first described when very minute quantities were inoculated, by which the period of disease was prolonged for nearly two weeks from the date of inoculation. April 20, Nos. 84 and 85 were inoculated with 5 drops of a culture derived from mouse No. 78. No. 84 died in two days, and No. 85 died in six after inoculation. In both the characteristic bacteria were present in spleen and liver. At the same time Nos. 82 and 83 were inoculated from the culture obtained from the blood of mouse No. 77. No. 82 died two days after, and No. 83 seven days after, inoculation. In the latter case the longer time had allowed the formation of coagulation necrosis in liver and great enlargement of the spleen.

This new microbe, identical morphologically with the bacterium of hog-cholera already described, produces a disease in mice which is practically the same as that produced by the latter microbe.

The effect of these two bacteria is the same on rabbits. May 22 a young rabbit received subcutaneously an equivalent of $.001^{cc}$ of the eleventh culture (mouse) four days old. No symptoms of disease appeared until June 5, fourteen days after inoculation. It was then very quiet, refusing to move and breathing with some effort. On the following day it was found dead. The autopsy revealed the following lesions:

At the place of inoculation was found a yellowish-white mass resting on the muscular tissue and covering an area about 2^{cm} in diameter. This mass, consisting of necrosed tissue, did not crumble readily between the forceps. The superficial veins in the vicinity were dark and distended with blood. On the contiguous abdominal wall there was a patch about 2^{cm} in diameter closely studded with small extravasations. These were found isolated as far as the lowest ribs on the same side. In the abdominal cavity there was a small quantity of stained serum. The intestines and bladder were lightly glued to each other and to the abdominal walls. The spleen but slightly augmented in size. The liver studded with minute isolated whitish points of coagulation necrosis. Lungs mottled with a bright red throughout. In the spleen and liver the bacteria inoculated were abundant. A culture in nutritive gelatine from the liver grew precisely like former cultures. Two cultures in beef-infusion peptone were turbid on the following day, and had a complete membrane.* Both were pure cultures of the motile bacterium inoculated.

A young rabbit inoculated May 28 with a comparatively large quantity ($\frac{1}{8}^{cc}$) of the thirteenth culture (mouse) was found dead June 3. The local and general lesions were the same as those above detailed. The bacteria were present in considerable numbers in spleen and liver.

In liquid cultures from blood of heart and liver the motile bacterium only was found, forming a surface membrane. Cultures in gelatine were equally satisfactory. The lesions produced by this bacterium resembled those produced heretofore by the bacterium discovered in the East very closely. The spleen, however, was not markedly enlarged.

Effect on pigeons.—Two young pigeons were inoculated April 23, beneath the skin over the pectorals, each with $.6^{cc}$ of a culture from a mouse. They appeared unaffected until April 27, when the feathers became ruffled and the birds moved about with difficulty. They became worse, exhibiting the usual appearances of pigeons inoculated with the hog-cholera bacterium; feathers much ruffled, so as to give the birds a puffed appearance, tail feathers drooping, head drawn in and depressed. Discharges of a mucous character. One was found dead April 30, the other died in the course of the same day. In both the pectorals presented the parboiled appearance due to the local effect of the culture and previously described. In one bird the bacteria were abundant in the liver, few in the spleen; in the other there were but a few in both organs. Finally, liquid as well as tube cultures in gelatine were successful in containing the bacterium inoculated. Another pigeon inoculated at the same time, which had been fed with spleen unsuccessfully some weeks previously, did not become sick. After two weeks it was killed, and in each pectoral an elongated sequestrum was found surrounded by a membrane and evidently in process of absorption. Another pigeon previously vaccinated and inoculated with the bacterium of the East, and now inoculated with this bacterium from Nebraska, remained perfectly well. Two other pigeons were inoculated April 24, for the sake of comparison, one with $\frac{3}{4}^{cc}$ of a liquid culture of the Eastern, and the other with the Western variety. Both pigeons exhibited the characteristic symptoms above described. The former died April 30; the latter recovered. When killed later

*This bacterium differs from the one described in forming a surface membrane on liquids.

only a small sequestrum was found at the seat of inoculation. In the former, bacteria were found in spleen and liver. A tube culture in gelatine from liver and a liquid culture from blood of heart were both cultures of the Eastern germ. The bacterium failed to show any pathogenic effects when injected beneath the skin of two guinea-pigs. The same culture which was promptly fatal to a rabbit had no effect whatever on a guinea-pig inoculated at the same time.

Whether we are here confronted by a very slight attenuation or weakening of the virus with reference to guinea-pigs, due to prolonged cultivation in artificial media, with an occasional rejuvenation by its passage through a susceptible animal, or whether the difference in activity between it and the bacterium from Eastern outbreaks of the disease is in reality due to a permanent physiological difference, remains to be determined by additional experiments.

In order to determine the effect of inoculation upon pigs at the Experimental Station, bits of two spleens from Nebraska were introduced beneath the skin of each thigh and the remainder fed to the same animals on March 16. A slight swelling at the place of inoculation soon subsided. As no results followed, the same animal was fed April 28 with portions of the spleen of four or five pigs which had died of hog-cholera at the Station. It was found dead May 4. Without giving the autopsy notes in detail, it is sufficient to state that among other lesions the large intestine and ileum were more or less ulcerated.

May 12, two pigs (Nos. 234 and 237), were inoculated each with about 3½^{cc} of a seventh culture obtained originally from a mouse. One-half was injected beneath the skin of each thigh. There being no indications of any disease after this inoculation, No. 237 was fed July 10 with portions of viscera from cases of hog-cholera, and was found dead July 15. No. 234 was fed July 25, and died from the effects August 8. No. 219 received May 28 10^{cc} of a liquid beef-infusion peptone culture, one-half into each thigh. At both places a small tumor developed, which did not disappear. This animal seemed unaffected by the inoculation, and was fed, together with No. 237, July 10. Both died on the same day. In both animals there was considerable superficial necrosis in the cæcum and colon, and complete necrosis of the mucosa of the major portion of the ileum. In No. 219 there was an encysted mass about the size of a marble in the subcutaneous connective tissue at the place of inoculation, freely movable. On section a grayish-white cheesy mass, partially converted into a liquid in the interior, could be easily peeled out of a capsule, the inner surface of which was considerably reddened. In Nos. 237 and 219 the spleen contained the bacterium of hog-cholera, as determined by cover-glass preparations. No. 234 was not examined. The subcutaneous inoculations having proved unsuccessful thus far, a pig was fed June 4 with the viscera of a rabbit which had died from the inoculation, and the organs of which contained the bacterium in abundance. June 9 a second rabbit was fed to the same pig. July 20, one month and a half later, the animal being apparently in good condition, it was fed with the viscera of a pig which had died of hog-cholera at the station. After some days of marked debility it was found dead August 9. It presented the lesions consequent upon a general systemic invasion of the virus, greatly augmented spleen, deeply congested lymphatic system, hemorrhagic foci in lungs, and extensive necrosis of cæcum and upper colon.

The negative results of these few experiments must not incline us to reject the conclusion that the microbe under consideration was actually the cause of this outbreak of swine disease in Nebraska. When we remember how closely it resembles in its culture reaction and its pathogenic effect upon smaller animals the bacterium which was demonstrated to be the cause of the disease as observed for over a year at the Experimental Station, the evidence from the standpoint of to-day becomes too strong to be set aside. We must also remember that the culture was obtained early in March, and was kept for inoculation experiments without re-enforcement from any fresh cases of disease for several months, and that the disease is only exceptionably produced by subcutaneous inoculation. Our information concerning the attenuation of this virus under cultivation is very meager, although it is highly probable that any microbe adapted to a parasitic existence will suffer by artificial cultivation.

In order to determine whether the disease could be produced by feeding the bacterium from Nebraska in liquid cultures, two pigs (Nos. 383 and 384) were fed, each with about 250^{cc} of a beef-infusion culture after being starved for over twenty-four hours. No. 383 received previous to the ingestion of the culture liquid about 1 liter of beef broth to which 1 per cent. sodium carbonate had been added. The feeding took place on the evening of December 19, 1886. On the following evening No. 384 was dull; on the next day it did not eat, was dull, and its bowels relaxed. It continued in this way, with poor appetite and manifesting general debility, until the ninth day, when it was killed for examination, which gave the following facts:

Stomach rather pale; the mucous membrane of small intestine much reddened. The mucosa of large intestine, from cæcum to rectum, very dark red in large patches, resembling in some places punctiform and diffuse extravasations. A few whitish diphtheritic patches in the cæcum; no ulceration. On section of kidneys a moderate number of punctiform extravasations were found limited to the basal portion of the pyramids. Beneath the pleura the surfaces of both lungs were covered with pale red spots not larger than a pin's head. On section they could also be seen. Other organs not changed. Six liquid cultures from blood and spleen remained sterile. In this case the local lesions were very mild compared with those produced by the bacterium from Illinois and the East. In order to determine whether the bacteria themselves, which had been cultivated for nearly nine months, had lost their virulence for rabbits, a black rabbit received hypodermically into the thigh $\frac{1}{4}^{cc}$ of a culture in beef-infusion peptone one day old. The culture liquid was covered by the usual membrane characteristic of this variety.

The rabbit died January 4, 1887, five days after inoculation. The germ, therefore, was still as virulent as ever for rabbits. At the point of inoculation the blood vessels of the connective tissue and delicate fascia covering the muscles on the inner aspect of the thigh were injected and tortuous. There was no extravasation, however, and on careful inspection what appeared to be so was resolved into arborescent injections of very minute vessels. The fascia was but slightly thickened. The muscular tissue covered by it had a whitish aspect, and when cut into it was found necrosed for a depth of several millimeters and over an area of 3 or 4 square centimeters. The neighboring lymphatic of the knee-fold was enlarged and infiltrated with blood throughout. Spleen enlarged three to four times, blackish, friable. Medulla of kidneys very deeply reddened, also inner portion of cortex. Liver shows six or seven large patches of a yellowish cast, representing regions of commencing coagulation necrosis. A large number of ecchymoses of the size of a pin's head on gall-bladder; on mucous surface the membrane is blackish. Similar extravasations beneath the mucosa of the rectum for a distance of 5^{cm}, and extending upon mesorectum; one of these is a projecting hæmatoma. Caudal and cephalic regions of both lungs dark red, airless. Beneath the pleura of these regions are still darker spots or ecchymoses. The pleura covering the remainder of both lungs is dotted here and there with dark spots, varying in size from a pin's head to 10^{mm} diameter. The characteristic bacteria very numerous in spleen, less so in liver; few in blood from the heart.

A gelatine and liquid tube culture were made from the spleen and liver, and a liquid culture from heart's blood. In the tube the tracks of the needle were soon covered with colonies. In the liquid cultures only the motile hog-cholera bacteria were found. In two days every tube had a complete membrane, which became slightly thicker a few days later.

From the liquid culture prepared from the spleen one day old a large white rabbit received hypodermically into the thigh .05^{cc}. The culture was diluted in sterile beef broth and $\frac{1}{4}^{cc}$ containing the above amount of culture liquid was injected. The rabbit seemed well and active until it was found dead on the eighth day after inoculation. The local lesion involved only the subcutaneous tissue, in which there were ecchymoses and greatly enlarged vessels. At the place where the virus had been deposited a small nodule had formed, consisting of a whitish, pasty mass. The lymphatic of the knee fold near by was enlarged, with dark red cortex. The internal organs, markedly changed as usual, were the spleen, liver, and lungs. The spleen was many times enlarged, dark, friable, crowded with bacteria. The liver was similarly enlarged. On its caudal surface there was a diffuse discoloration, which, on closer examination, was proved to be coagulation necrosis. It had invaded the acini from the portal system, leaving the central portion still intact (Plate VI, Fig. 2). On the cephalic aspect this network of necrosis was replaced by larger solid yellowish white masses. In two places near the border of the liver the necrosis involved five to six contiguous acini, converting them into pale hyaline cylinders. The entire parenchyma was thus more or less changed, as shown on section. The bacteria injected were very numerous in this organ. The lungs were generally emphysematous. The margins were dark red, with darker points, probably hemorrhagic. On section these were found throughout the lung tissue for $\frac{1}{2}^{cm}$ from the border. Bacteria in moderate numbers. Two liquid cultures from spleen and liver contained on the following day the injected bacteria, with the membrane beginning to form.

The disease caused by this germ in its duration, symptoms, and lesions, in rabbits and mice, cannot be distinguished from that caused by the bacterium of Eastern hog-cholera. It is, moreover, entirely different from rabbit septicæmia,* in which no great enlargement of the spleen, no coagulation necrosis in liver, nor inflammation of lungs is present.

Pig No. 384, fed with No. 383, was dull on the following day, with relaxed bowels. It remained more or less unthrifty for several weeks after feeding.

Thus far the feeding experiments had not been conclusive, and a final attempt was made, which proved successful.

A flask containing between 500^{cc} and 600^{cc} of sterile beef infusion was inoculated from a culture (rabbit), and after standing six days in the incubator the entire amount was given to a pig which had not been fed for thirty-six hours. The culture liquid was covered with a thin membrane, and on microscopic examination contained only the motile bacterium. The animal became dull and weak, eating little. The bowels were loose on the fourth day. On the fifth it was unable to rise, and on the sixth it was found dead. The autopsy notes are briefly as follows:

In abdominal cavity several hundred cubic centimeters of a reddish serum, a thin translucent exudate covering the peritoneum of the intestine, which is diffusely reddened. Between the layers of the mesentery, along the line of attachment to small intestine, an abundant translucent gelatinous exudate. Spleen very dark on section; the surface dotted with elevated points of extravasated blood. Liver congested. Lungs normal with exception of a few lobules, which are simply collapsed.

Almost the entire digestive tract was found involved. Around the cardiac orifice a zone of mucous membrane about two inches in width was covered with whitish diphtheritic patches. Isolated ulcers in duodenum. About 6 or 7 feet of the lower portion of the small intestine very much thickened, the mucous membrane covered with a thin sheet of necrosed tissue, whitish, brittle. The cæcum and portion of the colon greatly thickened, and covered with a thick layer of necrosed tissue very rough and brownish. Near rectum necrosis gives way to closely set, isolated, roundish diphtheritic elevations of a whitish color, which leave a raw surface when scraped away.

These lesions were therefore as intense as any produced by feeding pure cultures of hog-cholera bacteria obtained from the East. The

* Journ. Comp. Medicine and Surgery, VIII (1887), p. 24.

identity of the two bacteria from Nebraska and the East was thus completely established.

In the liver and spleen the bacteria were few, for a cover-glass preparation from each organ did not show any after some searching. Liquid cultures from the blood (heart), spleen, and liver were turbid on the following day, and all contained the motile oval bacterium. Within four days complete membranes had formed on the surface. The differential character of the bacterium had not changed, therefore, in passing through the organism of the pig. That the bacteria were very few in blood from the heart was indicated by a gelatine tube which had been inoculated several times with a platinum wire dipped in blood; no colonies were visible on the fourth day. Of three liquid cultures, each inoculated with a loop of blood, two remained sterile. It was presumed that the liver would contain the largest number, inasmuch as the portal circulation received its blood from the seat of the disease. This assumption was confirmed by the very abundant colonies surrounding a piece of liver tissue which had been dropped into a tube of nutrient gelatine.

In order to make certain of the pathogenic powers of the cultures obtained from this case of feeding the tube culture from the liver was used to infect two rabbits. The skin on the inner aspect of one thigh was carefully shorn and disinfected with .1 per cent. corrosive sublimate. An incision was made through the skin, and with a loop dipped in the surface growth of the culture a minute quantity was introduced into this pocket. The larger of the two rabbits was found dead on the fifth day. The lesions were briefly as follows:

Slight amount of pus at the place of inoculation. Neighboring inguinal glands enlarged and infiltrated with blood throughout. Surrounding vessels much injected and very tortuous. Liver very friable, spleen dark and enlarged; both dotted with points and stellate spots of coagulation necrosis, especially numerous on the caudal surface of the liver. Both organs contained the bacteria of hog-cholera in large numbers. Lungs deeply congested, perhaps hypostatic. A small number of ecchymoses beneath pleura; very few bacteria in kidneys and heart's blood.

The second rabbit was found dead on the sixth day. The lesions were the same, if we except the more pronounced coagulation necrosis in the liver (Plate VI, Fig. 1) and its absence in the spleen. The bacteria of hog-cholera were distributd as above; very abundant in spleen and liver; lungs normal.

Gelatine-tube cultures from spleen and liver of these rabbits confirmed the microscopic examination. Liquid cultures from the blood contained the motile bacteria, which had formed a brittle surface membrane on the second day.

Differential characters of the hog-cholera bacterium from Nebraska.—The bacterium, when stained on cover-glass preparations from the spleen and other viscera, closely resembles the one found in the disease prevalent in the East, so that it is impossible to distinguish them in this way. Both stain well in an aqueous solution of methyl-violet in from two to five minutes, and show a well-stained narrow periphery around a pale center. This may be due to the presence of a dense envelope obstructing the inward movement of the coloring matter. In the last report an opinion was expressed that it might suggest the presence of an endogenous spore, but that the other evidence did not seem to warrant such a view. The experiments of the present year have not changed these views. The illustrations given in the last report apply equally well to the microbe from Nebraska.

A few minor differences revealed in the various culture media indicated that the two microbes were not alike in every way, and brought up the very interesting question of the variation of species of bacteria and the influence of such variation on the severity of epidemics.

The first difference was observed in liquid cultures. Within twenty-four hours after inoculation from the spleen or blood the culture liquid became turbid, and upon its surface a complete membrane was present in nearly every case. This whitish membrane is not homogeneous, but made up of patches of varying thickness, and when shaken, slowly settles to the bottom in lumps and flocculi. The microbe of Eastern outbreaks does not form a membrane within several days after inoculation, and then only when the tube remains perfectly quiet. It appears as a whitish ring attached to the glass, and is rarely found covering the entire surface. When a number of successive inoculations are made a week apart the later cultures are quite apt to form membranes after a few days' standing. Thus one microbe forms a membrane very speedily; the other only occasionally, and then quite tardily.

In these liquid cultures both exhibit, during three or four days after inoculation, *very active spontaneous movements.* Sometimes masses of five to ten bacteria may be seen moving actively to and fro and at the same time revolving about themselves.

In the same culture liquid the microbe from Nebraska seemed to grow more vigorously, so that at the end of two or three days the liquid became turbid, and the deposit in the bottom of the tube was very abundant after one or two weeks.

Both fail to liquefy gelatine. A very slight but significant difference was observed in this medium also. It was found that when line cultures were made on plates of gelatine, in order to test the purity of liquid cultures, the microbe from Nebraska failed to develop, while the microbe from the East invariably grew as described in the preceding report. This observation was made so uniformly with every culture that it became later a means of distinguishing the two forms when the cause of this behavior became known. Such lines, after a few days, appeared as an aggregation of mere points under a 1-inch objective, and did not enlarge, or else there was no indication of any growth whatever.

Later, another quantity of nutrient gelatine was prepared, which, on boiling, threw down a very fine precipitate, uniformly clouding the gelatine. A few drops of acetic acid added to it when liquefied by heat dissolved the precipitate completely. It seemed probable that the precipitate was some alkaline phosphate or carbonate, and in fact the reaction with litmus paper was more alkaline than with the gelatine previously used. In this medium the bacterium from Nebraska grew very well both on plates and in tubes, and the bacterium from the East grew much better than in the previous preparation of gelatine, thus showing that an alkaline medium is best for the bacterium of hog-cholera, and that the Nebraska variety is by far the more sensitive, and fails to multiply unless the reaction is fairly alkaline. On gelatine plates the colonies are somewhat darker and more coarsely granular when viewed by transmitted light than those which develop from the Eastern variety.

On the surface of beef-infusion peptone agar-agar made slightly alkaline with potassium carbonate both bacteria grow very vigorously when kept in the incubator at 95° to 100° F. On potato both grow as a dirty straw-colored layer at the ordinary temperature, so as not to be distinguishable. (Plate V, Fig. 3.)

From the comparative plate cultures and from potato cultures both bacteria, when inoculated into liquid media, showed the characteristic difference already mentioned. On the following day one culture would be covered with a membrane, the other not. In milk both multiply without producing any macroscopic change.

This bacterium is likewise killed by a temperature of 58° C., as the following experiment shows: Five tubes containing sterile beef-infusion were inoculated from a liquid culture ten days old, obtained from a mouse. Four of these were placed in a water bath at a temperature of 58° C., and retained there for fifteen, twenty, twenty-five, and thirty minutes respectively. These, with the check-tube, were placed in the incubator. Next morning the check-tube was turbid and the liquid capped by the characteristic membrane, consisting of the oval bacterium. The four heated tubes remained permanently clear.

Hog-cholera in Illinois caused by the same bacterium.

A herd was found September, 1886, a few miles southwest of Sodorus, Champaign County, Illinois, in which a number of animals had already perished from what was supposed to be hog-cholera. The disease had existed for months, and the affected animals usually lingered for several weeks.

Two pigs about four months old were chosen from this lot, which were so weak as to be scarcely able to stand or move about, and killed by a blow on the head. Owing to the disadvantages of the situation no thorough autopsy could be made. In what we shall denominate No. 1 the superficial inguinal glands were very much enlarged, purplish. In the thorax the caudal portion of both lungs was completely solidified. On section the hepatization had a variegated pale red appearance. The smaller bronchi were plugged with a white tenacious mass. A few bands loosely attached the lungs to the costal pleura. In the abdominal cavity the various organs seemed of normal size and color. The large intestines were filled with dry hard fecal masses. On opening them about four or five ulcers, ½ inch across, were found in the cæcal portion; the mucous membrane itself was pale, with a few specimens of *trichocephalus* attached to it. The stomach was empty, the mucosa pale, and pyloric region bile-stained.

In No. 2 the lungs were in the same condition, the pleurisy slightly more marked. In the abdomen the spleen was four or five times the normal size, very soft, and gorged with dark blood. In the small intestines lesions caused by *echinorhynchi* were present. In the intestine, which was empty, the only lesion noticeable was a patch of ulceration involving the mucous crypts at the base of the ileo-cæcal valve. Stomach as in No. 1.

The major portion of the spleen of No. 1 was removed with sterile instruments and transferred to a sterile bottle plugged with cotton wool. Within four or five hours bits of this spleen were carefully excised after thoroughly scorching the surface with a heated platinum spatula, and placed in tubes containing nutrient gelatine. Cover-glass preparations gave negative evidence as regards the presence of bacteria. Within two days minute whitish points could be seen in the depths of the gelatine. The hot weather had liquefied the gelatine and allowed the bit of spleen to sink into it. Small surface patches of a very gelatinous appearance were also present. On returning to the laboratory at Washington the colonies in the four gelatine tubes thus prepared were found to be made up of the oval motile bacterium of hog-cholera, identical with the bacterium described in the preceding report microscopically and in its growth in gelatine and other culture media. There was not even a single differential character by which this germ might be distinguished from the one demonstrated to be the cause of hog-cholera last year.

In order to test its pathogenic effect on small animals and to make comparisons a number of animals were inoculated simultaneously from the same liquid culture. This was obtained as follows: One of the original gelatine tube cultures was used as the starting-point and from it a liquid culture inoculated. On the following day a gelatine-plate culture was prepared from this, and when the colonies had de-developed sufficiently a tube of beef-infusion peptone was inoculated from one of them. In this way a liquid culture was obtained from the progeny of a single germ, although the preceding cultures had been found pure.

Three days later (October 4) the following inoculations were made: Two mice, $\frac{1}{2}^{cc}$ each; 1 guinea-pig, $\frac{1}{8}^{cc}$; 1 pigeon, $\frac{1}{8}^{cc}$; 2 rabbits, $\frac{1}{4}$ and $\frac{3}{16}$ respectively; and 2 pigs, 5^{cc} and 3.5^{cc}. Of these animals the pigeons, the guinea-pig, and the pigs remained well. One of the mice escaped several days after inoculation; the other remained apparently well until October 18, two weeks after inoculation, when it was found dead. This long period of incubation and sudden death were characteristic of hog-cholera. An examination confirmed the nature of the disease. The spleen was enormously enlarged with a mottled grayish and bright-red surface. The liver very large, dark red, and dotted with minute whitish points of coagulation necrosis, found so uniformily in inoculated mice last year. Both liver and spleen contained the oval bacterium in large numbers. The lungs were deeply congested.

Both rabbits succumbed on the seventh day, about eight hours apart. The lesions were also the same as those observed heretofore. In No. 1, at the place of inoculation, there was a small area about $\frac{1}{4}$ inch in diameter over which the fascia covering the muscles was infiltrated and thickened. There was no peritonitis, but the fat about the kidneys contained patches of injected capillaries. The spleen was very much tumefied, its dimensions being 6^{cm}, 1^{cm}, $\frac{1}{4}^{cm}$. It was very soft and dark. The liver was large; rather pale. On its surface were scattered whitish points and patches of coagulation necrosis, most numerous about the portal fissure. Kidneys but slightly reddened. The lungs were deeply congested; the pleural surfaces were mottled everywhere with blood-red points and patches. The stomach was normal. In the duodenum, at the pylorus, a band of hemorrhagic deposit encircled the tube. For $\frac{1}{4}$ inch farther the mucosa was covered with petechiæ.

In the spleen, liver, lung, and kidney the bacteria of hog-cholera were very abundant; in blood from the heart quite scarce. Cultures in nutrient liquids from liver and blood proved pure. The movements of the bacteria were exceedingly active when examined in a drop suspended from a cover-glass. The tube cultures in gelatine from the spleen and liver contained the same bacterium.

In the second rabbit *rigor mortis* was marked an hour after death. Locally a thick pasty infiltration had formed in the subcutaneous connective tissue, surrounded by injected vessels. The spleen, liver, lungs, and kidneys presented precisely the same lesions as were found in the first rabbit. There was a slight amount of serum in peritoneal cavity, not containing bacteria, as a tube of beef infusion inoculated from it remained sterile. The extravasation at pylorus was limited to a small patch. There was, however, a circumscribed area on serosa of large intestine covered with petechiæ. The bacteria were abundant in spleen and liver; absent in cover-glass preparations of kidney, lung, blood, and peritoneal fluid. A liquid culture of blood contained the motile bacterium only. Tube cultures in gelatine inoculated from the spleen and the liver also proved pure.

These autopsies, the microscopic examination of the organs, and more especially the invariably pure cultures from each animal, confirmed the supposition that the microbe obtained in Illinois was the same as the one causing hog-cholera in the East. The fact that neither pigs nor pigeons nor guinea-pigs died does not in the least weaken this conclusion. The experiments on preventive inoculation show clearly that large doses of liquid cultures can be borne with impunity by the majority of swine when introduced beneath the skin. The microbe may have been of a less virulent variety than the one with which inoculations were made last year. On the other hand, a most virulent case of hog-cholera was produced by feeding pure cultures, as the following notes will show:

A pig was kept without food for over twenty-four hours. A 2½ per cent. solution of sodium carbonate in meat broth was then given to it. Of this it consumed about one liter, taking thus about 25 grams of the salt. It was then fed with about 50^{cc} of gelatine cultures and 100^{cc} of liquid cultures of the hog-cholera bacterium obtained from rabbits which had succumbed to inoculation; one was obtained from the original gelatine culture of the spleen made in Champaign County, Illinois. The animal was found dead December 4, scarcely three days after feeding. This was the briefest period of illness thus far observed. The lesions were very pronounced. Pyramids of kidneys deep red throughout; glomeruli visible as dark points. Lungs pale, not fully collapsed. Right heart filled with semi-coagulated blood. Liver gorged with blood. Mucosa of stomach intensely reddened, especially along fundus, and covered with a thick layer of tenacious mucus. Mucous membrane of ileum similarly affected. Peyer's patches exceedingly dark red, showing through serous coat. The elevated border gives each a slightly concave boat-shaped appearance. The colon also deeply congested, almost hemorrhagic in patches, filled with a small quantity of semi-liquid feces. The rectum still filled with consistent masses. The mesenteric glands congested.

The feeding had thus produced a very severe inflammation of the digestive tract, so severe, in fact, that the animal died before the ulceration or necrosis had begun. The diagnosis was further confirmed by obtaining pure liquid cultures from the spleen, the liver, and blood from the heart. The bacteria were not sufficiently numerous in these organs to be detected by the microscope. To make sure that the carbonate of soda had no corrosive effect another animal was treated precisely in the same way by starving and feeding a solution of the salt. No ill effects whatever were manifested.

In order to test the specific pathogenic character of the bacterium obtained from this animal a large rabbit was inoculated subcutaneously with about ⅛^{cc} of a liquid culture from the blood. On the sixth day the rabbit was lying on its side; abdominal breathing very labored. It was found dead on the next day. Slight thickening of the subcutaneous tissue and fascia covering the thigh muscles at the point of inoculation. The muscular tissue covered with minute ecchymoses around the infiltrated patch. Small quantity of serum in the peritoneal cavity. Spleen very large, blackish, exceedingly friable, and crowded with bacteria. Liver enlarged; interlobular tissue pale; the entire parenchyma very soft and brittle. Dotting both surfaces of all the lobes are small grayish-white patches, involving one, two, or three, rarely more, acini, and bounded very sharply by the acini themselves. Peculiar figures are thus formed, three contiguous ones giving the patch a clover-leaf appearance. On section they are found to extend to the depth of one or several acini into the parenchyma. The great majority of these masses of coagulation necrosis involve lobules on or near the surface. Only a few are in the depths of the organ. When such a whitish mass is spread on a cover-glass and stained innumerable bacteria of hog-cholera make their appearance. The rest of the tissue is likewise crowded with them. Beneath the pulmonary pleura are large purplish patches of extravasation, which on section extend deeply into the parenchyma. The lung tissue is in general congested. Blood from the heart contained very few bacteria. No cultures were made.

A pipette filled with heart's blood from pig No. 1 (Sodorus, Ill.), as described in the first annual report, and sealed, was opened about three weeks later. Want of time had prevented earlier examination. Two liquid cultures were inoculated from the contents of the pipette, which were dark and firmly clotted, without any odor whatever. On the following day both were clouded, and contained the motile bacterium of hog-cholera growing on gelatine in the same manner. One of the cultures contained in addition a streptococcus, which was eliminated by making plate cultures and inoculating fresh tubes from a single colony. A second pipette furnished a pure culture of another pathogenic microbe, probably the cause of the lung disease. This will be described in detail farther on.

From the spleen of No. 2 cultures were made as above. Small pieces were dropped into tubes of gelatine with the usual precaution. One tube remained permanently sterile. In two others liquefaction began after several days. A rather large bacillus was found in both tubes, in one associated with a microbe to be described later. Pieces of the spleen from the culture containing this bacillus alone were placed beneath the skin of two mice. Both remained well. This bacillus, therefore, had no pathogenic effect upon these animals. It was probably a germ accidentally present in the spleen during life rather than a contamination of the cultures. No further attention was paid to it.

The bacterium of hog-cholera was not therefore obtained from the spleen of No. 2. Nor was it present in a pipette of blood obtained from the heart. The autopsy notes will indicate that the intestinal lesions were limited to a single patch of ulceration at the base of the valve. Whether this was due to hog-cholera cannot be said. Nevertheless the absence of the bacterium of hog-cholera from the internal organs in chronic cases, or its great scarcity, has been a matter of common observation in our investigations of this disease. The disease is in fact over, and only the lesions remain. It resembles in this respect typhoid fever in man.

The presence of another microbe in this animal, however, even more virulent in its effects upon animals than the bacterium of hog-cholera, gives it a peculiar interest, as indicating the existence of two totally distinct diseases in the same herd and even in the same animal.

To illustrate the negative results often obtained in this disease it seems advisable to give the *post mortem* notes of another case of genuine hog-cholera observed at a place but a few miles from the herd from which Nos. 1 and 2 were taken. In this herd the animals were slowly dying of a chronic malady lasting weeks. None of those alive seemed very ill excepting one, which, when incited to run, would move a short distance and then lie down. Yet when an attempt was made to catch it it showed considerable strength, scarcely warranted by the extensive lesions found at the autopsy. It was killed by a few blows on the head. The following facts were noted down:

The superficial inguinal glands very large and of a pale red. In the peritoneal and pericardial cavity a small quantity of serum; blood clots readily; lungs normal. In the cæcum the mucous membrane is converted into a continuous yellowish necrotic layer. The remaining portion of the large intestine, containing but little food, is studded with isolated ulcers from 1^{cm} to 2^{cm} ($\frac{1}{2}$ to $\frac{1}{4}$ inch) across, showing on the surface concentric brownish and yellowish rings. These ulcers are visible as opaque whitish patches under the serous coat, which are surrounded by zone of newly formed injected vessels. The ulceration, being thus deep, indicated a disease of some weeks' duration. These lesions accorded very well with those observed at the Experimental Station.

The spleen, which was preserved in a sterilized bottle, contained no germs visible on cover-glass preparations. A pipette of blood was sterile, neither liquid nor solid cultures manifesting any growth after inoculation. Of about six tubes of gelatine, each containing a bit of spleen tissue, all but two remained permanently sterile. One of these contained a feebly growing motile bacillus, harmless to both mice and rabbits. The other contained a liquefying microbe not further examined.

EXPERIMENTS DIRECTED TOWARDS PRODUCING IMMUNITY.

On page 219 of the Second Annual Report of the Bureau of Animal Industry an account is given of an experiment demonstrating the very important fact that pigeons may be made insusceptible to the strong virus of hog-cholera by the subcutaneous injection of liquid in which the bacteria had multiplied and had afterwards been destroyed by heat.

In order to confirm the remarkable result there obtained a second experiment was tried in the same way. Three pigeons were inoculated at three different intervals indicated in the table below with 1^{cc} of heated culture liquid in which the bacterium of hog-cholera had been multiplying for sixteen, eleven, and fouteen days, respectively. Three additional pigeons received only two doses from cultures sixteen and fourteen days old, respectively. The culture liquid used was beef infusion containing 1 per cent. peptone. The tubes described in the First Annual Report of the Bureau were used unless otherwise stated. The liquid was injected beneath the skin covering the pectorals on both sides of the keel. Three pigeons were reserved as a check upon the experiment. All heated cultures used were tested by inoculating fresh tubes, which remained invariably sterile. Six days after the last inoculation with heated virus the nine pigeons were inoculated each with ¼^{cc} of the eighth culture, two days old, from the spleen of pig No. 156. On the following day two of the three check pigeons were found dead. The rest were apparently undisturbed. The third check pigeon, which was not affected by the inoculation, differed from the rest of the pigeons in having a differently shaped trunk, a long curved beak, large ruffled masses over the nostrils, and nearly invisible iris. It was snow white. It was supposed to have some of the characters of the carrier pigeon. Leaving this bird out of account, this experiment was as conclusive as the preceding in demonstrating the protective power of devitalized cultures.

In the two dead pigeons the pectorals presented a parboiled appearance over an area about 2^{cm} by 3^{cm} (1 by 1½ inches). On section the discoloration extended into the muscular tissue for from ¼ to ½ inch. Nothing characteristic in the internal organs. In both the œsophagus was filled as far as the pharynx with regurgitated food. This phenomenon had been observed in former cases.

Number of pigeon.	February 19, inoculation with heated virus.	February 24, inoculation with heated virus.	March 2, inoculation with heated virus.	Total.	March 8, inoculation with strong virus.	Remarks.
	cc.	cc.	cc.	cc.	cc.	
16	1	1	½	2½	¼	Well for several weeks after.
17	1	1	1	3	¼	Do.
18	1	1	1	3	¼	Do.
19	1	....	1	2	¼	Do.
20	1	....	1	2	¼	Do.
21	1	....	1	2	¼	Do.
22	....	....	....	....	¼	Dead March 9.
23	....	....	....	....	¼	Do.
24	....	....	....	....	¼	Well.

Since the product formed during the growth of the bacteria is not destroyed by the heat necessary to destroy the life of the bacteria themselves, it became necessary to determine whether the evaporation of the culture liquid in a water bath at the temperature of boiling water would destroy this product.

Recent investigations point to an alkaloid or ptomaine resulting from the multiplication of bacteria in liquids. It seemed advisable, therefore, to determine whether the substance producing immunity in pigeons was related to or identical with the ptomaines thus far examined. If the boiling temperature destroyed the power of producing immunity, the substance possessing this property must either be easily volatile or decomposed at this temperature. The cultures used were renewed from day to day, so that the seventh culture would indicate that the seventh tube had been inoculated from the sixth, and that the original culture from the spleen of the animal was not more than seven or eight days older than the seventh.

In the following experiment two pigeons received two injections of heated cultures, two received injections of cultures which had been evaporated on a water bath to one-half or one-third the original volume and restored to this volume by the addition of sterile distilled water, and two were reserved as checks. The cultures used were from eighteen to twenty-three days old. All received these injections beneath the skin of the right pectoral. Five days after the second inoculation each received beneath the skin of the left pectoral ¾cc of the ordinary unattenuated culture. On the following day one of the check pigeons was dead and one sick, as shown by the ruffled plumage and quiet position. Those which had received the heated culture were both well and remained so. Of the two which had received the evaporated culture one was well, and the other sick, which died two days later. From the blood from the heart a pure culture of the bacterium of hog-cholera was obtained. A few bacteria were found in cover-glass preparations of the liver and blood. The dead muscular tissue of the pectoral was already beginning to separate as a sequestrum.

This experiment seemed to point to a partial destruction of the element producing immunity during the process of evaporation.

Number of pigeon.	April 26.	April 29.	Total.	May 3, inoculation of strong virus, twelfth culture, two days old.	Remarks.
				cc.	
30	1½cc evaporated culture.	1½cc evaporated culture.	3cc evaporated culture.	¾	Sick May 4; dead May 6.
31	....do	....do	....do	¾	Well.
32	1cc heated culture.	1cc heated culture.	2cc heated culture.	¾	Do.
33	....do	....do	....do	¾	Do.
34				¾	Dead May 4.
35				¾	Sick May 4; recovered May 12.

A number of other experiments were made, which are tabulated below. In some the culture liquid was evaporated on the water bath to dryness and again diluted in sterile water. In others the culture liquid was simply heated to 58° C. to devitalize it. This was tested, as before, in every case by inoculating sterile infusions therefrom. In a few experiments the age of the culture was limited to three days.

The results of these experiments show that evaporated cultures are less efficacious than heated ones; also that a single injection is not protective. A period of two days between consecutive inoculations seems to be sufficient to protect. It will be observed that the experiments were most uniformly successful in the winter. As the warm weather approached the birds became less susceptible, so that the checks failed to take the disease in some experiments. In the winter they usually died within twenty-four hours after inoculation with strong virus. Grains of corn in the beak and œsophagus indicated partial regurgitation of food from the crop. Later on the birds lived longer. The feathers became ruffled and gave them a puffed appearance. They stood in a corner of the coop with head drooping, the tips of the wing separated from each other more than normally, the tail feathers touching the ground. The birds were conscious of movements about them, and would, when approached, regain for a time their normal position, relapsing into the former relaxed attitude soon after.

Experiments with pigeons.

Number of experiment.	Number of bird.	Heated virus, 7 to 8 days old.		Strong virus.	Remarks.
		May 29.	*May* 31.	*June* 2.	
I	1	1 cc.	1 cc.	.75 cc.	Well June 9.
	2	1	1	.75	Do.
	3	1	1	.75	Slightly ill; recovered June 9.
	4	....	....	.75	Ill next day; dead June 7.
		May 26.	*May* 29.	*June* 1.	
II	1	1 cc.	1 cc.	.75 cc.	Ill after first inoculation; very thin; dead June 8.
	2	1	1	.75	Became sick June 3; still worse June 9; dead June 12.
	3	1	1	.75	Well June 9.
	4	....	....	.75	Do.
		Evaporated virus, 7 to 8 days old		Strong virus.	
		May 20.	*June* 1.	*June* 4.	
III	1	1 cc.	1 cc.	¼ cc.	Well June 9.
	2	1	1	¼	Do.
	3	¼	1	¼	Do.
	4	....	....	¼	Sick June 5; still so June 9; dead June 14.
		Heated virus, 7 to 8 days old.		Strong virus.	
IV	1	1 cc.	1 cc.	¼ cc.	Well June 9.
	2	1	1	¼	Do.
	3	1	1	¼	Do.
	4	....	....	¼	Dead June 5.
		May 26.		*May* 28.	
V	1	1 cc.	....	1 cc.	Very sick June 2; dead June 3.
	2	1	....	1	Very sick June 2; recovered June 9; dead June 13.
	3	1	....	1	Well June 3.
		Evap. virus.	Heated virus.	Strong virus.	
		May 26.	*May* 29.	*June* 1.	
VI	1	1 cc.	1 cc.	¼ cc.	Very slightly ill, but apparently well June 9.
	2	1	1	¼	Do.
	3	1	1	¼	Do.

Experiments with pigeons—Continued.

Number of experiment.	Number of bird.	Evap. virus.	Evap. virus.	Strong virus.	Remarks.
VII	1	1 cc.	1 cc.	$\frac{1}{4}$ cc.	June 20, well; July 1, well.
	2	1	1	$\frac{1}{4}$	Do.
	3	1	1	$\frac{1}{4}$	Do.
	4	....	....	$\frac{1}{4}$	Slightly ill.
		Heated virus.	Heated virus.	Strong virus.	
		June 12.	*June* 15.	*June* 18.	
VIII	1	1 cc.	1 cc.	$\frac{1}{4}$ cc.	Well July 1.
	2	1	1	$\frac{1}{4}$	Do.
	3	1	1	$\frac{1}{4}$	Do.
	4	....	....	$\frac{1}{4}$	Do.

In order to determine whether such very susceptible animals as rabbits and guinea-pigs could be made immune by heated cultures three rabbits were selected, two of which were inoculated with heated cultures and the third kept as a check. The culture liquid used consisted of about 2 per cent. Liebig's meat extract and $2\frac{1}{2}$ per cent. peptone, neutralized with sodium carbonate. Contrary to the former method, the cultures were made in Erlenmeyer flasks, and the liquid was not more than 1^{cm} deep. Considerable evaporation took place through the cotton-wool plug, which was covered with tin-foil. Thus it was presumed the bacteria would multiply more abundantly because of the greater amount of air to which the surface of the liquid was exposed. When the cultures were fourteen days old they were heated to 58° C. to destroy all life, their sterility subsequently being tested by reinoculation into fresh tubes. Rabbits Nos. 3 and 4 received subcutaneously into the thigh on April 24 and 28 and May 1 1.5^{cc} of this culture liquid. May 6 the three rabbits (Nos. 2, 3, 4) were inoculated subcutaneously with an equivalent of $\frac{1}{300}^{cc}$ of a fourteenth culture of the bacterium of hog-cholera. Nos. 2 and 3 were found dead May 12. No. 4 died on the morning of the same day.

All, therefore, succumbed to the inoculation with strong virus in about six days, those having received about 4.5^{cc} of the heated culture as quickly as the check animal.

In No. 2 (check) there was slight necrosis of the muscular tissue at the place of inoculation. Small amount of serum in the peritoneal cavity. Spleen enlarged, very dark, and friable. The bacterium of hog-cholera was present in large numbers in cover-glass preparations of the spleen and liver, fewer in kidneys, the cortex and pyramids of which were deeply congested. A liquid culture from the heart was found pure microscopically and when grown on gelatine plates.

In rabbit No. 3 local necrosis more pronounced than in No. 2. Ecchymoses on the contiguous wall of the abdomen. Large intestine loosely adherent to bladder, the latter to abdominal wall; mesenteric vessels distended with blood; spleen very soft, dark; bacterium of hog-cholera very numerous in spleen, less so in liver. A gelatine tube culture from the spleen pure.

In No. 4 the local lesion was similar to that in Nos. 2 and 3. The liver studded throughout with very small punctiform or stellate grayish-white masses of coagulation necrosis. A large abscess filled with white creamy pus and with a well-defined wall fills the major portion of the right lung. Several small abcesses present. The bacteria of hog-cholera were abundant in spleen and liver. A liquid culture of blood from the heart and a gelatine tube culture from the liver were both pure cultures of the same bacterium. No immunity was thus obtained by the injection of this quantity of devitalized culture liquid.

A similar experiment was tried with three guinea pigs, the same cultures being used. Nos. 5 and 6 received subcutaneously into the thigh 1^{cc} April 21, 24, and 28. The culture first used ten days old, those used subsequently fourteen days old. May 5, one week after the last injection, the three animals were inoculated with an equivalent of $\frac{1}{1000}$^{cc} of a thirteenth culture in beef-infusion peptone two days old. The check animal (No. 7) and one inoculated animal (No. 5) both died May 16, eleven days after inoculation with strong virus. They were well and active to within a few days before death, when they began to crouch together and breathe heavily. In No. 5, at the place of inoculation, two small glands were enlarged, and a cavity was found containing soft, dirty grayish material, showing no cellular structure under the microscope. It was very likely a product of coagulation necrosis. The spleen was enormously enlarged, its dimensions being 2 by 1 by $\frac{1}{4}$ inch. The liver was dotted with grayish points and patches of coagulation necrosis. Kidneys pale, soft, enlarged. Lungs of a deep red. Both liver and spleen crowded with hog-cholera bacteria. A gelatine tube culture from the spleen pure. In No. 7 the local lesions were confined to an enlargement of the lymphatics, otherwise the lesions were identical with those of No. 5. One cover-glass preparation from spleen and liver revealed no bacteria, but a liquid culture from heart's blood and a gelatine tube culture from the spleen were both pure. In both rabbits and guinea-pigs the local lesions were more pronounced in those previously inoculated with heated virus. The third guinea-pig remained well. A second inoculation with $\frac{1}{8}$^{cc} of a liquid culture May 22 was also without effect, as it was well and active June 2.

Tests with heated virus on pigs.

In order to test the effect of heated cultures upon pigs the following experiments were made March 1: Two animals (Nos. 162 and 173) received hypodermically each 9^{cc} of a second and third culture, twelve and thirteen days old respectively, which had been devitalized by heat. March 9 a second dose of 9^{cc} was given in the same way, using a fifth and eighth culture eighteen and fourteen days old respectively. These cultures were made in beef infusion containing 1 per cent. peptone, excepting one, which contained about 2 per cent. of blood serum in place of the peptone. After the second inoculation of No. 162 a swelling appeared on one side. Both were fed with viscera infected with hog-cholera, and placed with sick and dying pigs in a large infected pen. No. 162 was found dead March 29 and No. 173 April 5. The appended table and notes give a summary of the experiment:

Number.	March 1.	March 9.	Total.	Fed.	Died.	Number days after feeding.
	cc.	cc.	cc.			
162	9	9	18	March 19	March 29	10
173	9	9	18	March 19	April 5	17

No. 162. Subcutaneous fatty tissue much reddened. Mucous membrane of stomach considerably ulcerated; of small intestine deeply congested. For 8 or 10 feet above the ileo-cæcal valve the mucous membrane of ileum is completely necrosed. Large ulcers in cæcum and upper portion of colon.

No. 173. Subcutaneous fatty tissue slightly reddened. Petechiæ under pulmonary pleura. Extravasations under serosa of cæcum and colon. Inflammatory adhesions of large intestine with walls of abdomen. A patch of extravasation beneath peritoneal layer of dorsal abdominal wall nearly 2 inches across. Spleen very much enlarged and softened. The mucous membrane of large intestine and several feet of ileum necrosed and breaking down. Fundus of stomach deeply congested.

This experiment clearly showed that this method was no protection to the animal when the latter was infected by feeding.

It now became necessary to determine whether this method would confer immunity upon animals simply exposed to the disease by cohabiting with diseased animals in infected pens. Observations made upon other diseases by investigators, and by us upon this disease, seem to lead to the inference that it frequently depends on the quantity of virus introduced into the system whether the disease will make its appearance or not. In feeding this quantity is considerable; in simple exposure in infected pens to diseased pigs the amount of virus taken into the body with the food and drink is necessarily in small and repeated doses. The following experiment was therefore planned:

Four pigs (Nos. 163, 164, 177, and 196) were inoculated March 13 with heated virus, each receiving $4\frac{1}{2}^{cc}$ beneath the skin of each thigh. The cultures in beef infusion with 1 per cent. peptone were about fifteen days old when heated. The second inoculation was made March 16 from a culture in an Erlenmeyer flask about eleven days old, and containing about 50^{cc} of culture liquid. Each animal received 10^{cc} as before.

March 31.—These animals, together with two check pigs (Nos. 195 and 201) were placed in a large infected pen. Within a period of three weeks from this date at least fifteen pigs died of hog-cholera in this pen. The two check animals died on the 14th and 19th of April, respectively. Of four vaccinated animals only No. 163 showed signs of the disease, and gradually developed into a chronic case, dying of general debility on May 1. The three other vaccinated animals remained apparently well for months after, although constantly exposed to the disease in the infected pen.

Pig. No.	Vaccination.		Exposure.	Died.	Number of days after exposure.
	March 13.	March 16.			
	c.c.	c.c.			
163	9	10	Mar. 31	May 1	31 days.
164	9	10	....	....	
177	9	10	Mar. 31	July 23	3 months and 23 days.
196	9	10	Mar. 31	July 7	3 months and 7 days.
195	....	....	Mar. 31	April 19	19 days.
201	....	....	Mar. 31	April 14	14 days.

Autopsy notes.—No. 163. Spleen not much enlarged; texture firm; effusion into pericardial and thoracic cavity. Lymphatic glands enlarged, but pale; two ulcers in stomach; small intestine normal; mucosa of cæcum and colon studded with many extensive and deep, yellowish ulcerations. On cover-glass preparations of the spleen only a few bacteria could be seen. Two liquid cultures inoculated from the same organ remained sterile. No colonies appeared in the gelatine tube inoculated with blood from the heart. A few developed in the tube inoculated from the spleen.

No. 195. Spleen greatly enlarged; gorged with blood; very friable; shreds of a fibrinous exudate on serosa of intestines; much serum in abdominal cavity; petechiæ on epicardium of auricles; small anterior lobes of lung hepatized; mucous membrane of gall bladder ulcerated; extensive ulceration and inflammation of mucous membrane of cæcum and colon. Hemorrhagic inflammation of kidneys.

No. 201. Spleen but slightly enlarged; lungs extensively hepatized; intense congestion and commencing ulceration of the mucosa of large intestine; stomach and portion of ileum similarly congested. Though no bacteria were found on a cover-glass preparation, a pure culture was obtained by carefully dropping a piece of spleen tissue into a culture tube. This was tested on gelatine.

After apparently resisting the infection for several months the remaining pigs (Nos. 164, 177, and 196) were transferred to a clean pen. No. 177, not very thrifty, began to decline, and finally died July 23. Among the most prominent lesions were a plastic exudate on the epicardium and numerous large old ulcers in the large intestine. The mucosa itself was extensively pigmented. No. 196, on removal from the infected pen, seemed in good condition, but it died July 7, after some days of unthrifty condition. In this case the mucous membrane of the large intestine was pigmented, and there were what appeared to be cicatrices of old ulcerations. In all of the large serous cavities there was considerable effusion. In cover-glass preparations of the spleen there were no hog-cholera bacteria to be seen, but numerous bacilli resembling those of malignant œdema.

A second experiment was made in the same way upon Nos. 197 to 200, inclusive, and No. 157. March 24 each animal received in the thigh about 10cc of a mixture of heated cultures in beef infusion with 1 per cent. peptone about fourteen days old. March 29 an equal amount was injected, one-half into each axilla, these cultures being about fifteen days old. These animals were kept until April 20, when all but No. 157 were placed in the large infected pen. From that date on pigs died of the disease almost every day, so that the infection must have been quite thorough. Unfortunately no check animal was exposed at the same time. In these animals the slight swelling at the seat of inoculation disappeared in a few weeks.

They remained well, with the exception of No. 199, which became emaciated and was found dead May 19, about one month after exposure. The three remaining animals were apparently unaffected nearly two months after exposure. At this time No. 197, which appeared rather thin, was killed, to determine if any ulcerations were present. But the mucous membrane of the intestine was entirely normal, with no indications of former ulcerations.

Pig No.	Injection of heated virus.		Time of exposure.	Remarks.
	March 24.	March 29.		
	cc.	cc.		
197	10	10	April 20	Killed June 10. Healthy.
198	10	10	April 20	Well June 10.
199	10	10	April 20	Died May 19.
200	10	10	April 20	Died July 12.
257	10	10	May 25	Died June 28.

Autopsy notes of No. 199.—Slight extravasation in subcutaneous connective tissue. Spleen somewhat enlarged, filled with blood, friable; considerable effusion in peritoneal cavity. Right lung in part hepatized; pleuritic adhesions to chest-wall; hemorrhage in and about pelvis of kidney; lymphatic glands purplish; extensive and deep ulceration of the mucosa of large intestine.

Pig 197, killed for examination, was very anæmic. There was some pale serum in abdominal cavity. The kidneys and lymphatic glands showed evidence of chronic inflammation. The lungs were exceedingly pale. No evidence of inflammation or ulceration in any portion of the intestinal tract.

It must be borne in mind that these animals were constantly exposed for a period of several months to the virus of the disease, and that a continual struggle between the organism and the invading parasites must have been going on, which naturally would tend to lower the vitality. Such severe conditions as these are probably never realized among herds.

The later history of No. 200 does not, however, bear out the first supposition that complete immunity was attained. After being continually exposed in the infected pen from April 20 to June 21 it was removed to a clean pen, where it continued to grow very weak. It died July 12. The autopsy revealed a plastic pleurisy over the right lung and a fibrinous exudate upon the epicardium. The mucosa of the cæcum was extensively necrosed; in the colon the ulcers were isolated; the solitary follicles were very prominent. A small bit from the epicardial exudate was placed beneath the skin of two mice. One of them died on the eighteenth day. The spleen was greatly enlarged. Numerous hog-cholera bacteria were present in this organ and liver. The epicardial exudate of the pig must have contained but very few, for they could not be demonstrated in cover-glass preparations. The long period of time from the inoculation of the mouse to its death is also evidence of a very small quantity of virus.

No. 157, inoculated with the rest, became quite lame in the hind limbs, so that it was thought best not to expose it to the disease in the infected pen for the time being. It soon recovered its power of locomotion, and was transferred to the infected pen May 25 and removed therefrom June 28. In the new pen it grew rapidly weaker and died June 28. On *post mortem* examination the right lung was found entirely hepatized and adherent to the chest-wall. The mucosa of cæcum and colon was studded with large and deep ulcers; that of the fundus of stomach was deeply congested.

It became desirable to determine whether repeated subcutaneous injections of heated cultures until a large amount had been introduced into the system would be more efficacious in producing immunity. For this purpose the culture liquids were concentrated, by using a 2 per cent. solution of meat extract with 2 per cent. peptone for some of the injections; for the remainder a 2 per cent. solution of peptone in beef infusion. The cultures were made in Erlenmeyer flasks, plugged with cotton wool.

The table given below gives the date of the injection and the quantity used each time. It will be noted that Nos. 191 and 194 received two, Nos. 216 and 218 three, and Nos. 219 and 221 four doses each of the heated culture liquid. The injections were made two days apart, the exposure in the infected pen and among diseased animals about one week after the last inoculation. Nos. 220, 232, and 235 were placed in the infected pen at the same time, to determine the virulence of the infection upon pigs which had not received any injection.

Pig No.	Heated virus.				Total.	Exposure in infected pen.	Remarks.
	April 20.	April 22.	April 24.	April 26.			
	cc.	*cc.*	*cc.*	*cc.*	*cc.*		
216	9	8	7½	....	24½	May 4	Died May 17.
217	9	8	7½	8	32½	May 4	Died May 19.
218	9	8	7½	....	24½	May 4	Do.
221	9	8	7½	8	32½	May 4	Died May 23.
191	....	....	10	8	18	May 4	Do.
220*	....	....	....	....	18	May 4	Died May 17.
232*	....	....	....	....	....	May 4	Died May 23.
235*	....	....	....	....	....	May 4	Died June 12.
194*	....	....	10	8	18	May 4	Died June 19.

* Checks.

All of the inoculated and control animals died within periods ranging from thirteen to nineteen days, only one living thirty-nine days, and this one a control animal. Of those that had received two doses, No. 191 died May 23 (nineteen days after exposure), with considerable ulceration in cæcum and colon. No. 194 died May 19, with extensive and deep congestion of the lymphatic glands in general, of the kidney, stomach, and large intestine. In the latter, ulceration was not yet begun. No. 216, which had received three doses, died very unexpectedly thirteen days after exposure. The lesions were of the hemorrhagic type, involving extravasations and ecchymoses of the intestinal tract, more especially of the large intestine, heart, lungs, lymphatic and subcutaneous fatty tissue. Ulceration in large intestine very slight, the congestion being intense. No. 218, treated like the former, died fifteen days after exposure. The lesions were like those of No. 216, but not so severe. Ulceration as yet very slight.

Nos. 217 and 221, which had received four injections, died fifteen and nineteen days after exposure, respectively. The lesions in No. 217, which died very suddenly, were of hemorrhagic character, the ulceration in the cæcum and colon being quite superficial. In No. 221 the ulceration was more pronounced, the general congestion and extravasation much less so.

Of the control animals the lesions of No. 220 were of the hemorrhagic type, resembling those of No. 194 very closely. In No. 232 there was extensive ulceration of the mucous membrane of the large intestine. In No. 235, which lived for thirty-nine days after exposure, the mucosa of the cæcum and upper portion of the colon was involved in complete necrosis nearly 5^{mm} thick. Beyond this the necrosis took the form of isolated ulcers. Owing to the depth of the ulceration inflammatory adhesions had formed between the cæcum and adjacent organs. There was no reactionary swelling of the inoculated animals at the point of injection.

Those animals in which the disease took the hemorrhagic type succumbed very suddenly, as if the invasion had taken place in a single day. In those animals in which symptoms of weakness and loss of appetite appeared some days before death the well-defined lesions were as a rule limited to the large intestine in the form of ulcerations. The former cases represent a class in which the bacterium invades the entire vascular system; in the latter the absence of a general congestion and extravasation seems to indicate a more local multiplication of the specific disease germ in the intestinal tract.

This mode of vaccination, as shown by the results recorded, did not prove to be any protection to the animals, as they died, most of them, within a brief period after exposure from a very acute attack of the disease.

The spleen examined in about one-half of these cases contained the bacterium of hog-cholera, usually in large numbers. From a few, cultures were made in which the bacterium was found pure.

A second experiment was tried, in which each animal received hypodermically 40^{cc} of heated culture liquid in two doses. The cultures were made in beef infusion with 1 per cent. peptone, the growth being killed by a temperature of 58° C. the third day after inoculation. The flasks used were shaped like Erlenmeyer flasks, a glass cap being fitted over the flask by means of a ground-glass joint, which contracted into a straight narrow tube, plugged with glass wool. The removal of a cotton-wool plug was thus avoided, the cap being removed for inoculation. This culture flask affords better ventilation and a more rapid evaporation of the culture liquid than does the culture tube with the bent ventilating tube.

The following table gives all the facts necessary for an understanding of the experiment and its results:

Pig No.	Heated virus.		Total.	Exposure in infected pens.	Remarks.	Days after first exposure.
	June 14.	June 17.				
	cc.	cc.	cc.			
231	20	20	40	June 21	Died July 7	16
233	18	20	38	June 21	Died July 9	18
266	20	20	40	June 21	Died July 9	18
280*				June 21	Died July 8	17
267	20	20	40	June 21	Died July 6	15
268	20	20	40	June 21	Died July 10	19
269	20	20	40	June 21	Died July 10	19
270*				June 21	Died July 9	18

*Check.

It will be seen that all the experimental animals died, inoculated as well as check animals, within a few days of one another, death taking place about sixteen to eighteen days after the first day of exposure. A brief synopsis of the *post mortem* appearances will not be amiss in this connection:

In No. 231 the spleen was very much enlarged and gorged with blood. The intensely congested mucous membrane of the cæcum and colon was dotted with small superficial ulcerations. In No. 233 the congestion of spleen, and ulceration with congestion of the large intestine, were also very marked. No. 266 presented the same lesions. The ulcers in the cæcum were from ½ to ¼ inch across. No. 280 (check) differed from the preceding cases in presenting severer lesions; greatly enlarged and congested spleen and lymphatic glands, entire superficial necrosis of the cæcum and upper portion of colon, with intense congestion of the mucosa of the entire colon and great thickening of the walls; extensive extravasation of blood beneath the mucosa of duodenum.

Of the second lot of four treated in the same way, No. 267 presented very severe lesions, consisting of intense congestion and extravasation, involving the spleen, lymphatic glands, lungs, and kidney. The left lung was almost entirely adherent to costal pleura. There was considerable hemorrhage in the pelvis of both kidneys. The large intestine was least changed, the mucosa being slightly ulcerated and containing some hemorrhagic spots and points. This animal was first to die out of this lot of eight. In No. 268 the congestion involved the lymphatic glands generally, and the mucosa of the large intestine, which was extensively necrosed in its upper portion. No. 269 resembled No. 267 in the severity of the lesions. The lungs were not affected, however, while the ulceration of cæcum and upper colon was very extensive and deep. No. 270 (check) presented extensive ulceration of the large intestine and a greatly enlarged spleen. In five cases the spleen contained the bacteria of hog-cholera more or less abundantly. In two none could be seen on one or two cover-glasses. No local swelling had developed at the points of injection in any of the inoculated animals.

In this experiment no immunity was produced, since the animals succumbed to the infection very quickly and showed themselves very susceptible, as indicated by the severe lesions of the internal organs in general.

The foregoing experiments, aimed at producing immunity by the injection of the chemical products or ptomaines, were, as a whole, unsuccessful with reference to pigs, although successful upon pigeons. If larger doses of culture liquid had been given and in separate doses extending over longer periods of time the results might have been positive even upon pigs. The cost of the culture fluid being too great to make the experiment of practical value on a large scale, no further attempts were made in this direction for the present.

As the etiology of this very virulent disease had been sufficiently demonstrated by the experiments reported last year, no particular attention was paid to a determination of the presence of the bacteria of hog-cholera by cultures. Usually the spleen was examined by means of cover-glass preparations whenever time allowed, and in most cases large numbers of the specific bacteria were present. In the many cultures from spleens made from these and subsequent cases to carry out the inoculations none other than the motile bacterium of hog-cholera appeared in these cultures. At the same time many minor experiments upon mice were made for various purposes, and in all the characteristic lesions described in the second report were found associated with the specific bacterium.

Inoculations with unattenuated cultures.

While the tests for conferring immunity upon pigs by the injection of heated virus were being carried on it was thought advisable to experiment in the same direction with the unattenuated cultures themselves. A lot of animals were at first inoculated twice with very small quantities, the period between the two inoculations being about two weeks. This time was sufficient to reveal any disease which might have been induced by the inoculations. Two weeks after the second inoculation the animal was infected either by feeding the internal organs of pigs which had died of the disease or by exposing it to the sick and dying in an infected pen. It was soon found that the inoculations were by no means protective in whatever way the virus entered the system. Feeding usually produced cases of the most acute character and with the most severe and extensive lesions. The doses of inoculated cultures were gradually increased in quantity without yie ding any better results. Of a large number of animals subjected td inoculation only five took the disease unmistakably as a consequence of the operation.

This method of protective inoculation having failed with unattenuated cultures, there seemed no necessity for attempting any investigations with attenuated cultures. The experiments, including tables and *post mortem* notes, are given *in extenso* as they were made. In reading them over it will be noticed that the virus was cultivated chiefly in liquid media, and the solid media, more particularly nutritive gelatine, were only employed to test the purity of the cultures. Whenever these cultures were used for inoculations they were previously tested on gelatine plates by drawing a platinum wire, dipped into the culture, through the gelatine layer two or three times before the gelatine had become solid. Among the hundreds of cultures thus tested in the space of several months not one was found impure. Series of cultures extending up to the tenth generation were usually carried on by inoculating fresh tubes each day. The last culture tested as described above gave precisely the same colonies as the first in all the series thus far prepared. The culture tube described in the First Annual Report of the Bureau was used almost exclusively for these cultures in liquid media. The advantages and accessibility of cultures in liquids for purposes of inoculation; the readiness and ease with which quantities or doses may be determined, finally, certain characteristics of growth in liquids, place this method on a level with, if not above, that of solid cultures for experimental purposes. For diagnostic purposes solid media are to-day a *sine qua non* of bacteriological work.

Experiments—Pigs Nos. 152, 167, 168, and 175 were inoculated with pure cultures in beef-infusion peptone as follows: On January 23, one drop of the seventh culture, derived from the spleen of pig No. 114; on February 8, with ⅛cc from a culture derived from a guinea-pig (No. 4). Both cultures were diluted in sterile normal salt solution in such a way that 1cc of fluid was injected each time. The inner aspect of the thigh near Poupart's ligament was chosen. The liquid was introduced beneath the skin into the subcutaneous tissue with a hypodermic syringe. There was no perceptible swelling at the site of either inoculation, excepting in No. 175, in which there were two nodes, each of the size of a walnut, at the seat of the first inoculation. In order to test the extent of the immunity which these inoculations may have conferred, feeding the viscera of pigs which had succumbed to hog-cholera was resorted to, the animals being transferred to the large infected pen for this purpose. Nos. 168 and 175 were fed in this way March 5, and two animals not inoculated (Nos. 158 and 159) were fed with them. All four died, the two vaccinated animals in about twenty days, the others in about fifteen days after feeding. March 13, Nos. 152 and 167 were fed with two check animals Nos. 176 and 190. These four also died of hog-cholera; the two vaccinated ones averaging twenty days, the others eleven days after feeding. The inoculation may be said to have simply retarded death from five to nine days. A table gi ing a summary of these facts is appended, together with a brief description of the *post mortem* appearances:

Pig No.	January 23.	February 8.	Fed with hog-cholera viscera.	Died.	Days after feeding.
	Drop.	*cc.*			
152	1	⅛	March 13	April 3	21
167	1	⅛	March 13	April 1	19
168	1	⅛	March 5	March 28	23
175	1	⅛	March 5	March 22	17
158			March 5	March 21	16
159			March 5	March 19	14
176			March 13	March 23	10
190			March 13	March 25	12

Autopsy notes.—No. 152.—Skin of limbs and abdomen dotted with purple spots; on abdomen general reddening. Points of extravasation and ecchymosed spots throughout the subcutaneous connective and fatty tissue and on gastro-splenic omentum. Superficial inguinal glands greatly enlarged and congested. Spleen enlarged, filled with blood, and very soft. Petechiæ on epicardium. Numerous lobules of the lungs collapsed. Glomeruli of kidneys appear as deep red petechiæ. In cæcum and upper portion of colon extensive and deep ulcers. A few in the ileum near the valve. The mucosa of the stomach, small and large intestine, thickly covered with dark red points or petechiæ.

No. 167.—Dying, and hence killed by a blow on the head. Spleen swollen, friable; epicardium dotted with points and spots of extravasation. In lungs a few collapsed lobules. Lymphatic glands generally very deeply congested, similarly the mucous membrane of fundus of stomach and the kidneys. Large ulcers in cæcum and upper portion of colon.

No. 168.—Subcutaneous and subperitoneal tissue contains numerous ecchymoses from ⅛ to ⅜ inch in diameter. Spleen enlarged, gorged with blood, friable. Petechiæ on epicardium. Lungs not collapsed; its parenchyma contains numerous deeply congested areas from ¼ to ½ inch in diameter. Kidneys enlarged, with extravasations on surface and in parenchyma. Cortex of lymphatics in general deeply congested. Extensive, almost continuous, ulceration of cæcum and upper portion of colon, in part blackish, the remainder of the large intestine being the seat of severe inflammation and extravasation. Mucous membrane of stomach similarly involved.

No. 175.—Subcutaneous tissue dotted with pale red spots. Tumor at the place of the first inoculation firm throughout, pale yellowish. Superficial inguinal glands, as well of those of thorax and abdomen, with purplish cortex. Spleen tissue still firm, dotted with numerous bright red points, but slightly enlarged. Beneath the entire epicardium and endocardium many extravasations. Cæcum and upper portion of colon extensively ulcerated. Serous surface of large intestine dotted with extravasations.

No. 158.—Subcutaneous fatty tissue deeply reddened. Spleen slightly enlarged. Lymphatics in general with deeply congested cortex. Adhesive peritonitis matting the various viscera together and to abdominal walls; fibrinous and serous exudate abundant in the abdominal cavity. A few lung worms present. Cæcum and colon extensively ulcerated; rectum congested. Serous surface of this tract dotted with extravasations. Fundus of stomach deeply congested.

No. 176.—Slight reddening of skin and subcutaneous fatty tissue. Cortex of lymphatic glands in general deeply congested. Spleen much enlarged and surface dotted with numerous bright red elevated points. A few petechiæ on endocardium and epicardium. Lungs deeply congested throughout; kidneys likewise inflamed. Stomach slightly reddened at fundus. Small intestine also slightly congested. Serosa of large intestine dotted with extravasations. The mucosa of cæcum and small portion of colon one mass of necrosed tissue. Walls thickened.

No. 189.—Extensive and deep reddening of skin of abdomen, throat, and limbs. Subcutaneous tissue only slightly reddened; spleen enlarged, gorged with blood, friable. Besides the general congestion of the lungs there are small darker areas, representing hepatized lobules. Bronchial glands and those along lesser curvature of stomach swollen and gorged with blood; the other lymphatics only moderately congested. Besides a small number of ulcers throughout the large intestine the mucous membrane is deeply congested and dotted with occasional hemorrhagic points. Kidneys extensively inflamed; on section the cortex shows extravasations.

No. 190.—Considerable reddening of the skin of abdomen and ventral aspect of limbs, very slight in subcutaneous tissue. Spleen greatly enlarged; dark purple; blood flows freely on cutting into it; very soft. Lungs contain regions of congestion and hepatizations, possibly due to the presence of a few lung worms. Lymphatic glands near stomach, the bronchial and superficial inguinal glands deeply congested. Other glands only slightly congested. Mucous membrane of stomach extensively congested; a large patch of extravasation in fundus; large intestine severely inflamed, with occasional extravasations; no ulcerations.

In these animals the lesions of a severe type of hog-cholera were manifested both by severe inflammations and hemorrhages of the viscera and the extensive ulcerations. It seems very probable that the bacteria begin their ravages after the food has reached the large intestine, where it remains for a time. The absence of anything but a small quantity of semi-liquid matter in the small intestine indicates the rapid passage of food from the stomach into the large intestine. The bacteria are protected from the gastric juice by the muscular and cellular tissue in which they are imbedded, and are thus able to pass through the stomach without being destroyed. The diagnosis of hog-cholera was confirmed in every case by finding the specific bacterium in cover-glass preparations of splenic tissue and obtaining therefrom pure cultures in liquid media and in gelatine.

In conjunction with the first series of inoculations, two pigs (Nos. 149 and 161) were inoculated at the same time, as follows: January 23, with 1^{cc} of the seventh culture in beef-infusion peptone derived from the spleen of No. 114. No reaction at the place of inoculation in No. 149; a tumor as large as a marble in No. 161. On February 8 both received a second injection of 1^{cc} of the second culture in beef-infusion peptone derived from pig No. 165. Two swellings as large as a chestnut at the place of the second inoculation in No. 149; in No. 161 also a considerable thickening was present. No. 149 was fed March 5 with four of the preceding series; No. 161 on March 13 with the remainder of the preceding series, and some to be subsequently spoken of. Both died of hog-cholera. The accompanying table and brief autopsy notes explain themselves:

Pig No.	Inoculation.		Fed.	Died.	Days after feeding.
	January 23.	February 8.			
	cc.	*cc.*			
149	1	1	March 5	March 24	19
161	1	1	March 13	April 14	32

No. 149.—Slight reddening of the skin and subcutaneous connective tissue; the nodes produced by inoculation firm, pale yellowish, only one showing softening within; spleen considerably enlarged and full of blood; ascarides in gall bladder, which is ulcerated; mucous membrane along fundus of stomach intensely congested; the mucous membrane of cæcum and upper portion of colon one mass of ulcers; in the remainder of colon they are isolated; kidneys congested.

No. 161.—Great emaciation; spleen enlarged and gorged with blood, very soft; all excepting the posterior region of each lung hepatized and the bronchi filled with a thick creamy mass, which consists almost entirely of pus corpuscles; lymphatics but slightly congested; adhesions between adjacent coil of large intestine and bladder; cæcum and colon studded with large deep ulcers; valve greatly enlarged; intense congestion of mucous membrane of fundus; cover-glass preparations from the spleen of both contain the charactteristic oval bacerium. Gelatine and liquid cultures from the same organ were pure.

The comparatively large dose of strong virus used for vaccination was not capable of protecting these animals from the disease communicated by feeding. There was no suspicion of disease caused by the vaccination when they were fed, and the time intervening was sufficient for the development of the disease from the injected virus.

Pigs Nos. 151, 169, 170, and 178 were inoculated as in the preceding experiments on February 8 and 23 with $\frac{1}{8}^{cc}$ of a beef infusion peptone culture derived from a guinea-pig and the seventh culture from the spleen of a pig in the same medium. The dose was diluted in salt solution so as to make 1^{cc} of liquid. In No. 151 the second inoculation produced a tumor about 1 inch long and $\frac{1}{2}$ inch thick. The first was scarcely noticeable. In No. 169 the first inoculation resulted in a bean-like nodule; the second produced several of the same size. In No. 170 neither inoculations showed more than a very slight swelling. In No. 178 both inoculations produced rather extensive swellings.

On being fed with the viscera of pigs known to have died of the disease all took the disease and died; two on March 13 and the remaining two on March 19, one in thirteen, one in eighteen, and two in twenty-two days after feeding. A table summarizing these facts and brief *post mortem* notes are appended:

Pig No.	Inoculation.		Fed.	Died.	Days after feeding.
	February 8.	February 23.			
	cc.	*cc.*			
151	⅛	⅛	March 13	March 26	13
169	⅛	⅛	March 19	April 10	22
170	⅛	⅛	March 13	April 4	22
178	⅛	⅛	March 19	April 6	18

Autopsy notes.—No. 151.—Purplish spots on skin of abdomen and paler ones in subcutaneous tissue. Inoculation tumor cuts like cheese; yellowish white. Extravasations under endocardium and epicardium; left lung mottled from congested areas; cortex of lymphatic glands congested; those of meso-colon and lesser curvature of stomach dark purple throughout; kidneys pale; hemorrhage into pelvis of left kidney; extravasations into mucosa of stomach; moderate number of ulcers in cæcum and colon; large quantity of blood in the lower six or eight feet of ileum and in the large intestine; clotted in the former tube, where the mucous membrane is deeply congested.

No. 169.—Small tumor on the left side, the place of the second inoculation; spleen enlarged and congested, with large hemorrhagic infarcts; considerable effusion in the large serous cavities. Besides the general congestion of lungs, there are scattered throughout its parenchyma hemorrhagic foci. Hemorrhagic inflammation of kidneys manifested by bright red glomeruli throughout its cortex; lymphatics in general deeply congested; numerous petechiæ in stomach, small and large intestine. In cæcum and colon large, deep ulcers.

No. 170.—Redness of skin of abdomen; nothing at places of inoculation; spleen enlarged, friable, full of blood; abdomen, thorax, and pericardial cavity contain much yellow serum, congestion of the lungs with darker hemorrhagic foci throughout; anterior lobes collapsed; kidneys enlarged, with a few extravasations on surface and in parenchyma; mucous membrane of stomach and intestines covered with many hemorrhagic points and spots. In large intestine, including rectum, numerous old ulcers, some 1 inch across. Lymphatics in general extensively congested.

No. 178.—Died quite unexpectedly. At the place of first inoculation two firm whitish masses; spleen enlarged. friable; its substance contains hemorrhagic infarcts; extravasations beneath both serous surfaces of the heart; congestion of lungs, with numerous darker hemorrhagic foci; lymphatic glands of abdominal cavity very dark and gorged with blood; extensive ulceration about the ileo-cæcal valve, in the cæcum, and colon; in the lower portion of colon and in the rectum numerous small extravasations. Hemorrhage into pelvis of both kidneys.

The *post mortem* determination of a severe type of hog-cholera in these four cases was confirmed by finding in the spleen of each animal, by means of cover-glass preparations, numerous specific bacteria of this disease. Cultures in liquid media made from every spleen were found pure when examined microscopically as well as on gelatine plates. This experiment likewise proved the inefficiency of small quantities of non-attenuated virus introduced beneath the skin in preventing an invasion of the micro-organisms from the alimentary canal.

A third lot of four pigs (Nos. 117, 171, 172, and 174), between three and five months old, were inoculated as before with .2cc each from the second beef-infusion peptone culture derived from the spleen of No. 159. On March 1 they were inoculated with .2cc from the second culture derived from the spleen of No. 156. In No. 117 there was a slight swelling after the first and one as large as a chestnut after the second inoculation. In No. 171 a mass 1½ to 2 inches long and three-fourths inch in diameter was found at site of the first inoculation. There was but a small nodule at the place of the second inoculation. In No. 172 two lumps, like small marbles, formed after the first inoculation; after the second only a small nodule formed. In No. 174 the reaction after the second inoculation was manifested by an irregular tumor about 2 inches long and one-third of an inch in diameter, the reaction at the place of the first inoculation being less marked.

Of these four, two (Nos. 117 and 172) were fed with the viscera of pigs dead from hog-cholera, together with two control animals (Nos. 192 and 193), on March 19. The rest (Nos. 171 and 174) were simply placed in the large infected pen March 22, with those that had been fed with infectious matter. Below the result is given in a tabulated form. It shows that all the animals succumbed to the disease, those simply exposed by contact with the sick as well as those fed. Of the inoculated animals, those fed died in twenty-one and eighteen days after feeding; those exposed, in twenty-two and twenty-five days respectively. Those not inoculated died twelve and eleven days respectively after feeding. Here, likewise, we notice the prolongation of life in the inoculated pigs.

Pig No.	February 13.	March 1.	Date of feeding and exposure.	Died.	Days after exposure and feeding.
	cc.	cc.			
117	.2	.2	Fed March 19	April 9	21
171	.2	.2	Exposed March 22	April 13	22
173	.2	.2	Fed March 19	April 6	18
174	.2	.2	Exposed March 22	April 16	25
192*			Fed March 19	March 31	12
193*			do	March 30	11
195*			Exposed March 31	April 19	19
201*			do	April 14	14

* Checks.

The lesions found at the autopsies of these pigs are briefly as follows:

No. 117.—Extensive reddening of the skin of abdomen; great enlargement of spleen, which is gorged with blood, very soft; petechial discolorations on surface of lungs and on section; large intestine studded with broad deep ulcers as far as the rectum; a few in ileum.

No. 171.—Skin over ventral aspect of body deeply reddened; hemorrhagic spots under peritoneal covering of diaphragm and large intestine and under capsule of kidneys; lungs congested, containing numerous dark hemorrhagic lobules; part of anterior lobes collapsed. The spleen very large, dark colored; nodes slightly raised above surface, shown on section to be hemorrhagic infarcts; lymphatic glands generally highly congested; petechial spots on surface and in cortex of kidneys; hemorrhagic foci throughout mucosa of stomach and intestines. About four large ulcers in cæcum and colon.

No. 173.—Reddening of skin of ventral aspect of body and of subcutaneous tissue generally; firm, pale yellow cheesy masses, surrounded by a thin membrane, at place of inoculation; engorgement of spleen and lymphatic glands; extravasations in parenchyma of kidneys. In cæcum and colon numerous deep ulcers, some coalesced. Mucosa of stomach generally congested, and that of intestines thickly dotted with petechiæ.

No. 174.—Deep reddening of skin of abdomen; encysted cheesy mass at site of first inoculation; great enlargement of spleen; prominent red points on surface; effusion into abdominal cavity; anterior lobes of lungs collapsed, remainder normal; lymphatics highly congested; three large ulcers in cæcum; valve thickened and ulcerated; petechiæ numerous throughout mucosa of stomach and intestines.

No. 192.—Reddening of skin of ventral aspect of body and of subcutaneous tissue; spleen swollen, full of blood, friable. Atelectasis of the small anterior lobe of each lung; ulcers on the mucous surface of gall bladder. Cortex of lymphatic glands congested; mucosa of large intestines congested; numerous ulcers in cæcum and upper colon.

No. 193.—Subcutaneous connective tissue considerably reddened; spleen but slightly enlarged, not much softened. Mucous membrane of stomach, of large and small intestines, deeply congested; contents of large intestine fluid, chocolate colored.

In cover-glass preparations from the spleen pulp of these animals numerous bacteria of hog-cholera were found in each preparation. Both gelatine and liquid cultures from every spleen proved to be pure cultures of the bacterium of hog-cholera.

The diagnosis made on *post mortem* was thus confirmed by microscopic examination and culture.

To determine the effect of a single inoculation, on February 13 two pigs (Nos. 115 and 160) received subcutaneously each 1^{cc} of the second beef-infusion peptone culture obtained from the spleen of a pig. In No. 115 a tumor as large as a marble was found at the seat of inoculation March 9. In No. 160 the tumor was elongated, about 2 inches long and three-eighths of an inch thick. No. 115 was fed with viscera taken from cases of hog-cholera March 19. No. 160 was simply exposed to the disease by being transferred to the large infected pen. No. 115 died April 8. No. 160 recovered and was well May 6. The detailed account of this experiment is appended:

Pig No.	February 13.	Date of feeding and exposure.	Effect.	Days after feeding.
	cc.			
115	1	Fed March 19	Died April 8	20
160	1	Exposed March 22	Recovered	....

Post mortem notes.—No. 115.—Firm, pale yellow tumor at seat of inoculation, encysted; center undergoing softening. Spleen tumefied, very dark and friable. A few extravasations beneath serous coverings of heart. In cortex of kidneys numerous hemorrhagic points; cystic degeneration of right kidneys; advanced ulceration of cæcum and colon; scattered petechiæ in mucosa of stomach and small intestine.

No. 160.—Was very low for a time, beginning with April 1. It was barely able to stand and its appetite was poor. It rapidly recovered, however, and was gaining flesh in May. Whether the animal was suffering from hog-cholera or from the *Sclerostoma pinguicola* (kidney worm), with which some of this lot were found affected, cannot be said.

In order to determine whether a single injection of a comparatively large quantity of culture liquid, while not inducing the disease, would protect against the disease itself, the following experiment was performed:

Four pigs (Nos. 202, 204, 205, and 212) were inoculated April 2 with 1½^{cc} of a seventh culture in beef infusion with 1 per cent. peptone one day old. Four additional pigs (Nos. 206, 207, 208, and 209) received but 1^{cc} of the same culture. The remaining four of the same lot (Nos. 203, 210, 211, and 213) were reserved as checks upon the experiment. Of these, Nos. 203 and 213 had a temperature of 106° F., and hence were suspected of disease. This suspicion was soon confirmed after they had been placed in a pen alone. Both had a severe diarrhea, one dying April 11, the other April 13. The lesions were confined to the mucous membrane of the large intestine, which was dotted with numerous elevated lemon-yellow tough masses $\frac{7}{16}$–$\frac{1}{8}$-inch across, simulating ulcers. On close examination, however, this impression was dispelled. These tough masses were easily removed *in toto* from the mucosa, which presented a slight depression without any loss of substance. They were evidently exudates from the mucosa and perhaps diphtheritic. There were no bacteria in the blood or in a bit of spleen dropped into a culture tube. No development took place in either tube.

Of those inoculated with 1½^{cc}, two died from the immediate effects of inoculation. No. 204 died in eleven days and No. 212 in seven days. In No. 204 a tough tumor had formed at the point of inoculation on each side. The mucous membrane of the large intestine was completely necrosed and the spleen enlarged. In No. 212 local swelling was present on one side. The stomach and large intestine were deeply congested, with points of commencing ulceration in the latter. In both animals the bacterium of hog-cholera was present in cover-glass preparations of the spleen. Nos. 202 and 205 seemed to remain unaffected by the inoculation. One month and a half later both were exposed to the disease in the large infected pen. A month later they were removed with others to a clean pen, after having apparently resisted infection. No. 202 was gradually wasting away and died July 24, more than two months after exposure. In the large intestine were cicatrices of healed ulcers and such as were healing. The severest lesions were in the lungs. Both were adherent by means of bands to the costal pleura, and were extensively hepatized. No. 205 was alive and well August 15.

Of the second lot, which had received 1^{cc} of the same culture, the results were nearly the same. Two succumbed to the inoculation, one died of infection, and a fourth survived. No. 208 died fifteen days after inoculation. Besides the inoculation swellings, enlarged and congested spleen, the mucous membrane of the large intestine was covered with extensive deep ulcers and the walls much thickened and softened. The corresponding lymphatics in the meso-colon deep purple. No. 209 died in six days after inoculation. There was general congestion and extravasation of blood in the internal organs, involving the entire mucous membrane of the alimentary tract, especially the large intestine, the lymphatics and serous membranes, the spleen and kidneys. Ulceration had not yet begun. In both animals the spleen was crowded with bacteria and furnished pure cultures of the specific germ.

Nos. 206 and 207 were not affected by the inoculation. They were exposed with the preceding lot, as indicated in the table. No. 207, after apparently resisting the contagion in the infected pen for a month, died July 18, after having been in a clean pen since June 21. The extensive necrosis of the mucous membrane of the cæcum and upper portion of colon, with the absence of any acute inflammation elsewhere, gave evidence of a chronic case of hog-cholera. No. 206, though still alive, is emaciated.

The two remaining check pigs, which were exposed with the preceding animals in the same infected pen, both died of hog-cholera. No. 211 found dead June 21. The most marked changes were a small number of ulcers on a pale mucous membrane scattered over the cæcum and colon. No. 210 lived a month longer than its mate. The existence of hog-cholera was demonstrated by a general necrosis of the mucous membrane of the cæcum and an extensive pigmentation in the remainder of the large intestine. The lungs were adherent in places and much congested.

When we gather together the facts presented by this experiment we shall find a certain number of interesting deductions springing therefrom. In the first place we note the peculiarity of the intestinal lesions of the two animals which died from some unknown cause, presumably not hog-cholera. We next point to an additional demonstration of the specific nature of the bacterium of hog-cholera, for out of eight inoculated four died, and the age of the lesions corresponded well with the length of time elapsing between inoculation and death.

Those animals which resisted the inoculation were in part protected, as two among four were still alive on August 17, and the remaining two died, probably from effects of the ulceration, months after exposure.

Pig No.	Inoculated April 2.	Died from inoculation.	Exposure in infected pens.	Removed from infected pens.	Remarks.
202*	1½ cc. cult. liq		May 18	June 21	Died July 4.
204	....do	April 13	May 18		
205	....do		May 18	June 21	Alive Aug. 17.
212	....do	April 9			
206	1 cc. cult. liq		May 18	June 21	Alive Aug. 11, but unthrifty.
207	....do				Died July 18.
208	....do	April 17			
209	....do	April 8			
203†					Died Apr. 11, from some unknown disease.
210†			May 18	June 21	Died July 21, of hog-cholera.
211†			May 18		Died June 21, of hog-cholera.
213†					Died Apr. 18, from same disease as No. 203.

* These animals were one and a half months old at date of inoculation. † Checks.

Having determined that even large doses of liquid cultures of the bacterium of hog-cholera can be borne without producing the disease in most cases, it was thought advisable to make two inoculations of strong virus, a first one with a small quantity and a second with a large quantity.

First inoculation, April 21: Nos. 214, 227, 223, and 222 received ¼cc of a third culture in beef infusion containing 1 per cent. each of peptone and glucose. The liquid was diluted with sterile salt solution so as to make ½cc. It was injected, one-half beneath the skin of each thigh.

Second inoculation: After waiting two weeks in order to determine whether the inoculation had not produced the disease, a second injection was practiced May 6, the thirteenth and fourteenth culture of the same series being used for this purpose. The animals received 1cc, 1½cc, 2cc, and 2½cc, of the culture liquid respectively. No untoward results following the injection of these large doses, they were transferred to the large infected pen May 25.

A second lot (Nos. 226, 228, 215, and 229) were treated in precisely the same way and at the same time, excepting in receiving ⅛cc for the first dose instead of ¼cc.

Pig No.	First inoculation April 21.	Second inoculation May 6.	Exposure in infected pen.	Time of death.	Days after first exposure.
	cc.	cc.			
214	¼	1	May 25	July 1	37
227	¼	1½	May 25	June 27	33
223	¼	2	May 25	July 2	38
222	¼	2½	May 25	July 1	37
226	⅛	1	May 25	July 3	39
228	⅛	1½	May 25	July 31	49
215	⅛	2	May 25	July 10	46
229	⅛	2½	May 25	June 27	33
224*			May 25	Aug. 4	71
225*			May 25	June 27	33

* Checks.

No. 214 being in a dying condition July 1, was killed. In the cæcum and colon were found very large, deep, blackish ulcers upon a pale mucosa. The case was evidently one of chronic hog-cholera. A pure liquid culture of the hog-cholera bacterium was obtained from the spleen.

No. 227 died June 27. The lymphatic glands were deeply congested; the mucosa of large intestine was generally pigmented and covered with large blackish ulcers,

Small yellowish ulcers were also found in the ileum. The points of injection were occupied by encysted, partly liquefied masses.

No. 223 was found dead July 2. At the points of injection encysted masses were found, the contents of one of which were discharging through an opening in the skin. The mucosa of the entire large intestine deeply congested. Scattered ulcers of varying age and size in the cæcum and colon. Bacterium in spleen.

No. 222, after a period of unthriftiness, was found dead July 1. The autopsy revealed a chronic broncho-pneumonia, with pleuritic adhesions of right lung. The mucous membrane of the cæcum and colon, besides being studded with a large number of broad shallow ulcers, was deeply and uniformly congested, the congestion involving also the lower portion of the ileum. On both thighs an encysted semi-liquid mass indicated the seat of the inoculation. This case suggests the probability of a double infection, the first represented by the ulceration, the second by the more recent inflammation of the mucous membrane.

Of the second lot, which had received $\frac{1}{8}$cc of the first inoculation, all succumbed to the infection. No. 226 died July 3. The characteristic lesion was extensive ulceration, together with deep congestion of the mucosa of large intestine. Encysted masses at the points of inoculation. A considerable number of bacteria of hog-cholera in the spleen.

No. 228 died July 13. In this animal the mucosa of cæcum and colon presented a continuous mass of necrosed blackish tissue, the ileo-cæcal valve being enlarged to twice the nomal size. A few scattered yellowish ulcers in the lower portion of the colon. No. 215 died July 10, probably affected in the same way, though no *post mortem* examination was made.

No. 229 died June 27. In this case the lymphatic glands were in general deeply congested; ecchymoses beneath the serous membranes. Pigmentation of the mucous membrane of the stomach, duodenum, ileum, and large intestine from former extravasations. Several large ulcers on the valve and some others in colon. Ulcers in the cardiac portion of the stomach. Encysted masses at the point of inoculation.

Nos. 224 and 225 were penned with the above eight animals as checks. No. 225, after being sick for a few days, was found dead June 27. The mucosa of the cæcum and upper half of the colon is extensively pigmented and ulcerated, the lower half deeply congested. The ileum is also ulcerated for 5 or 6 feet from the valve. Many of the ulcers are so deep as to have produced inflammation of the serous membrane and thickening of the intestinal walls. The other check (No. 224) lived over two months after exposure, being unthrifty during this period. On *post mortem* the mucosa of large intestine was considerably pigmented and scars of healed ulcers were present. A large suppurating wound of the lower jaw, involving the bone, may have contributed towards the fatal issue.

These inoculations having failed to produce immunity from natural infection, a second experiment was tried by augmenting the dose of strong virus used for the second inoculation. Thus Nos. 239, 242, 244, and 245 received each $\frac{1}{8}$cc for the first inoculation May 27, No. 243 being retained in the same pen as a check. Of these No. 239 died of hog-cholera as the result of the inoculation. The remaining three, received two weeks later, on June 10, 2cc each of strong virus. The cultures were prepared in beef infusion with 1 per cent. peptone. They were usually the third or fourth culture, not more than one day old. A second lot (Nos. 240, 254, 255, and 256) were inoculated at the same time and in the same way, with this exception, that the second dose was increased to 3cc. On June 24 all were placed in the large infected pen.

No. 239 died June 2, within six days after receiving $\frac{1}{8}$cc of the culture and as a result of the inoculation. The lesions were those of a very acute case, engorged spleen and lymphatics, intense congestion of the mucosa of the large intestine and of the intestinal tract in general. The lungs were likewise engorged and dotted with extravasations. This animal was eating and apparently well on the morning of death. The spleen was crowded with the bacterium of hog-cholera, and pure cultures of the microbe were obtained from it.

No. 243 died July 17. The characteristic lesions of hog-cholera were found in it; extensive ulceration of the cæcum and colon; engorgement of spleen and lymphatic glands with blood. Encysted masses at the point of inoculation. No. 224 succumbed July 9 with practically the same lesions, besides the presence of a considerable quantity of serum in the abdominal cavity.

The check to this lot died July 18. The depth of the ulcerations in the cæcum and colon had implicated the serous covering, so that adhesions had formed between the cæcum and abdominal walls. Punctiform ecchymoses on serosa of ileum; the mucosa not affected. The mucosa of cæcum was found completely ulcerated, the necrosis stopping abruptly at the edge of the valve; in the colon the necrosis resolved itself into large isolated ulcers.

Of the second lot No. 240 died July 10. At the place of inoculation a firm pale yellowish mass about one inch long was found. The lower portion of ileum, the cæcum, the upper portion of colon, contained ulcers of different sizes. The duodenum was occluded by a clot of blood. No. 254 died the same day with lesions of a similar character. No. 255 died July 20. The spleen in this case was greatly augmented in size and gorged with blood. The right lung was congested and adherent to wall of thorax; considerable effusion in this pleural sac. The cæcum and upper portion of colon covered with deep blackish ulcers. A few small ulcers in ileum.

Pig No.	First inoculation May 27.	Second inoculation June 10.	Exposure in infected pen.	Time of death.	Days after first exposure.
	cc.	cc.			
239	½			June 2†	
242	½	2	June 24	July 17	23
244	½	2	June 24	July 9	15
245	½	2	June 24		
243*			June 24	July 18	19
240	½	3	June 24	July 10	16
254	½	3	June 24	July 10	16
255	½	3	June 24	July 20	26
256	½	3	June 24		
253*					

*Check. †From inoculation.

The foregoing experiments demonstrate the important fact that pigs cannot be made insusceptible to hog-cholera by subcutaneous injections of pure cultures of hog-cholera bacteria. This method, which was originally suggested and applied by Pasteur to anthrax and *rouget*, therefore fails in this disease. The experiments have been sufficiently varied and extended to leave no doubt as to this point. The subcutaneous injection of large as well as small quantities of culture liquid, either once or twice, left the animal as susceptible to natural infection as before inoculation, and in a few cases produced a virulent type of the disease. We have already dwelt upon the important fact that the disease can be produced by feeding when subcutaneous inoculation fails. This may also explain the failure of protective inoculation. The disease exerts its severest effects locally upon the mucosa of the large intestine, and in only a few cases is it a real septicæmia. The bacteria have the power of rapid multiplication within the vascular system only when exceptionally virulent. Subcutaneous inoculations of cultures, in which they may have become attenuated, are of little avail, because they are speedily destroyed in the connective tissue, leaving only a slight local swelling behind. Other lines of investigation must therefore be followed out before any practical results can be obtained.

HOW CAN HOG-CHOLERA BE PREVENTED?

The measures which must be adopted to prevent the introduction and spread of hog-cholera depend upon our knowledge of the disease as it appears in herds, and more especially upon a study of the cause. This we have demonstrated to be a microscopic plant organism belonging to the class of bacteria, and resembling in a general way those organisms which are the cause of infectious diseases among men. Of this disease the only reliable diagnostic lesion is ulceration of the large intestine, or the presence of the bacterium in the body of the affected animal, and whatever follows can only apply to the disease produced by this specific organism or bacterium.

It has been shown in this and preceding reports that the disease spreads from one animal to another of the same herd until sometimes only a small percentage of unthrifty animals remain. It extends from one herd to another, and may be carried long distances. The presence of the specific bacterium has been demonstrated in such widely different regions as the District of Columbia, Illinois, and Nebraska.

The fact that one animal takes the disease from another does not explain how the virus is transferred. Is it carried directly from one to another in the air, or is it deposited in the soil by one animal to be taken up by another? Is it introduced through a wound in the skin? Is it taken up by the lungs from the inspired air, or is it introduced with the food and drink? These questions cannot be solved by simply observing the disease in herds, hence numerous experiments detailed in this and the preceding report have been directed to a solution of these questions, upon which some rational rules for prevention may be based.

The disease is perhaps never communicated by injuries of the skin, by bites and wounds obtained in other ways. Large quantities of liquid containing the virus can be introduced beneath the skin without fatal results. In the great majority of pigs a local swelling is the only effect.

Whether the lungs serve commonly as an entrance to the virus cannot be definitely stated. All experimental evidence points the other way, and in a large percentage of cases the lungs are intact, while the large intestine is severely ulcerated. We have shown that blood and tissue which have been dried for two months may contain bacteria, which readily multiply when placed in proper media. Hence the dust from pens where the disease exists may contain many bacteria, which, on reaching the lungs, multiply and produce the disease. It is our intention to continue experiments which may throw more light upon this mode of infection.

Perhaps the most common source of infection is the food and drink. That is, the virus enters the alimentary canal, and there produces such extensive ulceration that the animal sooner or later succumbs from gradual exhaustion, septic poisoning, or peritonitis. Or the virus immediately enters the blood from the intestines, multiplies in every organ of the body, and causes death in a few days, or even hours. Such sudden deaths usually occur at the beginning of severe epidemics. Pigs which are fed with the internal organs of those that have died of the disease almost invariably take the disease in a very severe form, and die within one or two weeks after infection. To demonstrate that it was the specific bacterium of hog-cholera in these internal organs, and not some other element, pigs were fed with liquids which contained only this organism, and they produced the most severe disease. These demonstrations, together with the commonly observed fact that the disease seems to exist in the large intestine only, prove conclusively that the virus is introduced largely with food and drink.

It has already been stated that the most common seat of the disease is the large intestine. The food after leaving the stomach passes in a liquid condition through the small intestine, so that this never seems filled; in fact, its only contents are a coating of semi-liquid matter over the mucous membrane. It passes through the small intestine quite rapidly, but on reaching the large intestine the undigested remains become more consistent, because the liquid is reabsorbed, and are kept here for some time. The bacteria, if not destroyed by the gastric juice, pass quickly through the small intestine, but in the large intestine they begin to multiply and attack the mucous membrane, which they destroy. Hence the feces or discharges of diseased pigs, wherever deposited, scatter larger or smaller quantities of the virus, which may induce the disease over and over again. The discharges, then, must be looked upon as the chief vehicle for the virus when the disease has taken hold of a herd. Pigs endowed with the well-known habits will not hesitate to avail themselves of the opportunity of becoming infected whenever it is offered. But the discharges are not the only means by which the virus is disseminated and kept alive. We have shown that the bacterium constituting the living virus is a very hardy germ, and one endowed with great powers of multiplication. In the laboratory it has grown luxuriantly in milk and on boiled potato. It grows slightly in hay infusion, even in urine not neutralized. The temperature throughout the summer in most of the States is sufficiently elevated to permit the growth of the bacterium in these various substances, since a temperature of 70° F. is amply sufficient, and temperatures above this point simply favor the rate of increase of the quantity of virus. Even in good drinking water the virus will increase for four or five days and remain alive for months.

There is consequently very little about a pen in which the virus, when scattered in the discharges of infected animals, will not increase in quantity and form a more potent source of infection. It will multiply in the wet soil, in the drinking water, and in the semi-liquid food. A gallon of milk inoculated with a minute portion of infectious material and allowed to stand through a warm night in midsummer might be sufficient to produce the disease in at least a dozen animals if fed to them on an empty stomach.

Such are the external conditions which may favor the extension of hog-cholera. The condition of the animals themselves is of great importance in favoring or preventing infection. When pigs are fed with liquids in which the specific bacterium only is present, those that have been deprived of food for some time previous take the disease, while those whose stomachs contain food that is undergoing digestion do not take it readily. If, besides starving the animal, they are fed with some alkaline solution by which the alkalinity of the stomach is increased, the pathogenic effect is still more pronounced. Any disorder of digestion by which the secretion of gastric juice is diminished or checked and the mucus is increased in quantity will increase the susceptibility of the animal to infection, because the alkalinity of the mucous membrane will favor rather than destroy the virus. Any mode of feeding which produces constipation and overdistension of the large intestine is likely to favor the disease, as the virus is retained for a longer time. It multiplies there and destroys the mucous membrane before it is discharged. Keeping these facts in mind, we may formulate a few rules, which must be carefully observed if the disease is to be kept in check.

In the first place, there should be no communication between infected herds and such as are still free from the disease. The virus may be carried in various ways, even on the shoes of persons. A small quantity thus introduced may multiply in the soil and water until it becomes a center of infection for many animals. Streams into which sick animals have dropped discharges or in which dead ones have lain must be considered as vehicles of the disease for all herds below the source of infection. This is especially true in warm weather, when the virus multiplies very rapidly and extensively.

When the disease has appeared in a herd, the ground upon which the animals lived at the time must be considered as infected, and it is much safer to remove all the well ones to uninfected grounds than to simply remove the sick ones. But how are we to know that the disease has gained a foothold in the herd? It is quite common for the disease to announce itself by a few sudden deaths. The stricken animals may seem well a day, perhaps only a few hours, before death. Such animals should always be immediately destroyed by careful deep burial, or by burning, which is much better, for the bodies are as a rule crowded with the specific poison of hog-cholera. In order to remove any doubts as to the precise nature of the disease, it is best to examine such animals before burying or burning them. This should be done in a secluded place which pigs cannot reach, and the ground thoroughly disinfected, as will be described later. The disease in the sudden cases can be easily recognized. The spleen is as a rule very black and enlarged. Spots of blood from the size of a pin's head to a quarter inch or more will be seen in the fat under the skin, on the intestines, lungs, heart, and kidneys. The lymphatic glands are purplish instead of a pale pink. When the large intestines are opened they are found covered with these dark spots of blood more or less uniformly and entirely. Often the contents are covered with clotted blood. Any or all of these may be considered as signs of the disease in its most virulent form. In these animals the virus has penetrated into all of the vital organs, and they should be immediately removed and destroyed. It must be borne in mind that for any animal to consume portions of these carcasses would be certain death; that the blood and fluids from these dead bodies contain the virus, and when scattered over the soil or thrown into streams they simply distribute the virus, allow it to multiply, and all the other animals are thereby put in the way of becoming infected.

In many outbreaks the early cases do not succumb so rapidly. They grow weaker, lie down much of the time, eat but little, and usually have diarrhea. Most of such cases may linger for weeks, meanwhile scattering the poison in the discharges. The disease may be recognized in these cases as soon as they are observed to act suspiciously, and there should be no delay in determining at once the nature of the disease. When the animal has been opened the large intestine should be carefully slit up and examined, beginning with the blind or upper end. There will be seen roundish yellow or blackish spots, having an irregular depressed, sometimes elevated, surface. These are well shown in the Second Annual Report of this Bureau, p. 246, or in the Annual eport of the Department for 1885, p. 522. These spots correspond to dead portions of the mucous membrane, and they are frequently seen from the outside as soon as the animal is opened. Sometimes the membrane has been entirely destroyed. Its appearance is well shown on Plates I and II of this report. These slow, chronic cases are apt to spread the disease in the bowel discharges, for in them the virus is chiefly located.

Having determined the existence of the disease, it may not be possible to remove the healthy animals to uninfected quarters after the sick ones have been taken away. Under such circumstances thorough disinfection should be practiced at once. Among a large number of substances tried in the laboratory only a few were found to meet the requirements of rapidity of action combined with certainty and cheapness. Carbolic acid seems to be useless, as it is expensive, and a considerable quantity is required to destroy the germs. Thus experiments in the laboratory have shown that to kill the virus in liquids 1 part carbolic acid in 100 parts of water is required, whereas 1 part of mercuric chloride in 75,000 parts of water is sufficient. The best disinfectant is therefore mercuric chloride, also called mercuric bichloride and corrosive sublimate. As it is a violent poison to man and animals, it should be very carefully handled. In order to make a solution which is strong enough to act rapidly and with certainty, 1 part of the substance should be dissolved in 1,000 parts of water. This is best accomplished by adding half an ounce to about four gallons of clear water, preferably rain-water. As a pound of corrosive sublimate retails at about 70 cents, the cost of the disinfectant is very small. This solution, which should be made in wooden or graniteware vessels at least half a day before use, should be applied by means of a broom or brush to the flooring, sides, and covering of pens in which diseased animals have staid. All utensils used about the pens, as well as the troughs and other things containing food, should be carefully washed with the solution and afterwards rinsed thoroughly in pure water. Ten minutes' exposure to the disinfectant solution is sufficient for all purposes. As the corrosive sublimate solution attacks many metals, iron and tin utensils should be disinfected with boiling water instead of the mercuric chloride solution.

The bowel discharges should be made innocuous by pouring upon them corrosive sublimate solution or mixing them with powdered chloride of lime. In general it may be stated that whatever has come in contact with diseased animals or their discharges should first be disinfected before healthy animals are brought in contact with them. In using the corrosive sublimate solution we must bear in mind that it is poisonous to animals as well as to man, and that to get the desired effect no large quantities need be applied. The surface need simply be moistened with it in order to be disinfected. A spray apparatus, by means of which a spray is deposited, would be most convenient, but such apparatus is expensive and not readily procurable. It is always desirable to moisten the bodies of dead animals with the disinfectant before removing them. Any virus adhering to the surface of the body is thereby destroyed and the danger of disseminating it avoided.

When the disinfectant is not at hand much can be done with boiling water, which immediately destroys the virus. Scalding the troughs and other articles is perhaps better than the use of the corrosive sublimate, especially if they are immersed in the boiling water or flooded with it. Some good may be done by scalding bowel discharges and the flooring of pens, although by doing so the virus which is not destroyed is carried away by the cooling water, which may later on favor its multiplication. In any case it is best to use for pens the sublimate solution first and then scald them.

As it is quite impossible to disinfect the soil with any degree of certainty, it is very desirable that in a herd in which the disease has appeared the still healthy animals be transferred to fresh ground and kept confined. In this way the dangers arising from an infected soil are averted. For a like reason animals should be kept from streams which have become polluted, as it is impossible to disinfect them.

Hence a dry soil, without standing pools of water, should be chosen as long as any suspicion of the disease exists.

Great care should be bestowed upon the food, especially that of a liquid character, which, when infected, will permit the multiplication of the virus and may infect large numbers. Cleanliness in this respect is perhaps the simplest and most universal rule which can be laid down. This simply means that the food should not come in contact with the bowel discharges of diseased animals; that it should not be allowed to stand for more than a few hours before it is consumed; and that the troughs used for feeding should be scalded at least twice a day when there is a suspicion that the virus may be among the animals.

It may seem too laborious or perhaps superfluous to carry out such directions as these. They may be incompatible with the present methods of hog-raising in many parts of our country. They are, however, the only means at present available by which the spread of the virus may be checked. They prevent the soil from becoming saturated with it, and every exertion made towards disinfection destroys so much, and continued efforts may finally destroy it altogether. Moreover, if the disease does appear while measures of prevention are being carried out, it is not so apt to become very destructive, for the severity of the disease depends, as a rule, upon the quantity of virus taken into the system. If this is allowed to accumulate on all sides, much will find its way into the stomach and intestines and cause the most severe disease.

We do not know whether the virus can live in the soil through the winter, but it seems highly probable. Hence thorough disinfection practiced will lessen the chances for a reappearance of the disease in the following year.

The investigations in regard to vaccination as a means of prevention have not yet led to any results which can be practically utilized, and therefore are still being carried on. The ordinary methods of attenuation, as practiced by Pasteur in obtaining a vaccinal virus for anthrax and *rouget*, are inapplicable in this peculiar disease, for the unattenuated virus itself is incapable of conferring immunity. The experiments demonstrating this fact are found on another page. Hence any attenuated virus is still less capable of accomplishing this end.

The use of certain medicines internally to act as preventives may prove of some value, and it is our purpose to carry out some experiments in this direction as well.

The treatment of this disease, as of the great majority of infectious diseases, after it has gained a firm hold upon the animal, is not only useless but dangerous; for the animal can only serve to spread the disease. The ulcerations produced in the large intestines can only heal slowly if they are not too extensive, while medicines are of no avail. Those who insist upon a cure for well-pronounced cases of hog-cholera, in which the bowels have become ulcerated, should look upon the disease of typhoid fever in man, in which ulceration also occurs. Through centuries the best physicians have been treating this disease, yet none has ever ventured to assert that he had a cure for these ulcerations. They take the best care of the patient and allow nature to heal the ulcers. Even then they frequently find their patient snatched away at the very threshold of recovery.

PRELIMINARY INVESTIGATIONS CONCERNING INFECTIOUS PNEUMONIA IN SWINE* (SWINE-PLAGUE).

In prosecuting investigations in the West in order to determine whether the disease which has been described in these reports as hog-cholera existed there also, the lesions characteristic of this disease and the specific bacterium were found in Illinois and Nebraska. At the same time another microbe was found, resembling in its microscopical characters the microbe of rabbit septicæmia very closely, and associated with disease of the lungs—a chronic pneumonia—in the few cases which were examined. Although the investigations concerning the nature of this microbe, its distribution, and the losses it produces, are scarcely begun, we venture the conclusion that it produces an infectious pneumonia in pigs, and that its effect may perhaps be spent upon organs other than the lungs. This conclusion is based upon the facts recorded in the following pages.

Among the *post mortem* examinations made in the State of Illinois in July, 1886, the following are worthy of attention:

In Marion County, a few miles from Patoka, a herd was found, July 7, of which about ten had died and an equal number were still alive. Through the kindness of the owner several pigs, which were evidently diseased, were killed by a blow on the head. In No. 1 the superficial inguinals were greatly enlarged; ecchymoses were found in the subcutaneous fatty tissue in large numbers on the omentum and the epicardium. The lymphatic glands were as a rule enlarged and purplish, the spleen augmented in size, the major portion of the lungs hepatized, and the remainder interspersed with hemorrhagic foci. The mucous membrane of the stomach and the large intestine was ecchymosed, that of the latter presenting here and there deep ulcers, especially on the ileo-cæcal valve. Cover-glass preparations from the spleen of this case contained no bacteria of any kind. A tube of gelatine into which a bit of spleen had been dropped remained sterile. No. 2, from the same herd, also killed at the time, was affected with a suppurative pyelitis of the right kidney, causing inflammatory adhesions of the large intestine. The mucous membrane of the latter was dotted with innumerable petechiæ and a few ulcers. Cover-glass preparations from the spleen of this animal were equally negative. A tube of gelatine into which a bit of spleen tissue was dropped began to liquefy very slowly. It contained a bacillus and a large oval coccus.

No. 3, from the same herd, killed, had its lymphatic glands generally enlarged and purplish, the spleen dotted with numerous blood-red elevated points, lungs with large carnified areas. The mucous membrane of the large intestine was merely congested. No bacteria seen in cover-glass preparations of the spleen, and a gelatine culture made as before remained sterile.

Several miles east of Champaign, Ill., the disease was appearing in a herd, the owner of which very kindly permitted us to make what examinations we thought advisable. On July 8 two autopsies were made. In No. 4, dead since last night, the lymphatic glands generally were enlarged and purplish. The subcutaneous fatty tissue stained yellow. The peritoneal and pericardial cavity contained a considerable amount of yellow serum. The only other marked lesion observed was an enormous enlargement of the spleen, which was very dark and pulpy. The mucous membrane of the alimentary canal apparently intact. These lesions did not point to hog-cholera. Cover-glass preparations of the spleen were negative. A piece dropped into a tube of gelatine slowly liquefied the latter. A bacillus was found in it, not pathogenic.

A pig (No. 5) which was observed to be very weak, although able to move about when disturbed, was killed for further information. In the subcutaneous tissue over the abdomen were numerous ecchymoses. The inguinal glands were greatly enlarged, cortex purplish, some lobules deeply congested throughout. The abdominal cavity contained a small quantity of colorless serum; the spleen considerably tumefied and covered with blood-red raised points. The lymphatic glands about the

---

*We shall call this disease swine-plague, in distinction from hog-cholera, just described. See introductory remarks to Diseases of Swine, p. 603.

stomach, as well as the bronchials, were deeply congested, the cortex infiltrated with blood. The epicardium was dotted over its entire surface with minute extravasations. The mucous membrane in the fundus of the stomach and of the entire length of the large intestine covered with closely-set extravasations. Cover-glass preparations, as well as cultures of the spleen, were entirely negative.

Reports of swine-plague from Geneseo, Henry County, made it advisable to make a few *post mortem* examinations in this section of the State, in order to make sure of the nature of the disease. The losses were very heavy, involving in many places the greater part of the affected herd. July 11 several autopsies were made in a herd about 3 miles from Geneseo. In this herd the disease had been observed about nine days before. At the time three or four large animals had died during the night and a number of others were ill.

No. 6.—Adult black male, in good condition, no signs of decomposition. In the peritoneal cavity there were ecchymoses beneath the peritoneum of the dorsal wall, near the caudal end of the kidneys, at least an inch in diameter. The spleen was enlarged and congested. Whitish patches showing through the serosa of the large intestine were afterwards found to correspond with ulcerations of the mucous membrane. The lymphatic glands in general with congested cortex. The left lung completely solidified, blackish, and everywhere adherent to chest wall. On forcing the ribs apart the lung tissue broke as a watermelon would; from the broken surface a blackish frothy liquid exuded. A portion of the right lung was in the same condition. A fibrinous deposit on the epicardium indicative of pericarditis. In the alimentary tract the mucous membrane of the fundus of the stomach is darkened with extravasations on the ridges of the folds. In the large intestine the mucous membrane is completely covered with punctiform extravasations, in part converted into pigment. In the cæcum and colon are isolated disk-shaped ulcers about one-half inch in diameter, slightly elevated. The center is dark, surrounded by a broad yellowish margin, giving the whole a button-like appearance. On section a whitish tough tissue is found to make up the ulcer and extend to the peritoneum, where it appears as a whitish patch when viewed from the serous surface. Cover-glass preparations of the spleen negative. Two portions dropped into a tube of gelatine and agar-agar respectively gave rise to cultures which will be described in detail farther on.

No. 7.—A small shoat, having shown signs of disease for a few days, was killed by a blow on the head. The superficial inguinal glands were enlarged and reddened. Both kidneys dotted on the surface with minute petechiæ. On section a few are found in medullary portion. The spleen is dotted with a few blood-red elevated points. Cover-glass preparations of the spleen negative. Cultures remain sterile.

No. 8.—Large black sow; died last night. Adipose abundant. In this animal the spleen was enlarged, the medullary portion of kidneys deeply reddened, lungs normal. The mucosa of the large intestine was entirely covered with minute elongated spots of pigment, representing former extravasations. Cover-glass preparations of spleen also negative. A gelatine tube containing a portion of spleen contained a micrococcus. Bits of the spleen introduced beneath the skin of the dorsum of two mice made them ill for a few days. Both finally recovered.

Besides the cultures mentioned in the autopsy notes at least ten others were made at the time by piercing the spleens with a platinum wire and then piercing with it tubes of gelatine or drawing it over the surface of tubes of agar-agar. None of these showed any signs of growth, thus confirming the supposition, derived from the examination of cover-glass preparations, that the specific microbes are either entirely absent from the spleen or else are present in very small numbers.

The lesions found in all but three cases, in which the ulceration of the large intestine was present, were not sufficiently uniform to warrant the diagnosis of hog-cholera. Viewed by the light of later observations, it seems highly probable that the remainder of the animals were affected with a different malady, due to the presence of the microbe to be described later on. The ecchymosis of the large intestine and the congestion and tumefaction of the lymphatics generally differed from the lesions which we have found in hog-cholera. The absence of bacteria from the tissues is also suspicious. There was moreover a partial cirrhosis of the liver in most of the animals examined which we have never encountered in hog-cholera. We must remember, however, that of these eight cases five were killed, perhaps in the early stages of the disease, before the lesions were well marked. Leaving these observations for future interpretation, when more cases have been examined we will proceed to a description of the bacteriological investigations.

In a few among a large number of tubes bacteria were present. Nearly all were found harmless when inoculated into animals very susceptible to hog-cholera. In two tubes inoculated with bits of spleen from No. 6 two microbes were found which deserve attention.

One grew in both tubes, which was more carefully examined, because it resembled the bacterium of hog-cholera very closely. In liquid media it is actively motile and simulates the form of a bacillus. When stained, however, each individual is resolved into a pair of ovals or very short rods with rounded extremities. A deeply stained narrow border surrounds a comparatively pale body. There seems to be slightly more stained material at the two extremities than in the bacterium already fully described in the last report. It seems a trifle longer than the latter form, but on attempting to confirm this impression by measurement the dimensions were found practically the same. Sown on gelatine plates the colonies appear within twenty-four hours and grow quite rapidly. The deep colonies are spherical, with smooth outline and homogeneous disc. The surface colonies appear as irregular patches, spreading very quickly, and, as a rule, growing far more vigorously than the deep colonies. In tubes containing nutrient gelatine the isolated colonies in the depth of the needle track may grow to the size of pins' heads. On the surface a flat, thin, pearly layer rapidly extends from the point of inoculation, and in from one to two weeks may have covered the entire surface. The margins are irregularly scalloped and lobed, the entire layer often simulating the frost flowers on windows or lace work (Plate V, Fig. 2). On potato, a thick straw-colored shining layer of nearly smooth surface forms, which grows very vigorously and gradually covers the entire cut surface of the potato with a layer 2^{mm} thick. This growth is brighter in color and more abundant than appears in the potato culture of the bacterium of hog-cholera. Cultivated in liquids, such as beef infusion with 1 per cent. peptone, the medium becomes very turbid within twenty-four hours. A thin pellicle appears, which soon becomes a thick membrane. A cream-colored deposit forms and accumulates to a considerable extent, while the liquid remains turbid. It will be remembered that the bacterium of hog-cholera grows very feebly in comparison.

No resistant spore state was found, for tubes exposed to 58° C. for fifteen minutes remained sterile; those exposed ten minutes became turbid. The pale, unstained central portion of the bacterium simulates very strikingly the appearance of an endogenous spore, yet they all succumb to the temperature of 58° C., as described. A peculiar property not common to the hog-cholera bacteria described is the coagulation of the casein of milk. If a tube of this liquid, sterilized by discontinuous boiling, be inoculated, it will be solidified within twenty-four hours. The coagulum, contracting later on, leaves a shallow stratum of watery liquid near the surface. The reaction is acid. Grown on gelatine a rather penetrating odor of decomposing flesh is given off. The bacterium of hog-cholera develops no odor whatever in cultures. This microbe, therefore, resembled the bacterium of hog-colera very closely in its microscopic characters, but differed from it in some of its physiological properties. This illustrates how important cultivation experiments are in the determination of specific differences. That it was not the bacterium of hog-cholera was shown by an utter want of pathogenic properties when inoculated into mice and rabbits. Pigs were inoculated and fed; cultures were introduced per rectum without any effect whatever.

In one of the tubes the motile bacterium just described was mixed with another microbe, which proved to be a very virulent germ. It was obtained pure as follows: A rabbit inoculated with the mixture from a liquid culture made from the original gelatine tube died in seven days, after showing signs of lameness for several days. The inoculated thigh was enlarged, the skin bluish. The subcutaneous connective tissue was of a leathery consistency. The surface of the muscular tissue on the inner aspect of the thigh was of a uniform yellowish gray; this change extended into the muscular tissue to the depth of 3^{mm} (one-eighth inch); the striated appearance was lost. This change also involved the deeper intermuscular septa of the thigh. On the abdomen the subcutis was infiltrated with a blood-stained serum. The local effect had thus been unusually severe. Cultures from the spleen, liver, and blood in gelatine tubes contained only the second microbe. The one above described had no power of invading the tissues of the rabit. That the microbe obtained from the tissue of this rabbit was pathogenic the following experiments clearly demonstrate:

With pure liquid cultures of this microbe three mice were inoculated. Two of these died within one and two days of inoculation. In the spleen of both peculiar torula-like forms were found, presumably the cocci in process of division, which was retarded by unfavorable conditions. Its effect upon a rabbit, however, was more pronounced. This rabbit died three days after a hypodermic injection of ½cc of a liquid culture. Beneath the skin of the inoculated thigh there was a translucent gelatinous exudate about one-half inch thick. The muscles of the thigh and of the contiguous wall of the abdomen were dotted with closely set punctiform and larger extravasations. In the abdomen they were very numerous on the large intestine along a zone nearest the abdominal wall. They were also found over the kidney and on the psoas muscle. Spleen not enlarged, dark; liver rather pale; acini well marked; the entire right lung and base of the left deeply congested; very few bacteria in the internal organs. Two liquid cultures of blood and one from liver contained the injected microbes. Gelatine cultures of blood, spleen, and liver developed into numerous colonies of the same microbe in the needle track.

Two pigs (Nos. 287 and 289) were inoculated September 11 from a culture of the rabbit. Each received beneath the skin of the thigh 2½cc of the culture liquid. No. 287 became dull and lost its appetite several days later; eyes discharging. September 28 the animal became delirious and ran blindly about the pen; dead next morning. The only observable lesions were local swellings two inches across and one-fourth to three-fourths inch thick, with centers which were beginning to soften. Blood very dark, not coagulated; a few petechiæ on epicardium. The liver was very pale, sclerosed; the medulla of kidney deeply reddened. No. 289 died September 21, after exhibiting the same symptoms; local swellings as above, without indications of softening; the connective tissue and fat of the whole body of a deep yellow color; liver very firm, bloodless, and of a peculiar yellowish red color throughout; medulla of kidneys deeply reddened; two large cysts in the right one. In neither case was the alimentary tract diseased. In both there was cirrhosis of the liver, producing in the second animal a general jaundice. From neither were cultures of the inoculated microbe successful, though blood from the heart, the spleen, and the liver were used. The tubes remained sterile.

Nos. 288 and 290, which had been retained in the same pen, did not contract the disease from the others, as would ordinarily happen in hog-cholera. No. 288 was fed with hog-cholera viscera October 12, and died from the effects December 4; cæcum and colon ulcerated. No. 290, fed at the same time, died October 28, the only visible cause of death being retention of urine.

This microbe was, therefore, fatal to mice, rabbits and pigs, producing in the pig an acute inflammation of the liver, leading to a marked cirrhosis and general jaundice.

The same disease found near Sodorus, Ill.—The same microbe was obtained from an outbreak in Sodorus, Illinois, several months later. On page 630 a description is given of two *post mortems*, in one of which (No. 1) the lesions were ulceration of the large intestine and a grayish hepatization of the lungs. From this animal the bacterium of hog-cholera had been obtained from the spleen. In the other animal (No. 2) the lung lesions only were present. Portions of the solidified lung tissue from No. 2, hardened in strong alcohol, were submitted to a microscopic examination. The tissue was infiltrated with paraffine, the sections treated with turpentine to remove the imbedding substance, and then stained in various ways. The smaller bronchi and air-cells were completely filled with an exudate, consisting of white blood corpuscles chiefly, and some larger pale cells, probably derived from the epithelium. This infiltration was exceedingly dense in many places; in others less so. The septa or alveolar walls were not perceptibly affected, but the capillaries were distended with blood corpuscles, and formed an unstained mesh-work around the deeply stained alveolar contents. The interlobular connective tissue was also infiltrated, and the lymphatic spaces distended and filled with a fibrillar network of coagulated lymph. When the alveolar contents were carefully examined with a one-eighteenth homogeneous objective, after staining the section in Löffler's alkaline methylene blue for several hours and decolorizing in one-half per cent. acetic acid, groups of very minute oval bacteria were recognizable, in size and outline like those obtained in cultures from the pleura. These groups were very large and extended through the depth of the section, a fact easily recognized by focusing up and down. They were found in all parts of the section, the bacteria themselves and the groups they formed being readily recognizable. No other bacteria could be detected, though the sections were searched over many times. Staining in aniline water methyl violet overnight did not bring these groups out so clearly as the stain above given. These groups, moreover, were present in those air-cells chiefly in which the exudate was but moderately dense.

The lesions of the lungs found in both pigs at Sodorus, Ill., were different from those occasionally found in *post mortem* examinations of hog-cholera at the Washington Experimental Station. In the latter the acute cases, characterized by hemorrhagic lesions in various organs, usually presented lungs which were dotted with dark red patches visible on the pleural surfaces and in the parenchyma. These were evidently extravasations into the alveoli, and etiologically the same as the extravasations found elsewhere. In the majority of cases lung lesions were entirely absent. When present they were usually associated with an abundance of lung worms in the bronchi. In many cases the small anterior lobes resting laterally upon the pericardium were collapsed (atelectasis), of the color of red flesh. This condition seems to stand in no direct relation to the disease itself.

The broncho-pneumonia found in the pigs above referred to extended over at least one-half of the lungs, involving the caudal portion of the base, resting on the diaphragm. The pleura was but slightly affected; a few adhesions and a more than normal quantity of serum on its surface constituted the visible changes. The lung tissue itself was airless, solid, of a grayish red, somewhat mottled. From the pleural surface of No. 2 two tubes of gelatine were inoculated by dipping into them a loop of platinum wire filled with serous exudate. The heat of the weather liquefied both tubes soon after, and within a few days the gelatine in one of them was densely crowded with small whitish points; in the other tube the colonies were fewer in number and consequently much larger. Both were, in fact, pure cultures of a non-motile oval bacterium, found identical in all respects with the microbe obtained from Geneseo, Ill., and already described.

Postponing the description of this microbe for the present, the following experiments were made in order to determine its pathogenic effect upon small animals:

From one of the original tube cultures in gelatine plate cultures were made, and from one of the colonies a tube containing 10cc beef-infusion peptone was inoculated. When two days old the following animals received subcutaneously portions of this culture: Two mice, $\frac{1}{8}$cc, $\frac{1}{16}$cc; two rabbits, $\frac{1}{8}$cc, $\frac{1}{2}$cc; two pigeons, $\frac{1}{4}$cc, $\frac{3}{4}$cc; two pigs, 4.5cc, 3cc. One of the mice was dead on the following day. In the spleen and liver were present oval bacteria and some quite long rods. The liquid culture from the blood remained sterile. The second mouse died in two days. A peculiar bacterium was present in spleen, liver, and blood, often irregularly fusiform and pyriform; most were cocci in pairs. A liquid culture from the blood of the heart contained the inoculated microbe only, and the identity of this germ with the one injected was confirmed by plate cultures.

Both inoculated pigeons died, one two days and the other four days after inoculation. In the former the pectoral muscle at the point of inoculation had a grayish-yellow parboiled appearance over an area of 1 to 1½ square inches and extending to a depth of three-eighths inch. In the second bird, which had received the larger dose, the local lesion was less marked. A thick pasty deposit had formed between the skin and muscle, slightly infiltrating the surface of the latter. No bacteria could be detected on cover-glass preparations in the blood or liver of either bird.

Both rabbits likewise succumbed, one four and the other five days after inoculation. The autopsies point out the radical differences between the hog-cholera bacterium and the coccus under consideration. Before death both animals lay on their sides, breathing slowly. In the one which died first (which had received the smaller dose) the inoculated thigh was enlarged and drawn up to the body, the fascia covering the muscles of the thigh and the contiguous abdominal wall were thickened into whitish opaque sheets; a small area of the thigh muscles was whitish, necrosed. In the abdominal cavity strings and flakes of coagulated fibrin in various parts, together with the reddened appearance of the peritoneum, indicated a severe peritonitis; the liver was dark, blood flowing freely on section; spleen scarcely enlarged. Beneath the serosa of large intestine a few patches of extravasation; kidneys deeply reddened to the tip of the papilla; lungs normal. The microbe was very abundant in the local infiltration, the peritoneal exudate, in the parenchyma of spleen, liver, and kindeys, as well as in blood from the heart. In these cover-glass preparations involution forms were very common. Liquid cultures from blood of the heart and the peritoneal exudate contained the microbe as it usually appears in liquids. Tube cultures in gelatine from the blood, peritoneal exudate, and liver contained very many colonies, growing in a somewhat characteristic manner, to be described later on.

In the other rabbit the local effect was equally extensive, and there was a more marked grayish discoloration of the thigh and contiguous abdominal muscles. Peritonitis less marked; no coagula present. The bacteria not so numerous in the organs, but very abundant in the peritoneal cavity. Liquid cultures from the latter and from blood were pure. Gelatine tubes, cultures from the liver and spleen, contained many colonies.

Rabbits, mice, and pigeons were thus shown susceptible when inoculated with the quantities above mentioned. Two rabbits were at the same time inoculated with large quantities of two other microbes obtained from spleens. Both remained unaffected. In one a small circumscribed abscess could be seen through the skin.

Of the two pigs inoculated (Nos. 330 and 331), No. 330, which had received the larger dose (5cc) died in nine days, after exhibiting the same symptoms as those manifested by the two former cases—debility, loss of appetite, inflamed eyes. In this animal there was a similar condition of the liver, together with a deep yellow staining of the connective and adipose tissue generally. Cultures negative. No. 331 died thirty-five days after inoculation. In this animal there was a less pronounced pathological change in the liver. Icterus present. No cultures were made.

In order to confirm and extend the preceding inoculation experiments a second series was planned in the same way. A beef infusion peptone culture, which had been derived from a single colony of the microbe on a gelatine plate and was twenty-four hours old, was used to inoculate of mice, pigeons, fowls, and white rats 2 each, 1 guinea-pig, and rabbit. The mice, which received $\frac{1}{12}^{cc}$ beneath the skin of the back, died in two and six days respectively. In the first one the spleen and blood were crowded with bacteria, and a liquid culture from the blood proved pure. From the second mouse no cultures were made; bacteria few or absent from the organs. Of the 2 pigeons, 1 inoculated with $\frac{1}{8}^{cc}$ was dead next day. At the place of inoculation in the pectoral the muscular tissue was whitish, parboiled for a depth of one-fourth to one-half inch; cultures from blood and liver sterile. The other pigeon, which received $\frac{1}{4}^{cc}$, survived. The white rats, receiving respectively $\frac{1}{8}^{cc}$ and $\frac{1}{4}^{cc}$ subcutaneously in the thigh, did not prove susceptible. The rabbit, which received $\frac{1}{8}^{cc}$ in the same place, died in three days, after showing symptoms like those in the preceding experiment. Locally the lesions were the same; thickening of the fascia more pronounced; lardaceous appearance of the surface of the muscular tissue; punctiform extravasations both on abdomen and on thigh as far as symphysis pubis. In the abdominal cavity the serous surface of the entire intestine appeared as if sprayed with blood, the extravasation being beneath the serosa and not visible from the mucous surface. Small intestine but faintly reddened; only a few delicate fibrils of exudation as yet visible; a few extravasations on capsule of kidney, which is deeply reddened throughout; spleen and lungs normal; liver invaded by *coccidium oviforme*. Cover-glass preparations of spleen, liver, and peritoneum contain the microbes in abundance; in the peritoneal exudate they seem as numerous as in a liquid culture. Cultures both in beef infusion and in gelatine from the blood and peritoneal fluid were pure.

The guinea-pig, which had received into the thigh a rather large dose, $\frac{1}{2}^{cc}$, succumbed on the sixth day. At the point of inoculation there is but a slight infiltration and thickening of the subcutaneous connective tissue. In the abdomen, both spleen and liver somewhat enlarged. Covering these a thin, translucent, gelatinous layer, easily scraped away, and particularly well marked on the liver. Lungs deeply congested, not collapsed, but showing the impression of the ribs. The pleura covered with a similar exudate. The internal organs contained scarcely any bacteria, but cover-glasses touched to the surface of lungs and liver showed the exudate, consisting chiefly of leucocytes, to contain large numbers of the injected bacteria. Gelatine cultures of blood and from the liver, a liquid culture from the blood, were pure. A liquid culture from the peritoneal surface of spleen contained also a motile bacillus. The contact of this organ with the very thin-walled large intestine may explain the contamination.

Of two fowls inoculated beneath the skin of the pectoral with $\frac{1}{2}^{cc}$ and 1^{cc}, respectively, the one which received the smaller dose died in five days. In this bird the local lesion was very extensive. On removing the thickened, discolored skin the large pectoral was parboiled in appearance throughout half its mass; the remainder of the muscle studded with small extravasations. The pathological changes involved also the smaller pectoral in points and patches, extending through one of the fenestra of the sternum to the membrane surrounding the coils of intestine. The serum between the two muscles crowded with the injected bacteria. The mucosa of the intestine below the duodenal portion, including the cæca and the rectum, was very much inflamed. The cæca and the cloacal portion of rectum of a very dark red. There were also occasional hemorrhages beneath the mucosa. The bacteria seem to be confined to the local lesion, for cultures from the blood and liver remained sterile. The second fowl remained ill, sitting quietly and not moving unless disturbed. It was killed nine days after inoculation. The local lesion presented the appearance of a more advanced degeneration, but was more circumscribed, and limited in its depth to the larger pectoral. The intestines and other organs were free from inflammation. Cultures from this bird remained sterile.

In order to determine whether there would be any difference in the mortality or the lesions, another mode of inoculation was resorted to. Instead of employing liquid cultures and injecting into the subcutaneous tissue with the hypodermic syringe, a gelatine culture nine days old was used and the inoculation made as follows: In three mice an incision was made through the skin at the root of the tail, and into the subcutis through this incision a loop of the gelatine culture, consisting of a mixture of gelatine and microbes, was introduced. With the same amount two guinea-pigs were inoculated beneath the skin of the abdomen, two pigeons and one fowl beneath the skin covering one of the pectorals, and one rabbit on the inner surface of the ear, near the tip, by puncturing the skin with the point of a lancet and inserting the mass into the wound thus made. Of these animals the two guinea-pigs, the rabbit, and two mice died. The pigeons and fowl remained unaffected.

The mice died three and four days after inoculation respectively. One guinea-pig died in five days. The subcutis of the ventral surface of body from neck to pubis was infiltrated with a sero-sanguineous effusion and thickened, the skin itself infiltrated. There was but little change in the internal organs excepting the liver, which was pale and very friable. No exudate indicative of peritonitis, although a cover-glass touched to the surface of the liver contained very many bacteria, which were few in number in liver tissue and blood from the heart. The second guinea-pig died on the eighth day with the same but less extensive local lesions, parenchymatous degeneration of liver and spleen. The rabbit's ear had a deep red blush on the day after inoculation; enlarged slightly and drooping backward. There were no marked symptoms of disease at any time. The animal died on the ninth day. There was an extensive inflammatory infiltration of the subcutaneous tissue and fascia over the sides of head, extending to the top, involving the ventral aspect of neck and extending to shoulders laterally. The subjacent muscular tissue was considerably ecchymosed. Peritoneal exudate absent. Degeneration of liver and spleen. Bacteria numerous in the local infiltration, very few in blood and organs. A liquid culture from heart's blood was found pure.

These results place fowls and pigeons upon the border line of susceptibility; that is, these animals may be destroyed by large doses, but are not affected by small ones. They also put rabbits, guinea-pigs, and mice among the susceptible animals, the first named being the most susceptible. In every case the inoculation seems to produce local lesions, the extent and severity of which seem to stand in an inverse relation to the number of bacteria found in the blood and the internal organs, and in a direct relation to the duration of the disease.

The foregoing inoculations were made from cultures derived from the pleural exudate of pig No. 2 (Sodorus, Ill.). The same germ was isolated from the spleen and blood of the same animal.

Three tubes of gelatine, into which bits of spleen had been put, began to liquefy. (It will be remembered that the spleen was enormously enlarged and softened.) One of these contained only a large bacillus, another the same bacillus and a microbe resembling the one under consideration. By means of plate cultures these were separated and a pure culture of this microbe obtained. By introducing beneath the skin of two mice bits of the spleen containing the two forms a pure culture of the same microbe was obtained from one of the mice which died three days after inoculation. Two mice, inoculated with bits of spleen from the culture containing the liquefying bacillus only, remained unaffected. From a vacuum tube of blood taken directly from the heart of the same animal pure cultures of the same microbe were obtained.

From pig No. 1 (Sodorus) two pipettes were filled with blood, obtained with every precaution directly from the heart. One of these tubes, opened three weeks later, was used to inoculate a liquid culture, which proved, when tested on gelatine plates, a pure culture of the same microbe obtained from the pleura, the spleen, and the blood of pig No. 2 of the same herd. In the other tube the bacterium of hog-cholera was found. It will be remembered that pig No. 1 had in addition to the ulcerations of the cæcum and colon, partial hepatization of both lungs, while No. 2 had merely the lung lesions. About a month later a liquid culture, made from a gelatine-tube culture of this blood, was used to inoculate a rabbit, only $\frac{1}{16}$ cc being injected subcutaneously into the thigh. The animal was found dead on the third day. The lesions were nearly identical with those observed previously after inoculation with this microbe—local thickening of the fascia, hemorrhagic markings of the muscular tissue, with superficial degeneration at the point of inoculation, ecchymoses on the contiguous abdominal walls, peritonitis indicated by a few stringy deposits on liver, as well as more than the normal quantity of serum. Cover-glass preparations of the spleen and liver revealed a large number of the injected cocci, which, stained in alkaline methylene blue, showed the polar stain very clearly. A cover-glass touched to the serous surface of the large intestine contained immense numbers of the same germ. Gelatine tube cultures of liver and heart's blood grew in the characteristic manner. From the blood culture a second rabbit was inoculated, as follows: The hair was clipped from the inner aspect of the thigh, which was washed with .1 per cent. solution of mercuric chloride. With a flamed lancet a little pocket was formed beneath the skin, into which a small quantity from the gelatine culture was introduced on a platinum loop. The animal sat quietly in the coop, eating but little, and breathing slowly for some days before death, which occurred ten days after inoculation.

Slight enlargement of the inoculated thigh. Subcutaneous tissue over the inner and caudal aspects of the thigh, on the abdomen beyond umbilicus, greatly thickened by inflammatory infiltration, which is of a soft, pasty consistency, grayish white. It is closely adherent to skin, but not to muscular tissue on abdomen, from which it may be easily removed. The muscular tissue beneath is dotted with punctiform extravasations. On the caudal aspect of the thigh the infiltration is closely adherent to muscular tissue as far as the pubis, involving the superficial muscular fibers, which are whitish, softened; the groin stained with a frothy, blood-stained serum; the superficial lymphatic gland on the same side enlarged to size of a horse-chestnut; on section whitish, lardaceous; the lobules of the gland appearing as pale red masses imbedded in it. The serosa of intestines and the liver coated with a glairy, translucent, grayish deposit, which may be drawn out into threads and peeled from the liver in a thin layer. This exudate contains very few cells, but immense numbers of bacteria, evidently in a state of active multiplication, as they are quite small, resembling oval cocci, and staining uniformly. Parenchyma of liver uniformly dark brownish; bile very dark greenish; spleen not enlarged; lungs normal; right heart filled with a translucent gelatinous clot; left, with dark liquid blood; mucosa of stomach, which contains considerable food, coated with a tenacious mucus; circumscribed hemorrhagic spots scattered over the right half of the stomach; very few bacteria in the parenchyma of spleen and liver.

In this case ten days elapsed between inoculation and death. The local lesion was very extensive, the peritonitis advanced. According to previous experience the difference between this and the preceding case was due entirely to the mode of inoculation. There is also another difference worthy of note. In the preceding rabbit the bacteria showed very beautifully the stain at the ends of the short rod; in this one they did not show it clearly at all.

This microbe was therefore present in the pleural cavity, in blood from the heart, and in the spleen of one pig, and in the blood of another. It is highly probable, judging from the microscopic examination of the diseased lungs, that if circumstances had permitted a thorough examination of the lung tissue itself by means of cultures and inoculation experiments, the same results would have been obtained. This, however, was quite impossible under the circumstances.*

This microbe, from Geneseo, Ill., also found associated with completely hepatized lungs, was without doubt the same as the one just described, when we take into consideration microscopical characters and those brought out by culture and inoculation. This microbe had not yet been tried upon fowls. In order to confirm still further the results already given the following experiment was tried:

October 30, two pigs and two fowls were inoculated with the microbe from Geneseo, and an equal number with that from Sodorus, Ill. The pigs received subcutaneously each 5^{cc} of a beef-infusion peptone culture. Of the four only two died. One of these had been inoculated with the microbe from Sodorus. On the third day both eyes were discharging, the animal looking unthrifty and becoming weak and thin. It died on the eighth day. In brief the lesions were as follows: Fat and connective tissue in general yellowish. Both ventricles of heart filled with large washed clots and semi-coagulated blood. Liver very firm, of a dirty red-lead color. On cutting

---

*Very recent investigations of the disease in the District of Columbia have confirmed these statements. The pathogenic bacteria are limited almost exclusively to the diseased lungs.

into it a gritty sensation is transmitted to the hand. Venous stasis of the abdominal vessels. Other organs and intestinal tract normal. Cultures failed to detect the microbe in the spleen, liver, and blood.

No. 363, inoculated with 5^{cc} from a culture of the microbe obtained from Geneseo, Ill., showed inflammation of the eyes a few days after, which disappeared in a week. At the same time the animal looked unthrifty. It had apparently recovered two weeks after inoculation, when it again became unthrifty and weak. The abdomen became enlarged and it was unable to rise. Found dead December 27, nearly two months after inoculation. At each point of inoculation on the thigh an encysted mass was found in the subcutaneous tissue as large as a marble. The contents were softening and inclosed by a fibrous wall. Lungs hypostatic. Pulmonary vessels and right heart filled with a firm clot. Liver very much contracted, especially the lobes on the right, and streaked with depressed lines and furrows. The peritoneal covering on the cephalic aspect was very much thickened, in some places uniformly, in others in a mesh-work corresponding to the interlobular tissue. The acini of this side were very small. On the caudal aspect they were in some places very large and bulging. On section this transition from large below to small above could be easily traced. Gall bladder filled with a thick prune-juice-colored bile. Inflammatory adhesion between rectum and cæcum. The mucous membrane of the large intestine of a dull red color, probably due to a passive congestion. No ulceration anywhere to be seen. The intestine itself was very much distended with dry, half-digested feces of a yellowish hue. Four liquid cultures made from blood of heart remained clear.

This case is interesting in that the inoculation caused a cirrhosis of the liver, which became indirectly fatal by destroying in great part the normal functions of this organ.

Both fowls inoculated with the microbe from Sodorus died. One of them, which received $\frac{1}{2}^{cc}$ of the liquid cultures into the pectoral muscle, had a temperature of 110½° F. next day. It began to grow weak rapidly, the temperature remaining high, and it died on the ninth day. The only lesion was the parboiled condition of the pectoral muscles. No growth in cultures from the liver. The other fowl, which had received but $\frac{1}{2}^{cc}$ of the culture, lingered in the same condition, becoming very emaciated. It died on the seventeenth day. The inoculated pectoral muscle very pale and infiltrated with serum. Yellowish necrotic masses embedded in it. Extravasations beneath serosa of duodenum, also beneath corresponding mucosa. The mesentery streaked with petechiæ near the vessels. Terminal portion of rectum dilated, filled with yellowish semi-liquid matter; mucosa of this region intensely dark red.

One of the fowls inoculated with $\frac{1}{3}^{cc}$ from a culture of the microbe from Geneseo died on the fourth day. Extensive serous infiltration and tumefaction of the inoculated pectoral, which is firm, whitish, parboiled in appearance; mesentery adjacent to pectorals slightly inflamed; slight congestion of duodenum.

This case demonstrates a similarity of pathogenic power of the two cultures both upon pigs and fowls. In these cases the local infiltration contained the microbe in abundance, but cultures from the blood and liver remained sterile. It seems that it has not the power to multiply in the internal organs, though producing exceedingly severe local lesions sufficient to cause death. The lesions which the subcutaneous injection of the microbe produces in pigs were so uniform and yet so peculiar, that it seemed necessary to add a few more experiments to those already made.

November 18, two pigs (Nos. 374 and 375) received hypodermically 5^{cc} (one-half into each thigh) of a beef-infusion peptone culture two days old, derived from a gelatine culture (rabbit) about one month old. Three pigs were placed with these to determine whether the disease was infectious. In both animals two days after inoculation the sclerotic became deeply reddened. This congestion was followed by discharge, which gummed the lids together for a part of the time. In about a week these symptoms gave way and the eyes became jaundiced. The eyes of the three check pigs were not affected. No. 375 died November 25, one week after inoculation. The subcutaneous connective tissue of a deep yellow color. The points of inoculation occupied by cysts filled with a blood-stained serum. Blood black, partially coagulated. Hypostatic congestion of lungs. Purplish spots beneath pleura and in parenchyma; some lung worms present. Liver very pale, bloodless, very tough. The sclerosis general and the contraction of the connective tissue has made the caudal aspect very concave. Removed from the body it resembles india-rubber, as it retains the same form in whatever position it is laid. Gritty sensation when cut. The gall bladder filled with semi-liquid, dark brown bile, resembling plum juice, surrounding a mass of putty-like consistency and of the same color. The papillar opening of the common duct into the duodenum contained a plug of gelatinous mucus, and when the duct was slit open it contained mucus only. The walls were not even bile-stained; the secretion of bile had ceased some time past. When the liver was cut the section was of a dirty reddish-yellow color throughout; no blood flowed from the vessels; when scraped the cellular elements of the acini came away readily, leaving the tough interlobular tissue *in situ* as a honey-combed mass.

Sections hardened in alcohol and stained in alum-carmine showed a large amount of connective tissue as compared with the normal liver. This increase was general. In the parenchyma of the lobules there were circumscribed areas in which the protoplasm of the cells stained very feebly, while the nuclei were either shriveled or else replaced by a group of granules. The characteristic trabecular structure in these areas was more or less destroyed. Almost every lobule examined contained these altered regions, which were situated as a rule near the periphery.

There was a very marked venous stasis of the portal circulation, characterized by an overdistension of the vessels, bringing even the smallest into view. The vasa recta of kidneys very prominent, giving the pyramids a bright red appearance. Serum in the abdominal cavity of a deep yellow. This yellow tinge is present in the fat around the base of the heart. The urine deep yellow, the mucosa of bladder stained with the same color. The urine readily gives, with Gmelin's test, the colors characteristic of the bile pigments. The intestinal tract normal throughout, save what changes arose from the general stasis of the portal circulation. The stomach empty and coated with a viscid mucus.

The injected microbe which without doubt caused these lesions could not be found. Three tubes of culture liquid were inoculated each with three to four drops of the blood from the heart. They remained sterile. Bits of spleen and liver about $\frac{1}{2}^{cm}$ cube were dropped into tubes. They also remained sterile.

No. 374 lived longer, became very weak and stupid, and finally was unable to rise. Eleven days after inoculation it died. At one of the points of inoculation there was a firm, tough tumor. The lesions were very similar to those just given, but less pronounced. There was but slight icterus of the connective tissue. Serum in pericardial cavity and fat about heart stained yellow. Urine gives very easily the reaction for bile pigments. Lungs hypostatic. Both sides of heart filled with black coagula. Liver in the same condition as that of No. 375. Gall bladder as above. The common duct was patent and still bile-stained. Venous stasis of portal system but slightly marked. Intestinal tract normal. Four liquid cultures of blood from the heart remain sterile. Into one a large coagulum had been dropped. Two pieces of liver and two from the spleen fail to induce any bacterial growth whatever in the liquids into which they are dropped. The check animals remained well for a month after.

The uniform success in producing most severe cases of hog-cholera by feeding pure liquid cultures of hog-cholera bacteria to pigs which had been deprived of food for 24 to 36 hours led to the inference that the same result might be expected from the microbe of pneumonia, provided it was at all capable of being infectious by way of the intestinal tract.

December 19.—Two pigs (885, 886) were deprived of food for 32 hours. No. 886 then received a liter of beef broth containing 10 grams of sodium carbonate to increase the alkalinity of the stomach. Each was thereupon fed with 250^{cc}. of a culture of the pneumonia microbe in simple beef infusion six days old. This dose was mixed with beef broth to make one liter. Up to the time of writing (January 27) not the slightest disturbance in health has been manifest. Three pigs fed about the same time and in the same way with cultures of hog-cholera bacteria all succumbed, with very severe lesions of the intestinal tract. (Page 31.)

This microbe had thus produced, when injected beneath the skin in quantities not less than 5^{cc} of culture liquid (beef infusion with 1 per cent. peptone neutralized), an acute cirrhosis of the liver in seven out of ten pigs. The pathological changes in most cases were so severe as to check the formation of bile entirely. We must provisionally accept the theory that the injected microbes exert their pathogenic power chiefly upon the liver. Perhaps the germs are deposited there by the blood current and cause an acute inflammatory hyperplasia of the interlobular tissue. In contracting, the portal vessels and bile ducts are compressed so as to become impervious. This produces a venous congestion of the abdominal organs, which pour their blood into the portal vein, and a generalized icterus, caused perhaps by the retention of the bile elements in the blood, as well as their reabsorption from the liver. Meanwhile the bacteria themselves are destroyed in the tissues, so that at the death of the animal none can be found even by means of the most delicate methods of cultivation.

That the three pigs which did not succumb to the inoculation were not affected is not warranted, as the following experiment shows: A pig was inoculated by injecting into the trachea a culture of this microbe. The pig remained well for several weeks, when it was killed for examination. At the autopsy it was found that owing to the thick layer of fat in the neck the injection did not enter the trachea. A tumor almost as large as a hen's egg had formed by the side of the trachea. Its center was already softened. The organs were apparently normal with the exception of the liver, which is extremely pale and bloodless, showing signs of cirrhosis.

GENERAL CHARACTERS OF THE MICROBE CAUSING PNEUMONIA IN SWINE.

In cover-glass preparations from the organs of animals which have died from inoculation, and of which the rabbit presents the best advantages for study, the microbes appear as oval bodies, measuring about 1 to 1.2 micromillimeters in length and .6 to .8 micromillimeter in breadth. When stained by some aniline, such as an aqueous solution of methyl violet or an alkaline solution of methylene blue, their appearance is very much like that of the microbes of rabbit septicæmia. The two extremities of the longer axis are deeply stained. Between these colored masses a transverse band remains transparent, without any color. This unstained portion may vary between one-fourth and one-half of the entire optical area of the oval. It is limited on either side by a very delicate, stained line (Plate III, Fig. 2; Plate IX, Fig. 1).

It is probable that this appearance arises during the elongation of the coccus preparatory to a transverse division into two, and that the width of this unstained area depends upon the stage of the process. Among the cocci there may be seen in cover-glass preparations of liquid cultures rodlike forms as broad as the cocci, imperfectly segmented, and attaining in a few cases a length of 15 to 20 micromillimeters. These filaments must be regarded as involution forms of the cocci, due to a want of power of division; for such a form is frequently of varying width and the extremities irregularly tapering; moreover, the cultures containing them are invariably found pure when tested on gelatine plates. This abnormal growth is not confined to cultures. It is found in cover-glass preparations made directly from the tissues of animals which have succumbed to inoculation with pure cultures. They are common in mice and rabbits. In the former animals they assume a bacillar form occasionally, in rabbits a form staining very irregularly and resembling swollen diplococci. In the earlier experiments with this microbe these abnormal appearances were very puzzling. Inoculation of liquids with these bacteria gave invariably the same form. Gelatine tube cultures and the colonies on plates always proved the same. It became necessary to conclude from these results that, although fatal to these animals to a very high degree, this particular coccus does not find the best conditions for multiplication in these animals; or else it may be found that some slight variations in the manipulation of cover-glass preparations, a too rapid drying or a greater heat applied to the dried film, may cause changes in the microscopical appearances of the stained germ. Whatever the reason may be, the striking fact remains that in some rabbits the bacteria on cover-glass preparations are regular and uniformly stained at both extremities; in others they are irregular in outline and the staining is not characteristic.

If a neutralized beef infusion with 1 per cent. peptone be inoculated with this microbe a faint opalescence pervades the entire fluid on the following day. There is no membrane present at this stage, nor after several weeks. A pure liquid culture of this microbe is easily distinguishable from that of the hog-cholera bacterium. The latter is more opaque, and when the tube is shaken rolling clouds are formed. This is not seen in the faint opalescent liquid of the former. It will also be remembered that after one or two weeks a ring of deposit forms about the tube at the surface of the liquid in the culture of the hog-cholera bacterium. In a few cultures an incomplete surface membrane may also appear. It multiplies more abundantly, therefore, in this medium than the more delicate microbe under consideration.

If a drop from a culture one day old be examined with a $\frac{1}{12}$ homogeneous objective *no spontaneous movements* can be observed. When dried and stained in an aqueous solution of methyl violet or other aniline, the microbes are best studied, as regards their form, at the circumference of the dried film, where they have been drawn together in large numbers by the slow drying of the drop. The microbe appears in the form of an oval coccus, about .6 to .7 micromillimeter long and .4 micromillimeter broad. The small size makes the exact measurement very difficult. Besides these there are smaller and larger forms measuring 1 micromillimeter in length. The great majority of forms correspond with the dimensions first given. Those around the border of the dried film usually show the characteristic stain at the extremities with the unstained band between. The remainder are usually so small that this cannot be made out, or else they are in that stage of growth when division has not yet begun, and are uniformly colored.

If a minute portion from the organs of a rabbit, or from a culture of this microbe, be shaken up with nutrient gelatine, barely liquefied by a gentle heat, and the mixture poured on plates, the colonies will become visible to the unaided eye in about two days, provided the temperature does not fall below 70° F. They are round, with pale homogeneous disk, when examined with transmitted light. Their growth is slow, and at the end of a week they vary in diameter from $\frac{1}{8}$mm to $\frac{1}{2}$mm. Their appearance at this age is peculiar (Plate IV, Fig. 3). Each colony is provided with a border of varying width, usually not exceeding one-fourth the radius of the colony. This border is paler than the central portion, and sharply separated from it by a circular line, sometimes slightly eccentric, as in the illustration. The central disk is usually somewhat granular at this stage. The colonies when growing on the surface of the layer of gelatine spread quite rapidly, and soon are four or five times the size of the deep colonies. The margin of the more or less circular patch is very thin and sharp, and slightly wavy. This microbe *does not liquefy the gelatine* at any time of its growth.

In tubes containing nutrient gelatine the microbes carried by the needle into the depths of the gelatine develop into spherical colonies which do not become larger than $\frac{1}{2}$mm in diameter (Plate IV, Figs. 1, 2). The surface growth is quite vigorous. It spreads as a pearly white circular patch in all directions from the point of inoculation. This patch is not convex, but uniformly thick, usually with a wavy or scalloped border (Plate V, Fig. 1, *b*). The growth is very slow as a rule, varying with the temperature of the room. It requires several weeks for a disk a few millimeters in diameter to form, and from one to two months for one 5mm to 10mm. When viewed obliquely very faint concentric markings may usually be observed on this pearly growth. There are some slight differences between the tube cultures of the microbe of genuine hog-cholera and this organism, which are entirely expressed in the surface growth (Plate V, fig. 1, *a*, *b*). In the second annual report the tube culture of the bacterium of hog-cholera was figured as having very minute deep colonies and scarcely any surface growth. Later observations showed that if a more alkaline nutrient gelatine be used the growth is far more vigorous; the deep colonies are much larger and the surface growth abundant (Plate VI, Figs. 4, 5). It presents either as a compact convex pearly disk or button, or as a very irregular flat patch, sending out ragged prolongations over the surface of the gelatine.

This microbe grows upon blood serum from the cow. On the surface the growth is very thin, scarcely visible. In the needle track a dense opaque mass forms. On the condensation liquid in the bottom of the tube a whitish, brittle membrane is present. Repeated efforts to induce growth on potato have thus far failed. In milk its multiplication is not very great when compared with the other microbes. It is capable to a certain extent of multiplying in tubes from which the air has been exhausted and in which the ordinary saprophytes remain dormant. When exposed to a temperature of 58° C. for fifteen minutes it is invariably destroyed. This is true of the bacteria taken directly from the animal as well as of those in liquid cultures.

This microbe is easily killed by drying, three days being sufficient, whether it is taken from cultures or from the tissues of the dead animal.

Upon sterilized cover-glasses a drop from a liquid culture two days old is allowed to dry under a plugged funnel. On the third day a tube of beef infusion, into which one of these cover-glasses had been dropped, remained clear. On the sixth, seventh, and ninth days tubes were inoculated in the same way, which also remained clear.

Exudate from the peritoneal surface of the liver of a rabbit which died from inoculation was dried on cover-glasses and tested in the same way. The exudate contained immense numbers of microbes. One tube inoculated after four hours' drying, two after one day, and two after two days became opalescent and were found pure cultures. Two inoculated on the third, fourth, and fifth day remained clear.

The multiplication in ordinary drinking water was tested as described for the hog-cholera bacteria. The latter, very hardy, as the experiments showed, remained alive in large numbers for months. The microbes under consideration showed themselves almost incapable of living and multiplying in such water. In fact, it is very probable that many are destroyed in being transferred into it from nutrient media.

On November 20 a tube containing sterilized Potomac drinking water was inoculated from a culture two days old. A plate culture immediately prepared to determine the number of germs transferred was lost by accident. Judging from preceding experiments, there could not have been less than 50,000 in 1^{cc} of the water. Plate cultures containing $.1^{cc}$ of water were made two and three days after inoculation. Nothing grew upon either plate. On the sixth day a tube of beef-infusion peptone was inoculated from the water. The liquid remained clear.

On November 27 a tube containing sterilized Potomac drinking water was inoculated from a liquid culture of the microbe twenty-four hours old. A plate culture made immediately after the inoculation showed two days later that each cubic centimeter of the water contained after inoculation about 140,000 microbes. After standing for two days at a temperature of 22° to 25° C. a plate culture made with about $\frac{1}{300}^{cc}$, which should have contained at least 500 colonies, showed none whatever. December 6, nine days after inoculation, $\frac{1}{8}^{cc}$ was added to a tube of beef infusion peptone. On the following day this tube was turbid and contained the microbe only. Hence a few individuals were still alive on the ninth day. A plate culture was made from the same water twenty-four days later by adding $\frac{1}{8}^{cc}$ to the gelatine before pouring it upon the plate. No colonies grew. Finally a tube of nutrient liquid, to which $\frac{1}{8}^{cc}$ was added on the twenty-seventh day, remained clear. Hence all the microbes were practically dead before a month had passed, and the great majority perished, without doubt, a few days after being mixed with the water.

The appearances and morphological differences of the microbes discovered in hog-cholera and in the infectious pneumonia which we now call swine-plague, are illustrated by the photo-micrographs reproduced in Plates VII, VIII, and IX. The microbe of hog-cholera is seen in Plate VII, Fig. 1, as it appears in the tissues of the body. Most of the germs in this case are sufficiently elongated to be classed as bacilli. In cultures where more rapid multiplication occurs the microbe is shorter and assumes an oval form (Plate VII, Fig. 2). The microbe from the Nebrasba outbreak of hog-cholera, referred to above, maintained a distinctly rod-like form, however, even in liquid cultures (Plate VIII, Fig. 1). The micrococcus of swine-plague, which is plainly oval in the tissues and in the blood, as shown in Plate IX, Figs. 1, 2, becomes very nearly or quite spherical in liquid cultures (Plate VIII, Fig. 2). This is also very nearly the form seen in gelatine cultures.

The following comparative table sets forth briefly the differences between the bacterium of hog-cholera and the microbe which has been found associated with pneumonia in pigs and described in the preceding pages:

HOG-CHOLERA BACTERIUM.	MICROBE OF PNEUMONIA.
Morphological and biological properties.	*Morphological and biological properties.*
1. Ovals varying in length from 1.2mm to 1.8mm.	1. Ovals varying in length from .8mm to 1.2mm. (In both species the size is very variable, according to the stage of growth and division and the culture medium.) This microbe is in general much smaller than the bacterium of swine-plague.
2. Stains around periphery, with a slight increase in the width of the stained border at the extremities; observed chiefly in the tissues of animals. In cultures may stain entirely.	2. Stains in process of division at the two extremities only.
3. *Motile* in liquids.	3. *Non-motile* in liquids.
4. Grows actively on potato.	4. Growth on potato fails. Growth in nutrient liquids more feeble; on gelatine almost as vigorous.
5. Resists drying for one to two months.	5. Resists drying only a few days.
6. Multiplies for a time in drinking water, and remains alive at least four months.	6. Does not multiply in drinking water, and is entirely destroyed in a few weeks.
Pathogenic effects.	*Pathogenic effects.*
1. In small susceptible animals subcutaneous inoculation causes but slight local reaction.	1. Local reaction usually very severe and extensive.
2. In mice it always produces a disease lasting from eight to sixteen days; spleen enormously enlarged; liver enlarged and containing numerous foci of coagulation necrosis.	2. Mice destroyed, but not invariably, in two to six days. No characteristic lesions.
3. In rabbits the disease produced by inoculation of small quanties of culture liquid into thigh lasts from six to nine days. Great enlargement of spleen; enlargement of liver and centers of coagulation necrosis. Local lesion: circumscribed necrosis of muscular tissue. Lungs usually have hemorrhagic foci or more extensive lobular pneumonia.	3. Same mode of inoculation destroys life in from three to six days. Extensive local sero-sanguineous, later purulent infiltration and thickening; plastic peritonitis; spleen not enlarged.
4. Same mode of inoculation destroys guinea-pigs, with a few exceptions. Lesions quite the same as in rabbits. May live fourteen days.	4. Guinea-pigs somewhat more refractory; extensive local lesions as in rabbits; occasionally plastic peritonitis; die in four to six days; spleen not enlarged.
5. Pigeons destroyed by large doses. Bacteria in internal organs.	5. Pigeons also susceptible to large doses. Bacteria absent from internal organs.
6. No fowls destroyed by inoculation.	6. Large doses kill fowls. Very extensive local infiltration and destruction of muscular tissue.
7. Pigs are either not affected by hypodermic injection, or else a severe disease follows, characterized by hemorrhages in all organs. Bacteria present in large numbers in internal organs.	7. Large doses cause acute sclerosis of liver, with icterus. Bacteria absent.
8. Feeding cultures after starving for a day produces extensive necrosis of mucous membrane of large intestine; inflammation and occasional ulceration of stomach and ileum.	8. Feeding cultures produces no effect whatever.

The inoculations apply to subcutaneous injections of small quantities of liquid cultures, in mammals on the inner aspect of the thigh, in birds on the pector[illegible]

MORE RECENT OUTBREAKS OF INFECTIOUS PNEUMONIA.*

Recently specimens were received from an outbreak of infectious pneumonia in Iowa. According to information obtained by Dr. N. H. Paaren in January, 1887, a disease of swine prevailed during the fall and winter of 1885–'86, and during the same period of 1886–'87, which was limited chiefly to the four counties of Worth, Mitchell, Cerro Gordo, and Floyd, along the Shell Rock River. Specimens of lung tissue were obtained from Cerro Gordo County, although the disease was almost extinct at this time (January, 1887).

At Mason City Dr. Paaren examined a number of dead hogs at a soap factory, which had been brought together from different parts of the surrounding country. In these animals the lungs were uniformly diseased, the digestive tract normal or but slightly congested. The liver also was diseased in all examined.

From these observations it would seem that the disease prevalent in Iowa was the infectious pneumonia which has been described in the preceding pages, and not the real hog-cholera. The following experiments tend to confirm these views:

Pieces of lung tissue sent from Cerro Gordo County were partly immersed in a blood-stained liquid which must have exuded from the lungs. The animal was frozen solid when the tissues were removed. Both pieces of lung tissue had a faint, not putrescent odor. They were of a red flesh color. The tissue seemed completely airless. Cover-glass preparations showed the infiltration to be made up almost exclusively of small round cells, with an occasional epitheloid cell amongst them. Careful observation demonstrated the presence of very minute oval bacteria, varying slightly in length. The longest (perhaps not more than 1^{mm}) stained only at the extremities. There were no other bacteria visible to indicate any advanced decomposition. In one of the pieces the knife had been passed through an irregular cavity in the lung substance as large as a marble, lobulated, bounded by a membrane, and partly filled with an inspissated substance easily crumbled, and consisting entirely of round cells. There was also marked pleuritis. The pleura of the portions sent was thickened, and a spongy membranous exudate, about $\frac{2}{3}^{mm}$ thick, had formed, which consisted also of small round cells exclusively.

A number of plate cultures were made by shaking up pieces of lung tissue and pleural exudate in gelatine and pouring it on plates. These plates were, as a rule, negative. Inoculations into animals proved more successful, however.

Two mice were inoculated by placing bits of the lung tissue beneath the skin at the root of the tail. One mouse died on the second day. Internal organs unchanged; no local reaction; no bacteria to be seen on cover-glass preparations of spleen and liver.

The second mouse died on the third day, though apparently well the day before. In this animal the spleen was very dark and enlarged; liver also much congested. In these two organs, as well as in the blood from the heart, oval bacteria were present in large quantities. Plate cultures and liquid cultures of blood proved them to be the immotile oval microbe already described.

Two rabbits had been inoculated at the same time by placing a bit of the lung beneath the skin of the thigh on its inner aspect. One of them died in five days. The

---

* Lately a disease of the lungs, probably identical with the infectious pneumonia under discussion, came to our notice in the District of Columbia, from which the same microbe was obtained. A detailed account must be reserved for future publication.

local reaction, very slight, was limited to a small mass of pus in the subcutaneous tissue. The muscular tissue was not involved. The internal organs were also unchanged, but in all of them the microbe already described was present in immense numbers in the spleen and liver, fewer in heart's blood and kidneys. Gelatine cultures from spleen and liver and two liquid cultures of heart's blood contained only the specific microbe. The second rabbit remained well.

Two mice inoculated subcutaneously with a liquid culture derived from a gelatine tube of the above rabbit died within twenty hours, though each had received but $\frac{1}{4}$cc of liquid. The spleen and liver crowded with the injected microbe.

From a tube culture in nutrient gelatine a tube of beef infusion was inoculated, and on the following day a rabbit was inoculated hypodermically into the thigh with a few drops, and two pigeons, beneath the skin of the pectoral, with $\frac{1}{4}$cc to $\frac{1}{2}$cc from the same culture. In the former bird the needle entered the pectoral muscle. The rabbit was found dead next morning, not longer than eighteen hours after inoculation. At the place of injection a few ecchymoses and distended vessels on the inner surface of the skin. A lymph gland near by deeply reddened. A few threads of fibrinous exudate on coils of intestine. Lungs hypostatic. Immense numbers of bacteria in liver, spleen, and heart's blood, most of them showing the characteristic stain at the ends.

The pigeon which had received $\frac{1}{4}$cc into the pectoral died in twenty-four hours. In this bird the pectoral was discolored, parboiled for a depth of one-half inch and over an area of about 1 square inch. The subcutis was filled with a reddish serous effusion, the skin slightly thickened. Innumerable bacteria in this local lesion. Fatty degeneration of liver. A small portion of each lung deeply congested. Vessels of duodenum and testes injected. Immense numbers of bacteria in blood from the heart, in the liver and lungs, showing the characteristic stain at the ends very well. The other pigeon was not affected.

The fowls inoculated with $\frac{1}{4}$cc of a liquid culture of this microbe remained unaffected. Similarly two pigs, which had received each 5cc beneath the skin of the thigh, remained well.

Specimens from the Mason City soap factory were like the first. The lung tissue was enlarged, solidified, and of a pale reddish color. When sections were made into this airless mass the cut surface showed a reddish ground, in which were embedded whitish specks about $\frac{1}{2}$ to 1 micromillimeter in diameter. These protruded slightly, giving the surface a granular appearance. They could be lifted out, and when crushed upon a cover-glass and stained small round and larger epitheloid cells were found to make up the mass. Bacteria of different kinds indicated *post mortem* multiplication.

These lesions were therefore very much like those found in Illinois, and there is no reason to doubt that they were caused by the same agency. In all of the lungs thus far examined from which the same microbe was obtained the vesicular portion of the lungs was filled with a cellular exudate, partly derived by a desquamation of the alveolar epithelium and partly by an infiltration of cells from the blood.

Two rabbits inoculated by rubbing some of the scrapings from the cut surface of the lung tissue into a wound made on the inner surface of the ear remained well. One mouse inoculated as above died next day. No bacteria in the organs. Blood cultures remain sterile. A third rabbit was inoculated by placing a bit of lung substance beneath the skin of the thigh and closing the incision with a stitch. The animal remained well.

No positive results were thus obtained from this specimen. The source of the animal, the time of death not being known, it is not at all improbable that this specific microbe may perish in the animal body a certain time after death through frost and other agencies. It is not, moreover, to be denied that only certain portions of the lung tissue are, at a given time, the seat of active bacterial growth. These portions may not have been sent to us.

It seems that this hitherto unrecognized disease in swine is far more prevalent in the Western States than was at first supposed. It therefore becomes necessary to inquire more carefully into the distribution of these two maladies and to determine whether they do not frequently exist in the same localities.

The microbe from Iowa outbreaks showed a greater virulence, as a few drops of culture fluid were sufficient to destroy mice and rabbits in less than twenty-four hours. Whether such differences are sufficient to account for the varying severity of the disease in different localities remains to be determined by more extended observation. The fact that the subcutaneous inoculation of cultures did not affect two pigs may be due to a want of power to develop in the internal organs. This is virtually the case in the disease, as it appears naturally among swine. Though the lungs may be extensively diseased, the blood, spleen, and other internal organs are practically free from bacteria. The disease seems to be caused by inhaling or aspirating the specific bacteria, which exert their destructive effect in the alveoli and smaller bronchi, and do not in reality enter the blood of the affected animal. The final test will rest upon the possibility of producing the specific lung disease by means of inhalation experiments which are now being carried on.

RECENT FOREIGN INVESTIGATIONS IN INFECTIOUS SWINE DISEASES.

The investigations by foreign observers during the past year upon infectious diseases of swine, and more especially their causation, have led to some interesting results, which deserve careful consideration. In the Second Annual Report of this Bureau it was pointed out that the disease known in this country as swine-plague, or more commonly as hog-cholera, was wholly different from the disease known on the Continent as *rouget* and *Rothlauf*. Not only are the lesions different, but the micro-organisms producing them wholly unlike in their microscopical and biological features, as well as in their pathogenic effect upon animals. Thus far *rouget* has not been found in this country. The conclusions reached last year, though doubted by those who seemed to consider all infectious or contagious diseases of swine identical, are unshaken. All efforts at practicing preventive inoculation in hog-cholera with virus derived from *rouget* must not only be looked upon as absurd in the light of present knowledge, but as dangerous, inasmuch as a new disease may thus be introduced into our country from abroad.

The important lesson taught by these investigations lies on the surface. Infectious diseases in which the gross pathological effects differ quite constantly in the same species of animals should not be classed as identical until so proved by the most rigorous methods that scientific research possesses.

On page 226 of the Second Annual Report of the Bureau (1885) a brief mention was made of a disease found once by Löffler in Germany, which presented as the most marked lesion an enormous œdema or swelling of the skin of the neck. It is caused by small ovid bacteria, calling to mind by their appearance the organisms of septicæmia in rabbits, especially when in the process of division, although but half as large. Inoculation with these bacteria produced speedy death in rabbits, mice, and guinea-pigs, as well as pigs. Rabbits died within twenty-four hours; mice lived a few hours longer; guinea-pigs died on the second and third day after inoculation. In all animals there was a sero-sanguinolent effusion into the subcutaneous tissue of the entire abdomen, extending to the axilla on the one hand and the inguinal region on the other. Muscular tissue infiltrated with the same reddish effusion. Pigeons, fowls, and rats remained unaffected after the inoculation. One of the three inoculated pigs died on the second day with the following lesions: "Skin of abdomen bluish red. Enormous œdema of the skin. Lungs hypostatic. Mucosa of stomach deeply reddened. Spleen unchanged. Kidneys parenchymatous. Mesenteric glands not swollen."*

More recently this same infectious disease among swine in Germany has been carefully described and studied by Schutz,† and as it has many features in common with the disease which has been separated from hog-cholera in the preceding pages, it deserves a somewhat careful analysis here.

The author first obtained the microbe causing this disease by placing beneath the skin of small animals bits from spleens of pigs which had presented symptoms of *rouget*. The spleens were putrid, but the pathogenic microbe was found alone in the bodies of the inoculated animals,‡ the putrefactive germs not having the power of penetrating beyond the wound in which they are placed. In this way he inoculated 2 mice, 2 guinea-pigs, 1 pigeon, and 1 rabbit. The mice died on the second and third day. The bacteria found in the organs of these mice have the form of ovals, and are easily stained by watery solutions of aniline colors.

> When stained with gentian violet they show in their central portions an unstained region surrounded by a layer stained blue. The thickness of this layer is greater at the poles, so that the extremities appear more deeply stained than the sides. When deeply stained they appear uniformly blue. As these organisms stand between micrococcoci and bacilli, they may be called bacteria. They are 1.2^{mm} long and .4^{mm} to .5^{mm} broad. They multiply in the following manner: They become twice as long as broad, show distinctly rounded extremities, and stain like the organisms of rabbit septicæmia and fowl-cholera, so that between the deeply stained ends about one-half or a third of the entire length remains unstained. Careful examination shows, however, that the colored end pieces are connected with each other by a fine line which passes from one to another on each side. The end pieces then separate and the median portion disappears. The former are at first spherical, but very soon assume an oval form. Hence from every organism two new individuals arise by division, in which by careful staining the uncolored central portion is easily distinguished from the colored periphery. If the process of multiplication is very rapid, as in pigs and rabbits, the organisms do not attain the size given above, but divide before the unstained median piece becomes distinctly visible. Under these circumstances the organisms of the succeeding generations are smaller, only one-half as large as, or even smaller than, those which have resulted from the slow division of the bacteria. The younger generations are frequently extraordinarily small, plainly oval, however, and staining uniformly in gentian violet. * * * They do not execute any spontaneous movements.

This description applies very well to the microbe found by us in pigs with lung disease. It points out the folly of expecting to determine a specific form with the aid of a microscope and an aniline stain only, when we reflect how many different forms of one specific microbe may be met with, according to the rapidity of multiplication, which in turn depends upon the medium in which they grow.

We will continue with the author's statement. The rabbit died on the third day. From the inoculated ear an inflammatory swelling had spread over the entire head and neck, due to an extensive effusion of a turbid liquid into the subcutaneous connective tissue. Enlargement of neighboring lymphatics. Bacteria in the blood and all

---

* Arbeiten a. d. kaiserlichen Gesundheitsamte, I, S. 377.

† *Loc. cit.* S. 376.

‡ The bacterium of hog-cholera as found in Nebraska was obtained pure in the same way as described elsewhere in this report (p. 623).

organs, especially numerous in the subcutaneous effusion. The two guinea-pigs and the pigeons remained well. Gelatine tubes inoculated with this germ show no signs of liquefaction at any time. With a pure culture on gelatine the author inoculated two mice, one rabbit, and three pigeons. The mice died on the first and second day after inoculation respectively. The lesions were as follows: "Slight œdema and hyperæmia of the subcutis. Swelling of the lumbar, inguinal, and mesenteric lymphatic glands. Large intestine filled with feces; spleen considerably enlarged. Parenchymatous inflammation of liver, kidneys, heart, and muscles. Portion of blood coagulated; the remainder coagulates on exposure to air. Bacteria in all the organs."

The rabbit died on the second day after inoculation. Besides local and general lesions already mentioned, there is an implication of the respiratory apparatus (tracheitis and bronchitis hemorrhagica). To these lesions we cannot attribute any specific character whatever. They are very likely due to proximity to the point of inoculation (ear). If the animal had been inoculated in the thigh they might have been absent. The pigeons remained well.

Two pigs were inoculated with beef-infusion peptone culture, obtained from a mouse, each receiving subcutaneously the contents of a Pravaz syringe. On the following day a considerable tumefaction of the thigh appeared. The skin over the swelling was dark red. Both animals were so weak as to be scarcely able to walk. No appetite. Breathing accelerated. One of them died twenty-four hours after inoculation. At the autopsy the following changes were observed: Infiltration of skin, connective and muscular tissue at the point of inoculation, with a red turbid effusion; the skin tough and thickened. About 55cc of turbid yellow liquid in the peritoneal cavity. The other changes given by the author do not point to any specific lesions, and are omitted. The bacteria were found in the exudates and in all the organs, especially numerous in the effusion at the point of inoculation. The other pig died forty-eight hours after inoculation. In this animal the local swelling was also very extensive and severe. Bacteria in all the organs.

The lesions indicated that the bacteria had at first multiplied and exerted their pathogenic effect at the point of inoculation, and thence had spread over the entire body by way of the blood and lymph channels.

The author calls attention to the great resemblance between the inoculation disease produced by him and by Löffler, and considers the cause the same in both cases.

A pig which had been made insusceptible to *rouget* by vaccination was inoculated with a pure culture of this oval bacterium. It died in two or three days, with extensive local swellings where the inoculation had been made. Bacteria in all the organs; especially numerous in the spleen. This case illustrated the fact that an animal made insusceptible to one disease is not necessarily protected against the virus of another.

Schütz was unable to produce the disease by feeding, as the following shows: After starving a pig for twenty-four hours it was fed with bouillon in which 5 per cent. sodium carbonate was dissolved, and half an hour later with one liter of blood and pieces of flesh from a pig which had succumbed to inoculation. The animal seemed slightly ill for a few days, but recovered.

In continuing these investigations an epidemic came to his notice in which the early symptoms were diarrhea, sometimes bloody. At the same time the hind legs became stiff, so that the animal lay most of the time. On the sixth and seventh day the back became weak, so that in walking the animals swayed to and fro. They then were scarcely able to reach their food without tumbling over. In a few the ears became red. In all the breathing became labored and hurried. In some twitching and convulsions appeared before death, which occurred on the eighth to the tenth day. Without giving the complete autopsy notes it will suffice to say that there was nothing abnormal in the intestinal tract. The stomach was considerably bile-stained. The lesions were limited to the thoracic cavity. In the pericardial cavity about 36 grams of an opaque reddish fluid. Pericardium and epicardium glued together by small quantities of a warty, stringy, elastic substance:

Both lobes of the left lung, with the exception of the upper border and the four lobes of the right lung, tough and airless (hepatized). In both pleural sacs about 64 grams of an opaque reddish-yellow fluid, mixed with flakes of fibrin. The pleura covering the hepatized portions was rough, dull, clouded. These were in general of a dark grayish red, with interspersed, circumscribed patches of various size and form and grayish-yellow or reddish-yellow in color. * * * On the cut surface of the hepatized portion grayish-red and reddish-yellow areas could be detected, which were sharply marked off from one another. They corresponded to the circumscribed patches on the pleura, were very friable, partly with a pale luster, partly granulated. They occupied larger volumes of lung tissue, or were sprinkled as scattered foci in the grayish-red portions. Their extent was limited by the course of the larger bronchi and blood vessels. The surface of the grayish-red portions was also granulated, of a faint lustre, and clouded. In these there appeared numerous, more prominent, reddish-yellow spots, corresponding to the inner portions of the lobules. They were either isolated or gathered into small groups. The interlobular tissue was filled with a cloudy reddish fluid. In the softer portions of the lung the pleura was smooth, transparent. The cut surface was smooth, shining, and here and there provided with small diffusely dark red spots; resistant. On compression a very fine foam poured out upon the cut surface. The bronchial lymphatics were enlarged; their capsules reddened.

In a second animal the lesions were the same, almost the whole lungs hepatized. These animals had therefore suffered from an acute pleuro-pneumonia, involving the pericardium in the first animal. The yellow regions correspond to necrosed tissue, which, extending to the surface, produces inflammation of the pleura. In cover-glass preparations of the lung tissue the oval bacteria were found in large numbers. The author infers from the lesions that the bacteria had been aspirated into the finest bronchioles and alveoli and there produced pneumonia. They were also found in the pleural and pericardial cavities. The remaining internal organs contained but few. With portions of the hepatized lungs six mice, five guinea-pigs, two rabbits, two rats, two pigeons, and one fowl were inoculated. The mice and rabbits died in the usual time, and presented lesions already described. Three of the guinea-pigs died on the fourth, fifth, and eighth day respectively. In the two first mentioned the subcutis and muscular tissue at the point of inoculation (abdomen) were infiltrated with a bloody, clouded liquid; in the third animal—an old one—an extensive hemorrhagic and purulent infiltration was present. One of the pigeons died on the third day. The point of inoculation in the subcutis over the pectoral muscle was infiltrated with a fibrinous, purulent mass, containing a few bacteria. These were very scarce in the internal organs. One of the rats died on the seventh day with lesions similar to those of the older guinea-pigs. Very few bacteria in the internal organs. With bits of lung tissue from another pig which succumbed to the same infectious pneumonia the following animals were inoculated: two rabbits, guinea-pigs, pigeons, and fowls, and one rat. The rabbits died in one day, the guinea-pigs in two and five days respectively after inoculation. The two pigeons, which had received comparatively large doses, died in one and two days respectively. The rat and fowls were not affected.

The author also introduced pure cultures directly into the lung tissue of a pig through the chest-wall by means of a hypodermic syringe. The animal died in less than three days. On *post mortem* examination the lungs were necrosed at the point of inoculation; there was severe and extensive pleuritis and pericarditis. Bacteria were very numerous in the affected organs, but very scarce in other organs. In another experiment a pig confined in a box was made to inhale the spray of a liquid culture for several hours on two consecutive days until 500^{cc} had been used up. The animal was killed eleven days later, after having shown marked symptoms of lung disease. The same mortifying pneumonia as that described was found at the autopsy.

Schütz also describes a case in which there was a condition of the lungs, lymphatic glands, and other organs closely resembling tuberculosis. Caseous degeneration of these structures was followed by a gradual loss of strength, leading to death. In this animal there was a caseous degeneration of the various joints of the posterior limb, enlargement and softening of the lymphatics. The oval bacteria were present in large numbers in the caseous contents of the glands. The effect upon small animals when inoculated with this caseous mass was precisely the same as that produced by lung tissue or cultures from former cases.

The disease disappears at the beginning of winter to reappear again in the spring. The losses sustained by one owner from the disease in a single year were very heavy, two hundred pigs having died. It was found in regions a considerable distance apart, which led Schütz to infer that it was a widely distributed disease.

The relation of hog-cholera to this disease.—A careful perusal of this brief synopsis will convince even those who have only observed the gross pathological lesions that are constantly met with in hog-cholera, or who have read the *post mortem* notes as reproduced and summarized in this and the preceding report, that this new disease described by Schütz has nothing in common with hog-cholera. We regard the description of the disease as given in these reports as the basis for this statement, because the hundreds of cases examined in the laboratory were invariably associated with the same etiological factor—the same bacterium which has been minutely described, and which is at once distinguishable from the microbe described by Schütz. Leaving aside the many differences, a glance into the microscope will show us an actively motile bacterium on the one hand, and on the other a non-motile bacterium. Our investigations have already shown the existence of another bacterial disease in swine, which may even be associated with hog-cholera, in the same herd and in the same animal. From the present standpoint of our information it would be presumably absurd to rely upon *post mortem* examinations in different parts of the country without at the same time making bacteriological investigations, in order to decide the nature of a certain class of symptoms and lesions. We have almost invariably found severe intestinal lesions in hog-cholera, producing ulceration and often complete death of the mucous membrane of the large intestine, involving in the severest cases a similar destruction of the mucous membrane of the ileum. In the autopsy notes given by Schütz the alimentary canal is invariably intact or the slight changes due to general causes. The lesions are limited entirely to the thoracic organs, where the lungs are primarily affected by a "multiple mortifying pneumonia." Thence the disease may involve the pleura and the pericardium.

In hog-cholera, lung lesions are quite secondary and only rarely seen. In the severest hemorrhagic type of the disease we have almost always observed hemorrhagic *foci* scattered through the lung tissue, but these were no more numerous or more extensive than the extravasations found in most of the other viscera. It is quite easy to believe that such cases surviving the first severe attack may develop a pneumonia by the gradual extension and confluence of the separate foci. In all cases where the causation of such lesions is a matter of doubt bacteriological investigation must now decide.

Relation of infectious pneumonia to this disease.—It is of considerable importance to find out what relation this microbe of the German *Schweineseuche* bears to the one which we have recently found in pigs as the cause of infectious pneumonia. Morphologically they are evidently the same. So far as their growth in culture media and their biological properties have been observed there seem to be no grounds for regarding them as different species. As to their pathogenic properties we find some marked differences. The evidence which has been brought forward in the preceding pages that the microbe there described is the cause of a pneumonia in pigs, which is therefore, from an etiological standpoint, wholly different from hog-cholera, is not yet conclusive, and will require further investigations. Yet the facts there recorded are strongly in favor of the view that we are dealing with a hitherto unrecognized disease. The microbe was obtained from three outbreaks hundreds of miles apart. In the animals examined pneumonia was present. In the one outbreak hog-cholera was also present, as demonstrated by the lesions and the specific bacterium. The presence in the same herd of two diseases, and even in the same animal of two wholly different microbes which produce them, complicates matters very greatly. The disease described by Schütz as *Schweinesueche* is essentially a localized disease, involving the lungs only. There are no lesions of the intestinal tract. Is, then, this *Schweineseuche* the same as the pneumonia which we have found? Let us compare for a moment the microbes. Both destroy mice, the microbe of *Schweineseuche* more speedily and invariably. The same may be said of rabbits. Inoculation on the ear caused death in one to three days, according to Schütz. The same mode of inoculation produced death with the American form in nine days, and even subcutaneous inoculations do not prove fatal in less than three days.* Guinea-pigs are only in part susceptible to both microbes; pigeons to both when large quantities of virus are introduced into the system. Fowls are killed by the American form in large doses. Schütz does not report the use of large doses with these birds. Both produce extensive pathological changes at the point of inoculation in the susceptible animals.

*The microbe obtained from Iowa is more virulent than this, and resembles more closely the German form. These lines were written before this had been investigated.

When we come to their effect upon pigs after subcutaneous inoculation marked differences are manifested. Pigs inoculated by Schütz died from one to three days after inoculation. Besides producing rather severe local reaction, the bacteria had multiplied in all the internal organs and were easily demonstrable in cover-glass preparations. Those inoculated with the American form at the experimental station died in from one to two weeks. The quite constant pathological change consisted in acute contraction or cirrhosis of the liver, followed by jaundice. The bacteria had been meanwhile destroyed, for cultures from such cases remained sterile. Feeding either in cultures or in animal tissues failed to produce the disease. Schütz succeeded, however, in producing pneumonia from inhalation of cultures. Our experiment failed, perhaps, because the spraying was not continued long enough.

These differences, apparently very wide, may after all depend simply upon a difference in virulence; and it may be possible for us to obtain from other outbreaks a microbe which is as virulent as the one described by Schütz. There is every reason to believe that this mircobe loses its virulence very speedily in artificial cultures. This may have modified somewhat the results, since several weeks elapsed between the time the cultures were prepared from the affected animals and the time when the pigs could be inoculated therewith.

Schütz* and others† are inclined to regard the microbe of *Schweineseuche* identical with the one which has been found to produce septicæmia in rabbits. In this connection it is of interest to mention briefly some experiments‡ made with a microbe obtained from rabbits, which seems to be closely related to, if not identical with, the microbe of rabbit septicæmia as described by European observers, and may perhaps be a modified form of the microbe found in pigs. This it resembles in form and mode of staining at the two extremities, but it is, as a rule, somewhat larger. It also differs in forming a more or less complete membrane at the surface of the culture liquid two or three days after inoculation. In its effect upon animals, that upon rabbits is especially characteristic. It destroys them within two days when injected hypodermically. There is a slight purulent infiltration at the seat of injection, varying in intensity with the duration of the disease. The bacteria are present in large numbers in all the internal organs, giving the disease the character of a true septicæmia. Fowls are insusceptible. Of seven pigeons inoculated, three died; of four guinea-pigs, one. Mice are less susceptible than rabbits, but more so than guinea-pigs.

We must regard this microbe as more virulent to rabbits and less so to other animals than the one found in pigs. As regards its effect upon the latter no extended experiments were made, excepting to note that doses of 1^{cc} culture liquid produced no effect upon two animals. Perhaps future experiments may throw more light upon the relation of this microbe to the disease of swine, which we must consider, at least for the present, as a hitherto unrecognized infectious pneumonia.

---

* *Loc. cit.*

† Huppe: Ueber die Wildseuche u. ihre Bedeutung für die Hygiene. *Berliner klinische Wochenschrift*, 1886, No. 44.

‡ For a detailed account, see the *Quarterly Journal of Comp. Medicine and Surgery* for January, 1887.

UNITED STATES NEAT-CATTLE QUARANTINE.

The Superintendents of the various neat-cattle quarantine stations report the names of the importers and the number and breed of each lot of animals imported during the year 1886, as follows:

LITTLETON STATION, MASSACHUSETTS.

DR. A. H. ROSE, SUPERINTENDENT.

Date of arrival.		Name and post-office address of importer.	Port of shipment.	Name of breed.	Number of animals.
Feb.	18	B. Schuurmans, Littleton, Mass	Antwerp	Holstein	16
	18	John C. Christie, Windom, Minn	Glasgow	Black Polled Angus	12
	26	J. B. Warren, Larchwood, Iowa	Liverpool	Welch-Dean	18
Mar.	17	Kirby & Cree, Fort Stanton, N. Mex	Glasgow	Black Polled Angus	71
	17	George Bruce, Newport, Dak	do	do	4
	31	John B. Goodwin, Beloit, Kans	do	do	21
May	10	John Kemper, Galesburgh, Ill	do	do	6
	14	Smiths, Powell & Lamb, Syracuse, N.Y.	London	Holstein	22
June	27	William Hanks, Iowa City, Iowa	do	Red Polled Angus	19
Aug.	17	C. Furness, Boston, Mass	do	Holstein	62
Oct.	14	C. L. Rea, Carrollton, Mo	Glasgow	Galloway and Black Polled Angus.	75
	24	Mr. McKay, Fort Wayne, Ind	do	Galloway	21
	24	Mr. Montgomery, Arlington, Ill	do	do	24
Nov.	24	James Symington, Golconda, Nev	do	Highland and Black Polled Angus.	44
	24	Lyulph Ogilvy, Greeley, Colo	do	do	1
Dec.	11	John Cunningham, Dalbeattie, Scotland	do	Galloway	84

GARFIELD STATION, NEW JERSEY.

DR. A. M. FARRINGTON, SUPERINTENDENT.

Date of arrival.		Name and post-office address of importer.	Port of shipment.	Name of breed.	Number of animals.
Jan.	9	Sluiter Bros., New York city	Amsterdam	Holstein	71
	27	Robert Burgess, Wenona, Ill	Liverpool	Aberdeen-Angus	7
Feb.	18	P. Admiraal, Garfield, N. J	Amsterdam	Holstein	27
	24	Anderson & Findlay, Lake Forest, Ill	London	Aberdeen-Angus	11
Apr.	20	G. F. Taber, Patterson, N. Y	Hull, England.	Red Polled Angus	6
	30	French Bros, Cincinnati, Ohio	Rotterdam	Holstein	25
May	1	F. Von Schuembach, Perry, Tex	Hamburg	Simmenthal	4
	5	W. H. Johnson, Center Rutland, Vt	London	Jersey, 17; Guernsey, 3	20
	24	do	do	Danish	1
	26	R. Deibel, Garfield, N. J	Amsterdam	Holstein	42
June	21	Sluiter Bros., Garfield, N. J	do	do	51
	21	C. E. Brackbill, Strasburgh, Pa	do	do	49
July	2	G. F. Taber, Patterson, N. Y	Hull, England.	Red Polled Angus	8
	29	Dr. J. M. Curtis, Wilmington, Del	Amsterdam	Holstein	28
Aug.	12	Thomas Brown, Ellenswood, Kans	London	Hereford	1
	26	J. H. Offord, Topeka, Kans	do	Red Polled Angus	31
	31	Charles Le Vesconte, Hastings, Minn	Bristol	Jersey	25
Sept.	7	Smith & Lockwood, New York, city	Havre	Normandie	1
	9	E. M. Knox, New York city	London	Jersey	4
Oct.	18	E. N. Howell, New York city	do	Guernsey	10
	28	W. M. Sneed, Memphis, Tenn	do	Holstein	15
Nov.	6	J. McLain Smith, Dayton, Ohio	do	Red Polled Angus	8
	15	Richard A. McCurdy, New York city	Liverpool	Kerry	1
	26	Edward Kemp, New York city	do	do	11
	27	A. N. Martin, New York city	London	Jersey	1
Dec.	11	Wm. Hanks, Iowa City, Iowa	do	Red Polled Angus	45
	27	E. N. Howell, New York city	do	Guernsey	1

PATAPSCO STATION, MARYLAND.

Date of arrival.		Name and post-office address of importer.	Port of shipment.	Name of breed.	Number of animals.
May	5	George G. Ware, Clearwater, Dak	Liverpool	Hereford	12

Whole number of cattle received at the various stations from January 1, 1886, to January 1, 1887.

Littleton station	495
Garfield station	504
Patapsco station	12
	1,011

Table showing the number of cattle received at the various quarantine stations for each month of the year 1886.

Months.	Littleton, Mass.	Garfield, N. J.	Patapsco, Md.	Total.
January		78		78
February	41	38		79
March	96			96
April		31		31
May	28	67	12	107
June	19	100		119
July		36		36
August	62	57		119
September		5		5
October	120	25		145
November	45	21		66
December	84	46		130
Total	495	504	12	1,011

Table showing the different breeds of cattle and the number of each breed imported during the year.

Name of breed.	Number.	Name of breed.	Number.
Holstein	408	Aberdeen-Angus	18
Black Polled Angus	115	Simmenthal	4
Red Polled Angus	117	Guernsey	14
Galloways and Black Polled Angus	75	Normandy	1
Galloways	129	Kerry	12
Jerseys	47	Danish	1
Highland and Black Polled Angus	44		
Welsh Runts	13	Total	1,011
Hereford	13		

No infectious or contagious disease appeared among the animals quarantined at the above stations during the year.

Respectfully submitted.

D. E. SALMON, D. V. M.,
Chief of Bureau of Animal Industry.

Hon. NORMAN J. COLMAN,
Commissioner of Agriculture.

DESCRIPTION OF PLATES.

ATE I.—Ulcerated cæcum of a pig inoculated with blood from a case of hog-cholera. The entire mucous membrane has undergone necrosis. Near the valve, in the upper portion of the figure, the early stage, that of ecchymosis, is still to be seen. The valve is slit open to show the intact mucosa of the ileum. This figure also serves to illustrate the appearance presented by the cæcum and colon when pigs have been fed with pure cultures, the only difference being that in the latter case the necrosis is at first superficial. In the figure it involves the entire thickness of the mucosa, having begun in the submucosa, whither the bacteria have been carried by the blood.

ATE II.—Ulcerated cæcum of a pig fed with viscera from a case of hog-cholera. The cæcum is slit open to show the mucous membrane quite uniformly necrosed, with isolated deeper ulcerations. The ileo-cæcal valve is very much thickened, the mucous membrane ecchymosed and ulcerated. The lymphatic glands of the meso-colon and in the angle formed by the entrance of the ileum into the cæcum are purplish, with cortex engorged with extravasated blood. They illustrate the condition of the lymphatics of both thorax and abdomen in the acute hemorrhagic form of the disease.

TE III, FIG. 1.—Cover-glass preparations from the spleen of a rabbit inoculated with the bacterium of hog-cholera from Nebraska. Stained for a few minutes in an aqueous solution of methyl violet, mounted in xylol-balsal. Drawn with camera lucida, Zeiss $\frac{1}{12}$ homogeneous, ocular 8. x 1110 The bacteria are seen among diffusely stained cells. They are chiefly in pairs, in some of which the process of division is not yet completed.

FIG. 2.—Cover-glass preparation from the liver of a rabbit inoculated with the microbe of pneumonia in pigs. Stained in an alkaline solution of methylene blue. Mounted and drawn as stated in Fig. 1. The colored portion is confined to the two poles, the central region remaining colorless.

TE IV, FIG. 1.—Culture twenty-eight days old in a tube of nutrient gelatine of the microbe causing pneumonia in pigs. The culture was prepared from the internal organs of a rabbit which had been inoculated from a culture obtained originally from Geneseo, Ill.

FIG. 2.—Culture eleven days old of the same microbe obtained from Sodorus, Ill. Both natural size.

FIG. 3.—Colonies of the same microbe on a gelatine plate seven days old. x 60. The pale peripheral zone, which appears after three or four days in beef infusion peptone containing 10 per cent. gelatine, together with darker granular nucleus, is very constant.

FIG. 4.—Gelatine tube culture from the blood of a rabbit inoculated with a culture of the hog-cholera bacterium from Sodorus, Ill., ten days old.

FIG. 5.—Tube culture of the hog-cholera bacterium inoculated from cultures of the spleen obtained from Sodorus, Ill., fourteen days old.

In Figs. 4 and 5 the two modes of surface growth of the hog-cholera bacterium are illustrated, both distinguishable from Figs. 1 and 2. See Plate V.

FIG. 6.—Colonies of hog-cholera bacteria on a gelatine plate four days old x 100.

TE V, FIG. 1.—Surface growth in gelatine tubes, enlarged two diameters.

a. Bacterium of hog-cholera, growing as an irregular patch, flattened, with a jagged margin and occasional slender branches, and as a convex rounded head.

b. Microbe of pneumonia, growing as a very thin pearly patch, with lobed margin, often showing faint concentric lines when viewed obliquely. *a*, twenty days old; *b*, twenty-six days old.

FIG. 2.—Gelatine tube culture of a bacterium which resembles the bacterium of hog-cholera very closely, but which differs in its physiological properties, and which has no pathogenic effect on animals. Found associated with the microbe of pneumonia in the spleen of a pig (Geneseo, Ill.). Culture about a week old. The surface growth is very vigorous, covering after a time the gelatine completely. The peculiar mesh-work shown in the figure is a constant character.

FIG. 3.—Growth of the bacterium of hog-cholera on potato twelve days after inoculation.

PLATE VI.—Coagulation necrosis in the liver of rabbits inoculated with cultures of hog-cholera bacteria.

FIG. 1.—Cephalic aspect of the liver of a rabbit which was found dead on the sixth day after inoculation. The lighter spots are groups of acini destroyed by the growth of bacteria. The larger patch to the left shows groups of acini in which the necrosis has involved only the peripheral zone of the acini.

FIG. 2.—Liver of rabbit which died on the eighth day after inoculation. The caudal aspect is shown with two extensive patches of commencing necrosis. In both only the peripheral zone of the acini is involved, giving the discoloration a mottled appearance.

PLATES VII to IX inclusive.—Photo-micrographs of the bacteria producing hog-cholera and swine-plague. Made with the Zeiss camera, using the new $\frac{1}{12}$ apochromatic homog. immersion objective, projection ocular No. 4. Magnification 1,000 diameters. The preparations, stained either in Bismarck brown or fuchsin, were mounted in Canada balsam. Illumination from an incandescent electric lamp.

PLATE VII, FIG. 1.—Bacterium of hog-cholera. Cover-glass preparation from the liver of a rabbit inoculated with cultures from Illinois. Stained for one hour in an aqueous solution of Bismarck brown.

FIG. 2.—Liquid culture of the bacterium of hog-cholera from Illinois. Stained in Bismarck brown.

PLATE VIII, FIG. 1.—Bacterium of hog-cholera from Nebraska. From a culture in beef infusion less than twenty-four hours old, inoculated from a colony on a gelatine plate. Stained for one hour in an aqueous solution of Bismarck brown.

FIG. 2.—Micrococci of swine-plague. From a culture in beef infusion about twenty hours old. This culture was obtained from a gelatine tube culture of effusion and plastic exudate in the pleural cavity. The lungs were extensively hepatized. Stained for one hour in aniline water fuchsin.

PLATE IX, FIG. 1.—Cover-glass preparation from the liver of a rabbit inoculated with a bit of lung tissue obtained from an outbreak of swine-plague in Iowa, January, 1887. Stained in Bismarck brown for one hour, decolorized in ½ per cent. acetic acid for a few moments. Note the polar stain.

FIG. 2.—Cover-glass preparation from the blood of a pigeon inoculated from a culture of the microbe of swine-plague from Iowa. Stained in aniline water fuchsin.

PLATE X.—Contagious pleuro-pneumonia. Lung of a diseased steer from Phœnix Distillery, Chicago, Ill.

PLATE XI.—Contagious pleuro-pneumonia. Lung of a cow slaughtered in Baltimore, Md.

PLATE XII.—Contagious pleuro-pneumonia. Lung of a cow slaughtered in Baltimore, Md.

Calf-Raising on the Plains.

PLATE I.—Ready for "cutting out."
PLATE II.—"Roping" and "cutting out."
PLATE III.—Roping a steer to inspect brand.
PLATE IV.—Throwing a steer.
PLATE V.—Branding a steer.

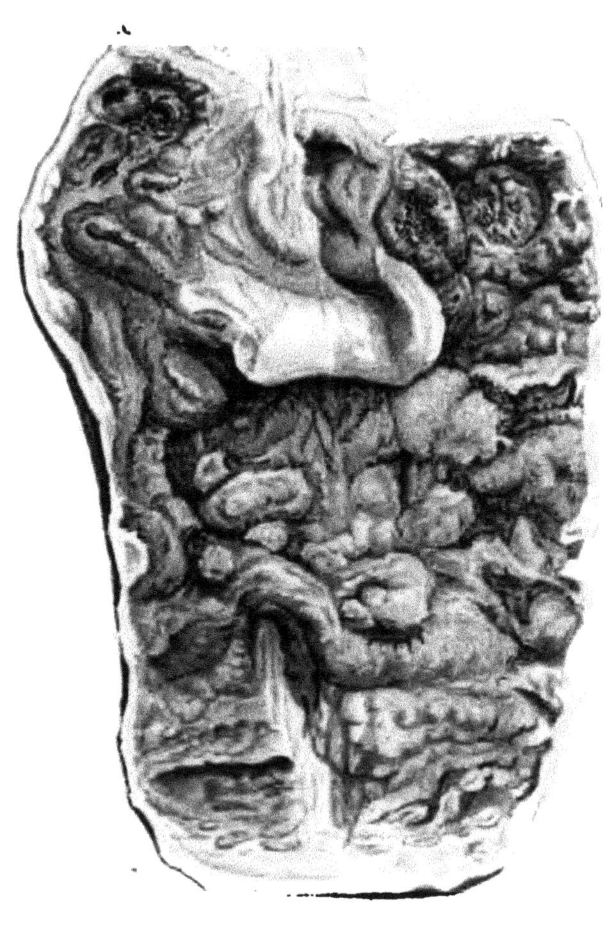

HOG CHOLERA [illegible]

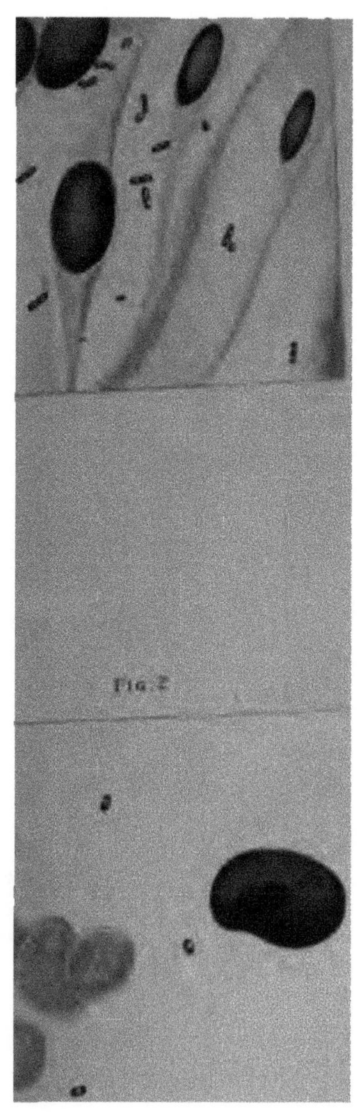

Fig. 2

Fig. 5.

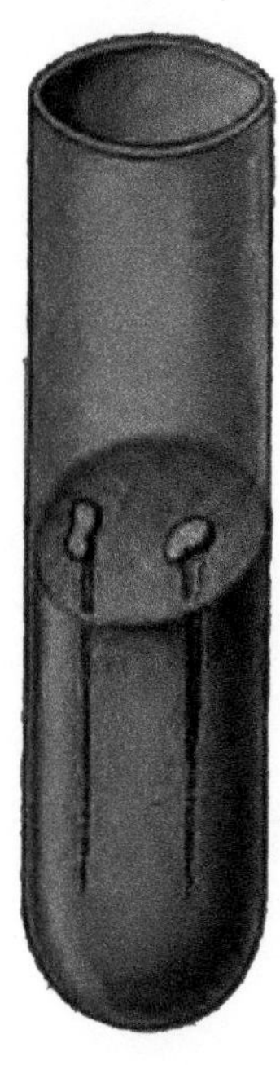

Fig. 6

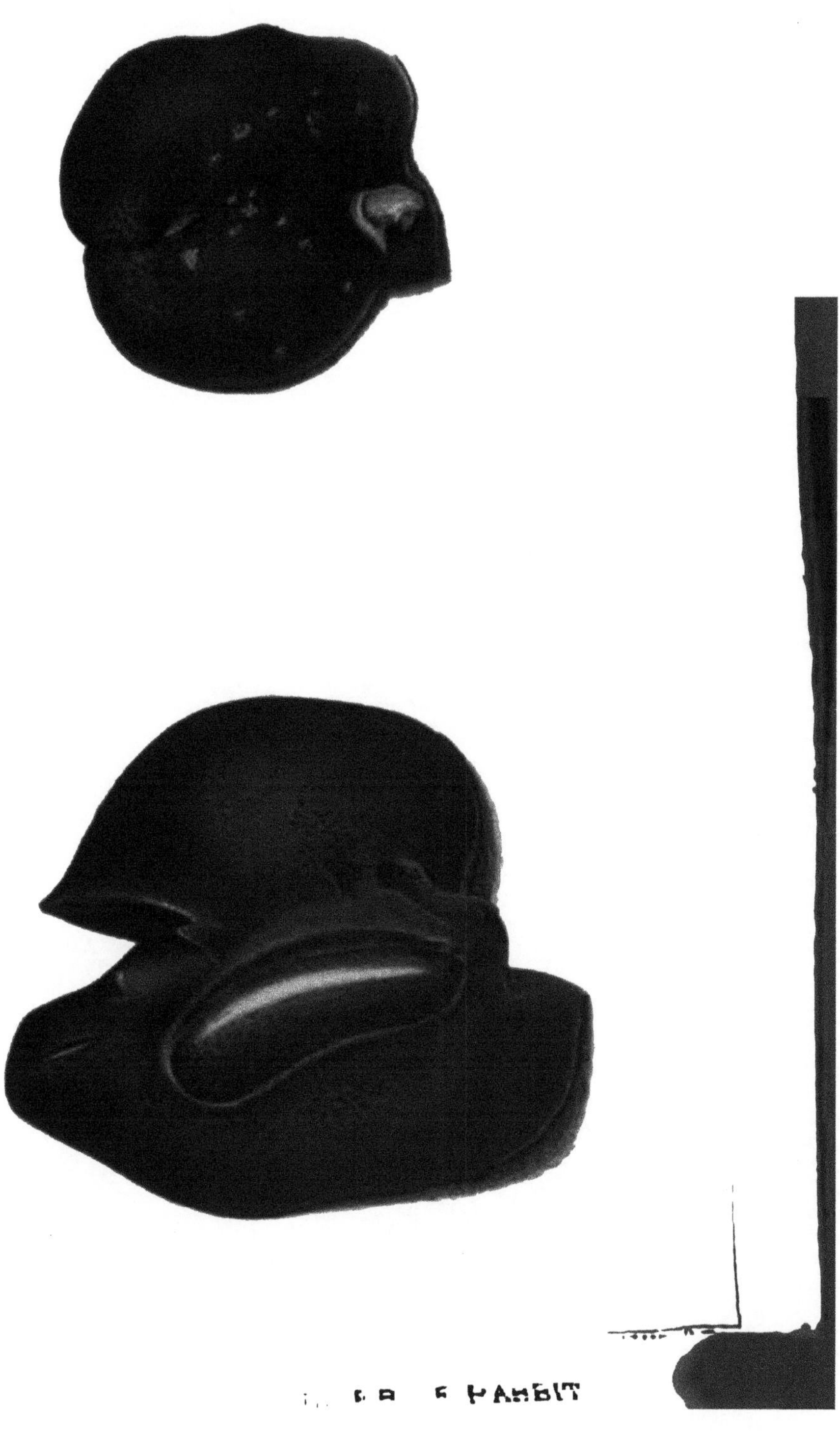

[illegible] RABBIT

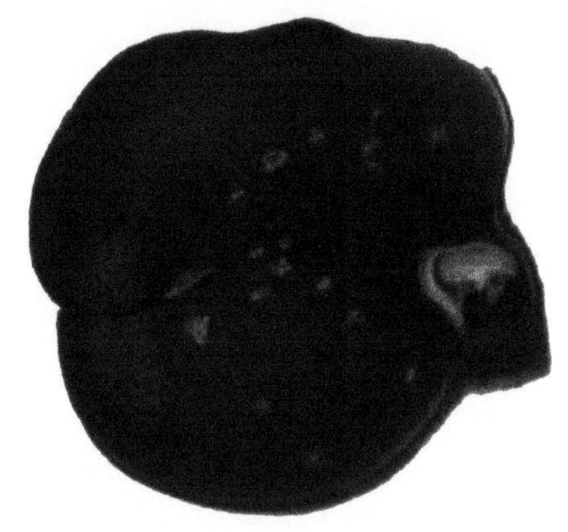

[illegible] CHOLERA [illegible] OF RABBIT

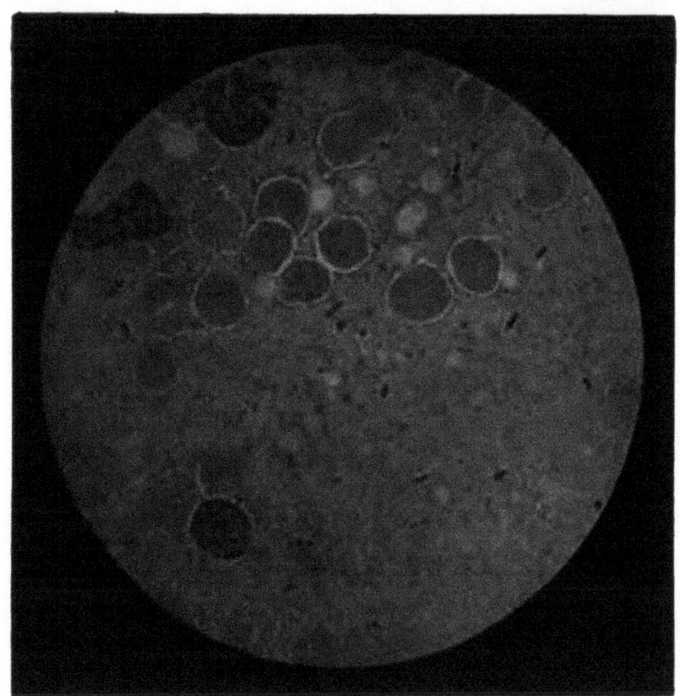

FIGURE 1.

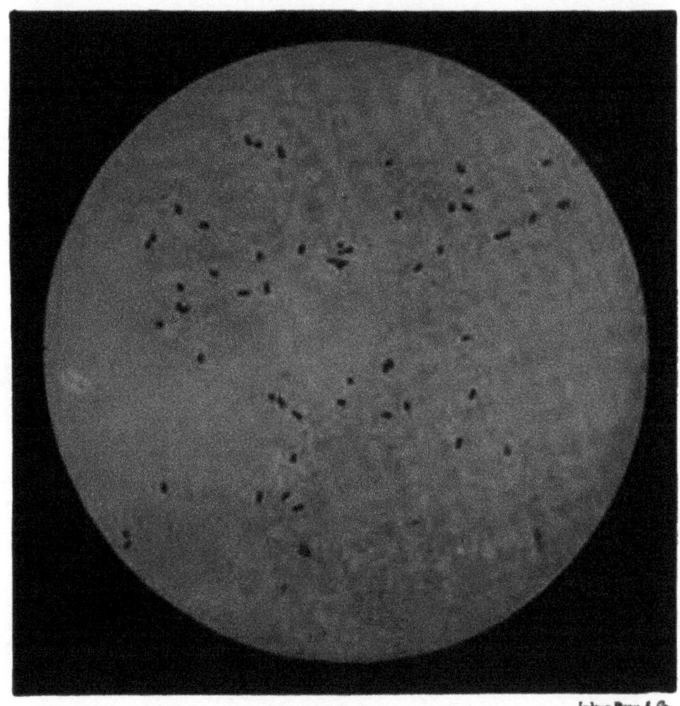

Julius Bien & Co

FIGURE 2.

HOG-CHOLERA

Plate IX

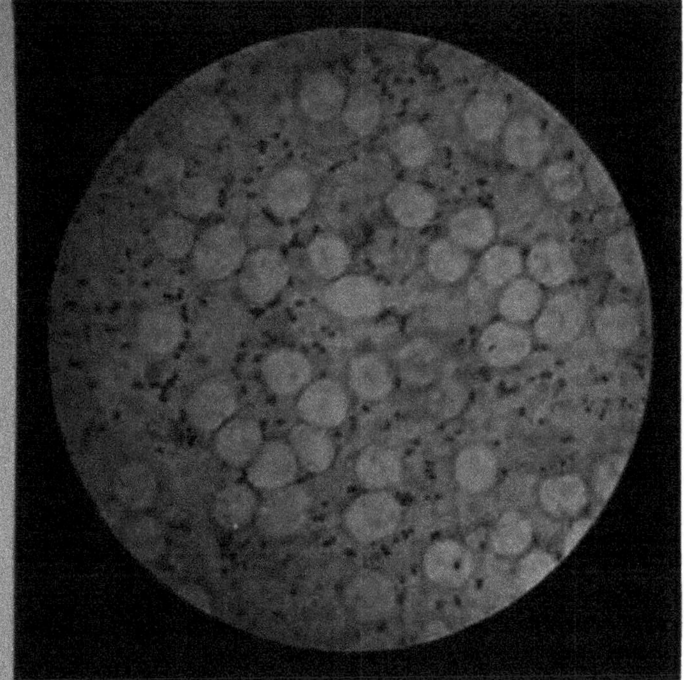

Figure 1.

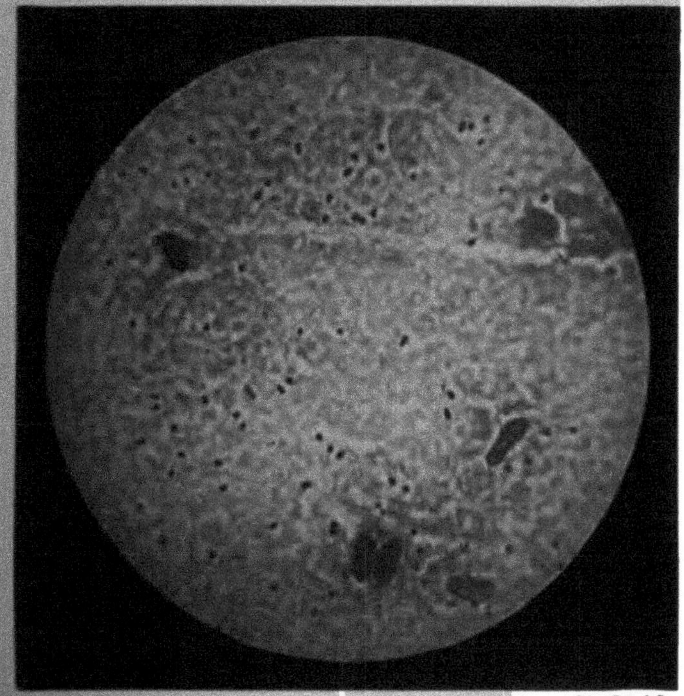

Julius Bien & Co

Figure 2.

SWINE-PLAGUE.

Plate IX

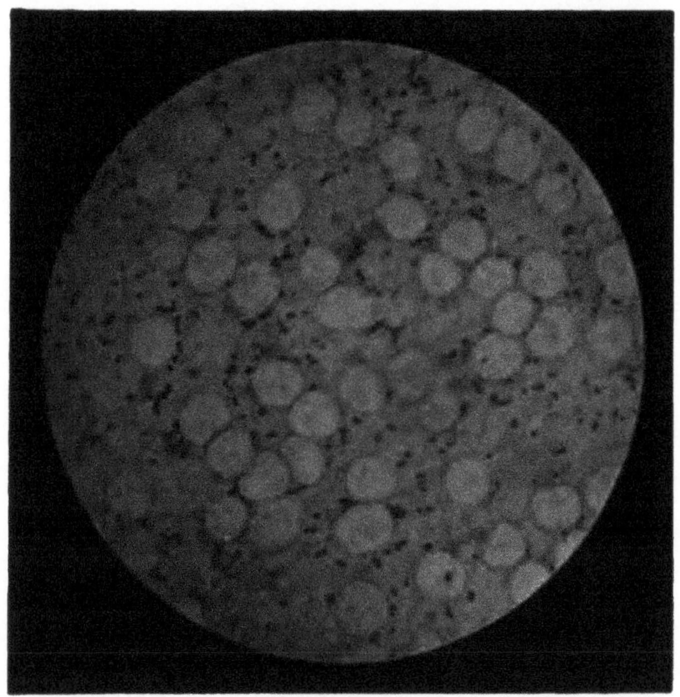

FIGURE 1

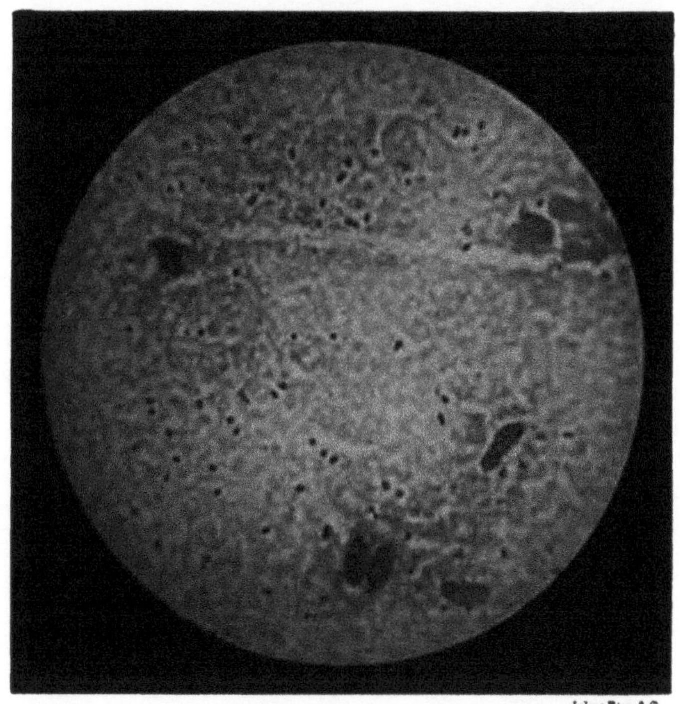

Julius Bien & Co

FIGURE 2

SWINE-PLAGUE.

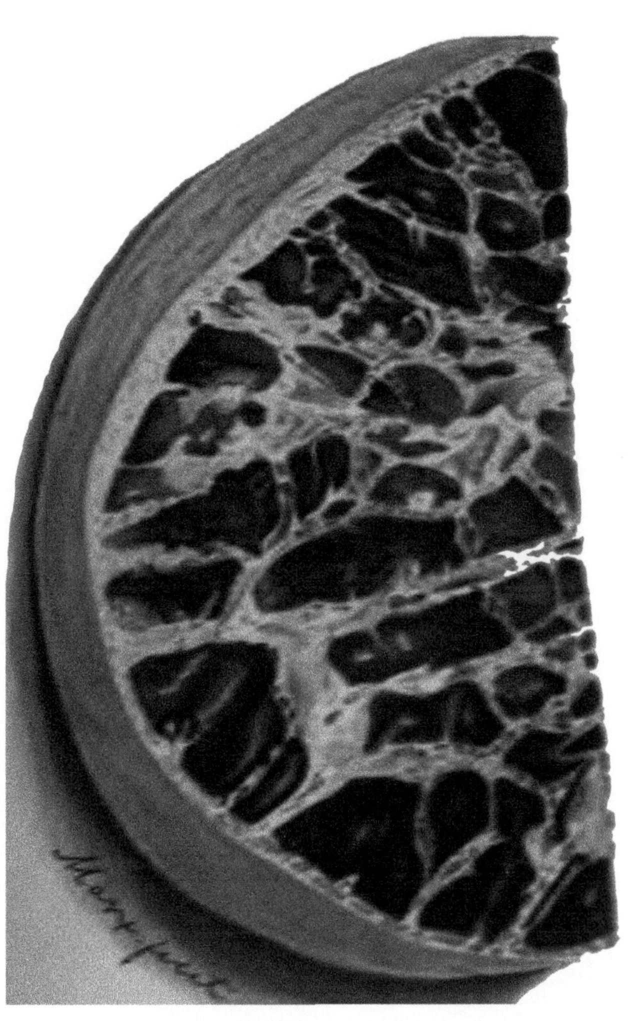

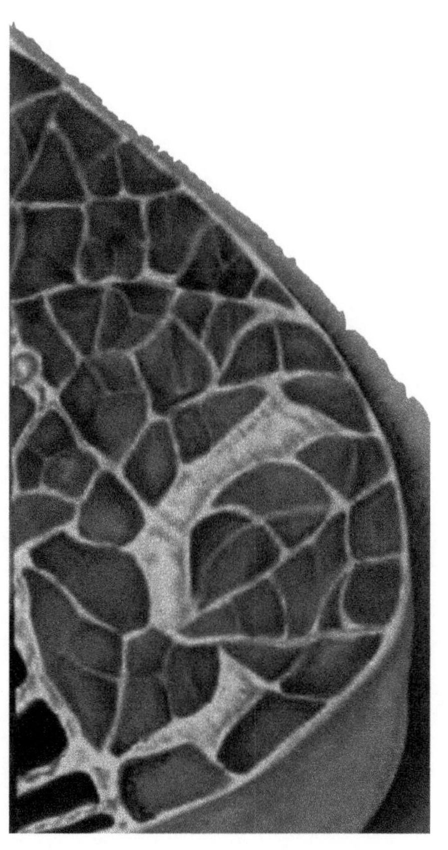

CONDITION OF THE CATTLE-RANGE INDUSTRY.

Hon. NORMAN J. COLMAN,
Commissioner of Agriculture:

SIR: At this time, when every citizen of the United States is disposed to study the question of the meat supply of the land, there seems no more appropriate way of introducing my annual report than by a summary of the cattle interests of the plains.

CONDITION OF THE RANGE.

A general depression of the cattle interests of the whole country set in with the year 1885, and it has continued up to the present time, growing worse from month to month, until almost a total stagnation in ranch trading has resulted. A glance at the prices paid for beef cattle in the great market centers of the East shows an almost continuous decline in value for two years, and a present price so low as to leave literally no margin between the cost of production and the market quotations. All grades of cattle have been affected, but in this as in all other articles of commerce the inferior quality sustains the greater depreciation. For reasons that will be made plain hereafter in this report, the range beef of the West has been, as a general rule, thin in flesh, and consequently sold at the lowest figures. The average decline in values, covering the period named, is fully $15 a head on all of the beef crop of the plains. This, as a natural result, has caused a shrinkage of the fortunes of the range men, and at the same time kept new men from entering into the business, thus causing the stagnation of trade in ranch properties above referred to.

Happily for all concerned, the climax of depression seems to have been reached, and a general feeling of hope in the future is beginning to spring in the breasts of the range men. This hope is very largely based on the fact that beef production is decreasing while the demand is steadily increasing. Population is rapidly increasing in all parts of the world, noticeably so in the United States, and with that increase is developed a proportional increase in beef consumption per capita. On the contrary, the range area of the United States is annually growing less. In Texas, Kansas, Nebraska, and Dakota this is notably the case, caused by the westward movement of the farmers and the enactment of laws prohibiting the running of cattle on the open plains.

This same condition exists in Oregon, Washington Territory, and California, where thousands of settlers are crowding into the edges of the range.

In time this border country, along the line between the permanently arid or range region and the agricultural, will produce as many and perhaps more cattle than when it was used exclusively as a range, but the transition period will be one of non-production. Generally speaking, the persons who settle on this questionable area are poor men who have no cattle, and whose utmost exertions will be required for years to simply produce food and raiment for their families. Again, the land taken from the range, if capable of grain production, will be wholly devoted to that use for a number of years, because new land makes a crop every year. By the time the cream has been taken off and the conditions changed, so as to make this belt a stock country, the population will have increased to such an extent as to more than balance the gain in cattle thus produced, so that we are justified in figuring this detachment from the grazing area as permanently gone.

Another reason for the hope that the tide has been out to the full length of the ebb is the fact that in all branches of trade and manufactures in the East there is a very perceptible revival setting in. Periods of activity and depression follow each other in all branches of trade or productive occupations as regularly as ebbs and flows the tide, and that a return to prosperous conditions for the beef-producing industry will follow the present unsatisfactory relations of that industry is as certain as that sunshine follows cloud.

The actual condition of the range country to-day is far better than is generally believed to be the case, even among rangemen themselves. The country bordering on the hundredth meridian, and extending from Dakota to Texas, suffered a very material loss in its herds during the winter of 1885–'86; and the spring and early summer of 1886 proved so dry as to cause starvation to thousands of cattle in western Texas and on the border of New Mexico. Outside of these the losses for last year were comparatively light.

The 1st of December, 1886, ushered in a winter range well cured and reasonably abundant, from the Gulf of Mexico on the south to the British Possessions on the north, and covering the entire arid belt from east to west. The only exceptions to this rule are to be found in a small area reaching from northern Wyoming up into Montana for a short distance, and lying east of the base of the Rocky Mountains. Besides this belt there is a part of central and western Nevada that is short of winter range, caused by the lack of snow-fall on the mountains last winter and the consequent forcing of the herds into the winter range in search of water during the late summer and early fall. No serious losses will be sustained in either of these districts unless the winter proves to be more severe than the present prospects indicate.

There will be losses, of course, all over the range. There must, of necessity, always be. But they are not likely to be of any such proportions as to overcome the percentage of profit. There are many old cows on the range, having been kept to too great an age because of the high price of young stock a few years ago. Among these there will be the heaviest losses, but many ranch men are prepared to feed them, and thus carry them through. Upon the whole, the outlook at the beginning of 1887 is decidedly hopeful so far as range conditions are concerned.

One of the most serious conditions of the range country to-day is the

DANGER FROM OVERSTOCKING.

Every acre of the arid belt is full of stock. From the foot of the Sierra Nevada Mountains east to the grain fields of the Missouri and

Mississippi valleys, and reaching from the extremes of the north and south, there is absolutely no spot where an unoccupied range can be secured for anything like a large herd of cattle. During what may very properly be termed the cattle boom, from 1880 to 1885, every breeding animal from Texas to Montana was saved, and the increase has spread out over the whole land. When the ranges were new, and grass was more abundant than cattle, fat animals were the rule everywhere, both in winter and summer. But the rapid increase has caused the winter range to be more or less eaten out in the summer, and the summer range is kept down so that in the autumn, when the fat is laid on by eating the cured grass, there is not enough to satisfy all the vast herds without going such long distances to water as to prevent the rapid taking on of fat. The result is that we are turning off feeders instead of beeves from most of our ranges in the fall, and the stock cattle go into winter in good condition, rather than fat, as formerly. Here lies the danger. If an animal goes into winter with a great roll of tallow inside to act as a steam heater for keeping up the animal heat it can endure an untold amount of cold and exposure without material damage. But if it goes into winter plump and round, yet without the full supply of tallow, the animal heat must be kept up by the daily food supply, which is not always obtainable. Hence the greater liability to loss.

The corn belts to the east are so near that our steers may be ripened on grain with a profit; but if we permit our herds to so increase that the cows and young stock all go into winter thin, we have no means of preventing heavy losses when a severe winter comes, as is liable at any time to happen. Safety lies in the direction of reducing rather than increasing our holdings.

But with breeding herds there is a continuously strong temptation to save the cows and heifers, hoping for a good winter, until calamity comes. This must be avoided by selling cows and spaying heifers until there is no surplus of stock on the range over what is absolutely safe against the storms of any winter.

The hard winters are what we must provide against. The good ones need no provision. A given area will carry through the year double the number of cattle when the summer is favorable for the growth of grass and followed by a dry autumn and mild winter that it will carry when the summer is dry, the grass short, and washed out by fall rains, to be followed by a winter of more than common severity. Yet this last-named condition is the one to be provided against, for there is the danger. Range men are beginning to realize that this is the vital question, and the next few years will witness a great change in this direction. The herds will be reduced. Until that time the danger-line will not have been passed. The only means whereby the range product may be increased is

ARTIFICIAL WATER SUPPLIES.

There are many high table-lands and ridges dividing the watersheds of the streams that flow from the mountains, where the grass is abundant, but the absence of water after the early spring renders it unavailable for stock. The sinking of wells on these ridges and plains, and the erection of windmills and tanks, would convert millions of acres of good grass into beef where now it is lost. But this would require a very considerable outlay of money which, under our land system, stockmen are slow to risk. There is scarcely a doubt, however, but the time is near at hand when this will be done, for the reason that the increased thrift of the herds will more than repay the expense. Well-boring has been tried, and in many instances has proven satisfactory, and each year will, undoubtedly, witness more and more of it, until all of the waste places are made productive. Let the good work go on, for it adds immensely to the comfort of the great herds that wander over the grassy plains, and will lead them up to winter's gate in much better condition to stand the stormy blasts.

While the above conditions are almost universal in the range country, it is particularly true of the great Southwest. A very large per cent. of New Mexico and Arizona consists of far-reaching mesas, or high plains, where there is a prolific growth of the celebrated black gramma grass, but no water save in the short seasons of rain. There are millions of acres of this kind of land now wholly unproductive that could be utilized for range purposes if an artificial water supply could be obtained at a reasonable cost, thus adding thousands of head of choice beef animals to the yearly output of the plains country. In a few instances stockmen have gone on to these high plains and sunk wells, putting up windmills, and arranging a system of troughs for watering their stock. One good well, properly provided with tanks so as to store the water and fill the troughs therefrom as needed, can be safely counted upon to furnish water for one thousand cattle. But to provide against accidents it is necessary to have the well supplied with an extra pump and a horse-power that can be used when the wind fails or the machinery gets out of order.

Experienced range men all admit that the lack of water, both in summer and in winter, is one of the greatest sources of loss to the cowman. It causes a double loss. First, the lack of a sufficient supply of water daily and within convenient reach causes a slow growth in the young animals and prevents the rapid ripening of the matured ones. Second, it sends many more into the winter thin in flesh, and the absence of tallow leaves them unable to endure the hardships of an exceptionally severe winter. Hence, this is a problem requiring careful thought by stockmen themselves and some consideration at the hands of the Government, whose duty it is to aid in every practicable way the increase of the food supply of the nation.

WINTER RANGES.

The arid region, as a range country, is absolutely safe under all ordinary circumstances if only stocked to its capacity; but a range that affords feed for one thousand cattle ought not to be expected to carry two thousand head. The grasses of this region generally spring early on account of the winter snow-fall and the spring rains, then cure as they stand, and make the best of fall and winter feed; but there must be enough of it to supply the herd. There is enough of the range country bare of snow, or with so slight a covering as not to cover the grass, always accessible to cattle for them to live upon and do well, if the grass has not been eaten down too short. The winter range should be reserved for the winter. If cattle are allowed to graze in summer over the winter feed they eat off the seed and tramp it down, so that the most nutritious portion is gone when most it is needed. Besides, if the grass remains standing it is not so apt to be covered up by the snow. There is always more or less wind on the plains and sweeping around the hill-sides. The tall stems of grass that extend above the snow are caught by the wind, and in a few moments the motion creates an opening about it that permits a current of air to rush in, generating sufficient force to soon lay bare the ground and form a whirlwind that drifts and twirls until a large area is freed from its covering, and the cattle are enabled to get their fill. With the grass trampled down the wind passes over the smooth surface, and a much higher wind is necessary to lift the snow-fall than is required where the tall grass is caught as above mentioned.

The rule to be adopted in the matter of stocking a given range should be its capacity under the most unfavorable circumstances. A dry summer and short grass are liable to be followed by a hard winter. The number of cattle that will live and do well under these circumstances should be looked upon as the maximum that the range will support in safety, and no more should be placed thereon. During favorable years a larger number could be kept, but no one can tell when the good or bad years are coming. So the only safe plan is to be content with this number, and get the benefit of the extra good years in the greatly increased growth of the cattle. In the early days of the cattle industry on the plains the losses were extremely light and the cattle were always fat. Winter and early spring beef could be gathered from every herd. Why? Because there was an abundance of grass for grazing all the year. The grass grows just as well now as it did then, but there are too many cattle to eat it, and the winter range is more or less disturbed during the summer months. Absolute safety means a considerable reduction of the number of cattle now on the open ranges, if recourse is not to be had to hay-feeding, which in most cases is only partially practicable—that is, can only be done for a part of the herd. With the proper reduction of numbers the herds would be more profitable, the investment considered better than at present for the reason that losses from the inclemencies of the season would be unknown, and the growth of all the animals would be increased 20 per cent. at a low estimate. The temptation to overstock is very great, but range men must learn to withstand the temptation.

RANGE TENURE.

The question of range tenure is one that has caused considerable discussion of late, and is likely to become a matter of very great importance to the entire range country. This matter could be easily and speedily adjusted by the General Government if it would take hold of it and distribute the holdings under some uniform and reasonable basis of leasing. But opinion is greatly divided on this subject in the West, and in the East a general objection is raised. Many Eastern people believe that there is no arid region suited only for grazing, and assert that the whole of the great plains should be left open to the farmer who may desire to take up a 160-acre homestead. Under these circumstances the presumption is that the range country will remain as now, open to the herds of all who desire to occupy it. It remains, then, for the occupants themselves to adjust the question of range rights by some mutual agreement that will insure safety to their herds and protect them against the intrusion of others.

Experience thus far seems to point to "water rights" as the key to the solution. The great bulk of the range country is covered by the land laws of the United States, and title can be secured only to small areas of land, and this by actual settlement or improvement under the desert act that make land ownings very expensive. Water holes and running streams are scarce and widely separated, and in consequence but a small proportion of the plains and mountains will ever be secured by virtue of occupancy or improvement under any of the present laws. The hardships and expense incident to securing title to these watered lands are far in excess of their real value, and no one would think of making the effort but for the fact that their ownership carries a sort of squatter-sovereignty title, or a right of occupancy to the waste lands lying back of the water. Without access to the water the plains and hillsides in the rear are entirely valueless; they will produce no crop but grass, and this is only valuable by reason of the herds thereon being able to go down to the water at will to slake their thirst.

There would seem to be but one standard by which to measure the range rights of ranch men as between themselves, and that is their individual water rights. There is vastly more arid than watered land, and if each ranch man was held to that number of cattle for which he owned a necessary supply of water, there would be enough grazing territory tributary to maintain his herd with safety and profit. But even should this become recognized as the basis of settlement for this vexed question, its execution could only be properly entrusted to the local associations. There is such a wide difference in localities very near together as to the quantity of both water and grass, that the stockmen of one section would not be competent to sit in judgment on the claims of another. It is a subject beyond the reach of State or Territorial legislation, and can only be reached by arbitration, compromise, and general consent. This would be reasonable, fair, and honest between man and man. Of course there are no statute laws under which the provisions of such an agreement could be enforced; but individual and business honor between the parties would be a reasonable guaranty of its fulfillment if once generally entered into. Beside, under the widespread regulations of the stock associations of the range, the plan could be very generally made a success by reason of the rules of working that all are required to live up to under the penalty of forfeiture of membership and associated benefits. This rule has been adopted in a few districts, and the results have, so far, proven satisfactory. In some cases where, for instance, the public lands have not been surveyed, and there is absolutely no way in which titles to land can be secured, this rule might work a hardship. Actual possession in such cases would have to be recognized as ownership until the conditions were changed.

This is really a matter of grave and growing importance, and should receive the serious thought of all range stockmen until this or some other plan is hit upon to govern the question of "how many cattle shall be placed on a given range area?" Its proper solution bears directly on the main proposition, safety to our herds, and the one of all others that most concerns the future and the permanency of the industry.

SANITARY SUGGESTIONS.

Like the balance of the United States, the range country is more or less nervous over the existence of contagious pleuro-pneumonia in some of the States east of the Mississippi River. Western men realize the grave danger to the plains cattle should the germ of any contagion once be brought in, and while they have faith in the honesty and good intentions of the Bureau of Animal Industry and its agents, they know that until the law is so amended as to give them authority to slaughter all diseased and infected animals there is danger of its being carried to the herds of the unfenced ranges of the plains. There are but two agents of the Bureau to cover the range country from Texas to Montana. This is so wide an area that nothing like a proper surveillance can be made by the employés personally. But by co-operation with the cattle-growers' associations and the live-stock sanitary authorities a very complete system of inspection may be secured.

Every State and Territory in the range country has a State or Territorial stock association, and the officers of these organizations are in the fullest sympathy with the designs and efforts of the Bureau. Most of these range States and Territories have sanitary boards, or veterinarians with full power to act in emergencies, and most of the States immediately east of the range have created by law sanitary boards. Thus a network of co-operation may, by proper effort, be secured to guard the frontier and watch the range. Texas and Dakota are without adequate live-stock sanitary laws looking to protection. Governor Ross, of Texas, has made an earnest appeal to the legislature to pass suitable laws on this subject, and with the strong support of all the cattle men of the State it is believed the necessary laws will be passed this winter. Dakota is also making an effort in this direction.

The stock associations are made up of the best men in the West, and their influence is potent in shaping legislation. By cultivating the closest relations of co-operation with these associations their united labors may be secured to mould or aid in shaping uniform legislation under the reserved police powers of the States and Territories, of such stringency as to be a real protection. In this way it is hoped a much greater degree of safety may be secured.

The railroads are another adjunct of strength that may be secured with little trouble. Every railroad leading to the range has a direct interest in the cattle of the plains, amounting to from 20 to 30 per cent. of the entire cattle investment. Interviews with the managers of several of these roads justify me in saying that they will fully co-operate with the Bureau agents and the sanitary boards in all legitimate efforts to keep diseased or exposed cattle from moving west. By the union of action thus outlined, and the promulgation of uniform rules and regulations covering the entire range frontier, it would be rendered comparatively easy for the railroad employés to effectively co-operate with the sanitary boards by giving notice of all stock distined for the west, when not accompanied by the proper bills of health.

The entire Western country may and should learn a lesson from the course pursued by the officials of Wyoming Territory. The law of that Territory makes the veterinarian a sort of autocrat, with full authority to quarantine everything at the border not showing unquestioned evidence of freedom from disease or exposure thereto. A clearly understood set of rules have been adopted, and their non-fulfillment is cause for quarantine. A simple examination of stock by an expert and his certificate of health is no evidence that there has been no exposure. If any difference, there is more danger than from diseased ones. Diseased cattle are at once slaughtered or quarantined, and healthy ones kept from them. Exposed cattle may be allowed to mix with the herds, and by the time of the development of the disease hundreds of others may have taken on the contagion. Safety to the West means absolute quarantine against all eastern cattle unless they can give proof positive as to both their freedom from disease and exposure thereto. Any system adopted that falls short of this will be a serious mistake, and one liable to cost the range country the total destruction of its herds.

It is hoped, of course, that Congress will pass some effective law to strengthen the hands of the Bureau, so as to enable it to rid the country of disease and the suspicion of disease. But in that event the West will be called upon to exercise greater care than ever. It may be taken for granted that the Government will not pay over three-fourths the value of sound cattle, where they are killed by reason of exposure to disease, and not to exceed $160 for pure-bred animals, even should the most stringent laws yet discussed be passed. This leaves the margin between the real value and the appraised value under the law so great that unprincipled men will be tempted to buy and sell animals known to have been exposed, and ship them west for a higher price. Hence the avenues of commerce are liable to be more or less filled with this class of cattle, and renewed vigilance must be the watchword all along the line in the West.

Another good reason may be assigned for seeking the co-operation of the railroads. I will again cite Wyoming Territory. While her sanitary law is the strongest to be found in any section of the range country, and while little danger is to be feared from the entrance of cattle by rail, it would be found difficult to guard the entire eastern boundary against the crossing of grazing cattle. Dakota is now without any effective sanitary laws. Should none be enacted, that portion of Wyoming bordering on Dakota is open to the inroads of cattle from that Territory. At present there is no adequate Territorial law to prevent the shipment of diseased cattle into Dakota, and once in, there is nothing to prevent their roaming at will over the range. But with active co-operation with the railroads exact knowledge of every shipment of cattle may be secured and such details of information as will enable sanitary boards to learn of each shipment open to suspicion, thus giving the means of keeping watch over them, although in another Territory, and keeping them from the boundary line.

The leading idea in the minds of the people who labored most to organize the International Range Association was protection against the approach of bovine diseases, and the present officers of that organization are alive to the importance of the work. They will be found willing and active supporters of the Bureau of Animal Industry in all of its efforts in the way of keeping diseases from the plains. The West has the means in its own hands to erect an effective bar to the entrance of contagious disease, but in order to do so it must be diligent and leave no weak places. Union of all the forces is the only safe plan.

FOREIGN IMPORTATIONS.

About December 25, 1886, R. G. Head, president of the International Range Association, addressed the following letter to the Secretary of the Treasury:

SIR: In behalf of the International Range Association I have the honor to request you, under section 2494, Revised Statutes, to prohibit the importation of all cattle into the United States from all foreign countries where contagious cattle diseases exist.

The cattle raisers of the West are a unit in favor of such action, which is in harmony with the position taken by the Farmer's Congress at its annual meeting held in Minneapolis last summer, and the Consolidated Cattle Growers' Association at their recent meeting held in Chicago.

It is very generally conceded that the quarantine regulations relating to the importation of cattle into the United States do not afford sufficient protection against the introduction of diseased cattle into this country, and when the history of the outbreaks of contagious bovine diseases in other countries is considered, and the fact borne in mind that the admission to the open range of the West of a single infected animal would in all probability result in ruin to our great industry, on which the nation depends in a great measure for its food supply, it becomes apparent that immediate action should be taken in the premises.

I would respectfully call your attention to the fact that the Canadian and Australian authorities have prohibited the importation of cattle from Great Britain on account of the fear of the introduction of disease, which action suggests to us the necessity of placing similar safeguards around the health of the cattle of our own country. I would suggest, further, that in view of the fact that large sums of money will most likely be appropriated for the examination of disease where it now exists in our borders, the work should be rendered effective by preventing its further introduction.

R. G. HEAD,
Pres't. International Range Association.

To Hon. DANIEL MANNING,
Secretary of the Treasury.

In this letter Mr. Head correctly voiced the views of the cattle men of the range country. The honorable Secretary of the Treasury, in answer, stated that information from the Department of Agriculture was to the effect that no infected cattle had passed our quarantine stations, and therefore he did not feel justified in stopping importations. While it is true that our quarantine laws are efficiently administered at our ports of entry by the Department of Agriculture, it is also true that the ninety days in which cattle are held in quarantine is not long enough to establish the fact of freedom from disease. It is but fair to assume that our escape from contagion is due more to the care exercised by importers in making their purchases in foreign countries than to the effectiveness of our quarantine laws. As evidence of the fact that these regulations are not deemed sufficient by Western stockmen, the Colorado Veterinary Sanitary Board has refused admission to cattle that had passed through our quarantine stations until after being held an additional ninety days outside the limits of Colorado. It is better to err on the side of safety than to take chances which involve possible ruin to the plains cattle industry.

RANGE REFRIGERATOR PLANTS.

There is at this time a general discussion all over the West of the question of refrigerator plants. The difference between the retail price of meat in the populous portions of the United States and the prices received for live animals by the range beef producers has caused much more than the ordinary amount of thought on the question of markets. All sorts of ideas, practical and impracticable, have been brought out, and the prospects are that a good deal of experimentation will be indulged in during the coming year. No man knows of course what the future may demonstrate, but in studying this question we can only reason of the future by the experience of the past.

A careful study of the history of the refrigerating business shows very clearly to my mind that before the range country can hope to kill all its beef at home the surrounding conditions must be changed.

Most of the efforts of the kind so far made have been failures. The trouble lies first in the difficulty to secure a market for the dressed beef, and second in the loss of the offal. In order to secure a steady market it is necessary to supply a regular output. This can not now be done, for the reason that the range can supply fat cattle but for a few months each year. The amount of labor and the great expense incident to opening and building up a market would have to be undergone each year as the slaughtering season commenced. Hence the competition with Eastern establishments, that can kill their regular supply each day in the year, would be unequal and wholly insurmountable. The contest is unequal in the second place, because the offal that is worthless in the range country is of sufficient value in the great market centers to pay all of the expenses of slaughtering. Therefore the range can look for no present relief on anything like a large scale at least from Western refrigerator plants.

When the irrigable valleys of the arid region are all put under ditch, and the production of hay and alfalfa becomes so general and abundant as to afford sufficient feed to enable ranchmen to hold their beeves through the winter and early spring, then we may hope for permanent slaughter-houses in the West. Then the operator can secure a regular supply of animals, and each day in the year keep his customers in supply. The range country will be at the disadvantage of losing most of the offal, for some time at least, for the reason that the products made from this are never in demand in new countries, and in order to find a market high rates of freight must be paid to the older States. But there will be a partial compensation in the overcoming of the shrinkage of the long haul alive.

There is one thing, however, that can be successfully done at present. Small packing-houses may be erected at many points in the range country with sufficient capacity to kill as many beeves as the local trade will support, thus retaining some of the live animals at home and overcoming the present practice of shipping to Eastern markets alive and paying freight back on the dressed beef eaten at most points in the range. At first these establishments will have to make some shipments of live animals from the corn belts during the winter and early spring, but gradually the hay product will increase to such an extent as to give hay-fed cattle all winter.

IMPROVED STOCK-CARS.

There is perhaps no one thing which would more surely or more speedily benefit the stock grower, and at the same time promote the public health, than improved facilities for the transportation of live stock. That the old-time death-pens have not been consigned to obscurity long ago is one of the marvels of the age. Railroads doubtless oppose innovation on the old methods because of the large amount of money already invested in common stock-cars. To be required to at once discard their use would involve a heavy loss; but I believe the railroad companies would be glad to make progress in the direction of better facilities if some means could be devised that would enable them to employ the rolling-stock already in existence. Cars have been invented which meet all the requirements from the shippers' stand-point; but their general use would not only require an immense outlay of money but would render the tens of thousands of cars now owned by the railroads practically worthless. In addition to this, most of the cars which have been constructed with the sole view of carrying live stock rapidly and in comfort can not be used for carrying return freights; and as the railroads can not be expected to haul these empty cars without compensation, a higher rate for their use must be exacted than if they could be utilized both ways. A device applicable to the old style stock-car would doubtless be generally employed, if it could be so constructed that it would permit of feeding and watering in transit, and could be readily displaced for the loading of return freights.

This is a subject of national importance, and demands at the hands of the General Government careful investigation.

RANGE CATTLE GROWERS' ASSOCIATIONS.

It is the tendency of the times for enterprises of like character to combine for the purpose of promoting the general good of the individuals engaged in them. The business of cattle raising has not been an exception to the rule. The first attempt in this direction of national importance was witnessed in the convention of cattle growers at Chicago, in 1883. This was followed by the national meeting at Saint Louis, in 1884, and by the meeting one year later at the same city, in 1885.

These meetings demonstrated that the methods of raising cattle in the Eastern States and in the arid region were so dissimilar that but little good was being accomplished by conventions composed of stockmen from both sections. This fact gave birth to the idea of an association of range stockmen, and the first meeting of this kind was held at Denver, in January, 1886. The result of this meeting accomplished but little more than proving the necessity of such an organization, but the second meeting, held in Denver in February of this year, resulted in perfecting an organization which, it is believed, will be of the greatest benefit to the business of cattle raising as conducted on the open ranges in the country west of the one hundredth meridian. An industry of such vast extent must necessarily be the subject of more or less legislation in the different States and Territories, and it is only by the aid of associations that its needs can be properly and forcibly presented or effective measures secured against the ravages of disease. Through these associations just and effective sanitary laws can be had and enforced, and oppressive legislation can be prevented; and, as an agent of the Bureau of Animal Industry assigned to duty in the arid region, I have felt that my efforts could be directed in no more profitable channel than by aiding the building up of these associations and co-operating with them for the general good of the industry.

There is nothing better understood among thinking stockmen than the importance of a close union of live-stock interests, both for protection and the general promotion of the good of the industry.

In the early days of the range cattle business, when stockmen were few and far between, when but few herds roamed at will over a wide expanse of territory, the business ran itself, and by force of circumstances was safe and remunerative. Many of the men engaged in cattle raising then are still in the business, but some of them find it very difficult to adapt themselves to the new conditions that surround them. Progressive stockmen a few years ago saw where the industry was drifting, and hoped, by the aid of associations, to mitigate approaching disaster.

Associations were hastily formed, and were immediately followed by the depressing effects that had been long accumulating. Some old-time cattle men, not knowing how else to account for their troubles, seized upon the associations as a convenient scapegoat, and they have been slow to overcome their prejudices against these organizations intended for the general good. In spite of these things the friends of associated effort have kept right on in their work, and to-day the absolute necessity for a union of range interests is almost universally recognized. Men have been educated to an understanding of the causes that have depreciated ranch and cattle properties, and realize that these causes can not be met and overcome except by presenting a united and organized front. They see that men engaged in other great enterprises have been driven to the same means of protection and defense.

The distilleries of the country were, a few years ago, pressed to the verge of bankruptcy. They found that the cause was an overproduction, and they at once proceeded to save their industry by forming a union which should control the manufacture and keep it at all times within the limit of the demand, and they were saved from ruin and placed upon a basis that gave to all a profit on their labor. Coal operators and iron manufacturers have had to submit their business to similar regulations. While the depression in cattle is not because of overproduction, the causes of depression are subject to regulation and control, and prosperity will not return until the cattle men unite their efforts in a close and systematic union, whereby the whole interest may speak and act. Such an organization is contemplated and is assured in the International Range Association.

The benefit to be derived from associations is not merely theoretical or speculative. Take, for instance, the Colorado Cattle Growers' Association, the oldest in the range country. Its usefulness has grown with every year of its existence. The record it has made stands as an unanswerable argument in favor of associated effort. The cost of maintaining it has been merely nominal to its members, and it has profited the industry hundreds of thousands of dollars. Its members would go out of the business if they could not have the benefits obtained through its agency. What this association is to the stockmen of Colorado, the Range Association can be made to the stockmen of the entire range country. The work of the latter will be different, because it will cover a larger field and deal with different problems, but its work is as essential and in every sense as important to be accomplished as that of an organization limited in its operations to a county or State. It is possible that there are yet stockmen who are too obtuse to grasp the situation, but it is as certain as anything can be that these men will not long survive the attacks being made upon their business, and that but a few years will elapse when the cattle business of the plains will be in the hands of the men who have the intelligence to understand its needs, and the courage, manhood, and liberality to do whatever is necessary to save it.

MOVEMENT OF CATTLE FROM SOUTH TO NORTH.

In my last annual report I called attention to the advantages possessed by the South for breeding and the North for fattening cattle. It is now generally conceded that the line dividing the range country into these two divisions is the southern line of Colorado. While in restricted localities, both North and South, conditions exist that favor success in both breeding and fattening cattle, they are only exceptions that establish the rule. In Southern breeding ranges, where breeding outfits are at work during the greater part of the year, steers are necessarily moved about and disturbed to that extent that they will not take on fat as when allowed to control their own movements. In the North on fresh ranges, with abundance of water and shelter during favorable years, satisfactory calf crops have been secured. Experience has demonstrated that during severe winters occasionally to be experienced the per cent. of losses falls on the she cattle and calves. A knowledge of these facts has caused prudent investors to take advantage of the natural condition of things, and to utilize Southern ranges for breeding purposes and Northern ranges for fattening, necessitating the annual movement of cattle from South to North. Owing to the drought which was so prevalent over the greater part of the range country last season, and the low prices that beeves were bringing in the markets of slaughter, Northern buyers limited their purchases of Southern cattle to a number that was considerably less than had been anticipated. The total number of cattle en route to Northern ranges last season that passed Trail City, in Colorado, on the Arkansas River near the Kansas line, was 184,052 head, as reported by the Colorado Veterinarian. The era of good feeling which was inaugurated at the range cattle growers' meeting a year ago between the stockmen of the South and North was fully secured by the labors of Mr. F. B. York, Arthur Gorham, R. G. Head, and myself, who were selected to adjust all questions which had been in controversy between the two sections. These gentlemen formulated the following agreement, which was signed by Messrs. York and Head:

Whereas, F. B. York, of Saint Louis, Mo., representing certain parties holding and ranching cattle along what is known as the Dallas trail upon the one side, and R. G. Head, of Colorado, certain drovers of Texas cattle upon the other, realize the great annoyance, the loss of property and general dissatisfaction affecting both parties hereto which have resulted from the movement of cattle in previous years over the various trails leading from Texas, and more especially during the year 1885, over what is known as the Dallas trail, which trail runs north from Wichita Falls, Tex., passing through the western portion of the Indian Territory, and from thence through the western portion of the Cherokee strip; thence to a point near the northwest corner of the Panhandle of Texas; and

Whereas it is believed that cattle from certain sections of Texas in their migration from the South to the North have imparted or communicated to the native cattle along the line of this trail with which they come in contact, splenic fever; and

Whereas the absence hitherto of any rules or requirements by which the movement of such trail cattle might be governed, with a view of respecting and protecting the rights, holdings, and property of each, has caused great inconvenience and given rise to murmurs of general discontent and dissatisfaction, to say nothing of the heavy expenditures of money and losses of property entailed upon all concerned, and interruption of interstate commerce which has followed:

Therefore, we, the representatives of the above-mentioned interest, have formally made and entered into the following agreement, and we firmly believe that by a strict observance of the same by all parties each and every interest involved will receive just and adequate protection; that friendly relations will be restored and cemented, and the general welfare of all concerned will be promoted to a high degree of satisfaction. The following is the agreement:

First. That all cattle driven or shipped from that portion of Texas lying west and north of the following line, which area it is believed is absolutely safe ground and free from contagion and infection, are to be permitted to pass over what is known as the Dallas trail through the Cherokee strip, without hinderance or restriction.

The following is the line: Beginning at the Red River, at the northeast corner of Wilbarger County; thence south along the east line of Baylor, Throckmorton, Shackleford, Callahan, and Coleman Counties to the Colorado River in the southeast corner of Coleman County; thence with the Colorado River to the southeast corner of Llano County; from thence along the east line of Gillespie County, the east and south line of Kendall County, the east line of Bandera County, the east and south line of Medina County, and the east and south line of Zavalla County; from thence due west to Eagle Pass, on the Rio Grande.

Second. All cattle moved from that portion of Texas lying east and south of the above-described line, and west and north of the following-described line, are to be permitted to pass over what is known as the Dallas trail, through the Cherokee strip, when driven the entire distance by trail from their native ranges, but when shipped by rail any part of the distance forty-five days must elapse from the date of being unloaded from the cars before an entry shall be made into the said Cherokee strip.

The restricted locality.—The following is the line to which these restrictions will apply: Beginning at a point on Red River in the northwest corner of Grayson County; thence south to Dallas, and from thence due south to Waco; thence south, following the line of the Missouri Pacific Railroad to its junction with the International and Great Northern at Taylor; thence southwest, following the line of said International and Great Northern Railroad, to Laredo, on the Rio Grande.

Third. All cattle moved from the remaining portions of Texas, east and south of the last-described line, shall be permitted to pass over the said tract through said Cherokee strip, after a period of sixty days, when driven the entire distance by trails from their native ranges; but when shipped by rail any portion of the distance a period of seventy-five days must elapse before an entry shall be made into the said Cherokee strip. In the absence of other evidence as to the lapse of time where cattle are driven by trail, the bill of sale and inspectors' certificate will be accepted as evidence, and where cattle have been shipped by rail the shipper's contract, showing the date of release from the cars, will be accepted as evidence.

Held to the trails.—All cattle driven over the said trail through the said Territory shall be confined strictly to the limits of said trail; and further, all cattle so driven shall pass through the chutes or lanes, erected along the line of the trail by order of the Dallas convention, and the ranch men along the route to cross the trail with their native cattle, so as to secure freedom from exposure to disease.

It is expected, and we most respectfully request, that Texas drovers will use all possible care in passing over the route indicated to protect the range interest, and not permit their stock to mix with the range cattle along the route where it is possible to avoid so doing.

F. B. YORK.
R. G. HEAD.

So far as my knowledge goes, this agreement was generally observed. There were two violations which were probably unintentional, and would not have occurred had time permitted full knowledge of the agreement to have been disseminated. These two herds were from the infected and prohibited districts of Texas, and were shipped to Harrold, Texas, and driven thence north, arriving at the Colorado line before the lapse of a sufficient length of time to purge them of infection. The Colorado authorities, obtaining information of the facts, promptly quarantined these herds, where they were held the required length of time.

The results of the drive were just as the parties to the contract anticipated. No splenic fever was developed anywhere north of Texas so long as the terms of the compact were lived up to.

After the violation of the agreement there were few Northern cattle, or these from north of the fever line, moved over the trail, and in consequence but little damage. There was one herd moved from the Indian Territory over the trail after the passage of the Southern herds mentioned as not complying with the agreement, and about twenty head of cattle died in consequence.

The experience of last year demonstrates very conclusively that if this agreement is honestly lived up to no trouble will follow. It also proves that its violation brings trouble, and that the agreement must be strictly enforced.

This demonstrates that the movement of cattle from even the infected districts of Texas to Northern ranges can be made without endangering the health of Northern cattle by the adoption of such restrictive measures as experience has shown will prevent the communication of the disease.

It affords me pleasure to say that general good feeling prevails among the stockmen of the arid region, and a willingness to comply with the necessary sanitary regulations, which is well illustrated by the following resolution introduced at the recent range cattle growers' meeting by Mr. Ike T. Pryor, of Texas, which was unanimously adopted:

Resolved, That we, as representatives of the range-cattle industry, do hereby recommend and request that all parties driving cattle from any State or Territory to anywhere quarantine regulations exist do faithfully comply with such rules and regulations as their respective sanitary boards may agree upon, and we heartily disapprove of any attempt to violate said rules and regulations.

WESTERN HORSES.

For the last decade the breeding of horses has increased very rapidly in all the Western States and Territories. This has been especially noticeable during the past few years. Seeing that ranges were largely overstocked, feed on some eaten off and short, and that recent winters have brought loss in cattle, there is a growing disposition among parties predisposed to investment in cattle to prefer the breeding of horses. This preference is induced not only by the large demand and remunerative prices paid for really good horses in large cities, but from the fact that however severe the winter, and however heavy the loss of other live stock, the percentage of horses reported dead is always very light.

When snow is not deeper than their knees, sheep will paw away the snow to reach grass, but other cloven-footed stock, especially cattle, will not paw through snow to reach feed. During deep snows cattle go to the hills where the wind has swept away the snow, leaving feed exposed, or where the grass is tall and projects above the snow. Unless the snow has laid on the ground a long time, and their noses have become sore from such continued use, cattle will "nose" and root down through snow to reach grass. If the snow is encrusted and hard on top they can not do this, but rely upon following the strongest of their band, and eating the grass exposed in the trail made by their footsteps. But range cattle are never known to paw away snow to reach feed.

On the contrary, horses will paw away snow several feet in depth and obtain grass at any time, where the depth of the snow does not reach up to their bellies. There is only one condition in which horses will not paw down to feed, and that is where the surface of the earth, under the snow, as sometimes happens, is covered with a sheet of ice several inches thick. This soon cuts away their hoofs, rendering them foot-sore and unable to paw for feed. Horses bite off the grass much closer to the ground than cattle, and will exist on short ranges where cattle would starve. It is because of their ability to obtain feed under unfavorable circumstances that horses thrive on the range, during winter, better than other range-bred animals. This fact, together with increasing demand and better prices year by year, has made the horse business of the West remunerative and attractive.

We can not answer why the demand for horses continues to increase year by year more rapidly than steam and electric motors are invented seemingly to supersede them. But the fact remains. Whatever the cause of the demand, it must be supplied from the best and cheapest source. Increasing sales of Western horses every year indicate that the demand will be largely supplied from the West. Recognizing the profit to be made in supplying this demand, Western stockmen have imported largely and bred to Percherons, Clydesdales, Cleveland bays, French coachers, Belgians, Hambletonians, Arabs, Morgans, Canadians, and every strain of pure-bred horses, not even slighting the Shetland, Iceland, and other pony breeds. To such general extent has this grading up been brought that the horse-breeding establishments of the West are now prepared to sell any class of horses desired, from the smallest pony for ladies' and children's use to the heaviest draft-horse for city trucks, stylish coachers, carriage horses, saddlers, serviceable, heavy, "all-round" horses for farm use, and thoroughbred racing stock. It is not the prophecy of an enthusiast, but a fact readily established by personal inspection, that the finest horses of the world are to come from our Western plains and mountain valleys.

One of the reasons of the superiority of Western horses is attributable to the dry, exhilarating, pure air, and an equable climate. The admitted superior constitution and endurance of Western range-bred horses is due largely to the fact that the colt, being born in mountains or valleys, frequently miles from water, is compelled to travel with its mother, before twenty-four hours old, on her journey for a drink, and this is thenceforward a part of its daily exercise. The horse is in many respects like a man. To be useful he must possess will power, and the roaming life on the plains imparts this characteristic to both.

Eastern horses have been bred in bondage generation after generation, while the range horse has known only the freedom and exercise of the range. The result is that the range-bred horse has "lungs of leather, hoofs of iron, and sinews of steel." Western horses are very much like the people—made up of all nations and in many instances better than those they came from.

When the Western stockman first recognized the increasing demand for horses his impulse was to improve his stock of natives by importing and breeding to the best thoroughbred stallions obtainable from the East, Canada, and Europe. While this has been so far productive of fine classes of grades and undeniable improvement and enhanced usefulness and value, there are certain qualities in both our native horses and native cattle which can not be bred away without losing some essentially good characteristics. We refer to their rustling qualities, reproductiveness, rapid breeding, and to the care and success of the mothers in raising their young, and to their ability for long-continued service and rough usage. It seems these well-known qualities of the original rough, range-bred native pony stock—the Mustangs, Marsh Tackeys, Cherokees, Sioux, and Cayuses—have something in them worth preserving, if possible.

In the general improvement and breeding-up, it may be well not to breed our range-horses too fine, or, as with cattle, it may be found that they will lose to a great degree their qualities of reproductiveness and ability to endure rough usage.

It will be seen, then, that this branch of animal industry, employing millions of dollars of capital, with brightest promises of producing millions more, merits the encouraging and protecting care of our Government. The East, with her great industrial centers, must look to the West to supply her with the draft-horses of commerce.

The farmers of the East have failed to so do in sufficient numbers, and they never can raise and supply a horse as cheaply as the West, because our range-bred horses are never fed until they are taken off the range at three and four years of age and put to work.

Peace is a thing devoutly to be prayed for, but it is a condition that has never existed continually in the history of any government. Therefore in time of peace it is wise to be prepared for war. In the event of war our Government would have of necessity to rely on the West to mount her cavalry, as the West is the only section to-day prepared to furnish horses in any quantity at all suitable for cavalry use; and while Western horses may not at this date fill the entire requirements of the present army standard for cavalry horses, there are hundreds of thousands of Western range-bred horses whose hardiness and endurance would be especially valuable for irregulars like the Cossacks of Russia, the Uhlans of Germany, and for mounted infantry.

It is said that France expends $3,000,000 annually in the improvement of her horses. Some encouragement from our Government, with a few years more of judicious breeding up to a proper standard, would enable our Western horse-raisers to supply an unlimited number of superb horses, entirely suitable to the standard and requirements for cavalry horses. Looking to the future of the horse business of the West, there are a few simple things that will continue to render the industry profitable for long years to come; first, freedom from disease; second, favorable climatic conditions; third, ability of horses to feed far back from water where grass is untouched and best; and fourth, the ability of horses to thrive where cattle can scarcely live.

So great is the confidence in the future continued profit of the Western horse business that one company, operating in Idaho and Oregon, "runs" 8,000 native mares on the range. The grades of these, bred principally from Percheron and Hambletonian stallions, when broken, are sold readily in eastern markets for street-cars, trucks, delivery-wagons, and carriages. From the stock of this one firm alone may be obtained well-broken and serviceable horses of any class for commercial and family use, and wherever tested their good lungs, powers of endurance, and sound feet have proved them especially valuable for service on the stone-paved streets of cities. In California the large amount invested in thoroughbreds in the Palo Alto stables implies confidence that the racing stock bred there will continue to maintain their reputation for producing horses that make fast time.

A further reason for the continuance of the range horse business is the ability of horses to feed far out from water. Horses will "use" dry stretches of range which could not be utilized for other live stock without the expenditure of large sums of money in affording artificial supplies of water. Owing to this fact horses can be run on the same range with cattle without detriment to the latter, and a large amount of grass thus economized that otherwise would rot on the ground and be wasted.

To realize the largest profits from Western horses breeders must put them on the market broken and gentled. Eastern buyers have neither the inclination nor the horse-taming experience to handle unbroke and range-bred horses. They desire to buy well-broken animals, ready for immediate service.

With the rapid development of the semi-arid lands on the border of the range country, and the consequently largely increased number

same as cattle men do. Most sheep herders load their mess-wagon in the spring and follow the flock all summer, never camping more than two nights in one place, thus putting them in the attitude of willing trespassers upon the range rights of their neighbors. This is the main cause of so much ill feeling toward them throughout the West. Should the question of range tenure ever be settled by Government rules, sheep and cattle men should be held to the same line of action—kept on their allotted area. This industry, being second in importance to cattle in the range country, demands from the Government its fostering care. The arid region possesses many advantages for successful sheep husbandry. The dryness of the atmosphere and the light dry soil prevents the appearance of the destructive disease so prevalent in the lower and damper countries.

The greatest obstacle in the way of success to the sheep men of the arid region has been their inability to realize from their muttons. The railroad rates for transporting sheep has been nearly if not quite as much for a single deck load as for a car of cattle, notwithstanding the fact that it is impossible to load to exceed 10,000 pounds on one floor, when 20,000 pounds would be permitted. The use of stationary double decks were so objectionable to the railroad companies that by common agreement some months ago they were prohibited. Stock cars thus equipped could not be utilized for carrying merchandise on return trips, and to remove and restore their temporary floors was expensive and injurious to the cars. This decision of the railroads was equivalent to an absolute prohibition to the traffic in fat sheep from remote points. The railroads, however, expressed a willingness to permit the use of double decks if an adjustable floor could be devised that would overcome the objections stated. This stimulated inventive genius, and the Missouri Pacific system is now using a deck invented by Olney Newell, of Denver, Colo., which is at once simple, durable, and cheap. The officers of the road express entire satisfaction with it, and I think its general adoption, or something equally good, will greatly benefit the sheep growers of the country.

FEEDING IN THE ARID REGION.

Under the old system of range production, feed for winter was only thought of in connection with the cow ponies kept up for every day use. Grass being everywhere abundant there was no apparent necessity for feeding, and the mortality was light. But with the rapid increase of the herds has come a shortage in grass and an increased mortality. This has caused an investigation into the subject of preparing feed for winter as a means of security. Years of experience among the farmers who have settled along the streams that here and there penetrate the arid region has fully demonstrated the richness of the soil and the wonderful hay-producing capacity of the land when once put into cultivation under irrigating ditches. Five tons of alfalfa can be raised from every acre that can be thoroughly irrigated, and heavy crops of almost every other known variety of grass. All kinds of hay cure so perfectly in this arid country that their nutritive and fattening qualities are something wonderful. Well-authenticated experiments at several points in the range country have established the fact that alfalfa, wild and tame clover, and our mountain bluestem grass, if fed under reasonably fair conditions in winter, will put on flesh at an average of two pounds gross per day for a period of three or five months. This without grain of any kind to mix with the hay.

These facts being generally known, there is a growing tendency to utilize all of the available lands for irrigation and the production of forage crops. Probably not more than one acre in two hundred of the entire arid belt is susceptible of being brought under ditch with the hope of getting an ample water supply. But the increased quantity of feed this small area is capable of producing would be sufficient to winter-feed one-fourth or more of all the cattle now grazing on the great plains. In time a system of water storage may be developed so as to save the vast volume that now runs to waste in winter (when not wanted), which will double the available supply. When this time arrives the risks of winter will have departed. Meantime each coming year will see more and more of the valley lands converted into meadows, and the hay crop so increased that thousands of beef steers may be fattened during the winter, or all of the weak members of the herd taken up and properly cared for. This will involve a very considerable outlay of money and labor, but as compensation it will give immunity from winter losses and a continuous growth from calfhood up, thus adding largely to the matured weight of each animal in the herd. Limited real-estate investments in connection with the herds, if made for hay lands, will give both permanency and security to the general investment.

CONCLUSION.

There are many other topics of which I might profitably treat, but to do so would render my report of unreasonable length. I have submitted my views upon subjects which seemed to me of greatest importance, with the hope that these suggestions may serve to promote the welfare of the live-stock industry.

I have traveled almost constantly over the range country since the date of my last report, and have co-operated with live-stock sanitary authorities and officers of associations in protecting the range-stock interests from disease.

H. M. TAYLOR,
Agent U. S. Bureau of Animal Industry.

DENVER, COLO., *February* 22, 1887.

THE CATTLE TRADE AND ALLIED INDUSTRIES OF MICHIGAN, WISCONSIN, AND TENNESSEE.

Hon. NORMAN J. COLMAN,

Commissioner of Agriculture:

SIR: The following are the results of my investigations of the present year as to the condition and importance of the cattle trade and allied industries of the States of Michigan, Wisconsin, and Tennessee:

MICHIGAN.

In its natural conditions the State of Michigan was not well adapted to stock-growing. The circumstances affecting the commerce, manufacturing, and other industries of the State were not such as tended to rapidly develop farming, nor were they likely to foster the growth of the live-stock interest. The lower or southern tiers of counties were on the lines of travel along which the tide of immigration flowed before the completion of the through lines of railroad in Canada. In those southern counties were located the railroads which first crossed the State connecting the east with the country beyond the timbered region; the result was that those counties were settled at a comparatively early date. But the larger part of the State was at one side of the course of travel, and formed as it might be described, a cove or bight beside the stream of immigration, into which only a small part of the great current eddied, the rest flowing on toward the newly discovered and far more tempting prairies of Illinois and the west. Thus the settlement of Michigan has gone on slowly. Of the 36,655,200 acres of land in the State, only 12,207,220 acres were, in the year 1885, included in farms; and even of the land in farms only 7,280,775 acres were at the time named improved, the remainder being covered by forest. Yet, Michigan offers advantages to the farmer, and especially to the dairyman. The State is within easy reach of large markets, has good soil and a comparatively equable climate, in which the extremes of temperature that occur in some of the prairie States are never felt. The water supply is abundant and good, and droughts seldom, if ever, occur.

The State is without a single mountain, and no hills worthy of the name are seen in the southern part or lower peninsula. Rising by very slight grades from the low flat lands at the head of Lake Erie and along the rivers Detroit and St. Clair, and the low shores of Lakes St. Clair and Huron, the land nowhere reaches an elevation greater than is needed to give the drainage required. A very large part of the interior is a rolling clay soil, covered by vegetable mold; but on the west side of the State and in the northern end of the lower peninsula there are considerable tracts of sandy land. On the shore of Lake Michigan this land has become famed as a profitable fruit-growing region. That part of the State lying north and west of the Straits of Mackinaw and Lake Huron is known only as a region of copper, iron, and timber. Little farming is done there, and the few cattle kept are raised for the purpose of supplying their owners with milk and butter, for use in the yoke, or for replenishing the stock. There are in the eleven counties of the upper peninsula, from which reports have been received, only 2,866 milch cows and 3,530 other cattle, being 1.2 cows and 1.6 other cattle for each 100 acres included in the farms of those counties. In the year 1880 there were in those eleven counties 1,760 cows and 2,726 other cattle, the population having been 85,030 at that time.

Fifty years ago nearly all of the surface of the State of Michigan was covered by heavy forests. Having no means for learning the character and extent of the prairie regions of the West, then comparatively unknown, the people of Michigan had no idea of the value their timber would have within a quarter of a century. Many of them did not even know that vast and fertile fields lay ready for the plow only a few days' journey away. Most of the pioneers had not been taught to believe that a farm could be made in any way other than by the exceedingly laborious and tedious one of clearing away forests, digging up stumps, and cutting down bushes that sprang up in the clearings until at last the forest should be finally subdued and the fields yield harvests in plenty and comparative ease. As in all somber forests, the forage in Michigan was of inferior quality and scant in quantity, having little nutrition for stock. That which grew on the sedgy margins of the ponds or on the boggy marshes was little or no better than that which grew under the trees. So small was the supply of food for the stock of the pioneer, that tender trees were often felled that the starving animals might gnaw the twigs and bark to keep themselves alive until spring should cause the scanty crop of grass to grow again. Scattered throughout the State are many small lakes, on the shores of which sedges sprang up early in the spring, and a little pasturage appeared on the banks of streams where clear spots were, but in the most favored places there was little to encourage stock-growing.

Lying as it does in the midst of great bodies of water, Michigan is usually covered in winter by deep snows. They come early and stay late. The vapors which rise from the broad expanses of water, warmed by summer suns and by the heat of the earth beneath their depths, meet the chilling north winds of autumn, and are driven over the land, to fall in thick blankets, that protect the fields of grain and the trees and vines. In spring the lakes are covered by floating fields of ice, that grind along the base of the hills of frozen spray on the shores. These cool the winds of early spring, as the chill waters do later, and retard the thawing of the snow. They keep back the springing of the grass and the opening of buds until after the open prairies of the West are ready for the plow. While these causes serve to discourage stock-growing, they have operated to make Michigan one of the best fruit-growing States in the Union. Yet despite all obstacles Michigan was eleventh in a list of forty-seven States and Territories, in the year 1884, in the number of milch cows, and twenty-first in that of oxen and other cattle owned by their people.

As in all forest regions, the pioneer had no desire to own more cattle than were required to answer the immediate demands of his family. Almost invariably a cow was taken with the family to the new home to supply milk. In most cases a yoke of oxen was also driven into the wilderness, hauling the household effects to their destination and afterward helping to clear the ground of logs and stumps and in plowing and other farm work. For these few animals the stalks of corn raised furnished a goodly quantity of forage; for other food wanted they hunted in the woods. As the cow could furnish a large quantity of food for the family more directly and with less attention from her owners than was required for the production of a like quantity of food by the aid of the other stock, there was a general desire to increase the number of cows as fast as forage could be got for their support. Comparatively little beef was eaten by the pioneers. Game was for years abundant, as it is even now in some parts of the State that have been settled for years. Venison and other game supplied much of the meat eaten during the early days by the farmers, and pork to a large extent took the place of game as the latter became scarce. This has usually occurred in other wooded regions, because the domesticated pig can, like his wild ancestors, get in forests from roots, nuts, and fruits a large part of, if not all, the food needed, and fatten where horned cattle could scarcely find food enough to sustain life. In Michigan the growing pigs roamed at will in the woods, as they do even now where the forests have not been cleared away, getting no other food than they found for themselves until autumn came and maize was fed to fatten them.

As settlers entered the State and forests gave way to cultivated fields villages appeared, towns grew, and railroads gave facilities for sending the products of the farms to market. All these created a demand for products which had before been of comparatively little value. Farmers found a ready sale for the butter and cheese they made, and as these articles could be produced with little or no addition to the labors of the men, and were more easily disposed of than the more bulky products of the farm could be, there was naturally a disposition to increase the number of milch cows rather than to raise stock for beef. The result is that of the whole cattle supply of the State in the year 1885 fully 47.8 per cent. were milch cows; only eight other States—Maine, Massachusetts, Rhode Island, Connecticut, New York, New Jersey, Pennsylvania, and Delaware—showing as large a percentage of milch cows in their herds. All of of the States named have easy access to or have within their borders large markets in which milk and butter meet ready sale.

PASTURAGE AND FORAGE.

Of the 36,655,200 acres of land in the State of Michigan, there were in the year 1885 only 12,207,220 in farms, the rest having been almost entirely in woodland in its natural condition, except so far as the axes of the lumberman had cut out the larger trees. Of the land included in farms, only 7,280,775 acres were improved, the remaining 4,926,445 acres being woodland pastures. The forage in these wood lots is not invariably poor, but in few if any tracts of forest can pasturage be found as good as that of the open prairies of the West. The larger part of the pasturage of Michigan is in fields that have been cultivated and seeded. The forage thus obtained is supplemented by the growths found in the cultivated fields a[illegible] the crops have been removed each year. The clovers, timothy, and some blue-grass are the staple plants found in the pastures. They thrive well in all parts of the State, even in the extreme northern part of the lower peninsula, the climate there being much modified by the large bodies of water near.

Of hay there was produced in the State in the year 1884 some 1,648,665 tons from 1,365,834 acres, the average yield having been 1.21 tons per acre, the acreage and the average yield having been greater than in any previous year except 1883. The average yield of hay per acre for the seven years ended with 1884 was 1.23 tons; the average number of tons harvested per annum during that period having been 1,362,935. In the same period the average area planted to maize was 780,352 acres, from which an average yearly yield of 40,978,611 bushels was obtained, or 52.5 bushels per acre. In the year 1884 the area in corn was 802,988 acres, from which an average of 59.1 bushels was harvested.

Oats form an important forage crop in Michigan. In the year 1885 there were 717,854 acres in oats in the State, from which 25,841,525 bushels were harvested, being an average of 35.98 bushels per acre. The straw from the oats crop forms an important addition to the forage supply, as do the corn-stalks also. The latter are usually cut when the corn is harvested, and are carefully stacked, housed, or otherwise protected from the weather, instead of being allowed to remain standing as they grew, to be eaten by the stock or trampled under foot, as they are in the prairie States.

Hay, corn-stalks, and straw form the major part of the rations of the stock of Michigan, as of other States; but these are supplemented by barley, of which grain an average of 37,576 acres per annum was grown during the seven years ended with 1884, the average yearly yield having been 808,145 bushels, or 21.5 bushels per acre. Pease are also fed in a few instances. In the year named above 851,410 bushels of pease were grown on 42,529 acres. It can not be said that pease form a very large part of the food supply, but there seems to be no reason why they should not be fed much more freely, except that many farmers seem to think that pease are worth more in the market than they are as rations for stock. Apples have often been feed freely to the cattle, especially in years when the apple crop has been large and prices so low that the owners of orchards thought that they would not be paid for the labor and expense of gathering and marketing the fruit. Bran, roots, oil-cake, and oil-meal are used to a large extent in some of the older dairy districts of the State.

WATER SUPPLY.

Throughout all Michigan the water supply was abundant in the early days of the State; but as a large part of the water was from swampy places the quality was not always good. The effect of the drinking of water tainted by soaking in the rotting vegetation of swamps was often tasted in the milk and butter. No worse effect seemed to follow than a slightly offensive taste and odor. Cattle seldom showed symptoms of the milk sickness that proved so disastrous to cattle and to human beings in Indiana and Illinois in early days—symptoms which occasionally appear even now. Michigan has few large rivers and none of great length. In the south the St. Joseph rises near the town of Hillsdale, in the county of that name, and flowing westward empties into Lake Michigan. Rising within a few rods of the source of the St. Joseph, the river Raisin flows eastward to Lake Erie. Twenty-five or thirty years ago both streams, like all others in this part of the State, were clear and pure, fed by

long the greater part of their courses. The volume of water as diminished since the forest was cleared away. Some of the butaries to the rivers mentioned now fail in the latter part ummer months, and become series of stagnant pools; but ot so generally the case as in the prairie States.

alamazoo, the Grand, and the Saginaw are the other large in the southern half of Michigan, and the Au Sable and stee drain the northern part of the lower peninsula. All of rs mentioned, and the smaller ones scattered through the e fed by innumerable tributaries intersecting every section in the State. In nearly all parts of Michigan many little found, around the edges of which grow reeds and coarse nd grasses. These ponds or lakes are fed by cold and pure and never become stagnant. The water in nearly all of cool and palatable. Usually the bottoms are sandy or . No better watering places for stock could be devised, as als never become stuck in the mire, never lack for an abun- pure and cool water, and find in the ponds a pleasant refuge flies and heat. Altogether, Michigan may be said to be as plied with water fit for stock as could be wished. In every he State an ample supply of good well water can be found at te depth; in some places flowing wells have been made by few scores of feet. It seems to be more than probable that erations will pass away before the general supply of flowing ll be much lessened, as the forest disappears slowly.

upper peninsula the water supply is unsurpassed in quality, through rocky channels from springs in hills so covered by that they will probably remain practically undisturbed for y it seems scarcely likely that so rugged a district will be- farming region before the whole prairie country of the West e become occupied by farms.

DISTRIBUTION OF CATTLE.

higan the growth of the cattle interest has been rather slow, s already mentioned, as compared with the growth of the erest in some parts of the Western States; yet it has been le as compared with the increase of the number of cattle in ed States as a whole. It is worthy of note that during the ared with 1870 there was a gain of 14 per cent. in the cattle f Michigan, whereas in the same period the supply of cattle hole country showed a decrease of 7 per cent. The table llows shows the changes made in the supply of cattle in the ited States each decade since 1850 and since the census of taken, and the percentage of increase from time to time

Years.	Milch cows.	Working oxen.	Other cattle.	Totals.	Per cent.
[illegible]	6,385,094	1,700,744	6,693,069	14,778,907	......
[illegible]	8,585,735	2,254,911	14,779,373	25,620,019	.73
[illegible]	8,935,332	1,319,271	13,566,005	23,820,608	*.07
[illegible]	12,443,120	993,841	22,488,550	35,925,511	.50
[illegible]	13,501,206	(†)	29,046,101	42,547,307	.15

* Decrease. † Added to "other cattle."

It will be seen that the check received by the cattle industry during the decade in which the great civil war occurred has not yet been recovered from. The rate of increase in the cattle supply during the ten years ended in 1860 was 7.3 per cent. per year. In the next following decade it was only seven-tenths of 1 per cent. per annum, and since 1870 the rate of increase has been only 4.33 per cent. per year, although the cattle business of the Western plains has in the last fifteen years made the greater part of its growth. From these facts it seems to be safe to conclude that the supply of beef and of dairy products is not likely to so greatly exceed the requirements of the future as to lead to any marked decline in prices of these products.

The progress of the cattle interest in the State of Michigan, since the completion of the first trustworthy census of the agricultural industries of the United States, is shown by the statement which follows:

Years.	Milch cows.	Working oxen.	Other cattle.	Totals.	Per cent.
1850	99,076	55,850	119,471	274,497	.....
1860	179,543	61,680	238,615	479,844	.75
1870	250,859	36,499	260,171	547,529	.14
1880	384,578	40,393	466,660	891,631	.63
1881	311,300	....	322,231	633,531	*.19
1882	310,596	....	317,874	628,470	*.01
1883	315,927	....	322,228	638,155	.02
1884	334,869	....	354,841	689,710	.08
1885	348,412	....	379,981	728,393	.06

* Decrease.

In the table above given the figures presented for the years 1881 and later are from statistics furnished by the Secretary of State. In those years the working oxen were included in the account of "other cattle."

Of the eighty counties reported in Michigan six had less than an average of 1 milch cow for each 100 acres of improved land; twenty had between 1 and 2 cows per 100 acres; thirty-eight had over 2 and under 3 cows, and sixteen counties had over 3 cows for each 100 acres improved. Of other cattle three counties had, in 1884, less than 1 cow per 100 acres; fourteen counties had from 1 to 2; twenty-six had from 2 to 3, and thirty-seven had 3 or more for each 100 acres of improved land. Only one county in the upper peninsula showed the possession of 4 cattle other than milch cows for each 100 acres. The distribution of cattle in the State in the year 1884 was, according to very full figures furnished by the Hon. H. D. Conant, Secretary of State of Michigan, as shown in the statement which follows. For convenience the report has been arranged to show a grouping in five geographical divisions, of which the mineral and forest district of the upper peninsula forms one.

SOUTHEASTERN COUNTIES.

Counties.	Improved land.	Milch cows.	Per 100 acres.	Other cattle.	Per 100 acres.
	Acres.				
Clinton	300,977	8,594	2.8	9,789	2.9
Genesee	344,222	11,273	3.3	11,278	3.3
Gratiot	215,985	6,082	2.8	6,088	3.7
Hillsdale	312,424	9,608	3.1	12,097	3.9
Ingham	284,188	8,066	2.9	8,914	3.1
Jackson	356,244	8,615	2.4	9,245	2.6
Lapeer	308,565	8,643	2.8	10,922	3.5
Lenawee	370,256	13,496	3.6	14,799	4.9
Livingston	321,859	7,501	2.3	8,608	2.7
Macomb	263,686	10,254	3.9	8,276	3.1
Monroe	278,855	9,288	3.6	8,482	3.0
Oakland	458,601	12,910	2.8	11,858	2.5
Saginaw	254,191	9,955	3.9	10,629	4.2
Sanilac	298,895	9,131	3.0	12,370	4.1
Shiawassee	264,720	8,240	3.1	8,110	3.0
Saint Clair	328,979	12,327	3.7	13,009	4.0
Washtenaw	387,964	10,873	2.8	11,607	3.0
Wayne	241,902	11,309	4.7	7,863	3.2
Total	5,592,463	176,360	3.2	188,594	3.3

SOUTHWESTERN COUNTIES.

Counties.	Improved land.	Milch cows.	Per 100 acres.	Other cattle.	Per 100 acres.
Allegan	337,273	11,608	3.4	11,565	3.4
Barry	276,120	6,718	2.4	7,759	2.8
Berrien	274,767	7,792	2.8	7,719	2.8
Branch	284,945	8,327	2.9	9,513	3.3
Calhoun	371,191	9,560	2.6	10,955	2.7
Cass	270,466	62,241	2.3	7,499	2.8
Eaton	304,809	9,953	3.3	11,548	3.8
Ionia	311,172	8,352	2.7	9,367	3.0
Kalamazoo	296,940	7,208	2.4	8,781	2.9
Kent	393,106	11,414	2.9	10,596	2.7
Montcalm	188,805	4,941	2.6	5,701	3.0
Muskegon	85,033	2,350	2.8	2,387	2.8
Ottawa	196,280	9,070	4.6	8,336	4.1
Saint Joseph	288,977	7,143	2.5	7,807	2.7
Van Buren	266,835	6,874	2.6	6,840	2.6
Total	4,146,809	117,601	2.8	126,163	3.0

NORTHEASTERN COUNTIES.

Counties.	Improved land.	Milch cows.	Per 100 acres.	Other cattle.	Per 100 acres.
Alcona	15,321	286	1.9	300	2.5
Alpena	32,731	483	1.8	559	1.7
Arenac	27,502	582	2.1	731	2.7
Bay	86,307	3,288	3.8	3,422	3.9
Cheboygan	46,801	706	1.5	725	1.6
Crawford	22,788	176	0.8	234	1.0
Gladwin	13,567	310	2.2	422	3.1
Huron	225,419	6,657	2.9	9,802	4.3
Iosco	21,941	498	2.3	811	3.7
Midland	64,123	1,635	2.9	1,919	3.0
Montmorency	10,290	80	0.8	126	1.2
Ogemaw	41,271	371	0.9	510	1.2
Oscoda	31,568	167	0.5	242	0.8
Otsego	20,164	216	1.1	209	1.0
Presque Isle	49,682	827	1.7	1,042	2.1
Roscommon	4,916	59	1.2	78	1.6
Tuscola	266,567	8,248	3.1	9,205	3.5
Total	980,968	24,584	2.6	30,517	3.1

NORTHWESTERN COUNTIES.

Counties.	Improved land.	Milch cows.	Per 100 acres.	Other cattle.	Per 100 acres.
	Acres.				
Antrim	54,857	1,092	1.9	1,428	2.6
Benzie	47,041	770	1.7	891	1.9
Charlevoix	59,196	975	1.6	1,235	2.1
Clare	28,080	498	1.8	681	2.4
Emmett	68,088	680	1.0	676	1.0
Grand Travers	78,168	1,678	2.1	2,313	3.0
Isabella	120,517	3,202	2.6	4,410	3.6
Kalkaska	42,422	544	1.2	724	1.7
Lake	32,790	522	1.7	792	2.4
Leelenaw	88,308	1,603	1.8	2,246	2.5
Manistee	55,470	1,332	2.4	1,522	2.7
Manitou	7,155	170	2.4	242	3.4
Mason	56,750	1,342	2.3	1,673	2.8
Mecosta	106,474	2,476	2.3	3,295	3.1
Missaukee	32,407	664	1.8	1,023	3.1
Newaygo	135,352	3,311	2.4	4,308	3.2
Oceana	110,407	2,734	2.5	3,989	3.6
Osceola	109,988	2,320	2.1	3,347	3.1
Wexford	51,584	1,055	2.0	1,506	3.0
Total	1,285,059	26,988	2.1	36,246	2.8

UPPER PENINSULA.

Counties.	Improved land.	Milch cows.	Per 100 acres.	Other cattle.	Per 100 acres.
Alger	1,102	17	1.5	27	2.5
Baraga	7,060	117	1.7	120	1.8
Chippewa	35,107	392	1.1	610	1.4
Delta	21,472	430	2.2	483	2.2
Houghton	15,900	206	1.3	185	1.2
Keeweenaw	3,420	67	2.0	103	3.0
Mackinac	30,044	250	0.8	252	0.8
Marquette	24,921	522	2.1	659	2.6
Menominee	48,518	639	1.3	753	1.5
Ontonagon	6,208	193	3.1	291	4.7
Schoolcraft	7,272	33	0.4	38	0.5
Total	201,919	2,866	1.2	3,530	1.6

SUMMARY.

Districts.	Improved land.	Milch cows.	Per 100 acres.	Other cattle.	Per 100 acres.
	Acres.				
Southeastern	5,592,463	176,380	3.2	183,524	3.3
Southwestern	4,146,809	117,601	2.8	126,163	3.0
Northeastern	980,968	24,584	2.6	30,517	3.1
Northwestern	1,285,059	26,988	2.1	36,246	2.8
Upper Peninsula	201,919	2,866	1.2	3,530	1.6
Total	12,207,218	348,399	2.9	379,980	3.1

The relations which have existed between the population of the State of Michigan and the cattle supply of the State at various times, suggest the changes that have taken place in some of the industries of the State. They also recall the changes that have resulted in the dairying and beef-producing interests of other States, as well as of Michigan, from the settlement of the grassy plains of the States west of Indiana. In the census of 1850 it was shown that Michigan had then 250.6 milch cows, 139.2 working oxen, and 300.5 other cattle for each 1,000 of her population. In the census of 1860 there were 239.7 milch cows, 82.3 working oxen, and 318.5 other cattle for each 1,000 people then in the State. In 1870 the census showed that the number of milch cows was 211.8 of working oxen 30.8, and of other cattle 219.8 per 1,000 of population, and in 1880 the supply of cows rose to 235 per 1,000 inhabitants, the number of working oxen had dwindled to 24.7, while of all other cattle there were 285 per 1,000. The total supply of cattle of all classes in the State in 1850 gave for each 1,000 inhabitants then in Michigan 690.3 animals. During the next following decade the number shrank to 640.5, and in the ten years during which the civil war made so serious inroads upon the live-stock supply of the whole country there was a further falling off to 402.4 cattle to each 1,000 people. Between the years 1870 and 1880 there was a tendency to restore the supply to the old standing, and the number of cattle rose to 544.7 per 1,000 inhabitants. The whole country had in 1880 some 716.3 per 1,000 inhabitants; but while Michigan had 171.6 fewer cattle of all kinds than the general average of the country, in the total supply of milch cows per 1,000 people she falls only 13 short of that general average.

In the year 1880 the State could muster only 24.7 working oxen for each 1,000 people, while in 1850 there were 139.2. Of cattle of this class there were then in the whole United States only 19.8 for every 1,000 people. The largeness of the supply in Michigan of stock of this kind is accounted for by the fact that considerable numbers of yoke cattle are used in Michigan in lumbering, which forms the occupation of many of the people of this State, and also in the task of clearing away the forests and converting the lands into cultivated farms. This work is going on at a reasonably rapid rate. It is worthy of note that, whereas in nearly every other State there has been a marked falling off year by year in the supply of working oxen, there was an actual increase of 10 per cent. in the number in Michigan between the years 1870 and 1880, the increase having amounted to 3,894. Between the years 1860 and 1870 the supply shrunk very nearly 41 per cent., or 4,126 animals. In this connection may be mentioned the fact that between the years 1860 and 1870 the number of farms in the State was increased by the addition of 36,364 farms, or 58 per cent. Between 1870 and 1880 the increase was 55,222, or 56 per cent. Assuming that the rate of increase in oxen has been maintained during the six years which have passed since the gathering of the last census, there should now be in Michigan 42,816 yoke cattle. If the rate of increase in the number of farms had been kept up in the same years, there would now be in the State 205,755 farms; but the report of the Secretary of State shows the existence of less than 150,000 in 1884.

CHARACTER OF THE CATTLE.

A very large number of the cattle in Michigan are of the common or unimproved class, only 138,500, or 19 per cent., having in their veins the blood of improved or purely bred animals. The common stock is rather larger and of better form and quality than are those of some of the timber-covered States of the Gulf region; but they are inferior to the native or unimproved cattle of the prairie States, where the forage has been more abundant than it is in Michigan. A number of herds of purely bred cattle have been in the State for some years, and have had great influence upon the general character of the cattle of the neighborhood where they have been kept. This work of improvement began by the introduction of Shorthorns many years ago; but little progress was made before the end of the late war. Then high prices and ready sale for beef and for dairy products stimulated the cattle industry greatly, and at the same time gave promise of means with which to pay for the stock required in the work of improvement. In the years following 1865 a marked activity was observed in the movement of purely bred cattle into the State, and this lasted until the financial reverses of 1873 and following years checked the work for a time. Jerseys, Ayrshires, and Holstein-Friesians, Devons, Galloways, and Shorthorns were taken to many places where no cattle of pure breeding were before kept; and although the fluctuations in the markets for dairy products and for beef have tended to retard the work of improvement, the result from those importations has already been of great value to the commonwealth. A careful canvass of the subject in the year 1884 showed that the cash value of the cattle of Michigan was not less than $7,068,900 more than it would have been had no good blood been introduced. It will be apparent that if the improvement of 19 per cent. of the stock caused an increase of more than $7,000,000 in their value, the increment of value in the whole supply, if good bulls had been used to the exclusion of all others, would have been equal to fully $37,204,720. To have effected that improvement, and to keep up the breeding of the stock, about 8,700 bulls would have been an ample supply. At $500 each, that number of bulls would have cost $4,355,000. This would have left a gain of $32,850,000 in the actual productive value of the stock.

Ayrshires were introduced in Michigan between ten and fifteen years ago, but seem to have failed to win the lasting favor of the farmers, for only a very few animals of that race are mentioned by correspondents, and only one or two herds of purely bred Ayrshires are noted as being kept in the State. The State Agricultural College has long kept a few Ayrshires, and for several years herds were maintained in Clinton and one or two other counties.

Shorthorns are mentioned as having been taken to the southeastern counties of Michigan fully forty years ago. It is not unlikely that grade cattle sired by Shorthorn bulls went to that district even earlier, and that no record was made of the importation. Washtenaw and Livingstone Counties obtained purely bred Shorthorns twenty years ago. Other southern counties were only a few years later in importing animals of that breed, but movement in the direction of improvement had not much force before the year 1875. In Michigan, as in most other States, the breed named spread more widely and rapidly than did any other race, except, perhaps, the Holstein-Friesians. There was in the size, color, and readiness to fatten exhibited by the Shorthorns that which readily attracted the attention of farmers and led them to try the cattle. The genuine worth of the stock gave sufficient reason for continuing to use them. The race has many warm friends among the farmers and dairymen of Michigan.

In the year 1852 an importation of Galloway cattle into Canada was made from Scotland. This led to the purchase, in Canada, by the Agricultural College of Michigan, in 1854, of a Galloway bull. This animal was used for some time at the college, and left a large number of descendants. Since his purchase the college has always had a representative of the Galloway race on its farm. The next importation of stock of that breed was made by J. N. Smith, of Bath, and George Coleman, of Howells, who were for years almost the only farmers in the United States who owned representatives of the breed. From this center the Galloways spread slowly. People seemed to feel a prejudice against the stock because they were hornless and black. Since the year 1875 several herds of Galloways have been established in widely separated parts of the State, and the breed seems to have become firmly established in the good opinion of those who know them. The principal centers of supply of Galloway cattle in Michigan have been in the counties of Ingham, Clinton, Livingston, and Lapeer, three of them adjoining, and all near the center of the most populous and longest settled part of the State. The introduction of the breed in each of the counties named, and the establishment of herds of considerable size and value there, are clearly traceable to the influence of the importation, by the State Agricultural College, of the bull Victor, in 1854—a curious but by no means solitary instance of the important changes that may be made in an agricultural industry by an act which may in itself seem to be unimportant. For several years the Galloways were sold at figures not much above those for which other cattle of like weights and quality were sold in Michigan; but in the year 1881 there was an improvement in prices and demand, which grew stronger until 1884, and gave very liberal profits to those who owned animals of that breed. There was a decline in the selling value of these, as of all other pure breeds of cattle, after the year 1883, but purely bred Galloways continue to bring fair figures.

In view of the fact that more working oxen are used in Michigan than in any other State in the North, excepting Maine, the fact that few Devon cattle have been owned or bred in Michigan is noteworthy, as the Devons have long been celebrated as being the most docile, active, and generally useful of cattle for the yoke. In 1840 a few animals of that race were taken to Oakland County, in southeastern Michigan, by Mr. P. R. Leach; ten years later a Mr. Leach introduced Devons in Macomb County. A herd or herds of this race were taken to Lapeer County, in eastern Michigan, and are still to be found there. No reports of the presence of Devons in other parts of the State are made by correspondents.

The first herd of Hereford cattle, established in southeastern Michigan, of which any information has been obtained from correspondents, was the one taken to Oakland County in 1864 by Hon. Edwin Phelps, who has also introduced Holstein-Friesians and other purely bred cattle there. Other Herefords were taken to the center of the State in 1878, and one lot was located in the eastern part of Michigan in 1878. Other herds followed quickly until representatives of the race were to be found in various parts of the State. It is evident that the breed has found much favor with practical and intelligent farmers and breeders of that State, for the number of registered cattle has been increased by importations as well as by births, and the number of grade animals begotten by Hereford bulls is already large enough to be worthy of especial note. There is evidently a clear appreciation of the value of this stock as a profitable breed to keep for the purpose of furnishing bulls of pure blood to cattle owners of the West. Prices of Hereford bulls of good breeding have been uniformly higher than have those for bulls of almost any other breed, and the demands of the market seem to have been constant despite the decline in prices of beeves and of common cattle generally within the last three years.

Holstein-Friesian cattle seem to have been next to the Shorthorns in general popularity in Michigan. Naturally they appear oftener in the counties below the middle line of the State than they do north of that line, as a large percentage of the dairying done in Michigan is in the southern three or four tiers of counties. The Holsteins readily won a good position in the opinion of the farmers and dairymen, as their yield of milk was both large and of good quality. This consideration is especially important to those who sell their milk to cheese or to butter factories, as many do in Michigan. It is said by some correspondents that while an annual yield of 4,000 to 4,500 pounds is as much as even good cows of no defined breeding will give per year, a half-breed cow, sired by a good Holstein-Friesian, may be confidently expected to yield an average of 6,000 pounds to 8,000 pounds of milk per year for as many years as the common scrub cow would give milk. If it be assumed that the milk be sold at an average of 75 cents per 100 pounds the milk of the common cow would bring each year $30 to $33.75, while that from the half-breed Holstein-Friestein would bring in $45 to $59. The differences in favor of the better blood will be from $15 to $25 per year. As a good bull may easily average forty calves each year for at least five years it will be seen that, assuming that half of the calves be bulls and worthless, the increased productive value of the heifers begotten by each bull over the value of a like number of common or scrub heifers would be equal to from $300 to $500 each year. If these figures, based upon the statements of men who have had experience with cattle of the classes mentioned, are correct, then the actual cash value of the improvement effected by using a Holstein-Friesian bull of good breeding has been from 50 to 75 per cent. It is further apparent that if the increased selling value of the yearly yield of a cow, sired by such a bull, is $15 to $25, the total increase in value of her milk will be $120 to $200, for cows properly cared for will give milk for at least eight years. If the bulls should average a get of even ten heifers per annum for five years it is apparent that the actual total value of the services of each bull would be $6,000 to $10,000. This is more than even the ardent advocates of the dairy breeds seem to claim as the result of good breeding, but it is the logical deduction from statements of observed facts of practical dairy farming.

Jersey cattle seem to have been less popular than Holstein-Friesians have been in Michigan. The importations of Jerseys to the State began earlier than did importations of the other race, but there appears to have been considerable difference in the movement of the two breeds, and the number and size of herds of the two breeds in the State is by no means equal.

At or near Dexter, Mich., there is a herd of Aberdeen-Angus cattle, the only one of the kind in the State. This herd was imported in 1884. In the central part of the State is a herd of Norfolk cattle, taken there in 1881. If there are in the State other purely-bred cattle than those named above, the fact has not been mentioned by correspondents.

DAIRY PRODUCTS.

Michigan is a butter-making State. The product per cow is 36.3 pounds, or 56 per cent. greater than the average product of butter per cow in the whole United States. Per capita of population of Michigan, the yield of butter is 7.6 pounds, or 47 per cent. greater than the production per capita of population for the whole country. In Michigan, as in the country generally, the farmers make by far the larger part of the butter; but in cheese-making the factories do nearly all of the work. As has been stated on a preceding page, the cows in this State are quite generally kept for the purpose of furnishing to the family the butter and milk required for use at home. When there is more milk than the family can use, butter is made. When there is more butter than the family requires the surplus is taken to market. As butter is always readily salable, and as nearly every farmer's wife can make butter, and does usually without calling in the aid of the men, the churn has been depended upon to supply a considerable part, if not all, of the groceries needed by the family. In 1850 the output of butter for each person in the State was 17.77 pounds; in 1860 it was 20.7 pounds; in 1870 it had fallen to 20.61 pounds, and by 1880 it had risen to 23.74 pounds per capita. The cheese made in 1850 would have furnished 2.54 pounds; in 1860 there were 2.2 pounds; in 1870 only 1.96 pounds, and in 1880 there were 2.42 pounds for each inhabitant in the State.

The subjoined table exhibits the growth of the butter and the cheese production of the State, and shows the relative importance of the output of the farms and of the factories:

Years.	Butter.		Cheese.	
	Farm.	Factory.	Farm.	Factory.
	Pounds.	*Pounds.*	*Pounds.*	*Pounds.*
1850	7,065,878	....	1,011,492	....
1860	15,503,482	....	1,641,897	....
1870	24,400,185	....	670,804	1,650,997
1880	38,821,890	43,216	440,540	3,513,045

It will be observed that in the year 1870 the total production of cheese reported was 2,321,801 pounds. In 1880 the production had risen to 3,953,585 pounds, which was equal to 10.3 pounds for each milch cow in the State. This was one pound per cow more than the cheese output of 1870. The influence of the establishment of factories upon the making of cheese on the farms was most marked, the quantity made on farms having fallen from 1,641,897 pounds in 1860 to 670,804 pounds in 1870, between which dates the cheese factories began operations in Michigan. The decrease in the home production of cheese was 971,098 pounds.

While the establishment of the factories drew from the farms some 1,925,000 gallons, or 16,940,000 pounds, of milk, in 1870, and 35,161,812 pounds in 1880, yet the quantity of butter made by farmers in the last-mentioned year was nearly 39,000,000 pounds. This was equal to 31.4 pounds for each of the population of the State at that time, and to 161.6 pounds per capita for each person engaged in farming in Michigan. The increase in the quantity of butter made on farms in 1880 over that thus produced in 1870 was 14,421,705 pounds.

The average quantity of milk sold and of butter and of cheese produced per cow, and the supply of each for each one of the population of the State at various dates, are shown below:

Milk, butter, and cheese made in Michigan.

Years.	Milk.		Butter.		Cheese.	
	Per cow.	Per capita.	Per cow.	Per capita.	Per cow.	Per capita.
	Pounds.	*Pounds.*	*Pounds.*	*Pounds.*	*Pounds.*	*Pounds.*
[illegible]	....	....	70.80	17.77	10.15	2.54
[illegible]	....	....	80.85	20.70	9.16	2.54
[illegible]	79.88	16.88	97.27	20.61	9.25	1.96
[illegible]	431.69	10.61	101.05	23.74	10.28	2.[illegible]

No statistics showing the quantity of milk sold in 1850 and in 1860 are at hand. In the year ended with June 30, 1860, it was estimated that the total quantity of milk produced in the whole United States was equal to an average of 3,960 pounds per cow. This would have given 710,990,280 pounds as the total milk yield at that time per year.

The relation in which the butter and cheese production of Michigan stood, at the several periods named, to the entire yield of those articles in the United States is shown by comparison of the above with the subjoined statement:

Butter and cheese produced in the United States.

Years.	Butter.		Cheese.	
	Farm.	Factory.	Farm.	Factory.
	Pounds.	*Pounds.*	*Pounds.*	*Pounds.*
1850	313,345,306	....	105,535,893	....
1860	459,681,372	....	103,663,927	....
1870	514,092,683	277,709	53,492,153	109,435,229
1880	777,250,287	29,421,784	27,272,489	215,885,361

In addition to the above dairy products, 13,033,267 pounds of condensed milk, valued at $1,547,588, were made by the factories during the year ended with June 30, 1880. Michigan is not credited with having produced any of that supply of condensed milk.

The figures given above serve to show that the butter made in Michigan would have furnished 1.4 ounces per diem for each of the population of that State, whereas the entire supply of butter produced in the United States in 1879–'80, would have furnished only 0.07 of an ounce per diem for each inhabitant of the whole country. The smallness of the supply reported by the United States census is, in part, accounted for by the fact that the butter and cheese used by persons engaged in farming did not enter into the account from which the figures above given are quoted. Assuming that this was invariably the case, there would have been an average supply of 22.5 pounds per annum for every person in the land, not on farms, likely to use an appreciable quantity of butter. This would have been very nearly 1 ounce per day for each. That quantity would have been scarcely more than would be consumed by moderate users of the article; but great quantities were exported from this State, therefore many people must have gone with a much smaller supply.

Consideration of the facts stated in the foregoing pages leads to the conclusion that, while Michigan already heads many of the States in the development of her dairy interests, there are good reasons for the opinion that far greater development will be seen within a few years. The climate is by no means unfavorable to dairying; for, while the snows may be deep, the temperature in winter is so modified by the great watery reservoirs of heat on three sides that the winters are mild and equable as compared with regions farther west where the snowfall is less. All cultivated forage plants common to the Northern States thrive in Michigan, clover being an especially good crop in many places. The water supply is good in most parts of the State, and in many places is of a purity unsurpassed if not unequaled by the natural water supply of any other region of like area in the Middle States. Market for all the products of the farm is within easy reach of almost any part of Michigan, and a large number of competing lines of transportation afford the competition needed to keep rates of freight within reasonable limits, while the rapidly growing towns, the lumbering camps, and other domestic establishments absorb a very important part of the output of farming products, especially of butter.

In the year 1880 there were in Michigan 74 cheese factories. In these 88 men and boys sixteen years old or older, and 23 women and girls fifteen years old or older, were employed at an average of $16 per month. The value of materials used in the cheese factories was $200,152, and in the butter factories it was $1,114, making a total of $201,266, which, added to the wages paid, made an expenditure of $222,369. The products of the cheese factories were valued at $292,971, and those of the butter factories at $1,994, making a total of $294,964, the difference being $72,596, or an average of $981 for each. It is not easy to arrive exactly at the cost of the production of butter and cheese on farms, as in those instances where accurate account is kept of the items that go to make up the total cost, there is almost invariably much more intelligent management of all details, including care of stock, land, and milk, than is commonly seen on farms, consequently the result obtained by such observers serve to show not what the average is, but what may be done by the aid of better management. In a general way it is stated by correspondents that the average cost of keeping a milch cow in fair condition throughout the year is between $30 and $35. It is at once evident that if the average yield of butter per cow was 101.05 pounds, the whole yield should sell for 29.7 cents per pound to barely meet the cost at $30. With the cost at $35 the butter should sell at 34.7 cents per pound to pay expenses. This would leave the buttermilk, the manure, and the calves to pay for the labor involved, interest on the capital invested in the stock, and for deterioration in value of the cows. As the latter are fattened when they become too old for further milking, and are then sold to the butcher, the item of deterioration in milking value is less than it would be if no use could be made of the cows other than for butter-making.

Of the actual profitableness of butter-making in Michigan, when carried on under the conditions necessary for the production of a really good article and for putting it into the possession of the consumer, there is no apparent reason for doubt. Where the land has been clear from weeds, sour grasses, sedges, and other noxious forage plants, and cultivated plants have been introduced in their stead, Michigan is admirably fitted for dairying. It is known that a number of farmers in the State find ready sale at 30 to 35 cents a pound for all the butter they can make during the whole year. By taking advantage of the influence of good breeding they have greatly improved the yield of milk by their cows, both in quality and quantity, and by care over their pastures and water supply, by painstaking watchfulness over the operations of butter-making, and by dealing directly with consumers, they have established a reputation which is sufficient warranty for the excellence of their butter, and have got a return which has made them rich. If there is any reason why all the farmers of Michigan can not do as well as these have done it has not been discovered

BEEF PRODUCTION.

With the exception of those herds of highly-bred animals kept for the purpose of supplying pure blood for the improvement of stock, the cattle of Michigan are, as a general rule, kept for milk and butter production. All these animals eventually find their way to the butcher, for when they cease breeding, or fail in their yield of milk, so far that they are no longer profitable in the dairy, they are fattened and sent to market, or slaughtered for home consumption. As losses from accident or from disease are very few, it may be said that very nearly all of the supply of cattle in the State are in the end used for beef. Considerable numbers are shipped from the State to eastern markets, although it will be seen that even if the entire supply of cattle in the State last year had been slaughtered, and had averaged 900 pounds in gross weight, or 500 pounds of dressed beef, there would have been only 231 pounds of beef per capita for all of the inhabitants of the State. That would have afforded 10.2 ounces of beef per day for each inhabitant; but as the annual calf crop in the State will certainly not exceed 348,400 in number, and as 25 per cent. of those calves are killed before they reach the age of one year, it follows that there are not more than 261,300 beeves each year to slaughter. If it be assumed that beeves will dress an average of 540 pounds of beef each, there will be 86.2 pounds per capita of population. This would give to each person less than half an ounce of beef per day. It is one of the curious facts of the cattle traffic that while Michigan does not produce beef enough to furnish half an ounce per day to each of her inhabitants, and while that supply is lessened by the shipment of cattle to other States, large quantities of beef and other meats are imported from the large beef-packing centers of the West, to supply the demand for local consumption. This is accounted for by the fact that the dealers in meats in the railroad towns in Michigan can obtain from those beef-packing centers such steaks, roasts, and other cuts as will best supply the wants of their customers. Such cuts are taken from the carcasses of cattle in the beef-canning establishments, usually from those in Chicago, and are packed in boxes, which are in turn put into refrigerators and sent by express to their destinations. By this plan a dealer in a town in the extreme eastern part of Michigan can order by telegraph in the afternoon of one day the meats required for the trade of the next day. The order will be filled and the meats shipped by express, perhaps at 10 o'clock in the night, and at 7 o'clock the next morning, or 14 hours after the order was given, the meats will have reached the shop of the dealer. They will have been cut into the sizes and shapes most suitable to the wants of the customers of that particular dealer, and will be of such quality as his experience has taught him will be wanted. The advantage of this system is, to the dealer, that he is relieved of the necessity of making journeys in the country for the purpose of buying stock; that he is saved the expense, care, and loss attending the operation of a slaughter-house; he is saved the necessity for selling at low prices rough pieces and the less desirable parts of the beeves, and has little or no tallow or bones to cut off and sell, or to throw away. As he can carry on his business with less assistance than he could if he slaughtered his own cattle, and with much greater ease with his reduced force, the saving is great. This enables him to sell meats of good quality at lower prices than he would find it necessary to charge if he bought stock near his town and dressed them himself. The consumer finds his advantage in the fact that he gets meat that has been handled under the most favorable conditions practicable in the present state of knowledge of the business; he is benefited by the fact that he can have a choice from as great a range of quality as can be found in the great markets, and by a reduction of prices of such meats as he may select. Thus the consumer gets meats of better quality than local slaughterers can afford at like prices.

A large quantity of dressed beef is sent in the form of quarters to local dealers in Michigan as to those in other States. From these the dealer cuts such meat as his customers want. Using beef thus obtained from the great markets the local dealer saves the expenses of maintenance of a separate slaughter-house, and of men who would be needed for the operations of buying stock and driving them to the slaughter-house, and for killing and dressing the animals when there; he also has some benefit from the saving effected in the great slaughtering establishments, where nothing is permitted to go to waste, and where skilled labor constantly employed and machinery combine to reduce the cost of every operation to the lowest possible point.

At a first thought it appears that one effect of this system of supplying people with beef must be a reduction of prices of living beeves in the country, and that farmers who raise cattle must be losers to that extent; but there is a doubt as to whether this does result. The general supply of beeves in the country can not be directly affected by the change in the method of furnishing consumers, while the greater economy in the operations of converting the animals into cuts suited to their wants and the consequent reduction of cost serve to increase the consumption of beef. The larger demand is at once felt in the greater markets, and through them is instantly communicated by telegraph to buyers of cattle in the interior. As there is a keen rivalry between buyers in almost every part of the land, prices advance immediately even in remote districts. In the end the demand for beef must be increased by anything which will lower its cost, and with a stronger demand there should be an advance in prices, and will be sooner or later.

In the lower tiers of counties of Michigan there has been, in the opinion of correspondents who are in position which enables them to judge correctly, an improvement of from 10 to 75 per cent. of the cattle by the introduction of the blood of purely-bred stock. The number thus improved appears to be equal to nearly or quite 39 per cent. of the whole supply. This indicates a rapid progress during the last five years, and is some 3 per cent. more than was shown by investigations made by the United States Department of Agriculture two years ago. It is more than likely that the additional 3 per cent. has been improved by the influence indicated since those investigations were made. Probably there are now in the State 250,000 cattle having some of the blood of pure stock in their veins; of these it is likely that 180,000 may be described as high grades of some milking breed. As the Holstein-Friesians have been introduced in many localities, it may be assumed the increase in number of improved cattle will result in a corresponding increase in the production of beef, for while the purpose of using bulls of that race is primarily to add to the yield of milk, the result is a development in size that makes the grades much more valuable for beef than the native or scrub stock. In those counties where good bulls have not been used the general average weights of the beeves is given as ranging from 700 to 900 pounds. In districts where good blood has had an influence, the weights are quoted as being 1 000 to 1,300 pounds each, with some at 1,400 to 1,600 pounds. On this point a correspondent in Oakland County, writes:

> In making my estimate of the live weight of beef cattle of this county I did not take into consideration animals kept for other purposes and finally turned to beef, such as working oxen, milch cows, and bulls. I think their average weight would probably bring the average of all beef cattle raised in this county to 800 pounds, live weight. The cows are mostly fattened by dairymen, who buy the farmers' best cows and feed them well as long as they pay for milk. Then they fatten the cows and turn them into beef. The practice of selling the best cows and breeding from the poorest during the last ten years has so lowered the grade, that good cows are very scarce among breeders of common cattle. As a rule breeders of common cattle are poor feeders. More than half the common cattle wintered here for pasturing the next summer weigh less on May 1 than in the fall before, when they went into winter quarters.
>
> E. R. PHILLIPS.

Few cattle are taken to Michigan for grazing or for fattening; on the other hand, goodly numbers of calves and other young cattle are sent to Chicago and other markets, from which they are distributed among the farms in the Western States. Some farmers in the southeastern corner of the State buy store steers from Chicago or from the northern counties, but the number of animals so introduced has never been large. No calves have been taken to Michigan to grow up, but many of the calves born in the State are slaughtered for veal, the number thus disposed of being from 10 to 75 per cent. of the whole number born. The few steers bought for grazing are usually two-year-olds, while stock a year older is usually selected for feeding fully for fattening. As a rule the final fattening begins in the late autumn or in the winter, the purpose being to mature the stock and sell it before the heavy farm work of spring begins. Even then they are seldom fully fattened, most of them being turned off weighing 1,000 to 1,200 pounds. A few farmers, however, send to market beeves weighing 1,500 to 2,000 pounds, and of excellent quality.

No good reason has appeared for supposing that beef can not be grown in Michigan at a fair profit. Indeed, it is not apparent that beef raising in the lower half of the lower peninsula can not be generally made as profitable as that branch of farming has been and is in northern Indiana, Illinois, Iowa, and the country north of those States. It is true that in Michigan the snows are deep, but the cold is not often so intense as it is frequently in winter in the prairie States. As a corn-growing country Michigan has proved much more productive than have the United States as a whole; yet it does not appear that unusual effort has been made to increase the average yield of corn per acre. The clovers furnish an abundance of forage, and timothy, orchard, June, and blue grasses flourish in all parts of the State where introduced. It is true that the pastures may be covered for weeks by snow, but it is not impossible to demonstrate that the loss of the winter grazing, which is so largely depended on in the Middle States, is nearly or quite compensated for by the increased saving in and value of the manure and in the economy effected by feeding straw and other coarse fodder, which, it is claimed by some, is fully as nutritious as is most of the winter pasturage east of the Missouri. Animals well housed from cold and stormy weather make a growth which is rapid enough to go far to make up for the loss of the use of the pastures in winter. Yet between 23 and 25 per cent. of the calves born in the State are sold at prices ranging from $5 to $15 per head, and averaging a few cents over $7 each;

and the whole supply of cattle in the State seems to be actually smaller than it was six years ago. Many calves and other young cattle are sent each year to Chicago, where they mingle with others of their class, and are sold to farmers and feeders from Iowa, Missouri, and other States west of Indiana. The stock thus sent from Michigan goes to the western farms, there to graze until two or three years old. Then they may return to Chicago, to be sold as "stockers" or as "feeders," or they may be served with full rations of grain on the farms where grazed, and be there fully matured for market.

In the year 1880 the United States census stated that the total value of the 13,807,000 acres of land then in Michigan farms was $499,103,200, or an average of a fraction less than $39 per acre. Last summer correspondents writing from many and widely separated neighborhoods stated that lands were valued at prices which ranged from $10 to $125 an acre. The average value was near $55 per acre in what may be properly called the farming or settled part of the State, where cleared and cultivated farms occupy the greater part of the land. The usual rate of interest paid for money is 7 per cent. The price of corn-stalks ranged from $2.50 per wagon load to $6 per acre. The cost of attendance in winter is, as in summer, scarcely to be separated from the cost of the other farm operations of the seasons, as few farmers keep so many beeves as to require the especial attendance of more men than would be needed for carrying on other operations of the farm. In a region where the fattening of beeves is seldom carried on in such a way as will enable the feeders to arrive at the actual cost of the several items, there is great difficulty in ascertaining the average cost of beef. Enough has been stated by correspondents to warrant the belief that the average profits gained, exclusive of the manure made, by fattening beeves in Michigan, will not exceed $5 to $8 per head. Manure made when cattle are fattened in barns, as is usual in Michigan, on ground grain, roots, hay, and other fodder, is more highly valued in this State than it is in States farther west.

It may safely be assumed that the average cost of fattening 100 bullocks would, under good management in winter, be about as follows:

100 steers, at $38	$3,800.00
1800 pounds hay each, at $10 per ton	900.00
1200 pounds grain each, at 80 cents per 100	960.00
Salt, say	7.50
Interest on above outlay, at 7 per cent	80.85
Total cost	5,748.35

The 100 steers would probably weigh about 1,250 pounds each at the end of 100 days of feeding. At $5 per cental they would sell for $6,250. Deducting from that sum the cost, as shown above, there would be a profit of $5.02 on each steer. But if the price should be only $4.60 per cental, the cost as above estimated would be paid, and the feeder would have interest at the rate of 7 per cent. per annum for 100 days on the amount paid for the stock, and interest at the same rate for 50 days on the value of the food given to the cattle. In addition he would have the manure made by 100 beeves in 100 days, which would more than pay for the labor of feeding the steers. It is possible that just now, when prices of beeves are extremely low, cattle of the weight mentioned would bring no more than $4.50 per 100 pounds in the markets of Michigan; but prices are almost invariably higher in early spring than they are at the beginning of win-

[illegible] and give a profit on cattle even where there has been no great [illegible] weight. The increased consumption of beef and dairy prod[illegible] resulting from a rapid growth of population and wealth seems [illegible] sufficient guaranty that prices of cattle and their products [illegible] not often, nor for any long periods, be much lower than those which have been current during the last two years.

DISEASES.

Michigan is one of the most fortunate of the United States so far as diseases of cattle are concerned. There have been very few losses of cattle from any ailments. A few cases of splenic or Texas fever appear nearly every year among stock exposed to cattle recently brought from the coast of the Gulf of Mexico or the low-lying regions adjacent. There is some tuberculosis among the stock, as in many other States; but attention has seldom been called thereto, and the extent to which it exists is unknown. Milk fever attacks some of the cows, but cases of the kind are comparatively rare. Only one case of actinomycosis, or lump-jaw so-called, is mentioned by correspondents, all the others reporting that they had known of no cases of the disease. Anthrax or black leg seems to be equally rare. In fact the whole State may be said to be almost entirely free from all diseases of cattle. The appearance in 1884 of contagious pleuro-pneumonia in [illegible] and the immediate conveyance of the malady to [illegible] States created a feeling of alarm in Michigan, which [illegible] the passage of an act providing for the creation of a live-stock [illegible] and for taking measures for preventing the introduction [illegible] of infectious and of contagious disease in Mich[illegible]. This act was approved June 10, 1885. The text of the act was [illegible] Second Annual Report of the Bureau of Animal [illegible]. The authorities of Michigan, acting under [illegible] of that law, have recently declared quarantine against [illegible] County, Ill., in which county the city and stock-[illegible]

[illegible] counties of Michigan are in a pe-[illegible] three of the principal lines of railroad [illegible] sent to the East pass through those [illegible] animals are taken from Chicago or other [illegible] Michigan for grazing, for fatten-[illegible] stock in transit from points outside [illegible] trains for feeding or for rest [illegible] this fact may be due the freedom [illegible] diseases. There is, however, [illegible] cattle will result in Michigan as [illegible] dumping of manure and bedding from [illegible] over adjoining lands, or from [illegible] carrying of stock from point to point

---

WISCONSIN.

[illegible] Wisconsin presents widely-varied char-[illegible] large expanses of rich, rolling [illegible] some instances these were large [illegible] forests. In most cases they were [illegible] widely over broad prairies. Along the banks of the streams flowing through this region grew woods which covered the narrow valleys or made a belt of timber winding through broad and shallow vales in which the streams flowed slowly. Small lakes abound in the southern and eastern parts of the State, their shores sloping gently to the water. The soil is fertile and easily cultivated, being, as a rule, free from stones. These parts of the State have been longest cultivated, as they were nearest the great routes of immigration pouring from the East past the head of Lake Michigan toward the West. For twelve or fifteen years after the development of the agriculture of Wisconsin began, Lake Michigan afforded the principal means of communication with the East, and the chief means of transportation of the products of the State to market. Naturally the lands near the lake were settled before other regions more remote from lines of travel became occupied. In those eastern and southern counties grain-growing as a special feature of farming began about a quarter of a century ago, giving way to stock-keeping and dairying. The result is that agricultural interests have made greater progress there than in other parts of the State, and the region has become famed for the excellent quality and large quantity of its dairy products. The twenty-one counties in the southeastern division of the State, having 787,637 cattle, produced, in 1885, of butter, 19,164,433 pounds, valued at $3,170,098; of cheese, 28,441,376 pounds, valued at $2,637,692; and slaughtered 129,210 cattle, valued at $3,480,155. In detail these products were as shown by the following table:

SOUTHEASTERN DISTRICT.

Counties.	Cattle.	Cattle slaughtered.		Butter.		Cheese.	
	Number.	Number.	Value.	Pounds.	Value.	Pounds.	Value.
[illegible]	25,531	3,578	$84,083	447,517	$82,801	1,168,698	$96,480
[illegible]	37,360	7,153	237,407	1,056,419	161,018	165,027	16,234
[illegible]	80,847	12,082	346,543	1,970,674	294,348	876,909	75,589
[illegible]	64,983	7,148	183,097	1,323,460	215,932	1,701,692	166,806
Fond du Lac	87,868	10,173	248,150	1,305,345	196,968	2,437,363	207,662
[illegible]	68,651	11,312	300,047	925,406	154,005	3,204,686	301,990
Green Lake	17,327	2,331	74,530	419,172	61,818	64,370	7,106
[illegible]	45,407	9,044	162,227	1,105,079	193,307	3,014,106	275,661
[illegible]	19,202	4,298	122,750	726,006	157,329	149,572	7,026
[illegible]	40,552	3,801	79,872	609,350	69,911	2,631,770	240,859
[illegible]	13,417	1,063	46,077	945,728	32,120	650	56
[illegible]	10,343	4,564	111,975	761,808	158,007	75,760	6,983
[illegible]	19,206	2,738	55,759	597,087	91,060	1,044,807	136,546
[illegible]	28,421	4,314	185,003	716,292	131,151	9,700	911
[illegible]	53,800	12,061	441,185	1,767,819	298,490	406,301	36,606
[illegible]	34,477	9,349	131,136	558,022	90,136	7,323,518	717,609
[illegible]	43,640	8,842	248,978	1,432,572	279,940	2,217,999	181,965
[illegible]	29,332	1,778	44,758	562,607	79,153	467,682	40,480
[illegible]	28,993	6,007	153,663	1,282,307	220,487	315,770	26,482
[illegible]	17,826	2,647	54,198	479,937	73,113	164,952	16,469
Winnebago	81,868	6,087	161,782	800,961	148,884	879,404	79,511
Total	787,637	131,201	3,534,570	19,164,423	3,350,402	28,478,900	2,984,814

The southwestern part of Wisconsin is rather more rugged and broken in surface than is the eastern part of the State. The streams have generally cut deep channels in the rich soil and friable rock, much of it sandstone. These become deeper and narrower as the Mississippi is approached, and have often abrupt, if not precipitous boundaries. Near the great river the land is in many places cut into high spurs by the waters which flow into the Mississippi or its tributaries. The tops of these spurs have generally one level, and were crowned and their sides clothed by oaks, and are to this day in many places. Yet the land on their tops is fertile, producing good crops of grain and grass, while in the valleys luxuriant crops grow. The early settlement of the western part of the State was promoted by the facilities for transporting goods and people by boats on the Mississippi and those of its tributaries which were navigable in Wisconsin. The speedy development of agriculture was also fostered by the demand created by the industries carried on upon the rivers and their shores. The Mississippi River and others flowing into it afforded easy means for sending farm produce to market in the large towns and the lumber camps upon their banks. In later years railroads were built to give direct communication with the great ports of Lake Michigan, and through them with the larger markets of the East. Yet cattle-growing and dairying grew less rapidly than in the more favored southeastern quarter of the State, and in 1885 there were in the 11 southwestern counties, covering 3,949,592 acres, 363,974 cattle, or 9.2 cattle for each 100 acres. This was twice as many as the whole State could show per 100 acres of its entire area. Of their cattle supply the southwestern counties slaughtered last year 53,115 cattle of all ages, the value of which was placed at $1,594,158. Of butter they produced 8,954,166 pounds, valued at $1,349,048; and of cheese, 1,726,509 pounds, valued at $154,504. The total value of the cattle products mentioned from these 11 counties was, in the year 1885, $3,097,710. The distribution of the cattle among the several counties of the district under consideration, and the butter, cheese, and beef produced by each county, is represented by the table which follows:

SOUTHWESTERN COUNTIES.

Counties.	Cattle.	Cattle slaughtered.		Butter.		Cheese.	
	Number.	Number.	Value.	Pounds.	Value.	Pounds.	Value.
Adams	10,662	2,090	$48,505	272,320	$41,025	1,402	[illegible]
Crawford	20,935	2,282	60,598	368,157	45,584	190	[illegible]
Grant	68,174	10,835	369,949	2,047,751	321,682	137,165	[illegible]
Iowa	54,310	6,482	284,375	1,215,696	198,707	164,040	[illegible]
Juneau	18,581	1,940	41,635	335,574	46,813	18,370	[illegible]
La Crosse	19,710	3,961	107,742	480,089	79,005	108,392	[illegible]
La Fayette	58,639	9,488	348,738	1,170,717	181,871	190,898	[illegible]
Monroe	24,908	2,578	57,560	619,394	80,290	11,295	[illegible]
Richland	27,068	2,632	57,776	686,767	90,236	748,903	[illegible]
Sauk	34,274	4,888	119,505	992,876	163,228	282,678	[illegible]
Vernon	31,698	3,974	97,745	765,366	98,017	46,186	[illegible]
Total	363,974	53,115	1,594,158	8,954,166	1,349,048	1,726,509	154,504

The northeastern quarter of Wisconsin has been favored by easy communication by water with the larger markets of the west shore of Lake Michigan and with those of the East. Before railroads were constructed to connect Chicago and other Western cities with the Atlantic coast, vessels entered the excellent harbors of northeastern Wisconsin, bringing pioneers to clear away the forests and make farms, and taking away the lumber and such farm products as were not needed on the farms and in the lumber camps and sawmills near. Before railroads from the south penetrated the northeast the lumber and the mining interests of northern Wisconsin and the upper peninsula of Michigan had made very heavy drafts on the farms for beef, pork, butter, and meal, flour and other products of the farm, wherewith to feed the workmen, and for grain and hay with which to feed the stock employed. When the railroads were completed the demands on the farmers increased rather than diminished, notwithstanding the roads carried from the south large quantities of provisions. But nearly all of northeastern Wisconsin was covered by a heavy and valuable forest. The labor of clearing the land for cultivation has been exceedingly arduous, and much of the land was hilly. As in all heavily timbered regions, the native growth of plants was not such as were suited to the wants of domestic animals. Indeed, there were very few native forage plants, and these few afforded little nourishment. It was necessary to cultivate forage for cattle, horses, and sheep; consequently the live-stock interest developed much less rapidly than it did in the southern half of the State. Another reason for the slow settlement of northern Wisconsin lies in the fact that during the last thirty years the railroads passing to the southward of Lake Michigan have carried the great stream of emigration far to the south of this region, which has appeared less tempting to the pioneer than are the open prairies of the West lying ready for the plow. It is a question whether the forest lands of northern Wisconsin, covered as they are by dense growths of timber of great value, will not, during the next coming half-century, yield a larger net income than will be obtained from the lands of the most favored farms of the prairies; but it can not be claimed that there is much in the natural conditions of the northeastern part of the State to encourage stock-growing and dairying.

In the fifteen counties in the northeastern quarter of Wisconsin there were 175,912 cattle of all ages in 1885. During that year 16,917 cattle, valued at $359,205, were slaughtered, in the same time 3,467,944 pounds of butter were made, valued at $524,371, and 1,745,111 pounds of cheese were produced, valued at $143,172. Adding these items, we find the cash value of the output of the cattle interest of these fifteen counties for the year named amounted to $1,026,748. This was equal to $1.27 per acre of the improved land in the region under consideration. A detailed account of the cattle and cattle products of the several counties in the northeastern quarter of the State is given below:

NORTHEASTERN COUNTIES.

Counties.	Cattle.	Cattle slaughtered.		Butter.		Cheese.	
	Number.	Number.	Value.	Pounds.	Value.	Pounds.	Value.
[illegible]	24,330	3,294	$69,920	511,008	$73,208	663,181	$51,708
[illegible]	12,492	1,112	20,967	242,151	37,581	1,400	130
[illegible]	71	....	....	....	....	....	....
[illegible]	2	....	....	940	285	....	....
[illegible]	19,002	584	11,368	317,660	33,986	139,179	12,286
[illegible]	1,941	61	2,018	30,122	5,459	....	....
[illegible]	1,480	138	3,092	14,877	2,678	....	....
[illegible]	17,525	1,657	28,687	292,450	39,277	4,817	504
[illegible]	3,032	346	8,822	97,383	22,981	....	....
[illegible]	7,219	755	15,076	106,440	30,577	10,786	1,012
[illegible]	30,331	3,329	78,312	654,774	98,563	768,073	64,715
[illegible]	14,755	1,580	39,964	371,604	63,007	600	75
[illegible]	11,080	528	10,995	160,042	18,268	680	60
[illegible]	24,156	3,048	66,708	541,063	80,707	136,435	12,512
[illegible]	8,500	558	13,436	137,424	22,198	500	60
Total	175,912	16,917	359,205	3,467,944	524,370	1,745,111	143,172

Northwestern Wisconsin is largely occupied by forests, and lumbering has formed the occupation of a large percentage of the population. The country is well watered, the valleys are fertile, and there has been a very considerable growth in stock-growing and dairying. For all products of the farm, especially for those in the condensed and easily transported shape of butter and cheese, a good demand was found at an early day in the rapidly growing settlements of Minnesota, in the lumber camps of the Lake Superior region and of Minnesota, and in the towns along the banks of the Mississippi River. The development of the northwestern part of Wisconsin began rather later than did that of those parts lying near Lake Michigan, but it can not be justly said that the development has been slow. In 1885 that division of the State possessed 216,258 cattle, and produced 4,653,898 pounds of butter, worth $806,884; 565,904 pounds of cheese, valued at $49,448; and slaughtered 20,144 cattle, of the value of $493,551. These several amounts aggregate $1,349,883. The growth made by the cattle interest of this district, and by the dairying branch of that interest especially, promises to become such as will give this region rank with others more favored by nature than this has been. The winters are not exceptionally severe here. The land is as a rule sheltered from the cold and strong blasts which sweep the open prairie country. Water of the purest quality is always found in plenty. Cultivated grasses grow well wherever introduced and give large crops. Fuel and land are comparatively cheap, and means for transportation to near markets are not wanting. In not a few of the counties composing this region the advantages favorable to stock-growing and dairying have been recognized, as is shown by the progress made in those industries indicated in the following statement of the butter, cheese, and cattle products:

NORTHWESTERN COUNTIES.

Counties.	Cattle.	Cattle slaughtered.		Butter.		Cheese.	
	Number.	Number.	Value.	Pounds.	Value.	Pounds.	Value.
Ashland	348	....	....	....	....	....	....
Barron	9,791	641	$15,796	296,685	$44,307	....	....
Bayfield	131	5	110	....	....	....	....
Buffalo	24,953	2,290	56,057	362,779	55,872	116,874	[illegible]
Burnett	4,906	92	1,749	68,448	7,371	1,847	191
Chippewa	12,033	1,331	31,120	319,471	70,840	....	....
Clark	15,782	1,283	38,331	338,525	50,700	65,[illegible]	[illegible]
Dunn	22,590	2,011	48,117	468,744	78,054	22,019	2,084
Eau Claire	15,094	841	19,945	357,508	63,997	46,600	3,679
Jackson	16,291	1,717	30,078	508,921	105,019	10,980	1,110
Pepin	6,764	691	17,025	170,774	24,577	7,416	767
Pierce	22,208	2,778	70,109	471,612	75,793	74,975	7,719
Polk	14,407	1,145	29,238	292,874	50,138	36,793	3,637
Price	574	96	2,397	....	....	....	....
Saint Croix	20,716	2,098	55,182	509,101	96,662	159,608	14,410
Taylor	1,447	18	508	23,750	4,299	....	....
Trempealeau	28,844	3,117	68,842	535,201	80,394	22,380	2,344
Total	216,258	20,144	493,538	4,653,898	806,884	565,904	49,448

DAIRYING.

The history of farming in Wisconsin resembles that of Indiana, Illinois, and others of the States, in that for years after the first settlement wheat-growing was the chief purpose and occupation of the farmers. In a few years the fertility of the soil became so far exhausted that large yields were the exception rather than the rule. New and richer fields were opened in the newer West to compete with the worn-out soil of the States east of the Mississippi, and the railroads assisted the farmers of the new frontier in their rivalry with those farther east by giving rates that were little if any higher than the Middle State farmers were charged for carrying grain to the sea-board. These circumstances drove the Wisconsin farmer into a search for some plan which would restore the fertility of his soil, and would at the same time give profitable returns for the labor and money invested in the farm and its work. This change began some thirty years ago, about the time when the completion of railroad lines from the Atlantic coast to the Mississippi gave fresh impetus to immigration to the West, and thus aided the opening of thousands of new farms on the rich prairies beyond the Mississippi. Other causes arose to compel a change of methods of farming in the State. Thirty-six years ago Wisconsin had only 183,433 cattle of all kinds. Of these only 64,339 were milch cows. From the milk of these were made on farms 3,633,750 pounds of butter and 400,283 pounds of cheese. Small as was the total number of cows there were yet 210.7 milch cows for each 1,000 people then in the State. Many of the farmers were from New York and other Eastern States, where they had been accustomed to the processes and profits of dairying, and they therefore naturally turned their attention to that branch of farming when wheat-growing ceased yielding fair returns.

Early in the year 1867 a co-operative cheese factory was opened in Jefferson County. It is believed that this was the first establishment of the kind in Wisconsin, in which there were then between 250,000 and 300,000 cows. From that time the dairy business grew rapidly and prospered exceedingly, making rich many if not all of those who engaged therein, until every farm in several counties, and most of the improved farms in the southern half of the State, were conveniently near one or more cheese or butter factories. In 1872 the dairying branch of the farmers' business had grown to so important proportions in the State that need was felt of the organization of a body for the promotion of that industry, and the Wisconsin Dairyman's Association was formed that year. Under its auspices a dairy fair was held in Milwaukee in 1875; another exhibit was made at the Centennial Exposition in Philadelphia in 1876; in 1877 a show was made in Chicago; in 1878 yet another was made at the International Dairy Show in New York, and in 1882 the association carried on another dairy fair in Milwaukee, and has since exhibited successfully in other places. Annual meetings are held by the association, at which the general interests and the important details of dairying are discussed carefully by intelligent observers of much experience. The result is that the association has done effective work for the promotion of the interests of dairymen and farmers.

The growth of the dairy business of Wisconsin during the last thirty-six years is shown by the table which follows:

BUTTER AND CHEESE.

Years.	Butter.				Cheese.			
	Farm.	Factory.	Per cow.	Per capita.	Farm.	Factory.	Per cow.	Per capita.
	Pounds.	*Pounds.*	*Pounds.*	*Pounds.*	*Pounds.*	*Pounds.*	*Pounds.*	*Pounds.*
[illegible]	3,633,730	....	50.4	11.9	400,283	....	6.3	1.3
[illegible]	[illegible]	....	67.0	17.5	1,104,300	....	5.4	1.4
[illegible]	[illegible]	2,500	72.9	21.8	1,591,798	1,606,783	10.6	3.1
[illegible]	[illegible]	469,291	70.7	23.8	2,281,411	17,258,913	40.6	14.9
[illegible]	[illegible]	866,107	41.8	23.2	3,858,015	29,620,995	33.5	13.9

Of the butter reported in 1880 as having been made in factories, 103,281 pounds were from skim-cheese factories, which made 446,919 pounds of cheese in the same year. In 1880 sale was reported of 231,381,398 pounds of milk, of which 181,841,161 pounds were used by factories. It will be observed that the increase in the product of butter between 1880 and 1885 was equal to 10.7 per cent., and that in the annual production of cheese was 71.4 per cent.

The statement above given shows, in the columns under the heading "per cow," the average product of butter and of cheese per cow. Under the heading "per capita" is shown the average number of pounds of butter and of cheese the whole amount made in Wisconsin would have furnished for each of the inhabitants of the State at the several dates named. It will be noted that between 1870 and 1880 the average yearly production of butter per cow had fallen off 2.2 pounds, the average yield of cheese per year for each cow having in the same period shown an increase of 30.2 pounds. In the decade under consideration the average supply of butter per capita of population for the year rose 4.5 pounds, and the yearly supply of cheese per capita was increased 11.8 pounds. In the figures for the year 1885 there is apparent a decrease in production of butter and cheese per cow, but as these figures are based upon returns made to assessors, and as such returns are usually lower than those which would be furnished to enumerators of the general census of the United States, there is room for the belief that the falling off is only seeming, and that accurate returns would disclose an actual increase of the production per cow.

The relation borne by the cattle supply and the cheese, butter, and beef production of the several groups of counties into which the State is naturally divided may be seen by reference to the account presented below:

BUTTER, CHEESE, AND CATTLE PRODUCTS.

Divisions.	Cattle.	Cattle slaughtered.		Butter.		Cheese.	
	Number.	Number.	Value.	Pounds.	Value.	Pounds.	Value.
Southeastern	787,637	131,201	$3,534,570	19,164,428	$3,170,098	28,441,376	$2,627,691
Southwestern	363,974	53,115	1,594,158	8,954,166	1,349,049	1,726,509	154,804
Northeastern	175,912	16,917	359,205	3,467,944	534,871	1,745,111	163,173
Northwestern	216,258	20,144	493,551	4,058,898	806,384	565,904	49,446
Total *	1,543,781	221,377	5,981,486	35,940,431	5,860,402	32,478,900	2,994,814

* Two counties, Sawyer and Washburn, not included in the above, have 118 cattle.

The value of the dairy products of Wisconsin in 1885 was equal to 34 per cent. of the value of the living cattle in the State.

CATTLE SUPPLY.

In the State as a whole there were in the year 1885 some 34,359,246 acres. Of this 8,115,333 acres were improved land, 3,660,198 acres were woodland in farms, and 4,583,715 acres were unimproved land in farms, making a total of 16,359,246 acres in farms. The value of this farm land was $393,556,146, or an average of $24.06 per acre. Of pine and hard wood forests there were 16,080,000 acres, much of which will become in due time fertile, arable land. Lakes of clear, fresh water cover some 1,920,000 acres. There were in the year named 136,108 farms, on which 60,285 men were hired at an average yearly wage of $141.81. In addition to these men 272,216 persons were employed in agriculture, making a total of 332,501 people so occupied, out of a total population of 1,563,423. Of the whole population of the State, 583,534, or 37.3 per cent. were workers. The value of the farms and farm products in 1885 was $568,187,288, while that of the manufacturing establishments and their products was only $193,700,167.

Of live stock Wisconsin had last year 1,196,200 swine, valued at $4,472,658; of sheep and lambs there were 1,429,137, which were valued at $2,353,015; of horses and mules there were 398,132, of the value of $31,049,563, and of cattle there were 1,548,899, valued at $26,062,598.

The total value of the live stock mentioned was $63,937,834, or one-third of the value of all the manufacturing establishments in the State and their products for the year mentioned. Of hogs, 1,047,156 were slaughtered in 1885, valued at $10,323,776; of sheep, 296,802 were slaughtered, having a value of $793,018, and 221,337 cattle and calves were butchered, their value having been $5,981,486; making the entire value of stock slaughtered in Wisconsin during that ye $17,098,280. This was nearly 10 per cent. of the value of all the manufacturing establishments in the State at the time, and their products for the year. The yield of butter and cheese in the State in 1885 was valued at $8,745,217. This makes an average of $26.30 per capita for the people engaged in agriculture in Wisconsin. If to that be added the other money income from live stock for that year, the average per capita will be raised to $177.70. As the total valuation of the agricultural products of Wisconsin for the year 1885 was placed at $174,631,142, it follows that 14.8 of the entire farm income came from live stock alone. Of the whole income derived from live stock, cattle furnished 57 per cent.

The extent of the supply of cattle in Wisconsin from time to time during the thirty-six years in which trustworthy statistics have been obtainable is shown in the subjoined table. A fact worthy of note is that there was an increase in the number of cows and cattle, other than working oxen, from 1860 to 1870, in which decade the supply of cattle in many other States decreased. Of working oxen there were fewer in 1880 than in 1870, in which year there were not much more than half as many as in 1860. At the last-mentioned date there were in the State 93,652 animals of this class. That was more than double the number in Wisconsin in 1850, when the settlement of the State had really not been much more than fairly and fully begun. In the years immediately preceding and following 1860 the work of opening new farms was going on with great vigor, and oxen were in request in every part of the State. They were of great assistance in clearing the land of logs and stumps, and in plowing it afterward. As the land became subdued and the work of cultivation became easier, and as the highways became reasonably smooth for travelers, quickness in draft animals became more important and more desired than massive strength was; therefore the powerful but slow ox gave way to the horse. A like course of events has been seen in every State in the Union, and the ox is now seldom used except in heavily-timbered regions, where lumbering is carried on. It is not unlikely that in a few years the use of yoke cattle in the ordinary work of the farm will be scarcely remembered, except in a few hilly, wooded regions. From time to time efforts have been made in this country to reawaken the interest in the use of oxen in the yoke; but, although their case is not without some good arguments, such efforts have signally failed. A quarter of a century ago nearly every farmer's boy was taught to train and to drive oxen skillfully; but now it is doubtful whether a quarter of the farmers' boys can put a yoke on a pair of oxen.

Between the years 1850 and 1860 the number of milch cows in Wisconsin increased more than 300 per cent. In the ten years ended in 1870 the increase was a little more than 50 per cent. In the next following decade the growth of the supply was a little over 55 per cent.; and in the five years next following the gain in numbers was fully 41 per cent. Should the last mentioned rate of increase continue until 1890, Wisconsin will have over 954,000 milch cows. The relation each class of cattle has borne to the whole cattle supply of the State each census year is shown in the table given herewith:

SUPPLY OF CATTLE.

Classes.	1850.	1860.	1870.	1880.	1885.
Milch cows	64,339	203,001	308,377	478,374	676,636
Working oxen	42,801	93,652	58,615	28,762	....
Other cattle	76,293	225,207	331,212	622,005	867,263
Total	183,433	521,860	698,204	1,129,141	1,543,899

The relation of the cattle supply of Wisconsin to the total population of that State has been comparatively uniform during the last forty years. In 1850 there were in the State 600.6 cattle of all classes for each 1,000 inhabitants. Of these 210.7 were milch cows, 140.1 were working oxen, and 249.8 were other cattle. More than half of the entire cattle stock were either giving milk or working in the yoke. Although there were 93,652 working oxen in the State in 1860, yet the immigration had been so great that there were only 120.7 for each 1,000 people in the State. At that time there were 261.6 milch cows and 290.3 other cattle, a fact which gauges the interest people then felt in stock-growing and dairying, and the progress they were making in increasing their herds. In 1870 they had raised the number of milch cows to 292.4 per 1,000 inhabitants, and in 1880 this was yet further increased to 363.6 per 1,000 people. The total number of cattle in the State for each 1,000 of its people was 858.4 in 1880, which is much higher than the number of cattle per 1,000 inhabitants in most other States east of the Mississippi. In this fact is evidence that Wisconsin is entitled to high rank as a stock-growing, and more particularly as a dairying State.

In character the cattle of Wisconsin resemble generally those of Michigan, as the general conditions of surface, forage, and water supply of Wisconsin resemble those of the other State named. Forests still cover the northern parts of both; their southern halves have become rich farming regions; both border on one great lake, which has furnished facilities for the cheap and easy transportation of products to market, and both have great water-ways on their eastern and their western borders, into which their drainage flows. But while in 1884 Wisconsin had 194,480 cattle in which the influence of good breeding was apparent, and Michigan had at that time 170,215 high-grade cattle, yet only 16 per cent. of the Wisconsin cattle were improved, while 19 per cent. of those of Michigan were grades. One cause which has tended to retard the improvement of the cattle of Wisconsin, as of other States, is mentioned by several correspondents. One writing from Beloit, Rock County, says:

The railroads are very generous with exhibition stock, but extortionate on purchases of improved stock. I shipped three head and three calves over the Milwaukee and Saint Paul and the Illinois Central Railroads to El Paso, Ill. The freight charge was $44.65. One of the lot was an imported heifer. Enough has been paid for freight charges on her to buy several common cattle. On one of my cattle, brought from Galesburgh, Ill., I had to pay $17 freight. I often have to pay first class for 2,000 pounds for transportation of a six-months-old calf. More favorable rates of freight on breeding stock will be a benefit to the whole community. The rates of freight from Janesville, from which point most cattle from Rock County are shipped, and from Beloit to Chicago, are $22 per car load. The rate charged for the transportation of a single cow, heifer, or bull from Beloit to Chicago, only 95 miles is $6.60; by express the rate is $12. The railroad tariffs, with their double and quadruple weights, and one and a half first-class rates, are a serious bar to the ready interchange of good cattle among farmers and breeders, and a great detriment to the whole community, producers and consumers alike.

From Dodge County a correspondent writes:

Most beeves sent to market from Lowell and adjoining towns in Dodge County are shipped from Reeseville to Chicago. The rate of freight from Reeseville to Chicago is $22 per car-load. The rate charged for the transportation of a single cow, heifer, or bull from the town named to Chicago is $1 per cental for each 100 miles. A great many milking cows are sent from Reeseville.

Another wrote, under date of August 13, as follows:

I do not fully understand your position, but hope you have power, opportunity, and disposition to help the whole community, through improvement in the breeding, care, and handling of meat-producing animals. Stock cattle and calves should be shipped at half rates, also breeding cattle, and the tariff on shipments of lots of a few animals each ought to be sweepingly reduced. For example, freights from this place to Puget Sound are now $210 per car by one line, $374 on another, and $[illegible] on a third; the latter rate for a car 35 feet long, which is the smallest size that will carry the 20,000 that must be paid for.

There seems to be no reason for doubting that a liberal, even a generous, policy as relates to rates on purely-bred stock wanted for breeding purposes would greatly accelerate the improvement of stock of various kinds in every part of the States. Breeders of purely-bred animals would be encouraged to greater efforts to produce and sell such breeding stock, for their sales would doubtless be largely increased by a considerable reduction of the existing rates, which are so high as to be considered in many cases almost prohibitory. New and remote districts, which are now practically closed to many breeders, would be thrown open to them by such reduction of rates. By such a course as is suggested the interest of many owners of common or inferior stock in the work of improvement would be aroused, and they would be led by the low rates of freight to buy stock with which to improve that they now have and to increase their herds and flocks. This would quickly add to the volume of freight furnished by the farms, and the railroads would thus be repaid richly for any concessions they may make in rates on purely-bred stock. This view has been held by some railroads, and they have favored in many ways the introduction of good breeding animals into the country from which a large part of their freights come. The results have been most satisfactory to the farmer and to the railroads.

Of the 1,543,900 cattle in Wisconsin, 16 per cent., or 247,024, are high grades. The bulls that have caused the improvement were Ayrshires, Holstein-Friesians, Jerseys, and a few Guernseys, of the milking breeds, and Shorthorns, Devons, Galloways, and Red-Polled Norfolks. Shorthorns appear in every quarter of the State and are favorites among the farmers in nearly every county where beef-growing or dairying is practiced. Shorthorns were taken to the southeastern counties at least as early as 1850; Devons were introduced in some of the eastern counties about thirty years ago; a few Jerseys appeared in southeastern Wisconsin in 1853, and as they proved to be valuable butter-makers they won favor, and there are now in that region considerable numbers of grades having a strain of the blood of that race. About 1878 Holstein-Friesian cattle began to be looked on with favor by Wisconsin farmers and dairymen, and the breed has increased very rapidly in numbers and in popularity. It is, perhaps, the most generally popular race of cattle in the districts where dairying forms an important, if not the chief, occupation of the farmers. Galloways have gained a footing in several parts of the State. All or nearly all of the herds of Galloways in Wisconsin sprang from one taken to Waukesha County in 1870 by Peter Davy. Those were the first Galloways ever seen west of Lake Michigan. They descended from those which were imported by Mr. J. N. Smith, of Michigan, from Canada. Long before these Black-Polled cattle were imported by Mr. Davy there was near Boscobel a family of White-Polled cattle, having black spots on their legs. These were descendants of a white hornless cow taken to that district by a pioneer from Ohio. The cow gave birth to a bull having her own characteristics and proving to have strong power for impressing his peculiarities upon his offspring. The family grew and spread over the adjoining counties, but was at last permitted to die out, although the stock had many good qualities.

Ayrshires won a high place in the regard of dairymen and others in Wisconsin, particularly in those neighborhoods where cheese-making was an important industry, because the milk of the Ayrshires is rich in casein and in butter. In a meeting held by the Wisconsin Dairymen's Association in Appleton, in 1877, the statement was made by Mr. W. C. White that from a herd of 50 cows, of which the greater number were half Ayrshire, an average of 530 pounds of cheese, worth $58.30, and 73 pounds of butter, worth $21.90, were made one year, the total income per cow having been $80.20.

The value of the improvement effected by the use of animals of pure breeding on the cattle of Wisconsin was in 1884 estimated as being $7,330,100. Yet only 16 per cent. were thus improved. It is clear that if the value of 16 per cent. of the cattle was thus increased by the amount named, fully $45,813,125 might have been added to the wealth of the cattle-owners by the use of like influences on all of the 84 per cent. of unimproved stock. But it has been stated by a dairyman of long experience that his best cows gave an average yield worth $92, and his poorest $43 per annum, respectively. The difference in his case was $49 per cow per year between the best and the poorest. Assuming that the average yearly income from the best cows is only $80, and that from the inferior stock is $50, it will be seen that the difference is fully 62½ per cent., instead of the 26 per cent. assumed in the estimate of 1884. Experience in cheese and butter factories has shown that improved cows have produced a yield of milk worth $20 per annum more than the general average, and fully $35 more than the yield of the poorest cattle. Assuming that the value of the annual yield of the 563,400 inferior or unimproved cows was increased $20 each by an infusion of good blood, the gain would be $11,368,000 per year. If the term during which the cows would yield milk be ten years, the actual value of the improvement of those now unimproved would be $113,680,000. It is apparently the sincere opinion of many correspondents that results quite equal to those set forth above may be attained by the use of bulls of one or more of the so-called milking breeds, combined with careful feeding and good management generally, and that such results are within the reach of every intelligent farmer.

Less information has been gathered regarding the value of improvement of beef cattle in Wisconsin, for the reason that, while many farmers seem to think they can find or breed cows well adapted to milk-giving and to beef-producing, the many intelligent observers upon whose correspondence the above estimates are based seem to have kept in mind the one purpose of dairying to the almost entire exclusion of beef-growing.

BEEF PRODUCTION.

While the chief income from the cattle interest of Wisconsin is derived from butter and cheese, a very considerable sum was obtained last year from the cattle and calves slaughtered. This sum, $5,981,486, was $131,084 more than the receipts for butter. The total receipts for dairy products in 1885 was $8,835,216, or only $2,853,730 more than came from beef and veal grown in the State. Much of this was an incidental income from the business of the dairy farmer, who raised the male progeny of his cows for beef; but the major part of the money was earned by breeding cattle expressly for beef, or by buying store stock and grazing and fattening them. In raising beef Wisconsin seems to be able to compete on favorable terms with neighboring States which are apparently more highly favored naturally. Of hay there were produced in 1885 in the State 2,306,335 tons, valued at $13,218,215, or $5.73 per ton; of maize there were 37,718,394 bushels, worth $12,576,561, or 33.3 cents per bushel; of oats there were 43,047,410 bushels, valued at 25.5 cents per bushel, or $11,008,507; and of roots 1,646,176 bushels, valued at $305,814. The average yield of corn per acre was 37.5 bushels, of oats 33.3 bushels, and of roots 154.3 bushels. From statements made by correspondents located in various parts of the State, it appears that the actual cost of producing beef in Wisconsin is nearly as follows, interest being from 5 to 8 per cent. per annum, and land in farms valued at an average of $24 per acre. It is estimated that of all the land in farms in Wisconsin, an average of 6 acres will be required for one year for each cow carrying a calf, and three years for that calf before it will have reached the age at which steers are usually put on full rations. The average results throughout the whole State would therefore be about as shown in the following account:

Service of bull	$1.00
Interest on value of land, 4 years, at 7 per cent	6.72
Interest on value of cow one year	2.24
[illegible]8 pounds hay per day, 180 days, at $5.78 per ton	9.28
[illegible]0 bushels corn, at 33.3 cents	29.97
Interest on cost of bullock, 180 days	.35
Interest on cost of feed, 90 days	.37
Salt	.10
Total cost	52.03

Assuming that beeves thus grown and fattened will average no more than 1,300 pounds in weight, the owner will be repaid for the actua. cost if he receives $3.85 net per central therefor. As steers of that weight usually sell for at least 4 cents per pound, it appears that good profits may be derived from beef growing in Wisconsin.

Mr. M. T. Dill, living in Pierce County, in northwestern Wisconsin, furnishes the following information as to the cattle interest in that county:

The cattle are a mixture of all breeds, or what I call mongrel. The few purely-bred cattle kept here are Shorthorns and Jerseys, introduced ten or twelve years ago. It is probable that not more than 2 per cent. of our cattle not purely bred have one-half or more of their blood from purely-bred animals. They are generally kept for beef, only about 40 per cent. being kept in dairies. About two-thirds of the cattle fattened in our county are brought here from the timbered regions east of this county. The store cattle introduced for fattening are usually three-year-old steers. No calves or other young cattle have been brought here from the States south and east of Wisconsin, but, on the contrary, large numbers of our young cattle have been shipped to Montana.

Twenty-five per cent. of the calves born in this county are slaughtered for veal, prices for such calves ranging at from $5 to $8 each. For grazing we bring "stockers" here during the summer from May to August. For fattening we buy "feeders" between the 1st of September and December. When the purpose is to ship to Montana, we buy steers eight to eighteen months old; but when full feeding is intended we purchase those three to four years old. We usually begin the final fattening of our cattle in March or April, that we may send them to market in April or May when they are three to five years old. Of stock for local market 75 per cent. are sold when only partly matured, or "grass fat," Shorthorns or their grades being marketed when one or two years younger than inferior or mongrel cattle can be matured. The average weight of the beeves alive when marketed is about 1,200 pounds. Beeves not used to supply our local demand are sent to Chicago, to Minneapolis, or to Saint Paul.

In this region farming lands are worth about $35 per acre; grazing lands, $15. The rate of interest on loans secured by land or cattle is 8 per cent. per annum. On the farms where grown corn in the ear is worth 30 cents per bushel, corn stalks are worth $2 per acre; hay is worth $5 to $8 per ton; straw or other like forage has only a nominal value, most of it being burned in the fields. The charge for pasturage accords with the value of the land.

In fattening cattle it is usual to feed about eight bushels of corn per month, and about 900 pounds of hay. Where wheat-screenings, bran, or oats mixed with corn are fed, we give eleven to fifteen bushels of the mixture per month. When on pasturage alone, the cattle gain about thirty pounds per month. When fed with corn, and not on pasturage, the average monthly gain in weight is, in my experience, about five pounds. There is, however, a marked difference in the rate of increase per bushel between cattle of different ages. For example, yearlings and two-year-olds gain more in weight on hay alone than three-year-olds will gain on feed; and the latter will gain more on grain rations than the former will. I should think that the difference in the last-named cases would be nearly or quite 25 pounds. When stock are fed in winter, the average cost of attendance per head for wages of men, if there are, for example, 100 bullocks, would be $160 for the herd; their board would be worth $80, and the keeping of two horses required for hauling feed would be $60, making the total cost of these items $300, or, say, $3 per head. In summer, when the stock are on pasturage, the cost of maintenance is about $150 for the herd of 100, one man being in charge of the whole. In winter, fattening cattle are usually housed; therefore no hogs fatten on the droppings of the stock. Cattle are usually fed in winter here in order to use up coarse feed on the farm, and because they can be cared for then with less outlay than would be required in summer if full feeding were to be followed.

In our neighborhood, in which I intend to include Pierce County generally, stock is watered from wells; therefore the sources from which our cattle obtain water do not become impure or stagnant. The county consists of rolling prairie, free from forest growths. All of our pastures are dry and undulating, on the mounds and ridges of which wild or native grasses abound, while clover and timothy are most commonly found on the tilled land.

There are no diseases among our cattle. I have lost only one animal during the last ten years, out of a herd of from 500 to 600 head. There have been no losses from anthrax, or black-leg, nor from milk sickness, Texas fever, nor from lung worms. We have had four or five cases of lump-jaw, or actinomycosis.

From the above information it appears that in raising and fattening a herd of 100 beeves the cost would be, in Pierce County, about as follows, the items being interest on the value of the land in pasture for the whole year, for the breeding stock, since it is used for no other purpose, interest on the value of the bulls and cows from which the steers are gotten, and rations for the three months of winter during which the breeding herd should be fed on grain and hay. The steers, from birth to the time they will be ready for full feeding, require the produce of from four to six acres of land, including pasturage, hay, and other food. At the end of that time they will receive 8 bushels of corn and 900 pounds of hay, or their equivalent, per month, for from four to six months. The account should then be about as follows:

Interest on value of 3 bulls, worth say $50 each, one year	$9.00
Corn for bulls, six months, 144 bushels, at 30 cents	43.20
Hay for bulls, six months, 16,200 pounds, at $6.50 per ton	52.65
Interest of pasturage, one year, say 15 acres, at $15 per acre	14.62
Interest on value of 110 cows, valued at say $25 each, one year	178.75
Interest on value of land for pasture for cows, one year	58.62
Corn for cows, say three months	79.20
Hay for cows, five months	1,320.00
Pasturage of 100 steers, three years, five acres each	1,462.50
Interest on value of 100 steers, three years	371.44
Hay for 100 steers, six months, 900 pounds per month each	1,755.00
Corn for 100 steers, six months	1,440.00
Total	6,779.98

The above shows that highly-fed steers, born of equally well-fed cows and fully matured at the age of three years and six months, would cost an average of $67.80. If sold at 4½ cents per pound alive on the farm where fed they would, if 1,500 pounds in weight, bring the sum they cost. The fact is that animals of such weight and quality as would be produced by so thorough a system of management as is indicated by the above account usually sell for more than 4½ cents per pound, but even if they did not sell for more, the gain the farmer would make by marketing his hay and grain on his own farm, thus saving the cost and the waste of attending the hauling of those crops to market, the full use that he would make of his pasture lands that might otherwise be unproductive, and the constant enrichment of his lands would give him a liberal reward, even if he did not pasture the stock on lands owned by others and lying open as commons. It is not claimed that as good results as are indicated above can be obtained without good management, but that beef growing can be carried on profitably in northwestern Wisconsin seems to be established.

Mr. James O'Neill, of Clark County, in northwestern Wisconsin, says in a letter relating to pastures and cattle growing in that county:

> We have a few Shorthorns, Jerseys, and Holsteins, but nearly all our cattle are "natives" of excellent quality. Farmers raise a good many oxen for use in lumbering. One acre of land here will pasture a cow and another will put her through the winter.

From Walworth County, in southeastern Wisconsin, Messrs. L. and M. A. Brown write:

> Our cattle are generally of mixed breeding of natives and Shorthorns, Jerseys, and Polled Angus [probably Galloways were meant]. The established races of purely-bred cattle kept here are those named above, and Holsteins. The Polled Angus were introduced in 1883, the Holsteins in 1878, the Shorthorns in 1870, and

the Jerseys in 1880. About 15 per cent. of our cattle have a trace of the blood of the stock mentioned. Seventy-five per cent. of our cattle are kept for dairying purposes, only about 300 cattle a year being brought in from Chicago for grazing or for fattening. As a rule the stockers thus secured are one-quarter or one-half Shorthorn. No calves or very young cattle from other States have been pastured or fattened here. Such stock as are brought here come in the summer, and are pastured until autumn, andr oughed through the winter. Two-year-olds are usually bought for grazing and three-year-olds for fattening. For the latter purpose cattle are bought in September or October, and the fat stock are sent to market in March or April, at the age of three or four years. About 60 per cent. are sold when only "grass fat;" when they are one or two years younger than were the cattle marketed in like condition ten or fifteen years ago. We send our beeves to Chicago.

Fifty per cent. of the calves born in this county are killed for veal, selling at about $6 per head as an average.

The cash value of the farming land in this region is $75, and of the grazing land $40 per acre. Where money is borrowed, and the loan secured by land or cattle, the rate of interest is from 6 to 8 per cent. per annum. Corn in the ear is worth $10 per ton; cornstalks standing in the hill are worth 50 cents an acre, and $3 when cut up. Hay is worth $4.50 to $6 per ton, straw $2 per ton, and pasturage 50 cents per month. In fattening a bullock we feed 10 to 12 bushels of corn per month and about 600 pounds of hay. Straw, cornstalks, and other forage we do not feed to fattening stock. On such feed as we have mentioned cattle gain from 30 to 40 pounds a month, the average increase in weight of fattening cattle for each bushel of corn fed to them while on pasture being 5 pounds, and 4 pounds when on dry feed. Of foods other than those named above, barley and oats are commonly used for fattening stock. When cattle are fattened in winter, the average cost of attendance per head is, for wages $1.50, and board of men and keep of team $1, making a total of $2.50 per head. In summer the cost is not more than one-quarter as much. Our cattle are housed in winter and one hog for each bullock is allowed to follow fattening cattle, and makes from one to two pounds' growth a day. It is our opinion that cattle fed in summer while having access to pasture will take on one-quarter more fat on the same feed of grain and at a quarter of the cost of care.

Our water supply is from flowing springs, from streams, from ponds having inlets and outlets, and quite often from wells. These seldom become stagnant. The lands along the water-courses are sometimes flat, in which case water is taken from wells for the stock. Often the land is rich and covered with small timber. The pasturage is partly on such lands and partly on prairie openings. In our cultivated grasses are included timothy, red-top, and white and red clover.

Of diseases we know few instances. There is an occasional case of milk-sickness in cows, but not over 1 or 2 per cent. die of that malady. That is the only disease affecting our cattle, except an occasional lump-jaw or big-head.

The readiness with which milk can be sold for cash in nearly every county of Wisconsin has tended to check the development of the dairying as well as of the beef-growing interests of the State. The milk can be sold for an average of nearly or quite 1 cent per pound. A calf can use from 20 to 25 pounds of milk per diem during the first six months of its life. It is clear that if permitted to do so, the calf would soon consume a quantity of milk equal in market value to the price the animal would bring when six months old. Calves are sold for prices ranging from $3.50 to $15 each, the price depending on the age and the nearness to the larger markets. Consuming 20 pounds of milk per day, the calf would, in seventeen days, use up milk worth $3.50; to consume milk worth $15, sixty days would be required, at 25 pounds of milk each day. In view of these facts it is scarcely surprising that farmers prefer to sell their calves, even though they know that they will find it necessary to buy cows to keep up their herds. It is asserted that nearly or quite 200,000 calves have been slaughtered in a single year in Wisconsin, and that the result of this wholesale killing of stock, which might have become most valuable to the dairyman, has been the sending from the State of large amounts of money for the purchase of cows that might better have been raised within the State.

The unvarying testimony of correspondents in Wisconsin is that no diseases of a serious nature have appeared among the cattle of that State. A few report the existence of lump-jaw, but say that only a few cases have been known. From Kenosha, a correspondent writes that milk-fever, blackleg, and consumption have been known in that county, but that cases of lump-jaw (*actinomycosis*) have not been seen there during the last ten years. It is evident that several correspondents mistook the inquiry, "Have losses from so-called milk-sickness occurred?" for an inquiry as to the prevalence of milk-fever. One writes from Dodge County that milk-fever is quite commonly seen there; "in fact, it is the only cow disease we have." Another gentleman writing of the same county estimates the loss from that malady as amounting to about 1 per cent. of the cows in bearing.

MARKETS.

While large quantities of the cattle products of Wisconsin have been absorbed by local demands, by far the greater part have gone to markets outside of the State. Within the last five years many young cattle have been drawn from Wisconsin to increase the herds of the plains of Dakota or the valleys of Wyoming and Montana. This demand arose some five years ago, and quickly grew to considerable importance, dividing with Chicago the trade in stockers or store cattle, of which that market had before enjoyed almost the whole. Great numbers of young cattle still go to Chicago, where they are bought by men who make a business of purchasing and selling such stock after assorting it to suit the wishes of their customers. From Chicago the animals may go to the States east, south, or west of that place, or may even return to Wisconsin, perhaps to the very county from which they were sent for sale. Saint Paul and Minneapolis have long been markets where a considerable part of the surplus stock of Wisconsin has been sold, particularly that from the western part of the State.

Since the establishment in Chicago of the business of sending to interior points dressed meats in refrigerators or in ice-boxes, exports of cattle from Wisconsin have increased, although it does not appear that there has been any very large growth of the business of beef production, the increase in exports having been in the movement of young store stock to the northwestern Territories and to other markets. In Wisconsin, as in other States, retail dealers in meats have found it cheaper and better to order quarters of beef, or roasts, steaks, or other choice cuts from the packers, rather than pay the expense of maintaining small slaughter-houses at local and often inconvenient points. This peculiarity of the meat traffic is seldom found in places away from the more important lines of railroads, over which express companies send cars at convenient intervals.

Not many years ago the prejudice against Wisconsin dairy products was so strong in the Eastern States, and even in Milwaukee and Chicago, that butter and cheese bearing a Wisconsin brand was almost unsaleable in those markets. But in time the quality of the goods became so improved that they gained favor with consumers despite the prejudice that existed, and certain brands of dairy goods from Wisconsin are so highly esteemed that they are in demand at all times, and at prices much above those for which butter or cheese may be bought in the open market. This reputation exists in the remote eastern cities of this country, and is known even in Europe.

It is not an unusual matter for farmers in Wisconsin to supply to families in the larger cities of the north all the butter those families may need throughout the year. Such contracts or arrangements, for there is often no written contract or agreement, sometimes run on for many months, the butter furnished being of the best quality and the price higher than the current rates in the markets where the consumers live. This method of supplying consumers with butter might be indefinitely extended with advantage to the producer, and pleasure and even profit to the consumer, for it is much more profitable to buy sweet, pure butter at a high price than it is to accept an inferior article at a lower figure. Dealers in butter assert that the public has become far more exacting in regard to the quality of butter than it was before the sale of oleomargarine became general, demanding that the article offered shall be uniform in color and sweet in flavor and odor. At the same time people are seemingly willing to pay a price as much higher than those of ten or twelve years ago as they demand that the quality shall be better.

While there has been great improvement in the operations of making butter, and some has been brought about in the handling of the product in the market, much remains to be done before good butter can be safely entrusted to commission men and other dealers. It is not exaggerating to say that more injury is done to butter by the ignorance or carelessness of dealers than by any other cause. Although it is now well known by every person of ordinary intelligence that butter is more readily damaged by bad odors than is almost any other food, or by coming in contact with contaminating substances, yet much if not most of the butter sent to market is stored in dark cellars or musty basements, where the odors of rotting wood, decaying fruit, vegetables, fish, and other unpleasant things fill the air. In Chicago and other large cities are places in which butter and cheese alone are sold, and in many if not most instances these butter stores are in basements where the floors rest on or are very near the ground, which has become soaked with drainage. There is no ventilation and no escape for the accumulated odors of sewer-gas, rotting wood, and foul drainage. No butter could be kept pure and sweet in such a place. The injury done to the dairy interest by the exposure of butter to such influences as are indicated above has been enormous and inexcusable, for the only reason that can be given for putting butter in such places is that they are cool.

TENNESSEE.

By those who know its natural advantages Tennessee is regarded as one of the most favored of all the States. Naturally divided into eight great districts, having each its own peculiar geological formation, altitude, climate, and soil, the State shows as many and as marked differences in its agriculture. Along the Mississippi River on the west is a strip of alluvial bottom land 220 feet above sea level. This contains 900 square miles of exceedingly fertile land, largely covered by forests of massive trees under which is an exuberant growth of underbrush, cane, and other vegetation. The climate in this low-lying region is almost tropical in its heat, and where the forest has been cleared away and the land cultivated most abundant crops have been grown. There are here many swamps, lakes, lagoons, and sluggish streams. Of the whole region little is more than a few feet above the level of the surface of the Mississippi River, by which a large part of the whole tract is overflowed. As a stock raising region, it is scarcely necessary to say, it is not likely to reach prominence.

WEST TENNESSEE.

Rising gently from the bluffs, 400 feet above tide level, which define the eastern edge of the bottom lands of the Mississippi, is a plateau reaching eastward to the Tennessee Ridge which bounds the west side of the valley of the Tennessee River. This ridge has an altitude of 600 to 700 feet. The surface of this plateau is broken into hills, among which are fertile valleys in which cotton and corn can be grown successfully, but the soil is generally loose, and, although rich, it is easily exhausted by unskillful or careless farming. Nearly every farmer in the district raises such stock as may be required for use at home, and usually has some to sell. The cattle are described as being generally, almost universally in fact, natives or scrubs in which some faint traces of the influence of good blood may be sometimes seen. Only a few animals of pure breeding have been taken into this region; those introduced being Shorthorns, Holsteins, and Jerseys. Of the improved cattle imported the greater number have been Shorthorns from Kentucky, Ohio, and Virginia.

Generally the land is dry and rich, yielding large crops of red-top, blue grass, timothy, and clover. Herds grass (red-top) and orchard grass grow well here, and the latter is more highly valued than blue grass is by the stock owners. It is more than likely that this whole plateau might be easily converted into a most prosperous stock-growing country by covering the hills with the various forage plants which thrive so well there. Herds grass and timothy are said to yield an average of 2 tons to the acre in several of the counties of this tract. Among the wild grasses growing there is one called swamp grass, of which cattle are very fond and which resists the effects of drought well. Bermuda grass gives an almost inexhaustible supply of forage in those places where it has been introduced, and orchard grass and winter rye afford good pasturage in winter. There is in the natural conditions of this large area enough to assure the people of a successful result if they choose to make stock-growing an important branch of their business. The climate is favorable, being so mild that cotton is profitably grown in nearly every county. The warmth of the summers might make profitable butter production difficult except in winter, but the other conditions are favorable, and good markets would not be distant. Pure and cold water comes from springs in many of the hill-sides, and some of the lakes and streams are fed by water from springs of unsurpassed purity. Comparatively little attention has been given to dairying, and the total sales of butter from the counties on the plateau have been small. The supply of cattle in the twenty counties of West Tennessee at the time of the taking of the last United States census, was 6,918 working oxen, 96,458 milch cows, and 135,490 other cattle. During the year ended at the time of the taking of that census, 836,326 gallons of milk were sold, and 5,002,043 pounds of butter and 4,694 pounds of cheese were marketed. All of the butter, cheese, and milk was from farms, no cheese or butter factories having existed in that region. It will be noted that the average quantity of milk sold per cow was 3.5 gallons; the output of butter averaged 51.85 pounds, and the sale of cheese averaged .05 pounds per cow. At that time the general average yield of butter per cow for Tennessee was 58.9 pounds, and for the United States it was 62.5 pounds, while the average yield of cheese for each cow in Tennessee was 0.33 of a pound, and per cow in the whole country was 2.2 pounds, the highest average for any one State having been in Vermont, where it was 7.12 pounds. It will be seen that the quantity of butter sold per cow was only 3.6 pounds less than the average for the entire country, including the famed dairy regions of Vermont, where the average was only 116.3 pounds per cow.

A detailed statement of the number of cattle of the several classes, and of the quantity of milk, butter, and cheese sold from the farms in the twenty counties in West Tennessee at the time above mentioned is given herewith. It is to be regretted that all efforts to obtain more and later information as to the product of sale of dairy products have failed. It is due to the officers of the Bureau of Agriculture of Tennessee and other gentlemen of that State to add that they have been earnestly striving to obtain the creation of a law that will make the collection of statistics relating to the agriculture of Tennessee comparatively easy and certain. It is not easy to gauge the value and influence such information would probably have upon those who may be seeking homes where the climate, soil, and other conditions are favorable to stock raising, dairying, or other agricultural operations. Observations extended over twenty-three years showed that the mean number of days that were free from frost was 173 per year, and the mean number that were free from killing frosts in that period was 189. This was at an elevation of 500 to 600 feet. Ice sometimes forms to the thickness of 6 or 7 inches in favorable situations in the northern part of the State, but the usual thickness is from 1 to 2 inches.

The cattle supply of West Tennessee and the sale of dairy products at the date of the latest collection of statistics regarding those branches of agriculture is shown below:

PLATEAU COUNTIES.

Counties.	Working oxen.	Milch cows.	Other cattle.	Milk.	Butter.	Cheese.
				Gallons.	Pounds.	Pounds.
Carroll	347	4,974	5,433	2,977	373,748	234
Crockett	107	3,351	4,089	16,986	252,154	316
Fayette	135	7,182	11,384	690	233,790	50
Gibson	77	6,584	8,969	5,167	458,223	2,706
Haywood	154	5,292	7,730	67,737	247,026	100
Hardeman	452	5,916	8,806	2,347	230,838	....
Henry	242	4,726	4,681	3,478	391,478	30
Madison	170	4,907	7,425	17,385	243,581	14
Weakley	199	5,223	7,040	1,079	352,866	290
Total	1,883	48,155	65,467	118,371	2,780,694	2,740

In the next natural division lying east of the plateau there are five counties, of which Hardin and Decatur lie partly in the west valley of the Tennessee River. The supply of cattle and the dairy output of those counties were as follows in 1880:

RIDGE COUNTIES.

Counties.	Working oxen.	Milch cows.	Other cattle.	Milk.	Butter.	Cheese.
				Gallons.	*Pounds.*	*Pounds.*
Benton	729	2,673	3,898	....	144,101	125
Decatur	558	2,251	3,750	....	120,425	75
Hardin	807	3,674	5,738	....	143,069	....
Henderson	615	4,854	6,829	....	257,514	....
McNairy	840	4,806	6,923	156	281,099	90
Total	3,637	18,458	26,033	156	967,258	290

West of the plateau are the counties on the bluffs bordering on the bottom-lands through which the Mississippi River flows, and the county of Clay, which consists entirely of bottom-lands. The supply of cattle in those counties, and the quantities of milk, butter, and cheese sold from farms in them, as given by the last census report, were as below:

BLUFF COUNTIES.

Counties.	Working oxen.	Milch cows.	Other cattle.	Milk.	Butter.	Cheese.
				Gallons.	*Pounds.*	*Pounds.*
Dyer	270	3,985	7,257	1,860	302,991	....
Lake	98	1,484	2,088	22	43,710	....
Lauderdale	250	4,709	7,265	1,849	234,157	....
Obion	367	4,578	7 669	5,402	269,297	....
Shelby	221	10,040	11,923	190,212	327,966	360
Tipton	192	5,099	7,236	19,454	236,010	300
Total	1,398	29,845	43,390	217,799	1,814,131	660

Writing of the cattle business of the southwestern part of Tennessee, particularly of the beef production of that part near Fayette County, a correspondent states:

Our cattle are mainly scrubs, but a few Jerseys and Shorthorns have been kept here, at least since 1883. The percentage of cattle having an infusion of the blood of pure cattle is too small to estimate. Our cattle are kept for general purposes of the farm, most of the cows being milked. No stock is brought here for fattening or for grazing. About 10 per cent. of the calves born here are slaughtered for veal, for which use they are usually valued at $5 each.

For grazing we generally prefer steers of two to four years' growth, and for full feeding we get those from three to five years old. These are fattened through the winter months and sent to market in the early spring. They are all what may be called "grass fat," and range in weight from 300 to 1,000 pounds. They are sold at Memphis. Our lands are worth from $3 to $5 per acre, and the legal rate of interest on loans is 6 per cent. per annum. Very little, if any, corn is fed in this region. Our pastures are rolling, dry, and sandy, and the pasturage consists largely of broom sedge and Japan clover. The water for stock is frequently found in pools, and is stagnant in warm weather. The disease most commonly found in this part of the country among the cattle is murrain; in fact, it is the only one.

From the northern part of West Tennessee Mr. H. C. Pearce writes:

Jerseys, Holsteins, and Shorthorns have been brought to this section, and our stock are beginning to show traces of the influence of the imported animals. About 25 per cent. of our cattle not purely bred have half or more of their blood from purely-bred animals. Cattle are kept here for milking and for beef production combined, no animals being kept exclusively for either of those purposes. No cattle are brought here from abroad for grazing or for feeding, but those born here are kept until mature, very few calves being killed for veal. Cattle fit for sale are usually sent to market in early spring, 75 per cent. of the beeves going when grass fat. In fact, little or no attempt at fattening stock is made here. Our market is found in New Orleans, Memphis, Louisville, Saint Louis, and Mobile. For the few calves sold for veal the sellers get $5 to $7 per head.

Farming and grazing land is worth here from $8 to $10 per acre, and the legal rate of interest is 6 per cent. per annum. Corn in the ear is worth, at times, 60 cents a bushel, and hay $15 to $20 per ton. For straw, cornstalks, and such fodder there is no established market price. In the few instances where cattle are fed here cotton-seed meal is used. Fall and winter feeding pays best here for the reason that prices of beef are much better in the Southern markets in the spring. Our stock get their supply of water from springs, streams, and pools; the latter sometimes become stagnant in warm weather. The lands adjacent to the sources of water supply are generally flat, of rich soil, and covered by a dense growth of bushes and trees, but our pasturage is generally on dry, undulating land, where redtop, timothy, blue-grass, clover, and other forage grows. Of diseases we have seldom any cases.

MIDDLE TENNESSEE.

At a point about 100 miles east from the Mississippi the Tennessee River crosses the southern boundary of the State of Tennessee and flows due north across the whole width of the State, and forms the dividing line between western and middle Tennessee. The valley of this river is narrow, very fertile, and not thickly settled, being swampy and low, and is near the western border of the highlands that form the western part of middle Tennessee. These highlands surround the great central basin, which is regarded as the garden of the State. This rim or table-land has a total area of some 9,300 square miles, and an elevation of 900 to 1,000 feet on the west, and a somewhat greater altitude on the east side of the basin. On the south the Elk River cuts through the highlands and flows into the Tennessee; the Duck River crosses the whole width of the great central basin from the east and makes its way through the highlands on the west to the Tennessee River, which it joins at a point not far from the middle of the line formed by the last-named stream between the northern and the southern limits of the State. Near the northern edge of the basin the Cumberland River flows to the westward, draining all the northern half of the valley and the western part of the Cumberland table-land which bounds middle Tennessee on the east. These highlands are generally of a clayey, siliceous soil, most of which is productive, but is somewhat broken without being mountainous. In some places the surface is of rounded hills, between which are wide valleys; in others it is cut by deep ravines through which flow clear streams, but as a whole it may be described as a great plain of productive soil and well adapted to farming, especially to stock-growing and dairying. To this industry the hills and ravines would offer no obstacle, while the cool and pure streams would be a decided advantage.

The most remarkable of the great natural features of Tennessee is the valley, or basin, inclosed by the highlands or terraces described. This valley is from 50 to 60 miles wide and 100 miles long. The soil rests on limestone and slopes to the northwest, forming a gently undulating field of great richness, on which blue-grass and other forage plants grow vigorously and of excellent quality. There is not a swamp on its entire serface, every mile being perfectly drained by the bright streams which find their way to the Tennessee or the Cumberland; and every crop known north of the 35th degree of latitude can be produced in this valley or in the highlands surrounding it.

Corn, rye, barley, and all the cultivated forage plants flourish. Of the grasses growing in this grand valley there is a great variety. Among them is one that has been of immense benefit to the peopl of the State, as it covered the open country and grew among the trees, wherever the sunlight penetrated, when the first white men entered the country. It clothed the high table-lands, the hills, and the sandy lowlands, furnishing abundant pasturage from April to August to the stock of the settler. It still covers a large part of tho land of Tennessee, and affords forage on which thousands of cattle live, with little or no expense to their owners, during the summer months. Nimble-will is a perennial and indigenous grass, which makes a good growth and is very nutritious. It springs up on limestone lands, where the sunlight has been let in among the trees, and furnishes abundant pasturage during five or six months of each year. Crab-grass gives fair fall pasturage, springing up quickly in cultivated fields after the regular crops have been harvested. The grass which is believed to be likely to become one of the most valuable of all the forage crops of Tennessee is blue-grass. It thrives in every field and in the open forests of the limestone districts, covering the ground with a thick carpet of food on which stock of all kinds fatten. It is believed that blue-grass may be profitably introduced into almost every county in the State, and that to the great central region of highland and valley it will prove to be of almost illimitable value. Timothy, red and white clovers, alfalfa, Hungarian grass, herd's grass, meadow oat grass, orchard grass, and others, are all grown here most successfully; in short, those who know this broad central plain of middle Tennessee and the terraces surrounding it assert that here is a region that will fully equal the best parts of Kentucky in stock-growing, whenever the people shall have taken advantage of the natural conditions by which this part of the State is so greatly favored. It is a curious fact that while in Tennessee there are so many grasses which would afford a heavy yield of hay, if properly managed to that end, very little hay is made in the State, although prices for good hay seldom fall below $15 per ton and often rise above $20.

It was but natural that where the conditions were so favorable to stock-growing as they were in middle Tennessee good cattle should have been introduced at an early date. From time to time importations were made of animals of pure breeding from Kentucky, Virginia, and other States, and even from Europe. Ayrshires were imported to increase the milk, butter, and cheese p u g capacity of the native stock; Devons were taken in to add todthei[illegible]alue of the stock for general purposes; and more Shorthorns were taken into the State than all representatives of other established breeds taken there would number. Jerseys won much favor in some parts of the State, and herds of Jerseys in Tennessee have become known in all parts of the land. The improvement of the cattle of the State was checked, if it was not entirely stopped for years, by the late war; but the cattle interest has more than recovered its old standing as to numbers, and is better off than it was before the war in regard to the quality of its stock, many Shorthorn, Devons, Jerseys, and Holsteins having been taken there within the last ten years. Holsteins seem to have met no little favor from owners of stock in Tennessee of late, for many correspondents mention the introduction of animals of that race in their respective neighborhoods as having been made within the last five years.

For some reason not apparent there was a decline in the cattle interest of Tennessee from the years 1850 to 1870. This falling off in numbers is shown by the statement which follows. The same statement shows that between the years 1870 and 1880 there was a marked increase in the number of cattle in the State.

Classes.	1850.		1860.		1870.		1880.	
	Number.	Population.	Number.	Population.	Number.	Population.	Number.	Population.
Milch cows..........	250,456	249.7	249,514	224.8	243,197	194.3	303,905	197.0
Working oxen	86,255	86.0	102,156	92.0	63,970	50.8	27,312	17.7
Other cattle.........	414,051	413.0	413,060	372.2	335,929	264.7	452,457	293.3
Total..........	750,762	748.7	764,732	689.0	643,096	511.5	783,674	508.0

It is worthy of note that while there was an increase of 60,708 in the number of cows in 1880 over that of the milch cows of 1870, the number of oxen declined some 36,600 in the same period. In the relation of the supply of cattle to population, as shown in the columns under the proper heading in the above table, the cattle interest has shown a constant decrease since the first trustworthy statistics were gathered. In 1885 there were in Tennessee 249.7 milch cows, 86 working oxen, and 413 other cattle for each 1,000 inhabitants then in the State. They made a total of 748.7 cattle of all classes for each 1,000 people in the State, or three-quarters of a beast for each. In the year 1880 there were only 197 milch cows, 17.7 oxen, and 293.3 other cattle, or a total of 508 cattle for each of the inhabitants. In the year 1884 the Department of Agriculture reported that in Tennessee there were 779,826 cattle, of which 313,742 were milch cows. This indicated a shrinkage of 3,848 in the supply of cattle of all classes, but there may have been more than that number roaming, uncounted, among the mountains of the State.

Two years ago it was ascertained that of the whole supply of cattle in the United States 18 per cent. were high grades. It is not to the discredit of Tennessee that the cattle of the State were, so far as the number of high grades is concerned, fully up to that percentage. In the average value of that improvement of her cattle the State was above the average, as the improvement in the Tennessee stock was valued at 38 per cent., while that of the country as a whole was only 35 per cent. In this respect Tennessee was tenth among the States, Kansas ranking first. The increase in the market value of the stock of Tennessee from higher breeding was estimated as having been $4,180,401. At that rate the increased value of the entire supply would have amounted to $27,235,600, if all had been half-bloods or better.

No complete information has been gathered relating to the cattle and cattle products of middle Tennessee since the United States census of 1880 was compiled. That census showed that there were in the forty counties in this district 12,193 working oxen, 124,402 milch cows, and 185,226 other cattle. From farms were sold 433,914 gallons of milk, 8,018,478 pounds of butter, and 33,968 pounds of cheese. De Kalb County had more cows than had any other one of the twen y counties; Wilson County, in the northern part of the great basin and only a few miles east of Nashville, had more cattle of all classes than had any other county in middle Tennessee, and sold more butter than did any of the others. This county was third among all the counties of the State as to the number of cattle and first as to the quantity of butter sold. Jackson County, in the extreme northeastern part of middle Tennessee, had more working oxen than had any other county in the State. The distribution of the cattle among the counties of this division of the State, and the quantity of milk, butter, and cheese sold by the farmers of each, is shown in detail below.

LOWLAND OR BASIN COUNTIES.

Counties.	Working oxen.	Milch cows.	Other cattle.	Milk.	Butter.	Cheese.
				Gallons.	*Pounds.*	*Pounds.*
Bedford	90	5,199	8,909	5,151	354,868	1,781
Cannon	285	2,404	2,548	788	162,308	720
Davidson	34	6,251	8,668	304,156	443,745	4,614
De Kalb	610	7,297	3,088	....	167,272	....
Giles	185	5,776	9,318	9,256	404,038	1,080
Jackson	1,[illegible]	2,327	2,934	1,350	176,489	....
Marshall	88	3,765	5,954	649	412,969	1,406
Maury	120	6,280	9,081	15,576	392,551	1,796
Moore	45	1,289	1,776	505	77,914	641
Smith	615	3,027	4,961	....	221,361	140
Rutherford	99	9,785	9,702	18,656	438,043	1,118
Sumner	119	4,653	8,651	4,450	[illegible]	218
Trousdale	71	1,150	2,176	959	74,496	44
Williamson	77	5,152	7,677	6,558	374,587	2,508
Wilson	142	6,086	10,107	8,707	598,498	567
Total	3,854	67,874	96,505	371,009	4,551,343	16,868

In the lowland or valley counties the average production of butter in excess of the requirements of the farmers was 67.55 pounds per cow, and of cheese sold from farms the average quantity per cow was one-quarter of a pound. Of Rutherford, Cannon, and Wilson Counties, in the eastern and northern part of the great fertile basin, Messrs. W. B. Earthman & Co. say:

The lands are generally rolling, with very few swampy places, and mostly having a red clay subsoil. On these lands blue-grass, herd's, orchard, red-top, timothy, and wild grasses flourish. The water supply is from springs, streams, and wells, and is pure. Under so favorable conditions diseases are never found among the cattle, unless a few cases of "hollow-horn," caused by hollow stomachs, are diseases.

The cattle of the counties named are good milkers and fair beef cattle, Short-horns, Devons, Jerseys, and Holsteins having left their impress on the stock. Shorthorns were brought here in 1868 or 1870; J. W. Sparks introduced Jerseys in 1872, and J. W. Oliver the Holsteins in 1885. Cattle here are generally kept for beef-growing, only about 10 per cent. being kept for dairying purposes. Few of the calves are killed, and for those they do kill the butchers pay from $5 to $10 each. No cattle are brought into these counties from abroad for grazing or for fattening; but in the spring the surplus stock is sold to Kentucky and Virginia graziers.

Our two-year-olds and three-year-olds are put on good pasture, and four-year-olds are fed from November until May or June. Then they are sent to market in Nashville, Louisville, New York or New Orleans. Twenty-five per cent. are thus sold when they are only partly matured or "grass fat," and averaging about 1,000 pounds.

As to prices, land ranges in value from $25 to $100 per acre, the average being about $40. Corn is worth, on the farms, 35 cents per bushel, but standing corn, grain and stalks, is worth $10 per acre; hay is worth $10 per ton, straw $4 per ton, and pasture 80 cents a month. In feeding, we give 10 bushels of corn per month and 750 pounds of hay. Three-year-olds gain 33 per cent. more than two-year-olds do on the same quantity of food. Cotton-seed is fed here, and is equally as good as corn. The cost of attendance on a herd of cattle in fattening is about 50 cents per head per month in winter and 10 cents in summer, but we think that winter feeding is 50 per cent. better than summer feeding. We always house our cattle in winter, but it is not generally done here.

HIGHLAND COUNTIES.

Counties.	Working oxen.	Milch cows.	Other cattle.	Milk.	Butter.	Cheese.
				Gallons.	*Pounds.*	*Pounds.*
Clay	775	1,508	2,141	520	91,991	....
Cheatham	115	1,468	2,647	1,250	108,936	....
Coffee	247	2,341	3,278	17,008	147,[illegible]	345
Cumberland	235	1,492	2,771	....	51,088	2,385
Dickson	394	2,967	4,619	1,257	178,128	218
Fentress	494	1,615	3,204	....	96,104	725
Franklin	286	3,048	4,472	2,646	170,291	1,035
Grundy	265	869	1,138	1,122	25,827	3,[illegible]
Hickman	126	2,809	4,844	840	202,449	75
Houston	214	925	1,297	5,405	59,414	194
Humphreys	330	2,644	4,574	....	155,072	1,[illegible]
Lawrence	261	2,320	3,082	47	130,[illegible]	[illegible]
Lewis	100	568	808	52	27,207	[illegible]
Lincoln	169	5,204	8,726	14,658	261,240	2,[illegible]
Macon	199	1,867	2,787	90	110,908	[illegible]
Montgomery	371	3,382	4,437	9,168	212,406	[illegible]
Overton	869	3,078	5,015	66	171,248	[illegible]
Perry	321	1,829	2,646	2,398	91,543	[illegible]
Putnam	597	2,270	3,778	....	135,856	120
Robertson	27	2,975	3,822	702	198,272	[illegible]
Stewart	580	2,617	3,818	60	142,013	....
Van Buren	184	650	1,406	410	68,847	[illegible]
Warren	311	2,725	4,059	4,672	195,413	[illegible]
Wayne	558	2,996	4,766	102	164,427	78
White	261	2,421	5,506	408	170,830	1,[illegible]
Total	8,330	57,066	88,721	62,815	3,467,135	17,148

A gentleman living in Montgomery County, in the northwestern corner of Middle Tennessee, states that the pastures there are dry, some being on the rich bottom-lands and others on the rolling ground. There is some forest, and many pastures are in part covered by trees and bushes. Timothy, herd's-grass, blue-grass, and all other agricultural grasses grow there. On these pastures disease is almost entirely unknown, a few cases of "big jaw," locally known as "snake bites," being the only malady known there. He says:

I have been raising cattle here for years, keeping about seventy-five head on hand all the time. I have had splendid success. I think cattle will pay well in this county; it is a sure thing with me. I have some Shorthorns, but ours are mostly scrub stock. Our stock get water from springs and running streams, although in some parts of the county stock water is scarce. In making beef we in this country usually buy our stockers in spring-time, taking two-year-olds when we can get them. For full feeding we prefer three-year-olds or four-year-olds, which we begin feeding about the 1st of January, sending the fat stock to market in April. I think it better to feed in winter, if one has sheds, for in summer the flies trouble stock greatly, so that they will not feed well. When we are feeding we have hogs follow the steers, one hog to three bullocks. The pigs make 1½ pounds of growth per day, which is clear gain. Three-fourths of all the stock fed here is sent to market (Clarksville or Louisville, Ky.) when only grass fat. Those marketed off the grass will average 500 pounds in weight, while the stock we feed go at 1,000 to 1,200 pounds. Most of the cattle here are what are called scrubs, but are of a healthy, hardy nature. In 1880 some Jerseys were brought here, and in 1882 Shorthorns were introduced, and have done something toward the improvement of the cattle of this corner of the county.

None of the stock here is kept for dairy purposes alone, but those who are acquainted with the advantages offered by Tennessee, and with the conditions necessary to success in factory dairying, believe that good profits can be made in co-operative butter and cheese making here. A cheese factory was built in Clarksville, in this county, in the spring of 1885.

About one-twentieth of the calves born here are sold to the butcher before they are a year old, generally bringing $5. Land here is worth from $5 to $25, some as high as $40. Interest is from 6 to 10 per cent. per annum. Corn is worth $1.50 per barrel, or 30 cents a bushel; corn-stalks, $1.50 an acre; hay, $15 per ton, and straw, $8 a ton. Pasture is charged for at the rate of $1.50 per month at times, and is scarce at that. In fattening steers we feed 10 bushels of corn and 250 pounds of hay. Sometimes bran and oats are fed. On such rations our stock gain 30 pounds per month. When cattle are fattened in winter here the cost for wages is about $1 a head per month for attendant and 50 cents a day for keeping the team. Cattle are never housed here, but they should be.

Another careful observer writes from Hickman, which is, like Montgomery, a highland county, as follows:

The cattle most commonly found in this part of Tennessee are scrubs. The cows weigh at maturity 750 pounds; steers, 1,000 pounds. There are some grade Shorthorns, Mr. S. L. Graham having laid the foundation of a Shorthorn herd here in 1869. In this county not over 1 per cent. of the cattle not purely bred have half their blood from any pure race. The cattle are used for all purposes, old cows and steers going for beef. All the females are used for dairying as long as they yield a profitable quantity of milk. About 300 cattle a year are brought here, usually from Nashville, for grazing. They are Shorthorn grades and scrubs. They are brought in in autumn or in spring. If they are Shorthorns, two-year-olds are selected for grazing and a year older for fattening. If scrubs, then they should be a year or two older than the others. When stock are to be fed in winter, the final fattening begins in November, and the ripe beeves are turned off in May. If they are summer fed they are sold about the middle of December, full feeding having begun in September. Fully 75 per cent. are sent to market when grass fat. Except in the cases where Shorthorns and their grades are fed, cattle are not sent to market at any earlier age than were those raised here ten or fifteen years ago. Grades are marketed as two-year-olds and three-year-olds; the scrubs as four-year-olds or older. When sent to market the scrub weighs about 800 pounds, while Shorthorns and their grades average 1,300 pounds. Most of our beeves go to Nashville and to Memphis.

Land is valued here at $15 to $20 per acre and interest is 6 per cent. on good security. Corn is worth 30 cents per bushel and hay $20 per ton, while straw is sold at $5 a ton. In fattening, all the hay the stock will eat is given, and 8 quarts of corn or a like quantity of cotton-seed meal are given per day. On such pasturage Shorthorns make from 30 to 60 pounds gain in weight per month. I can not say what difference there is in the increase in weight between yearlings and cattle of other ages, but the one-year-old bullock will increase faster than the three-year-old, but not faster than the two-year-old. I prefer the two-year-old.

I have not been systematic enough to say what the average cost of attendance is per head for wages, maintenance of men, and of horses or other teams used in hauling food for cattle. I feed, say, fifty steers, and it costs, counting as above, say, 3 cents per head per day. In summer the cattle cost nothing except to salt, or if fed, say, $1. When fed on whole corn the cattle are followed by hogs. It seems to me that the advantage of summer feeding must be obvious, as it takes less to produce a given weight. Winter feeding costs more per head, owing to rains, cold, and other causes.

Our pastures are generally on dry and rolling land, where a variety of wild grasses grow in the woods and red clover, herd's-grass, blue-grass, and orchard-grass abound.

Of diseases, there are scarcely any among the cattle of Hickman County. One season some Alabama cattle were introduced and caused severe loss among the native cattle. No losses from anthrax, from milk sickness, lung worms, nor actinomycosis have been known here. On two occasions I had ophthalmia in my herd, especially among the calves and young stock. Some cases were in 1883, and a little last year.

EAST TENNESSEE.

There are in East Tennessee three great natural divisions. That on the west is formed by the Cumberland Mountains or table-lands, which are the coal-bearing fields of the State. This region is from 35 to 40 miles wide, containing about 5,100 square miles, having a mean elevation of 2,000 feet above the sea, and is 1,000 feet above the eastern highlands of Middle Tennessee, which it borders. It is fully 1,300 to 1,400 feet in mean elevation above the great fertile and populous central valley of Middle Tennessee. The Cumberland table-lands have comparatively few streams, the chief one being the Sequatchie, which flows along the western base of Walden's Ridge, which divides the Cumberland region from the great valley of East Tennessee. The Sequatchie empties into the Tennessee River at a spot a few miles only from the place where it crosses the State line on the southern line of Marion County. The mountains of the Cumberland country are as a whole well covered by nutritious grass, which affords good pasturage during eight or nine months of each year. They are swept by breezes from the southwest and west, which make them cool, comfortable, and healthful ranges in the hottest weather. In winter the stock easily find shelter in the hollows between the hills from cold winds from the northwest, toward which the surface of the region as a whole slopes. In the mountains of nearly all of this range stock may be successfully pastured at a cost even less than that of keeping cattle on the plains of the far West, for in the Cumberland Mountains there is little need of herding, nor of the expensive and frequent "round-ups" required on the open range of the western plains. Owners of stock in East Tennessee have the additional advantage of being so near the great markets of the Atlantic coast that the cost of reaching them with fat beeves is trifling as compared with cost of putting into those markets cattle grown on the plains of Texas, New Mexico, or other western Territories and States. The gains which can be made from stock-growing in Tennessee are so great, and the country appears to be so much better fitted by nature for this business than for profitable cultivation, that there is cause for the wonder expressed by intelligent Tennesseeans that beef-growing has not become the most important if not the sole occupation of most of the inhabitants. The country is so sparsely inhabited that by far the greater part of the land may be used for pasture. There were in 1880 only 8.9 people per square mile. At that time they had 6.78 cattle per square mile, or 773 head per 1,000 inhabitants. For each head of cattle there were 94.4 acres of land.

The distribution of cattle in the seven counties lying wholly or in part on the Cumberland Mountains, and the quantity of milk, butter, and cheese sold from farms in each of those counties during the year covered by the last census of the United States, were as stated below. It is regretted that all attempts to gather later trustworthy information of this kind have failed, although earnest efforts have been made by the Bureau of Agriculture (Mines and Commerce of Tennessee) to fully cover the ground:

TABLE-LAND COUNTIES.

Counties.	Working oxen.	Milch cows.	Other cattle.	Milk.	Butter.	Cheese.
				Gallons.	*Pounds.*	*Pounds.*
Anderson	237	2,034	3,317	96	101,958	820
Bledsoe	207	1,564	5,193	49,572	77,451	363
Marion	438	1,606	4,359	407	73,881	....
Morgan	323	1,371	3,016	451	54,222	494
Scott	598	1,896	3,351	1,230	86,963	....
Sequatchie	112	728	2,069	1,600	46,667	55
Unicoi	228	824	1,117	60	34,615	150
Total	2,135	10,020	22,422	53,416	475,757	1,884

Anderson County lies partly on the Cumberland Mountains and in part in the edge of the great valley of East Tennessee. The county is exceedingly broken in surface, and contains much land that, while it is rich in mineral resources, is poorly adapted to farming or for pastoral purposes. Nevertheless the county contains 13.4 cattle per square mile, which is very nearly double the number per square mile possessed by the Cumberland region as a whole. Of its entire supply of cattle 36.4 per cent. were milch cows, while of all the cattle in the seven table-land counties 28.9 per cent. were cows. Of butter Anderson County sold from her farms an average of 50.1 pounds, the average quantity per cow in the seven counties having been 45 pounds. This superiority over the other counties is doubtless due to the fact that Anderson County is near Knoxville, and has felt for a long time the influence of a good market for the products of the dairy. Yet, with all the advantage of good markets, little improvement in the quality of the stock of the county has been attempted.

Sequatchie, Marion, and Bledsoe Counties have running through their entire lengths the narrow and originally fertile limestone valley of the Sequatchie River. Farmers in this valley have allowed their cattle to graze at will on the mountains, which shut off every harsh wind and afford abundant pasturage. From this long valley there is no outlet except by tedious ways over the steep rocks of Walden's Ridge to Chattanooga, 50 or 60 miles away, or down the valley to Jasper, in Marion County, almost as far distant. The chief crop grown in the valley was for many years, if it is not now, indeed, maize, which was fed to swine and cattle. When fat these were driven in great numbers over the mountains to Chattanooga, and from that point were shipped by rail to market. In this, as in the other counties in which this valley lies, stock-growing has for many years been recognized as being the most profitable of all farming operations possible to the inhabitants. The stock are driven in March or April to the mountain pastures, where they remain until November, coming home in good condition for market. The only cost is that of herding and salting.

The eastern edge of the Cumberland Mountain system forms one of the borders of the remarkable valley of East Tennessee, which is a broad, nearly flat trough having a deeply corrugated bottom. The wrinkles or folds in the rocks which underlie this valley seem to have been formed by the upheaval of the Unaka chain of the Appalachian Mountain system. These rocks appear to have been in part worn away by waters of which the Tennessee River, flowing through the entire length of the valley, is the representative. These left long narrow ridges and deep confined furrows occupying the whole bottom of the great valley, all trending, with the mountains on each side, from the Virginia line west-southwest to the southern limit of the State of Tennessee. The valley is watered in every part by swift, pure streams which never fail, and grass grows in the orests and on the hills wherever sunlight falls. The hills furnish abundant pasturage in summer for the cattle, and the cost of pasturing a bullock through the year is nominal. The winters are warmer in this valley than on the mountains on either hand, for all northerly and cold west winds are cut off or thrown high above the valley by the ridges on the northwest, which rise from 600 to 1,200 feet above the bottom of the valley. The latter slopes regularly toward its southwestern end. which is some 600 feet lower than is the upper

County was first, Sullivan County, in the northeastern corner of the State, was second, and Greene County was third.

Doubtless the fact that Knoxville, the most important town in the valley, offered a ready market for dairy products, did much if not more than any one cause to encourage the development of dairying in Eastern Tennessee, and to put Knox County in the first place among all the counties of the valley in the quantity of milk, butter, and cheese sold; but others have ascribed the marked advance of the dairy industry there to the fact that the pastures have been carefully improved and extended, and to the other fact that numbers of Jersey cattle have been introduced, and have greatly increased the butter-producing powers of the general supply of cows. The importation of Jerseys had another effect usually noticed where purely-bred stock of any kind are taken into a neighborhood. Their appearance was followed by greater interest in the stock on hand, and the example set by owners of animals of great value led breeders of the common stock to give more liberal rations and better shelter and care generally to their cattle. Still, although Jerseys and a few Holstein-Friesian cattle have been taken to this valley, very few, if any, farms are devoted to dairying exclusively or even largely.

It is estimated that fully 20 per cent. of the cattle in the northern half of the great valley of East Tennessee have been improved by the influence of good blood. Some estimate the percentage of improvement as including many more cattle, one gentleman stating that 90 per cent. were grades; but this is obviously an error. It is known that Durham cattle were taken to this region fully fifty years ago by several planters; Jerseys were taken in thirty-five years ago by C. W. Chatterton, Devons ten years ago, and Holstein-Friesians in 1884, by C. M. McGhee. The last-named gentleman says of the cattle interest of the valley:

Seventy-five per cent. of the stock is unimproved, hardy, healthy, and good "shifters." The grades among our stock have touches of the blood of the Shorthorns, Jerseys, Devons, and Holsteins. Our cattle are generally grown for beef, and we have very few dairy farms. Every farmer, and almost every head of a family, keeps one or more cows. No cattle have ever been brought here for grazing or for fattening, but the calves born here are carefully saved, only a very small per cent. being sold for veal. The cattle raised on small farms are collected by the larger farmers, taken to the mountains east or west of us, or pastured on valley lands. In September quite large lots are collected, and at two years old are sold to Virginians as stockers. Therefore we prefer yearlings for grazing. Our best farmers winter two-year-olds on hay and stalk fodder; begin feeding grain in March, put them on grass in May, and sell them as fat cattle in the last half of June. Seventy per cent. are sold as stockers. The introduction of good blood and better management than of old has enabled us to market our cattle at least a year younger than they were marketed ten or fifteen years ago. Our beeves are shipped to Virginia or to Maryland.

Farming and grazing lands are worth $25 per acre; mountain lands, $2. Corn is worth 60 cents per bushel and hay $20 per ton here. The water supply of East Tennessee is pure spring-water. We have no swamps nor malaria. It is a model country. Orchard-grass, blue-grass, red-top, and clover are the forage plants most commonly found on our grazing lands. Of diseases of cattle none are known here, except an occasional case of milk sickness near the mountain foot-hills. Several years ago some Florida and Texas cattle in passing through killed all cattle that followed them in pasture. In fact, it may be said with truth that our cattle are absolutely healthy.

Mr. Thomas P. Graham, writing of the northern counties of the valley, says:

On pastures alone our cattle make from 80 to 100 pounds growth per month. They weigh from 1,100 to 1,800 pounds when turned off, being largely red or roan

Shorthorn grades. We never kill any calves here, keeping the males for beef and the heifers for breeding. They cost us nothing more than a little care and an occasional salting, say once or twice a week. We usually provide them with open sheds for shelter in winter. We do not use any grain in fattening except a little corn sometimes we use green or winter pasturage. As the sons in the family or the owners of the stock attend to cattle, no account of the cost of attendance can be given. It is nominal.

From Grainger County Mr. A. X. Shields writes:

Probably one-third of our cattle are one-fourth to one-half Shorthorn blood. About three-fourths of them are sent to market when grass fat, going usually to Petersburgh or to Norfolk, Va., or to Baltimore. Corn is worth 65 cents a bushel and hay $15 per ton. In addition to these we feed oats, barley, bran, and shorts. The cost of attendance on our herds is nominal; in fact, there is no data from which to estimate it. Winter feeding for market does not pay well here, and summer pasturing is much preferred. Our cattle are turned on good pasturage in February, and between April and the middle of June are sold. Orchard, timothy, red-top, and a mixture of blue-grass and clover are our forage plants. In 1884 some murrain appeared here; perhaps 20 head died in this section; otherwise the stock has been perfectly healthy.

It appears that a few stockers are taken from the mountains of western North Carolina to the valley counties of East Tennessee for grazing, and that of the matured beeves many are sent to market grass fat. Baltimore, Philadelphia, Cincinnati, Charleston, and Atlanta are all markets to which cattle from this region are sent. Mr. J. W. Taylor, jr., of Grainger County, states that corn was worth 65 to 75 cents per bushel, hay $15, and straw $2.50 per ton. Of corn, 20 bushels, and of hay, 150 to 200 pounds per month are required in fattening a bullock fully. The cost of keeping cattle in summer is almost nothing. Mr. Taylor corroborates fully the statements of others about the healthfulness of the cattle.

A few cases of black-leg (anthrax) appeared in one of the counties adjoining Hancock County in 1884, and occasional cases of murrain have been seen in the northern part of the valley. In a letter, Mr. M. D. Fleener says that in Hancock and neighboring counties little feeding of cattle is done in summer, as cattle will live and fatten without it. The cost of caring for a bunch of cattle during the winter will not, in his estimation, exceed $13 to $15. Cane seed, pumpkins, and meal are the additions to the usual rations of corn, hay, and fodder, given to fattening stock.

The easternmost division of Tennessee consists of that part which lies on the western slope of the Unaka range of mountains, and has an area of 2,000 square miles of a mean elevation of 5,000 feet. In this division are seven counties, in which there were, in 1880, of population, 85,671, and of cattle, 46,586. This shows that there were an average of 23.3 cattle per square mile, while the population was 42.8 people per square mile. This is evidence that the people of these rocky counties have found that grazing is the most profitable branch of agriculture they can follow, and that they have adopted it more completely than have the people of the great valley, where there were only 15.4 cattle and 31.9 people to the mile. Moreover, the mountain counties sold an average of 11.9 pounds of butter per capita of population in the year covered by the last United States census, while those of the valley counties sold 11.5 pounds per capita, and those of the table-land counties sold 10.4 pounds. It is true that most of the counties in this division extend into the valley, but even there they are mountainous.

The supply of cattle in each of the mountain counties is given in detail in the accompanying statement, as is also the quantity of milk, butter, and cheese sold from each:

UNAKA MOUNTAIN COUNTIES.

Counties.	Working oxen.	Milch cows.	Other cattle.	Milk.	Butter.	Cheese.
				Gallons.	*Pounds.*	*Pounds.*
Blount	236	3,204	5,296	3,852	214,884	3,010
Carter	248	2,069	2,560	200	118,899	65
Cocke	627	2,808	4,633	....	160,147	2,395
Johnson	176	1,787	2,886	....	82,658	1,977
Monroe	296	3,121	5,186	315	157,138	782
Polk	265	1,805	2,135	10	98,094	560
Sevier	301	3,101	4,538	306	197,209	1,646
Total	2,143	17,480	27,238	4,683	1,019,008	10,385

Testimony furnished by scores of observing witnesses, living in widely separated parts of the State, and thoroughly acquainted with the natural and the artificial conditions affecting the cattle interests, shows that Tennessee affords many and great advantages to those who breed cattle for beef alone, or who make dairying their occupation. While the climate of the mountains differs from that of the valleys, and that of each of the great valleys is in some degree different from that of the others, the climate of the whole State is comparatively mild and equable. The synclinal axes of the valleys lie almost exactly in the line of the winds which blow, during the major part of the year, from the southwest, bringing warmth and moisture from the Gulf of Mexico, to raise the temperature, make the winters spring-like in their mildness, and prevent the drying of the pastures in summer. The ridges and the mountain ranges rise as barriers to completely shelter the valleys by turning aside the northwest winds, which are the only cold ones that blow over the country west of the Appalachian system of mountain ranges. In nearly every part of the State the mountains are covered by wild grasses which afford good pasturage, which is in much of the State as yet free to all who choose to drive their herds to the range. The cultivated grasses thrive wherever the ground has been properly prepared. In the valley lands, particularly on the bottom-lands, timothy grows luxuriantly, and yields heavy crops of excellent hay. The clovers and lucerne thrive on land having loose subsoil, and other forage plants furnish an abundance of food for stock, while grain is grown in the valleys to supplement the fodder in feeding fattening cattle and those in the dairy. The water supply is unlimited in quantity, and of a quality that can not be surpassed. Lands and labor are cheap, and the cost of living is not great, therefore the cost of herding stock and of raising grain and forage for cattle is light, while the nearness to market gives to the Tennessee cattle-owner very great advantage over the stock-raisers of the remote Southwest, who must, in fact, compete in the markets of the Atlantic coast with the stock-owners of this and other States east of the Mississippi.

Hay may be made in nearly every valley in Tennessee at small cost; yet in the census of 1880 the State was credited with the production of only 186,698 tons of hay, which was less than a quarter of a ton for each of the 783,674 cattle of all classes then in the State. In 1870 the hay crop amounted to 116,582 tons, or about 360 pounds per head of cattle at that time in the State; in 1860 the hay crop was 143,499 tons, which was a little less than 270 pounds per head for the cattle in the State. In 1850 less than 200 pounds of hay for each of the cattle then in Tennessee was made, the total yield of hay having then been 74,091 tons; from which it appears that considerable progress has been made in hay production, and that there may be reason for the belief expressed that the time will come when plenty of hay will be made in the State to liberally feed all the cattle through the winters.

Dairying has made considerable progress in Tennessee. Previous to the year 1880 no account was found in the census reports of the General Government of the manufacture of cheese in factories. In the report of 1880, however, it was shown that there was made in the State 3,600 pounds of factory butter, and 9,000 pounds of factory cheese. The growth of the dairy interest is shown by the figures which follow:

Years.	Butter.		Cheese.		Milk.	
	Farm.	Factory.	Farm.	Factory.	Quantity.	Per cow.
	Pounds.	*Pounds.*	*Pounds.*	*Pounds.*	*Gallons.*	*Gallons.*
1850	8,139,585	....	177,681	....	....	....
1860	10,017,787	....	135,575	....	....	....
1870	9,571,069	....	142,240	....	3,586,137	14.7
1880	17,886,369	3,600	98,740	9,000	3,688,607	26.6

The circumstances described above are fully as favorable to the development of dairying as the best known in States that have long held the foremost places in the dairying industry in America, with the one exception that in those States there have been, in the many populous towns they contain, a greater number of active home markets than Tennessee possesses. But Tennessee has several lines of railroad crossing the State, and the Mississippi River on the west to furnish ready means of transportation for her surplus productions. There seems, therefore, to be ample grounds for the belief, confidently held by many Tennesseans, that their State is destined to become widely known as one of the leading butter and cheese producing States of the Union.

Respectfully submitted.

EDWARD W. PERRY.

CHICAGO, ILL., *January* 1, 1887.

CALF-RAISING ON THE PLAINS.

HON. NORMAN J. COLMAN,
Commissioner of Agriculture:

SIR: Persons who have never seen the west bank of the Missisissippi are nevertheless able to maintain from their own experiencs and observation that this is a very large country. But there are very few people who really comprehend how large it is. And the first thing which will impress one who makes the range of industry of the United States the subject of investigation will be the immense area over which it is extended and in which it must, for many years at least, be recognized as a leading interest. Drawing a line from Galveston northward to the southwestern corner of Manitoba, and making due allowance for the purely agricultural part of Texas, everything west to the summit of the Sierra Nevadas may be classed as included in the range country. This is an area containing a million and a half square miles, or a thousand million acres, and (not counting Alaska) is about one-half the total area of the United States, and equal in extent to thirty-seven States as large as Ohio.

In different portions of this vast area are presented almost every possible variation of surface and physical features—level plains in one place, mountains in another, great stretches which can be classed properly neither as plain nor mountain, low valleys, and high plateaus. Every variety of soil is also presented, from coarse gravel and shifting sands, in which scarcely any vegetable growth can be maintained, up through every possible grade and shade to the deep alluvium of the valleys and the rich mold on the mountain benches. But there is one common climatic condition which in one respect gives this area a similar character throughout. This is the scant rains in the late summer and autumn, whereby the growth of the native grasses is arrested, and they become dried and cured into natural hay as they stand, constituting a winter feed which is impossible in more humid regions. It is this peculiarity which distinguishes the range country from all others, and which renders the range industry possible. But for this peculiarity it would be impossible for cattle to subsist in the open air more than half the year.

THE NATURAL GRASSES OF THE RANGE COUNTRY.

There is an almost endless variety of native grasses growing in different localities. At the New Orleans Exposition there was a display of about 200 different grasses found in the State of Texas, and an equally large collection has been made of the grasses native to Colorado. Even of the principal grasses there are of each several varieties. Many of these grasses, however, from their limited growth and narrow range, are of little importance in a grazing sense. One of the principal grasses is the gama-grass (commonly known as the mesquite or buffalo), the *Bouteloua oligostachya* of the botanists. Another is the buffalo or false mesquite, the *Buchlœ dactyloides* of the botanists. Another prominent grass is blue-stem or blue-joint (*Agropyrum glaucum*). Then there are the so-called bunch-grasses in great variety, of which *Ericoma cuspidatata* is the principal and most widely disseminated, growing from California to the British Possessions, and eastward through the interior to the Missouri River. Rye-grasses also flourish in some localities.

All of the grasses named are of slight growth, but highly nutritious. Their quantity can be largely increased by the application of water where conveniences exist for irrigation, but not to such an extent it is thought as to give as good returns for the expense and labor as can be afforded by tame grasses. The blue-stem especially responds most liberally to the application of water, but it has been noticed that its quality suffers greatly, and that it is reduced in nutritive value below that of timothy hay—whereas grown upon non-irrigated land it ranked much higher. As it constitutes the main winter feed, a season favorable to a luxuriant growth will in some measure impair the excellence of feed on the range during the succeeding winter months.

A VAST AREA MUST BE PERMANENTLY DEVOTED TO GRAZING.

Much of the great area of land embraced in the range country is of course capable of cultivation. There are numerous fertile valleys in the more mountainous portion and vast stretches upon the plains which by irrigation can be made suitable for successful agriculture. But deducting these there remains a vast area—the major part of the whole—which can not be farmed; at any rate until through increasing population the rewards of agriculture become so much greater than at present as to justify new methods and much greater expense being put upon the land to render it productive, than would be considered practicable in the light of present experience and conditions. This great area must either remain idle and unproductive or be given over to grazing for a period of time sufficiently great as to justify this being regarded as their permanent use. That they will not be permitted to remain unproductive in this practical age, when men are everywhere seeking avenues for the employment of both capital and labor, is quite certain. In fact, these lands are practically pretty well stocked already, possibly excepting restricted localities here and there. Some few Indian reservations, seemingly large when considered by themselves, but insignificant in area when compared with the whole grazing country, remain to be covered with herds as the Indian question is again adjusted to meet the fresh requirements of the white man. But, aside from these, there is nowhere room which some one does not claim and consider very well stocked.

There may be, as has been suggested by some writers on this subject, considerable changes to come over the range industry as time progresses. But it will always remain a range industry, and necessity in one way and another will bring about an increase in its production. If the larger owners give way to those of smaller pretensions, the land will likely be more closely utilized than at present, and more cattle raised to a given area. If, on the other hand, the large owners absorb the holdings of the smaller, it will be through an acquisition of the actual title of such land as will secure absolute control of the ranges. The increased investment will not only stimulate but fairly compel improvement in methods and greater care to secure the highest possible product. And the result will be the same—more cattle.

THE SUSTAINING CAPACITY OF THE RANGE.

In estimating the carrying capacity of the range, it is generally calculated that 40 acres should be allowed to a steer. But the calculation is a very rough one, and there is nothing certain about it, although it is likely much too high. There are locations on the high "divides," so remote from water, that while affording excellent grass but little of it can be utilized, and is not sought by cattle except in seasons of great scarcity. Then there are great plains of disintegrated rock and loose, shifting materials, which produce little useful vegetation. There are plains where the soil and water are impregnated to a damaging degree with alkalies. There are great ranges of abrupt mountains, where the country is so broken and much of it is so steep and high as to be practically useless, and where the grazing areas are practically confined to the valleys or parks on occasionally favorable slopes. As a rule, there are few stock ranges in which at some point there is not more or less, and often a great deal, of comparatively unproductive land. So no one knows just how much it does take to graze a steer, and whether it be 40 acres in one place and less than 40 in another will depend upon the local conditions and the season. The Texas State Land Board is said to have calculated 10 acres to be sufficient in the case of lands belonging to that State, but the cattle men claim 30. Possibly there is a medium between the two which more nearly represents the true point.

There are now not far from 10,000,000 cattle maintained upon the range. With one to each 40 acres, the range is capable of sustaining [illegible],000,000 head. And if it should be demonstrated that it has a higher average maintaining capacity than one steer to each 40 acres, the range stock can be correspondingly increased. The difference of a single acre would permit of an increase of a million head in the aggregate number of cattle. However, in considering these totals and the possibilities they suggest, a large deduction must be made for the millions of sheep and horses also maintained upon the range, and which, in proportion to their numbers, limit the number of cattle maintained in their vicinity. But whether 40 acres are required or less than 40 acres, one thing is quite certain, that it takes a great deal more than any one who has never been upon the range would suppose. The native grasses are not strong and luxuriant growers, and even if moisture and all the conditions of soil and surface were favorable would not produce heavily. And as their period of growth is confined mainly to the spring and early summer, when they are stimulated by an occasional rain they produce very little in point of weight and bulk, and their admirable quality is not sufficient to compensate for their lack of quantity. These matters controlling the sustaining capacity of the range are important in forming any correct estimate of the business; for whether a person has one steer or a thousand, he must have room on a scale to which the sober agricultural experience of older and in many respects more favored regions is quite a stranger.

FAIR-SIZED HERDS ESSENTIAL TO SUCCESSFUL BUSINESS.

There is an old saying that "one should not carry all his eggs in one basket," but if circumstances require that they all go into one basket it would seem to be prudent that the basket be large and that there be plenty of eggs. In that event there is a likelihood that some of them will remain unbroken in any contingency. The rangeman, through the force of circumstances, is compelled to place all his eggs in one basket—he can produce nothing but live stock. If there comes a season of drought, which diminishes the feed and prevents a due proportion of cattle from getting fat and renders inevitable heavier losses than usual the succeeding winter, he can *recoupe* from no other crop. If the market is unfavorable for his one product he has no other to sell. If beef is low in price he has nothing high in price. If the time to sell is unpropitious and money is to be made by holding he can not wait. If there comes a disastrous storm everything he has is exposed. His cattle are drifted far away by storms and may or may not be wholly recovered, and certainly not without considerable expense, and losses are often encountered which would bankrupt an Eastern farmer. Under such circumstances the range man has only one recourse—to raise enough cattle to make his business renumerative despite these disadvantages. And he must have room for this additional stock and must maintain a herd out of proportion, in point of numbers, to what would be necessary on inclosed farms in the Eastern States.

Then there are certain incidents of the business growing out of the wandering and intermixture of cattle of different owners, which fix a limit to which it would seem the range interest can be subdivided among many owners, and which require, if it be conducted successfully at all, that it be upon a certain scale. One must at least be allowed, first, the maintenance of enough cattle to return the cost of the least help, horses, and other expenses, with which a small herd can be managed and the annual losses made good; and, second, enough additional cattle to make a living business. This much would constitute a very small owner in the arid regions—one not in position to make or aspire to a large income—but he would be considered a large owner and a large occupier of land in any other region.

To what extent public policy will favor larger operations than those described is a matter of opinion upon which many people differ and which it is not the purpose of the present paper to discuss. However, it is worthy of remark, in leaving this branch of the subject, that a very large proportion of range men now in the country are doing a business not above that outlined, and a very considerable proportion of remaining range men have a business not greatly exceeding these limits. The number of large owners counting their cattle by the thousands of head is very small.

It is not impossible that, as the settlements encroach from the east and the settlements upon irrigated lands multiply and widen upon the west (for more and more land seems coming under the irrigated process without any visible increase in the volume of the streams) the conditions now surrounding the range industry will be greatly modified, especially throughout that large section of country located east of the mountains. If ordinary agriculture can not everywhere be carried on, something, perhaps, in the way of cattle forage may be raised in situations where it is now thought to be impossible.

New grasses, too, may be introduced; and, in short, the business brought nearer the conditions which prevail in the older States, such as cattle receiving care in winter and perhaps subject to more restraint, if not actually maintained in inclosed pastures, during the summer. But, without speculating further upon these altered conditions which the future may have in store, it is the present purpose to give some account of the business as it is now conducted, under the conditions, natural and otherwise, by which it is at present surrounded.

THE RANGE—HOW MUCH LAND SHOULD BE OWNED.

Taking things as he finds them, about the only course a rangeman can pursue, whether he owned few cattle or many, is to turn them out and let them run. Cattle when turned out in this way, unless they attempt to regain an old range, which they seldom do if removed any great distance from it, unless driven by stress of weather or feed, are not likely to pass beyond natural boundaries. Thus, if turned out upon a water-course, they are not likely to pass over the "divide" to another, unless it be near by, but may generally be found somewhere upon the slopes or water-shed of the stream upon which they were originally placed, or wandering to the next stream, are likely to remain there. They seldom pass over a high mountain, and especially if much timbered. So, when a ranchman turns out cattle he has a tolerable conception of the boundaries within which they will ordinarily graze, and within which most of them will, under usual conditions, be found. This he terms his "range."

He should have a home ranch or headquarters, which should be located at such point as will permit of the range being worked and overlooked with the greatest convenience. Here are corrals for holding cattle and branding, and some accommodations provided for the horses which do not happen to be with the herd. Of course water is an indispensable requisite here, and, if possible, a location is secured adjacent to natural meadows where hay can be cut for the winter feeding of weak cows, the horses which may be kept up, and such other stock as can be taken care of in this way. These natural meadows are generally in the valleys or "bottoms," as they are termed, of the streams, which, while perhaps showing no continuous flowing water during most of the year, are marked by a line of "water holes," where the water comes into view, and carry more or less water under ground, which in favorable soil and situations rises to the surface through capillary attraction, in sufficient quantities to sustain a luxuriant growth of grass. There is very little water found beyond the beds of the streams, and springs, such as occur at frequent intervals in the East, are of rare occurrence in the grazing regions, except in the more mountainous portions.

Some additional land, beside that embraced in the home ranch, should be owned at other points on the range sought to be occupied, but where the number of cattle owned is small and the operations of the owner correspondingly restricted, the water and land of the home ranch is all that is generally sought to be acquired. Owners of large herds, whose cattle naturally graze over a wide expanse of country, say from 25 to 100 miles, or even more, from one extreme to the other, have several ranches located at convenient points upon the range. Many of these, however, are only designed for temporary occupancy, and are simply provided with "dug-outs" for the men (a cave-like house, half under ground, the earth from the excavation forming the roof and sides), and other appliances on a similarly crude scale. These owners of the larger herds endeavor to acquire the title to as much of the land on their range containing water as they possibly can, not only for the purpose of preventing the location upon their range of other herds, which would shorten the supply of feed for their own stock, but also because the ownership of water, according to range customs, gives a better right than could otherwise be claimed to maintain cattle upon the adjacent grazing lands.

It is not considered just the thing in any locality already stocked with cattle, to turn out an additional number without owning some water in the vicinity. But there are people engaged in the business who do not own any land whatever, and occasionally there are those who do not even have a ranch or headquarters, and who give the business no further attention than to attend the "round-ups." Of course such persons must make arrangements to work with some one else. In localities where water is very abundant its ownership is not considered as carrying with it the same grazing privileges as where it is more scarce. And the ranges are in some of these localities already so fully occupied, at least in the estimation of those already there, that strenuous objection is made to the turning out of more cattle, even though the owner may acquire land with water.

THE BOUNDARIES OF RANGES NOT DEFINED.

The ranges of different people are not separated from those of other persons by any definite boundaries, but on the contrary overlap each other in every conceivable manner, and the ranges of the larger owners contain within their boundaries those claimed by many small owners. If the country bordering on the west shore of Lake Michigan, for instance, were a grazing country, and divided into ranges according to the manner in which the arid region is occupied, it might be imagined that some large owner would have cattle grazing all the way from Chicago to Milwaukee, and back perhaps 50 miles west of the lake, and would call this his range. Another man would have his cattle between Chicago and Waukegan, and he would call this his range. Another man, as his range, would name the country between Chicago and Racine. Another man, the country between Waukegan and Milwaukee. Still another might name a narrow belt extending westerly from the lake between Racine and Waukegan. And so the country would be occupied as ranges to its maintaining capacity, each person defining the boundaries of his own range to suit himself and extended enough to sustain his stock, without any reference to what others may regard as their ranges. When a person speaks of his "range," he does not mean to be understood as naming any particular scope of country in which he has or claims exclusive rights, but simply as indicating the boundaries within which most of his cattle will be found under ordinary conditions of weather and feed.

As a rule, the owners of few cattle and the owners of large herds prefer that their c shall be kept somewhat distinct, or at any rate not too muchattlermixed. Accordingly most persons owning but few cattle prefer a location in a broken or hilly country, or in some park or elevated plain encompassed by mountains. Here cattle have more natural protection in case of storms; there is very little danger of their drifting far, and they are more immediately under the owner's eye. And, if the number is not too large, an effort is made to see them all at frequent intervals, and it is the common practice to search the contiguous ranges as often as possible, and drive to their own proper range such cattle as may have wandered. In such broken or hilly country, abounding in ravines and gulches, there is generally water sufficient for stock purposes at convenient distances, and several owners of small herds will settle in as closely to each other as they think desirable. The limited area over which their small herds range, the personal attention they are able to give them, and the knowledge of where this or that "bunch" was last seen, as well as their thorough acquaintance with the country and of the grassy slopes or protected "draws" where cattle are most likely to be found, enable these men to keep a very close track of their business, and to find and care for their animals with more facility than where herds are larger and more widely dispersed. It would be difficult to make a satisfactory "round-up" in such localities where there are so many obstacles to the vision, and so many inequalities and depressions to screen cattle from observation. And the habit these smaller owners have of continually passing among the cattle is not agreeable to the views of the owners of large herds, who do not like to have their cattle moved or disturbed. It is inconvenient, too, in other ways, to have their herds too much intermixed. And so, while the owners of small herds prefer the broken and hilly country, the owners of larger herds seek the more open plains.

CATTLE DRIFTING OR DRIVEN BY STORMS.

Here the cattle drift far and wide. Many miles intervene, oftentimes, between watering p aces, and in na ural grazing, even in the absence of storms to drive them, cattle often wander considerable distances. If feed happens to be short in one locality, as from local drought or overstocking it sometimes is, many cattle are apt to travel as far and long as there is any new country in sight, until a region of better food is encountered. And in winter, when severe storms occur, they turn their heads in an opposite direction and travel before it until some natural shelter is found or the storms subside. It is not unusual for them to cover 100 miles or more before they come to a halt; and as no attempt is made to bring them back before spring, a succession of storms carries them farther and farther away from home, until finally their progress is arrested by some natural obstacle, like a river with a course across that of the prevailing winds. Here they drift up stream or down, sometimes alternately, depending upon which course will bring them most relief from the chilling blast. A northwest wind will send them down stream, for instance, and a northeast force them in the contrary direction. Under unusual stress they will undertake a crossing. The owners have very little definite conception of where they will find them, and as they do not know precisely how many animals they own, or possess any accurate knowledge or description of each animal, they never know how many have been sacrificed to the fury of the elements, or when the whole of the remainder have been recovered. And, in point of fact, would get few of them back but for the comity prevailing among stockmen and the unique system of working the ranges which has been devised to overcome just such obstacles as these to the successful conduct of the grazing business.

But under any system it will readily be seen that a very considerable number of cattle must be lost. The cattle may be driven on to territory where the grass has been destroyed by fire and starve to death after the storm has passed; their movement during a storm may be interrupted by a lined wire fence and many perish; weaker animals may not possess sufficient vitality to endure the exposure; and all may suffer from the lack of water; and thus the danger of heavy losses is an element in the business (even if the losses do not always occur) against which the range man must insure himself, and which must be considered in any estimate of its advantages and profit. One who has his capital exposed to such perils should not be expected to content himself with the moderate returns which, by common consent, are regarded as ample for those who view the world and its belongings from the safe stand-point of an investment in Government bonds,

THE LOSSES ON RANGE CATTLE.

The losses on range cattle are estimated by those in interest anywhere from 3 to 5 or 6 per cent. The estimate seems a low one, but it is only an estimate, and in point of fact there are no means for arriving at any accurate knowledge of what the real losses are. For very obvious reasons, there would be a disposition upon the part of ranch men to underestimate the losses. Even if no one desired to sell, it is human nature to put the best foot forward, and men are everywhere reluctant to admit to themselves that serious losses or mistakes have been made. There is one thing, however, which tends to increase the death-rate much below what would be expected from a comparison with the losses sustained on farm stock. That is, the absence of aged animals on the range. On the farms cows are kept along from year to year on account of some peculiar value as breeders or of special excellence in the dairy. But range men have long since found that old animals will not endure the vicissitudes of the range, and all such are carefully selected out at the "round-ups" and sent to market. So, the animals exposed to the inclemencies of the unfavorable season are those of such ages that they should have their vital powers most vigorous and active and be best able to endure exposure. The storms which cause the losses occur at a season when there are not many very young calves, and if such do die they do not enter into the estimates, because owners do not yet know of their existen e. Then the estimated losses, even if approximately correct, are the *average* losses.

Those which fall upon individuals are frequently very heavy, even in seasons which are favorable generally, and they are more severe in the case of cattle which have been newly brought upon the range, coming late in the season in comparatively low condition, and in the case of cattle (and especially young cattle) the first season from the Eastern States. So, while the losses in the case of cattle which have been for some time upon the range may be small, those that are "through cattle," *i. e.*, cattle which have come through from the extreme Southeastern States that season, may, and oftentimes do, count up to 15, 20, or even 25 per cent., depending upon the season, the character of the range upon which they have been turned, and the opportunities the cattle may have had to recuperate from the effects of their journey before winter sets in.

FIRES UPON THE RANGE.

When fires occur upon the range, as they sometimes do, especially in seasons of unusual rain-fall and more than usual luxuriant grass, great stretches of country, perhaps 100 miles from one extreme to the other, are burned over. Cattle driven by the storm into such a burned territory would certainly starve, unless the storm should prove of sufficient duration to urge them across it. For when the storm subsides the cattle come to a halt, and if in a region affording no feed would wander aimlessly around within a few miles of where they happened to be, and soon perish. Accordingly, precautions are taken to prevent cattle drifting upon extensive burned tracts, and when this can not be prevented, they are generally followed on the first let up of the weather and driven out upon the opposite side.

INCLOSED PASTURES—WINTER FEEDING.

If the cattle should be confined in inclosed pastures the business would be deprived of its greatest element of uncertainty, relieved from much of the expense with which it is now burdened, and in every way be placed upon a more satisfactory basis. *If*—but it is a big if in this instance, not a mere stumbling-block, but a veritable mountain in the way, which it seems impossible to avoid until the future brings some of the changed conditions to which reference has been made, and which may or may not follow remotely in her train. In the first place, no one will or ought to be permitted to erect fences and make extensive inclosures on the public domain. In the second place, the carrying capacity of the land is so limited and so much would have to be inclosed to maintain a herd of only fair proportions, even in the most favorable of seasons, that it is doubtful if the expense of making and keeping up the fences would not more than overcome all the advantages which, under the most favorable circumstances, could be realized from their employment. It will be understood that, aside from the mountain districts, the country furnishes nothing in the way of fencing materials, that everything has to be brought in by rail, and transported considerable distances by wagons after reaching the range country. So nowhere else does fencing cost as much as here. And, finally, fences introduce some new difficulties peculiarly their own, and are, besides, an element of danger to the cattle of the owners as well as to those of other stockmen.

If a drifting herd encounters a fence in a storm its progress is arrested, and, unable to move forward and unwilling to move backward in the face of the storm, the cattle stand still or move but little along the line of the barrier, and a large percentage freeze to death. The fences, therefore, would often serve to hold cattle to be starved if some effort were not made to relieve them. Fires sweeping over a few miles are not of rare occurrence; and while these small affairs make no perceptible difference in the available feed of an open range, they would serve to destroy, for that season, the feed in an inclosed pasture which happened to be within their limits, and compel the removal of the cattle.

The amount of feed upon the range, and consequently the carrying capacity, depends upon the rains which fall during the growing season. And these are by no means equally distributed, as the storms by which they are accompanied sweep across the country in belts, not always favoring the same strip of territory in successive seasons, giving the normal amount of moisture in one locality and depositing very little in another. So, after having provided an inclosed pasture, the owner would find that some seasons, owing to local droughts, it would be comparatively worthless, and he would rest under the disadvantage of never knowing in advance, so as to calculate upon them, when these unfavorable seasons would occur.

The same peculiarity marks the course of the winter storms, and belts of snow 10 to 20 miles wide extend for some distance across the plains, while on either side is bare ground and good feed, which the cattle, unrestrained, will find. Confined within a pasture in the snow belts the cattle will be unable to find subsistence and must inevitably perish. If released to seek feed they are turned loose at the very season when the owner hoped to have them confined, and all the expense of "rounding up" and the dangers and losses of drifting must be met, the same as if no pasture had been provided. And having incurred the expense of fencing a pasture, which could not be depended upon to save a dollar in the expense of management or avert any of the losses usually attendant upon the business, the owner must maintain a sufficient force of men during the winter to "round up" the cattle whenever an unusual snow occurs, and get them outside of his inclosure before they starve to death; and if fencing were general, the coveted feed would likely be within some other person's inclosure or beyond it where it could not be reached; so that inside the fence or outside the cattle might fare very poorly. Fencing, with present conditions, does not seem feasible, and the only practical course to pursue with cattle seems to be to let them roam at pleasure, following their own instincts.

At any rate, unless some provision can be made for winter feeding, the general experience of the range appears to be against the practice of placing cattle behind fences. If provision is to be made for winter feeding a less number of cattle under one management would be a necessity, and while from a large number of owners and better cattle the quantity of beef produced might be as great or greater than now, the industry of its production would cease to be a range industry. With what has been accomplished in the past in the way of rendering the whilom "American Desert" productive, no one will attempt to fix a limit to the developments of the future. But at the present time, regarding the matter from the standpoint of present experience and methods, no one can see just how or when it will be possible, as a general thing, to winter feed in inclosures for the cattle which are able to fpedvthemselves in the arid region.

THE CLIMATE AND STORMS OF THE ARID REGION.

With reference to climate the grazing regions are much the same throughout, possessing a degree of uniformity in this respect much greater than would be supposed, considering their wide stretch from north to south, and the difference in the altitude of different sections. This is doubtless mainly due to the lack of humidity in the atmosphere. During the summer months the temperature, as measured by the thermometer, rises in the middle hours of the day fully as high as would in any other climate be consistent with tolerable comfort. But here the heat is seldom felt to be as oppressive as elsewhere, and is certainly less debilitating in its effects. There is an almost constant refreshing breeze, often a good strong wind, and the air contains so little vapor that a rapid evaporation is maintained on all moist surfaces, and perspiration disappears as quickly as it is formed, absorbing and carrying off the heat from all animal bodies. The nights throughout the season, when they are so oppressive elsewhere, are deliciously cool throughout the grazing regions, refreshing the healthy system and restoring the vital powers to their perfect tension. The autumn comes on early, and the delightful Indian summer of other regions is here prolonged far into the winter months. There are but few days in the year when the sun is not at some time visible, and days and weeks of clear, bright weather lengthen out, oftentimes into months, with scarcely a storm (if winds are excepted) to interrupt the almost unending succession of pleasant days.

Taking the winter months, though more storms occur, the climate is simply incomparable, and a majority of the days are scarcely paralleled by the finest days of the later autumn. The air is a little more crisp, a chill comes on towards evening, and deepens into a sharp freezing temperature as the night proceeds. But the morning comes as if one might imagine another summer was at hand, and the bright skies and balmy air impart a tone to nerve and spirit such as no other region can give. And even the cold, when it does come, if the air be not in too rapid motion, is of that dry nature which robs it of half its terrors.

But while this is the rule, the picture is sometimes subject to very rude changes. Near by are lofty mountains, around whose summits the weather for the continent is chiefly made, and occasionally a sample is dropped close at hand, quite different from that which is ordinarily experienced. And so it occurs that the grazing regions are subject to sudden and extreme alterations of temperature, and storms of great severity sometimes occur. They are not frequent, however, or greatly protracted, for the low degree of humidity in the atmosphere is such that heavy snows are rare, and such phenomenal falls as are sometimes experienced in the East are impossible. When snow storms occur, accompanied by a low temperature and a heavy wind, the cattle drift badly, as has been already described, and it would be impossible for any living thing to face them for any length of time. But many snow-storms occur—in fact, the majority are of this character—which are not accompanied by sufficient wind to move the cattle to any great extent. The mantle comes down with no more disturbance of the elements than is common in other regions. Such storms, however, are much lighter in volume than are usual elsewhere, and seldom lay so long upon the ground that one fall comes down upon another.

The region is eminently a windy one, and within a day or two after the storm has gone the wind is pretty sure to come, and often the storm brings the wind immediately in its train, and simply retreats as it advances. The wind catches up the light snow, whirls it around in every direction, wearing it out as it were, until it seems largely absorbed by the atmosphere, and piles much of the remainder in great drifts in the low places. The sun, too, seems to possess unusual power in this clear air. And between the wind and the sun bare spots quickly appear upon the southern exposures, and these enlarging under the same influences miles and miles of southerly slopes facing the sun are soon free from snow, giving the cattle a chance to feed.

Where the wind does not quickly succeed the storms, however the case is not so favorable, for the sun thaws the top of the snow and congealing at night, a surface is presented upon which the ordinary winds do not rapidly work, and the snow is likely to remain for some time or disappears very slowly, unless a "chinook" comes to the range man's relief. The peculiar wind to which this name is given comes from the southwest, and occurs at intervals during the winter months, but does not blow with any regularity. It comes with variable strength, sometimes almost akin to a gale, and is as warm and genial as if coming from a region of perennial summer. Neither snow nor ice will long withstand its touch, and whirling into every hollow and behind and around every ledge of rocks or obstruction, it cuts away the snow wherever it hides. When the "chinook" reigns, shade and sunshine, night or day, are all the same, and everywhere the work of frost destruction goes on. It is wonderful to observe what this wind can do in the way of getting rid of snow. In a few hours it will remove a covering which in the Eastern States would not disappear in several weeks of the most favorable winter weather.

THE TRYING TIME FOR CATTLE—FEEDING HAY IN WINTER NOT PRACTICABLE.

The cattle endure the winter storms very well, and also the occasional periods when deprived of feed. But if the winter has been one of frequent and severe storms, or if the previous season was unfavorable to an abundant food-supply, so that they do not go into the winter in good condition, they come out considerably the worse for wear in the spring. Indeed, the condition upon which they enter the winter has almost everything to do in determining the manner in which they endure its privations, and range men, therefore, are especially solicitous about feed in the fall, and careful that cattle are not moved or traveled or unnecessarily disturbed late in the season. If there are no bad spring storms then cattle pick up quickly as soon as grass starts, which in favorable seasons it will do sometimes in April. But there sometimes occurs an unfavorable spring after a bad winter, and the storms which then come upon cattle, when thin and weak, tell more severely upon them in the way of losses than any which have been before encountered. The spring storms are usually wet, if not rain, damp snow, or a mixture of both rain and snow, and they are usually more sluggish about clearing up than the winter storms. The animals, wet to the skin, and chilled through from the unusual and continued loss of heat consumed in the evaporation of water with which their coats are saturated, have their powers of endurance sorely taxed, and it is right here that the most serious losses among acclimated cattle occur.

These storms are especially severe upon weaker animals, whose vitality has been strongly drawn upon and powers of resistance well nigh exhausted by the winter's exposure. Cows which have suckled calves until late in the fall, or perhaps into the winter months, generally give out, if at all, on these final trials, and calves coming too early in the season have a tough time of it if such weather is encountered.

It is scarcely practicable to secure hay with which to feed range cattle in case of emergency. There are only occasional localities where hay in quantity can be cut, and to range men in general it is a very scarce commodity. And even were it in sufficient supply the cattle could not be secured and the hay fed at such times as cattle need it most. For, at the first appearance of the storm, when the icy particles first come riding upon the wind, their instincts teach them to move, and it would be almost impossible to stop or turn them back against the hourly increasing storm. And, generally, at such times, the weather is such that it would not be safe for anyone to expose himself to it for any length of time. Besides, if range cattle are rounded in a few times and fed hay, they are prone to linger around the place where they have been fed, or in sight of the stacks, and manifest a reluctance to return to distant grazing even after the ground is bare and the last vestige of the storms have disappeared, and in their self-imposed abstinence very seriously impair their condition.

With a small number of cattle and a locality where hay could be cut in quantity, winter feeding would be possible with cattle confined in inclosures of such moderate size that they could be quickly gathered when wanted and conveniently dispersed. But for large herds it is not practicable to winter feed, and throughout most of the range country hay can not even be secured to feed small herds. Such range men as can secure hay generally do so, but its use is mainly restricted to weak cows, or cows with early calves, to bulls if any are kept up, and to the small number of horses in actual use, and no effort is made to winter feed the general herd.

Horses, by the way, endure the range conditions better than cattle, and it is a cold day when they are compelled to leave their accustomed grounds or suffer from want of feed. The horse will paw away the snow which covers his feeding-ground, appearing to understand perfectly what he will find beneath it and how to reach it. With cattle the case is different. If the snow conceals the feed they do not seem to know what has become of it, and if, in trampling about, accident exposes some of it, they do not seem encouraged to search for more in its vicinity. They could either root or paw, but these resorts seem to be beyond their instinct or reasoning powers.

MAKING A START—THE MATTER OF BRANDS.

In starting in the range business, a location having been selected, the first step is to secure a herd of females. If only a few are required they can be picked up readily here and there from the owners of small lots, who are willing to sell almost any way. But if a large number is desired it is not so easy to obtain them, for the owners of considerable herds, although they may have a surplus of the very kind of stock desired, are unwilling to sell animals of their brand to remain on the range. They wish to be in position to maintain that every animal on the range bearing their brand belongs undeniably to them. And this they could not do if they made the practice of selling cattle to all comers. The brand would then lose its significance as an indication of ownership. Some protection against this confusion might be secured by counterbranding, *i. e.*, giving an additional brand, whenever an animal is sold, to indicate that fact. But this is not a complete protection, though often practiced, since there is no way of detection should the counterbrand be dishonestly applied by some other person. So if one desires to purchase a number of females already in the range country, he will generally be compelled to purchase some brand outright (many range men have several different brands), or go to some distant part of the range country, where an owner may be willing to sell in view of the removal of the cattle to such a distance that none of them will find their way back to the locality where his remaining cattle graze. Or, as it is more generally done, contracts are made for young cattle to be brought up from Texas, or heifers are brought in from the Eastern States. And for stocking the more northeasterly ranges, Oregon and Montana have contributed a great many young cattle.

The cattle to stock the range having been delivered, the new owner places his own brand upon them in addition to the others they already bear. If, however, he has bought an entire brand, which would pass to him the ownership of all cattle bearing it, whether few or many, or whether delivered or undelivered, the rebranding is not necessary, and the owner contents himself with simply placing his own brand upon the increase. And sometimes even this course is not pu su , but the calves are continuously given the same brand as their mothers, and the brand thus kept alive.

Brands, it may be stated, are devised by the owners to suit their own taste or fancy. They are almost infinite in variety, and many of them fairly hideons in proportions. Size, however, is an element which can not be entirely ignored, for the branding tool must contain sufficient metal to hold the heat for some little time, and the lines of the design must therefore possess a certain width. Then they must be a certain distance apart to prevent the different parts from burning together. Thus the letters O or S, if made of considerable size, can be very clearly shown in a brand, and even such more complicated lines, as in the figure 8; but if these were made quite small the whole inner portion of the characters would be burned, and the brand would simply become a blotch, and any resemblance to the design employed traced with difficulty from the outer borders. And in another respect good size is important, as it must be sufficiently distinct to enable it to be made out clearly with the steer on the run and at some little distance away. Cattle will not remain quiet and allow a person to approach and examine their brand at his leisure, but whoever desires to examine their brand on the range must make his own opportunity as best he can, have a good horse and the nerve to ride it.

To facilitate the reading of brands under these difficulties different persons place their brands in a different position, some upon the shoulder, some upon the side, some upon the thigh, some on the right side and some on the other. Then it is only necessary to examine such brands closely as are in the right position. Some range men, for a similar reason, cut off the tip of one ear or the other, or cut bits or notches on the sides, or cut slits in the dewlaps, so that one or two particles of skin hang pendant. But while brands must be necessarily of good size, there is no reason why they should cover the whole side of an animal, and sometimes both sides, as is often the case.

There has been much written concerning branding from a humanitarian standpoint. It is undoubtedly an act of cruelty. But if cattle are to run at large in the grazing country it seems necessary that a brand shall be imposed for the purposes of identification. It is not necessary, however, to use brands so large as those usually employed. Neither does it seem necessary to use so many brands, and much of the rebranding could be dispensed with.

There is another aspect of the branding question which is worthy of serious consideration in the matter of the value of the hides from branded animals. The brand affects the fiber of the hide, and no process of tanning will restore it to the same excellence as the unbranded portions. So when an animal is covered all over with these heavy brands—shoulders, sides, and thighs on both sides scarred and seared everywhere from the effects of the barbarous red-hot iron—the greater value of the hide for leather is destroyed. Good leather of no grade can be made from it. It lacks the smoothness necessary to the finer grades of leather, and it is wanting in that uniform strength and closeness of texture equally necessary in the heavier grades. It has recently been stated by competent authority that the commercial value of many hides are impaired several dollars each by the unnecessary or careless use of the branding-iron. Certainly there is room for a great reform in reducing the size and number of brands, and in placing them on the most undesirable part for leather making, without depriving the range man of any of the protection or much of the convenience which he secures through the branding system.

A brand, when selected, can usually be recorded with some authority designated by law. In Colorado, until recently, the brands of each county were recorded with the county clerks of the several counties. Now, however, by recent law, they are recorded with the secretary of State, and a brand book, containing a description of all the recorded brands in the State, is published by State authority. When duly recorded a brand becomes the personal property of the owner, and he is protected by law in its exclusive use. No one but he can use or record the same brand, or introduce the same as evidence in any court of justice. The recorded brand upon an animal is made prima facia evidence of its ownership, and in case of suit in court, if either party proves his brand to be upon the animal the identification and ownership is regarded as complete, and can only be overthrown by direct proof that the brand had been wrongfully applied. So, if a man brand his cattle with a brand which some other man had previously used and recorded, he would simply place the other man in position to claim his cattle, and himself under obligations to prove, in every case, his own ownership as against the brand. No man cuts off his own nose, and no one adopts another's recorded brand.

THE NUMBER OF BULLS NECESSARY.—TOO FEW PROVIDED.

In turning out bulls upon the range, not less than one should be provided for each twenty-five females, and even a greater proportion of bulls would be much better, and insure a heavier calf drop. As a matter of fact, however, there are but few range men who maintain bulls in the proportion of one to twenty-five cows, and many of them fall sadly short of this limit. This is one of the matters in which an intensely "economical" person can very largely appropriate the result of a neighbor's superior enterprise and public spirit, and it is to be regretted that so many range men are willing to make a little off their neighbors in this way. When bulls are turned upon the range there is no way of controlling them in the matter of whose cows receive their services. If every owner maintained bulls of equal quality and number in proportion to his females, then it would make little difference, for each one would bear a burden and share an expense in proportion to benefits received. But, when one man turns out a proper number of bulls, and another but a few, some one has acted very meanly, and there are many peop on the ranges who are not above it. The man who turns out bu few knows that most of his cows will owe their calves to his neighbor's bulls, and that his own bulls are not capable of serving a correspondingly large number of cows in return. The failure of th one party to turn out his proportion reduces the proportion of bulls upon the range, and this means a reduction in the calf drop, from which the range men who have turned out the proper number must suffer in the same measure as the shirks. It is very exasperating to have neighbors of this character, but many have them, and it greatly discourages the liberality of those who are disposed to be liberal to see themselves persistently imposed upon in this way by men whose indignation would flash in an instant if any one were to describe their conduct as dishonest. Some range men, too, when their neighbor has turned out a due proportion of improved bulls, of which their cows will receive the common service, endeavor to satisfy unkind gossip while still gratifying their innate meanness of spirit by turning out their proportion of bulls in the shape of the cheapest and most inferior animals they have been able to buy. They thus get half the benefit of the good bulls upon the range, and their neighbor pays for both of them.

Nothing could be imagined more discouraging than this to the effort and disposition of enlightened and liberal men to improve the character of range cattle, by the employment of a better class of bulls. But if all range men were fair and just in this matter, it is undeniable that many of those who turn out the largest number of bulls would turn out in still greater proportion than now, and that all would be encouraged to secure better bulls, and thus the character and value of the entire range stock be placed in the way of more improvement than it is likely to know while men are permitted to prey in this way upon their neighbors.

One peculiarity which renders a larger number of bulls more necessary upon the range than elsewhere, is the nature of cattle to separate into "bunches." No matter how numerous, they are not often seen in vast herds spread over the plain, but rather in small groups of varying numbers. In certain conditions of the feed or weather these bunches may be close together, but are generally separated at considerable distances. With one bunch of cows there may be two or three bulls (though in such cases if the bunch is small the master animal drives the others away), while other bunches of cows will be without a bull. Often a bull will bunch with two or three or a half dozen cows, when the complement assigned him is at least twenty-five by every honest calculation, and perhaps forty or fifty in the actual state of affairs on the particular range. Sometime attention is given to the breaking up of these little bunches, and bringing the bulls into more general association with the cows in the herd, but generally very little is attempted in this line, unless in the cases of bunches which happen to fall under notice in the course of other range work.

THE MANAGEMENT OF BULLS.

It is the general practice on the range to let the bulls run with the herd the year around. Lately there has been some attention given to separating the bulls from the herd in the fall, and close herding them in some locality where the feed is better than usual, or confining them in small inclosures where they can be fed, and restoring them to the herd about July 1. There is a great advantage in this practice, or would be if it were generally pursued, as it would prevent any calves being dropped so early in the spring as to be exposed to bad storms, and the bulls, being maintained in better heat and condition, would give more calves and better ones, and there would be much less mortality among the bulls. But while there is danger of too early calves with bulls always in the herd, the number dropped at this unfavorable season is not large, for both cows and bulls are weak and thin, and there is not much disposition to exercise the procreative powers until both get again into condition, which does not ordinarily occur until the close of June, which is about the most advantageous time for range calves to be sired. So the bulk of the calves, anyway, will come about the right time. But it is best to separate the bulls and keep them out of the herd if practicable, for some calves are seen under the contrary rule to come at a season of the year when there is danger of losing not only them but their dams also.

The mortality among bulls is very great when they are allowed to run out. In some cases, when the losses in the general herd will fall below 5 per cent., the mortality among bulls may mount up to five times that much. A bull that has been hard worked during the fall months, following the cows and wearing off the fat of which he should be accumulating a store, is in poor shape to go through the winter. Bulls more sluggish in disposition, and serving less cows, will stand the winter in better shape, oftentimes as well as a steer. But if a bull winters like a steer it is likely due very largely to the fact that he passed the summer and fall much like a steer. So it is often the case that the very bulls which succumb to the stress of the winter are the very ones which are most valuable on the range, and those which survive are the ones which could be spared the best. If bulls could be gathered and fed all this would be obviated. But it involves a good deal of labor and expense to gather and distribute them again, and many authorities on range matters maintain that, from a purely financial point of view, there is no advantage in gathering, and the practice of the range is certainly against it—*i. e.*, does not follow it—the owners of the largest herds allowing their bulls to run, and turning out a certain proportion of new ones each season.

It has been urged as a desirable innovation in the general management of range bulls that each person gather and feed the bulls he finds in his own immediate locality, regardless of brand and ownership, turning them out again at the same place at the proper season, charging the owners as ascertained from the brands with their keep. This would save most of the expense attending the gathering and distribution of bulls, but it is quite obvious that such an arrangement, while perfectly fair and of mutual benefit, could only be entered upon through personal agreement. It is a practice pursued in a few instances by owners of contiguous ranges, but so far has failed of general adoption.

Referring again to the unusual mortality among bulls, it may be stated that in addition to the relative condition in which different animals entering the winter, the manner in which they endure its privations is controlled, also, in a large degree, by the local conditions of the range as to feed and water, or that portion of it in which they happen to be located. There is also as strong a constitutional difference in individual cattle to withstand exposure as ther is in the constitutional powers in the same regard of individua men. The losses in bulls were formerly much less than now, show ing how powerful a factor abundant feed is in safely carrying the through the winter season. When the range was indifferently stocked there was good feed everywhere, and even if a bull did hap pen to work then in the fall, and enter upon the winter in low con dition, the chances were that he would pull through. Now, how ever, with feed so short that it is practically impossible to maintai condition during the winter months, to say nothing of improvement there are many chances against a thin bull which were not counted in the early days of the range industry.

This increase in the mortality of the bulls, growing as the range became more fully occupied and the feed shorter, at first led range men to suspect there was a lack in the hardihood of the bulls; but later experience and a wider observation has satisfied the most intelligent that the principal trouble has been a decrease in the sustaining power of the ranges.

A large number of bulls are bred in the range country or in the near-by agricultural districts; and these bulls, reared at a high altitude and within or on the borders of the range country, are turned upon the range when past one year old to two. Bulls raised in the East should be a year older, as the transition from the farm to the range and from one altitude to another is pretty sure to be followed by considerable interruption of normal health and vigor, and, in the case of young animals, results in more or less arrest of development which is seldom regained. Bulls raised east are, for this reason, of very little actual service the same season as introduced upon the range. It would be best to bring them into the range country during the fall or early winter and keep them in inclosures where they can be appropriately cared for until the proper time arrives for turning them with the cows, which is about the middle of the summer. Bulls handled in this way become thoroughly acclimatized during a period when their services are not required, and are, besides, under the owner's immediate care and eye, and can receive any attention which may be necessary during this trying period. But, nevertheless, many range men delay the purchase of bulls until about the time they need them, and until grass upon the range is such that they can turn them out without any previous preparation. It is short-sighted policy, however, as they get but few calves, and while they go through the summer well enough, they are of little use until the next season, and if no winter care is given their numbers are certain to be very much decimated.

PURE-BRED VS. GRADE BULLS FOR RANGE PURPOSES.

For the open range the preference seems to be for grade bulls instead of pure-breeds. The latter are as a rule finer in the bone, heavier fleshed in proportion to bone, do not stand fatigue so well in good flesh (for a bull on the range must be something of a traveler), and many believe do not stand the winter so well. But while this is perhaps the general opinion it is by no means universal, for pure-breeds are often turned out with the other cattle and endure the season as well as other bulls. Possibly this result may be due largely to he extent to which the particular range happens to be stocked, and co nsequently better than average feed. But range men, as a rule, have not yet given pure-bred bulls a sufficiently general trial to fully settle the question of their superiority for range purposes. It seems to be an impression among them that the better the bull for other purposes the less chance for his successfully enduring the privations of the range, and the poorer the bull the more certain is he not to succumb to any of the vicissitudes of weather or food supplies. And while this may not be true in its complete sense, there is some real foundation for it, since it would be impossible for very heavy animals to cover the long distances which are sure to be attempted when they are caught upon the high plateaus by a sudden storm. But the range men do not wish the poorest animals, while afraid of the best, and accordingly have settled upon a mean between the two in the shape of grades. Their greater cost, which not only calls for a heavier outlay at the start but renders the matter of winter losses much more serious, is also a great drawback to the more general use of pure-bred bulls.

The range man, when he loses pure-bred bulls, always takes note of that fact, and from their greater value bears the matter more in mind, while the loss of grade and ordinary bulls is scarcely thought of, and is accepted as a matter of course, or as one of the things which can not be avoided. The pure-breeds are taken with some apprehension that perhaps they may not endure the strain; and when one of them dies that fact is taken as proof that these apprehensions were well-founded, and no allowance is made for the probability that a grade bull would have died under similar circumstances. The loss of a very few pure-bred bulls is sufficient to convince many range men that they will not answer for range purposes. But the loss of no number of grade bulls will serve to awaken any suspicion that they are at all lacking in adaptability.

As has been before observed, the pure-breeds have not been tried on a sufficiently extensive scale to settle the question of their adaptability for range purposes adversely, and if they could be had at equal cost they would likely come into more extended use upon the range, for then there would not be such a disparity between the losses when reduced to dollars and cents. Where the slightest attention can be given to feeding or pasturing in winter, there can be no question as to the great advantage of pure-bred bulls over any other, no matter what may be thought of them under other conditions.

But regardless of the superior character of the calves sired by purely-bred bulls, and also regardless of the fact (if that were established) of equal power to endure the seasons, it is not likely that pure-bred bulls will receive the preference of a majority of range men. Many range men persistently neglect to turn out bulls in the proportion of one to each twenty-five females, the lowest estimate that common experience has shown to be at all consistent with the hope of a tolerable calf-drop, and scarcely any one turns out bulls in excess of this proportion. This shows that there is a too general disposition among range men to economize upon the bull question. So long as this is the feeling and practice among them, it is not to be expected that pure-bred bulls will be selected for range purposes in preference to grades, with a difference in their cost, no matter how slight it may be. Many of them even carry this economy to a discrimination as between grades, buying those which can be had for the least money per hundred head or per car-load, regardless of the fact that they may possess but a small fraction of improved blood. And so long as these men buy grade bulls, for any reason, they will persuade themselves that they are the best. But it is probal that, considering their enhanced cost and some little extra at and care bestowed upon them, the general employment of pu but bulls upon the range would not only be practicable and f but of millions of dollars advantage annually to the range in

Another matter affecting the manner in which bulls broug the range country are able to meet its conditions, is the ma which they have been previously maintained, especially dui season immediately preceding their removal. Many of the: been fed very largely upon corn and accustomed to being ho warm buildings. To bring in such bulls to be turned at on the range, perhaps when feed is not abundant and the season ent or very hot, is sure to be followed by unfavorable result which no breed of cattle would be exempt. As pure-bred bu more likely to have had this extra care and feed, there is mo ability of them disappointing purchasers. Breeders who are bulls intended for sale on the range should adopt a course of n ment having this end in view, and not send the young bull range handicapped with a disadvantage which not only injur but brings their breeders and the breed they represent into di Probably buyers would be amply compensated for their extra if they gave the selection of bulls more of their personal att and were careful to satisfy themselves that the youngsters ha reared under somewhat natural conditions, and not forced al too abundant supplies of corn.

THE CALVES—THE PERCENTAGE OF INCREASE.

Calves should come in the spring, after all danger of bad has passed, say after the 1st of May. They should be weaned tober, early enough to give the cows time to get into fair co before winter sets in. If weaning is delayed until cold w neither calf nor dam are in the best condition for the winter ure. The cow will in such case be thin, and the calf not suffi accustomed, from previous habit, to do as well as he should do exclusive grass diet. Early-weaned calves get accustomed wholly upon grass while the weather is mild and pleasant a fore there is any extra strain to withstand winter exposures. a consequence, are in the best possible shape to endure thes they come. If weaning occurs in very cold weather the teats cows are in danger of being frozen, especially in the case of co [illegible] quantity of milk. However, heavy [illegible] [illegible] weaning time. In most large herd [illegible] run with the cows [illegible] This [illegible]

[illegible]

until long after the proper time, while those again in calf are more prompt in this particular.

The natural increase in a herd of cows varies of course with the season and the range, and with other conditions, to which reference has been made. In the northern ranges the average is estimated at from 50 to 60 per cent. Perhaps it should be larger, but there are several influences which operate to keep it within these limits. First of these may be mentioned the scarcity of bulls upon the range; second, the bunching of bulls with small numbers of cows, by which the effective use of such as are present is greatly circumscribed; third, the small attention given to weaning calves in proper time, whereby many cows fail to get in calf every season, and can only be depended upon for calf in alternate seasons; and, finally, the chasing and worrying of the cows resulting from the bringing in of an unusual number of steers to the range. In the earlier days the percentage of increase was much greater. The country was more scantily stocked; cows were not worried and annoyed to the same extent as now; feed was everywhere more abundant, and the condition of cattle more favorable to breeding. And each range man, instead of relying so much upon his neighbor to furnish him with bulls for his cows (for he had few neighbors and perhaps none), realized that the number of calves was directly dependent upon the number of bulls he turned out himself, and accordingly his self-interest prompted him to provide a suitable number. And it is noticeable that at this time pure-bred bulls were in larger request and proportionate use. Nothing was heard concerning their lack of hardiness or adaptability in any respect until people commenced to crowd in upon the range, and occupiers began to study how few and how cheap bulls would answer to serve their neighbors' cows.

HOW THE ROUND-UPS ARE ARRANGED.

In turning cattle loose upon the open range to wander over square leagues of territory in grazing, and be driven hundreds of miles by the stress of storms, and, under all conditions of weather, and feed intermixed with the innumerable cattle of other owners, a person would have small chance of ever recovering them or deriving benefit from their increase, if dependent wholly upon any efforts of his own to either separate or keep track of them. The fabulous search after a needle in a haystack were a simple task compared with this. From the top of a ridge the owner might come into view of a hundred or more cattle, scattered over more ground than he could cover with a day's riding. When all were visited and their brand inspected, he might find one or more of his own and pass on to fresh ground the next day, to look over, perhaps, the same lot of cattle, and miss those which have passed behind him in the night, or to his right or left the day before. To overcome this difficulty and to render it possible for each man to regain his own, a co-operative system of working the range, or "rounding up" the cattle, has grown up among rangemen, and is now throughout the West, if not all the range country, sanctioned and conducted by legal regulations. Colorado, for instance, is divided into twenty-three round-up districts. The whole State is not embraced, as in the agricultural sections, and in some of the mountain country round-ups are not necessary. But there is provision made for new districts whenever, from extending interests or other causes, there may arise occasion for the same. Each round-up

in the round-up, where the neighbor relieves him and performs a similar service in return. A small owner often joins himself without pay to the "outfit" of a neighboring large owner, in consideration that his few cattle be handled and brought along with the other cattle of the "outfit." In short, there is all sorts of doubling up and co-operation among the parties working the range which either interest or convenience may suggest.

Each outfit has its own separate camp, herds separately from all the others its own horses, which, according to the district, are provided in the proportion of from three to ten to each man, so that each one can have a fresh horse each day, or part of a day, as circumstances may require. It is hard work on horses and not a light one on riders. Each outfit, when the cattle are brought in and separated, takes charge of its own cattle. In this matter, however, there is generally more or less combination between the outfits, those from the same section of country handling and holding their cattle in common, only separating them when they approach the boundaries of their respective ranges.

Strangers present from other ranges, looking for cattle which may have strayed from their proper grazing grounds, are furnished with meals, according to the custom of the range country, by any of the outfits, at 50 cents per day. They have their own bedding, as does everybody in the range country, and are privileged to share in whatever sleeping accomodations may exist, which is generally such as may be found under a wagon. They arrange for their cattle to be held in the herd of some person who will take them as near as possible to the point where they properly belong. This they are able to do without difficulty, in consideration of the contribution of their own services to the outfit, for the comity between stockmen is of the most liberal and generous character. One who dispenses favors to a stranger this month may be seeking precisely similar ones himself, or his men may be, at the hands of some other strangers next month. And the sense of mutual dependence upon mutual favors makes men wondrously liberal in their dealings with others.

The owners of large herds, whose cattle naturally graze or drift over wide areas, generally have "outfits" at all the round-ups in the country over which their cattle are likely to drift, and perhaps some representation like that just described at those still more remote.

HOW THE ROUND-UP WORK IS DONE.

The country throughout the district having been gone over many times before, is thoroughly known in all its features; every ravine and water-hole and peculiar place almost has a local name, and a very good opinion can be formed from previous experience of the rapidity and ease with which it can be worked. If much broken, or abounding in ravines or inequalities, it can not be passed over as quickly as where the surface is smooth or gently undulating.

Everything being in readiness the foreman designates a stretch of country to be worked that day, and assigns to the different men the portions which they shall work, so distributing them that they ride every valley, pass along every ridge, scour every ravine and depression, and bring the whole country into view. All the cattle found, no matter who may own them or what brand they may bear, are gathered up and driven to the headquarters camp. After the men had separated to their work camp was broken and moved during the day by those in charge to a point previously selected and convenient to the place where the labors of the day will terminate. The men detailed by each "outfit" to care for the horse herds or the cattle herds it may carry along of course move with the camp, but at such a leisurely gait as to give the animals in charge the best possible chance for grazing.

Towards the close of the afternoon the force commence to arrive at the new camp with the cattle which have been gathered during the day. These are divided, under the direction of the foreman, as they come in, into such number of bunches, considering the number of cattle and men to do the work, as will render the "cutting out" most convenient and expeditious. The foreman designates an "outfit" to commence "cutting out," and assigns the bunch it shall work, making these assignments until all the bunches are being worked. When an "outfit" is through with a bunch it notifies the foreman, who turns it over to the inspection of some other "outfit," but the last parties "cutting out" must hold the bunch until relieved. And so on, in turn, each outfit is given an opportunity of going through and "cutting out" its brand of cattle from each bunch.

Sometimes, when the number of cattle is not too large and the time is abundant, or perhaps help in short supply, the cattle are all rounded into one bunch, and each "outfit" takes its turn, as assigned by the foreman, in "cutting out." But in either case the results achieved and the general plan of work is the same.

CUTTING OUT THE DIFFERENT BRANDS.

A bunch of cattle being assigned an "outfit" to work, part of the men give their attention to the task of keeping the bunch of cattle from breaking up and scattering, while the others, mounted upon horses which are often reserved especially for this purpose, do the "cutting out." It is not the safest sort of work imaginable, for the cattle are excited and in more or less rapid motion. Occasionally an animal, grown desperate, will show fight, and still oftener one is rushed along by the irresistible force of those pressing behind. Horses often receive fatal injuries, and a rider unhorsed would be in danger of being trampled or gored to death by the excited animals before his companions could come to his rescue. Both rider and horse should understand the work and appreciate the danger. An intelligent, well-trained horse will appreciate his peril, and adopt some course to avoid the herds or crush before the rider could possibly guide him. And an expert rider, when a shock seems inevitable, will generally manage to protect his horse from the fatal thrust of the horn by interposing the heavy stirrup and thick housings of leather, which are a distinguishing feature of all range saddles.

Mounted as well as circumstances will permit, the rider plunges boldly into the seething mass of cattle, on the lookout for brands belonging to or represented by the "outfit" to which he belongs. As soon as an animal bearing any of the desired brands is discovered the horse is ridden straight at it with all possible speed. The horse soon comprehends which animal the rider has selected, and with very little guiding will follow it through all the turnings and deviating courses it may make. And the steer or cow retreating, with the inevitable rider at its heels, and receiving a blow from the whip as often as within reach, or whenever its speed is slackened, soon discovers there is no safety among its fellows, and permits itself to be rushed from among them. This is termed "cutting out."

As fast as animals are separated from the bunch they are driven to the particular herd of the outfit to which they belong. But not in the leisurely way in which cattle are driven in the East, horse and steer on the walk. Range cattle can not be driven in this manner, unless many are together, as, from their semi-wild and distrustful state, they are always reluctant to leave the immediate locality, or the companions which they may happen to have, so they are put through on the jump. If not headed in the right direction they are pursued with less rapidity until turned in the direction desired, and once headed that way are urged along so fast that they have little chance to turn to the right or left.

As the riders pass to and fro through the bunches "cutting out" particular animals, from the pursuit of which they allow nothing to turn them aside, their eyes are ever on the alert to discover whether there are other animals of the same brands present, which will in turn be cut out.

When all the bunches have been carefully looked over by each one of the outfits, and all the brands represented have been separated and secured, there are some cattle left which are turned loose at that spot. These cattle are either those which belong upon the range which have been worked during the day, and are therefore already at home, or strange cattle from some distance, bearing brands not represented at the round-up.

Sometimes a memorandum is made of these "strange" brands, and the owner hears of them through the associations. Brands, too, are extensively advertised in the range newspapers, and cowboys are perpetually on the lookout for animals bearing advertised brands, and notify owners of the locality where animals off their proper range may be found, receiving generally some slight compensation for recovered animals.

HOLDING THE HERDS.

The next day, and each succeeding day, the camp is moved and a fresh stretch of country covered, until the whole district is finished, which will be in from four to six weeks after the commencement. And all these special herds into which the gathered cattle have been divided are driven along within a convenient distance. They are allowed to scatter considerably in the day-time, in order to graze and obtain water, but they are kept distinct. At night they are rounded into bunches more or less compact, and guarded. Ordinarily it is not much trouble to hold the cattle at night, as they lie down for most of the time, getting up perhaps once or twice to feed, and they soon discover they are watched and lie down again. A dark night calls for more vigilance and a larger number of guards, and the reliefs are increased. When a bad storm occurs at night, accompanied by much thunder and lightning, the cattle sometimes become alarmed and much less manageable. On such occasions it frequently requires the services of all hands to keep the herds from breaking away, or stampeding.

As the round-up progresses and passes over the several ranges, the respective owners drop out such cattle belonging to them as may have been previously gathered and brought to that point. Those gathered from that time forward, belonging to the ranges which have been left behind, must be carried along until the whole d is finished.

Long before this time the round-up has assumed, if the a large one, very imposing proportions, and the thousa cattle and horses, and hundreds of men and trains of wagons stitute in the aggregate a spectacle to be remembered.

The district finished, the "outfits," comprising the roun separate, each returning as best it can their cattle to their own r Those who go to distant points, or to about the same distr country, join their herds for the drive, separating the cattle the first person's range is reached. Generally these herds, if consolidated at the close of the round-up, have been held in co the round-up was progressing. The several herds, as they at the close of the round-up, vary from a few hundred many thousands. Five to 8,000 head are contained in some herds which separate at the close of the round-up in a trict.

THE BRANDING—THE MOTHERLESS CALVES.

As the cattle are cut out at the close of each day's work an tunity is presented for counting and dividing the calves to the re ive owners. When a cow is cut out of the bunch if her calf at her side the rider can tell from her appearance whether she has a calf, and instead of being rushed away to her proper herd, the case of steers, she is allowed to remain near the bunch, bu vented from rejoining it, and in a short time if she has a calf p it will likely come out at her call and join her. The cuttin completed, each owner proceeds to brand his calves, though times this is deferred until the close of the round-up. To br calf one cowboy catches him around the heels with a lariat, i handling of which constant practice gives much proficiency. lariat being attached to the horn of the saddle the youngster is ged to the fire. Assistants confine his head and with the tight ually prevent his struggles until the brand is applied. Stee branded in much the same way. Only one lariat is thrown ov head and another around the heels, and the horses pulling b opposite directions throw and stretch out the animal to be ope upon, and hold him securely until the operation is completed. horses get so accustomed to this work that they will keep the taut and the animal stretched out upon the ground without a tention from the riders, who can even descend from the saddl handle the irons.

The irons are heated in fires made mainly of cold chips, dried droppings of the animals are known in range parlance. are heated as hot as they can be made and applied quickly firm hand. Great skill is required in the use of the branding to burn just deep enough to produce a clear, distinct brand, an too deeply, which would impair to a greater or less degree it bility. Particular care must be observed also to prevent th from being moved in the struggle of the animal. At the ranch cattle are branded in the corrals, sometimes in the way desc and sometimes "chutes" are provided, into which the anima driven and so confined as to render their struggles futile, and r the brand standing.

In the bunch of cattle remaining each day after each outf cut out its brands there will generally remain a few uncl cows and their calves. These cows are cut out under the direction of the foreman, and the calves of each one identified in the usual way, and each unclaimed calf is given a brand similar to that of the mother, irons with which running brands of any pattern can be given being carried for this purpose. In this way the owner of the cow, no matter how far she may be from her proper range, is certain that her increase will receive his brand, and if he ever gets on track of her or her increase, will recover both.

After all this is done there will remain some motherless calves, *i. e.*, those which have become separated from the dams, or where mother or calf or both have become so excited that they refuse to recognize each other. These are termed "mavericks," as are also any animals of any age found upon the range without a brand. These are sold to the highest bidder, and the proceeds constitute a fund out of which the expenses of the round-ups are defrayed. Sometimes this sale is made on the ground and sometimes it is made in advance before the round-up commences.

DISPUTED OWNERSHIP AT THE ROUND-UP.

If at any time a dispute arises between different persons as to the ownership of an animal, as is sometimes the case when brands similar in outline have been unskillfully applied, the foreman appoints a committee from among those present to examine the brand and award the animal. There is no appeal from the decision of the committee, which is final for all the purposes of the round-up. But of course this only determines the right of possession for the time being, and the matter of actual ownership, if either party is dissatisfied, is determined in the usual manner in the courts.

THE FALL ROUND-UP FOR BEEVES.

The round-up described is the spring round-up. There is another in the fall, which is completed just before the commencement of the shipping season. It is not attended with so much labor, and so many cattle are not moved as in the spring round-ups, because but few cattle have left their proper range in the interval, and herds have not likely become so widely scattered during the summer months as in winter. Its principal object is to facilitate the gathering up of beeves, which are thus brought upon their own range where the owner can readily collect them when ready for shipment. The fall round-ups, however, are conducted in the same way and under the same authority as those made in the spring.

NECESSITY FOR CO-OPERATION—KEEPING OUT NEW-COMERS.

Every man has a right to attend the round-ups and get his cattle. The foreman, being an officer of the State, could refuse no man the privilege of looking through the bunches of animals bearing his brand. But if disposed to shirk his proportionate share of the work, no one would join in with him in holding and driving the animals after he had cut them out, and so he would have to furnish men enough of his own to attend to every detail connected with his cattle, and this would, unless in the case of very large owners, call for much more help than would be required under any other circumstances. And if any one should be regarded with dislike there is nothing to prevent the workers, if they should observe an animal bearing his brand, from leaving it where they found it and not bringing it in.

There is probably no business in which individuals are so fully dependent upon co-operation with their neighbors as in the gathering and handling of range cattle upon the round-ups. If one were left dependent entirely upon his own efforts, in the present crowded condition of the range, it would certainly be a task involving much labor and expense to undertake the gathering of the cattle. And at the very best its results would be uncertain. One would never know when the work was accomplished. It is now proposed in many quarters that the range men already upon the range, as a means of preventing outsiders from bringing cattle into districts already regarded as fully stocked, shall take advantage of this dependence upon their favor and refuse these new-comers membership in their associations and decline to work with them upon the range and at the round-ups. It is also proposed to use the same means to compel range men already upon the range to observe what are regarded as the rights of others. With proper co-operation in this respect among the members of the existing associations, there is no doubt that a "pressure" can be exerted which in no case is to be despised.

THE PROPORTION OF BEEVES SHIPPED—SUPPLEMENTAL FEEDING.

In the earlier days of the range industry, when the country was new, cattle few in number, and feed everywhere, figuratively if not actually, "knee deep," pretty much everything upon the range got fat, and the proportion of beeves shipped during the course of the season was perhaps as high as 75 per cent. of all the animals of suitable ages. And they were in condition so early in the season that the bulk of them were safely marketed during July and August. Now, however, as was stated by Secretary Sturgis, of the Wyoming Association, at the forming of the International Association, in consequence of the closer stocking of the ranges and the less abundance of feed, the beeves are not in proper condition for shipment until September and October; and even at this later date only from one-third to one-half are in condition to be sold as beeves. So each year, as the range industry expands and more cattle are brought and reared upon it, there is a constantly increased proportion which must go to market in a half-fat or lean condition and be brought to the desired finish and ripeness in the agricultural States, where grain and hay for that purpose are available.

From the unsatisfactory market which at times prevails for this class of cattle, and is very likely to prevail at the time when thin-range cattle are being marketed in large numbers, many of the larger companies have sought to escape by arranging with the distilleries of the Western States to feed their surplus. Others, in turn, not finding in this quarter a satisfactory remedy, have erected feeding establishments at points where hay and corn are always abundant and relatively cheap, and are trying here the experiment of feeding their own cattle. They can be held in this way under daily and, it is asserted, economical improvement until a satisfactory condition of the market is reached, and are then so near to it that they can be quickly rushed in and disposed of. And everywhere throughout the range country there is much anxious discussion as to the feasibility of securing feed in favorable situations, or by the cultivation of alfalfa or other supposed drought-resisting grasses, to bring into shipping condition at least a portion of the range cattle which are now rushed to market in thin order.

PRECAUTIONS AGAINST IMPROPER SHIPMENTS—DETECTION OF THEFT—THE INSPECTION SYSTEM.

To complement the round-up system there is also a system of inspection in vogue in the arid region by which, as far as possible, all cattle are overlooked when about to be marketed. But for the inspection system, cattle straying far away from home would be almost certain to fall into the hands of dishonest persons and be shipped to market. Or they might be driven surreptitiously from their own ranges by rustlers, as the range thieves are called, to distant shipping points, where they could be safely put aboard the cars. But while a dishonest person may steal cattle with greater ease in the range country than elsewhere, and perhaps get with his plunder farther away from the scene of his crime, it is more difficult here than elsewhere to dispose of animals acquired in this way. The inspection system not only protects the rightful owners of cattle from the operations of dishonest persons, but also from the mistakes which are made in the shipment of large lots of cattle, whereby some wrong brands are often unintentionally included. In Colorado the inspection system is provided for by law, and the governor annually appoints an inspection committee of nine members, selected from the different portions of the State, and who are required to be stockmen actively engaged in business on the range. They serve without pay, and do not even receive back such expenses as they may incur. The committee employ all the inspectors and as many as they may regard necessary, not exceeding ten at any one time. They are limited in their expenditures on account of inspection to $5,000 per year. During the active shipping season inspectors are kept at all the stations along the different railroads where cattle are unloaded for feed and water, and during the remainder of the year at Omaha, Pacific Junction, and Kansas City, and at such other points as, from time to time, may seem necessary.

Each inspector has a brand book, in which all the known brands or those which ordinarily enter into the commercial movement are described. The person in charge of cattle in course of shipment is provided with a list of the brands borne by the cattle under his charge. The inspector examines each lot, sees that the cattle of each brand correspond in number with the description on the lists, and makes a report to the State committee, showing the brands and number of the different lots of cattle inspected by him, the names of the shippers, the dates of shipment, and the name of consignors. So, if any one suspects some of his cattle have been shipped out by others, here is a record which will enable him to trace the matter. If the inspector finds brands not upon the list, or which are not registered as the brand of the shipper, he requires a receipt to be given for the particular animals, which is returned with his report, and the owner of the brand is notified through the committee. If the owner of the brand has sold these cattle to the shipper, the matter will, of course, end there, but if not, he will know where to look for their proceeds. The shipper can not well deny the receipt, and the law makes him the agent of the owner in disposing of the animal, so he can not well retain the proceeds. If the shipper is not known to the inspector to be responsible, or if he refuses to give a receipt the inspector may make such entry upon the shipping bills as will require the sale of the animal for account of the brand, the proceeds to be held officially until ownership is legally determined. Or he may take the animal itself, sell it on the spot, or forward it with some other shipper. And for this purpose he is authorized to replevy animals if they can be obtained in no other way. It is very seldom that an honest shipper will refuse to comply with the inspection requirements, and there have only been two or three instances in years where the committee have been compelled to pay damages on account of inspectors taking possession of wrong animals. Usually shippers, when they find they have other brands along than their own, prefer that such entries be made upon the shipping bills as will cause the animals described to be sold separately, and the proceeds remitted direct to the owner, or, if his correct address is unknown, to the State Cattle Growers' Association, where he can obtain them. This course saves the necessity of the shipper giving any further attention to it. So, every little while, stockmen are receiving checks from the Cattle Association, or from commission merchants, for cattle which had strayed off to some distant range and found their way to market along with some other person's cattle. The Colorado Cattle Growers' Association has now in its hands, awaiting claimants, the proceeds arising from the sale of 25 or 30 head of cattle, of which the owners of the brands are unknown. Sometimes one range man makes an arrangement with another to market any of his beeves which drift upon the other's range, and the inspection system discloses to him just how many of such were shipped. Perhaps the first intimation he may get that any have gone forward is the receipt of a check from a commission merchant in Chicago or Kansas City, for the proceeds of 2 or 3 head which have been sold for his account.

The Colorado inspectors save to the owners the proceeds of from 300 to 400 head of cattle per year. This is the direct benefit. Indirectly the benefits are much greater, for, but for this check upon the indiscriminate marketing of cattle, dishonest persons would be encouraged to pick up and ship as many of other people's cattle as possible. Under this system, the last thing a cattle thief would think of doing would be the shipment of cattle out of the country. To drive them some distance and keep them, altering the brands, which can sometimes be successfully done, or selling them to a local butcher, perhaps as equally dishonest as himself, or killing them himself and peddling the meat, is about the only way of disposing of stolen stock. The Wyoming inspectors, during the year 1885, inspected 320,597 head of cattle on the railroads and at the Indian agencies, recovering 2,828 head of cattle shipped by others than their rightful owners. Of this number, 1,222 head were found at Council Bluffs, and 931 head at Minnesota Transfer, near Saint Paul. The greater proportion of these were likely shipped by arrangement between the owner and the shipper, but in the absence of an inspection system, they could have been successfully shipped by anybody without any arrangement, and detection would have been practically impossible. The figures given as the work of the Wyoming inspectors probably include re-inspections, not only of Wyoming cattle, but of all range cattle, for the same lot may be looked over by more than one inspector. These are, therefore, gross figures, while those given in connection with the Colorado inspection exhibit the net result, after

-inspection, the cattle of other lo-
es when remittances are made by
wners.
lition to the inspectors outside the
nver, Pueblo, and Leadville, and
r orders from one part of the State
have their cattle inspected before
ess explanation necessary while ca
le are sold from one point on the
generally insist that they shall be
pection makes the interests of both
y law, are required to preserve the
ter, and inspectors regularly visit
these hides, and report the brands.
s of stolen cattle are detected, the
ous and perfect that the stealing of
ns, and dishonest men are deterred
a tax of 1.15 mills on all the cattle
for the support of the inspection
themselves, through their State
t detective system, and have able
st the regular officers in the prose-
aling. The inspection system of
from that in Colorado, which ha
everywhere these systems are des
uards, and in one way or another
sarily vary somewhat in methods
iar to each section.

MEN AND HORSES REQUIRED.

he range is mainly confined to an
. The cattle in cold weather suffer
water than from any other cause.
d down the streams during severe
e at convenient distances, through
here should be more of this done
oor substitute, and during most of
are of it. With open water at fre-
a larger area in grazing than when
stant, and of course get more feed
cattle are brought into the ranches
are helped along with feed, and
served, are growing more and more
ne ranches which are capable of
At some ranches, too, more or less
e horses kept out of the herd also
gregate, the winter's work is light,
are maintained than in summer.
h holes and miry places in which
g lost if assistance is not at hand to
re often visited.
, and consequently the expense of
e intelligence of the management
and decreases in proportion as a
ler one management. Thus, upon

THROWING A STEER.

THE DISEASE KNOWN AS "STAGGERS" AMONG HORSES IN VIRGINIA AND NORTH CAROLINA.

Hon. NORMAN J. COLMAN,
Commissioner of Agriculture.

SIR: In accordance with your directions I visited the eastern part of this State and a portion of the State of North Carolina, to investigate the nature and cause of the disease called "blind staggers," which proved fatal to so many horses during the past summer. I arrived in Suffolk, Nansemond County, Va., on the 2d of November, and upon inquiry I was informed that there had not been a case of "staggers" in that locality for at least six weeks, but it had prevailed in an extremely fatal form to an alarming extent during the summer and early fall. I learned that Dr. John T. Kilby had lost several horses, therefore I called upon him to get what information I could concerning the disease. Dr. Kilby was born in the town of Suffolk, and is a practicing physician of many years' experience. He said:

I have owned horses for over forty years; remember an outbreak of this disease in 1867; many horses died that year; I lost 2 horses myself. I think it is safe to say that over 100 horses died within a radius of 25 miles. There was another outbreak in 1876 or 1877, but it was not so fatal. I never knew it to be as fatal as this year. I am certain that over 200 horses have died within a radius of 25 miles. I lost 4 horses this year, 2 of which died in Suffolk, and the others died in the country. Of course there are isolated cases of it every year, but a very rainy season is always followed by a general outbreak of the disease. I have no idea of the cause; believe it to be due to some epidemic influence. It is rapidly fatal. Some animals die within six hours after first symptoms; others last as long as four days. I gave large doses of aloes, calomel, tartar emetic, and jalap, followed by half-pound doses of epsom salts and enemas, but could get no action from the bowels. The symptoms of the 2 that died here were somewhat different. The mare when first attacked became blind. She would stagger about, or press her head against any object, or lean her body against the stall or house. In the case of the colt, his hind parts would sway from side to side; would fall and could not arise without assistance; lost control of his hind parts, but had good use of his front legs until he got very weak. He fell three days after he showed the first symptoms, and was conscious up to within an hour of death; no signs of coma until an hour before he died. I was present when a man held a *post-mortem* examination of the colt. He took out the brain, and it seemed to be all right, although I must say that I did not examine its structure—only looked at it superficially; did not examine the spinal cord. The left lung was very much congested. I fed corn, oats, bran, hay, and corn-fodder. I have no feed that was here during the prevalence of the disease. My hay was moldy. All my feed was raised in the vicinity, except the bran.

In the symptoms given by Dr. Kilby it will be seen that in the case of his mare the cerebral disturbance predominated, whilst in the case of the colt, from the symptoms furnished one would suppose the lesions almost entirely confined to the spinal cord. This being the case, it is not surprising that he saw nothing materially wrong with the brain, but I am certain that if the spinal cord had been properly examined sufficient evidence would have been discovered to satisfactorily account for the weakness of the hind parts and the inability to rise. I am equally certain that a carefully conducted *post-mortem* examination of the brain would have discovered grave lesions in the case of the mare. The doctor informed me, after inquiry had been made, that the colt was on the left side when he died. This fact easily accounts for the left lung being more congested than the right. It was a hypostatic congestion. Dr. Kilby informed me that the gentleman who examined his colt was a citizen of Suffolk, a Mr. William M. Atkinson, whom I called upon immediately and obtained the following information: Mr. Atkinson keeps a boarding, livery, and training stable. He kept in his stable during the summer an average of 8 horses; had no case of the disease; did not use any feed raised in the vicinity, except some fodder a year old. When the disease first appeared in the neighborhood, he commenced to feed hot and cold mashes and a little hay; says he held *post-mortem* examinations on 11 horses that died of the disease and found the brain all right in every case. I asked him if he understood the anatomy of the brain. He said he did not, but the brains he examined looked like a hog's brain, and he thought they were all right. He said he found the lungs black in every horse, and consequently he concluded that the animals died of a lung disease. (I found a great many people who were of the opinion that the disease was an affection of the lungs, but of course they did not recognize the fact that congestion of the lungs is an ordinary complication of cerebral affections.) Mr. Atkinson says that the disease was almost entirely confined to the horses kept on the low lands; he said 4 horses were sent to him from the low country, where the disease was prevailing; he fed them on mashes and they were not affected. He stated that the horses that died in Suffolk were owned respectively by a doctor and a liveryman, and they could have contracted the disease from being fed in the swampy country. He said he did not know of a horse to die where the feed was good. I will give the following statement in his own words, which is significant:

Walter Wills wrote to me what to do as a preventive, and I advised him to feed mashes. He lost none. He owns 6 horses, and lives in a district on the river where other farmers lost horses.

He also stated that Dr. Kilby sent a colt from Suffolk to Mr. Putnam's, where it died, and Mr. Putnam lost 2 of his own. There is much valuable information contained in the statement of Mr. Atkinson, but his *post-mortem* examinations were worse than useless, and I found this to be the case generally, because the persons who held the examinations were incompetent, owing entirely to their ignorance of pathology.

I next visited Mr. George W. Nurney, liveryman, Suffolk, who said:

I kept about 30 horses in my stable during the prevalence of the disease; had no sickness in my stable. All my feed was from the West, except about 100 bushels of oats. I know this disease exists in this vicinity more or less every summer, but never to the extent of this year. I lost 1 horse from it in 1876.

Mr. R. W. Nelms, liveryman, Suffolk, said:

I lost 3 horses, only 1 of which died in Suffolk. One fell dead on the road while in harness; could not say that he had the "staggers," but supposed he had. The one that died in Suffolk became dull and stiff, walked "straddling" to one side, ate to the last; could turn the head to one side only; first noticed something wrong about 12 o'clock; horse died same night. My horses grazed, and were fed feed raised in this section and also feed from the West. Some of my hay was undoubtedly damaged. My animals were fed everywhere in the surrounding country.

Mr. H. P. Pinner, who is the proprietor of a livery and sale stable in Suffolk, I found to be a man who had given this subject much intelligent study. His statement is worthy of careful thought, and is given as follows:

I averaged 11 horses in my stable during the summer; had no cases of the disease. I fed Western hay, old corn, and old oats; I used no feed raised this year. I think the disease was an affection of the brain. A horse affected will stagger and breathe very heavy when down, and apparently die from suffocation while in spasms. I remember the outbreak of 1876, and then as now no man lost a horse who had good feed raised the previous year. I had a farm then on the banks of the Nansemond, and had a barn full of feed saved from 1875, which I fed to my horses. I did not have a sick one. I sold hay that I raised in 1876, which was very inferior. Persons who fed it lost horses. I am convinced the cause is in the feed. There were no persons who lost horses on the higher farms about here, because all the high land is on the sand ridges, where they raise principally peanuts and corn. All their fodder is from six to eight months old before it is used. The only places where horses have died from "staggers" to my knowledge is where new feed has been used.

On November 3d I visited Berea Church, 10 miles from Suffolk, where a conference was in progress, and consequently there was a large gathering of farmers from the neighboring country. I soon discovered that the reports of the great loss of horses from the disease had not been exaggerated. The following are the statements of some of the farmers with whom I conversed. I will give the statements as near as possible in their own words, but, of course, much of the information was elicited by questioning.

Mr. Mr. R. Williamson said:

I lost 2 horses. The first affected was a mare. She was sick three days; had a staggering gait behind, but at first straddled with front legs; hind part would swing from side to side; she leaned to left side all the time; would prop herself against barn or other object; get spasms and fall every time, and then throw herself about violently and nearly knock her eyes out. I first saw my horse leaning against the stall, right side. I backed him out, and he fell in the passage-way; had slight convulsions, and died six hours after. I fed new hay and oats for a month before the deaths occurred; the oats were moldy. I do not feed many of these oats now. The horse that died so suddenly had a ravenous appetite.

Mr. W. H. Harrell said:

I had no disease amongst my horses this year, but have lost one from "staggers" every year except this for the past eight years. They would get stupid, stagger about, or lean to one side against anything near them. This year I fed on feed that was raised last year; therefore they had no feed of this year's growth.

Mr. E. E. Lee said:

I lost one horse this year. I found him leaning against the stable. I took him out, when he reeled around for awhile and fell, and became completely paralyzed, and did not get up again; died very suddenly. I noticed a difficulty in swallowing in horses I have lost before. I have taken a bucket with a certain quantity of water in it, placed it before them, and they would put their mouths in the water and act as if drinking, but no water would be gone from the bucket. My horses did not graze; I fed on new hay and corn raised in the vicinity; I had some hay that was very much damaged, which I used for bedding; the horse that died ate some of it. I notice this disease appears in the wet, hot, and sultry seasons. I have known it to occur in such seasons for the last sixty years.

Mr. Amos Wilson said:

I lost some with what I would call "sleepy staggers," and others with "blind staggers," and others when they could not swallow. I always lost horses when I fed new oats in wet seasons.

I inquired particularly if any mules had been lost from "staggers," and several persons informed me that Mr. D. Shriver had lost two; therefore I was anxious to meet this gentleman. I was soon introduced to him, and he made the following statement:

The first mule that died was twenty years old, and the day before it died it seemed a little dull and consequently it was not worked much; was put in stable and given feed, some of which was eaten; went to the stable next morning and found the mule dead; seemed as if death took place suddenly, as the mule was propped against manger when it fell. A neighbor opened the mule, and said the cause of death was the rupture of a blood vessel. The second mule that died was seven years old. I first noticed that the mule could not eat; would chew food and try to swallow, but could not. It would eject the food from the mouth, and when it would try to drink the water it would return through the nostrils. There was a lump under the jaw; there was a copious discharge of matter from the nose and mouth. We smoked the head with pine tar and corn-cobs. Stood up until the last and fell dead. An examination after death revealed a tumor in the stomach containing matter of the consistency of hog brain.

From the above symptoms we can certainly conclude that the second mule was not affected by the "staggers." The symptoms point to strangles. In the case of the first mule there is a possibility that the verdict of the person who held the *post-mortem* examination was correct; if so, neither one of the mules was affected with staggers.

Mr. W. T. Frisbee said:

My brother and I farm jointly. Lost two horses this year. The first was an old animal; refused the feed; when brought out inclined the head to one side; kept going around in a circle; would not go straight forward; would back sidewise; left her leaning against door at night; next morning found her continually turning in a circle in the cotton patch; she soon fell and laid in a stupor until a short time before she died, when she strained a little and then died quietly. The other horse was seven years old; showed much the same symptoms. We examined them after death and found the lungs bloodshot and black; liver looked black; there was very little feed in the stomach; bladder full of urine. Fed on blade fodder and corn; noticed no smut or mold on it. We have lost over $2,000 worth of horses from this disease in the last ten years.

Mr. Frisbee said that the horses did not have any feed of this year's raising, to his knowledge, but he stated his brother knew more about the matter than he did. It is more than likely that the animals were either grazed or had been fed some hay, oats, or corn of this year's crop.

Mr. James T. Ramsey said:

I lost one horse seven years old. First appeared weak in the legs; would reel around and whinny very loud (delirium); he fell, and when lifted him up stood until 12 m., when he fell again and could not be gotten up; he appeared to be very blind; struggled very much; died that night. I fed oats of this year's crop, also old corn and fodder; my oats had been wet with rain after it was cut and was not perfect. I lost a horse four years ago with same disease.

Capt. T. R. Gaskins said:

I lost a mare this year. I noticed her reeling; she staggered and fell; died same night. I fed old corn and fodder, and oats of this year's raising.

Mr. Elisha Everett said:

I lost two horses this summer. A mare died first; she was down and struggling before we knew that anything was wrong; we got her up with assistance and took her out of the stable; discovered she was perfectly blind. We poured water on her head, which gave her relief; when we would stop the water she would reel around in one direction; she fell and died; she only lived twenty-four hours after we first noticed that she was sick. The horse we noticed to be sleepy and sluggish for three or four days; then he began to reel around and stagger and lean up against things, like a drunken man exactly; he fell, and we could not get him up; died soon after. I fed corn and fodder, and oats that I raised this year; they were damaged some by rain. I particularly notice that when we have heavy rains there are numerous cobwebs on the ground and trees, and always in those years there are more deaths from staggers than any other season. I remember this disease for years past.

I talked with many other gentlemen at Berea Church who had suffered losses by this disease, and there were many in the church engaged that I did not get an opportunity to see, who, I was informed, lost one or more horses during the summer with the staggers.

A number of times during the day I was informed that a Mr. Putnam had had considerable experience with the disease, and held many *post-mortem* examinations of horses that had died in the neighborhood. As I was desirous of getting his views on the subject we drove to his farm, about six miles from Suffolk. I may as well state that Mr. Putnam has something of a reputation in the vicinity as a "horse doctor." In fact, he told me that he "knew as much about practical horse doctoring as any other man." He did not put in a claim to theoretical knowledge, however. He said:

I lost some horses last summer; the first sick one I noticed could not get its head to the ground; there was a difficulty in swallowing; when he attempted to drink the water it would return through his nose; he would hold his mouth in the water for half an hour at a time and try to drink, but he could not; he breathed very hard; could not drench him; he would pick a little grass, chew it, and quid it; he stood very droopy until fourth day and then got in between some trees and roots and stood against the bank; fell on the fourth night and died the next; struggled a little before he died. The next attacked was a mare. She appeared weak across the loins; when down she could not get up again without assistance; the second day she got down and we could not get her up again without great assistance, when the breathing was very quick; her back was dry and hot. Next day she got down and struggled considerably for six hours and died that night. Another horse we first noticed sick in the stable in the morning. We brought him out and had much difficulty in leading him across the lawn, as he was inclined to turn to the right side and would not go straight; we finally got him to a cool shed about 20 yards from the stable; he leaned up against the barn and stood there until 2 o'clock, p. m., when he fell; he died that night about 7.30 o'clock without a struggle. I held a *post-mortem* on the first horse; the lungs looked very slimy on the outside; did not cut into them, but there appeared to be matter around them; stomach contained very little food. I held a *post-mortem* on a yearling colt belonging to a neighbor; found lungs all right; stomach looked healthy, but all along the large gut there were tumors from the size of a buckshot to size of a walnut; some were hard and others contained a greenish water. I don't think I ever lost one before except when I lived in North Carolina, when I lost one by staggers. I fed corn, hay, and fodder; my horses grazed on the lawn; also fed some pea-nut hay. I fed some early corn of this year's crop; fed a great deal of last year's millet. The horses died in this neighborhood in July and August. One of my colts had the disease and I cured him.

It is not certain that he first animal of Mr. Putnam's was affected with staggers; it might have been laryngitis or strangles. There is no doubt about the other two. I was informed that Mr. Putnam was the gentleman who held the *post-mortem* examination on the mules of Mr. Shriver.

Many horses and mules were in the neighborhood of Berea Church tied to wagons and trees. I examined the feed they had before them and I did not find one specimen that I could call first class; all was more or less affected with mold or rust. I was informed that there are as many mules in this neighborhood as there are horses, and still I could not hear of an authentic case of staggers in a mule. This fact is worth considering. The mules and horses are generally kept in the same stables and subjected to the same conditions and treatment. Another fact I wish to call attention to is this: No matter what ailed a horse or mule it was supposed to be affected with this disease; but this is easily accounted for when we take into consideration the panic-stricken state of the communities that were affected by the disease. One old gentleman, who lives in the vicinity of Berea Church, remarked:

We suffered heavier losses than the people of Charleston. Of course our houses were not destroyed by an earthquake, but just think of the thousands of dollars worth of horses that were lost in this neighborhood.

I tried to get a fair estimate of the losses in the neighborhood, but it was impossible to do so without visiting every farm. The lands of the people with whom I conversed to-day are situated between the Nansemond River and the Dismal Swamp—all flat land; wherever there is running water it is from the swamp running into the river. Many of the animals drink the water from the ditches, but the horses get their water from the wells, which average from 15 to 20 feet in depth. During the months of July and August the swamp was full of water, and, as a consequence, the water in many of the wells and ditches was even with the ground. On the opposite side of the Nansemond the banks are generally higher, and the losses from staggers were very few in comparison.

On November 4 I drove to Isle of Wight County. On my way there I passed through the village of Chuckatuck, 10 miles north of Suffolk, where I was introduced to a gentleman named Mr. G. W. Brittain, who said:

I saw five cases of the disease called staggers. The general symptoms they showed were a drooping of the head; they would press their heads against stalls or mangers, lose the use of their legs, fall, afterwards get convulsions, struggle violently, and die. These cases were on five different farms on the lowlands; one case was owned on a sand-ridge farm, but was worked and fed on the lowland; all were fed on feed produced in the vicinity. Have known outbreaks of the disease in former years; when the outbreaks are general they always follow a wet season; I remember an outbreak in 1867 and another in 1876. Twenty-three horses have died within 5 miles of here this season, according to my count. Only one mule died—that was Mr. Lattimer's.

These deaths occurred mostly on Barrett's Neck, a strip of land between the Nansemond River and the Chuckatuck Creek. I have good authority for stating that considerably more than twenty-three died on this neck of land. Afterwards I met Mr. B. F. Lattimer, the death of whose mule is mentioned above. He said:

I lost one mule in March. He seemed dull for two days, and then got down and would not get up again; he could eat some up to the time he died; when down the head was drawn back and the tail up; legs were stiff; jaws seemed stiff; bowels did not move; noticed the washer extended over the eye. I lost another mule the latter part of August. First noticed her unusually wet with perspiration when she came from the threshing-machine; next day she seemed stiff, as if foundered; she would try to drink, but the water would come back through the nose; swollen under the jaw, which swelling increased until she suffocated; before she died she could not breathe through the nostrils; she would get down and could not be gotten up without difficulty. The mate to this mule appeared to be affected the same way about two weeks after, but recovered. I keep four other mules and four horses on same farm. I fed corn and fodder of last year, and orchard grass and clover of this year's crop which was damaged some, but would be considered good for this year.

The first mule lost by Mr. Lattimer may have died from a spinal affection, but I am inclined to think it was affected with tetanus. I do not for a moment suppose the second mule was affected with staggers, although it is the general opinion of the people in the neighborhood that it had the disease.

Mr. N. N. Pitt, who lives four miles north of Chuckatuck, said:

I lost three fine horses. First one that died when brought out of stable would [illegible] lean to one side; it scrambled about 15 feet, fell, and died; all showed [illegible] symptoms. I fed last year's corn and fodder; two grazed; one most all the [illegible], the other was fed at other places, and was fed here oats of this [illegible] All died between the 3d and 13th of September. All the horses that [illegible] ridges about here were worked and fed on the lowlands.

I next visited the farm of Mr. Mills Rogers, jr., which is situated across the line in Isle of Wight County. Mr. Rogers was away from home, but I met his son, who said:

We lost a colt two and a half years old. It would walk around in a circle; could not hold him still; he would get down and go into convulsions; would make several ineffectual attempts to get up, and would finally do so; he was sick two days; went perfectly blind before he died; finally got down and could not get up. We fed fodder and corn and oats of this year's raising; grazed some on clover and some on wild pasture.

Mr. Rogers reported eight horses that died on this side of Brewer's Creek within 1 mile, viz: Pitt, 3; Pruden, 1; Mayo, 1; Ashby, 1; Cutchins, 1; Rogers, 1. He heard of no cases back on the sand ridges, and said that very few horses had died in Isle of Wight County. The farms on which horses died in this neighborhood are along the bank of Brewer's Creek, which empties into Chuckatuck Creek near its mouth. The land is damp and wet at seasons. Dr. G. A. D. Galt, a physician of Benn's Church, Isle of Wight County, said:

I have seen cases of it in former years, and am of the opinion that it is cerebro-spinal meningitis. I did not see any of the cases of this outbreak; there were only two cases in my neighborhood. I did not go near them, as I thought the disease contagious. The cases were nearly all in the necks between the creeks.

On November 5 I went to Portsmouth, where, I was informed, the postmaster, Mr. Lindsay, had lost some horses. I called upon him, and he took me out to his farm and gave me the following information as to his losses:

I lost five head. Two very valuable colts died in August; a mule died in September. I saw all when they were suffering, except the mule. I can not say that the mule died with the staggers, but it was said he did. I have lost horses almost every season by this disease for twenty-five years. It has been a common disease down in North Carolina, where I was raised, for at least forty years to my recollection. I believed it to be caused by malaria. I thought the hot sun had something to do with it; therefore I kept my horses in the stable during the sunshine, and turned them out on pasture at night, but they died all the same. They were also fed on hay and corn.

Mr. Lindsay has two stables, one distant about 35 yards from the other. One stable contained five and the other ten horses. The three that died on this farm were kept in the stable that contained the five. I was informed the stable got damp before the animals died. None of the horses in the other stable were affected, nor were the two horses that remained in the damp stable. All the horses in both stables were fed and treated the same. On our way to the farm we met the man who had charge of the mule when it died. He said the mule had a swelling in the throat, and lived nine days after it was first attacked. From the conversation with this man, I concluded that the mule was not affected with staggers. I remarked to Mr. Lindsay that I had not heard of a case where imported feed had been used. He replied that several such cases had occurred in Portsmouth, and gave me the names of W. & J. Parker and C. L. Dougherty. I called at the business place of Messrs. Parker, and met one of the firm, who said:

We lost a large draft horse about the 5th of August. He was in fine condition; was at the wharf for a load when he began to perspire and tremble; we put him in the stable; he was sick all the week and died the following Sunday. He was not blind at any time, but stood up until he fell dead, carrying the partition down with him. His bowels were regular during the whole week. Several times I noticed him throw his head back as if he was trying to shake off a fly. We held no post-

mortem examination. We fed hay, oats, and meal from the West. For a week before he died we fed from a load of millet hay raised on our farm, which is about 10 miles from Portsmouth. The farm is flat land, and surrounded by the Nansemond River and the west branch of the Elizabeth River. There is a swamp within a short distance. The horse doctor who attended him left the impression with me that the horse died with staggers.

Mr. Parker then called in the hostler who attended the horse during his sickness, who said:

The horse doctor said he had pneumonia; he did not cough; when first noticed that he was sick he would lay down and wallow; after the first day he would stand quiet wherever I put him; he would stand very quiet all the time after the first day; would drink, but would not eat.

I do not think this horse was affected with staggers—more likely an abdominal trouble.

I next called to see Mr. C. L. Dougherty. He was not at home, but the gentleman in charge informed me that the horse died of lockjaw, and I must say that, from the history of the symptoms furnished me, I am inclined to believe he was affected with tetanus. He died the last week in September. Mr. W. J. Davis, livery-man, Portsmouth, said:

I averaged twenty horses in my stable during the summer; I did not have a case of staggers in my stable; I did not use a particle of food that was not imported from the West, and I think that is the reason I did not have any of the disease.

As I was anxious to discover a case of the disease in a large town where the feed is procured from feed-stores, and consequently raised in the West, I made inquiries in every direction, but I failed to find a single case. I was told that a certain horse doctor in Portsmouth had had great success in treating the disease. I went to see him and he made the following statement:

I cured eighteen cases out of nineteen I treated for the disease, only one of which was in Portsmouth and owned by L. H. Pearson; the balance were in the country. I did not see the one that died, but I sent the medicine to him, and the man only got one dose down the horse before it died, and I can not count that a case. I do not call the disease staggers. I think it is malaria, because I treated it for such and the horses got well.

I went immediately to see Mr. L. H. Pearson, from whom I received the following account of his horse, mentioned in the horse doctor's statement:

I had an animal sick; drove her about 15 miles the evening before she got sick; she appeared as well as usual; about 12 o'clock next day I noticed she was uneasy; would look back at her flanks as if in pain; would walk around, then lie down and groan and grunt like a person; she would paw continually when standing up, then lie down and roll over from side to side; at 5 o'clock same evening she was as well as ever.

It is hardly necessary for me to say that I did not follow up any more of the cases of this horse doctor, who treated a case of ordinary spasmodic colic for a malarial fever, but, as I have remarked in another place, every sick horse was supposed to have the prevailing malady, even by that intelligent (?) fraternity, the self-made horse doctor. From a farmer or a business man I could always get a plain statement of facts, but from those fellows who pretended to have almost supernatural knowledge of the diseases of the horse I could never get anything but garbled accounts, accompanied by a superabundant quantity of volubility and pedantry.

I called upon Dr. H. F. Butt, of Portsmouth, who had given the subject much consideration, and his views are well worth recording. He said in substance:

I have seen at least a half a dozen cases. They appear dull, drowsy, and sleepy; some are indisposed to lie down; they have convulsions and delirium; I think it is undoubtedly an affection of the cerebro-spinal system, caused by the surroundings, feed, or water.

On the evening of November 5 I returned to Norfolk and visited many of the stables. I also went to some stables in Norfolk on the morning of November 6, but I could hear of no case of staggers that had died in this city. I met a gentleman who lives 7 miles east of Norfolk, near Ocean View, who lost a horse, showing the following symptoms: "Became weak; would stagger; walk in a circle; get crazy fits; rear up and fall down; fits would last ten minutes at a time; died three days after first signs of sickness." This gentleman, Mr. Woodcock, stated that he fed corn raised this year. He also said other horses had died in the neighborhood. His horse died two weeks ago. This was undoubtedly a case of encephalitis, but might have been the result of any of the causes which produce the sporadic form of the disease.

I conversed with many other people on the subject, but I give the above statements as fair specimens of the information to be obtained. Of course I heard many wild accounts, from which nothing could be learned, therefore I did not waste the time to take notes of them. There is no doubt there are many horses lost from this peculiar malady every year in the localities visited by me, and we have ample evidence that every wet season is followed by a general outbreak that destroys many thousand dollars worth of horses. We must bear in mind that I was through a small portion only of the affected districts in Virginia (to be more accurate, only a few sections of three counties was visited by me), and while I heard accounts of the havoc the disease played in other counties of eastern Virginia I was credibly informed it prevailed even to a greater extent in portions of the eastern counties of North Carolina. I have been told by gen m in whom I place confidence that more horses died during the past summer in Gates County, N. C., than in Nansemond County, Va. I was also informed that many were lost in districts around Albermarle Sound and other places on the sea-board of North Carolina. Joseph Lasitter and G. B. Bryan, who are at present engaged in the horse business in Richmond, Va., but formerly conducted a sale stable in Kinston, N. C., which is at least 40 miles from the coast, state that they have known the disease to exist in Lenoir County, N. C., for years. Yesterday I met a Mr. Mitchell, proprietor of a sale stable in Kinston, N. C., who stated that many horses died in that vicinity this year from staggers. Later I extended my investigations into North Carolina, the results of which will be found below.

Before I visited Nansemond County, Va., I thought the reports were exaggerated, but before I had spent a day among the farmers of that county my mind was disabused of that idea. No class of horses is exempt. They are all liable to the disease, from the highly-bred trotting stock of Mr. Lindsay down to the scrub, raw-boned animal that drags a truck cart.

It is amusing to hear the many different theories advanced regarding the cause of the disease. It is generally admitted that the heaviest losses occur after a very wet season, therefore the cob-web theory has many advocates; but this theory is easily disposed of when we know that horses that are kept in the stable all the time contract the disease as quickly as those that are on pastures covered with cob-webs. There are others who say the cob-webs are full of little bugs which are eaten by the horses and cause the trouble, but the same objection is opposed to the bug as to the cob-web itself. It is not due to the effects of the sun, as claimed by some, as the experience of Mr. Lindsay and many others sufficiently proved. We can not accept the malarial theory in the face of the fact that malarial fevers occur in many places where this disease is never known as enzootic. The symptoms of the disease are not those of malaria. Malaria prevails among the human beings of Portsmouth and Norfolk, but I was not able to discover a record of a single case of staggers in either of those places after searching for nearly two days. It is not due I am inclined to think to the same cause that produces Southern cattle fever, because native horses, both young and old, die even before those brought from the West, but like the cattle fever it disappears after the first cool weather. This point needs further investigation, as I find some people who think it due to the same cause, although the symptoms are entirely different, and the cattle fever exists in many places where staggers has never made its appearance. Some think it is caused by atmospheric influence. This is a very easy way to account for any disease, but we must look for something more tangible as the cause for the malady in question.

There are a few, and they are very few, who think it is contagious. It is almost useless for me to state that I do not entertain this opinion. There is no evidence whatever in support of this, but everything against it. Take, for instance, the cases where the horses were worked and fed on the low lands and kept in the same stable with the other horses on the sand ridges, and died without communicating the disease ; or take the experience of the towns of Suffolk, Portsmouth, and Norfolk, where horses were driven to and fed daily from the affected districts, and still there is no evidence that the disease was communicated. The affected districts were circumscribed, and horses owned in them were constantly taken to places where the disease never appeared. It would only be waste of time to further consider the contagiousness of the malady. There are people who attribute the cause to the dew on the pasture, but I object to this on the same ground that I object to the cob-web and bug theories. It can not be caused by any particular species or natural order of plants. It has occurred when any one of the usual kinds of feed has been entirely omitted, timothy hay, clover hay, millet hay, corn and corn fodder, oats, bran, and straw, grass of different kinds, and other green food, pea-nut hay, and rag weed, marsh and orchard grass, any one of them has been fed or has not been fed, and still the animals contracted the disease. But of one thing I am convinced, and that is, we must look to the feed for the cause, and look only to the feed raised in the section where the disease exists, and look to the feed raised the same year the disease exists. I am positive that here alone we will find the cause that produces this extraordinary enzootic malady. I will admit that the water may contain, as some assert, a poisonous something having the peculiar properties of conveying the disease, but even if it does, the feed contains those properties to a hundred-fold greater extent. This must be admitted when we consider the large number of horses that were fed on Western feed, and even feed raised last year, that were not affected by the disease, although they drank the same kind of water, and from the same source as the water drank by the horses that died with staggers. If I am right in supposing the cause is with the feed, I am equally right in saying that it is the feed raised in the section where the disease exists, because I could not get the record of a single case of the malady in a horse where the feed had been procured from a feed store supplied from the West; and furthermore, I can say with as much truth that it is due to the feed raised on certain locations only of a given neighborhood. For instance, take the land along the creeks and rivers, and in the necks between them—here is where over 90 per cent. of all the cases have occurred. Then take the land a few miles back, on the sand ridges, and we have only the record of a few isolated cases for evidence that the disease existed there at all, and even in these few cases all facts go to prove that the affected animals got their feed on the former land. To a person accustomed to mountainous regions, or even a section of the country where the land is called rolling, this country would appear as level as a billiard table, but it is not so. It is true that a sand ridge here is only a few feet higher than the marshes and swamps; but great sanitary importance is attached to this fact by the inhabitants, and rightly so, I think. Apropos, from an advertisement of the town of Suffolk, I will quote the following:

The climate and situation of Suffolk are exceptionably favorable to health, as is shown by the low rate of mortality, which is estimated, after a close investigation of all available facts, at the low average of 16 per 1,000 inhabitants per annum, as also the longevity and generally robust appearance of the population. While some portions of tide-water Virginia are undoubtedly subject to malarious influences, owing to their low, level, and marshy surroundings, this charge can not be brought even remotely against Suffolk, which is "built upon many hills."

Suffolk is 17 and 23 miles, respectively, from Portsmouth and Norfolk by railroads, and Suffolk is only 46 feet higher than either Norfolk or Portsmouth, which are located not far from the edge of the sea. The neighborhood of Berea Church, where so many horses died the past summer, is near about half-way between Norfolk and Suffolk on the main driving road, and a person driving into Suffolk from there would not imagine that Suffolk was on higher ground than Berea Church, and still it is claimed that Suffolk is "built upon many hills," and so it is, but they are indeed small hills in a mountaineer's estimation. It will thus be seen that a little difference in the location of the land makes a great difference in the health of not only the human population, but of horses also. Remember, the disease is confined to circumscribed localities, patches along rivers, creeks, and the necks, which land is always lower than the sand ridges. Now, if it is certain that the cause is with the feed raised in the sections where the disease occurs, it is certain that the cause is produced almost simultaneously with the production of the feed, or at least produced at some time during the growth of the feed; and to cause the disease the feed must be used within a certain time—July, August, and first part of September, during the hot weather, for the "oldest inhabitants" all say that there are no cases after the weather gets cool. I conversed with gentlemen who live in "staggers districts," who had sufficient feed of the crop of 1885 to last them until three or four weeks ago, when they began using this year's crop, and they did not have a case of it. In fact, from all the evidence I could gather, horses fed on feed raised in 1885 were as ex-

[illegible] from the disease as those fed on Western feed, [illegible] that I did not hear of a case of staggers in a horse [illegible] feed raised this year, except Frisbee's; and I heard [illegible] where last year's crop was used exclusively [illegible] case of staggers occurred; but further investigation [illegible] before this can become an accepted fact.

The question may now be asked, What is the exact cause of the [illegible] In answer to this I can only say, I don't know. I [illegible] to jump at a conclusion after an investigation of only [illegible] that limited investigation made six weeks after the [illegible] the enzootic occurred. Bear in mind that I did not see [illegible] sickness, consequently, when I began my investigation [illegible] chaotic state as regards the disease in question. Any horse [illegible] that was ailing from the effects of any disease whatever [illegible] supposed to be affected with this strange malady; the theories of the people as to the nature of the disease were as varied as their [illegible] cause, and the absurdity of some of the causes advanced were only equaled by the villainous modes of treatment adopted in many instances, such as cutting three links from the end of the tail to draw the blood from the brain. This I know to be a fact, and I was informed by Mr. Pinner that the ears were cut off in some cases. Almost every horse doctor had a particular "reseet" that was supposed to be infallible. From what statistics I obtained I am satisfied that recoveries did not average 2 per cent. of the affected horses. Of course, there are many horses in the affected districts who were fed on this year's growth and escaped the disease, whilst other horses in the same stable contracted it and died, but this is not strange when we remember that no disease, even the most malignant, destroys all that are exposed to the cause. This point can probably be better explained when a thorough investigation has been made into the nature of the cause.

Although I say I do not know what the cause really is, I am confident that it can be discovered with the microscope, or even, perhaps, with a strong magnifying glass. This part of the examination must be carried on in the field at the time the disease exists—at the time the feed is producing the disease; then I am sure some definite conclusion can be arrived at. I am well aware of the fact that some authorities claim that smut will cause encephalitis, and [illegible] and rust will cause it, but if this alone was the cause of these enzootic outbreaks of staggers, then we would have the disease raging in the districts I have been through at the present time, because I did not examine a specimen of feed that was entirely free from smut, mold, and rust, and that feed has been and is now fed daily to the horses, but there have been no cases of the disease since the commencement of cool weather. It may be that cool weather destroys the activity of those fungi, but I think not, as it does not destroy the poisonous effects of ergot, another fungus. I certainly think the cause is in the nature of a fungus, as the fact of the disease being most virulent after a very wet season points, and the fact of it always appearing on low, damp, and marshy lands, further confirms this theory. But I think the particular fungus is a more delicate one than any of those mentioned above, so delicate, indeed, that cool weather destroys its activity, and probably destroys the parent germ, leaving nothing but the spores to undergo maturation at the next favorable season. If the cause is not due to a fungus [illegible] solution, then it is within the province of the chemist to [illegible] omething unusual in the composition of all the plants raised in hose sections. But I do not entertain this idea. I think the cause vill be discovered in the nature of a fungi, whose active principle is subtile, delicate, narcotic poison, which is taken into the system vith the feed—on the feed that it matures—and gains access to the irculation and is thereby conveyed to the great nerve centers and roduces its toxic effects like other narcotic poisons, with the acompanying train of symptoms. Before a very accurate account of he effects of the poison can be studied, however, the *post-mortem* esions will have to be studied by competent veterinarians.

As to the nature of the malady, I have but little doubt of its being cerebro-spinal affection; therefore I think the views of Professor Villiams on the cause of encephalitis are applicable here. In his rinciples and Practice of Veterinary Surgery he says:

> In Scotland it has been called "grass staggers," from the fact that it occurs hen the animal has been fed on green food; but ordinary green food does not duce it. I have very carefully noted every case which has fallen under my care r some years, and I find that grass, more particularly rye-grass, when it has ommenced to ripen, or when it has been cut and allowed to heat and ferment efore being used, is a fruitful source of this disease. I find that my observations e borne out by those of Professor Dick and others, and not only horses and cattle e liable to the disease from this cause, but sheep, and especially lambs.

In the same work the same authority quotes Professor Dick as aying:

> From what has been stated it will appear that, when rye-grass begins to ripen, a hange should be made in the food by placing the animals on other pastures. The rass should be cut before it has quite ripened, as it will be found in that state inocuous.

Professor Williams says:

> He then refers to a statement made by White, of Exeter, in White's Farriery, at the disease occurred in one farm in South Wales from hay made the previous ear (1800), and concludes that "it seems more than probable that the hay had een over-ripe when made, and that the process of withering had not destroyed the ritating or noxious, or perhaps narcotic, quality of the over-ripe grasses."

Professor Williams further says:

> I quite agree with Professor Dick that the disease is due to some peculiar narcotic inciple that is developed in the grass at the time, or which may be developed by e process of heating and fermentation when cut at an earlier stage of its growth, r every-day experience proves to us that food, even rye-grass included, has no efect in producing symptoms of cerebral disturbance when used in its ordinary conlition, and that it is only when in a transition stage, as it were, between grass and ay, that it seems to possess toxic qualities.

As will be seen from my point of study of this question, I quite gree with both Professor Dick and Professor Williams that it is due o a narcotic principle, but it is developed on the grass, and on no partiular kind of grass. But I did not hear of a suspicion of the disease xisting among cattle as staggers, and only a few thought it due to he same cause that produces Southern cattle fever. Then, again, is he fact that out of the hundreds that died in the sections visited by ne I obtained no positive evidence of the death of a mule with s aggers. We can at least say that mules are almost exempt from tthe ffects of the narcotic poison. Why? I can at present only say that erhaps it is on account of their nervous system being less suscepible to nervous impressions, and it seems to me that this fact is mportant, for should further investigation prove that mules are exmpt then much value in live stock can be saved by using more mules nd a less number of horses in the districts visited annually and periodically by outbreaks of staggers; for we must remember that the very next wet spring and early summer will be followed by a general outbreak of this disease, if the feed is used that is raised in those districts. What few cases of mules were reported shows conclusively that they were not attacked with staggers, and if they were suffering from the effects of the poison it certainly acted in a different manner from the way it produces its effects among horses, which is not at all likely.

The most important point for consideration now is how to prevent the recurrence of this disease in the future, and this, in my opinion, would be an easy matter (that is, if my views of the cause are correct) were it not for two reasons. First, it is impossible to make some people believe that the cause is in the feed. I have had specimens shown me which the persons claimed were sound and all right, and when I pointed out mold and even smut I was told that the feed was as good as any other. Just so long as people are as hard to convince, just so long are their horses liable to the disease. Second, there is another class who are differently situated from those who can make selections in the feed and the manner of supplying it to their horses. I mean that class of poor farmers who do not raise sufficient feed one year to last them until the return of cool weather, when the danger is passed. Some have hardly enough of nutritious feed to winter their horses upon, and they have to be fed from the growing crops of oats, grass, etc., from the time they begin to grow in the spring. Others wait until they can give nearly cured hay and sheaf oats. There are many who do not turn on pasture, but give their horses the new hay and oats. There is still another class who would run the risk of the disease before they would buy feed for their animals, even if they could afford it, when they had feed on their own places, and nice fresh feed too. My advice to those who have horses in the districts where the disease occurs is, during the hot weather, say from the middle of June to the middle of September, do not turn your horses out to graze on farms where animals have been known to die with staggers. Do not feed anything raised on such farms, during the same length of time. During the hot months, at least, I advise giving a bran or linseed mash or scalded oats five or six times a week. This will do no harm even if you do not fear staggers from your feed. All feed should be first class. If animals are not allowed to have anything grown in the suspected districts until after cool weather begins I think staggers will disappear as an enzootic. If the instructions are followed, and in spite of them, the horses die with staggers, then we will have to look elsewhere for the cause; but I think such will not be the case.

As regards the scientific nomenclature for this disease, I would prefer to wait until I have the opportunity of studying the lesions *post-mortem* before I act the part of a nomenclator. The symptoms in many cases prove beyond a doubt that the brain is greatly deranged, if not the seat of grave lesions symptoms exactly similar to those of cerebro-meningitis; whilst in other cases the most prominent symptoms are those of spinal affections. But we can not class this as the same disease, and from the same causes as epizootic cerebro-spinal meningitis, which occurs in cold weather in the crowded stables of the large cities, and it is not confined to localities where the "lay of the land" can be said to produce it with certainty. However, there are some symptoms very similar, the suddenness of the attack and the different deglutition which is seen in epizootic cerebro-spinal meningitis. In my inquiries I was particular on this point, because I desired to discriminate between the difficulty of swallowing in laryngitis, influenza, and strangles, which is due to local lesions, and that of epizootic cerebro-spinal meningitis, which is believed to be caused by paralysis of the glossal muscles and the consequent inability of the tongue to assist in conducting the water back to the pharynx. In the former cases the water gets as far as the pharynx, but on account of the pain caused by the contraction of the constrictors, or the local swelling, the act of deglutition can not be accomylished, and as the water once in the pharynx can not be returned through the fauces, it therefore enters the posterior nares and is returned through the nasal chambers. In the case of cerebro-spinal meningitis (epizootic), I do not think the water gets as far as the pharynx; the animal inserts his mouth deep into the water and makes desperate but ineffectual attempts to quench his thirst, but I have never seen water come out the nostrils, nor have I heard of a case where it did; and, furthermore, in many instances of the epizootic nervous affection the horse will get his mouth so far into the water that the nostrils are beneath the surface. I have heard of cases of staggers where difficult deglutition was a prominent symptom as expressed by inability to swallow water, where cough, difficult respiration, discharge from nostrils, and swollen glands were entirely absent. Many cases were reported to me where, in addition to the difficulty or inability to swallow water, the horse would exhibit every other symptom of nervous disorder, viz., stand with head resting on trough or in the manger apparently asleep, and when suddenly disturbed would be greatly startled; dull, stupid, and deaf; press head against objects; lean against the side of stall or stable; inability to walk in a straight line; head drawn to one side, pleurothotonous; inclination to move in a circle; individual inclination to move to one side and one direction only, some to the right, others to the left; when down, head drawn back and tail also, opisthotonous; paralysis; delirium. Death takes place while comatose, or terminate the most frantic paroxysms or convulsions, making it positively dangerous to venture near the afflicted to render aid. All these symptoms were given to me by non-professionals, who little understand how to interpret them, but their significance are unmistakable to a veterinarian, and I will here remark, that we often come in contact among the farmers with the most acute observers; nothing escapes their notice. One man actually told me: "The first I noticed that anything was wrong was a funny looking color in the back of the horses eyes." This is a prominent occurrence in epizootic cerebro-spinal meningitis, but I have heard of an authority on that subject who says it takes an ophthalmoscope to see it. If this be so, what a penetrating eye that farmer must have. Or for "cuteness" take the statement of the old farmer who said: "He began to reel around and stagger, and lean up against things like a drunken man exactly." I was particularly impressed by this remark, as I took into consideration the fact that a drunken man was under the influence of a narcotic poison, and I believe the affected horses were dying from a different, but, nevertheless, a narcotic poison.

I will not waste much time in considering the theory of those few [illegible] Suffolk who think the enzootic is an affection of the lungs. [illegible] they admit that the animal does not cough or exhibit other [illegible] symptoms of lung disease. They base their opinion alone on the fact that they found, *post-mortem*, the lungs black or bloodshot.

the great loss of horses throughout the eastern counties of North Carolina. The disease is by no means confined to these two States, as the following statement from Mr. G. B. Bryan shows. Mr. Bryan is an old and experienced horseman and has been engaged in the horse business exclusively for many years in the Southern States. He is a native of Kentucky, but his business has caused him to visit all sections of the South. He says:

My practical experience with staggers was principally in North Carolina, as I lived in a section there where the disease was very common. I noticed that the class of horses generally affected were hard worked, poorly fed, and badly cared for; but fine, well-kept animals were often attacked. All kinds of feed raised in that section is poor. I have never seen a case in a horse that was fed exclusively on Northern or Western feed. It is not necessary to turn a horse on pasture in order for him to contract the disease. L. M. Blakely, of Washington, N. C., owned a fine stallion worth several thousand dollars. He was confined to the stable all the time; never grazed any, and was well cared for in every respect. I saw to that. Much of his food was from the West, but he was also given food raised in that swampy country, and he died with staggers. Many horses died all through that section. I am of the opinion that the cause, whatever it is, is in feed raised there. I know of another case where a horse died of staggers in that neighborhood, that never run on pasture, but his food was raised in that county. I have known staggers to occur in epidemic form in South Carolina, Georgia, Florida, Mississippi, Louisiana, and Arkansas; worse some seasons than others, especially in years when there has been an overflow. In Kentucky we raise as many horses as are raised anywhere, and I never heard of staggers appearing as an epidemic, and I think the season is simply because we raise good horses and know how to appreciate good feed.

I visited Hog Island, in the James River, about 100 miles below Richmond, for the following specific reasons: I was informed that mules had been lost there. I knew the manager of the farm was a practical horseman, and although not a graduate in veterinary medicine, had practiced for many years in Petersburgh, during which time he was agent for the stock company who own the island and are engaged in stock raising on a large scale. I had heard the barns, stables, and all buildings were of the highest order, and I found them to be so. I knew the island was in tide-water, and therefore not subject to overflow from freshets. They raise all their feed on the island proper, which contains about eighteen hundred acres, one-third of which is marsh. The highest point is not more than 9 feet above the level of the river. The island, as a whole, will not average more than 3 feet above mean tide, and is not thoroughly drained at present. The present manager, Mr. Potts, was not in charge when the first case occurred. From those in charge at the time I obtained the following information:

There were on the island 12 horses and 6 mules, of which 5 horses and 1 mule died. The first horse died in June, and the second the latter part of August. The third animal to die was the mule. I will occupy neither time nor space by giving all the history of the symptoms furnished me, as I am confident that all three died of acute indigestion. Here is a specimen of the symptoms of one: "Look around at his side; paw; lay down; roll; sweat very much; suddenly got quiet; cold all over; trembles very much; after he died we opened him and found his stomach in rags, and the feed all over the outside of the guts." No veterinarian would have any trouble in diagnosing this case from such symptoms, or the mule from these symptoms: "Would roll over; get up; turn complete somersaults; fell and died; before she died she rattled in her throat; stuff came out of her nose and mouth." No *post-mortem* examination was held on the mule, nor do I think it was necessary to determine the cause of death. About the 4th or 5th of September 3 horses were noticed to be sick within three hours of each other. One fell whilst on the way to the field; another fell while ploughing. "They appeared very weak and were taken back to the stable; the third took sick in the stable." Just at this time Mr. Potts, who had been across the river, arrived and took charge of the horses. He had (and has now) entire management of the place. Mr. Potts preferred to write out his own description of the cases, and I therefore attach it to this, as follows:

I was called to see 3 sick horses. The first was a gray mare eight years old. I found her trembling and very weak in right hind leg; tail and head up, eyes staring, hard breathing, muscles twitching I had her led out of stable and with great difficulty held her up one hour. She was stiff as a board and fell to the ground; her jaws were locked tight. She never moved a limb after falling to the ground. She died about twelve hours after I first saw her. The other was a gray horse ten years old. He was standing, leaning up against the side of the stable, grinding his teeth; breathing very hard; weak in left hind leg; pulse seemed normal; his tail was up and eyes staring; did not seem to show any abnormal pain. Tried to move him, but found him stiff, and in turning him around he fell. After striking the ground he was stiff. His muscles were drawn, teeth set tight, breathing laborious. I gave him anodynes, when he limbered up and commenced grinding his teeth and struggling in spasms. At last he laid perfectly still and stiff, breathed hard, teeth and eyes set. He died in about half an hour after the mare.

The third was a gray horse about twelve years old. He was standing, leaning up against the side of the stall, breathing hard; seemed weak across the loins; refused to eat; his pulse was beating about thirty to the minute; his tail was up, but not so much as the other; he would be quite cold, then change to heat, then quick pulse, and so on alternately. I bled, and blistered him across the back; used hot water across the loins and gave cathartics and he began to improve. At night after the others had died we led him about; put him in another stall; he was very weak behind, but did not lie down. On the next day the cathartics operated. He seemed better and kept improving for about a week; then he was taken with weakness and trembling of hind extremities. We led to a convenient place and put him in slings. By this time he had lost all use of both hind legs and began to have spasms, tail and head up, teeth set tight, eyes staring and set, and in four hours he died.

As you will observe, there are symptoms in all three of the cases described by Mr. Potts that remind one of azoturia, but I made particular inquiry and found the horses had been working every day. All the feed raised on the island this year was inferior in quality, especially the oats, which were bad in the extreme—the mustiest I ever saw used for horse-feed. None of the animals were on pasture. Mr. Potts saw eleven cases this year showing same symptoms as the three described. The most remarkable thing about these cases is the simultaneousness of the attack; and this is not the only instance I have heard of where several were attacked at the same time on the same farm. In fact, Mr. Potts related another such instance occurring on the main-land not more than four miles from his place.

The principal object of my visit to Gates County, N. C., was to discover, if possible, if any mules had died showing well-marked symptoms of staggers. I had been previously informed that many horses died during the summer and fall in this county, and I found soon after my arrival there that I had been correctly informed. The gentlemen who lost horses in the vicinity of Sunbury fed this year's crops and some grazed, and the information adds no new facts that are not given above. I heard that Mr. J. F. Cross had lost a mule with staggers. I called to see him, and he stated in substance as follows:

I lost a mule last August; he slobbered considerably; had a hacking cough; discharged from the nose; sick three or four days; when turned around would grunt; stood with head down, and had every symptom of lung fever; I never *thought he had staggers.*

I certainly hold the same opinion as Mr. Cross.

Mr. J. W. Hill, 2 miles from Sunbury, "counted about 50 horses that died in Gates County this summer and fall. All the best horses died. All our feed is raised in the county." The symptoms he furnished of his own and other horses affected were those of staggers. He also stated that the farms on which horses died were mostly near the desert (swamp). Mr. J. B. Riddick, 4 miles from Sunbury, lost 2 bay mares in August which were undoubtedly affected with staggers. These animals were fed exclusively on last year's corn and fodder, and had not been on pasture for several weeks before they died, when they were turned out nights on oats stubble (new ground). Although both of these animals had eaten of this year's growth it was so long before their death as to make it a suspicion (if we admit the disease is caused by the feed) that last year's growth can contain e cause.

thMr. A. F. McCotter, Sandy Cross, Gates County, said:

> I lost a mule in July; was taken sick about 12 o'clock, suddenly; would lie down, roll over, and get up; look around at his belly; had hiccoughs; jump, rear, and fall; died eight hours after first noticed to be sick.

I visited every place I could hear of a mule having had the staggers, and I will give the symptoms, so you can judge for yourself whether or not mules are liable to the disease.

I wish to call attention to this fact, that horses that recover from this disease are affected with sequelæ, as they are in the epizootic form of cerebro-spinal meningitis.

In rare instances I would hear of horses that recovered from the disease, but almost always I was told "they were never the same horses afterward." To illustrate this point, as well as some other information of importance, I will give in his own words, as near as possible, the statement of an old gentleman (Reuben Nixon) who resides near Sunbury Cross:

> I have seen many cases of staggers, and I think I know the disease when I see it. One of my best horses died with it this past August; he seemed drunk; would turn round and round; lost use of hind legs and fell paralyzed; died three days after. I have seen the disease for sixty years, and have noticed in the years we have much hot weather more horses die than at any other seasons; there have not been as many die for the past twenty years as this year. In this county we always say the disease rages from August to October. When I was a boy two cases belonging to my father got well, but they never had the same sense afterwards. We could work them, but if you turned them too short they would stagger and fall.

Mr. A. F. Riddick, Belvidere, Perquimans County, N. C., lost a fine horse, with symptoms of staggers, in August. His father lost several. He said:

> I think the disease is most prevalent in seasons following hot, wet weather. Fifteen or twenty died during this season, and only one mule that we can say died from staggers. It was owned by Mr. Chapel, of Chowan County. I think there are as many mules as horses in this county.

I drove to Mr. William Chapel's, whose mule is mentioned above. He said as to the death of this animal:

> My mule died the latter part of August; I first noticed he was stiff all over; was sleepy; refused water; would not eat corn; was swollen over the eyes; legs were cold; jaws stiff; would grit his teeth; would lie down and get up easily; did not lose the use of hind parts; first seemed to be sick on Friday; Saturday night he fell and remained very quiet until he died.

Was this a case of staggers? The symptoms come nearer to those of staggers than any case I ever heard of in a mule, but I am inclined to think the mule did not have the disease. If he had a case of encephalitis it may have been caused by an injury to the head, as Mr. Chapel said he was swollen above the eyes, although he did not know how the mule could have been injured. I inquired for symptoms of lung trouble, but the above were the symptoms as I received them.

Mr. Chapel told me of a gentlemen who lived four miles further who lost a mule with staggers. We drove to his (Mr. Copeland's) farm, but he was not at home. Spoke to his wife, and she said that she had heard them say that the mule died from "grubs," and from the history of the symptoms she gave I am confident the mule was not affected with staggers. It seemed to be a violent case of indigestion, as the animal died within two hours after it was first attacked.

Dr. Thomas N. White, Perquimans County, N. C., has given this disease consideration for years. A synopsis of his views is as follows:

There are more or less cases every year: over 20 died in this immediate neighborhood this year. It is undoubtedly a cerebro-spinal disease. I think the cause may be traced to the quality of the feed raised on our lands, as we can grow rice on all farms in this vicinity, and consequently the land is damp; and, further, we know the disease always occurs to the greatest extent in wet seasons, and at such seasons our feed is of a very inferior quality.

Mr. Joseph White, Windfall, N. C., says:

We have the staggers in this vicinity every year, but it is most destructive every seven years. No mules were lost in this neighborhood, but many horses died with it this year.

Mr. C. W. Small, Durant's Neck, between the Little and Perquimans Rivers, says:

I know of 20 horses that died on the Neck this year with staggers. Mules are not affected with staggers. Our crops were very poor and feed was bad. One man lost 5 horses.

Mr. N. R. Zimmerman, Elizabeth City, is my authority for stating that many horses died in Pasquotank County, N. C., this year, but no mules that he heard of.

Edenton, Chowan County, N. C., is on Albemarle Sound, and I expected to hear of many losses in the vicinity, which surmise proved to be correct, but I could not hear of the death of a mule with this disease. Like every other place almost every man had a theory of his own, two of which I will give. Dr. George H. Coke, a resident physician of this place, says:

I have known the disease for years; lost a horse myself; it is undoubtedly an affection of the [illegible] system. I think the cause is in the low lands and wet s[illegible]. I never heard of a mule being affected with staggers.

Mr. White, of the Bay View Hotel, who is also engaged in farming, [illegible] farmers prevented the disease by not allowing [illegible] during the sunshine, whilst those who were [illegible] their horses to be on pasture during [illegible] losses in consequence. I wish to particu[illegible] to this, as many cases of the disease are re[illegible] animals were not exposed to the effects of the dew

[illegible] I was frequently referred to Dr. W. R. [illegible] County, as a gentleman of vast experi[illegible] South. I was informed that he [illegible] physician, but was noted as an extensive breeder of fine stock. I learned that his plantation was situated across the sound in Bertie County, N. C. I procured a sail-boat and was taken to his place. We discussed the matter thoroughly, and as he was quite conversant with all the points connected with the disease, I will give his views in full:

I have had considerable experience with staggers in horses, but never saw a case in a mule. It is a cerebro-spinal disease due to miasmatic influences. I have never known the disease to occur elsewhere than in miasmatic districts. I don't turn my horses out to pasture before 9 a. m., during July, August, and September, and they rarely suffer. We all graze. I begin to feed new oats about the 10th of July. August is the month the disease generally appears, and we rarely have miasmatic fevers among our people until then. I treat the staggers of horses the same as I treat hemorrhagic malarial fevers among our people. I always notice that staggers is ushered in by rigors, and if I get it in that stage I give calomel and aloes, followed by quinine, and the horses get well. This has been the experience of my father and grandfather. If the horse has a second chill the case is serious, and if a third, he dies. The disease occurs after a protracted drought, but invariably follows wet seasons. I think mules are not susceptible, and by their general use much loss could be saved. Three years ago I had 2 valuable stallion colts that I kept in the stable constantly. Accidentally they got out and broke into a corn and pea field, where they remained for forty-eight hours, during which time there was a constant fog, causing vegetation to drip with moisture. On the third day one was taken with staggers in an aggravated form, violent derangement from beginning; I used mercurial and aloetic purgative; blister to poll; applied ice constantly to head. No action from bowels. He died eight hours after. The other colt was not affected in the slightest.

Low lands, though they be drained by ditches, suffer more with miasmatic troubles than the sandy soil of pint ridges that percolate freely.

My reasons for thinking this disease a malarial affection are: It occurs only in malarial districts; it is ushered in with a chill, followed by fever, with a recurring chill and congestion of the brain; and our best results have followed our treatment for miasmatic fevers.

I treated one filly three times for staggers within sixty days, and she lived to be ten or twelve years old. I bought a horse in Baltimore and brought him to this section. He was here a very short time when he had a well-marked case of staggers, with more than the usual amount of drowsiness, but no violence. I used no counter irritation of cold applications to the head. I gave an active purgative, followed by a 400-grain dose of quinine. The horse recovered without further treatment. This horse, in the possession of another owner, had a similar attack the following year and died, not having had any treatment that I am aware of.

From Edenton I proceeded up the Roanoke River. For miles up from its mouth nothing but swamps on either side are seen, and in such country I would expect to find records of the disease, and it is almost needless to say I had no difficulty in obtaining evidence of great losses from staggers. Mr. Samuel Baynor, Plymouth, Washington County, N. C., says:

Never knew a mule to be affected. Over 50 horses died around here this summer. Three boarding horses died in my stable in September. All were fed on old food raised in this neighborhood. One had no new feed; he was a doctor's horse, and could not possibly have grazed for more than an hour at a time when tied at some house in the country. Heretofore I thought the disease was caused by the dew on the pasture, but this case makes me think otherwise. I opend him and several other horses that died with staggers, and found the neck of the gut that connects with the maw stopped up, and this, I think, is the cause.

From the symptoms given, these were cases of staggers, and here again rises the question: Supposing the cause *is* in the feed, was it the old feed, or the little grazing (one hour at a time, or perhaps much less; once, twice, three, or four times a week), that caused the disease? Now, as regards the "neck of the gut that connects with the maw stopped up," I must confess that I am at a loss to account for this entirely new and original theory; simply I do not understand what neck. Dunglison and Webster define the *maw* to be the stomach of an animal, and so I understand it; but I find the great majority of the people who use the term mean either the colon or cæcum. In this case the gentleman when using the term *maw* meant either the stomach or the cæcum, because the *neck* was small, and I think (although I am not certain, as I did not thoroughly understand his explanation), he referred to the termination of the ileum at the ileo-cæcal valve, and consequently meant the cæcum. Of course this might have been a complication, but an utter impossibility to cause the disease, and therefore I will not give it further consideration.

Williamston, Martin County, N. C., is in the neighborhood of a mile from the river, and is situated on high land. I was told that people suffer from malarial fevers, but there were no cases of staggers among the horses in the immediate vicinity of the town. Many cases occurred in the county, however, where the land is lower.

Mr. O. Burnett, Tarborough, Edgecombe County, N. C., proprietor of sale and livery stable, had lost no horses with the disease, and after investigation I failed to find a well-authenticated case in the town, although I heard of a great many that had died. With the exception of the interesting cases to be mentioned in connection with Dr. Jones's statement, I do not think any of them were pronounced cases; but many horses died with the disease in the vicinity of Tarborough, but no mules.

Mr. J. K. Grannis, of Tarborough, formerly of Fleming County, Ky., gives a most interesting statement, as follows:

> The year 1875 was a very wet one in Fleming County, and all our feed was very badly damaged. Streams were all flooded and crops spoiled. The year 1876 followed with a drought, and we lost many horses from staggers, and I think it was caused by the damaged feed raised the previous year and fed on stock during 1876. That is the only outbreak of any consequence that I know of in Kentucky.

This statement is more than interesting, as it points to the fact that feed raised the previous year will produce the disease during the hot weather of the following year, and it proves that the disease can be caused by the quality of the feed in an enzootic form. It also proves that the disease can be caused by the feed outside of the noted miasmatic localities of the South.

Dr. J. W. Jones, Tarborough, president of the State Board of Health, states that staggers occurs all over the eastern part of North Carolina. He never heard of a case in a mule; the horses die in the surrounding country; very few die in the town; knew of cases treated with quinine that died. Dr. Jones is very much interested in the matter, and will bring it prominently before the board at its next meeting. He lost a horse in November, 1885, and another in January, 1886, showing symptoms of staggers.

The only cases that died in the town of Rocky Mount this year were two horses brought in from Nash County. One died in March, the other in April. These were evidently cases of staggers, as I made the most particular inquiry as to symptoms. These four were of course sporadic cases, or not the same disease, as all evidence goes to prove that the enzootic occurs only in hot weather.

Mr. R. H. Gatlin makes the following statement, which bears directly on the question of the susceptibility of mules:

> I lost horses from the disease in 1867. This was a very wet year, and many horses were lost during the season. My wife's father had in pasture on the Roanoke River, near Hamilton, four horse colts and two mule colts. All the horses died, but the mules were not affected. Many neighbors had horse colts on the same pasture that contracted the disease and died.

Dr. L. L. Staton, Tarborough, says:

Have seen cases of staggers, and think it is a cerebro-spinal affection. I am satisfied that it is not caused by malarial influences; if it were malaria quinine would be an antidote, but I have used quinine with no more success than other treatment. I have given extremely large doses without effect. It is the general belief of this community that colts are more subject to the disease than the older horses, as the colts graze more than other horses.

I wish to call attention to the fact that in this country physicians know how to use quinine. I mention this for the reason that I was called to account, in a veterinary meeting a few years ago, for making the statement that I gave 2-drachm doses of quinine as an antipyretic. The gentlemen who almost accused me of maltreatment, it is needless to say, obtained their knowledge of quinine from writers of veterinary *materia medica* who resided hundreds of miles from where it was necessary to have practical knowledge. I will add that in certain cases I use it with success in much larger doses now.

I have personal knowledge of the disease in Nash, Wilson, Wayne and other counties of North Carolina, but I get no information that I have not reported about. I heard of instances where mules died, but when I came to investigate I invariably found that they died from the effect of some other disease, most generally an affection of the digestive organs. A gentleman related an instance of a wealthy planter in South Carolina who had tried for years to keep up a four-in-hand team for his wife, but the horses invariably died with staggers. As he was determined to have a four-in-hand he substituted mules for horses, and consequently had no difficulty in gratifying his desire. Gentlemen who have paid particular attention to the subject do not hesitate in saying that mules are not subject to the disease. Others will say there are two or three or four different kinds of staggers, and the mule was thought to be affected with one of the different kinds of the disease. Let no person imagine the mules are scarce in this country, for there are many of of them, and good ones, too. In some neighborhoods where we find staggers mules are in the majority, while in other localities they are in the minority. A mule is a very staple article in the South, and deservedly so, and I think if they were generally substituted for horses in those districts where staggers is sure to occur much could be saved. Of course I do not recommend that all the horses be sold off and mules procured in their stead immediately, but I mean when the farmer wants a work animal always get a mule, or when a horse dies with staggers replace it with a mule. Those who keep carriage horses could continue to do so, and could adopt the preventive treatment advised elsewhere in this report. I will conclude the mule question by saying, and I think the evidence will bear me out, that if mules are subject to the disease the percentage is so very small that it should be considered no more than any rare sporadic disease.

As previously pointed out, the higher locations in this region are not affected by the disease, unless it can be traced to feed brought from some of the stagger localities, if I may be permitted to use the expression, and I have been told by the adherents of the malarial origin of the disease "that it just happened so." Well, perhaps they are right, but it seems strange that it always happens so." Goldsborough, N. C., is located on high land, and I did not come across a case of the disease in the city (although there were some reported that turned out to be something else), nor in the immeditae vicinity of the city, but like every other section there were many cases in the county on the lower land. Mr. George D. Bennett, of Goldsborough, who is the proprietor of large sale stables, says that "it is caused by the treatment the horse receives; the horses that are brought here don't die until about the third summer."

I was often told that the disease was caused by "sorryness," and upon inquiry I learned that by "sorryness" was meant either starvation, carelessness, laziness, or general neglect, or all combined; and we must admit that a combination of the above sins causes a great deal of trouble and sorrow in this world, but they alone can not cause staggers in the horse. I have seen as nice stables and as well-kept horses down there as I have seen anywhere, and I would indeed be ignorant of my duty if I overlooked such important matters. There are, of course, many instances where surrounding circumstances make it appear that the animal died of "sorryness," but there are many more instances where the designation is not applicable under any circumstance whatever. How many intelligent planters have been for years striving by every means within their knowledge and power to prevent this dread disease? I met gentlemen whose tastes inclined them to breeding fine horses, but the prevalence of this disease compelled them, after severe losses, to give up the enterprise in despair. I do not for a moment pretend to say that those who think the disease is due to starvation and neglect are not honest in their opinions. Quite the contrary; I know they mean what they say; but I know also that those who hold such opinions are invariably persons who never lost a horse from the effects of staggers.

As previously stated, and further investigation has proved the assertion, it is not necessary for the animals to be exposed to either the sun or the dew on the pasture in order to contract the disease; furthermore, I do not see why those who firmly believe the cause to be miasmatic prefer to turn their horses on pasture at either one of the extremes, viz., night or mid-day, when experience teaches that morning and evening are the times we are less exposed to miasmatic influences in such regions. The heat of noonday and nightly emanations are to be feared most. By morning and evening I mean, of course, after the fogs have disappeared in the morning and before the mists appear in the evening.

If the cause is in the feed, then it is reasonably possible that feed raised one year will, or can, contain the active poisonous principle that causes the disease. I have but three instances of this year's outbreak to confirm this point, viz., Mr. Frisbee, of Nansemond County, Va.; Mr. Riddick, of Gates County, N. C., and Mr. Baynor, of Washington County, N. C.; and even in these cases the animals did have a little of this year's feed.

But the convincing evidence is the outbreak in Fleming County, Ky. The question will be asked, Was that the same kind of staggers that appears in this country every year? Why not? The same cause was in operation there, viz., moisture; the summers are as warm there as in Nansemond County, Va., I am informed, and we must, therefore, conclude that it was the same form of staggers that appears every year in the extreme southeast of Virginia, the eastern part of North Carolina, South Carolina, and the other Southern States, unless investigation proves that this disease is a fever, specific and peculiar to the South, and can not occur further north than a certain latitude; but until this has been proved we are bound to call all these cases of staggers. I have a letter from Mr. George R. Lands, of Boydtown, Mecklenburgh County, Va., informing me that staggers prevailed to a considerable extent in that section last year (1885), but that no cases have occurred this year. He states that 40 horses died within the range of his acquaintance. This certainly was a heavy outbreak, and a severe loss for a circumscribed section, "between the hills," as a gentleman informed me. I did not have time to visit the section, nor can I state the causes in operation; but I will say that I was surprised to hear that so large a number of animals di d in the section referred to, when I know it is not a swamp county. On the contrary, it is very hilly. A gentleman, Mr. Lucy, a horse-dealer, who visits that section often, tells me that these animals were lost along the river, and therefore the same cause may have been in operation that caused the disease in Fleming County, Ky.

I can trace instances of outbreaks of staggers throughout nearly all of my old works. In the index to "Gibson's Treatise on the Diseases of the Horse," edition 1750, I find: "Staggers, sometimes epidemical, 308." I turn to page 308, Vol. I, and it treats of a case of staggers, but says nothing about "epidemical," but on the margin of page 309 I read: "This happened about seventeen years ago in a very wet season, when horses were so clogged that many of them began to fall off in flesh before they were taken up." I think this is what he refers to, and if it is, it shows that a wet season was the cause of the disease becoming "epidemical."

Percival says:

> When my father first entered the service of the ordnance it was the custom to turn horses which had become low in condition, but were still well upon their legs, into the marshes, in order to recruit their strength. During the months of July, August, and September nothing was more common than an attack of staggers among these horses, which was naturally attributed to the luxuriant pasture they were turned into, combined with the dependent posture of the head and the sultry heat to which they were exposed.

This statement shows that low lands (marshes) cause the disease in other climes than the Southern States, and that it occurred there during the same months that it occurs here as an enzootic, but we must remember in the section we have to deal with we can not attribute the cause to the luxuriant pasture or the "posture of the head," because horses contract the disease standing in the stable, that eat from the manger oat, hay, corn, fodder, etc.

Blaine held the same opinion about staggers being caused by the dependency of the head. In speaking of "*Mad staggers* or *phrenitis*," he lays down as one cause, "feeding at grass with head dependent, etc." Now if the dependent condition of the head, while grazing, was a predisposing or exciting cause of staggers, it must be admitted that staggers would be an extremely common disease in the grazing districts, where it is seldom heard of, simply because it is the natural "posture of the head" while grazing.

Youatt considered staggers an apoplexy, and to prove it was thought to be contagious, and appeared as an enzootic in his time, I quote from his work as follows: "Let no farmer delude himself with the idea that apoplexy is contagious."

All the old farriers and veterinarians thought staggers was in one way or another connected with distention, or disease of the stomach, but our modern knowledge of indigestion combats this idea. My extensive experience with acute indigestion of the horse compels me to agree entirely with Professor Williams when he says, in speaking of the cause of encephalitis:

> Now, if engorgement of the stomach were the cause of the train of symptoms seen in this malady, then coma, delirium, or paralysis would be general in the majority of cases of engorgement seen in the routine of general practice, but this is not the case. Numerous instances of engorgement, impaction, even to the rupture of the stomach, constantly comes under the notice of the practitioner, but signs of any brain affection scarcely ever occur. We must, then, look to something more than mere impaction as the cause, and I think this will be found in the nature of the food.

The varieties of staggers met with in the South can hardly be the "grass staggers" of England, spoken of by Gresswell, as "paraplegia enzootica, or reflex paraplegia," because that form is supposed to attack animals at pasture only, and is prevented by removing to other fields.

I think I can safely say we can trace the disease as far back as there are writings on the diseases of the horse. This word staggers seems to mean anything or everything. The old writers applied the term to every nervous disorder, and our modern writers use it as a synonym for the disease they think it was originally applied to, and I must continue to use it, because the inhabitants of the country where it prevails use it for not only this well-marked nervous disorder, but for every other disease the nature of which they do not comprehend. Until the symptoms by which it may be recognized in all its forms and stages are set forth; until the characteristic *post-mortem* lesions are established by scientific veterinary investigations, and the disease properly classified, we must continue to use this term.

Veterinary surgeons who have been in practice many years meet with comparatively few cases of brain affections, and then mostly traumatic (such at least is my opinion), except the periodic outbreaks of cerebro-spinal meningitis (epizootic).

We all know that in our private practice there are many ordinary sporadic diseases that cause more deaths than any of the nervous affections. But here is the enzootic staggers prevailing year after year, destroying hundreds of horses (even in the few counties visited by me), and the disease not classified, nor its cause known, and consequently prophylactic or therapeutic treatment is experimental, to say the least. For reasons previously given, I do not think this disease is epizootic cerebro-spinal meningitis. Additional investigation enables me to say to a certainty that it will again appear in the same localities and on the same farms that it has appeared this year or in former years. This almost points to a disease as peculiar [illegible] South as [illegible] is to India, or as peculiar to the horses of the South as some fevers are to the human being. It may be as [illegible] the cause of splenic fever in cattle, but of a different nature. [illegible] not for the occasional outbreaks far from the localities where the disease always occurs we could say that it was peculiar to [illegible] sections of the South, but if the occasional outbreaks [illegible] then, of course, the same cause comes into exist- [illegible] circumstances, such as, for instance, unusually [illegible] rainy season and consequent high waters, or something else not understood. As diseases peculiar to certain countries [illegible] parts of certain countries must be studied where [illegible] disease be studied where its cause certainly [illegible], and as the South is almost destitute of veterinary surgeons, these investigations must be carried on by the Government, either State or National, or both, because the private practitioner (I do not know of one graduate in all the affected country) can not give up his practice and provide the necessary outlay to conduct the investigations. But one thing I wish to say, the investigator will nowhere find more willing hands to aid him. I never met a more grateful people. When I informed them that I was sent by the United States Government to investigate the disease, they seemed to appreciate the fact that at last there was some hope of relief from this scourge to their fine country. Of course I met many people who had strong opinions of their own on the subject, and they had a right to them. Some would even get angry when I would question the soundness of their views, but these were exceptions, and generally those who were strong adherents of the cob-web theory, or a few people who would not acknowledge that their feed was moldy after I pointed out the defect. Nor can I forget to mention a class of gentlemen in North Carolina who, in every possible manner, assisted me in my investigations and inquiries. I refer to the physicians, whose parting words almost invariably were, "If I can do anything to help you in your work, let me hear from you." With such a state of affairs the future investigator need have no fears of failure when be begins his work next summer.

I have previously stated that I had never heard it hinted that cattle were affected with staggers. In this connection I will state that Dr. Jones, president of the North Carolina State board of health, informed me that one of his cows died last summer exhibiting symptoms similar to those of his horses that died of staggers. It is more than probable that the animal was affected with sporadic encephalitis, as it is the only cow I have ever had occasion to record as having been affected with staggers since I have been engaged in the investigation of the disease. So sure am I that this disease does not affect cattle that I would not have mentioned the above case were it not for the fact of my attention being attracted by the following: In a valuable work, called Resources of the Southern Fields and Forests, by F. P. Porcher, M. D., Charleston, S. C. (?), I find among the description of plants, on page 599, "*Atamasco Lily* (*Amaryllis atamasco*, L.) Grows in damp soils; collected in Saint Johns; vicinity of Charleston, Ell. Bot. i, 384." This is supposed to produce the disease in cattle called staggers. From this we must infer that the cattle were affected with a disease called staggers, supposed to be caused by a plant, but the disease might be the popular "stomach staggers," and not an affection of the nervous system.

Elliott's Botany of South Carolina and Georgia, above referred to, edition of 1821, says: "*Atamasco-Stagger-grass*. Generally supposed to be poisonous to cattle, and produces the disease in calves called staggers."

Whether or not "stagger-grass" produces a disease called staggers is not the question at issue. The real question is, Do cattle suffer from the disease that affects horses, called staggers? This, I think, can be safely answered in the negative. If the nervous organization of mules is not sufficiently delicate to be affected by the poison, or whatever it is, that causes the disease in the horse, then we must admit that cattle are much less susceptible to its influences. In coming to this conclusion I am keeping in mind the fact that Southern cattle fever is caused by a vegetable germ, which has not been proved to affect any other animal. The derangement of the nervous system, in Southern cattle fever, and, in fact, all its symptoms, bear a striking resemblance to the hemorrhagic malarial fever of man.

As regards the paramount question, *i. e.*, the cause of this disease, I am satisfied that we must look to the feed for the cause. I am confident that this cause is in the nature of fungi, and that the fungi is produced where the disease occurs. Further than this I dare not venture at present. The only theory that has any ground for consideration, in opposition to this, is that of those who undoubtedly believe that staggers is due to miasmatic influences, and as their conclusion has been arrived at after much thought and observation, I must necessarily devote some attention to it. As there are different varieties of malarial fever, we will have to dispose of these in turn, in order to convince that in staggers we have not a malarial fever to contend with, and as malaria is given, at times, a rather broad and expansive meaning I will have to be more explicit. Those who contend that the disease is a malarial fever, invariably compare it with the malarial fevers of the human being. Well, let us do so. I am happy to say that the only variety of the malarial fevers that I ever came in contact with in a personal manner was that familiar variety called fever and ague. I "shook hands" with it often, but I have no desire to "shake" with it again, and from experience I can assert positively that it has no resemblance to staggers, and I think all who differ with me on the main point will admit there is no similarity between the symptoms of staggers and intermittent fever. Occasionally symptoms of remittent fever resembles staggers, such as drowsiness or delirium, but in staggers there are no remissions. There are symptoms of brain or spinal affection from the beginning to the termination of the disease, and in the rare instances where horses recover from the disease, there is almost certain to be some defect in the animal, showing that grave lesions of the nervous system existed during the progress of the disease in the system of the horse. I am informed that the people who live near some localities of the Northern lakes, suffer to such an extent with remittent fever, that it is there popularly called "lake fever." Why do we not hear of staggers in these places, occurring as an enzootic, if the staggers is identical with malarial remittent fever? We certainly must decide that staggers and remittent fever are not the same disease in different species. We will now consider that variety known as hemorrhagic malarial fever. To begin with, I will state that the first case of this disease ever recognized in the vicinity where I have been was in 1866. We have proof that staggers [illegible] in that section at least one hundred years ago. For [illegible] the statement of Mr. Nixon, who remembers the [illegible] and his father before him who experienced [illegible] we have the statement of the gentleman [illegible] had experience with staggers. But [illegible] hemorrhagic fever being a comparatively [illegible] that State, there are distinc[illegible] different causes. Hemor[illegible] are never absent in the [illegible] or coma are often [illegible] disappear without treatment, [illegible] showing that no [illegible] existed. The cerebral disturbance [illegible] liver, reabsorption of bile, or the effects of the malarial poison on the great nerve centers, or possibly may be caused by the condition of the blood itself. I have often witnessed these same symptoms in horses suffering with influenza, caused by derangement of the biliary apparatus. Hemorrhages are frequently passed with stools in the malarial disease, whilst in staggers the bowels are always inactive; the most drastic cathartics seldom move them. It is true, the urine is occasionally high colored, and may in rare instances contain coloring matter of the blood, but never blood in staggers, and in the great majority of the cases there appears to be a suppressing or retention of urine. Staggers occurs where there never has been a case of hemorrhagic malarial fever, *e. g.*, three or four counties in Virginia. Malarial fevers occur in many places in the South where staggers is unknown.

I have given a brief description of Hog Island, in the James River. It is a low, marshy island, and there have been no malarial fevers of any variety on the island for at least four years to the knowledge of the civil engineer, who has lived there that length of time, and he does not think there was ever any fever on the island. He reasons thus:

Here we are, right out in the open river. It is four miles across to the main land on one side, and a background of trees behind us on the other side, and the wind has full play up and down the river. If any malarial poison arises from the marshes the wind comes along and carries it away with a full sweep as soon as the poison ascends and before it has time to do harm.

This must be the explanation, because there are a number of men working at dikes in the fields around the marshes, erecting buildings, making roads, and laying tiles, and no cases of malarial fever occur, whilst on the other hand 3 horses were stricken with staggers within two hours, and I am certain some of the feed was tainted sufficiently to produce disease.

If staggers was properly classified we would have no difficulty in illustrating the difference between it and malarial fevers in a more lucid manner than has been attempted in this paper. The difference between malarial fevers and epidemic cerebro-spinal meningitis has been so thoroughly proved by Southern physicians that those who are acquainted with the facts do not consider the matter at all, and if staggers were known to be identical with epizootic cerebro-spinal meningitis the difference could be shown with as much ease.

By concluding that staggers is not due to miasmatic influences, I do not mean to infer that horses are not susceptible to malaria. I firmly believe that they are subject to malarial fevers, and I think I have seen cases of it. I merely hold the opinion that miasmatic influence does not cause staggers, and leave the question open whether horses are susceptible to malaria.

When I advance the idea that staggers may be caused by a fungus on the feed I do not mean to insinuate that I have made a discovery, because I have not. That part must be done by a specialist in that branch of botany, but the evidence of fungi is too plain to be overlooked by any one who thoroughly investigates this matter and all the circumstances connected therewith. I am well aware of the fact that the cryptogamic theory was advanced years ago to account for the origin of malarial and other epidemic fevers, and I know that veterinarians have held the opinion that certain outbreaks of cerebro-spinal meningitis were caused by fungi; but in connection with this disease the question of the cause is more circumscribed. The disease is of yearly occurrence in certain localities, and therefore there should be less trouble in getting the subject into a better light. The only thing certain about the matter at present is the fearful loss of horses annually; all else is theory or supposition. I have given you the facts as I have obtained them, along with my own observations. I have given the opinions of others as well as my own views, and have argued the questions according to my ability; not for the sake of argument, but to get the subject into a smaller compass so that in its consideration one would not have to cover so much ground.

In the absence of all knowledge of the pathology of this disease, and as it proves so rapidly fatal (with very rare exceptions), to advise a course of treatment is a speculation I do not care to indulge in at present. To try to prevent is the only course to pursue in the present state of our knowledge. In addition to the opinion I have given as regards the dietetic course I think should be followed, I will add: Horses (or colts) should not be put to or allowed any severe exertion during the hot weather; should be watered, fed, and worked regularly, and at the first sign of indisposition should be taken to the stable and let remain there quietly until the owner is satisfied nothing materially ails the animal; but should he observe any signs of staggering gait, blindness, drowsiness, or difficulty in swallowing water, then administer carefully from six to twelve drams of aloes (if there is much difficulty in swallowing, this is easier said than done), and enjoin perfect quietness; injections of from one to two ounces of turpentine in warm water into the rectum several times a day; cold applications to the head, warmth to the spine, etc., may be tried. It would be a good idea to watch the state of the bowels carefully, and at the first sign of costiveness administer a laxative, such as four drams of aloes, and this might be done with benefit in the neighborhoods where there is an outbreak. Give, say, four drams of aloes once a week to each horse, and to colts in proportion.

Respectfully submitted.

W. H. HARBAUGH, V. S.,
Inspector of Bureau of Animal Industry.

RICHMOND, VA., *December* 13, 1886.

THE CATTLE INDUSTRY OF CALIFORNIA.

Ion. NORMAN J. COLMAN,
Commissioner of Agriculture.

SIR: In accordance with your instructions, I proceeded to California October last to make an investigation of the cattle industry and e diseases affecting cattle in that State. The results of that invesgation are herewith transmitted to you.

Before the advent of the farmer California was an ideal cattle nge from the head of the Sacramento River to the southern line of e State. The broad valleys of the Sacramento and the San Joaquin retched for hundreds of miles to the north and south, covered here ıd there with groves of live oak and intersected with fine running reams.

Bordered on the east by the foot-hills of the Sierra Nevadas and on e west by the Coast Range, with dozens of offshoots at various anes, the landscape was more entrancing than artist's imagination uld paint. The valleys were one vast field of afalfa, clover, and ch grass, while the hills on the east were similarly clothed, and ose on the west covered with wild oats. The Coast Range of mountns, from a point of 100 miles north of the bay of San Francisco uthward, is a pastoral region. Its rounded sides, abrupt bluffs, and wering summits are carpeted with the most nutritious grasses, and 'ord a world of most excellent range for cattle. The table-lands, untains, and valleys in the country south of the headof the San ıquin are quite similar in character to the country above menned, save that in many parts the grass is less luxuriant, with occaal stretches of semi-desert.

efore the days of "forty-nine" the Mexican vaquero was there, hundreds of thousands of cattle roamed at will over the grassy ns or climbed the hill-sides.

evious to the influx of the gold hunters, the cattle were slaugh- for their hides and tallow, these being shipped by vessel around Horn to New York and Europe. This practice prevailed for years after the American settlement, because there were more than the market demanded. The population of the coast y increased and the gold mines naturally drew to them a porf those engaged in cattle raising, so that for a few years the were neglected and a very material decrease in the number of ccurred up to about 1854. About this time large numbers of w settlers engaged in the ranching business, and the herds multiplied. By 1862 there were so many cattle in the State question of a market was a very serious one. The annual ption was estimated at 400,000 head, and the annual increase ,000. The range being full, this annual surplus of 200,000 n had to be disposed of in some way. Accordingly cattle nventions were called at several places in the State during

THE BEEF PRODUCT NOT INCREASING.

From the most reliable sources the information is to the effect that the beef supply of the State is not increasing. This is no doubt largely due to the fact of the existence of the herd law on the statute book. Wheat is the staple product of the farmers, and millions of acres are seeded on the plains without fencing. The aftermath is lost to the farmer because he can not afford to herd the small bunch of cattle his means would enable him to buy. Were the wheat-fields fenced into suitable lots every tenant would keep more or less cattle, and the stubble would thus be utilized to such an extent as to greatly increase the beef output of the State. The grain is all cut by heading machines and a growth of straw from 15 to 24 inches tall is left standing on the ground. The long, dry summers cure both grain and grass so thoroughly that this grain stubble is sweet and nutritious, making the choicest of feed for all kinds of stock. Large owners of cattle and sheep frequently rent these stubble areas in the fall and herd their stock upon them. But the proportion so rented is small as compared with the total area.

STOCK FEEDING.

Contrary to the generally received opinion, California is not a desirable place to feed cattle in winter. Feed is abundant and reasonably cheap. All kinds of grain grow luxuriantly, and wheat, oats, and barley, cut just before reaching maturity, make the choicest of hay, and on most of the cultivated lands yield 2½ to 3 tons to the acre. Alfalfa is largely cultivated, and 5 tons to the acre is a low estimate for the three crops usually cut. Farmers assure me that they frequently get a yield of 7 tons to the acre, and sometimes as high as 8 or 9 tons. There is little or no trouble to properly cure and save alfalfa or other kinds of hay, and the amount put up is astonishingly large. The wonder is what becomes of it all. The explanation comes from seeing the vast quantities baled and loaded on the vessels leaving San Francisco for southern ports, where no hay is made.

Cattle grow exceedingly fat in the early spring on the natural pasture or alfalfa fields, and ripen into solid, choice beef on the natural grasses during the summer. But when the winter begins the heavy, damp atmosphere seems to destroy the bovine appetite, and animals put up for fattening are as dainty as spoiled children. Fat steers put up in the late autumn and fed on alfalfa will not shrink, but they will not put on additional flesh. To increase their weight ground feed must be given them, and great care taken not to overfeed. The reverse of this is true just over the State line in Nevada, where the winter climate is cold but dry. For this reason nearly all the wholesale butchers of San Francisco buy cattle in Oregon or Nevada and hold them in the Humboldt Valley during winter, where they are fed on alfalfa or native blue-stem hay. The feeding yards are convenient to the Central Pacific Railroad, so that on a few hours' notice shipments can be made as required to supply the needs of the trade. Well-authenticated statistics show that steers from two to four years old, put up in the fall at any of the Humboldt Valley stations and fed hay for four or five months in open lots, will fatten at the average rate of 2 pounds gross per day. It is also demonstrated that under reasonably fair conditions a long ton of alfalfa will lay on 100 pounds of meat and growth.

The California alfalfa undoubtedly contains as much of the fat-producing element as does that grown across the Sierra Nevadas, but the different results are due to climatic conditions. The dry, bracing air of the Humboldt Valley gives a continuous appetite, while the damp, warm weather in the valleys of California weakens or destroys the appetite. It may be, too, that the moisture-laden atmosphere west of the mountains, coming in contact with the cured hay, overcomes the crystallization of the solids of the sap that was produced by the curing process, thus causing partial fermentation or decay, and thereby lowering its fat-producing capabilities. It is true that the sugar, starch, gluten, etc., contained in the sap of the grasses are the main sources of fat production; and it is equally true that liquefaction of those substances after crystallization is rapidly followed by fermentation, which is only another name for decay, or burning, and every feeder of cattle knows they will not fatten on rotten food. We do not wish to be understood as saying that California alfalfa becomes rotten when winter sets in, for such is not the case. But the crystallized matter of the sap is so sensitive to the action of water that it is difficult to determine just how much depreciation is brought about by contact with continually moist air during the winter season. Hence it seems reasonable to attribute a part of the cause or reason why cattle on the coast do not fatten on hay to the partially destroyed elements that hay contains.

In searching for the direct cause of rapidly fattening herds in summer, and the strong tendency to a reverse condition in winter, we find it in the trade or prevailing winds. From spring to autumn the winds blow down the coast from the north, and their breath is a healing balm. The air is dry, and to breathe it seems life everlasting. From autumn to spring the winds blow continually from the equator, and with them come the evaporations caused by a tropical summer. The air is continually charged with moisture, and breathing in consequence seems heavy and unsatisfactory. Hence the tendency to a loss of appetite.

CATTLE IN CALIFORNIA.

The report of the secretary of the State board of equalization shows about 400,000 head of cattle in the State. This report is made up from the returns of county assessors and is very unsatisfactory, in fact, far from correct. In the absence of reliable statistics our only source of information is the butchers. After making deductions for beeves brought in from other States there remains about 300,000 head furnished by the State. This estimate is above that made by some who ought to know, but in harmony with the views of others who have equal facilities for learning the facts. So we give the State the benefit of the doubt. It is a good range herd that turns off 8 per cent. of its cattle for beef each year of steers and old cows. Of course, when the range is fully stocked and the entire increase has to be gotten rid of the beef product should be double this per cent. Giving California the credit for turning off many heifers and cows to the local butchers, and her crop of steers largely at two years old, as farmers will generally do, still the beef yield could not well be over 25 per cent. of the herds. On this basis there are to-day 1,200,000 cattle in the State. Taking the lowest estimate of persons who are in a position to form a reasonably correct opinion of the number of home cattle killed, which estimate is 250,000 head, we still have 1,000,000 cattle in the State. There is no doubt that this is below rather than above the actual holdings, and as the herds are generally well graded up the wealth of cattle is away up in the millions. Ordinary herds are selling at about $25 all round, which would place the total valuation at $25,000,000. Besides these there is close to $1,000,000 worth of fine cattle in the State, a number of breeders having the very best that are to be seen in the United States.

DAIRYING.

With the present system of gathering statistics in California it is impossible to give figures as to the dairy products of the State. The leading commission men who handle the product say that the production is about equal to the demand, or rather consumption. There is still a limited amount of Eastern butter brought in, but as much, if not more, California butter is shipped beyond the State lines than is imported from the States east and from Oregon. Point Reyes is the most noted dairy district in the State, and the butter therefrom is the very best. Generally throughout the dairy districts, which are usually bordering the coast on account of the sea air keeping the grass green later into the season, the lands and cows are owned by rich men and corporations, and leased out in numbers to tenants at so much a cow. The price varies from $15 to $25, owing to local conditions and character of cows. Most of the cows are a cross between the Jersey and Shorthorn, though of late a good many Holstein cows have been introduced on some of the ranches. The dairymen are largely made up of Swiss and Italians, especially on the large dairies. The average product of a cow is 175 pounds of butter a year.

December calves are the rule, because the grasses are better from March to June, thus aiding to keep up a generous flow at a time when it would otherwise be light. Butter made during the dry season—July to December—is white and requires a large amount of artificial coloring matter, if the cows are not to be fed on roots. The export trade is small but growing, Hong-Kong and Honolulu being the principal points, with some orders from the southern coast towns.

SAN FRANCISCO AS A MARKET.

San Francisco has always been a very satisfactory market for beef steers, but it is somewhat limited in its capacity. It has no refrigerated meat or canning establishments to speak of, and only aims to supply the local demand for meats, and such outlying points as can be reached within a few hours' time. There are no great stock-yards, like our eastern cities have, where buyer and seller meet. As a rule each wholesale butcher has a man on the road who visits the ranches and farms and buys the cattle before they leave home. They are there held and shipped on order as needed. Cattle are universally bought at so much a pound net weight, figured on a shrinkage of one-half. Ranchmen with large herds sometimes visit the city in advance and sell their cattle, but no one thinks of shipping in train loads on the open market and taking what buyers may offer. Such a course would be suicidal, for the reason that butchers are always supplied ahead by their country purchases, and there are no facilities for holding cattle in the city without heavy expense.

EXTENSION OF THE BUSINESS.

Cattle raising in California may be said to have reached its maximum. With the exception of one or two open ranges in the extreme south and well up in the mountains, the ranges are fully stocked. Of course the ranges are all fenced, save a very few in the mountain valleys near the borders of the State, and when a pasture is once stocked to its capacity the increase must stop. You can not turn out to rustle on the outside, for there is no outside open to the cattle.

Many of the pastures are located on lands worth $20 to $30 an acre for agricultural purposes, and these will soon be turned over to the farmer, for the reason that it will not pay to graze cattle on such high-priced land. The interest on the money value of the land and the sum invested in cattle is greater than the profits on the herds. There is comparatively little mixed husbandry in the State. Men either have fruit farms or wheat farms. The fruit raisers pay little or no attention to stock, and the great wheat farms are generally unfenced and rented out in parcels to men who have only a team and rarely stay on a place the second year. In fact, the majority of renters are only on the place from the time the plowing season begins, in December usually, until the harvest is over, in May or June. This leaves the only hope of the extension in cattle production to the small homesteaders, who are located along the foot-hills of the mountains and trying to build homes for themselves and families. These must engage in mixed husbandry. They must have a cow or two, and raise something for them to eat. These small operators will in time contribute something to the beef supply of the State, but the process is slow and will not neutralize the decrease caused by the conversion of grazing lands into wheat fields.

There will be no material increase in the beef product of the State until the present pernicious system of special farming, that so generally prevails in the State, shall have been changed into the more rational one of mixed husbandry.

CATTLE DISEASES.

The general impression abroad, and even among many cattlemen in the State, has been that little, if any, disease prevailed among the California herds. The fact is, however, that the Golden State has suffered to the extent of hundreds of thousands of dollars from the prevalence of diseases of various kinds among its cattle during the past fifteen years. In the early history of the cattle business there seems to have been very little trouble of this kind, if we can believe the statements of the pioneers. But judging from the recent experience of the cattle growers, there is ground for suspecting that in the olden time the ranchmen valued their cattle so lightly that they gave little thought to the condition surrounding them, and the loss of a small percentage from disease was looked upon as a natural consequence, and not thought of as being caused by disease at all—a natural loss, if you please, that was common to the business. In the course of interviews with perhaps a hundred of the leading stockmen of the State, 1868 is about as far back as we could learn of any disease. The same causes that now make sick cattle existed from the beginning of cattle growing in the country, and why there should have been an exemption in the early days does not appear. The above inference, that the diseases really did exist but were unnoted, is certainly confirmed by all the facts one can now discover.

SPLENIC FEVER.

Splenic fever, or what is generally known as Texas fever in the country east of the Rocky Mountains, prevails to a very considerable extent in California. My attention was first called to this matter by a gentleman whom I met on the cars while crossing the Sierra Nevada Mountains in June last. He incidentally mentioned the fact that he had lost a good many cattle from a cause he did not understand, and, on being asked for details, stated that in 1877 he bought 400 steers in Tulare, which were shipped to his pasture, near Stockton, 200 miles north, and turned out to graze with about 1,000 head of natives and Oregon cattle that had been in the field for several months. About twenty-five days after the Southern cattle were turned into the pasture the natives and Oregon cattle began to die, and within a few weeks 160 head died. These were all cattle that had cost him $40 a head, and the loss of $6,400 was rather startling. None of the Southern steers died or even showed signs of sickness.

Again, in 1885, his partner bought 200 steers from the same Tulare range, then owned by J. M. Craighton, and after shipping turned them into a pasture near Stockton with 400 Northern and native cattle. The experience of 1877 was had over again, 60 head of the Northern cattle dying in a few weeks, and the Southern cattle showing no symptons of disease. A few of the dead cattle were opened, and, in the language of the owner, "were found to have melt twice its natural size and soft like liver; the contents of the stomach were dry and crisp, looking like they had been partially burned. Some of the sick cattle passed bloody urine. Generally they would hump up for a day or two, sometimes three or four, then lie down with a raging fever and die in from six to twenty-four hours."

This satisfied me that it was the old-fashioned, straight, splenic or Texas fever, and I promised to make an investigation of the matter in the autumn. Calling on this gentleman at his home in October, he repeated his former statements, which were verified by the words of other responsible parties. The Southern cattle were all killed by the butcher, and in the language of one who assisted in the shop, "they were all right, save the melt (spleen) was nearly double size, and the meat seemed to be of an unnatural color next to the hide." "The meat was all consumed in the neighborhood, and no evil effects resulted." The owner of the cattle says there was no poison weeds of any kind in his pasture, and that he had more or less cattle grazing in it every year; never lost any except on two occasions, when Southern cattle were turned in and allowed to mingle with the natives, or those from further north. He feels certain that the Southern cattle gave off the disease.

A gentleman from San Francisco reports the shipment of a herd of cattle from Kern County to the northern end of the San Joaquin Valley, where they were placed in a pasture with native or Northern cattle, and as a result many of the Northern cattle died, while none of the Southern cattle showed symptoms of disease.

Most of the trouble with this fever has occurred south of San Francisco, probably for the reason that there have been but few shipments of southern cattle to points north of that city. The cities of Stockton, Sacramento, and other towns get their beef supplies from the local ranch men, or from Oregon or Nevada, and in consequence have no fear. The only shipments known to have been made to Stockton have developed fever, and every shipment from the south to points on the upper or northern San Joaquin have caused trouble with the northern cattle. As a rule the gentlemen who gave me their experience did so after a promise not to publish their names, and that promise I must keep. But Mr. Miller, of the firm of Miller & Lux, San Francisco, probably the richest cattle-raising firm in America, gave me most valuable information, and did not require the suppression of his name. Owning hundreds of thousands of acres of land in Kern County, and having ranch property reaching almost connectedly from there to the northern end of the San Joaquin Valley, all fully stocked with cattle, and being at the same time one of the oldest and most experienced wholesale butchers on the coast, his opinions and observations are worthy of credence. He says that Texas fever developed on his ranches in 1878, and has continued to give trouble more or less ever since; less this year than formerly. Many cattle died in 1878, and the losses ran up into the thousands of dollars. He had been in the habit of mixing cattle from Kern County with those on the San Joaquin. Since 1878 he keeps the southern cattle, when brought north, in fields by themselves. He thinks the disease was developed on the coast by starvation and change of early conditions, the range too much crowded, and so many cattle on a given area that the food is befouled and poisoned. The germ being thus created and the conditions in many places remaining the same, the infection continues. In support of this theory he cites the sickness near Mindenhall, a village in Alameda County, where, in 1877, all the cattle in the neighborhood died of a disease so similar in character to Texas fever that the veterinarians pronounced it identical with that which, in 1878, developed on his ranch, and the nature of which leaves no doubt as to its being the true splenic fever. No strange cattle had ever been taken into or out of this community, and the germs must have developed there. In 1878 it developed 40 miles south, on the head of Orestimba Creek, in Stanislaus County, and killed 600 cattle out of a herd of 900 in a few months. The spleen is always affected, very large, discolored, and soft. The other organs are affected differently in different cases. Generally the animal droops for a few days, eyes run and hair rough, fever high, and death follows in a few hours after the animal lies down. Mr. Miller says he has tried the doctors and all kinds of medicines, but the only relief that has been obtained is by corralling the cattle and starving them until they will eat a little bran mush. At the same time he mixes copperas with the water in the trough, making it very strong. They will drink a little, and in this way he has saved a few. Mr. Miller is satisfied that cattle grazing near the carcases of cattle that have died with the fever will take the disease, and accordingly he has issued peremptory orders for the burning of all dead cattle, and the grass in the vicinity of each one. The disease rarely, if ever, shows itself until the hot weather begins, and on the approach of winter subsides. Another feature is that the disease is not apt to develop on ranches where there has been no movement of cattle, save where it has been given off by eating grass around the carcasses of dead animals. This rule is not universal, as is instanced by the cases above cited in Alameda and Stanislaus Counties, but it is the general rule. Hence it is suggested the cattle should not be moved either north or south in the heat of the season, and that shipments should be made in the early spring or in the late autumn.

The area of "big melt" seems to be pretty clearly defined as extending from San Bruno, 10 miles south of San Francisco, on down the coast to the State line; but the infected area is not continuous. One ranch, extending a few miles, will give off the disease, while the next one is free from infection. So clearly is the area defined that one farm will be rented for the aftermath from year to year, while the adjoining one can not be rented at all. Experience has proved that from 10 to 20 per cent. of the cattle will die on the range of one field while none will even sicken in the other.

The Hon. William Dunphy has a 10,000 acre ranch on the Salinas River, 15 miles south of Solidad. He also owns a large ranch in Nevada. It has been his practice for years to ship over several hundred head of cattle from the Nevada range to the Salinas ranch in the fall to ripen for the early spring market. These cattle generally arrive about October 1, and are turned on the stubble-fields adjoining the ranch until the winter rains permit plowing to begin. Then they are turned on the bunch-grass and alfalfa pastures of his own ranch, and are thus in condition to fatten quickly after the rainy season has passed. Mr. Dunphy informs me he loses from 30 to 60 head of these cattle every year during the first forty days after their arrival, but none of the native or held-over cattle die. His experience is different from that of Mr. Miller and all the ranch men on the San Joaquin. Mr. Dunphy never burns or buries the carcasses of dead cattle, and never has experienced any losses from such neglect. Neither was there any trouble from the dead cattle in the two herds above named near Stockton. This raises an important question in my mind: Are the diseases that annually carry off a certain per cent. of Mr. Dunphy's cattle and those which killed the cattle near Stockton identical with that which yearly shows itself on the ranges farther south? Mr. Dunphy lost 30 head in October last, but unfortunately I reached the ranch after the last death had occurred and decomposition was so far advanced that a *post-mortem* was of no service, nor was I able to see a case on the more southern ranches. The disease had run its length previous to my visit, so I have no means of comparing the symptoms and *post-mortem* appearance of the disease as manifested in the two cases other than the statements of the non-professional men who examined them. These descriptions I have had from at least fifty men, and they all agree nearly that the only conclusion is that the disease must be the same. Yet here is the very important feature of inoculation from contact with a dead animal in the one case and total exemption in the other. The disease in one case is similar in character and in surrounding circumstances to what we all understand of the splenic fever east of the Rocky Mountains. One of the most distinguishing features of our true southern splenic fever is that cattle from south of the line of infection, when brought in contact with cattle north of that line, give off the disease but do not themselves take it on. Another feature equally well established is the fact that the cattle which sicken and die will not give off the disease while suffering with it or after death. I have seen hundreds of cattle die in Kansas and the Pan Handle of Texas with the splenic fever, and have seen many of them opened after death. After listening to the description of the disease on the Pacific by fifty or more men, as stated above, there remains no doubt in my mind as to the identity of the two diseases, but there are some conditions materially different and these may account for the apparently different results.

There are different types of splenic fever, and a *post-mortem* of cattle on the San Joaquin may establish the fact that the disease is of a different type from that experienced on the Salinas and near Stockton. My investigations this year were begun sixty days too late to enable me to lay all the facts bare. The different conditions above referred to may be briefly stated thus: In the case of the cattle near Stockton, it was extremes meeting—cattle full of the fever germ coming in contact with those that were totally exempt from such infection. The same is true of the Salinas trouble. The Nevada cattle were free from the disease germs, and on coming in contact with them on their new range they were so susceptible that death resulted, while the located cattle were proof against it by virtue of a sort of every-day inoculation. On the other hand, the San Joaquin cattle sickened in what has, for many years, been an infected country, on their own range, and under such conditions as, perhaps, made the disease more virulent. This is not given as a satisfactory explanation, but merely to show the different conditions. Nothing short of a thorough *post-mortem* will determine the true relations of the disease as it manifests itself every year in the different localities. Mr. Dunphy thinks his losses are occasioned by his cattle eating some kind of poison weed, inasmuch as the deaths always occur after the range is dry and a green weed, though poison, would be tempting. Why, then, would not the native cattle die from the same cause? I spent two days on his range and rode all over it searching for the poison weed, but failed to find it. It is not there.

One gentleman reports that a few years ago he bought 800 cattle in San Luis Obispo County. They were moved a few miles on to an alfalfa pasture. In ten or twelve days they began to die, and he lost 300 of them in a few weeks. They showed no signs of bloat, such as cattle do when they get sick from eating green alfalfa. His explanation of the symptoms is as follows: "They were droopy for a day or two; the hair was rough; some of them run at the eyes and all had high fever; after they had got down they died in from six to thirty-six hours; many of them passed blood both in the urine and the dung, and some in the urine alone." All of the cattle examined after death showed a spleen twice its normal size, and many of them had a diseased liver. "The contents of the stomach were hard and seemingly powder-burnt," was the way he expressed it. Those remaining alive were finally moved off to the mountains, where none died except those that were sick when they reached the new range. The neighbors, of course, called it the "bloody murrain." The gentleman who gave me this statement is a practical cattle man and seemed anxious to give all the facts. It was evidently not blackleg or anthrax, for there was an absence of such symptoms, and none of the sick ones recovered on the march to the new range, which would have been the case had anthrax been the trouble. Nor was it confined to young fat cattle. Old cows, big fat steers, and youngsters all alike were stricken. The pasture was evidently infected with some fatal disease, and all the ascertainable facts point to splenic fever. If not that, what was it?

This gentleman says he loses cattle to a greater or less extent every year from apparently the same causes, yet he thinks it is not "Texas fever." He attributes the origin of the disease to warm, dirty water, and to the fact that the grasses grow so luxuriantly that too many cattle are put on a given area—they befoul the feed to such extent that it breeds disease. The cattle referred to in this case were healthy

tremes of north and south and from the coast to the eastern boundary. Thousands of cattle die every year from this cause, and it is becoming a very serious question among small breeders. There seems to be several types of anthrax fever on the coast, and its general prevalence has caused the markets to be flooded with all sorts of nostrums, claimed to be preventives and remedies. Considering the natural conditions it is not strange that anthrax should be prevalent. Ordinary years the whole face of the country is one solid mat of the richest kind of food, and animals fatten without an effort. Wild oats, pea-vine, bunch grass, clover, and alfalfa cover hillside and valley, and the general profusion creates that indolence that always and everywhere causes stagnation of blood and great tendency to anthrax. The universal testimony of stockmen is to the effect that coast cattle, on being removed to the interior valleys, very frequently die, especially if the movement takes place during the summer months. The evidence is not sufficiently clear to warrant the expression of an opinion as to whether the disease in these cases is anthrax or some other fever. The losses are quite serious and enough to justify the fullest and most scientific investigation. The feed is generally better on the coast, and hence a great tendency to this disease. The following statement, made by a gentleman living on the coast, in San Luis Obispo County, is one of many such given me by reliable parties: He says that last year his farm lost $2,000 worth of cattle on one small dairy farm. About August they bought 20 cows from a neighbor, 7 miles distant, and moved them to their own place. The cows had been grazing on top of the coast mountains, at this point less than 3,000 feet high, with plenty of grass and good water. The premises to which they were moved were a few hundred feet lower and the grass was a little more abundant, with excellent water. The range consisted of bunch grass, clover, and alfalfa, recognized as the best to be found anywhere. No disease had ever shown itself on either of these farms, yet within a few weeks after the arrival of the 20 cows 16 of them died and a large percentage of the home cattle sickened and died also. The local veterinarians were employed and tried all remedies that could be heard of, but none of the cattle that were attacked were saved by virtue of medicine. Cows in calf sometimes threw off the fetus, and when this happened they always recovered. This discharged fetus was putrid and so offensive as to be unapproachable. No steer recovered, and no cow, except those losing the calf as above. A neighbor on an adjoining farm lost 25 cows out of 90, and half of the balance lost their calves. A post-mortem revealed conditions almost identical with those given in former statements—melt greatly enlarged and rotten, liver diseased, and contents of stomach dry and hard. In all cases there was a high fever. More or less trouble of this nature occurs every year—sometimes [illegible] little and sometimes quite serious.

Remembering that an area of country over which this trouble extends is very large, and that the cattle are well graded up, it can readily be seen that the annual loss amounts to a very large sum, and that the subject is one worthy of careful investigation.

PROTECTIVE MEASURES REQUIRED.

The [illegible] cattle interests of the State of California are virtually without [illegible] protection of any kind. The sanitary laws are so meager as to be [illegible]. The $30,000,000 invested in cattle is liable to be wiped out by the introduction of contagious diseases, and no man can raise his hand against the infectious animal that brings the plague. The coast line of our possessions on the Pacific is nearly 6,000 miles long, and there are many ports of entry to and from which foreign vessels may come and go. It is true that under the United States Treasury regulations San Francisco is the only Pacific port at which the importation of cattle is permitted. But there are dozens of other ports at which foreign vessels arrive and discharge and take on freight. It is not an uncommon thing for captains of vessels to carry a cow on shipboard when they have their families with them, and it is not a very wide stretch of the imagination to suppose that a single cow might be landed at some of the obscure ports from a sailing vessel, and that disease might follow. But this is not the grave danger. The maps and charts on file in the office of the Chief of the Bureau of Animal Industry at Washington show that almost the entire western shore of the Pacific Ocean is infested with rinderpest, pleuro-pneumonia, or some other contagious bovine disease. These diseased animals reach the coast, and in various ways the infection is liable to be carried on shipboard, though the cattle remain ashore. Vessels from any or all of these ports are liable to land on our Pacific coast and thus bring the infection to us. Nor is this all. British Columbia lies just over the way to the north, and her port of Victoria is liable at any time to receive an importation of diseased cattle. Many cattle from England, the hot-bed of infectious diseases, have in the past been landed there, and as the stock interests of that country grow more are likely to be required. There is simply an imaginary line between that country and Washington Territory, over which cattle pass and repass at will. With disease once carried east of the Gulf of Georgia on to the main-land, there would be nothing available but a shot-gun quarantine to keep them out of the United States. There is no law or treaty by which reciprocal quarantine could be maintained. South of California is a long line of coast in Mexico and Central America, with many ports and a very considerable traffic. On the other side are the ports around the Gulf of Mexico and the Carribean Sea. While Mexico and Central America are not importing many cattle, there is something done in this way every year, and with almost every country in Europe infected, it is a fair presumption that diseased cattle will sooner or later find entrance at some of those ports. There are hundreds of miles of boundary line on the north of Mexico entirely unguarded, and, as on the north, where cattle are continually changing from one side of the line to the other. Here, then, is a source of constant menace to the cattle interests of the Pacific, with no possible way of avoiding general infection should an outbreak occur in Mexico. There are no sanitary laws in force in that country by which the local authorities would be enabled to grapple with the disease and prevent its spread to the border and over the line. On the east there are seven States where pleuro-pneumonia now exists in an active form, and generally without adequate means of suppression. Railroads from all of the infected States reach out and connect with three main lines of transcontinental roads that terminate in California. The quarantine regulations in most of the States and Territories to the east are very imperfect, and with many diseased cattle already in the channels of commerce, it is uncertain when some of them will reach the Pacific slope and spread contagion broadcast over that fair land.

destroyed every cow brute on the island. Precautionary measures may be necessary to prevent the introduction of the germ of infection into this country.

GENERAL REFLECTIONS.

No part of the United States possessed more or greater advantages for cattle raising than did California when it was an open range country. Now, since it has become a farming country to a very large extent, it still has advantages in this direction surpassed by no State or Territory in the Union. The soil is wonderfully productive, and the hay crop produced even on the mountain sides is abundant almost beyond belief. The wonderful climate enables the farmer to cut and thoroughly cure as hay any of the grain crops, so that what in other regions is an inferior straw is there the best of hay. The growth is luxuriant everywhere, giving sufficient roughness to carry great numbers of cattle through the year with little or no grain, save while fattening for beef. Cattle can be matured there cheaper than in any other State where agriculture is the rule. Beef production in winter is not so cheap as in the arid regions east of the mountains, but fully on par with the Atlantic seaboard or the Mississippi Valley. A cold, dry atmosphere is most conducive to the laying on of fatness.

The existence of splenic fever on the Pacific coast makes it plain that this disease develops south of a certain parallel from the Atlantic to the Pacific, if we accept the belief of Mr. Miller that it was not brought in. There are curves and breaks in the line which are affected by local causes, such as mountain ridges and trade winds. It is certain that portions of Arizona and New Mexico, though south of the general fever line, are entirely free from this malady, but the reason is undoubtedly the altitude.

Whether splenic fever is a development of the coast, or whether it was imported, is a matter for serious inquiry. It was unknown, according to all information so far obtained, until about 1868. Since that time it has been an ever present trouble. Had the germ been imported at that time, it is doubtful whether it would have been destroyed for the reason that in many parts of the cattle country there is never any frost. In all of the regions east of the Rocky Mountains, where cattle die of the infection, taken from southern herds, there are winter frosts, and these destroy the germ. How long the germ would remain alive or active in the absence of frost is probably an unsolved question. At any rate, it is a new subject to me and one only understood (if understood at all) by thoroughly scientific men. Many of the valleys of southern California are low and inclined to be marshy. The thermometer marks 112° to 115° F. in the shade for months during summer, and the conditions would seem favorable to the development of the disease germ. This fact, taken in connection with the statements of practical well-informed cattle men on the coast, that no southern cattle had been brought in for years before the disease appeared, and then on foot and across the mountains under conditions that would have purged them, strengthens the belief in the development theory.

Respectfully submitted.

A. S. MERCER.

CHEYENNE, WYO., *December* 7, 1886.

THE LIVE-STOCK INTERESTS OF MARYLAND.

Hon. NORMAN J. COLMAN,
Commissioner of Agriculture.

SIR: In obedience to instructions received from you, dated October 1, 1886, to visit the counties on the Eastern Shore of Maryland with a view of ascertaining the condition of live stock, and to determine if any traces of contagious diseases exist among cattle, horses, or swine in these counties, I have the honor to submit the following report:

SOMERSET COUNTY.

I have visited every district of Somerset County, calling upon and questioning many prominent men in each district, visiting and inspecting many herds of cattle; also, visiting the salt marshes, where many hundreds of cattle are pastured, and I am pleased to say that no traces of pleuro-pneumonia, tuberculosis, or any other contagious disease is to be found in the county. The class of cattle kept in the county is of a poor grade, and generally not well fed or taken care of, but for all that they are healthy.

The horses are of better stock, better cared for, and healthy.

In regard to the losses by swine plague, it is a very difficult matter to get at the exact facts. The losses in the past ten years have been very great. Farmers are generally keeping as few hogs as possible, while many keep none, because of this disease. Thus the losses this year are less than in former years, though I believe the percentage of loss is as great now as ever, many losing from 50 to 75 per cent. of their herds, and some have lost all. For the past few weeks the disease has been raging fearfully, but is now dying out.

In Princess Anne district Mr. E. D. Read, who has a farm of his own and also has charge of Hon. Isaac D. Jones' farm, says his losses in 1885 were $1,000 from hog cholera—75 head. Mr. J. W. Crisfield lost 50 per cent. of his herd, valued at $90. Mr. E. Brinkley lost many last year and this year also.

In talking with a large number of persons they estimate the annual losses in this district alone at from $2,000 to $2,500, and I am quite sure this estimate is not too high.

In Mount Vernon district, the estimate made in the same way as above, the losses are placed at from $500 to $1,000 per year.

In Dames Quarter district the annual losses are from $500 to $1,000.

In Brinkley's district Dr. F. A. Adams, physician and farmer, gave much information. In 1885 he lost 19 hogs out of 22, valued at $75. In 1884 he lost 9 out of 25 head, valued much higher, because they were fat and ready to kill—$150. His neighbor, John Long, this year lost four-fifths of his herd—12 head—valued at $100. Mr. Wilkins, another neighbor, in 1884, lost $100, in 1886, $50. A. P. Ellis, in 1884, lost $150, in 1886, $75. C. C. Wetherel, in 1884, lost $75, in 1886, $25. J. T. Walters lost, in 1885, $150. His average losses for the past ten years have been over $25. Many others have lost yearly from $25 to $100 each by this disease in this district alone. Dr. Adams and others estimate the annual loss in this district at from $1,500 to $2,000.

In Dublin district Mr. William M. Costin, a large land owner, says last year he lost 45 out of 65 head, valued at $200. Two years ago (1884) his losses were $300, and for many years his losses have averaged from $200 to $300; says all farmers in the district yearly lose more or less of their stock. Fewer hogs are now kept than formerly because of this disease. He estimates the annual loss in this district at from $1,000 to $1,200. This estimate agrees with that made by Francis Barnes and many others.

In Fairmount district Mr. Albert Sudler says there is scarcely a farmer who has not had the disease on his place. His own loss last year (1885) was $60. Mr. Ross, a neighbor, lost $75. Mrs. Bozman lost $50; J. E. Sudler, $50; J. S. Sudler lost $200. Eighteen head of fat hogs belonging to other parties near by died, valued at $250. Mr. E. Handy, Mr. R. H. Walters, Dr. F. A. Turpin, John S. Sudler, and Albert Sudler, all of this district, estimate the losses at from $1,500 to $2,000 per year, and some were inclined to place it higher.

Estimates made by well-posted men in Crisfield district make the losses per annum for the past six years at from $1,000 to $1,200.

J. H. Miles (sheriff), W. H. Roach, T. L. Miles (county commissioner), E. J. Gunby, and L. T. Coburn say the losses in Lawson's district will average $1,200 per year.

In Tangiers district, which includes Deil's Island, the losses have been heavy this year and every year, until the people keep as few hogs as possible. Losses per annum average about $1,000.

These estimates are all made by noting down losses by men who have kept a large number of hogs, and but little note has been made of those cases where from one to five hogs have been lost. There are also many portions of the county partly covered by water that I have not considered it important to visit, where, I hear, the losses are considerable, considering the poverty of the people.

I feel confident that the annual loss to this county from hog cholera during the past ten years, including this year, will amount to from $12,000 to $15,000. In former years much pork was shipped from this county, and it was quite a source of revenue, but now it is difficult to raise what hogs they need for their own use.

It has generally been the custom here to let the hogs that have died from disease rot on the ground, sometimes near the pens and stables. Frequently they have been thrown into the streams, and thus spread the infection. Very few have been thoughtful enough to bury the carcasses. I have made it a point to impress upon all with whom I have talked the importance of killing and burying deeply all infected animals, at any rate to separate the sick from the well, and have tried to instruct them in the use of sanitary measures generally.

The people are discouraged in regard to the raising of swine. This is a great corn-growing country, and hog raising would be very profitable if it were not for this disease.

WORCESTER COUNTY.

I find the cattle throughout this county in a healthy condition. No traces of pleuro-pneumonia are to be found, and probably there never has been a case in this county. The cattle are nearly all of native breed, having been bred here for many years. They are small and of inferior quality. Very few cattle have been brought into the county from other counties or States.

The only disease I have heard of here occurred about five years ago, and that was what is known as Texas fever. It came from a herd of cattle driven from Northampton County, Va. (and native of that county), through and along the east coast of this county. These cattle themselves appeared healthy, but all along their route they scattered the seeds of disease, which very soon destroyed nearly all cattle along the line of march. The malady did not become fastened upon this county, and it died out soon, probably under the influence of frosts. Some other instances are known where cattle have been brought into this county from Northampton County, Va., and always with the same result. The farmers here are in continual dread of the disease. The outlet by railroad and for driving cattle to market from this infected district is through this county, and there seems to be no effective law to prevent it. That the disease permanently exists in Northampton and the lower portion of Accomac County, there is no reason to doubt. There is a tradition accounting for its existence in Northampton County. It is said that many years ago a vessel was wrecked on that coast with a cargo of hides from South America, and that these hides were washed ashore along the coast of the county. Since that time the disease has been known there, but never before. As my assignment for duty confines me to Maryland, I have been unable to investigate this tradition to prove its truth or falsity. The disease undoubtedly exists on the lower end of the peninsula, and is a continual menace to the lower counties of this State. The danger is great, and calls for thorough investigation and legislation to protect the farmers of Maryland from this scourge.

I find the horses of the county of good stock, and no disease among them.

Swine plague has existed in this county for many years. I have investigated every district in the county. Some years it has been very destructive; other years the losses are small, because the hogs are nearly all destroyed in some years, and the next year very few are to be found. Last year the losses were very great, probably three-fourths of the hogs dying in the county, while this year there are very few hogs to be found and the spread of the disease is less rapid, though in many instances heavy losses are reported. In making my investigations I visited Pocomoke City, and from there went thoroughly over the southern portion of the county, from there to Snow Hill for the central part, and thence to Berlin for the northern portion to the Delaware line.

In Pocomoke district I visited Senator S. K. Dennis, a very large land owner and stock raiser, Mr. M. R. Merrill, W. W. Brittingham, P. C. Outen, and many others. These men have all lost heavily every year for many years, including this year. They were unanimous in estimating the average annual loss in Pocomoke district from hog cholera at $2,500, and last year it was much greater.

In Stockton district, among those visited were Messrs. Moses Hudson, Thomas Lindsay, Henry Jones, and others. These men estimate the average annual losses at from $1,500 to $2,000, say $1,750, from hog cholera in this district alone, at least 50 per cent dying yearly.

In Snow Hill district, Messrs. J. C. Ellis, James R. Purnell, George Hayward, and others, all large farmers, estimate the average annual losses in this district at from $1,000 to $1,500; say $1,250.

In Atkinson's district, Messrs. George Dryden, E. A. Marriner, and others estimate average annual losses at $1,200.

In Colbourn district, Messrs. E. Curmean, E. B. Parsons, U. F. Shockley, and others estimate the average annual losses at $1,000.

In Newark district, Mr. W. T. Boston, formerly county commissioner, and others estimate the average annual loss in this district at $1,500.

In East Berlin district, F. J. Miller, James B. Dirickson, and many others say losses here are very heavy, probably reaching $1,000 annually. This is the smallest district in the county.

In West Berlin district, Messrs. John R. Purnell, James Whaley, T. G. Hanley, Gordon A. Marshall, and many others estimate the average annual losses at from $1,000 to $2,000; say $1,500.

In Saint Martin's district the losses have been lighter than any other. Mr. H. J. King and others estimate average annual loss at from $500 to $800; say $650.

Recapitulation of average annual losses in the county, made by the best farmers, and verified by careful inquiry:

District.	Amount of loss.	District.	Amount of loss.
Pocomoke	$2,500	East Berlin	$1,000
Stockton	1,750	West Berlin	1,500
Snow Hill	1,250	Saint Martin's	650
Atkinson's	1,200		
Colbourn	1,000	Total	12,350
Newark	1,500		

I am satisfied the above estimates are below rather than above the actual loss to the farmers of this county.

I find the farmers here largely interested in the raising of poultry for market. The disease known as chicken cholera has for many years prevailed, and the losses have been great. It is believed here that hog cholera and chicken cholera go hand in hand, and where one disease prevails the other is sure to be found.

WICOMICO COUNTY.

The following is the result of my investigations in this county. I find the cattle in a healthy condition. There is not now, nor has there ever been, any contagious disease among them.

The cattle of this county, like those of the other counties on this peninsula, are nearly all of scrub or common stock, and have been bred for many generations on this poor, sandy soil, with indifferent care and poor feed, until they have become very much deteriorated in size. Great numbers of working oxen are used. These animals are very quick of action, and travel with wonderful rapidity upon the sandy roads. They are very small, however, usually not weighing not more than 1,000 or 1,200 pounds per pair. Hundreds of these cattle are pastured upon the salt marshes along the bay and sea shores, where they frequently remain all the year without any other feed than the salt grass they get from these marshes, having no shelter or attention other than an occasional inspection from the owners. They are good rustlers and are remarkably healthy. Very few farmers have brought into these counties any of the improved breeds of cattle. The few who have done so have been fortunate in not importing disease with them.

The horses are of good stock, well cared for, and healthy.

The swine plague is the great scourge of this section, large numbers dying annually. This is a very good corn-growing country, and pork-raising used to be a very profitable business here—a source of considerable revenue. Now, however, large quantities of pork have to be imported into this section every year to supply the wants of the people.

In the western portion of this county, along the bay shore—the districts of Sharpstown, Barren Creek, Quantico, and Tyaskin—the disease has raged fearfully, fully 75 per cent. of the hogs having died from cholera this year. The disease first appeared in Sharpstown about the 1st of July, evidently coming over the Nanticoke River from Dorchester County, where it had been prevalent for some time before. From thence the disease passed along the country, near the bay and along the inlets and water courses, gradually working its way into the interior. In Trappe and Salisbury districts, on the Wicomico River, it has also been particularly severe within the last few weeks. In Parsons, Nutters, Pittsburg, and Dermis districts, in the eastern part of the county, the disease has been less severe this year, except along the Pocomoke River and its small tributaries. The cause of the disease moving so rapidly in the sections spoken of may be because many of the farmers are in the habit of throwing their dead hogs into the streams or letting them rot on the low lands, where the drainage carries the infection directly into the streams. It is thus carried rapidly to every farm below. I have tried to impress upon the farmers the dangers of this practice, and the importance of burying deep all the dead, and also the importance of killing all infected animals so soon as the disease is developed, and quarantining all those exposed, believing they might by this means curtail the ravages of this pest. Much might be done by passing laws compelling the burial of all dead animals, with heavy penalties for its infraction. I think it important that this matter be brought before the State legislature of Maryland at its next session for the purpose of getting such a law passed. Such a law, if enforced, would save much valuable property, and add much to the sanitary condition of the county.

In getting at the average annual loss by this disease I visited and consulted many prominent men in every district. Among them were the members of the board of county commissioners, Messrs. J. C. Phillips, James H. Farlon, Henry J. White, and W. H. Cooper, and Mr. Daniel J. Halloway, county treasurer; also, the judges of the orphans' court, Messrs. George A. Bownis, Robert Walter, and Isaac N. Horn. Farmers and others in Salisbury district consulted were Messrs. Lemuel Malone, Hon. H. W. Anderson, James Disharvon, D. L. Bruington, and J. D. Perdue. In Sharpstown district, Messrs. J. A. Bownis, J. W. Selby, W. C. Mann, and W. R. Nelson. In Quantico district, Messrs. L. J. Gale, J. M. Jones, A. J. Crawford, and J. T. Phillips. In Tyaskin district, J. F. Mizick, M. Toadvine, Dr. A. J. H. Lankford, and D. J. Elliott. In Trappe district, Messrs. W. J. Bownes, James H. Gillis, and J. J. Dulaney. In Dermis district, Messrs. John W. Davis, Hon. K. V. White, and W. L. Laws. In Parsons and Pittsburg districts, Messrs. S. P. Parson, M. H. Parsons, J. S. Baker, J. W. Riggen, L. J. Timmons, Hon. W. G.

Gordy, and others. In Nutters district, Mr. T. C. Morris and others. These men agree in stating that the losses in their different localities, annually, for the past five years, will average more than 25 per cent. This year the loss in the western half of the county has no doubt reached 75 per cent., while in the eastern half the loss has not been over 25 per cent.

The lowest estimates made by these men, as taken from my note-book, are as follows:

District.	Amount of loss.	District.	Amount of loss.
Salisbury	$1,500	Trappe	$2,000
Nutters	1,000	Parsons	1,650
Quantico	1,000	Pittsburg	1,600
Barren Creek	1,900	Dennis	1,050
Sharptown*	600		
Tyaskin	1,000	Total	13,300

* Small district.

This $13,300 is the lowest estimates made by districts of the average annual loss for the past five years. Many intelligent men place the annual loss at $20,000 and over, and from what I have seen in the past few days I am of the opinion that the loss this year will go over $20,000.

As in the other counties I have inspected, the farmers are discouraged as to the keeping of swine. The loss to the larger farmers is great, but the loss to the poorer people, who keep only two or three hogs for their own use as winter meat, is a very serious matter, often depriving them of animal food when they most need it.

DORCHESTER COUNTY.

The cattle of this county are in a healthy condition. I have found no traces of pleuro-pneumonia or tuberculosis among them. These diseases are not known here.

Nearly all cattle in this county are of native breed and inferior in size and quality. A few Shorthorn and Jerseys (mostly grades) have been brought in here, but none recently. These importations from other portions of the country have proved to be free from disease. The only disease among cattle I have heard of occurred about a year ago, on the farm of Charles H. Seward, in Bucktown district. He lost last year 12 head. It was very difficult for me to get at all the facts in the case, but I am convinced, after careful inquiry, that the disease was Texas fever. I carefully examined the remaining animals of the herd and found them healthy. Several months have elapsed since any were sick. Whether this attack was the result of contact with cattle from the South or of sporadic character, I am unable to determine. These cattle are frequently pastured on the salt marshes adjoining his farm, where many other cattle from a distance are often pastured. They may in this way have come in contact with infected animals.

The horses seem in a healthy condition. I am informed, however, that frequently of late years, during the months of August and September, a disease known as "blind staggers" appears in many parts of the county; that often 10 or 15 horses die in one neighborhood of this disease. Nearly all die that are attacked. The loss has been considerable in this county. The farmers seem to be entirely ignorant of the cause of the disease. It might be well to investigate as to the cause of the malady, during the season in which it prevails. I have heard of this disease in other counties south of this, and my attention has been so often called to it of late that I concluded to report it.

The swine plague, as in the counties above, is the serious trouble here. The disease has prevailed for many years, and this year it has been particularly severe in most of the districts.

In Williamsburgh district the loss is estimated at not more than 10 per cent., while all the other districts are estimated to have lost from 40 to 75 per cent. Districts along the water and large streams suffer more than those inland. Williamsburgh district lies entirely away from the water. This confirms the observations made here and in other counties, that the infection of swine plague spreads more rapidly along the water-courses. Whether this is because the farmers so frequently throw their dead hogs into the water, or whether the bacteria are propagated in the water, I am unable to determine without experimenting and thorough investigation. On this peninsula it is evident the contagion spreads much more rapidly through the water than through the air or over the land. I have visited every district, and have talked with numbers of the best farmers, getting their opinions and estimates as to their own losses and losses in their neighborhoods, taking notes of my conversation with every man. Could I know the number of hogs in the county or in each district I could form a very accurate estimate of the loss. Without these data I have estimated 3 hogs owned by each voter. This is here considered rather under than above the average. The value of hogs is also a difficult question to decide. I find in the Report of the Department of Agriculture that the average value of hogs for the State of Maryland, estimated in January, 1886, is placed at $5.95. To be within bounds, I have estimated the average value at $5.

In the following table the number of voters was obtained from the latest registration lists:

Districts.	Voters.	Estimated No. hogs, 3 to a voter.	Value at $5 per head.	Per cent. loss.	Total losses.
Fork	456	1,368	$6,840	.40	$2,[illegible]
East New Market	602	1,806	9,030	.50	4,[illegible]
Vienna	364	1,092	5,460	.40	2,[illegible]
Parson's Creek	452	1,356	6,780	.40	2,[illegible]
Lake's	364	1,092	5,460	.40	2,[illegible]
Hooper's Island	209	627	3,135	.50	1,[illegible]
Cambridge:					
First precinct	694	2,082	10,410	.50	5,[illegible]
Second precinct	724	2,172	10,860	.50	5,[illegible]
Neck	305	915	4,575	.40	1,[illegible]
Church Creek	278	834	4,170	.75	3,[illegible]
Straits	313	939	4,695	.40	1,[illegible]
Drawbridge	256	768	3,840	.50	1,[illegible]
Williamsburgh	242	726	3,630	.10	[illegible]
Bucktown	227	681	3,405	.60	2,[illegible]
Linkwood	278	834	4,170	.50	2,[illegible]
Total	5,764	17,292	86,460	......	[illegible]

From this table the loss would appear to be $39,780. We will then subtract from this the estimated loss in the first precinct of Cambridge district, which is composed of villagers, many of whom keep no hogs, and we have $39,780, less $5,205, leaving $34,575 as the loss for the county.

This may be thought a large estimate, but I am convinced I am within bounds. In every instance I have cut down the estimates made by the farmers from 10 to 15 per cent., except in Church Creek district, where every man I talked with (and they were many) estimated the loss this year at 75 per cent. or over, and in Williamsburgh district the loss was placed at 10 per cent. by all with whom I talked.

Large quantities of pork must be imported into this county this year to supply the wants of the people. Fattening as well as stock hogs are dying rapidly now, and many farmers have told me they are afraid to kill their own fat hogs though they appear healthy, fearing they may be infected and prove unhealthy food.

This county of Dorchester is the largest in the State. In former years the farmers have depended greatly upon their hog crop both for food and for revenue. They are now greatly discouraged, and if this disease continues to rage they will have to abandon the industry.

TALBOT COUNTY.

Talbot County is one of the richest and best cultivated counties on the Eastern Shore of Maryland. Many more cattle are kept here than in any county south of this. Quite a number of the farmers keep thorough-bred herds of Herefords and Jerseys. The general condition of the stock is good, and I find no disease of any kind among cattle. This freedom from disease is, however, to be wondered at from the fact that cattle purchased from the stock-yards at Baltimore are brought here by boat to supply the beef market at Easton. This is done almost weekly. Besides, many farmers are in the habit of purchasing stock cattle in Baltimore and other points for feeding during the winter. Very little of this business, however. has been done this winter, because the farmers have become alarmed by the reports of pleuro-pneumonia in all the stock-yards in the East. The authorities here, I believe, are considering the propriety of establishing a quarantine against Baltimore, Philadelphia, and Wilmington. Unless this is done there is great danger of an outbreak here because of the constant traffic with these cities in cattle.

The horses are all in healthy condition.

The swine plague here, as in other counties I have inspected, exists to an alarming extent. The disease has been in this county for many years, and this year has ravaged many portions of the county to a greater extent than ever. It has been very severe along Miles River, St. Michael's River, the Chesapeake Bay, the Choptank, and all the inlets and creeks from these waters, while in the northern part of the county, in Chapel district, there has been but little of it this year, though last year it was more severe in this part of the county. I visited every portion of the county, and found the people greatly alarmed at the losses sustained from the disease. They can not now raise pork to supply their own wants, but import large quantities yearly, while in former years much pork was annually shipped from here to the larger cities. The farmers are negligent and careless as to the disposal of the hogs dying from the disease, leaving them to rot upon the land or throwing them into the streams, by both methods spreading the infection broadcast. Some few, however, are thoughtful enough to bury the dead animals. This matter certainly calls for legislation.

In estimating the losses I have consulted with men of all classes in every district and neighborhood, and the percentage of loss I have placed at the lowest estimates made. The number of voters is as taken from the registration books. I have estimated 3 hogs owned by each voter, which is rather a low estimate for this county, and $5 the value per head.

The estimated losses are shown by the following table:

Districts.	Voters.	Hogs, three to a voter.	Value at $5 per head.	Per cent. lost.	Total value of loss.
Easton	1,606	4,818	$24,090	40	$9,636
Saint Michael's	1,015	3,045	15,225	50	7,612
Trappe	1,256	3,768	18,840	66	12,434
Chapel	823	2,469	12,345	20	2,469
Bay Hundred	492	1,476	7,380	60	4,428
Total	5,192	15,576	77,880	....	36,579

By the above table it will be seen that the total loss for this county for this year amounts to $36,579. This estimate is entirely within the limits.

CAROLINE COUNTY.

I find no disease among cattle in this county. In former years many farmers purchased stock cattle in the large markets for winter feeding, but this year, because of the reports of pleuro-pneumonia in and around our large cities, they have been afraid to make such purchases. By this caution they have very likely prevented the introduction of infectious diseases. The prevalence of pleuro-pneumonia in the country thus works a hardship upon the farmers of the county.

The horses are all reported healthy.

The swine plague that has been so destructive in other localities on this peninsula seems to have done very little damage in this county, as a whole.

This swine plague first made its appearance in this county in the fall of 1885, and is said to have been introduced by the purchase of a hog in Talbot County which was brought into Preston preçinct of Harmony district, No. 4. This hog was procured for feeding purposes. It very soon sickened and died, infecting the whole herd of the purchaser. It was afterwards learned that disease existed in the herd of the gentleman who sold this hog. From this one animal the disease spread to some of the adjoining farms during that fall and winter, and during the year 1886 it spread and infected nearly every farm within a radius of 4 miles. It is estimated that 50 per cent. of the hogs have died in this infected district, amounting to a loss of $3,000 or more.

From this point the disease is spreading, and will soon take in all the lower portion of the county.

The disease has also made a lodgment in Tuckahoe Neck, near Hillsborough, another part of the county. Mr. Jarrell and Mr. Lord, in this locality, have lost nearly every animal from their large herds. This is a recent outbreak, but from these farms the disease is likely to spread. The other parts of the county are entirely free from the plague. This is surprising when it is known that the disease prevails in all the counties adjoining this on the south, west, and north, and in Delaware on the east. It is quite possible the malady might be held in check in this county and much property saved by strict quarantine regulations and thorough sanitary precautions.

QUEEN ANNE'S COUNTY.

I find no disease among the cattle of this county. There are some fine herds of Herefords and Shorthorns, and many grade cattle of good quality. There is much interest taken here in the breeding of fine stock of all kinds. Many farmers have been in the habit, in years past, of buying stock cattle for winter feeding and have found it profitable; but because of the prevalence of pleuro-pneumonia in many sections of the country they have feared to do so this year. They are now feeding only such as are bred in the county, but this supply is entirely inadequate to their wants. They are hoping for national legislation to rid the country of this terrible plague.

Many fine horses are also bred in this county. The horse stock I found in healthy condition.

Finding so little disease among the swine in Caroline County, as stated in my last report, I had hoped to find but little in Queen Anne's, but I was disappointed. The ravages of swine plague in this county have been as great or greater than in any county I have inspected. There is no portion of the county exempt from it, and the losses have been very heavy in every part.

This year the disease has been more severe in the southern and western parts of the county, and the losses are here estimated at 75 per cent. or over. In some neighborhoods there is not a hog left.

Mr. T. A. Embert, merchant at Queenstown, says that this year he has not sold a pound of sage for sausage, nor a sack of salt for curing meat, while usually he has sold large quantities.

In the districts about Wye Mills, Wye Neck, Queenstown, and Kent Island there is scarcely a hog left. Above Centreville the losses this year have probably not gone above 55 per cent. This is an estimate by Mr. E. B. Emory, an extensive breeder of Shorthorn cattle, fine horses, Cottswold sheep, and Berkshire hogs. He has lost no hogs this year, but last year he lost 100 head of thoroughbred hogs, worth over $1,000; and in 1884 he lost over 300 head, worth over $3,000. His immunity from disease this year is attributed to his great care and the strict quarantine regulations enforced on his farm. After canvassing every part of the county I am of opinion that the loss for the whole county is this year at least 66 per cent.

According to the registration list of 1885 there are in this county 4,545 voters. If we estimate 3 hogs to the voter, as we have done in other counties, we have 13,635 hogs, and if we value them at $5 per head we have $68,175 as the value of the annual hog crop. Estimating the loss at 66 per cent., we have $44,995.50 as the loss to this county for the current year.

This is according to estimates made as I have usually made them in other counties, *i. e.*, 3 hogs to the voter and $5 per head. Now, in this county, it is invariably estimated that at least 5 hogs are owned by each voter. This would make 22,725 hogs, and they are taxed at $4 per head, two-thirds of their actual value, making $6 the value per head. This would make $136,350 as the total value of the usual hog crop. Sixty-six per cent. of this amount would make $89,991 as the loss for this year. If the latter estimate is correct, my reports for the other counties I have inspected are far below the mark.

The same carelessness prevails here as in other counties as to the care of the sick and disposal of the dead animals. No care is taken to separate the sick from the well; no quarantine regulations are observed, and the dead are left to decay on the fields or are cast into the streams. There is a wonderful amount of ignorance among farmers as to the infectious character of the disease. It is worse than folly to attempt to cure an animal when once attacked, for so long as he is sick or convalescing he is scattering the seeds of infection, and should he recover he is usually valueless. Could the farmers be induced to kill the sick and bury the dead this plague might be checked. But if the present course is pursued they must soon cease to raise swine. Stringent legislative measures only can stop the spread of the disease.

HARFORD COUNTY.

I commenced the investigations of this county January 19. My work has been much delayed, as I could make but a few miles a day because of bad roads and deep mud. Besides, there are kept in this county a vast number of cattle, both for dairy and feeding purposes. As this county is so near Baltimore, a great center of infection, it has required great care and minute inquiry to determine the true condition of affairs. Along the line of the Philadelphia, Wilmington and Baltimore Railroad and the Maryland Central Railroad there are many dairy farms, from which great quantities of milk are shipped daily to Baltimore, and in some places butter is made for the same market.

In other parts of the county winter and summer feeding of steers for beef is made a large business. In the northeast quarter of the county, on nearly every farm, will be found from 10 to 140 head of feeding cattle; large numbers are also fed in other parts of the county. This feeding of cattle is a yearly business and a source of great revenue. Naturally rich soil has been greatly improved by this custom, until Harford County is one of the wealthiest in the State. Many herds of Jerseys are found here, and some fine Holstein-Friesians for the dairy, and a few good herds of Shorthorns for beef.

I commenced my work at Havre de Grace, from there visiting the lower part of the county, and from thence up along the Susquehanna to the Deer Creek country, where are to be found some of the wealthiest and best-informed farmers of the State.

Nearly all the farmers cheerfully aided me in my investigations, and this was particularly the case with the members of the Deer Creek Farmer's Club, a society that has done much to advance the interests of the farmers of this county. From thence along the north line of the county to the Baltimore County line, and thence to Bel Air for the central and southwestern parts, the feeding cattle are in first-class condition. I found no disease among them of any kind.

These cattle are generally purchased at the stock-yards at Baltimore. Immunity from disease must be attributed to the careful daily inspections made in these yards under the direction of the live stock sanitary board of this State. A few cattle, however, are bought in Pennsylvania, and some are brought from Canada. The dairy stock are not generally so well cared for. In many instances cows are not well fed, and stables are in a bad condition. Thorough search, however, revealed no cases of pleuro-pneumonia.

Cows in this county are generally bred here, and very few are bought in Baltimore. I am confident that there is not at this time, nor has there been for the past year, a case of pleuro-pneumonia in Harford County.

In several herds, however, I found cases of tuberculosis. In every case but one the owners promised to immediately slaughter those I pointed out as infected, and I believe they have done so. In the one case, however, the owner could not be made to believe his cow (a registered Jersey) was diseased, as he said she was giving more milk than any other cow in his herd. As our laws take no cognizance of this disease, I could do no more than give advice. I am convinced there is considerable of this disease in the county. In several stables abortion prevails to a considerable extent, and this disease is thought by most cattle raisers infectious.

Mr. William Davidson, near Bel Air, had pleuro-pneumonia on his farm in August, 1885; all his cattle were killed by order of Dr. Ward, State veterinarian. Mr. Davidson disinfected his stables and allowed no cattle on his farm for one year.

He now has 14 cows and 15 steers, all in perfect health. Stables and yards in best condition. Mr. Quinby, a near neighbor, had disease at same time, and the cattle was killed by same officer. Kept no cattle for over a year. Now has 4 head, all in good condition. I believe these farms to be entirely free from infection now.

The people of Harford County are deeply interested in the cattle industry, and are anxious for national legislation for the eradication of contagious diseases.

Swine plague has prevailed here more or less for several years. In the years 1884–'85 the southern half of the county lost heavily — from 25 to 50 per cent. loss each year — but in 1886 but few hogs were lost. In the northern half, however, the disease prevailed in 1886. From careful inquiry I estimated the loss for the northern half at about 25 per cent. for 1886, and on many farms I found hogs still dying. This northern half embraces more than half the population. The registered vote of the county is 6,977. One-half of this, say, is 3,488. Counting three hogs to a voter, this would make 10,464 hogs at $5 = $52,320, total value of usual hog crop. Twenty-five per cent. loss makes $13,080, the probable loss for 1886. This is counting no loss for the southern half of the county; but as the loss in this part in 1886 has been from 3 to 5 per cent., it would make a total for the county of over $15,500. Generally the same carelessness prevails here as in other counties as regards the care of the infected and disposal of the dead animals.

My investigations were greatly facilitated by Mr. Alexander, of Bel Air, president of the live stock sanitary board, and Mr. Fulford. Among the most interesting visits made was the one to his splendid Berkshire breeding farm, where I found the sanitary arrangements good and stock in perfect health.

KENT COUNTY.

With Chestertown for a base, I visited every portion of Kent County. This is the greatest peach-growing county of the State. All the energies of the farmers seem to be centered on this industry. As a consequence, cattle raising has been neglected. Generally the cattle are badly cared for, and of inferior grade. A few good herds are found of Shorthorns, Herefords, and Jerseys. I found no pleuro-pneumonia, and no indication that it had ever been here. Some few cases of tuberculosis were found. In a few stables abortion prevails to quite an alarming extent.

The horses of this county are of good stock and have excellent care. The only disease found among them was distemper, which now prevails extensively in some sections.

In consequence of the immense peach crops raised here, the farmers keep great numbers of hogs, probably far more in proportion to the population than any other county in the State. Many farmers keep from 50 to 75 head, while quite frequently more than 100 were to be found on a farm before the swine plague got among them. This disease has prevailed more or less for some years. In 1885 a half district, along the Chester River and Chesapeake Bay, lost nearly its whole hog crop. In 1886 not more than 20 per cent died. But during the past year the other parts of the county have lost heavily. The disease was worse during the fall of last year, but I found some farms where hogs were still dying. I give below, in tabulated form, the losses by districts for 1886. I estimate the number of hogs owned by each voter here at 5 instead of 3, as in other counties. This is considered entirely within bounds by all with whom I have talked.

District.	Registered voters.	No. hogs, 5 to a voter.	Value at $5 per head.	Per cent. loss.	Total loss.
First	1,069	5,345	$26,725	50	$13,362.50
Second	857	4,285	21,425	75	16,068.75
Third	643	3,215	16,075	66	10,609.50
Fourth	1,146	5,730	28,650	50	14,325.00
Fifth	1,004	5,020	25,100	20	5,020.00
Total	4,719	23,595	117,975	......	59,385.75

It will be seen from the above table that the total loss for Kent County in 1886 was $59,385.75.

This is greater than any county I have inspected. I saw several farms where from 90 to 100 hogs were lost last year. Kent is one of the wealthiest in the State, but the swine plague is one of the most serious troubles ever experienced here.

ANNE ARUNDEL COUNTY.

Comparatively few cattle are kept in this county, the farmers mostly devoting their attention to the raising of vegetables and fruits for market. Stables, as a rule, are very poor, and but little attention is given to cattle, which are of poor quality and badly fed. In and around the city of Annapolis quite a number of cows are kept for dairy purposes.

In the city, Horn Point—a suburb—and Camp Parole, about three miles out, are the only places where any disease was found. A detailed report of the cases found here, the number that died, number killed, and the number in quarantine, has been furnished your Department by Dr. William H. Wray, under whose direction the first investigations were made.

There are now in quarantine at Horn Point five stables, in Annapolis City one herd, and one herd at Camp Parole. I have been unable to find any other infected herds, though as warm weather comes on other cases may develop.

This disease (pleuro-pneumonia) was evidently introduced here in July, 1886, by a Jew cow dealer named Joseph Stern, from Baltimore, who brought a few cows from Baltimore to this place by boat for sale and exchange. Every case of this disease here has been traced to this lot of cattle. The first one attacked was an animal sold to Mr. Joseph Beardmore, of Horn Point. Seven head of Mr. Beardmore's herd died, and 6 more were killed by Dr. Wray. All the other herds infected were from contact with cattle from Stern's importation. Mr. Stern sold cattle to other parties in the city and country. I believe I have traced every animal sold by him, and have examined them and the herds into which they entered, but found no disease except in the cases already reported. It is quite evident that some of the cows brought here by Stern had been exposed to infection in Baltimore, which did not develop till some time after the lot was sold and separated; hence some of them escaped the disease and the herds into which they entered were saved.

As Anne Arundel County is separated from Baltimore only by the Patapsco River, it was supposed there might be found some disease in the northern part of the county. As Dr. Wray, chief inspector of the work in Baltimore, is making close inspections of every stable within 10 miles of that city, I made at his request a careful inspection of that part of Anne Arundel County commencing at Brooklyn and out the various roads from that place for 10 miles. A detailed report of these daily inspections have been made to Dr. Wray and will appear in his report to you. I will only here state that I found no signs of pleuro-pneumonia and but two cases of tuberculosis. From hearing the reports of so much disease in Baltimore the people have been very cautious in their purchases, and as yet the disease has not got among them.

I found no disease among the horses of this county.

Swine plague has prevailed here for some years. In 1885 and 1886 it was particularly severe. In the southern portion of the county it is estimated that at least 75 per cent. of the hogs died in 1886. In all other parts of the county 50 per cent. were lost. There are in the county 6,842 voters. In the eighth, or southern district, there are 887 voters. This, at 3 hogs to a voter, would give 2,661 hogs, and at $5 per head $13,305 as the value of the usual hog crop for this district. A loss of 75 per cent. would make $9,978.75.

The other districts contain 5,955 voters, × 3=17,865 hogs, at $5 per head, $89,325. A loss of 50 per cent. makes $44,662.50. This, with $9,978.75 in the eighth district, makes a total loss for the county in 1886 of $54,641.25.

The disease still prevails, and I saw many infected herds. Very many farmers told me they would not attempt to raise hogs while this disease was so prevalent; they are discouraged. Very few having made pork for their own use last year, and with low prices for other crops, they can ill afford to purchase meats.

CALVERT COUNTY.

I have found no infectious or contagious diseases among cattle in this county. Tobacco is the principal crop here, and very few cattle are kept, except as work oxen. They raise very little hay; the stables are very poor, and often no shelter is provided for cattle.

The general condition of the cattle of this county is worse than any I have seen. I have learned of many instances of actual starvation. I was called to visit several farms where sickness was said to prevail, and as was supposed, from infectious disease, for sometimes several in a herd were sick at the same time. In every instance I found the cattle nearly starved; they had been turned out into the fields and had eaten largely of the dried grasses and weeds, causing impaction of the stomach and bowels, and imflammation of these organs.

The number sick and the number that have died was a surprise to me. In these cases I could only give advice as to treatment and care of stock.

No disease among horses. The horse stock here is very poor in quality.

The swine plague has caused severe losses. In 1886 the losses were very heavy. I am satisfied the percentage of deaths in the county reached at least 50 per cent., though in some sections it reached 75 per cent. There are in the county 2,395 voters; at 3 hogs per voter makes 7,185 hogs, and at $5 per head makes $35,925, value of usual hog crop; 50 per cent. loss gives us $17,962.50. This, I am sure, is a fair estimate of the losses sustained by this county for 1886.

SAINT MARY'S COUNTY.

The condition of stock in Saint Mary's is better than in Calvert County, but still is in rather poor condition. Tobacco and corn are the main crops here, but generally the land is stronger and more grass is grown and rather better care and attention is given to live stock, though I found some in very poor condition.

I found no contagious diseases among cattle. Very few cattle having been brought into this county of late, they have escaped the infection of pleuro-pneumonia.

The horses are healthy. On the farm of Dr. John M. Broome, and in the vicinity of his place (Saint Mary's City), for some years glanders prevailed. The disease was brought in from Baltimore. The losses sustained amounted to several hundred dollars. The killing of every infected animal some time since has finally put an end to the contagion. Had this course been resorted to at first many horses and a large amount of money might have been saved.

As in all the other counties, the swine plague has caused great loss. During the past year it has prevailed in all parts of the county; less severely, probably, in Chaptico district than in the other districts. I am satisfied the loss for the whole county for 1886 will reach 75 per cent. Estimating, as in other counties, this would make a total loss of $43,515.

I found that Dr. John M. Broome had reported on April 1 to your Department that the losses by swine plague last year amounted to over 50 per cent., but he authorized me to say that upon further investigation he was satisfied that he had made too low an estimate, and he believed it was really 75 per cent.

Upon investigation I found that the pork and bacon brought into the town of Leonardtown by boat, to supply the demand for the district, say of 10 miles around, amounts yearly to about $44,000. This has been a necessity lately, because of the great loss of hogs by disease.

The money thus expended has been taken from the sale of other products, and this amount represents but a small part of the county. The real loss to the people is really more than double my estimate.

CHARLES COUNTY.

The farmers of this county, like most other counties of southern Maryland, have given very little attention to the improvement of cattle, keeping comparatively few of any kind. Very few cattle have been brought into the county, and fortunately they have escaped pleuro-pneumonia. I find no contagious disease among this class of animals, with the exception of a few cases of tuberculosis. Cattle here are usually badly cared for, both as to food and shelter.

The horse stock is of better blood and well cared for, and in a healthy condition.

I visited every district and section of the county, making inquiries as to the condition of hogs. I find the swine plague has prevailed here for several years. In the years of 1885 and 1886 the losses were heavier than ever before.

So generally has this disease prevailed that many of the best farmers told me they had now entirely given up the attempt to keep hogs, and others are keeping as few as possible. Fearing the ravages of the disease this year, very few hogs are to be found in the county.

In some neighborhoods few hogs died last year, but in most cases these same sections lost heavily in 1885. In most districts the losses for 1886 amounted to over 75 per cent. Considering the small losses in some neighborhoods this percentage will be somewhat reduced. After careful investigation, I am of the opinion that the loss for last year for the whole county will amount to at least 66 per cent. In the county there are 3,898 voters. Estimating 3 hogs to a voter gives a total of 11,694. At $5 per head makes $58,470 as the value of the hog crop. Sixty-six per cent. makes the total loss $38,590.20 for 1886.

I feel sure this estimate is below the actual loss. Inquiry instituted among the merchants shows that the pork and bacon brought into the county to supply the wants of the people far exceeds my estimated loss.

With the very low prices realized from their staple crop—tobacco—they can ill afford to buy meats to supply their actual wants.

Among the poorer classes much suffering and want is the result of this disease among swine.

PRINCE GEORGE'S COUNTY.

Tobacco, wheat, and corn are the great crops raised here, and comparatively few cattle are kept, except near the District of Columbia and along the railroads leading into Washington, where large numbers are kept for dairy purposes.

In the southern and eastern parts of the county I found cattle healthy; no contagious disease except a few cases of tuberculosis, which is found here, as well as in every other section of the State, to a greater or less extent. The cattle usually kept in this county are of inferior quality.

After having examined the southern and central parts of the county from Upper Marlborough, the county seat, I changed my quarters to Bladensburgh, near the District line. In this section I expected to find pleuro-pneumonia, for I knew your inspector, Dr. Wray, had, within the last few weeks, destroyed three herds, one belonging to Mr. Elon Behrend, at Seat Pleasant, one to Mr. D. M. Nesbit, College Station, and one to Mr. S. B. Holton, Hyattsville. As these stables were several miles apart, I felt it my duty to examine very carefully all the cattle in this section of the county. To do this has taken much time. Most of the cattle here are purchased at the stock-yards or from dealers in Washington. Careful inquiry convinces me that pleuro-pneumonia has had a home in the District of Columbia and vicinity for many years, and very likely was brought here from the North during the war.

I could hear of many farms and dairies where this disease is said to have prevailed, more or less, for several years. Many dairymen have learned to diagnose the malady, and when it appears the sick cattle are disposed of at once. Owing to this practice, very few cases are to be found.

I have been able to locate the disease in but one herd, that of Mr. John W. Gregory, near Seat Pleasant, a short distance from the District line. His herd contained over 40 cows and young stock. Here I found several chronic cases, and much coughing all through the stable. Mr. Gregory told me that two or more years ago he lost several cows with pleuro-pneumonia, and had some animals now in his stable that had recovered (?) from the disease. These cows it was not difficult to find, and in my opinion were such as were liable to spread the disease, and I reported them to Dr. Wray, who, I understand, is about to destroy the whole herd. Every animal on farms near this place has been inspected, and many of them by Dr. Trumbower, but we have been unable to find any others diseased. I have also examined all animals near College Station and Hyattsville, and find no signs of pleuro-pneumonia.

They are liable to get disease here from the District of Columbia, where I have good reason to believe the plague has a foothold. I should be glad if the District could be inspected at the same time as the counties bordering thereon.

Much interest is felt in the county because of a few cases of glanders among horses lately discovered here. Some time in May or June Dr. Ward, State veterinary officer, condemned and killed 4 head belonging to Mr. Smith, near Hall's Station. On June 15 I found two more cases on the farm of Mr. A. O. Brady, near Forestville. I at once notified Dr. Ward, but before he arrived one of the [illegible] was appraised and killed under State law. [illegible] quarantine.

[illegible] for many years prevailed here, until the farmers [illegible] Farmers all over the county [illegible] raise them for fear of the disease. [illegible] visited in the State. Instead [illegible] I am sure there can not be found [illegible] as the number [illegible] we have a total value of [illegible] the losses last year [illegible] the very lowest, and [illegible] I believe this to be [illegible]

[illegible]

[illegible] W. Patterson, M. D.,
[illegible] Animal Industry.

THE "LOCO" PLANT AND ITS EFFECT ON ANIMALS.

SIR: I have the honor to submit the following report of the results of an investigation directed by you:

The work assigned me was the investigation of the disease known as "*Loco.*" This is a term which has attached itself to a certain disorder familiar to many Western ranch men. The term is by no means an inappropriate one. It is the Spanish expression for "foolish" or "cranky." While the term is used simply to designate a certain affection, it is intended, also, to convey a notion of one of the characteristic clinical symptoms of the disease. The same term is applied also to designate one or more species of plants, which are generally supposed to have some connection with the disorder. These are the *Oxytropis lambertii* and *Astragalus mollississimus.*

The term ("*Loco*"), then, is applied to both the disease and the plant supposed to produce it. The disorder is known throughout a very large section of the western and southwestern portion of the United States. It is known in the western portion of Kansas and Nebraska, and extends to Texas and Mexico, westward to California, and north to Wyoming, and probably to Montana.

The territory I visited during my investigations extends from the western boundary of Nebraska to Salt Lake, and from Cheyenne to El Paso. In addition to personal observation, I endeavored to gather from the most trustworthy sources what verbal testimony I could that would tend to throw light on this subject. With this end in view I visited the headquarters and camps of many of the most experienced ranch men in Colorado, New Mexico, and Texas. So far as I was able I attended the local and general meeting of stockmen, and by this sort of personal contact with the practical men of the plains I was able to summarize the experience and judgment of these men. I spent much of my time on the range and ranches, observing the peculiarities of the afflicted animals, and making frequent *post-mortem* examinations of animals that had recently died from the disease, or those that had been destroyed for that purpose.

As to the testimony of stock-owners, it is pretty uniform, as given by those who have had personal experience with the trouble. I found a number of ranch men, and especially those who have their land "under ditch" and cultivate their crops and care for their stock according to usage on farms further east, who had but recently heard the term "loco" for the first time, or anything concerning its significance. Others had witnessed, years ago, the same effect as we now attribute to eating the loco, but for which they had no explanation at the time. In other instances there was abundant testimony that the appearance of "loco" with any serious results was of recent date. This was notably the case on the foot-hill ranches back of Longmont and Greely, Colo.

Some of the most intelligent and observing horsemen, who had been in the business for a quarter of a century, had recently come to a knowledge of the existence of the malady. It would seem, from the evidence furnished by such men, that the cause, whatever it may be, had not been operative in their localities till a recent date.

It is the testimony of those who have known the loco plant for a number of years that it does not grow with equal luxuriance during successive years, and that in time it will almost entirely disappear from localities where it has been recently abundant.

On the other hand, its presence in many localities has but recently come to the notice of observing men.

The plant grows from a pointed tap-root that extends some feet into the earth. During the fall, winter, and spring months, a thick tuft of compound leaves radiate at the surface of the ground and frequently cover a circular space 8 inches or a foot in diameter. These leaves present a pubescent or downy appearance, and remain comparatively fresh and green during the winter. During the summer the plant sends up a number of slender seed-stocks to the height of a foot or more, and on the top of each is a small seed-pod, containing a number of minute black or dark brown seeds. One plant is capable of producing several thousand seeds. Such is the plant, and during the summer, when in full foliage, the ground may be entirely covered over for a considerable extent.

Its habit of growth, as I observed in most places in Colorado, was in detached bunches. Sometimes a number of tufts could be seen on a single square yard of land; in other instances it was necessary to search carefully over an acre or two to find a single tuft, while much of the country is entirely free from the plant. It seems to be most abundant in southern and southwestern Colorado, in some sections of New Mexico, in western Texas, and I am informed it grows in great abundance in Chihuahua and other portions of Mexico. During the winter and early spring months, when other vegetation is dead and dry, the loco plant presents a tempting appearance, quite in contrast to the short dry pasturage of the plains. Notwithstanding this fact, it is uniformly rejected as an article of food by all classes of animals under ordinary conditions. Animals that have not acquired an artificial taste for the plant can not be induced to touch it. Occasionally one meets with an animal that is possessed of the keenest relish for the plant. He persistently rejects all other forage, and if the loco is not abundant, he spends his time in the most diligent search over the range for the now favorite plant. I have seen a single animal miles away from any other individual of the herd, carefully searching as if for some lost object, and when a loco plant is found he would devour every morsel of it with the greatest relish. As soon as one plant was eaten he would immediately go in search of more, apparently oblivious to everything but the intoxication afforded by his one favorite article of food.

Animals possessed of the appetite do not always behave in this manner. If the herd is grazing on a range where the loco grows, the victims of the habit remain with the herd and move from place to place with them.

The habit of loco-eating once formed it possesses for the victim all the suicidal fascination of the "opium habit." The intemperate gratification becomes stronger, and voluntary reform, I believe, is absolutely unknown.

When animals that have not been too long addicted to the habit are confined and kept on food free from the plant in the course of time they will lose their appetite for it and reject it when offered. I have seen animals thus forget the habit in the course of two or three months. Old animals that have been loco-eaters for a considerable length of time do not readily lose the habit.

Animals that have this habit are said to be "locoed." No animal having the loco habit is in a normal physical condition.

All individuals do not show the same morbid symptoms; but all show similar structural changes, varying in degree and accompanied by a change from the normal physiological function.

All confirmed loco-eaters become physical wrecks. The symptoms do not develop rapidly, but a general derangement of the nervous system follows, which is usually accompanied with more or less disturbance of the digestive apparatus. There is general loss of nervous power; the animal becomes dull, spiritless, and inattentive. He wanders about in an aimless, half-dazed condition, except when searching for his favorite food.

Groups of afflicted animals will sometimes congregate together, when they present a peculiar spectacle of stupor and dementia.

In time loss of flesh and general prostration is followed by death. Some months are usually required for the disease to run on to a fatal issue.

I have seen animals that have shown some of these symptoms for years. This is true in those cases where the animal has suffered severely, and afterwards been placed in such circumstances that he could not gain access to the plant. Important tissue changes had already taken place, leading to alteration of nervous function, from which the animal would never recover.

The same thing is true of animals that are kept in inclosures, where the plant grows in limited quantities, and the animal is never able to get enough at any one time to bring on the more severe symptoms.

Animals that are affected with this passive type of the disease will present no abnormal appearance when running at large, or standing quietly in the stable or corral. It is only when put to vigorous exercise that the more violent symptoms are discovered. It not infrequently occurs that one of these passive-looking creatures, when put under the saddle, or even when a rope is thrown over him, suddenly begins to act as though he were possessed. Under the stimulus of this sort of excitement he is suddenly transformed into the most wild and frantic creature of which it is possible to conceive. This is not due to the unbroken condition of the animal, for old and well-broken saddle horses will behave in this manner. This intense nervous excitement may be witnessed in the more marked cases. When suddenly disturbed, an animal may be so affected as to present the most perfect spectacle of stupor and inactivity, yet where a rope is thrown down before him he will jump over it as though he were clearing a fence.

It is a generally accepted belief among ranch men that when a horse is once under the influence he never recovers from the effects of the plant, no matter whether he continues to have access to it or not. I do not think this is literally true, though there are cases that might lead to this sort of generalization. Here are three observed facts: First, none of the herbivora ordinarily eat the loco plant; second, when once the taste is acquired the animal takes to the plant with the greatest voracity; third, all loco-eaters are diseased—are locoed—and manifest a general uniformity as to symptoms.

These facts I made personal observation of in numerous instances, and this is in accordance with the almost uniform testimony of men who have had years of practical experience with the live-stock business on the plains. It may be said, however, there are those who hold there is no such disease as "loco," save when it exists in the brain of those who believe in its existence.

I endeavored, so far as possible with the time and means at my disposal, to ascertain what pathological conditions there were that might serve as an explanation of these phenomena. With this end in view I made a large number of *post-mortem* examinations with pretty uniform results. In every instance there was serious effusion in the lateral ventricles and well-marked hemorrhagic clots in the fourth ventricle. The arachnoid space in some instances was likewise filled with serous effusion. The liver was dense in structure, there evidently being an increase in the fibrous tissue. The contents of the stomach and intestines were semi-liquid in character, and not over abundant. In many of the subjects there was evident lack of nutrition. There was one very noticeable condition present in every case, viz., the presence of the larvæ of the bot-fly (*œstrus equi*) in most extraordinary numbers. There was not a single instance in which *post-mortem* examination failed to reveal immense numbers of the larvæ adhering to the walls of the duodenum. This condition I found to be uniformly present, whether the animal had died from disease or had been destroyed for the purpose of examination. The duodenum was in every instance so thoroughly choked by the presence of larvæ that serious interference with digestion might reasonably be expected. The question would naturally arise as to what connection this phenomena had with the disease, if any. Certainly the presence of the parasites would not account for the clinical symptoms, especially in those cases that were more or less clearly marked for years, as the larvæ would be dislodged and disappear from the alimentary canal at the expiration of a few months. I do not regard it as improbable, however, that the presence of the parasites have to do with the development of the abnormal appetite that leads the animal to crave what he would not otherwise touch. One of the well-recognized effects of intestinal parasites is a vitiated appetite. It is not usually considered that the presence of the larvæ of the bot-fly in limited numbers produces any appreciable disturbance. But in the cases referred to they were present in unusual numbers, and had affected a lodgment not in the stomach, their usual habitat, but in the duodenum. I am inclined to the belief that the conditions were such as might account for the appetite, but certainly nothing more than this.

In a few instances cattle have been found eating this "loco plant," and are affected in the same manner as horses. Sheep quite frequently become loco-eaters, grow stupid, emaciated, and eventually die.

I made a number of *post-mortem* examinations on sheep and found all locoed animals to be badly affected with tape-worm. I took 22 tape-worms from the intestinal tract of one sheep, selected from a bunch of loco patients. Sheep are affected much in the same manner as horses. When in a state of repose they are very dull and stupid, but manifest excitement when disturbed.

The loco tendency in the sheep may be accounted for by the pres-
ice of the tape-worm, in part, as the presence of the bot-fly larvæ
ay account for the depraved appetite in the horse. The explana-
on in both cases is of course largely theoretical, but there is cer-
inly a sufficient basis of observed facts to make the hypothesis a
asonable one. Taking it for granted that the presence of intestinal
ırasites furnish a satisfactory explanation for certain animals con-
ıcting the habit, there are doubtless other causes that exert an
fluence. It must be borne in mind that a very large percentage of
e animals in the section of the country we have under considera-
n procure their own subsistence directly from the wild range, and
ver have any prepared forage. On many ranges the pasturage
comes very short during the winter and spring, and hunger drives
o half-famished creatures to eat whatever can be found of vegeta-
e kind. This is more frequently the case since the ranges have
come more completely occupied, and it is a fact that I have else-
ıere referred to that the disease is now becoming known where it
ıs unheard of a few years ago. The losses in many localities have
own to be a serious matter. I was told by different ranch men that
e losses from this source absorbed all the profits there would other-
se be in the business. It is a difficult matter to give even an
proximate estimate on the loss from this cause. The animals run
large on the plains, and frequently the first known evidence of the
ease is the discovery of a carcass. No one can tell from what
use the animal died. Again, almost any ailment is likely to be
ıssed as a case of loco. An animal is found to be sick, and of
urse shows more or less stupor and lack of activity. This is put
wn as a case of loco. Outside of all this, the fact is painfully ap-
rent that a large number of animals eat the plant and that they
e all out of condition; that the habit becomes fixed when once the
ste is acquired, and that it uniformly leads to death if the animal
left to select his food on the range where the plant grows. It is
be presumed that the plant is possessed of some toxic property
at has a specific effect on the nerve centers, and that these effects
ve a marked tendency to remain permanent.

I am not aware that the poison, if the plant possesses such a prop-
ty, has ever been separated by analysis. I am unable to propose any
ry satisfactory remedy for the evil. So long as the animal runs
large where the plant grows, the evil is likely to continue. The
actice of cutting down and destroying the plant has been proposed,
d tried on some ranges. The results were reported on, favorably,
· some sheep men who had tried the experiment. This is, of
urse, a tedious and somewhat expensive method of prevention, but
not impracticable, especially for sheep ranges, where the animals
e not allowed to wander over a wide range of country. I am of
e opinion that this method may be profitably employed in locali-
's where the plant does not grow in great abundance. In districts
ere there are considerable areas, thickly covered, these could be
losed by a wire fence and other parts of the range could be freed
m the plants by cutting. Where the area is too great or the
ınt too abundant for the application of either of these methods, I
no alternative but to prevent the animals from ranging over such
tricts. The trouble is not a serious one on cultivated or inclosed
rms. The plant is rarely seen growing except on the unbroken
d. It is a comparatively easy matter to exterminate it in culti-
ted fields. I have not seen it growing either on plowed land or in

the alfalfa fields, or among the cultivated forage plants. Again, if the causes leading to the formation of the loco habit are such as I have above observed, animals kept on farms would be less subject to these influences than those that are free on the range. Better care, feed, and attention would materially lessen the number falling into the habit.

The disease is not an incurable one, though the administration of drugs is not likely to be followed by very satisfactory results. No drug is likely to overcome the habit, and so long as the appetite and the ability to gratify it remain, the animal will continue to grow worse. Besides, it is practically impossible to medicate the half-wild animals on the open plain. If horses are taken from the range and placed on good, nourishing diet, they will make slow recovery. Favorable results are more likely to follow this method of treatment if the animal is young and the habit not of long standing. I have seen many cases of partial or total recovery from this course of treatment. Special attention should be given to the destruction of intestinal parasites. They are especially abundant and harmful in this region of the country, and I have no doubt but thousands of supposed cases of loco poisoning are the results alone of intestinal parasites.

The winter is not the most favorable season for conducting such investigation. During much of the time I was employed the ground was covered with snow, and the work was necessarily much interfered with.

My time would not allow entering upon any system of practical experimentation. I therefore confined myself entirely to collecting the testimony of those who have had years of experience in the live-stock business, and to making such personal observations as I was able to make on animals that had voluntarily contracted the habit of loco-eating.

There is much need for careful experimental work in this field. A series of carefully arranged practical tests should be made, and the results fairly and faithfully recorded. It is a matter of serious import, especially to the breeders of sheep and horses on the open plains.

I trust the few observations I have been able to make may be followed by more extended and systematic effort, and that a practical solution of the trouble may be found for these enterprising stockmen of the West.

Respectfully submitted.

M. STALKER.

Hon. NORMAN J. COLMAN,
Commissioner of Agriculture.

beef has its origin in Chicago, another statement has been prepared number of tons (2,000 pounds) sent to eastern markets by Chicago question, No. 18, "What proportion does the dead-meat trade now b stock trade?" may be answered at the same time, in convenient form cluded in that table shipments of cattle from Chicago to the same ca for the same years.

Statement in tons of dressed beef received at New York between Ja and December 31, 1885, by months.

Months.	1882.	1883.	1884.
January	....		1,913
February	....		1,840
March	....		1,937
April	....		1,900
May	....		3,170
June	....		3,122
July	....		3,024
August	....		3,187
September	....		3,320
October	....		3,941
November	1,233		3,535
December	1,400		3,700
Total	2,633	10,365	31,930

In July of each year cattle from Texas and the plains of the Southw begin to reach the great live-stock markets named above. The arriv increase in number until they are joined, in August and later, by ca ranges of the States and Territories farther north. The receipts of the continue until December, at which time the supply from the plains c place is at once occupied in the market by the stock which has fattened of the pastures of the States east of the Missouri River.

Comparative statement of shipments of cattle and dressed beef from ing the calendar years 1880 to 1885, inclusive.

[Tons of 2,000 pounds.]

Whither shipped.	Items.	1880.	1881.	1882.	1883.
New York City	Cattle	[illegible]	[illegible]	[illegible]	238,823
	Beef	114	....	3,[illegible]	13,000
Boston	Cattle	81,914	[illegible]	[illegible]	33,020
	Beef	9,[illegible]	14,465	[illegible]	33,130
Philadelphia	Cattle	18,[illegible]	30,408	[illegible]	30,223
	Beef	....	30	[illegible]	9,023
Baltimore	Cattle	4,[illegible]	3,[illegible]	5,[illegible]	5,167
	Beef	....	....	1,[illegible]	4,100
New England States	Cattle	43,145	12,081	[illegible]	1,003
	Beef	[illegible]	[illegible]	[illegible]	52,936
New York State	Cattle	[illegible]	[illegible]	21,738	14,471
	Beef	....	18	[illegible]	16,005
New Jersey and Delaware	Cattle	1,340	1,017	1,[illegible]	1,523
	Beef	....	....	[illegible]	6,137
Pennsylvania	Cattle	1,050	1,[illegible]	2,[illegible]	2,523
	Beef	....	....	[illegible]	5,831
Maryland and South	Cattle	1,308	[illegible]	2,[illegible]	8,415
	Beef	....	....	[illegible]	2,877
Eastern Canada	Beef	....	....	....	....
Total	Cattle	416,[illegible]	[illegible]	[illegible]	[illegible]
	Beef	30,795	43,774	63,773	150,041

4. "Do those engaged in it carry on the trade on their own account stock or in meat, or as agents for others? If as agents, on what terms

This trade is in the control of firms using their own capital, owning t houses, and, in some cases, the refrigerator-cars used in the business. buy, kill, transport, and, in some places, even retail their meats to th At the termini they have built and own cold-storage rooms for their o are in almost every way independent of all outside dealers or agents so far as concerns the buying of the cattle in the markets of the West, the selling to the actual consumer in the East, and all intermediate transactions necessary to the business, except the hauling of the refrigerator-cars over the railways. I do not intend to convey the idea that the firms in the business do sell large quantities of their meats to the consumer, for they do not; but they are able to do so at any time. They do not carry on any part of the business as agents for others.

5. "How are the stock awaiting slaughter kept?"

Beeves and sheep are bought from day to day at the stock-yards named above. The supply is scarcely ever below the needs of the shippers of dressed beef or mutton; therefore there is never any need of keeping a supply on hand for the next coming day. On arrival in the stock-yards, usually at an early hour in the morning, the stock receives hay. After eating the hay they receive water in practically unlimited quantities. They are then, if sold, weighed and delivered to the buyer. His assistants drive the stock to the slaughter-houses near, and there they are killed, very often almost immediately after arrival at the slaughter-houses."

6. "Describe the yards, slaughter-houses, and appurtenances, sending plans and lithographs, where procurable."

The stock-yards of Chicago are the largest in the world, and may be considered representative yards; but they are perhaps less perfectly planned than are those built at a comparatively recent date in Kansas City, Mo. The latter are upon the sandy bank of the Kaw River, to which the drainage of the yards flows through the sewers of ample size. These sewers underlie nearly every street in the yard, as their branches underlie nearly every alley. The area covered by the yards is divided by the streets and alleys into blocks as nearly square as the nature of the ground permits. The blocks are subdivided into pens of various sizes by fences, made of strong cedar posts, deeply planted in the earth, and of pine planks 2 inches thick firmly nailed to the posts. The planks are 6 inches wide, and are surmounted by a broad plank 3 inches thick, extending along the entire length of the fences, including the tops of the many gates. This broad plank thus affords a continuous walk from one part of the yards to any other part, high above the ground. At frequent intervals elevated bridges span the streets and alleys, that there may be no necessity for descending to the level of the ground. To each block a letter is given to distinguish it from the others; as "Block A," etc. To each pen in a block a number is given. When a lot of stock is put into a pen a record is made on the books of the company operating the yards; as, for illustration, if a car-load of cattle were received for John Doe, the record would read, "16 cattle, John Doe, lot 34, Block C." At convenient places in the yards scales are placed for weighing the stock. These scales are made expressly for this purpose, and are each covered by a substantially built house. Of their capacity something has been said above. The pens are floored with pine planks 4 inches thick, resting on other planks of like description. The latter rest in turn, upon their edges, upon plank lying on the ground. In cases where the pens are not so floored they are paved or macadamized. For cattle pens no roofs are provided, but pens for sheltering hogs and sheep are roofed. In every pen is a water-trough of ample size, filled, when desired, from cocks in pipes connecting with a water-tank. In Chicago the water supply is taken from a stand-pipe 100 feet in height and 7 feet in diameter. This pipe is filled by engines driving strong pumps taking their supply from artesian wells, some 1,200 to 1,300 feet deep. The stock-yards of Chicago cover 360 acres.

The slaughter-houses are of brick. From the stock pens at one side of the houses an inclined plane 7 or 8 feet wide extends to the height of the second floor. Between the side of the building and the drive-way mentioned is a row of pens, each 8 feet long and 4 feet wide. Each of these pens connects by a strong door with the drive-way, and at the other end is another door, covered by a plate of iron, through which door access can be had to the interior of the slaughter-house. In the operation of the business cattle are driven up the inclined plane to the level drive-way, and a gate closed behind them. The gates of the small pens are open, and the cattle naturally enter to escape the crowd and the shouting drivers behind. Only one animal, or at most two small beasts, can enter one of these pens at a time. The door is closed behind the animal, and it finds itself imprisoned in a space so small that it can not turn itself around, but must stand with its nose close to the iron-clad door beyond which are the butchers. Over the heads of the beasts awaiting death is a running board or walk 1 foot wide. Along this goes a man armed with a rifle carrying a ball 44-100 caliber, or with a piece of iron pipe three-fourths of an inch in diameter, in the end of which a lance-shaped point has been fastened. With the rifle placed within a few inches of the head of the animal the trigger is pulled, and the heavy ball tears its way down through the medulla oblongata and the brain: or if the lance is used, the spinal cord is severed by its sharp edge. Either way causes

The larger concerns attend to this at their own expense, having ice and men ready at the stations where required. The cost depends upon the condition of the weather at the time the beef is in transit and also at the time of putting up the ice used. In a favorable winter ice can be housed in the North for less than one dollar per ton. From 1,000 to 2,000 pounds are placed in each car, the quantity depending on the season. During the hottest part of August last dressed beef was sent from Chicago to New York and to Boston in cars in which 900 pounds of ice were placed at Buffalo, and 600 pounds at Albany, to replace that which was put in before starting from Chicago. Several cars safely took their loads of beef from Chicago to New York using only 1,800 pounds of ice on the trip. It may be said that the average cost of icing will range from $5 to $7 per car at each icing station.

14. "Say how trains with chilled meats are run, the distances they run, their average speed, and the average cost per mile per ton or per body for carrying and keeping cool."

It is the custom with railroad companies carrying meats from Chicago to make up special trains carrying fresh meats and other perishable freight to the sea-board. Each day such a train, consisting of 20 to 30 cars, is made up, to which are added those containing butter, cheese, and fruits, all in refrigerator cars. Such trains run at the rate of 25 to 30 miles per hour, including stoppages. Trains not infrequently make the run from Chicago to Buffalo, 523 miles, in 36 hours, including one stop at Cleveland when it is found necessary to ice there. As Buffalo is a common point at which eastward-bound trains meet on their way from the West to New York and Boston, all refrigerator cars are examined there, and iced if re-icing appears to be required.

The tariff rate on dressed beef is 65 cents per cental from Chicago to New York. To this charge is to be added the cost of icing as given above. In answering the above questions, I have been largely guided by the conditions of the trade of Chicago, because this city has done by far the greater part of the dressed meat business of this country. In the year 1884 shipments of dressed beef from Chicago amounted to 694,026 carcasses, and they have since that time increased. Perishable property is, it may be added here, carried to the Atlantic sea-board in refrigerator cars named from points 1,000 miles or more west and southwest from Chicago, at which points the temperature ranges from 90° to 100° F. in the shade during the heated months. In trips through such heated districts new supplies of ice are put into the tanks of the cars three times in each thousand miles.

15. "Whether the meat ever arrives in bad condition. If it does, what is the cause, and the percentage of loss from this cause."

In the earlier days of this business, when people were experimenting for the purpose of overcoming the obstacle then met, some cargoes reached their destination in bad order, the cause having been imperfect insulation and the ignorance of employés; but it is now held that there is little if any risk of loss in shipping fresh meats or other perishable property. The percentage of loss of goods in refrigerator cars is too small to be estimated.

16. "What are the form and construction of the meat markets, and of the cold store attached; the rate of the market dues, and the charges per day for keeping meats in the chill-rooms?"

As the markets are largely owned or rented by private parties who make leases, when they do lease, upon private terms, no answer that would have value in another country or in other conditions, can be made. In a few cities stalls are rented by retailers from municipal authorities; but the rates and conditions vary greatly. In regard to the construction of the markets it may perhaps be well to try to answer by describing the retail market of one Chicago firm which ships large quantities of fresh beef to the Eastern States, to Europe, and to many interior points in this country. In the market referred to a counter extends the entire length of the room, the walls of which are frequently covered by a coating of whitewash, and the floor thickly carpeted each day with fresh, clean pine sawdust. Through the middle of the room is a row of square pine posts supporting the floor above. These posts are also whitewashed, and each has attached to it brackets which support bunches of fresh flowers during the seasons when flowers bloom in the open air. The top of the counter on which the meat is served to customers is of marble, smoothly polished. Behind the counter are rows of strong hooks upon which are suspended a few, and only a few, pieces of meat in a fresh state, most of the meats thereon being cured hams or bacon, or sausage. On the heavy cutting blocks under the rows of hooks the butchers cut such pieces as the buyers require. Immediately after the wants of the buyer are satisfied the quarter of beef from which the cuts have been taken is returned to the cool room from which it was brought. It remains there until another piece is wanted for another buyer. Scales are suspended behind the counter for weighing the meats as they are served to the buyers. The chill-room or cold store in which the meat is kept while awaiting the coming of buyers, has walls insulated by dead air spaces, or by other devices, and is kept cool by ice stored in proper receptacles so arranged that while the chilled air falls into the room below the moisture therefrom passes away without coming into contact with the meats. Great care is used in all cold store arrangements to prevent the cold air bearing moisture to the goods to be preserved, and so perfect are some of the cooling devices in use that not the slightest trace of moisture can be seen in the apartments where the goods are stored. In this room the ice is placed in a receptacle at one side. From the ice the cold air falls into a store room below, where it becomes slightly warmed by passing over the meats or other food placed there. The warm air rises through the open floor of the second chill-room, and thence through openings near the ceiling into the room where the ice is stored, to again make the round, as before. Arrangements are made so that the valves close in the openings near the ceiling the instant the door of either of the cold storage rooms is opened. The closing of the valves stops the current of warm air which but for this fall upon the ice and cause it to rapidly waste away. When the door is again closed the valve is opened and the circulation of air goes on as before.

17. "Describe the receiving of meat intended for sale in the market; the mode of selling and delivery."

Upon arrival of the train conveying the fresh meat the cars are run into a cold-storage establishment. The meat is carried into the cold-storage room, and remains there in a temperature of about 36° to 42° F. until wanted. As a rule the quarters are sold to retailers who come at an early hour in the morning, or who send in their orders in the afternoon of one day for the meats they want for the next morning. Wagons prepared for the purpose go about in the morning delivering the meats ordered by the retailers. In some cases hotel managers and others using large quantities of meat order one or two car-loads at a time, and keep the meat in cold-storage rooms until required for their daily business. Poultry and game are also kept in this way.

18. "What proportion does the dead meat now stand to the fat stock trade? Is the dead meat trade increasing and likely to increase?"

This question is in part answered by the reply to query No. 8. The traffic in fresh meats grew rapidly, but not steadily, almost from its inception. It must continue to increase, unless there shall be a revolution in trade affairs and in the desire of the people to obtain the best meats for the smallest outlay. During the last five years the growth of the trade in dressed beef has been as follows: From 1881 to 1882 the increase was 42.5 per cent. over the trade of 1880; in 1882 the gain was 50.8 per cent. over the traffic of 1881; in 1883 it was 127.5 per cent.; in 1884 it was only 28.6 per cent.; and in 1885 it was 25.2 per cent. The relation borne by the entire dressed beef trade of Chicago to the fat stock traffic of that city may be seen at a glance at the figures given in the second table sent herewith.

19. "What distances are live stock carried by rail, and are they taken out and fed on the journey? If so, how often?"

Cattle have been sent by rail from Oregon, on the Pacific coast, to New York, on the Atlantic sea-board. It is a law that cattle shall not be kept confined in cattle cars for a period longer than twenty-four hours without being unloaded for food, water, and rest. In the regions west of Chicago trains do not as a rule run at so high a rate of speed as trains maintain on railways east of Chicago. Such trains now run from 250 to 500 miles without stopping for feeding and resting the stock.

20. "What is the average cost of carrying a fat bullock per mile, by rail, for 100 miles and upward?"

From Kansas City to Chicago the distance is 500 miles, and the rate is $[illegible] per car-load for cattle, nominally 20,000 pounds, but really often or nearly quite 24,000 pounds. From Chicago to New York the rate charged is $110, the distance being 1,005 miles. The average number of cattle in a car-load is 16, the range being from 12 fat and heavy cattle to 20 thin and small ones.

Very respectfully,

NORMAN J. COLMAN,
Commissioner of Agriculture.

Hon. JAS. D. PORTER,
Assistant Secretary of State.

EXTRACTS FROM LETTERS OF CORRESPONDENTS.

SOUTHERN CATTLE FEVER.

A very destructive outbreak of southern cattle fever occurred among cattle in the vicinity of Marshall, Mo., in September last, occasioned by the introduction of a herd of cattle from the southern coast of Texas. Col. S. P. Cunningham, an agent of the Bureau of Animal Industry, made an investigation as to the cause and extent of the outbreak, and reported the results of his investigations as follows, under date of October 9:

On reaching Marshall, Mo., I found that over 100 head of high-grade cattle had been infected and had died of southern cattle fever. The outbreak had been occasioned by the importation of 88 head of southern Texas cattle which had been shipped in July last from Kansas City, Mo., to Marshall. I found the history of the trouble as follows: On July 22, 88 head of cattle, purporting to be Kansas calves, were landed at the depot at Marshall. They were consigned to a Mr. Conway, a cattle trader of Saline, by a party from Kansas City stock-yards. Mr. Conway refused to receive them as his property, but under instructions of the consignor, a Mr. Dorsey, an agent of Hunter, Evans & Co., he held them for Dorsey, and secured pasture for them until he could sell. The pasture secured belonged to Mr. J. L. Coyle, upon which Mr. Coyle had then 66 head of high-grade Shorthorn native Missouri cattle. In this pasture were also placed a pair of scales for neighborhood weighing. Before September 1, Coyle sold 20 head of the Texas cattle to Mr. Wetlack, of Marshall, at $10 per head. In transferring these cattle he drove them through the streets of Marshall, and located them in suburbs near town. A number of cattle coming to Coyle's scales to be weighed passed over the pasture grazed upon by the Texas cattle, contracted splenic fever, and died. Coyle, who had 66 head of native cattle in pasture with the Texas consignment, lost 49 head. Citizens of Marshall, whose milch cows came on the trail from Coyle's to Wetlack's pasture, lost some thirty-odd head from the fever.

This was the situation of affairs when I reached Marshall on Tuesday, October 5, at 10 o'clock a. m. Accompanied by Dr. Edwards, a veterinarian of Marshall, I at once proceeded to Coyle's pasture and held autopsies on animals that had recently died. Case No. 1 was a six months' old calf taken sick October 2. It was constipated and had high fever. Its ears drooped and its eyes were dull. There was straining with great efforts to pass urine, which failed. Death ensued October 4, at 7 o'clock p. m. The body was opened sixteen hours after death. The stomach was impacted with dry, hard food; liver inflamed, cuticle yellow and blood-shotten in spots; gall-bladder full of madder-like particles; main bladder filled with serum; kidneys almost destroyed; urinic poison. Death was, no doubt, caused by this poison. In case No. 2, the first indications of disease, as reported to me, were high fever and constipation; dull eyes and drooping ears; listless movements, with desire for solitude. Salt, lime, and belladonna administered for five days seemed to check the disease. A recurrence followed, and death occurred seven hours before autopsy was made. The liver was found congested; the manifold contained dry impacted food. The kidneys were rotten, and gall-bladder filled with madder-like particles. The main bladder was distended with bloody urine. Case No. 3 was a ten-year-old cow. She was taken sick on the morning of October 1, and died early on the morning of the 5th. The autopsy was held at 2 o'clock p. m., of the same day. All the lesions were indicative of a perfect case of splenic fever. The spleen was plainly and heavily involved. It weighed 5 pounds, just double the weight of that of a healthy animal. The gall-bladder, kidneys, stomach, and bladder were each vitally involved. The gall-bladder was full of madder-like particles; kidneys surcharged with urinic poison; bladder distended with bloody urine; stomach hard, dry, and impacted. This case I unhesitatingly pronounced pure, unmitigated splenic, coast, or southern cattle fever.

I saw numbers of other cases in various stages of the disease. Having fully and satisfactorily identified the disease, I next undertook to ascertain the extent of the damage and trace the outbreak to its origin. I found that Mr. Coyle, up to October 6, had lost 49 head of high-grade Shorthorn cattle, and had 17 head still sick. Various citizens of Marshall had lost 43 head, and 15 were still suffering with the malady. I found that the 20 head of cattle from Texas, purchased by Mr. Wetlack, and held at Marshall, were southern Texas yearlings, and that the 63 head from this bunch were of the same class. I then visited Kansas City and found that the 83 head had been shipped to Hunter, Evans & Co., at that point, by William Butler, of Karnes County, Tex. The consignment reached Kansas City July 20; were held on sale in Kansas City stock-yards until July 22, when they were sold by Hunter, Evans & Co., through a Mr. Dorsey, salesman for said firm, to Mr. Conway, of Marshall, Mo., and were so billed on Hunter, Evans & Co.'s books. I found that Mr. Conway had never bought the cattle, although so billed to him—that he, as agent, received them from Mr. Dorsey (an under salesman of Hunter, Evans & Co.), and placed them in the Coyle pasture, where they remained until he sold 20 of them to Mr. Wetlack, for which he received $10 per head; 63 of the animals brought but $6.50 per head, and were sent to Saline County, Mo. I further found that Dorsey paid but $3.60 per head to Hunter, Evans & Co., for these cattle; took them to Kansas City stock-yards, and thus spread the disease. The facts deducible from this investigation are: First, 83 head of coast cattle, bearing the germs of a communicable disease, were, without delay, shipped from Karnes County, Tex., in midsummer, to the Kansas City stock-yards, and consigned to a commission firm for sale; second, an employé of said firm shipped the cattle from the above-named yards to Marshall, Mo., without a bill of health; third, from this shipment southern cattle fever was communicated to over 200 head of Missouri cattle, worth $2[illegible] per head; that up to to-day 125 head have died, entailing not only a heavy loss upon the owners, but rendering the pastures in the locality unremunerative and grain unsalable. These facts are submitted for your careful and earnest consideration.

In this connection I desire to state that I took charge of the cattle trail and shipment north of cattle from Texas on May 1, 1886. Since then, I have superintended the movement of 235,000 head of Texas cattle to northern ranges. During that time not one case of disease appeared in transit, and no splenic or coast fever was disseminated. All this work must prove nugatory if the central marts of trade are permitted to be made vehicles for the dissemination of disease.

Dr. T. A. Edwards, of Marshall, Mo., writing to Col. S. P. Cunningham, under date of October 15, gives the following history of this outbreak of southern cattle fever and the results of his investigations as to the cause of the disease:

On or about July 23, last, one of our cattle men received from Kansas City, Mo., a bunch of Texas calves, from five to fifteen months old. These little fellows were driven through town to a pasture 1½ miles south, where they remained until July 31, when they were divided, and 20 of them again driven through Marshall and located in a pasture within the city limits. The other 63 head were taken 8 or 10 miles west of town. These animals were watered at the public tanks as they passed through the city. The man with whom they were first pastured had a herd of 90 or more of registered and high-grade cattle, which had access to the same pasture and pond of water as the Texas calves. About September 15 cattle in the pasture where the Texas cattle first stopped began to sicken and die, and the owner came to me with the request that I visit his cattle, hold a *post-mortem* on the two that had died, and prescribe for the 15 head then sick free of charge. This, of course, I refused to do. At this time I did not know that any Texas cattle had been shipped in. I did not see the sick herd until 35 or more of them had died, when, at the request of several of our stockmen, I held several *post-mortems* and examined many of the living, and pronounced the disease as that variously known as Texas, coast, or splenic fever. These cattle had no treatment and have continued to die until over 50 head have been lost, and the living continue to sicken. About September 23 the town cows that were exposed to this bunch of Texans, now pastured in the city limits, began to sicken and die, until only 3 or 4 now remain, and they are not well. One of the little Texas bulls, confined in the pasture in town, managed to creep through a small hole in the fence, and ran with the town cows about the commons, and thus succeeded in contaminating nearly every cow in town. Some time in August 15 head of fine beef steers were weighed on a pair of scales to which the calves had had access, and about the 28th of that month these cattle (which are now 8 miles north of this place with other beef cattle) began dying, and up to date 8 have succumbed. I do not know how many cattle west of here have died, but understand that all of the natives exposed in any way to the Texas bunch driven from here have been lost. None of the Texas lot have died. All of my examinations of the living sick animals, as well as the many autopsies I have made, have given me no room to doubt this malady as being what is known as southern coast, or Texas cattle fever, but I was in total darkness as to what the trouble really was—its true pathology, its cause, and its best treatment, until the 6th instant. At that time I carefully dissected a large, fat, red steer which had died a few hours previous. Do not understand me to assert that I have learned it all by this examination, for I simply learned then that previous examinations had taught me nothing. In some *post-mortems* the manifold was in a perfect normal condition; in others its contents were very hard and dry. In all I found the urine highly colored, and in some it looked as though it might be half blood. The kidneys, in some cases, seemed in a high state of congestion, and in others putrefaction was rapidly advancing. The liver was enlarged, congested, and engorged with bile. The gall-bladder was greatly distended, with a ropy, thick, dark matter, in some almost black, in others not so dark, yet in all lumpy and resembling thick molasses or soft soap. The spleen in the steer referred to was greatly enlarged and filled with semi-coagulated blood. The duodenum was engorged with duodenal matter, very heavily charged with bile. Such was the condition of things, roughly given, as they appeared to the natural eye; but not being satisfied with these examinations I decided to make a chemical and microscopical examination and send you the results. I took the weight of the spleen, which was 10 pounds. Then I placed in clean separate bottles a small piece of the spleen, liver, kidneys, and a small quantity of the bile and urine. These I brought home and analyzed chemically and microscopically, with the following results: Urine loaded with albumen; kidneys simply in a high state of inflammation, with an occasional spot of decay. A peculiarity of the spleen is that there seems nothing wrong with it save its enormous enlargement. It seems to be filled to its utmost capacity with semi-coagulated blood, which presents under the microscope nothing more than an engorgement, with both red and white blood globules, the red greatly predominating. The liver was enlarged, congested, and thoroughly saturated with bile. The bile was filled with serum. It was hard to determine which was the smaller ingredient, bile or serum. Now what must we conclude from this examination? Certainly that the trouble is not in the spleen, but in the liver or the portal circulation, and the trouble with the kidneys, spleen, and other organs is nothing more than we would expect from overtaxation, because of the liver not being able to do its part. In my opinion this disease is much like "dengue" (breakbone fever), or yellow fever in the human race, and, treated as such, I believe a great deal of good may be done.

In the latter part of September a number of letters were received from cattle growers in the vicinity of Middleburgh, Va., stating that a fatal disease was prevailing among cattle in that locality which it was feared was contagious pleuro-pneumonia. Dr. C. K. Dyer, an inspector of the Bureau of Animal Industry, was directed to make an examination of the afflicted animals and report the results of his investigation to the Department. His report bears date of October 1, and is as follows:

In my investigations of this outbreak I learned that on the 14th day of September Mr. E. T. Holton purchased, at the Chicago stock-yards, of Messrs. Wagoner & Bender (cattle brokers for Messrs. Conover & Herrick), 134 steers; that they were shipped from there and arrived at Summit Point three days after (September 17), and were then driven about 35 miles to the farms of the following-named gentlemen in this locality, viz: E. T. Holton, Fauquier County, 2 steers, both of which died in a few days; W. N. Tiffany, same county, 37 steers, 7 of which have since died and 3 are now sick; Hugh Tiffany, same county, 15 steers, 3 of which have died and 2 are now sick; Frank Ish, Loudoun County, 20 steers, of which 1 is sick; William Humphrey and Edgar Ish, both of Loudoun County, 30 steers each. Six animals on the above-mentioned farms were suffering with mild attacks of Texas fever, and would likely recover. No native cattle had been attacked.

An outbreak of southern cattle fever, notable for its destruction of valuable animals, occurred in the vicinity of Richmond, Va., during the latter part of September and the early part of October. W. H.

Harbaugh, resident veterinarian of Richmond, furnished the Department with the following history of the disease on October 9:

For a month past there have been numerous deaths in this vicinity among the cattle from what is commonly called "bloody murrain" or "red water." My business partner and myself have been consulted professionally in a few cases only. An outbreak occurred in the Westham herd of fine Jersey cattle, the property of Col. R. Snowden Andrews, at the Westham Granite Company's farm, about seven miles from Richmond, in Chesterfield County. I was called to the farm, and found a cow dying, and from the symptoms furnished me I suspected the nature of the trouble. I inserted the catheter and withdrew seven quarts of very dark-colored urine. This animal died within an hour after my arrival, while in a semi-comatose state. I was informed that a cow had died the day before showing similar symptoms. I prescribed treatment and left. About a week afterwards I was again called to the same farm, and when I arrived was informed that a cow had died about fifteen minutes before my arrival. This animal I discovered to be one from which I had removed the placenta on my former visit, she having had a premature birth. At that time she exhibited no symptoms of Texas fever. A few days afterwards (six days) I was again called, and found two of the cattle in a critical condition, one of which was the celebrated "Oxford Kate," which cost Colonel Andrews $[illegible]. I again examined the herd and found more affected. The temperature of the affected cattle ranged from 108° Fahrenheit (Oxford Kate) down to 104½° Fahrenheit. The pulse ranged from 90 to 100. The animals lost flesh very rapidly; would stand with arched backs, staring eyes; would pass quantities of urine, varying in color in the different animals, from light red to black; would not stand long at a time, but preferred to lie down. Oxford Kate was loose in a box stall, and toward the last, when she was so weak that it was difficult for her to assume the standing posture, she would struggle from a bed of nice clean straw back to the paved floor, which was wet with urine, and lie there in preference. She died at 9.45 p. m. October 6. The *post-mortem* examination commenced the following morning at [illegible]. As the hide was being removed the fat was observed to possess a peculiar glistening greenish tinge. Mr. Phillips, the foreman, very appropriately remarked: "It looks something like the greenish color in a copper boiler." In cutting through the inferior cervicle muscles to remove the side a most sickening odor was emitted. The cut surfaces were a very dark color. A noticeable absence of blood in all the vessels was not to be overlooked; ecchymosis was observed in the cavities of the heart. The lungs were normal, except a certain amount of hypostatic congestion of the right lung, which was easily accounted for, as she was lying on that side when she died. There was ecchymosis beneath the parietal and visceral pleura—a few spots only. The spleen was much thickened and elongated, and the greatest care had to be taken in tearing it loose from its attachment to the rumen and diaphragm, as it burst in several places, from which matter resembling "whipped" coagulated blood oozed out. The liver was enlarged and parts of it congested; when cut into it was of a dull, yellowish, coppery color; the cut surfaces, after being exposed for a few minutes, assumed a bright yellow color. The gall bladder was distended, with a thick, dark, semi-fluid granular looking matter, resembling much the dregs of a "black strap" molasses barrel. The rumen contained less than the ordinary amount of ingesta; the walls of the viscus seemed normal. Nothing abnormal was noticed in connection with the reticulum. The omassum was normal; the ingesta between the leaves was moist. The abomassum contained very little ingesta, which was washed off to expose the mucous membrane; parts of the mucous membrane were dark colored; there were upon it many red and "angry" looking spots and numerous ulcers, which, to a person who has seen the ulcers in the nostrils of a glandered horse, could not help being struck with the similarity; many spots could be seen on the lamellar folds of the membrane; not a few large ragged-edged ulcers were observed in the pyloric portion; some were oblong and some were quadrilateral in outline, the edges dark colored and even blackened, and gave one the impression that the membrane had been removed in patches with a very dull instrument—"sawed out," as it were. The external appearance of the intestines was dark; they contained much blood of a very frothy nature and of a sero-sanguineous consistence; the mucous membrane was easily scraped off with the finger nail. The urinary bladder contained a sedimentary deposit of a dull leaden hue, nothing like the appearance of the claret-colored urine she had been passing previous to her death. On the mucous membrane were clusters of red-crested, papilla-like elevations. The kidneys were very dark-colored, much congested, the corticle substance friable, and upon close examination dark spots could be detected beneath the capsule. The right, always the largest, was more than a third larger than the left. The uterus contained a four months old fetus.

As I held a *post-mortem* examination on the second cow that died I was confirmed in my diagnosis, and am perfectly satisfied that that of Oxford Kate was correct. Oxford Kate was a famous animal, and had a record of thirty-nine pounds twelve ounces of butter in a week.

SOUTHERN CATTLE FEVER—THE PERMANENTLY INFECTED LINE.

Referring to the investigations of this Department relative to the territory permanently infected with southern cattle fever, Mr. William King Kendall, of Tilden, Tex., writing under date of September 25 last, says:

A copy of the Agricultural Report for 1885 has been received, for which please accept my thanks. In offering thanks for this kindness, you will pardon me for referring to a subject of very great moment to the live-stock industry of this State, and one that I am pleased to see has been treated very exhaustively and fairly in the report before me. I refer to that of Texas or splenic fever of cattle. It is quite evident to every intelligent mind that no arbitrary line, based upon any defined degree of latitude or longitude, can be drawn defining the infected and non-infected sections of the State. This can only be determined after years of careful investigation. With a view of adding my mite toward the ascertainment of such facts, I am constrained to address you upon the subject. I believe the Department has done all that was possible under the circumstances to ascertain the nature of the malady, as well as the extent of the affected territory, and that in so doing it has been actuated by the best of motives—the public good.

Before proceeding to a discussion of the subject, however, I desire to disclaim any personal interest in range cattle. I would further state that I am not of those who unreasonably contend, against well-established facts, that no such disease exists in the State of Texas, but, on the contrary, think it quite likely that the entire section contiguous to the sea-board is permanently infected. Being thoroughly acquainted with that section, as well as with the southern half of the State, I am led to believe that the disease prevails farther inland in the eastern than in the western section of the State. I reach this conclusion from two reasons: First, from the fact that the low, level plains bordering the coast extend farther inland in the former than in the latter section; secondly, because the climate, geography, and vegetation of the two sections are radically different, and much certainly depends, in determining this matter, upon altitude and climate. There is still another fact I desire to state in this connection, which appears to me to demand more than a passing consideration, and it is a fact so universally recognized by all intimately acquainted with the live stock of the coast country that no one will be found to deny the statement. For thirty years I was a resident of the coast, and during that time was engaged in breeding native cattle upon the range, and was thus offered every facility for making observations. From the earliest settlement of that section to the present time a malady has prevailed among the cattle of that region locally known as murrain. The loss from this disease is much greater than is generally supposed or admitted. Upon one occasion I had a small herd in an inclosure, and the loss from the first of March to the following November aggregated just 10 per cent.; and I am persuaded, after many years of close observation, that the annual loss from this disease alone will not fall short of 5 per cent. When compared with the estimated losses of range cattle from all causes as usually published, this statement seems alarming; but it should be borne in mind that these estimates are absurdly inaccurate and misleading. By reference to Youatt and other veterinary authorities I find no similarity between this so-called murrain and that known to veterinary science, but do find a very close similitude between the symptoms of this malady and that of Texas or splenic fever as described by veterinarians. Again, it is a well-known fact that the liver of all cattle over one year of age throughout the coast country is more or less affected, showing lesions in this organ to a greater or less extent. After a residence of nine years in this country I never knew or heard of a case of this so-called murrain where the liver and other organs were found, upon examination, in a normal condition.

In conclusion, I would most respectfully submit that I am under the impression that the line suggested by the Department in the report before me, locating the infected district, will be found upon further investigation to be but partially correct. It is my impression, based upon the facts above cited, that a line beginning at Laredo, or perhaps farther south on the Rio Grande, and bearing eastward sufficiently to include a greater portion of Duval, and perhaps the entire county of Mc-

Mullen, and a portion, if not all, of Atascosa County north of [illegible] and thence converging until it should intercept the designated line [illegible] San Antonio, would embrace all additional territory free from the fear of [illegible] in the State of Texas.

Mr. S. P. Goodwin, of Savannah, Ga., referring to the permanently infected region of southern cattle fever, as pointed out in previous reports of the Bureau of Animal Industry, in a letter of recent date, addressed to Dr. D. E. Salmon, says:

I see by the maps that Georgia lies entirely within the permanently infected region, or almost so, as also does South Carolina. Such being the case, it would seem to be an easy matter to remove cattle from one part of the State to another without danger of fever. It is not so, however, for cattle brought to the coast belt from the region of Atlanta and Athens, in this State, from Charlotte, N. C., and as far north as Greenville, S. C., invariably die within a few months. It is an exception when one lives through the following summer after arrival. Milch cows brought here from Atlanta can not be sold at all if it is known they are from that point. It does seem there is less danger in bringing cattle here from any point along the coast belt as far north as Long Island than there is in a few hundred miles in the interior. For that reason I must think there is a coast belt region which has been overlooked. I have been trying some time to acclimate a Jersey bull, and lost three before I succeeded in bringing one through the summer. There is only one way to do it, and that is to bring them here in the fall, at six or eight months old, and the following summer feed them on laxative food, and not expose them to the sun at all. The Holstein appears to do better here than the Jersey. Of quite a number brought here there have been few deaths in acclimating.

ANTHRAX AND CHARBON.

Dr. L. E. Rockwell, of Amenia, N. Y., writing under date of January 27, 1886, thus speaks of an outbreak of anthrax among cattle in that locality:

Another outbreak of anthrax, or splenic apoplexy, has occurred in our town, this time at R. R. Thompson's. Four years ago the disease appeared in the herd of Frank Baylim, 2 miles east of Amenia.

A supposed outbreak of anthrax occurred in a herd of cattle belonging to C. Hibbard & Son, of Bennington, Shiawassee County, Mich., in January last. On the 15th of April Hon. H. H. Hinds, president of the Michigan Live Stock Sanitary Commission, wrote the Department, giving an account of the outbreak, and inclosed the reports of Prof. E. A. Grange, State veterinarian, and William Jopling, veterinary surgeon, of Owasso, Mich. The report of the former, which was made to the Live Stock Sanitary Commission on the 9th of April, is as follows:

On the 28th of February last I was requested to examine some cattle belonging to Messrs. Hibbard & Son, Shorthorn breeders, of Bennington, Mich., which were said to be suffering from some new disease. On my arrival at night I found the animal (an ox) dead. Being late in the evening a *post-mortem* was deferred until morning, when autopsy revealed the following lesions: Beginning with the mouth I found the skin upon the upper lip much abraded, exhibiting very angry looking sores, with evidence of considerable ante-mortem discharge from the nose. Examination of the nasal chambers showed the mucous membrane to be of a reddish-purple hue, with pus distributed along their course. Continuing, I found the mucous membranes of the larynx, trachia, and bronchial tubes highly injected. After having observed the lesions in the air passages, my attention was next directed to the alimentary canal, the mucous membrane of most parts of which presented a decided blush. The accessory organs of digestion (liver, spleen, and pancreas) did not present any marked deviation from health; the feces were normal. I then proceeded to make an examination of the urinary organs, and on making sections of the kidneys I found the mucous membranes of the uriniferous tubes in a highly injected condition. In the urine bladder was found a considerable quantity of a jelly-like mass, highly covered with blood, the mucous membrane of which was amply covered with petechial spots. Examination of the brain did not reveal [illegible] peculiar.

On my arrival in the evening, in addition to the dead ox, I was shown a heifer in the same stable decidedly sick, and upon examination I found a profuse discharge of tears from the eyes; nostrils injected; ears drooping; temperature about 106° F.; respiration much accelerated; pulse, say, 80 per minute; appetite little affected; bowels almost normal; urine natural. Next morning the animal seemed somewhat worse, and going from bad to worse, day by day, Mr. Hibbard killed it about the sixth day.

From what I saw, and from the history of the disease given me by Dr. Jopling, of Owasso, and Mr. Hibbard, in those animals which had died some time previous to my visit, I diagnosed the disease as "malignant catarrhal fever," but am somewhat at a loss to account for the cause of the complaint, as my brief investigation failed to discover anything in the sanitary condition of the premises, care, and management of the animals, or other circumstance which I could say was the cause of the disease. I stated to Mr. Hibbard that I did not think the malady was of a contagious nature, and its behavior since then would appear to confirm that opinion.

The following is the report made by Dr. Jopling on the history of this outbreak and the characteristics of the disease:

Case No. 1.—On the 20th day of January, 1886, I was called to see a thoroughbred heifer nearly a year old which had been sick for two days. Upon arriving at the farm, some 4 miles distant, I found her suffering from spasms, during which she would fall down and appear as if about to die, but would recover in a few minutes and get on her feet again. I found her temperature 106° F.; pulse very quick and weak; respiration about 40; visible mucous membranes reddened; a free discharge from nose and eyes, and traces of blood in the urine. She lived some ten or twelve hours from the time I first saw her. She had repeated spasms or convulsions until she died.

The *post-mortem* examination showed that the mucous membranes were the principal seat of disease. They were of a purplish red color, with slight ulcerations in the mouth and fauces. A part of the muzzle sloughed off. The mucous membranes of both the respiratory and digestive tracts were involved throughout. The lungs were slightly inflamed. The right side of the heart was distended with blood, and the opposite side empty. The spleen was slightly enlarged, and the mucous membrane of the bladder somewhat inflamed. These are the *post-mortem* lesions, as near as I can recollect them. Owing to the fact that aconite had been freely administered in the early stage of the disease, and not being able to account for the symptoms presented and the *post-mortem* appearances in a better way, I attributed it to an overdose of this medicine.

Case No. 2.—A grade heifer, coming two years old, was taken sick three weeks after the first one died. She died inside of three days, showing symptoms exactly similar to those seen in the first case. I did not see this animal, but Mr. Hibbard held a *post-mortem* examination, and said that the appearance seemed to be the same as in the previous one.

Case No. 3.—An ox, ten years old, was taken sick on the 24th of February. Had taken his feed as usual the previous night, and was found sick in the morning. I arrived there six or eight hours from the time he was first known to be sick, and found the symptoms as follows: Temperature, 107° F.; pulse, 80; respiration about 40; a free discharge from the eyes, and eyelids swollen; an abundant discharge from the nostrils also; urine bloody and passed frequently. As the disease advanced the symptoms became more aggravated. The temperature increased a little during the first day, and then decreased a little. The pulse got weaker and more frequent, and the discharge from the eyes and nose more profuse. The mouth was very sore and ulcerated. The muzzle sloughed off, and the animal before death presented an unsightly appearance. Professor Grange, State veterinarian, was present when the animal died. The *post-mortem* appearances were similar to those described in the first case. The mucous membrane seemed to be the principal seat of the disease.

Case No. 4.—A grade heifer, rising two years old, which had aborted some four weeks previous. She was taken sick on the 26th day of February, and died within a few days. In this case the owner said that while withdrawing the milk a short time previous to death the skin peeled off the teats; otherwise the symptoms were the same as in the other cases. No *post-mortem* was made.

Case No. 5.—An ox (mate to one previously mentioned) was taken sick on the 2d day of April, and died within three days. I did not see this animal, and no *post-mortem* examination was made.

In conclusion, I might state that the first animal taken sick was in stables about one-half mile distant from the others, while all stood in the same stable side by side. They were all very fleshy. In no case was there any cough, notwithstanding the great degree of bronchial irritation.

In writing to the Department, under date of [illegible], Mr. B. B. Eskridge, Pecan Point, Mississippi County, Ark., states that charbon has made its appearance among horses and mules in that vicinity.

GOITER IN CATTLE.

William H. Gribble, veterinary surgeon, writing from Gaylord, Otsego County, Mich., under date of July 8, thus speaks of the general presence of goiter among calves in that locality:

The majority (calves), as far as I can learn, are born with goiter (or, as the farmers term it, "big neck"), which constantly enlarges, and in a few days causes suffocation; in fact, many are born dead, and calves in utero are the same. I also find many horses with enlarged thyroid glands. Wells are scarce, and where [illegible] are are usually quite deep, so that cattle which roam at large obtain their water supply from lakes having no perceptible inlet or outlet. The country is now, being mainly covered with virgin timber, mostly rock maple, hemlock, pine, [illegible] wood, etc. I have given no time to the smaller flora, as summers are short and most of the winter food is brought in by railroads.

I find that cattle given well-water all winter still give birth to goitered calves. Again, a large number of cattle brought into this neighborhood from a distance seem to do well but a short time. They then lose appetite, flesh, etc., and gradually become skeletons and die. A few seemingly get well, but in a short time they are again attacked.

I have had no opportunity to make a *post-mortem* examination, but the few I have seen strangely impress me as the symptoms of tuberculosis. Still, I can not see how this can be the disease.

A Mr. Newsome, a homesteader, tells me that he has lost cattle since he has been here, and that every neighborhood has had goitered calves.

DEATH OF A COW FROM TUBERCULOSIS.

About the 1st of December, Mr. Thomas Eckles, of Olmsted County, Minn., informed the Department of an outbreak of disease among his cattle, and requested that a veterinarian be sent to make an examination and determine the character of the malady. Dr. [illegible] was instructed to visit his herd, which he did on the 7th of December, and at once forwarded the following report of the results of his investigations:

In accordance with your orders, per dispatch of the 4th inst., I visited the farm of Mr. Thomas Eckles, located about 2½ miles southeast from Eyota, Minn., who had kept four head of Shorthorn cows. The owner had bought a three years' old grade Jersey cow last October from a resident in Eyota, who said she was raised in the county. She was not known to have come in contact with any diseased stock. When purchased she was in lean condition, and was troubled with a cough, but only when feeding, and at no other time. Exercise would cause difficulty in breathing, and she would then act, as the owner says, like a horse with the heaves. As she did not improve in flesh, and as the owner was afraid to use what little milk she gave, he destroyed her. On opening her he found what he thought were signs of pleuro-pneumonia, and so reported. He says a portion of the left lung adhered to the ribs and diaphragm, and on cutting into the lungs he found numerous smaller and larger abscesses or cavities filled with thick yellow pus. The lungs weighed about 11 pounds, while the right lung was apparently healthy. The diseased lung was preserved in a frozen condition for inspection.

I found the surface of the lung of normal smooth aspect, with no signs of previous inflammatory action. The anterior half of the lung was enlarged. A section through this portion revealed large tubercular deposits in various conditions and stages, from cheesy to more solid and granular, gritty or calcareous, with abscess formation in cavities from the size of a bean to that of a goose egg.

The four other cows, which had been kept with the diseased one, I found to be in a healthy condition. No deaths from contagious disease among cattle are known to have occurred in this neighborhood or in this county. The above case was tuberculosis.

DISEASE AMONG CATTLE IN TENNESSEE.

In November last an outbreak of disease was reported as existing in a herd of cattle near Brownsville, Tenn., and the Department was requested to make an investigation as to the nature of the malady. Dr. N. H. Paaren was directed to visit the herd, make the necessary investigation, and report the results to this Department. His report bears date of November 29, and is as follows:

In compliance with the request contained in your telegram of November 24, to "proceed at once to Brownsville, Tenn., and meet live stock commission and investigate cattle disease," I started on the 25th instant and arrived there on the night of the 26th. The next morning I met Messrs. F. B. Snipes and J. V. Fulkerson, of the live stock commission, and A. J. McWhirter, commissioner of agriculture for Tennessee.

We proceeded at once to the farm of Mr. B. G. Allison, located 2¼ miles northwest of Brownsville, on which farm were kept 18 dairy cows, 1 bull, and 16 heifers under two years old. The owner stated that, since the 1st of August last, a number of young animals commenced to fall off in condition; that a number of them became more or less affected with diarrhea, from which most of them slowly recovered without medical treatment, while others remained in poor condition and considerably emaciated. In this condition I found about a half dozen of the animals on my arrival.

Since the 1st of August five of these young animals had died. Although none of them had suffered from cough, or any other symptom that might indicate affection of the respiratory organs, still the owner as well as some of his neighbors were afraid that the trouble might be due to pleuro-pneumonia, and the State authorities were asked to make an investigation.

In the lot were only three animals in poor condition. Auscultation and percussion revealed nothing but a normal condition of the internal organs. The temperature of the three were respectively 101½°, 102°, and 102¼° F. On a close external examination, I found these, as well as several other young animals, literally covered with lice.

At the suggestion of the commissioners, and with the approval of the owner, I shot the poorest one of the lot; exposed every organ of the body to full view; cut open the trachea and bronchial tubes; made incisions of the stomach, liver, spleen, kidneys, etc., and found nothing whatever indicating an abnormal condition, excepting such signs as are due to a state of general debility and emaciation, such as flaccidity of textures, bloodlessness, consequent paleness of muscles, etc.

The animals had been fed on whole corn and hay, which passed off in an undigested condition. I recommended chopped and ground or steamed food, with the addition of vegetable tonics; attention to bodily cleanliness, and the application of an ointment made of snuff and lard, or kerosene with lard.

SALT SICK IN CATTLE.

Dr. J. M. Abbott, Tuckertown, Fla., in a letter addressed to the Department in February last, says:

Your Department would confer a lasting blessing on Florida if it could find out the cause and discover a remedy for what old settlers call the salt sick in cattle. I have opened and examined several of my own animals that died of the disease, and in some cases found their lungs affected, in others the liver, and in a few the kidneys seemed to be the seat of the disease.

In answer to a communication requesting further information in regard to the symptoms and characteristics of this disease, Dr. Abbott wrote as follows:

During last year from 25 to 40 per cent. of the cattle in this county died of the sick or salt sick malady, as it is called. One of my friends lost 250 head out of a herd of 550 head. It was more general last year than for fifteen years past. The animals, when first taken, look sick; while they continue to eat they get poorer and poorer, and finally die of inanition, like a person afflicted with consumption. The liver of one of those I opened was diseased; in the second one I found the kidneys diseased, and the liver normal; the third one showed disease of the lungs, while the kidneys and liver were unaffected.

DEATH OF CATTLE FROM IMPACTION OF THIRD STOMACH.

In July last Mr. D. P. Cox, of Liberty, Amite County, Miss., lost a number of cattle by impaction of the third stomach. In a letter addressed to the Department he gave the following symptoms and characteristics of the disease:

The first symptoms are similar to those of a horse suffering with the colic. Their appetite seems good until about a day preceding their death. They do not linger more than five days, and die in a great deal of pain, bellowing loudly for several hours before death. They are constantly straining to have an action of the bowels, but pass a very small quantity of feces, and that is hard and black. Sometimes the discharge is whitish-looking matter mixed with a small quantity of blood. Horns hot, with drooping ears; their eyes lose their luster and are sunken. I opened one and found the liver and lungs of the proper size. The liver looked as if covered with something resembling brick-dust, and the lungs seemed red or bruised in places. The gall bladder was very large and full of a very dark fluid. The urinary bladder was empty. The third stomach or maniplus was packed very tight and hard and dry—dry enough to burn. The contents of the main stomach were rather of a fluid nature. The intestines were filled with gas and were streaked with blood as if badly inflamed.

BLACKLEG.

But few cases of the disease known as "blackleg" have been reported during the year. On the 20th of March last Mr. Charles Achatz, Granger, Minn., wrote the Department that an outbreak of the disease had occurred in his herd. He said:

I have about thirty head of cattle on the farm, and am becoming alarmed, as the disease (blackleg) appears very active. I have lost three animals within a week. The first one to die was a yearling heifer. She was seen limping on the 12th instant, and was found dead in the stable next morning. On examination I found her flesh as if it had been all bruised; her liver was mottled or streaked with light brown or yellow; the gall cyst was enlarged and filled with thin dark green fluid, and the spleen appeared as if it was composed of clotted blood. The manifold was crammed full of dry feed and was very hard. On the 17th instant a yearling steer died, and on the 20th instant I lost a two-year-old steer. I do not know what caused the outbreak. There has been no black quarter on the place for three or four years. The yearlings were fed on timothy hay and oats, and were in good condition. The two-year-old had access to the straw pile.

Mr. James T. Gerald, Globe, Gila County, Ariz., writing under date of June 21, gives the following description of the symptoms and *post-mortem* appearances of a number of calves recently lost by him by a disease supposed to be blackleg:

When first taken the animals seem stupid and refuse food and water. As the disease progresses they get lame in the right hind leg, and die in from eight to thirty-six hours. After death the manifold is found very hard and the fæces in the several folds very dry. Swelling on the right side of the neck close to the jaw. On opening this swelling the flesh is found to be of a dark purple color and quite spongy. The same can be said of the right loin near the backbone, and also stifle joint of right hind leg.

PROBABLY ACUTE INDIGESTION.

Early in June last the Department received a letter from Prof. Charles W. Dabney, of Raleigh, N. C., inclosing one from Mr. D. W. G. Benbow, of the same place, who had recently lost a number of valuable cows from a disease unknown in that locality. The stomach of one of the animals was forwarded, accompanied by the following description of the disease, prepared by Dr. R. M. Gregory:

The cow (a Jersey) from which this stomach and its contents were taken was seized by tetanic convulsions, with slight intervals between. The convulsions gradually grew more frequent and violent, and death resulted in half an hour from seizure. The symptoms present were those of strychnia poisoning, or that of ergot as detailed by Bartholow in his *materia medica* and therapeutics. This cow, and the others that were attacked and suffered very similarly, had been eating other foods mixed with cured rye for about a week. This food was very carefully examined and no diseased heads or ergot were discovered. The body was carefully examined and no marks of disease could be discovered. The lungs were very much congested, as was also the brain. The heart was filled, both sides, with blood clots. No inflammation of any organ was present. This cow would have given birth to a calf on July 18; so it seems that if the poison was ergot its poisonous effects were not exerted in bringing about abortion. Ergot is said to produce an inability to void urine when taken in large doses, but in this instance there was no such difficulty. The food in the stomach was well masticated and seemed to be in a normal stage of digestion. No symptoms of any trouble or suffering were shown previous to the convulsive seizures. During these convulsions the head was drawn back and the eyes seemed to protrude. The fecal matter passed was carefully examined and nothing abnormal was found.

RINDERPEST IN INDIA.

Hon. B. F. Bonham, United States consul-general to India, writing to the Secretary of State from Calcutta, under date of June 2, 1886, gives the following information relative to the existence of rinderpest among cattle in that consular district:

Referring to pages 439 and 440 of Consular Regulations of 1881, and to sections 2493 and 2494 of United States Revised Statutes, I deem it to be prudent and advisable, as a matter of some public interest perhaps, for me to communicate to you the fact that it is reported in Calcutta, that the cattle plague known as "rinderpest," generally understood, I believe, to be contagious, prevails in parts of the Madras Presidency, within this consular jurisdiction.

I inclose herewith for the information of the State Department, as well as that of all whom it may concern, an extract from this subject which I clip from The Englishman, a reliable daily newspaper published here, of date the 1st instant. As you are aware, large quantities of baled hides (dried and salted) are being shipped from India to the United States. Not being myself an expert on the subject of the liability of our cattle in America to contract the rinderpest from the importation of the hides of cattle which have died of that disease, I content myself with reporting the facts only as they come to my knowledge.

Since the receipt at this office of dispatch No. 22 of the State Department, of date September 3, 1884, on this subject, I am advised that no consular certificate of non-infection has been issued in connection with invoices of baled hides shipped to the United States from this consular district.

FATAL DISEASES AMONG HORSES.

Mr. A. G. Dawley, Elko, Elko County, Nev., in January last wrote as follows concerning a fatal disease prevailing at that time among horses in that county:

We have a new and very fatal disease which has lately attacked horses in this section of the State, and we are at a loss to know how to treat it. The disease is confined mostly to mares. The animal is generally attacked when in good condition. The first symptom is a breaking down in one hind leg, the use of which they lose almost entirely. The flesh shrinks away from around the hip and stifle joint. In the course of a month or so the disease will attack the other leg, and death soon follows. We have lost 40 animals by the malady in this county during the fall and winter.

In answer to this note Dr. Salmon stated that he was unable to reach a positive conclusion as to the nature of the affection, but suspected it to be connected with either the food or water supply. He further stated that his attention had never been called to so large a number of cases of paralysis occurring in the same herd of horses and asked for further information. In response to this request Mr. Dawley wrote as follows on January 19:

Since writing you on January 2 I have lost one mare with the disease. The disease certainly acts like paralysis, but I don't think it can be that, for in a number of cases it has attacked mares on the range that have never been handled or overworked. It has appeared in herds in this county separated by a distance of 100 miles. The cause may possibly be in the feed—some kind of poisonous weed, perhaps; but if so it would be hard to determine at present, as the snow has covered up the grasses pretty generally throughout the county. The water supply is excellent—pure snow water from the mountains.

Since my letter of the 2d instant I have met a resident of the county who resides about 80 miles distant. He had a herd of 80 head of horses, and two or three months ago 10 of his animals were attacked by the disease and 8 of them died. I have heard of no new cases since I wrote, and possibly the winter and cold weather may kill out the malady.

On the 25th of January Dr. Salmon replied to the above letter as follows:

I would like to say further in regard to the disease of horses in your vicinity, which appears to be a form of paralysis especially in horses, that it results from various causes. In an instance like the one under consideration, where so many animals are affected, it must of course be due to a cause which acts on nearly or quite all the animals in the herd, and those that are most susceptible of course show its effects.

The forms of paralysis in horses which are liable to affect a number of animals almost simultaneously may be grouped under two heads: First, paralysis due to an affection of the spinal chord, which may be caused by poison taken with the food, or by various internal derangements of the liver and kidneys; and second, by obstruction of the arteries which supply the limbs with blood. This, in Europe, has been found to be frequently caused by a parasitic worm which, in one stage of its existence, lives in the blood vessels. The plugging of the arteries is frequently seen in this country in individual cases, but I have never met with it where a number of animals were affected, nor where it has been caused by this parasite. Still, this is no reason for concluding that this parasite does not exist with us.

I would be very glad if you would write me more fully in regard to the symptoms. When one limb becomes more or less useless does this limb seem colder to the touch than the opposite limb? Have you noticed that the paralyzed limb retains its normal sensitiveness? You might test this by pricking it with a pin to determine if the animal feels in this as well as in the other limb.

Providing you have any more cases I would suggest that you put the animal in a stable and give it a good dose of physic, *i. e.*, about three-fourths of an ounce of Barbadoes aloes mixed with a little ginger. The aloes may be given made up into a ball, if you have any one who understands administering the ball; if not, it may be rubbed up and dissolved in hot water and given as a drench. In case the disease is caused by a poison, this would free the digestive organs from it, and would have a great tendency to relieve the spinal chord from its effects. I think physic, given in the early stages, would produce a decided improvement if the trouble is caused by a poison in the food.

In May last Mr. William Cooks, Saint Paul, Minn., forwarded the following communication to the Department:

At the request of several gentlemen interested in breeding horses in this State, I wish to submit the following: In the latter part of June and the early days of July, 1885, in haying time, a lot of mares and colts, numbering 29, were turned into pasture on the place of Mr. John Osborn, 7 miles from Minneapolis. There was a pond of water, but the water was very low, and the animals drank of it. Sickness soon appeared, and after two or three days' illness they would die, and finally the whole herd died, and evidently of the same malady. When they commenced going, some were moved into the city and some to other pastures; but these means did not change the fatal results. The animals had good appetites, and the bowels were in good order to within four or five hours before death. They would lie on their side and have very severe spasms or convulsions until relieved by death. There are weeds in the pasture, but loco weed was not the cause of death. Another breeder, more than 100 miles distant from Minneapolis, at the same time last year and up to now has lost 40 head of most valuable trotting mares and their colts.

In answer to a letter addressed by the chief of the Bureau of Animal Industry, asking for additional information as to the symptoms of this disease, Mr. Cooks responds as follows, under date of May 28:

The symptoms first noticed in a sick animal are, that it wants to be alone and leaves the herd. When you take it to the barn the bowels rattle continually. At the same time it passes wind, as a horse does with colic. Some were taken this way last September and died a week ago. I have a four-year-old filly now that was taken ill last September. She wintered nicely and is fat now. This filly is failing and will die. They feed up to within a few hours of death. When they lie down they are taken with violent pains, as if with colic, and never rally, and are in pain from two to three days. Horses on dry feed are not affected, but when turned on grass the trouble comes. There has been no neglect. These are blooded horses and have the best of care and attention. The disease, however, reaches the common farm horses just the same under like circumstances. The first we saw of this disease was about the beginning of July, 1885, and those then taken died quickly—sometimes three or four animals a day.

Early in June last Mr. Thomas Weaver, of Julietta, Nez Percés County, Idaho, wrote the Department concerning a very fatal disease then prevailing among horses in that county. He gave the symptoms and *post-mortem* appearances of the disease, as follows:

The first manifestation is a lagging behind the rest of the band, with staggering gait; the pulse is high but weak, indeed, can scarcely be felt; respiration short and quick. Some have cough, while others have no cough at all. The feces is hard and covered with slime. Toward the last swelling appears under the belly. They die generally within ten days after the first symptoms are observed, but they continue to eat up to the very last. We have opened a great many, and in all cases found about the same lesions. The lungs were inflamed in patches; the pleura, and, in fact, the whole inter-costal space was inflamed; the bowels were reddened in places; the liver was black, and the covering seemed rotten; the spleen was filled with black blood and enlarged to twice its natural size. The peritoneum was also inflamed, and that part covering the bowels was nearly all gone. All through their illness a rumbling sound may be heard in their bowels. Some have yellow-colored discharge from the nose. The afflicted animals seldom lay down. The disease prevails among range horses, and it prevails on almost every ranch.

August 14 last Dr. W. H. Cowell, Shawboro, N. C., wrote the Department, stating that the mortality among horses in eastern North Carolina was becoming fearful.

A severe mortality occurred among horses in the vicinity of Hampton, Elizabeth City County, Va., during the month of September last, from a disease which seemed to be new to the people of that locality. During the prevalence of the malady the Department was urgently requested to send a veterinarian to discover, if possible, the cause of the outbreak, and give such advice as might be necessary to check its spread; but at that time every inspector in the employ of the Bureau of Animal Industry was engaged in important investigations in distant States, and it was found impossible to comply with these requests. Mr. J. C. Phillips, statistical correspondent of the Department for Elizabeth City County, writing under date of September 18, gave the following symptoms of the disease:

We are very much troubled at this time with a disease among our horses. The general opinion is that it is blind staggers; others think it pneumonia. The symptoms are a loss of appetite, drowsy appearance, restlessness, a disposition to walk in a circle; always turning on the same side; turning in a shorter and shorter circle until the animal falls down and is unable to rise. The disease proves fatal in from twelve to thirty-six hours. It is very prevalent and very fatal. The horses have been carefully examined, and almost every treatment known or heard of has been tried, but with the same unsatisfactory results. We have had some of the carcasses examined to try and find out the cause and seat of the disease, but, having no veterinarian, everything has been unsatisfactory, and we are still groping entirely in the dark.

Mr. John S. Hamilton, Rappahannock Station, Culpeper County, Va., on the 18th of October last, informed the Department that a fatal disease was prevailing among horses in that locality, and requested that a veterinarian be sent at once to make an investigation as to the cause and nature of the malady. Dr. Kilborne, an in-

given each animal. Previous to the last injection each horse was drenched with one-half pint of linseed oil and three drams aloes (all we had at hand). In each case before giving the injection we were obliged to unload the rectum, which was impacted with the feces. Apparently dung was passed only when forced out by the feces behind. In the morning (October 22) the bay had a temperature of 100° F., pulse 40, and respiration normal; the sorrel a temperature 101⅘, pulse 55, and respiration very much improved. During the night both horses passed feces, softened by the injections; the laxative dose given by the mouth being too small to produce any appreciable effect. Upon leading the horses out in the morning they walked much more freely than the evening before.

The third horse visited had essentially the same symptoms (temperature 102° F., pulse 50, respiration slightly labored), except that he had been walked daily, had better control over his hind limbs, and moved more easily. In this case, also, all coarse food was removed and the diet restricted to mashes and scalded oats. The animal was given the warm-water injections but no laxative, there being none at hand. In the morning his condition was evidently improved. The first two cases appeared to have an abnormal craving for dry coarse fodder, and while being walked in the yard would avail themselves of every opportunity to pick dry weeds, but especially rag-weed. The acute symptoms of the animals that died, and milder course of the disease in the sick animals examined, was probably due to the fact that the former were allowed to remain in pasture and the latter were placed in the stable before symptoms of the disease appeared.

Although this immediate outbreak was limited to the seven animals above mentioned, other farmers in the county were reported as having lost several animals with apparently the same disease. At Rappahannock Station I met several farmers who had recently lost horses, usually with symptoms similar to those given above; but I was unable to learn of any others that were now sick. Unfortunately I had no opportunity of holding an autopsy to ascertain the condition of the internal organs. As far as could be learned every case of the disease occurred among horses at pasture, and in no instance was a stabled animal so affected. Some farmers had lost one or more at pasture, and fearing contagion had taken their horses from the pasture to the stable, where all remained healthy.

The pastures, when examined, were found to be very dry from a protracted drought. The grasses were dried and apparently dead. In this vicinity the pastures were mostly covered with an abundant rank growth of very dry, weedy rag-weed (*Ambrosia artemisæfolia*, L.; also popularly called Roman worm-wood, hog-weed, bitter-weed). The horses were compelled to feed largely upon this rag-weed, and, judging from the two cases above mentioned, they may have recently acquired an abnormal appetite for this particular coarse, indigestible fodder. Droughts of previous years have usually been accompanied by the loss of horses in this locality, and the more severe the drought the greater the losses. The symptoms were said to have been similar, so that, presumably, the cause was the same each year. The prevalence of the disease is, therefore, to be attributed to the drought, causing a great scarcity of the forage grasses, followed by feeding upon coarse, dry, indigestible aliment, but especially the rag-weed.

GLANDERS.

In February last Mr. Eugene Henderson, of Ferguson, Saint Louis County, Mo., informed the Department of the supposed existence of glanders in a couple of horses owned by a gentleman of that county.

Mr. C. E. Laherty, Colton, Whitman County, Wash., writing under date of May 3d last, gives the following symptoms of a disease which is no doubt glanders:

> I write you concerning a disease which is quite prevalent among horses in this county. Nearly every farmer has a horse afflicted with it. The symptoms are a running from the nostrils, accompanied with a swelling of the glands under the jaw—the lymphatic and sub-maxillary. In some animals the symptoms are those of farcy—that is, corded veins and farcy buds. By some it is called nasal gleet, while others contend that it is glanders. The discharge much resembles the white of an egg, and sticks to the edge of the nostrils. The membrane lining of the nose has been found to be covered with ragged-edged ulcers.

On the 1st of June last Mr. E. R. Bowen, of Red Wing, Minn., informed the Department of the prevalence of a disease among horses in that county which was supposed to be glanders.

Mr. Robert Neal, Temple, Bell County, Tex., writing under date of July 4th last, gives the following account of the prevalence of glanders among his horses:

The people of this whole neighborhood are frightened about the condition of my stock. A disease is prevailing among my horses which kills every one attacked by it. When first taken the animal looks droopy or sleepy. This condition lasts about three weeks, when the nostrils begin to discharge freely. Sometimes this discharge ceases from the left but continues from the right nostril until the animal dies. Frequently the nose bleeds—generally the right nostril—which will continue for about half an hour and suddenly cease. There is no blood mixed with the discharge from the nose. Lameness after a while in the hind legs sets in, and boils appear on the inside of the legs and under the belly. These boils attain the size of a hen's egg. When lanced they discharge a pus similar to that found in boils. The animal grows weak in the loins, and when it gets down it can not get up without assistance. The drippings from the nostrils swim on the water as would a feather. I have lost five mules by the disease and have four more which will no doubt die in a short time if something is not done to relieve them. I have a fine mare also sick, and a full-blooded Norman stallion purchased in Iowa, and which cost me a big sum of money. This last-named animal is very badly off. He has been bleeding at the right nostril, and his hind legs are badly swollen and full of boils. * * * The disease seems to be spreading all over the country. It has broken me up, and will ruin many others if not soon checked.

Mr. Neal was informed that the disease described above was glanders, and as there was no remedy for it the only alternative was to slaughter the animals as soon as the first symptoms of the malady appeared.

SPINAL MENINGITIS AMONG HORSES.

Elsewhere in this report will be found the results of Dr. W. H. Harbaugh's investigation of a disease known as "staggers" among horses in Virginia and North Carolina. Recently an outbreak of disease occurred among a number of horses belonging to Mr. W. W. Gordon, of New Kent County, Va., which was investigated by Dr. Bowles, business partner of Dr. Harbaugh. The results of this investigation, as communicated to him by Dr. Bowles, are thus given by Dr. Harbaugh:

There were 16 horses and mules on the farm, 6 of which were suffering from what Dr. Bowles positively diagnosed as epizootic cerebro-spinal meningitis. Three horses and 1 mule died; 2 mules are beyond recovery, if not now dead. The feed consisted of corn and fodder; fodder in a very bad condition. Dr. Bowles assigns the cause of the disease to the quality of the fodder. He advised change of feed and administered a cathartic to each one of the remaining animals not attacked, as a preventive measure.

New Kent County is situated north of the James River, and north of the district known to me as the "stagger district," and I therefore consider this matter of much importance, as it is another point in favor of my view of staggers, *i. e.*, that staggers and epizootic cerebro-spinal meningitis are not one and the same disease. You will also take note of the fact that in this outbreak the malady is as fatal to mules as to horses. Another point I wish to call your attention to is the occurrence of this outbreak during the past remarkable cold weather. Staggers occurs only during the hot months.

Dr. Bowles says this particular form is situated high up on the banks of the Pamunky River. From inquiries among the neighboring farmers he is of the opinion that epizootic staggers is an unknown and unheard-of disease in that section.

SWINE PLAGUE.

Mr. James H. Hardison, Salina, Kans., writing under date of February 19, 1886, says:

Last spring swine plague made its appearance among my hogs, and I lost about 700 head, large and small. I gathered up the remnants and bred them, and last fall I had about 200 pigs from them. They thrived well until about a month ago, when they commenced to die, and since then about 80 head have succumbed to the disease. The older animals still remain healthy.

In a letter dated March 11, 1886, Dr. Hamilton C. Kibbie, of Obng, Ill., writes that swine plague is prevailing as an epidemic among o hogs in that locality.

Dr. M. R. Trumbower, inspector of the Bureau of Animal Indusy, while on a professional visit to Pennsylvania in April last, found me cases of swine plague at Coopersburgh, in that State, which he ported as follows:

Mr. William Meyers, living 2½ miles east of Coopersburgh, Pa., purchased 4 sixonths' old hogs of Samuel Gehman, about the 15th of December last. On the 28th the same month he purchased 3 hogs of the same age of William Bartholoew. They were all placed in the same stable, which was divided into three apartcnts, the Bartholomew hogs occupying the south pen and the Gehman hogs the her two. All of these animals, excepting one of the Bartholomew hogs, which as smaller than the rest, made rapid growth. This one did not appear to be as rifty as the others. This one, which I will call No. 1, began to manifest difficulty breathing, coughed, and then appeared to swell on the neck and shoulders. It n quit eating almost entirely. A week later one of the Gehman hogs in the cond or middle stable began to lose in appetite and became stiff in its movements, ing inclined to lie in the bedding all the time. Mr. Meyers had been feeding oilke meal in milk and slops pretty freely, and thought he had foundered them, but e of his neighbors told him they had the corns (whatever that may be), and prosed to cut them out. Within a few days No. 3, a Bartholomew hog, was taken k, laid in the bedding and refused to eat. About this time Mr. Meyers noticed at 5 of the 7 head were stiff in front and the lower part of the shoulder was ollen, according to the degree of their illness. He then had the corns cut in l of them and administered sulphate of magnesia and fed them sulphur, saltter and gunpowder. He says they began to eat better but did not grow any. nce the middle or latter part of March they again began to grow worse, increasg in stiffness and turning violet and purple along the abdomen and neck. This substantially the condition in which I found them at my first examination yestery.

Bartholomew Pig No. 1.—Temperature 102.2°. Dyspnœa excessive, and very weak. e could only stand on her feet for about ten minutes after being raised up. Purple colorations on the lower surface of the chest, with circumscribed pointed pimples. reness on the snout, with cracking of the skin. Difficulty of deglutition, but eats aringly. Feces hard-balled; moist cough; swelling of the throat and shoulders; njectivia injected, and membranes pale with a bluish cast. She has had to be ised and pushed to the trough for the past ten days.

Gehman Pig No. 2.—Temperature 104°. Has to be raised and pushed to the trough. ed and purple blush on the abdomen. Slight cough; throat very little swollen; oulders swollen considerably; nose and lips cyanotic; eyes watery; eats some.

Batholomew Pig No. 3.—Temperature 103.5°. Eats moderately well; feces very y and coated; membrane of rectum very highly colored; swollen shoulders, and ry sore when she moves.

Batholomew Pig No. 4.—Temperature 102°. Eats well; eyes bright; ears pointed; iff gait.

Gehman pig No. 5.—Lame in one hind leg.

Gehman pigs Nos. 6 *and* 7.—Slightly stiff in front.

The following is a record of the temperature at 10 o'clock a. m., April 7: No. 1. 0.5°; No. 2, 103.2°; No. 3, 102°; No. 4, 101°. In all other respects about the same yesterday. No. 1 experiences considerable tenesma on defæcation, and the muus membrane of rectum dark purple in color. I examined the tongue, mouth, domen, and other parts to discover cysticerous cysts, but failed to find any evince of them. The swelling of the shoulders of all, the excessively painful moveent of the front limbs, and the swelling of the throat in three of the animals, led e to suspect the possibility of the existence of cysticerci. On the contrary, there the entire absence of foul breath in the one which is almost on the point of suffotion, no external evidence of cysts, no loosening of the hair, no brain symptoms. either is it likely that all seven should be affected with the disease and manifesting ch a similarity of symptoms. Parotiditis and tonsilitis are excluded by slowness the disease, as they have not changed for the better or worse within two weeks. favor of swine plague, the following reasons remain: The reported existence of ine plague last summer in the county from which three of B.'s hogs came (Mr. rtholomew purchased these animals near Little York, Hunterdon County, N. J., t December). Difficult breathing in two of the cases; constipation (persistent) all of them; the red and purple discoloration of the surface of the body, which not disappear on pressure. These, together with lesser significant symptoms, may int to a mild and chronic form of swine plague.

On the 2d day of July last, Dr. Trumbower reported the prevalence of swine plague on many farms in the vicinity of Patoka, Ill. On the 17th of the same month, it was reported as prevailing quite seriously among hogs in the vicinity of Geneseo, in the same State.

Mr. W. N. Hubble, Gonzales, Monterey County, Cal., writing under date of June 23 last, thus speaks of the ravages of swine plague among his own and his neighbors' hogs:

I have lost some 250 head of hogs from swine plague, and they are still dying, as I lost 2 to-day. There has been a heavy loss from the disease in this county. The greater part of those who have died have been sucking pigs, but the two that died to-day were large hogs. I have about 20, or perhaps 30 head now sick. The animals are running in a barley field with an abundance of water. The first symptom of illness is a cough. It is sometimes from one to three weeks before some of them show serious illness. Then the cough increases in intensity; the hog humps up its back; scabs appear about the eyes, and some of them go blind. At this stage they still have an appetite, eat well, but grow poorer all the time. I do not believe any of them ever recover, though some of them will live for a period of two months. The disease has been on this farm for years.

Mr. R. E. Eveleigh, Bloomfield, Ind., writing under date of June 24, says that swine plague has almost ruined the hog industry of that State.

Mr. C. C. Buckuld, Raccoon Ford, Culpeper County, Va., writes as follows under date of July 3 last:

This section of the State has been visited for several years past by a disease called cholera, which has destroyed a great many swine. Many of my neighbors have suffered from it, but until recently my own hogs have escaped the plague. I now have 4 or 5 which I fear are affected by it.

On he 8th of July last, Dr. J. Eugene Jarningan, Toby's Creek, S. C., writes as follows concerning the disease in that State:

Many farmers of this section are losing their swine by disease, and I have been careful to make many *post-mortem* examinations, and in all I found the same lesions, but in some better developed than in others. I found all the organs of the thoracic cavity in a healthy condition. The liver was always in a state of inflammation. In some specimens the gall-bladder was filled with an almost black, effusive, semi-solid liquid, too thick to flow out of the duct; in fact the duct seemed to be closed by the matter becoming solid in it. In some cases the descending colon or "Tom Thumb" was highly inflamed. The mucous membrane seemed to be rotten, of a dull, ashy-gray color. The inflammation generally appeared more severe near the end of the "Tom Thumb," or the attachment of appendix vermiformis. The kidneys were normal and the intestines filled with gas. These are all the lesions found.

The hogs are running in swamp pasture and on oat lands, and get plenty of oats and grass. The first symptoms I have noticed are sick stomach and vomiting, with a sort of "rash" about the head, ears, neck, and belly. In violent cases these attain the size of a No. 2 buck-shot. The eyes, or more properly the eye-lids, seem to be inflamed, as they frequently stick together so closely that they blind the animal. Around the eyes the skin has a rough, scaly appearance. This I find confined to the early stages of the disease. I have taken the trouble to kill animals at the various stages of the plague, so as to inform myself properly, and I will say that in the first stage the gall-bladder is filled with bile, not unlike the yolk of an egg; so yellow is it that the gall-bladder has the color of an orange.

Mr. D. S. Waddell, Saint Maurice Parish, La., writing under date of August 6, 1886, says:

In the spring of 1885 a disease attacked my hogs, killing 32 out of 35 head. It was an irruptive disease, and I give a history of the outbreak as follows: I had 5 grown sows with 30 pigs, all in good order. The first symptom was high fever, then cough (dry), then an irruption, swelling of the head, eyes closing, with foam exuding from the eyes; skin of the belly red; violent spasms; eyes oscillating, and tremor and twitching of the muscles as if under the influence of strychnine. About three days after the irruption they would die. If they went into water it rapidly hastened death. Some would get down on their knees and squeal terribly while the "fit" was upon them; others would come up, walk around, and die in a few seconds without a struggle. One sow escaped without any symptoms of the disease; two lived through, and where the irruption occurred white hairs grew out (they were black hogs). These two sows have since had two litters of pigs. Of the first litter, now shoats, one this spring (1886) had a "fit" and vomited. I made an incision half an inch long and about one-fourth inch deep in the back of its neck, and inserted about 8gr of morphine. It recovered, but carried its head with a twist. The sows appear well, but I notice one pig of the second litter in the last day or two has a cough. I forbade my sons handling these hogs, and my health being too feeble to make *post-mortem* examinations I can not give such information as will prove satisfactory. I will state, however, that the people around me at the time were sorely afflicted with measles, and I rather believe the hogs had that disease. Their bowels were in no way disturbed. I noticed that the tongue and the mucous membrane of the mouth appeared very red. Some of them were very restless—could find no position that would relieve them, and would lean against a fence until they would fall dead. All "panted" as if their lungs were congested.

Dr. T. W. Roane, of Tennessee, says that swine plague prevailed to a considerable extent in that State during May and June last, and that while it was equally as fatal "it was not so generally diffused as in 1884." He attributes the disease to the poison communicated by buffalo gnats. No doubt these gnats assisted in spreading the disease by innoculating the animals with the virus of swine plague, an infinitesimal portion of which was sufficient to set up the disease.

Dr. A. B. Bradbury, health officer of Delaware County, Ind., and Mr. John M. Graham, president of the Delaware County Agricultural Association, writing under date of August 27 last, states that hog cholera or swine plague is prevailing extensively in that county, and that the losses are very heavy.

Mrs. S. T. Henderson, Sloan, Woodbury County, Iowa, writes, under date of September 5, that hogs are dying by hundreds in that county of swine plague.

PARALYSIS IN PIGS.

Mr. George Jacobis, Philmont, Columbia County, N. Y., writing under date of January 4, 1886, says:

A disease hitherto unknown has broken out among swine in this vicinity. It is confined principally to pigs. The disease seems to attack the loins, the animal soon losing the use of its hind legs. I find the same symptoms described in the annual report of the Department of Agriculture for 1881-'82, by R. J. Donaldson, of Georgetown, S. C. In the South Carolina case the feed was ground rice. Here the feed has been corn.

DISEASE OF SHEEP.

Mr. Aquilla Denmead, Del Rio, Val Verde County, Tex., writing under date of February 20 last, gives the following account of a disease which has proved quite destructive to his sheep:

I have been a sheep raiser here in Texas for eight years, and have had no disease in my flock until about the 1st of last August. About that time my lambs and yearlings commenced to die at the rate of about two or three a day in a flock of 1,800. They become poor and would eat but very little, and finally got so weak that they could not stand up. I do not think that over 10 out of the number that were effected recovered. I thought they had got hold of some poisonous herb, and I gave those that seemed to be sick plenty of melted grease, but it seemed to do them no good. They did not stop dying until we had rain, which occurred about the middle of September. About the 1st of January they commenced to get sick again. They were affected in the same way, and soon commenced to die, which they are still doing. Those that are dying now are last year's lambs and two-year-olds next month. I did not think it was poison this time. I have examined a great

LAWS OF THE STATES AND TERRITORIES FOR THE CONTROL OF CONTAGIOUS ANIMAL DISEASES.

The following are official transcripts of the laws of all the States and Territories adopted since the publication of the Second Annual Report of the Bureau for the control of contagious, infectious, and communicable diseases of domesticated animals. The proclamations of the governors of the various States and Territories which have adopted quarantine measures to prevent the introduction of contagious and infectious diseases will also be found below:

ALABAMA.

AN ACT for the prevention and suppression of infectious and contagious diseases of horses and other animals.

SECTION 1. *Be it enacted by the general assembly of Alabama*, That it shall be the duty of any person who is the owner or possessor of a horse, mule, or other animal having the glanders or other fatal, contagious, or infectious disease, to keep such diseased animals away and removed from any public or other place where horses, mules, or other animals are usually kept in said counties, and also to keep such diseased animals at a distance from any common rendezvous for animals therein, whether such rendezvous or place of resort be maintained for public or private use and convenience; and any person refusing or wilfully neglecting to obey this provision of law, by bringing such diseased horse, mule, or other animal or causing the same to be brought to any rendezvous of animals or other place where the same shall be usually kept, shall be deemed guilty of a misdemeanor and may be indicted therefor, and upon conviction thereof, by or before any court of this State competent at this time to try and punish misdemeanors committed in said counties, shall be fined not exceeding $50 nor less than $5 for any violation of this law: *Provided*, That the prosecution and conviction of any person under this statute shall not be a bar to an action for civil damages against said person for loss or injury incurred by reason of the violation thereof.

Approved February 28, 1887.

ARIZONA.

AN ACT for the protection of domestic animals.

SECTION 1. *Be it enacted by the legislative assembly of the Territory of Arizona:* Five commissioners identified with the live-stock interests of the Territory of Arizona shall be appointed by the governor, who shall constitute the live-stock sanitary commission of the Territory of Arizona. Before entering upon the duties of his office, each commissioner shall take and subscribe the oath of office, and file the same with the secretary of the Territory; and each commissioner, before entering on the performance of his duties, shall execute a bond, to be approved by the governor, in the sum of two thousand dollars, conditioned that he will faithfully perform the duties of his office, and file the same with the secretary of the Territory. The term of office of said commissioners shall be for the period of two years from the first day of April, 1887, next succeeding their appointment, and the governor shall have the power to fill any vacancy in said commission. Said commissioners shall elect one of their number chairman, and the Territorial veterinary surgeon hereinafter provided for shall be *ex-officio* secretary of said commission.

The secretary shall keep a full and complete record of the proceedings of the commission, and make such report to the governor as may from time to time be required.

SEC. 2. The governor shall nominate, and, by and with the advice and consent of the legislative council, appoint a skilled veterinary surgeon for the Territory, who at the date of such appointment shall be a graduate in good standing of a recognized college of veterinary surgery, and who shall hold his office for the term of two years, unless sooner removed by the commission: *Provided*, That the salary of said veterinary surgeon shall on no account exceed the sum of two thousand dollars per annum, and fifteen (15) cents per mile for each mile necessarily traveled in the discharge of his duties; and the Territorial auditor is hereby authorized to draw his warrant on the Territorial treasurer for the said amounts, properly verified, to be paid out of the live-stock sanitary fund hereinafter provided for.

Before entering upon the duties of his office the Territorial veterinarian shall take and subscribe an oath to faithfully perform the duties of his said office, and shall execute a bond to the Territory of Arizona, in the sum of three thousand ($3,000) dollars, with good and sufficient sureties, conditioned for the faithful performance of the duties of his office, which bond and sureties thereto shall be approved by the governor, and said bond, together with his oath of office, shall be deposited in the office of the secretary of the Territory.

SEC. 3. It shall be the duty of the commission provided for in the first section of this act to protect the health of the domestic animals of the Territory from all contagious or infectious diseases of a malignant character, and for this purpose it is hereby authorized and empowered to establish, maintain, and enforce such quarantine, sanitary, and other regulations as it may deem necessary. It shall be the duty of any member of said commission, upon receipt by him of reliable information of the existence among the domestic animals of the Territory of any malignant disease, to at once notify the Territorial veterinarian, who shall go at once to the place where any such disease is alleged to exist, and make a careful examination of the animals believed to be affected with any such disease, and ascertain, if possible, what, if any, disease exists among the live stock reported to be affected, and whether the same is contagious or infectious or not; and if said disease is found to be of a malignant, contagious, or infectious character, he shall direct the temporary quarantine and sanitary regulations necessary to prevent the spread of any such disease, and report his findings and actions to the commission.

SEC. 4. Upon the receipt by any member of this commission of the report of the Territorial veterinarian, provided for in section two of this act, if said member shall be of the opinion that the exigencies of the case require it, he shall immediately convene the commission at such a place as he may designate, and if upon consideration of the report of the veterinarian the commission shall be satisfied that any contagious or infectious disease exists of a malignant character, which seriously threatens the health of domestic animals, they shall proceed at once to the infected district, ascertain and determine the premises or grounds infected, and establish the quarantine, sanitary, and police regulations necessary to circumscribe and exterminate such disease; and no domestic animal liable to become infected with the disease, or capable of communicating the same, shall be permitted to enter or leave the district, premises, or grounds so quarantined, except by authority of the commission. The said commission shall also from time to time enforce such directions and prescribe such rules and regulations as to separating, mode of handling, treating, feeding, and caring for such diseased and exposed animals as it shall deem necessary to prevent the two classes of animals from coming in contact with each other, and perfectly isolate them from all other domestic animals which have not been exposed thereto, and which are susceptible of becoming infected with disease; and the said commission, or any of the members thereof, and said veterinarian, are hereby authorized and empowered to enter upon any grounds or premises to carry out the provisions of this act.

SEC. 5. When in the opinion of the commission it shall be necessary to prevent the further spread of any contagious or infectious diseases among the live stock of the Territory to destroy animals affected with or which have been exposed to any such disease, it shall determine what animals shall be killed, and appraise the same as hereinafter provided, and cause the same to be killed and the carcasses to be disposed of as in its judgment will best protect the health of the domestic animals of the locality.

SEC. 6. Whenever, as in the fourth section of this act provided, the commission shall direct the killing of any domestic animal or animals, it shall be the duty of the commissioners to appraise the animal or animals to be killed, and shall make an inventory of the animal or animals condemned, and in fixing the value thereof the commissioners shall be governed by the value of said animal or animals at the date appraisement: *Provided*, That no animal or animals shall be slaughtered excepe ose affected with contagious pleuro-pneumonia of cattle, or foot and mouth dis-se, or such as have been exposed thereto.

SEC. 7. When the commission shall have determined the quarantine and other cessary regulations necessary to prevent the spread among domestic animals of y malignant, contagious, or infectious disease found to exist among the live stock the Territory, and given its order as hereinbefore provided, prescribing quarantine d other regulations, it shall notify the governor thereof, who shall issue his procla-ation, proclaiming the boundary of such quarantine, and the orders, rules, and gulations prescribed by the commission, which proclamation may be published by itten or printed hand-bills, posted within the boundaries or on the lines of the strict, premises, places, or grounds so quarantined, or by being published in the icial paper of the Territory: *Provided*, That if the commission decide that it is t necessary, by reason of the limited extent of the district in which such disease ists, that a proclamation should be issued, then none shall be issued; but the com-ssion shall give notice as may to it seem best to make the quarantine established

SEC. 8. The commission provided for in this act shall have the power to employ ch persons, and purchase such supplies and material as may be necessary to carry to full effect all orders by it given, as hereinbefore provided: *Provided*, That no borer shall be employed, nor material or supplies purchased by the commission, cept such additional labor, material, and supplies as may be necessary to carry to effect the quarantine and other regulations prescribed by the commission.

SEC. 9. When any animal or animals are killed under the provisions of this act order of the commission, the owner thereof shall be paid therefor the appraised ue fixed by the appraisement hereinbefore provided for: *Provided*, The right of lemnity on account of any animals killed by order of the commission under the visions of this act shall not extend to the owners of animals which have been ought into the Territory in a diseased condition, or from any State, country, Ter-ory, or district in which the disease with which the animal is infected, or to which has been exposed, exists; nor shall any animal be paid for by the Territory which ay be brought into the Territory in violation of any law or quarantine regulation ereof, or the owner of which shall have violated any of the provisions of this act, disregarded any rule, regulation, or order of the live-stock sanitary commission any member thereof; nor shall any animal be paid for by the Territory which me into the possession of the claimant with the claimant's knowledge that such imal was diseased, or was suspected of being diseased, or of having been exposed any contagious or infectious disease; nor shall any animal belonging to the United ates be paid for by the Territory.

SEC. 10. It shall be the duty of any owner or person in charge of any domestic imal or animals who discovers, suspects, or has reason to believe, that any of his mestic animals or domestic animals in his charge are affected with any contagious infectious disease, to immediately notify such fact, belief or suspicion to the mmission, or any member of it, and to the sheriff and county clerk of the county which such domestic animal is found; and it shall be the duty of any person who covers the existence of any contagious or infectious disease among the domestic imals of another to report the same to the sheriff and county clerk of the county which such domestic animal is found.

SEC. 11. Any person who shall knowingly bring into this Territory any domestic imal which is affected with any contagious or infectious disease, or any animal hich has been exposed to any contagious or infectious disease, shall be deemed ilty of a misdemeanor, and upon conviction thereof shall be fined in any sum not s than five hundred dollars or more than five thousand dollars.

SEC. 12. Any person who owns or is in possession of live stock which is, or which suspected, reported to be affected with any infectious or contagious disease, who all refuse to allow the Territorial veterinarian or other authorized officer or offi-s to examine such stock, or shall hinder or obstruct the Territorial veterinarian other authorized officer or officers in any examination of, or in any attempt to mine such stock, shall be deemed guilty of a misdemeanor, and upon conviction reof shall be fined in any sum not less than one hundred dollars or more than o hundred dollars.

EC. 13. Any person who shall have in his possession any domestic animal affected th any contagious or infectious disease, knowing such animal to be affected, or er having received notice that such animal is so affected, or who shall sell, ship, ve, trade or give away such diseased animal or animals which have been exposed such infection or contagion, or who shall move or drive any domestic animal in lation of any direction, rule, regulation, or order establishing and regulating arantine, shall be deemed guilty of a misdemeanor, and upon conviction thereof shall be fined in any sum not less than one hundred dollars nor more than five hundred dollars for each of such diseased or exposed domestic animals which he shall sell, ship, drive, trade, or give away in violation of the provisions of this act. *Provided*, That any owner of any domestic animal which has been affected with or exposed to any contagious or infectious disease may dispose of the same after having obtained from the Territorial veterinarian a bill of health of such animal.

SEC. 14. When any live stock shall be appraised and killed by order of the commission, it shall issue to the owner of the live stock so killed a certificate, showing the number and kind of animals killed, and the amount to which the holder is entitled, and report the same to the auditor of the Territory and upon presentation of such certificate to the auditor, he shall draw his warrant on the treasury for the amount therein stated, payable out of the live-stock sanitary fund and no other, as hereinafter provided for.

SEC. 15. The members of the commission appointed by the governor as hereinbefore provided shall receive three dollars per day for the time by them necessarily employed in discharging the duties required by this act, and each member of the commission hereinbefore provided for shall receive fifteen (15) cents for each and every mile actually travelled, which said per diem and expenses shall be drawn from the treasury out of the live-stock sanitary fund and no other, as hereinafter provided for, on the warrant of the auditor, to be issued on the filing in his office of an itemized account thereof properly verified.

SEC. 16. Whenever the governor of the Territory shall have reason to believe that any dangerous, contagious, or infectious disease has become epidemic in certain localities in other States, Territories, or countries, or that there are conditions which render such domestic animals from such infected districts liable to convey such disease, he shall, by proclamation, prohibit the importation of any live stock of the kind diseased into the Territory, unless accompanied by a certificate of health, given by a duly authorized veterinary inspector, and all such animals arriving in this Territory shall be examined without delay by the Territorial veterinary surgeon, and if deemed necessary placed in close quarantine until all danger of infection is passed, when they shall be released by order of the veterinary surgeon or the live-stock commission.

SEC. 17. The commissioners shall have the power to call upon any sheriff, under sheriff, deputy sheriff, or constable to execute their orders, and such officers shall obey the orders of the said commissioners; and the officers performing such duties shall receive compensation therefor, as is prescribed by law for like services, to be paid as other expenses of said commission, as hereinbefore provided; and any officer may arrest on view, and take before any magistrate of the county, any person found violating the provisions of this act, and such officer shall immediately notify the county attorney of such arrest, and he shall prosecute the person so offending according to law.

SEC. 18. Except as otherwise provided in this act, any person who shall violate, disregard, or evade, or attempt to violate, disregard, or evade any of the provisions of this act, or who shall violate, disregard, or evade, or atttempt to violate, disregard, or evade any of the rules, regulations, orders, or directions of the live-stock sanitary commission establishing and governing quarantine, shall be deemed guilty of a misdemeanor, and upon conviction thereof shall be fined in any sum not less than one hundred nor more than five thousand dollars.

SEC. 19. It shall be unlawful for any person or corporation to drive or transport, or cause to be driven or transported into the Territory of Arizona, any cattle from those States, Territories, or countries against which the governor has proclaimed a quarantine as hereinbefore provided for in section 16 of this act: *Provided*, That cattle in transit through the Territory on the railroads are not liable to any penalties attached to said act.

SEC. 20. The provisions of this act shall not apply to sheep and hogs, or to cattle when affected by the disease known as Texas, splenic, or Spanish fever.

SEC. 21. For the purposes of this act each member of the live-stock sanitary commission is hereby authorized and empowered to administer oaths and affirmations.

SEC 22. Any moneys collected as fines under the provisions of this act shall be paid into the Territorial treasury and be set apart and be known as the live-stock sanitary fund, and all expenses of said sanitary commission shall be paid out of said fund, and from no other.

SEC. 23. An act to prevent the introduction of diseased cattle into the Territory of Arizona, approved March 2, 1885, is hereby repealed, and all acts and parts of acts in conflict with the provisions of this act are hereby repealed.

SEC. 24. This act shall take effect and be in force from and after its passage.

Approved, March 10, 1887.

AN ACT for the protection of cattle against Texas, splenic, or Spanish fever.

SECTION 1. *Be it enacted by the legislative assembly of the Territory of Arizona:* No person or persons shall, between the first day of April and the first day of December of any year, drive or cause to be driven into or through any county or part thereof in this Territory, or turn loose or cause to be turned upon or kept upon any highway, range, common, or inclosed pasture within this Territory any cattle capable of communicating or liable to impart what is known as Texas, splenic, or Spanish fever.

Any person violating any provision of this act shall, upon conviction thereof, be adjudged guilty of a misdemeanor, and shall for each offence be fined not less than one hundred dollars and not more than two thousand dollars, or be imprisoned in the county jail not less than thirty days and not more than one year, or by both such fine and imprisonment.

SEC. 2. No officer, agent, employé, servant, or other person connected with or employed in the business or operation of any railway, common carrier, or other transportation corporation, company, or association shall ship or cause or permit to be shipped, or transport or cause or permit to be transported by means of the transportation afforded by such common carrier, railway, or other transportation corporation, company, or association, or deliver to any consignee or other person, between the first day of April and the first day of December of any year, within this Territory, any cattle capable of communicating or liable to impart what is known as Texas, splenic, or Spanish fever.

Any officer, agent, employé, servant, or other person connected with or employed in the business or operation of any railway, common carrier, or other transportation corporation, company, or association violating any provision of this act shall, upon conviction thereof, be adjudged guilty of a misdemeanor, and shall, for each offence, be fined not less than one hundred dollars or more than two thousand dollars, or be imprisoned in the county jail not less than thirty days and not more than one year, or by both such fine and imprisonment: *Provided*, That cattle in transit through this Territory on any railroad are not liable to the penalties attached to this act.

SEC. 3. It shall be the duty of any sheriff, under sheriff, deputy sheriff, or constable within this Territory, upon a complaint made to him by any citizen of the Territory, or otherwise having notice or knowledge that there are within the county where such officer resides cattle believed to be capable of communicating or liable to impart the disease known as Texas, splenic, or Spanish fever, to forthwith take charge of and retain such cattle under such temporary quarantine regulations as will prevent the communication of such disease, and make immediate report thereof to the live-stock sanitary commission; and such officer shall keep said cattle in custody as aforesaid until released by order of said live-stock sanitary commission; and no officer who shall take or detain any cattle under the provisions of this act shall be liable to the owner or owners of such cattle for any damages by reason of such taking or detention, or by reason of the performances of any other duty enjoined in this act.

SEC. 4. Whenever the live-stock sanitary commission shall determine that certain cattle within the Territory are capable of communicating or are liable to impart Texas, splenic, or Spanish fever, they shall issue an order to the sheriff or any constable of the county in which said cattle are found, commanding him to take and keep such cattle in his custody, subject to such quarantine regulations as they may prescribe, until the first day of December next ensuing, on which date they shall direct such officer to deliver said cattle to their owner or owners or his or their agent: *Provided, however*, That before any cattle so held shall be delivered as aforesaid, there shall be paid to said live-stock commission all the costs and expenses of taking, detaining, and holding said cattle; and in case such costs and expenses are not paid within ten days after the first day of December, the said officer shall advertise, in the same manner as is by law provided in cases of sales of personal property, that he will sell such cattle, or such portions thereof as may be necessary to pay such costs and expenses, besides the expenses of the sale; and at the time and place so advertised he shall proceed to sell as many of said cattle as shall be necessary to pay off the costs and expenses and the expenses of the sale, and forthwith shall pay over to the owner of such cattle or his legal representative any amount so received in excess of the legal fees and expenses of such officer.

Any officer performing any of the duties enjoined in this section or in the next preceding section of this act shall receive the same compensation therefor as is prescribed by law for similar services, to be paid as other expenses of said live-stock sanitary commission are paid by law.

SEC. 5. Any person or persons, as is specified in section one of this act, or any officer, agent, employé, servant, or other person, as is specified in section two of this act, violating any of the provisions of this act, shall be liable to any party injured through such violation for any damages that may thereby arise from the communication of Texas, splenic, or Spanish fever, to be recovered in a civil action; and the party so injured shall have a lien for such damages on the cattle so communicating the disease, such lien to be enforced in like manner as other liens may be enforced.

SEC. 6. In the trial of any person charged with the violation of any of the provisions of this act, and in the trial of any civil action brought to recover damages for the communication of Texas, splenic or Spanish fever, proof that the cattle which such person is charged with driving or keeping in violation of the law, or which are claimed to have communicated the said disease, were brought into this Territory between the first day of April and the first day of December of each year in which the offense was committed or such cause of action arose, from south of the thirty-seventh parallel of north latitude, shall be taken as *prima facie* evidence that such cattle were capable of communicating and liable to impart Texas, splenic or Spanish fever, within the meaning of this act, and that the owner or persons or person in charge of such cattle, had full knowledge and notice thereof at the time of the commission of the alleged offense: *Provided, however*, That if the owner or owners or person in charge of such cattle shall show by such certificate or certificates as shall hereafter be designated by the live-stock sanitary commission of this Territory that the said cattle have been kept since the first day of December of the previous year west of the east line of the Indian Territory and north of the thirty-sixth parallel of north latitude, or west of the twenty-first meridian of longitude west from Washington, and north of the thirty-fourth parallel of north latitude, the provisions of this section shall not apply thereto: *Provided further*, That the provisions of this section shall not apply to any cattle shipped or driven from Sonora, Mexico.

SEC. 7. Whenever two or more persons shall, in violation of this act, at the same time or at different times during the same year drive or cause to be driven upon the same highway, range, common, or pasture, within this Territory any cattle capable of communicating or liable to impart Texas, splenic or Spanish fever, they shall be jointly and severally liable for all damages that may arise from the communication of such disease at any time thereafter during the same year to any native, domestic, or acclimated cattle that shall have been upon the same highway, range, common, or pasture so previously traveled over by such mentioned cattle.

SEC. 8. Justices of the peace within their respective counties shall have criminal jurisdiction in all cases under the provisions of this act.

SEC. 9. It shall be the duty of the prosecuting attorney of the proper county to prosecute, on behalf of the Territory, all criminal cases arising under this act.

SEC. 10. All acts and parts of acts in conflict with the provisions of this act are hereby repealed.

SEC. 11. This act shall take effect from and after its passage.

Approved March 10, 1887.

AN ACT to prevent the prevalance of diseases among sheep.

SECTION 1. *Be it enacted by the legislative Assembly of the Territory of Arizona:* Within thirty days after the passage of this act the governor of this Territory shall appoint an inspector of sheep in and for each of the counties of this Territory. Such inspector of sheep shall hold such office till the first day of January, 1889, and until his successor is duly appointed and qualified. On the first day of January, 1889, and every two years thereafter, the governor shall appoint such inspector of sheep, who shall hold such office until his successor is duly appointed and qualified. Each inspector of sheep shall be a resident of the county for which he is appointed, and shall be the owner of at least five hundred head of sheep, and shall be a practical sheep man. Before entering upon the discharge of his duties he shall execute a bond, payable to the Territory of Arizona, in the sum of $1,000, with at least two good and sufficient sureties, to be approved by the board of supervisors, conditioned for the faithful discharge of the duties of his office. Each inspector may appoint one or more deputies, for whose official acts he shall be responsible. It shall be the duty of such inspector, at any time, upon the affidavit of any citizen of his county having or owning any sheep, that sheep owned by or in charge of any other person are affected with scab, scabies, or any other contagious or infectious disease, and that such owner or other person has been notified of the fact and fails to take proper steps to cure such diseased sheep, it shall be the duty of the inspector, without delay, to examine such sheep, and if he shall find such sheep to be infected with such disease, he shall take such sheep into his possession at once, and cure them or cause them to be cured. He may call to his assistance such aid as may be necessary for that purpose, and the owner or owners of such diseased sheep shall be liable to said inspector for all necessary expenses, costs, and charges incurred in curing the sheep, including a compensation of three dollars a day to such inspector for every day or part of a day in which he shall be necessarily employed, and fifteen cents per mile for each and every mile traveled to and from such place: *Provided*, That if such complaint shall be false the party complaining shall be liable to said inspector for said mileage and per diem, such sum to be recovered in any court of competent jurisdiction.

SEC. 2. Any person, company, or corporation bringing or causing to be brought into any county of this Territory any sheep or band of sheep, must first procure from some inspector appointed under this act a certificate that such sheep or band of sheep are sound and free from scab, scabies, and all other contagious or infectious diseases before entering said county, and any person, company, or corporation desiring to move his or their sheep from one county to another, shall procure from the inspector in the county in which he or they leave or enter a certificate of inspection or traveling permit, duly signed, that such sheep are free from said diseases. Any person violating the provisions of this section, upon conviction, shall be punished by a fine of not less than one hundred dollars nor more than two hundred and fifty dollars.

SEC. 3. Whenever, on examination of any herds or bands of sheep within any county in this Territory, said inspector shall find such sheep or any portion of them affected by any of said diseases, he shall forthwith take all and every necessary measure and precaution to prevent such diseased sheep from going or being within four miles of any other herd or band of sheep, and shall so notify the owner or owners of such diseased sheep. The owner or owners of such diseased sheep shall immediately proceed to treat such sheep for the cure of such disease, under the supervision of said inspector, and any person who shall refuse or neglect to immediately observe the directions of such inspector, as hereinbefore provided, shall be punished, on conviction, by a fine of not less than one hundred and not more than two hundred and fifty dollars.

SEC. 4. In case the owner or owners of such diseased sheep shall fail or refuse, for the period of thirty days, to treat such sheep under the supervision of said inspector, as is provided in section three of this act, or shall fail or refuse to keep such diseased sheep at a distance of at least four miles from all other herds or bands of sheep, then, and in that event, such inspector shall seize such diseased sheep, and shall proceed to keep them at no less a distance than four miles of all other herds or bands of sheep, and to treat them for such disease, and the cost of such seizure, keeping, and treatment, and the fees and mileage of said inspector, as provided in section one of this act, shall be a charge on the sheep so seized, and such inspector shall hold such sheep till such amount be paid. If such sum be not paid within ten days after the completion of such treatment said inspector may recover the same from the owner or owners of such sheep by an action in any court of competent jurisdiction: *Provided*, That no person or company shall be required to dip or treat a band of ewes, or any part of them, in which there are ewes with lamb, at any time from the 15th day of March to the 1st day of June in any year.

SEC. 5. The fees of inspectors of sheep shall be as follows: For inspecting, granting certificates and traveling permit, $3 each, and fifteen cents per mile for every mile necessarily traveled in making such inspection.

SEC. 6. Any person, company, or corporation violating any of the provisions of this act shall be liable in a civil action for all damages sustained by any person, company, or corporation in consequence of such violation.

SEC. 7. It shall be the duty of said inspector and his deputies to institute prosecutions for all violations of this act; but nothing herein contained shall prevent other persons from so doing.

SEC. 8. Upon the arrival of any herd or band of sheep in this Territory the owner or person in charge shall immediately report such sheep to the inspector of the county where such sheep may be for inspection. Upon a failure so to do, upon conviction, such owner or person in charge of such sheep shall be punished by a fine of not less than one hundred dollars and not more than two hundred and fifty dollars.

SEC. 9. All acts and parts of acts in conflict with this act are hereby repealed.

SEC. 10. This act shall take effect and be in force from and after the first day of October, 1887.

Approved March 10, 1887.

AN ACT concerning quarantining of animals.

Be it enacted by the senate and house of representatives in general assembly convened: Whenever any animal, supposed to be infected or to have been exposed to contagion, shall be quarantined by the State board of agriculture or its commissioners, pursuant to sections six and seven of part eleven, chapter one, title three (3) of the general statutes, the actual pecuniary loss caused to the owner thereof by being deprived of the use of any animal or animals not infected during the period of quarantine shall, upon the request of the owner, be ascertained by the commissioners upon evidence satisfactory to them, and the amount of such loss, certified to by the commissioners, shall, on approval of the governor, be paid by the State to said owner.

Approved, April 22, 1885.

DAKOTA.

AN ACT to suppress and prevent the spread of contagious or infectious diseases among domestic animals.

SECTION 1. *Be it enacted by the legislative assembly of the Territory of Dakota*: That the governor of the Territory is hereby authorised to nominate, and by and with the advice and consent of the council appoint, a competent veterinary surgeon, who shall be known as the "veterinary surgeon," and, on entering on his duties, shall take an oath to well and truly perform his duties, as provided by law.

SEC. 2. The duties of said Territorial veterinary surgeon shall be as follows:

(1) To investigate any and all cases of contagious or infectious diseases among cattle, horses, mules, and asses in this Territory of which he may have a knowledge, or which may be brought to his notice by any resident in the locality where such disease exists; and it shall be his duty, in the absence of specific information, to make visits of inspection to any locality where he may have reason to suspect that there is contagious or infectious diseases.

(2) To inspect, under the regulations of this act, all cattle, horses, mules, and asses which may be brought into this Territory, in any manner whatever, from or through such State, Territory or foreign country as the governor shall declare by proclamation in quarantine for purposes of inspection for contagious or infectious diseases. And after the making of such proclamation it shall be the duty of the owner or person in charge of any domestic animals or Texas cattle arriving in this Territory, from or through any State, Territory, or foreign country against which quarantine has been declared, to notify the veterinary surgeon without delay, and not to allow such animals, or any of them, to leave the place of arrival until they shall have been examined by the said surgeon, and his certificate obtained that all are free from disease; and no animal pronounced unsound from disease by the veterinary surgeon shall be turned loose or allowed to run at large, or removed or permitted [illegible] but shall be held subject to the order of the veterinary surgeon.

Any person failing to comply with this provision shall be deemed guilty of a misdemeanor, and, upon conviction, shall be fined not less than fifty (50) nor more than five hundred (500) dollars for each offense, and shall be liable for any damages and loss that may be sustained by any person or persons by reason of the failure of such owner or agent to comply with the provisions of this section: *Provided*, That the owner of horses, mules, or asses ridden under the saddle or driven in harness into this Territory, or the owner of oxen driven into this Territory under the yoke, and any person coming into this Territory with his team or teams, shall not be required to notify the Territorial veterinary surgeon, or await the inspection of such work-oxen, team, or teams, but he shall be liable for all loss or damage to any person or persons from or by reason of any contagious or infectious disease brought into this Territory by his animals; and no cattle, horses, mules, or asses shall be held in quarantine in this Territory for a longer period than ninety (90) days, unless contagious or infectious disease shall be found to exist among them.

SEC. 3. In all cases of contagious or infectious disease among domestic animals or Texas cattle in this Territory, the veterinary surgeon shall have authority to order the quarantine of the infected premises; and in case such disease shall become epidemic in any locality in this Territory the Territorial veterinary surgeon shall immediately notify the governor of the Territory who shall thereupon issue his proclamation forbidding any animal of the kind among which said epidemic exists to be transferred from said locality without a certificate from the veterinary surgeon showing such animal to be healthy. The expenses of holding, feeding, and taking care of all animals quarantined under the provisions of this act shall be paid by the owner, agent, or person in charge of said stock.

SEC. 4. In case of any epidemic diseases where premises have been previously quarantined by the veterinary surgeon as before provided, he is further authorized and empowered, when in his judgment necessary, to order the slaughter of any and all diseased animals upon said premises, and of all animals that have been exposed to contagion or infection, under the following restrictions: Said order shall be a written one and shall be made in duplicate, and there shall be a distinct order and duplicate for each owner of the animals condemned, the original of each order to be filed by the veterinary surgeon with the governor of the Territory and the duplicate given to said owner: *And further*, Before slaughtering any animal or animals that have been exposed only and do not show disease, the veterinary surgeon shall call in consultation with him two respectable practicing veterinarians or physicians, residents of the Territory, or, if this is impossible, then two reputable and well-known freeholders, residents of the Territory, and shall have written indorsements upon his order of at least one of said consulting physicians or freeholders, stating that said action is necessary, before such animal or animals shall be slaughtered.

SEC. 5. Whenever, as herein provided, the veterinary surgeon shall order the slaughter of one or more animals, he shall, at the time of making such order, notify, in writing, the nearest available justice of the peace, who shall thereupon summon three disinterested citizens, who shall be freeholders of the neighborhood, to act as appraisers of the value of such animals. Said appraisers, before entering upon the discharge of their duties, shall be sworn to make a true and faithful appraisement, without prejudice or favor. They shall, after making their appraisement, return certified copies of their valuation, a separate one being made for each owner, together with an accurate description of each animal slaughtered (giving all brands, ear-marks, wattles, age, sex, and class, as to whether American, half-breed, or Texan), to the justice of the peace by whom they were summoned, who shall, after entering the same upon his record and making an indorsement upon each, showing it to have been properly recorded, return it, together with the duplicate order of the veterinary surgeon, to the person or persons owning the animals slaughtered; and it shall be the duty of the veterinary surgeon to superintend the slaughter of such animals as may be condemned and also the destruction of the carcass, which latter shall be by burning to ashes, or burying the same, which burial shall not be less than 6 feet under the ground and shall include every part of the animal, including excrement, as far as possible, and the hide shall be so cut and scarified as to be useless. He shall cause the said slaughter, burning, or burial to be done as cheaply as practicable.

SEC. 6. The veterinary surgeon shall make a report at the end of every year, to the governor, of all matters connected with his work, and the governor shall transmit to the several boards of county commissioners such parts of said report as may be of general interest to the breeders of live stock. The governor shall also give information in writing, as soon as he obtains it, to the various boards of county commissioners, of each cause of suspicion or fresh eruption of disease in each locality, its cause, and the measures adopted to check it.

stroy or cause to be destroyed the same by burning to ashes or burying the same, which burial shall not be less than 6 feet under ground, and shall include every part of the animal, and the hide shall be so cut and scarified as to be useless. Any person or persons who shall fail or neglect to comply with this provision shall be guilty of a misdemeanor, and shall be punished by a fine not less than one hundred ($100) dollars nor more than one thousand ($1,000) dollars, or imprisonment in the county jail not exceeding six months, or by both such fine and imprisonment, and the owner or owners of such diseased animal or animals shall further be liable for any and all damages and loss that may be sustained by any person by reason of failing to comply with the foregoing provisions.

SEC. 12. The right to indemnity under this act is limited to animals destroyed by reason of the suspected existence of some epizootic disease, generally fatal and incurable, such as rinderpest, hoof and mouth disease, pleuro-pneumonia, anthrax or Texas fever among bovines, and glanders among horses.

SEC. 13. The indemnity granted shall be the ordinary value of the animal, as determined by the appraisers, without reference to its diminished value caused by the suspected existence of disease or by having been exposed to any of the contagious diseases last above enumerated. It shall be paid to the owner upon his application and the presentation of the proofs prescribed herein; and it shall be the duty of said owner to make such application within six months after the slaughter of the animal for which payment is claimed, failing which, such claim shall be barred by limitation. Such payment shall be made by the Territorial treasurer, as herein provided, and from the fund provided by this act; provided, however, that no bovine shall be appraised for a higher value than fifty dollars ($50), except registered pedigreed animals, which shall not be valued to exceed one hundred and fifty dollars ($150). No equines shall be appraised for a higher value than one hundred dollars ($100) except registered pedigreed ani uals, which shall not be valued to exceed $300.

SEC. 14. The right to indemnify shall not exist, and payment of such shall not be made, in the following cases:

(1) For animals belonging to the United States.

(2) For animals that are brought into the Territory contrary to the provisions of this act.

(3) For animals that are found to be diseased, or that are destroyed because they have been exposed to disease before or at the time of their arrival in the Territory, or for animals that have been shipped into the Territory from any infectious or quarantined locality.

(4) When an animal was previously affected by any other disease which, from its nature and development, was incurable and necessarily fatal.

(5) When the owner or person in charge shall have knowingly or negligently omitted to comply with the provisions of sections 8 and 9 of this act.

(6) When the owner or claimant at the time of coming into possession of the animal knew it to be diseased, or received the notice specified in the first clause of section 9 of this act.

(7) When the animal or animals have been brought into the Territory within 90 days immediately preceding the outbreak of disease among or upon them.

SEC. 15. The veterinary surgeon shall receive for his services the sum of $2,500 per annum, together with his necessary traveling expenses actually paid out when in performance of his duty. These payments shall be made from any funds in the Territorial treasury not otherwise appropriated, upon itemized vouchers signed and sworn to by him and submitted to the Territorial auditor, who shall draw warrants upon the Territorial treasurer for the amounts, if found correct, separate vouchers being made for salary and expenses. No person shall be competent under this act to receive the appointment of veterinary surgeon who is not at the date of his appointment a graduate in good standing of a recognized college of veterinary surgeons and of not less than five years' actual practice. He shall hold his office for years; he may be removed for cause by the governor, who shall also have power ill the vacancy as herein before provided. The appraisers herein provided for l each receive three dollars for each day or part of a day they may be actually loyed as such, which shall be paid from the Territorial treasury out of the stock unity fund hereinafter provided, upon vouchers which bear the certificate of justice who summoned them. The justice of the peace shall receive for his ces the fees provided by law for similar services, to be paid out of the county al fund. The veterinarians, physicians, or freeholders called in consultation veterinary surgeon shall each receive three dollars for each day or part of a day may be actually so employed, and five cents per mileage for distances sarily traveled, which sums shall be paid from the Territorial treasury out of tock indemnity fund hereinafter provided for, upon vouchers certified to by surgeon; and other incidental expenses connected with his work and in-

made his duty by this act, such as causing animals to be slaughtered and their carcasses to be burned or buried, and disinfecting infected premises, shall be paid from the Territorial treasury out of the stock indemnity fund herein after provided for, upon vouchers certified to by him under oath. Before entering upon the discharge of his duties he shall give a bond to the Territory of Dakota, with good and sufficient surety, in the sum of ten thousand dollars, conditioned for the proper discharge of the same. No constructive mileage shall be paid under this act, nor shall the veterinary surgeon receive any mileage.

SEC. 16. The liability of the Territory for indemnity for animals destroyed, and for fees, costs, and expenses incurred under the provisions of this act, in any year, is limited by and shall in no case exceed the amount especially appropriated for that purpose and for that period by the terms of this act; nor shall the veterinary surgeon or any one else incur any liability on the part of the Territory, under the provisions of this act, in excess of the surplus in the stock indemnity fund hereinafter provided; nor shall any act be performed or property taken, under the provisions of this act, that will become a charge against the Territory of Dakota further than to the extent provided by said stock indemnity fund.

SEC. 17. Hereafter it shall be the duty each year of the Territorial board of equalization, at the time of making the annual assessment, to levy a special tax, not exceeding one mill on the dollar, upon the assessed value of all cattle, horses, and mules in the Territory, to be known as the stock indemnity fund. Said tax shall be levied and collected by the several counties and paid to the Territorial treasurer in the manner provided by law for the levying, collection, and payment of other Territorial taxes. Said fund shall constitute the stock indemnity fund specified by this act to be used in paying for animals destroyed under the provisions thereof. It shall be used exclusively for that purpose, and shall be paid out by the Territorial treasurer as hereinbefore provided for.

SEC. 18. The veterinary surgeon shall select the place or places where stock shall be quarantined.

SEC. 19. All fines collected under the provisions of this act shall be paid into the Territorial treasury and placed at the credit of the "stock indemnity fund."

SEC. 20. The veterinary surgeon shall have the power to appoint from time to time, by and with the consent and approval of the governor, deputies (not exceeding five in number, at any time he can not personally attend to all the duties required by his office), at a salary not to exceed $5 per day for each day actually employed, to be paid out of said stock indemnity fund, and shall designate the county or counties for which each deputy is to act. All acts performed by such deputies shall have the same effect as if done by the Territorial veterinary surgeon.

SEC. 21. It is hereby made the duty of the attorney-general or district attorney of the respective counties to prosecute any case complained of for prosecution in any justice or district court within the jurisdiction of which any violation of this act may have been had; and on conviction of violating any of the provisions of this act the court may award, in addition to the penalties prescribed by law, and add to the judgment such attorneys' fees and costs of prosecution as the court may determine just in the premises.

SEC. 22. This act shall take effect and be in force from and after its passage and approval.

Approved, March 11, 1887.

AN ACT to prevent the spread of contagious diseases among sheep.

SECTION 1. *Be it enacted by the legislative assembly of the Territory of Dakota*, That the owner or the person in charge of any sheep which are now, or shall hereafter be, affected with the scab, or any infectious or contagious disease, shall keep the said sheep securely within some inclosure, or shall herd them at a distance of not less than six miles from all farms, corrals, sheds, or other established headquarters where sheep are kept or are being herded: *Provided*, That any person owning sheep affected with the scab, or any infectious or contagious disease, who prior to the passage of this act established headquarters, shall be allowed to range such sheep upon the public domain within six miles, in any direction, of such established headquarters: *Provided further*, That such sheep shall not be allowed to range within three miles of any other headquarters, unless the other headquarters be less than six miles distant, in which case such sheep shall not be herded nearer to the other headquarters than a distance equal to one-half of the distance between the two headquarters.

SEC. 2. It shall be unlawful for any person or persons owning sheep affected with the scab, or any infectious or contagious disease, to drive, or permit the same to be [illegible] any public highway, or within the distance of one mile of any such highway, or within six miles of any farm, corral, shed, or other established headquarters where sheep are kept or being herded.

SEC. 3. Any person owning sheep, or any one in his employ, shall have the right to examine any band of sheep that shall be driven within six miles of his headquarters, and any person or persons in charge of such sheep shall stop them and allow them to be examined, and shall render the necessary assistance in catching and examining them. If the person so in charge of such sheep refuse to render the assistance as above required, he shall be punished as hereinafter provided.

SEC. 4. Any person who shall knowingly carry or drive, or cause to be carried or driven, one or more sheep affected with the scab, or any infectious or contagious disease, into a herd of sheep belonging to another person, or shall knowingly carry, or cause to be carried, the "parasite" which causes such scab, or disease, and place it where another person is corralling or herding sheep, so that such sheep may become affected thereby, shall be adjudged guilty of a felony, and upon conviction thereof shall be confined in the Territorial prison not less than five years nor more than ten years, and be fined in any sum not less than $1,000.

SEC. 5. Any person who shall be convicted of the violation of the provisions of this act shall be deemed guilty of a misdemeanor, and shall be punished by a fine of not less than $100 nor more than $600.

SEC. 6. Any person violating any of the provisions of this act shall be liable in damages to any person or persons injured thereby, directly or indirectly, to be recovered in a civil action in any court of competent jurisdiction.

SEC. 7. This act shall take effect and be in force from and after its passage and approval.

Approved, March 11, 1897.

ILLINOIS.

AN ACT to amend an act entitled "An act to revise the law in relation to the suppression and prevention of the spread of contagious and infectious diseases among domestic animals," approved June 27, 1885, in force July 1, 1885.

SECTION 1. *Be it enacted by the people of the State of Illinois, represented in the general assembly*, That "An act to revise the law in relation to the suppression and prevention of the spread of contagious and infectious diseases among domestic animals" be amended so as to read as follows:

"SECTION 1. *Be it enacted by the people of the State of Illinois, represented in the general assembly*, That the governor shall, with the advice and consent of the senate, appoint three practical stock-breeders, not more than two of whom shall be members of the same political party, who shall constitute a board of live-stock commissioners, who shall hold their office in the order in which they are named, the first for one year, the second for two years, and the third for three years; and their successors in office shall be appointed for three years each. Before entering on the duties of their office they shall take and subscribe to an oath of office for the faithful performance of their duties as such commissioners, and shall file the same with the governor.

"SEC. 2. It shall be the duty of said board of commissioners to cause to be investigated any and all cases or alleged cases coming to their knowledge of contagious or infectious diseases among domestic animals, and to use all proper means to prevent the spread of such diseases, and to provide for the extirpation thereof; and in the event of reasonable ground for belief that any such contagious or infectious disease has broken out in this State, it shall be the duty of the person owning or having in charge any animal or animals infected with disease, or any other person having knowledge or reason to suspect the existence of such disease, to immediately notify said board of commissioners, or some member thereof, by communication to said board of the existence of such disease, and thereupon it shall be the duty of said board, or some member thereof, or authorized agent of the board, immediately to cause proper examination thereof to be made, and if said disease shall be found to be a dangerously contagious or dangerously infectious malady, said board or any member thereof, or the State veterinarian or any assistant veterinarian, shall order said diseased animals, and such as have been exposed to contagion, and the premises in which they are, to be strictly quarantined for such time as the board, or any member thereof, or such veterinarian may deem necessary, not to exceed thirty days, in charge of such person as the board, or any member thereof or such veterinarian shall designate, and they shall have the power to order any premises and farms where the disease exists, or has recently existed, as well as exposed premises and farms to be put in quarantine, so that no domestic animal which has been or is so diseased, or has been exposed to such contagious or infectious disease, be removed from the places so quarantined, nor allow any healthy animal to be brought thereon, except under such rule or regulation as the said board may prescribe; and said board shall prescribe such regulations as they may deem necessary to prevent such disease from being communicated in any way from the places quarantined. In all such cases of contagious and infectious diseases, the said board or, in case the number of animals shall not exceed five, any member thereof, shall have the power to order the slaughter of all such diseased and exposed animals. The said board shall have the power to cause to be destroyed all barns, stables, premises, fixtures, furniture, and personal property infected with any such contagious or infectious disease, so far as in their judgment may be necessary to prevent the spread of such disease, and where the same cannot be properly disinfected. When the board, upon a written report of the State veterinarian, or any of his assistants, determine that any animal is affected with, or has been exposed to, any dangerously contagious or infectious disease, the board, or any member thereof, may agree with the owner upon the value of such animal or property, and in case such agreement cannot be made, said board, or the member acting in behalf of the board, may appoint three disinterested citizens of the State to appraise such diseased animal or exposed animals or property. Such appraisers shall subscribe to an oath in writing to fairly value such animal in accordance with the requirements of this act; which oath, together with the valuation fixed by said appraisers, shall be filed with the board, and be preserved by them. Upon such appraisement being made, it shall become the duty of the owner to immediately destroy such animal and dispose of the same in accordance with the order of said board, or member thereof, and upon failure to so do, said board, or member thereof, shall cause such animal or animals or property to be destroyed and disposed of, and thereupon the said owner shall forfeit all right to receive the compensation allowed by said appraisers and provided for by this act. When the board, upon the written opinion of the State veterinarian, determines that any barn, stables, out-buildings, or premises are so infected that the same can not be disinfected, they may quarantine such barns, stables, out-buildings, or premises from use for the animals that may be infected by such use, and such quarantine shall continue until removed by the board, and a violation of such quarantine shall be punished as is provided for violations of other quarantine by this act.

SEC. 3. The governor shall appoint a competent veterinary surgeon, who shall be known as the State veterinarian, who, together with his assistants, shall act under the direction of said board in carrying out the provisions of this act. In the event of the inability of the said State veterinarian to perform all the work which he may be directed to do by said board of commissioners, he may, by and with the advice and consent of said board, appoint such other necessary assistant veterinarians upon terms not exceeding that paid the State veterinarian. The State veterinarian shall receive for his services the sum of $8 per day for each day actually employed under the provisions of this act, together with his necessary traveling expenses, to be certified to by said board of commissioners.

SEC. 4. Whenever said board of commissioners shall report to the governor that such diseases have become epidemic in certain localities in other States, or that their conditions exist which would render such domestic animals liable to convey such diseases, he shall, by proclamation, schedule such localities, and prohibit the importation of any live stock of the kind diseased into the State, except under such regulations as may be prescribed by the said board and approved by the governor. Any corporation or person who shall knowingly transport, receive, or convey such prohibited stock shall be deemed guilty of a misdemeanor, and, upon conviction thereof, shall be fined not less than $[illegible] nor more than $10,000, for each and every offense, and shall become liable for any and all damage or loss that may be sustained by any party or parties by reason of such importation or transportation of such prohibited stock. Such liability shall be recovered in any county in this State, into or through which such stock is brought, upon information filed in the circuit or county court of any county or the superior court of Cook County. Any person who, knowing that a contagious or infectious disease exists among his domestic animals, shall conceal the fact, or, knowing of the existence of such disease, shall sell the animal or animals so diseased or any exposed animal, or knowing the same, shall remove such diseased or exposed animals from his premises to the premises of another, or knowing the existence of such disease or exposure, shall drive, or lead, or ship, the same by rail car or steam-boat to any other place in or out of this State, and any person or persons who shall bring any such diseased, or, knowingly, shall bring any exposed animal or animals into this State from another State; and any person or persons who shall knowingly buy, receive, sell, convey, or engage in the traffic of diseased or exposed stock; and any person who shall violate any quarantine established under the provisions of this act, shall, for each, either, any, or all the offenses mentioned in this section, be guilty of a misdemeanor, and, on conviction thereof, or of any one of said acts, shall be fined in any sum not less than $25, nor more than $200, and imprisoned in the county jail until the fine and costs are paid, and shall forfeit all right to the compensation for any animal or property destroyed under the provisions of this act. Any veterinary practitioner having information of any such contagious or infectious disease in this State, and who shall fail to promptly report such knowledge to the board of live-stock commissioners, shall be fined not exceeding five hundred dollars, or be imprisoned in the county jail not more than one year for each offense.

"SEC. 5. Whenever said board shall become satisfied that any dangerously contagious or infectious disease among domestic animals exists throughout any municipality or geographical district in this State, and, in their judgment, it is necessary to quarantine such municipality or geographical district in order to prevent the spread of such disease into contiguous territory, they shall report the same to the governor, who may thereupon by proclamation schedule and quarantine such district, prohibiting all domestic animals of the kind diseased from being brought into or taken from such infected district; and such proclamation shall from the time of its publication bind all persons, and any violation of such quarantine regulations so established shall be visited with like penalties, which may be recovered in like manner as is provided for the violation of other quarantine, as provided in section 4 of this act: *Provided*, That nothing contained in this section shall be so construed as to prevent the movement of any animals of the kind diseased through such territory under such regulations as the board of live-stock commissioners may prescribe and the governor approve.

"SEC. 6. Nothing contained in this act, or any section thereof, shall be interpreted so as to prevent the removal or shipment of diseased or exposed animals, under the orders of the board created by this act, from one place to another by said board or its agents, by driving along the public highway or shipment on cars or steam-boats, when, in the opinion of said board, such removal is necessary for the suppression of such contagious and infectious disease.

"SEC. 7. Whenever quarantine is established in accordance with the provisions of section 3 of this act, valid notice of the same may be given by leaving with the owner or occupant of any premises in person, or delivering to any member of his family, or any employé over the age of ten years found on the premises so quarantined, notice thereof, written or printed, or partly written and partly printed, and, at the same time, explaining the contents thereof. Such quarantine shall be sufficiently proven in any court by the production of a true copy of such notice of quarantine with a return thereon of the service of the same in the manner above required. Any person violating said quarantine shall be guilty of a misdemeanor and punished as is provided for in section 4 of this act, and, on conviction, shall be liable for all damage that may result to other persons in consequence of such violation: *Provided*, That any one feeling himself aggrieved by such quarantine may appeal to the full board of commissioners, who shall thereupon sustain, modify, or annul said quarantine as they deem proper.

"SEC. 8. All fines recovered under the provisions of this act shall be paid into the county treasury of the county in which the suit is tried, by the person collecting the same, in the manner now provided by law, to be used for county purposes; and it shall be the duty of State's attorneys, in their respective counties, to prosecute for all violations of this act.

"SEC. 9. All claims against the State arising from the slaughter of animals, as herein provided for, shall be made to said board of commissioners, under such rules and regulations as they may prescribe, and it shall be the duty of said board of commissioners to determine the amount which shall be paid in each case on account of animals so slaughtered, which, in cases of animals of the bovine species, shall be based on the fair cash market value thereof for beef, or for use for dairy purposes, not to exceed $75 per head; and, in cases of animals of the equine species, on their fair cash market value, not to exceed $100 per head, and report the same to the governor; and the governor shall indorse thereon his order to the State auditor, who shall thereupon issue his warrant on the State treasurer for the same.

"SEC. 10. Said board of commissioners, or any member thereof, and the State veterinarian and his assistants, in the performance of their duties under this act, shall have power to call on sheriffs and their deputies, constables and peace officers, mayors of cities, city and town marshals, and policemen to assist them in carrying out its provisions, and it is hereby made the duty of all such officers to assist in carrying out the provisions of this act when ordered so to do; and said commissioners and the State veterinarian and his assistants shall have, while engaged in carrying out the provisions of this act, the same powers and protection that other peace officers have, and any such officer who fails or refuses to enforce the lawful orders and quarantine of said board, or any member thereof, or any veterinarian acting under them, in the proper execution of the powers conferred by this act, shall be deemed guilty of a misdemeanor, and punished as provided in section [illegible] of this act.

"SEC. 11. The said board shall co-operate with any commissioner or other officer appointed by the United States for the suppression of contagious diseases among domestic animals, so far as the provisions of this act and the appropriations made in accordance therewith will allow, in suppressing and preventing the spread of contagious and infectious diseases among domestic animals in this State.

"SEC. 12. It shall be the duty of said board of commissioners to keep a record of all their acts and proceedings, and report the same to the governor annually, or oftener, if required, for publication. The annual report shall include an itemized statement of all sums expended by them under this act, including a statement of all damages recommended by them to be paid for all animals slaughtered, and the amounts paid therefor.

"SEC. 13. The members of said board shall each receive the sum of $5 per day for each day necessarily employed in the discharge of their duties, their necessary traveling expenses, and other incidental expenses necessarily incurred in the performance of their duties under this act, to be paid on certified and itemized vouchers to be approved by the governor.

"SEC. 14. All acts and parts of acts inconsistent herewith are hereby repealed.

"SEC. 15. Whereas the live-stock commissioners are without power to suppress contagious and infectious diseases now existing among live stock in the State of Illinois under the present law: Therefore, an emergency exists, and this act shall take effect from and after its passage."

Approved April 20, 1887.

IOWA.

AN ACT to amend chapter 11, title 24 of the code, relating to contagious diseases in domestic animals.

SECTION 1. *Be it enacted by the general assembly of the State of Iowa*, That sections 4058 and 4059 in chapter 11, title 24 of the code, be hereby repealed, and sections 2 and 3 of this act be substituted therefor, and be known hereafter as sections 4058 and 4059 of the code.

SEC. 2. Be it enacted, "Section 4058. Any person or persons driving any cattle into this State, or any agent, servant, or employé of any railroad or other corporation who shall carry, transport, or ship any cattle into this State, or any railroad company, or other corporation or person who shall carry, ship, or deliver any cattle into this State, or the owners, controllers, lessees, or agents or employés of any stock-yards, receiving into such stock-yards or in any other inclosures for the detention of cattle in transit, or shipment, or reshipment or sale any cattle brought or shipped in any manner into this State which at the time they were either driven, brought, shipped, or transported into this State were in such condition as to infect with or to communicate to other cattle pleuro-pneumonia, or splenitic or Texas fever, shall be deemed guilty of a misdemeanor, and upon conviction thereof shall be punished by a fine of not less than three hundred dollars and not more than one thousand dollars, or by both fine and imprisonment in the county jail not exceeding six months, in the discretion of the court.

SEC. 3. Be it enacted, Section 4059. Any person who shall be injured or damaged by any of the acts of the persons named in section 4058, and which are prohibited by such section, in addition to the remedy therein provided, may bring an action at law against any such persons, agents, employés, or corporations mentioned therein, and recover the actual damages sustained by the person or persons so injured, and neither said criminal proceeding nor said civil action, in any stage of the same, be a bar to a conviction or to a recovery in the other."

Approved April 10, 1886.

KANSAS.

AN ACT to prevent the spread of disease among swine.

SECTION 1. *Be it enacted by the legislature of the State of Kansas*, It is hereby made the duty of every person who owns or has the control of any hog that has died of any disease to bury or burn the same within twenty-four hours after such hog has died; and any person who knowingly fails or refuses to comply with the provisions of this section shall be deemed guilty of a misdemeanor, and upon conviction thereof shall be fined not exceeding one hundred dollars.

SEC. 2. Whoever shall knowingly barter or sell any hog afflicted with any disease without giving full information concerning said disease shall be deemed guilty of a misdemeanor, and upon conviction thereof shall be fined not exceeding one hundred dollars.

SEC. 3. Whoever shall knowingly barter or sell any hog which has died of any disease shall be deemed guilty of a misdemeanor, and upon conviction thereof shall be fined not exceeding one hundred dollars.

SEC. 4. Whoever shall throw or deposit a dead hog in any river, stream, creek, or ravine shall be deemed guilty of a misdemeanor, and upon conviction thereof shall be fined not exceeding one hundred dollars.

SEC. 5. This act shall take effect and be in force from and after its publication in the official State paper.

Approved February 19, 1895.

AN ACT to prevent the selling or running at large of domestic animal or animals affected with any infectious or contagious disease.

SECTION 1. *Be it enacted by the legislature of the State of Kansas,* Any person being the owner of any domestic animal or animals, or having the same in charge, who shall turn out or suffer any such domestic animal or animals having any contagious or infectious disease, knowing the same to be so diseased, to run at large upon any uninclosed land, common, or highway, or shall let the same approach within one hundred feet of any highway, or shall sell or dispose of any domestic animal or animals, knowing the same to be so diseased, without fully disclosing the fact to the purchaser, shall be deemed guilty of a misdemeanor, and shall be punished by a fine in any amount not exceeding five hundred dollars, or imprisoned in the county jail not more than six months.

SEC. 2. Any person violating any of the provisions of this act, in addition to the penalties herein provided, shall be liable for all damages that may accrue to the party damaged by reason of said diseased animal or animals imparting disease.

SEC. 3. This act shall take effect and be in force from and after its publication in the official State paper.

Approved February 20, 1886.

MAINE.

AN ACT to extirpate tuberculosis, foot-and-mouth disease, pleuro-pneumonia, and all other insidious and contagious diseases that are now or may appear among domestic animals, and to facilitate and encourage the production of live stock and their products.

SECTION 1. *Be it enacted by the senate and house of representatives of the State of Maine assembled,* That for the purpose of facilitating and encouraging the live-stock interests of the State of Maine, and for extirpating all insidious, infectious, and contagious diseases now or that may be among cattle and other live stock, and especially tuberculosis, the governor of the State is hereby authorized and required, immediately after the passage of this act, to appoint a board of cattle commissioners, consisting of three persons of known executive ability, who shall be charged with the execution of the provisions of this act, and who shall be known and designated as the "State of Maine cattle commission," and whose powers and duties shall be those provided for in this act. The governor may, when in his judgment the public interests will permit, suspend the functions and pay of said commissioners; and, when in his judgment the public interests may require, he shall restore such functions and pay, of which suspension and restoration he shall make public proclamation. The salaries of said commissioners shall be at the rate of three dollars per day during the time they are actually engaged in the discharge of their duties as commissioners. The said commissioners shall respectively take an oath to faithfully perform the duties of their office, and shall immediately organize as such commission by the election of one of their number as president thereof, and proceed forthwith to the discharge of duties devolved upon them by the provisions of this act.

SEC. 2. That it shall be the duties of the said commissioners to cause investigation to be made as to the existence of tuberculosis, pleuro-pneumonia, foot-and-mouth disease, and any other infectious or contagious disease. And such commissioners are hereby authorized to enter any premises, or places, including stock-yards, cars, and vessels, within any county or part of the State in or at which they have reason to believe there exists any such disease, and to make search, investigation, and inquiry in regard to the existence thereof. Upon the discovery of the existence of any of the said diseases, the said commissioners are hereby authorized to give notice, by publication, of the existence of such disease, and the locality thereof, in such newspapers as they may select, and to notify, in writing, the officials or agents of any railroad, steamboat, or other transportation company doing business in or through such infected locality, of the existence of such disease; and are hereby authorized and required to establish and maintain such quarantine of animals, places, premises, or location as they may deem necessary to prevent the spread of any such disease, and also to cause the appraisal of the animal or animals affected with or that have been exposed to the said diseases, in accordance with such rules and regulations by them as hereinafter authorized and provided, and also to cause the same to be destroyed, except as hereinafter provided, and to pay, in case of diseased animals, the owner or owners thereof three-fourths of their value, as determined upon the basis of health before infection, and the full appraised value in case of animals exposed to either of such diseases, but not themselves actually diseased, out of any moneys appropriated by the legislature for that purpose: *Provided, however*, That they shall not pay more than two hundred dollars for an animal with pedigree recorded or recordable in the recognized herd-books of the breed in which the animal destroyed may belong, nor more than one hundred dollars for an animal not pedigreed: *Provided further*, That in no case shall compensation be allowed for an animal destroyed under the provisions of this act which may have contracted or been exposed to such disease in a foreign country, or on the high seas; nor shall compensation be allowed to any owner who, in person or by agent, knowingly and wilfully conceals the existence of such disease, or the fact of exposure thereto in animals of which the person making such concealment by himself or agent is in whole or part owner.

SEC. 3. That the said commissioners are hereby authorized and required to make record, and publish rules and regulations providing for and regulating the agencies, methods, and manner of conducting, and the investigations aforesaid regarding the existence of said contagious diseases; for ascertaining, entering, and searching places where such diseased animals are supposed to exist; for ascertaining what animals are so diseased or have been exposed to contagious diseases; for making, reporting, and recording descriptions of the said animals so diseased or exposed and destroyed, and for appraising the same and for making payment therefor; and to make all other needful rules and regulations which may, in the judgment of the commissioners, be deemed requisite to the full and due execution of the provisions of this act. All such rules and regulations, before they shall become operative, shall be approved by the governor of Maine, and thereafter published in such manner as may be provided for in such regulations; and after such publication said rules and regulations shall have the force and effect of law so far as the same are not inconsistent with this act and other laws of the State or United States.

SEC. 4. That any person or persons who shall knowingly and wilfully refuse permission to said commissioners, or either of them, to make, or who knowingly and wilfully obstruct said commissioners, or either of them, in making all necessary examinations of, and as to animals supposed by said commissioners to be diseased as aforesaid, or in destroying the same, or who knowingly attempts to prevent said commissioners, or either of them, from entering upon the premises and other places hereinbefore specified where any of said diseases are by said commissioners supposed to exist, shall be deemed guilty of a misdemeanor, and upon conviction thereof, or of either of the acts in this section prohibited, shall be punished by fine not exceeding one hundred dollars, or by imprisonment not exceeding ninety days, or by both fine and imprisonment, at the discretion of the court.

SEC. 5. That any person who is the owner of or who is possessed of any interest in any animals affected with any of the diseases named in section two of this act, or any person who is agent, common carrier, consignee, or otherwise is charged with any duty in regard to any animal so diseased or exposed to the contagion of such disease, or any officer or agent charged with any duties under the provisions of this act, who shall knowingly conceal the existence of such contagious disease, or the fact of such exposure to said contagion, and who shall fail within a reasonable time to report to the said commissioners their knowledge or their information in regard to the existence and location of said disease or of such exposure thereto, shall be deemed guilty of a misdemeanor, and shall be punishable as provided in section four of this act.

SEC. 6. That when the owner of animals decided under the provisions of this act by the proper authority to be diseased, or to have been exposed to contagion, refuses to accept the sum authorized to be paid under the appraisement provided for in this act, it shall be the duty of the commissioners to declare and maintain a rigid quarantine as to the animals decided, as aforesaid, to be diseased or to have been exposed to any contagious or infectious disease, and of the premises or places where said cattle may be found, according to the rules and regulations to be prescribed by said commissioners, approved by the governor, and published as provided in the third section of this act.

SEC. 7. That no person or persons owning or operating any railroad, nor the owner or owners or masters of any steam, sailing, or other vessels within the State, shall receive for transportation or transport from one part of the State to another part of the State, or to bring from any other State or foreign country any cattle affected with any of the diseases named in section two of this act, or that have been exposed to such diseases, especially the disease known as tuberculosis, knowing such cattle to be affected, or to have been so exposed; nor shall any person or persons, company or corporation deliver for such transportation to any railroad company, or to the master or owner of any vessel, any cattle knowing them to be affected with or to have been exposed to any of the said diseases; nor shall any person or persons, company or corporation, drive on foot or transport in private conveyance from one part of the State to another part of the State any cattle knowing the same to be affected with or to have been exposed to any of said diseases. Any person or persons violating the provisions of this section shall be deemed guilty of a misdemeanor, and upon conviction thereof shall be punished by fine not exceeding the sum of two hundred dollars, or by imprisonment not exceeding six months, or by both fine and imprisonment.

SEC. 8. That it shall be the duty of the several county attorneys to prosecute all violations of this act which shall be brought to their notice or knowledge by any person making the complaint under oath; and the same shall be heard in any supreme judicial court having jurisdiction in the county in which the violation of this act has been committed.

SEC. 9. That the said commissioners are hereby authorized to appoint or elect one of their number as secretary of said board, who shall receive a reasonable compensation for his services during the time in which, under the provisions of this act, the services of the said commissioner shall be required. The said commissioners shall make and preserve a full record of all rules and regulations promulgated under the provisions of this act, of all payments and expenses hereunder incurred, and all other transactions performed by said commissioners in the discharge of their duties, as herein provided; and the said commissioners shall, on or before the first Wednesday in January of each year during their continuance in service, and at other times as they may deem conducive to the public interests, or as they may be required so to do by the governor of the State, report to, full and accurate accounts of their expenditures and other proceedings under the provisions of this act, and of the condition of said diseases, if any, in the State, to be communicated by him to the legislature. Whenever the functions of said commission shall be suspended or terminated, it shall turn over to the secretary of the State all its books, papers, records, and other effects, taking his receipt therefor, and he shall remain the custodian of the same until such time as the functions of the said commission may be restored.

SEC. 10. That the commissioners shall have the power, and are hereby authorized, to employ skilled veterinarians, and such other agents and employés as they may deem necessary to carry into effect the provisions of this act, and to fix the compensation of the person or persons so employed, and to terminate such employment at their discretion; and they are authorized, out of the moneys by this act appropriated, to make such expenditures as may be needed for the actual and necessary traveling expenses of themselves and their said employés, stationery, expenses of disinfecting premises, cars, and other places, destroying diseased and exposed animals and paying for the same, and such other expenses and expenditures as they may find to be actually necessary to properly carry into effect the provisions of this act.

SEC. 11. That the moneys appropriated by this act shall be paid over to the secretary of said commission from time to time as the same may be found to be needed, upon requisition made by the said commissioners, and shall be disbursed by the said secretary of said commission only upon vouchers approved by said commissioners, or a majority of them. The said secretary shall, before entering upon the duties of his office, take an oath to faithfully discharge the duties thereof, and shall enter into a bond to the State of Maine, with sureties to be approved by the treasurer of State in such sum as he may designate for the faithful accounting of all moneys received by the said secretary of the commission under the provisions of this act.

SEC. 12. That for the purpose of carrying into effect the provisions of this act the sum of five thousand dollars, or so much thereof as may be necessary, is hereby appropriated out of any moneys in the Treasury not otherwise appropriated.

SEC. 13. That all acts and parts of acts inconsistent or in conflict with the provisions of this act be, and the same are hereby, repealed.

Approved March, 1887.

MARYLAND.

AN ACT supplemental to and to amend an act passed March thirty-first, eighteen hundred and eighty-four, chapter one hundred and fifty-seven, entitled an act to prevent the spread of infectious or contagious diseases among the live stock of this State.

SECTION 1. *Be it enacted by the general assembly of Maryland*, That a commission is hereby established, which shall be known under the name and style of "the State live-stock sanitary board," to consist of three commissioners, who are practically engaged in the breeding of live stock, who shall be appointed by the governor, by and with the advice and consent of the senate, immediately on the approval of this act, and biennially thereafter, at such time as executive appointments are required by law to be made, and who shall hold their offices until their successors are duly appointed and qualified.

SEC. 2. *And be it enacted*, That it shall be the duty of said board, as far as possible, to protect the health of the domestic animals of the State from all exotic, contagious, or infectious diseases, and glanders in horses, and for this purpose it is authorized and empowered to establish, maintain, and enforce such quarantine, sanitary, or other regulations as it may deem necessary, and shall maintain an office in the city of Baltimore, and be clothed with all the powers and duties imposed on the governor by the said act of eighteen hundred and eighty-four, chapter one hundred and fifty-seven, except the power to appoint a chief veterinary inspector; it shall institute and prosecute diligent inquiries in the several counties and ascertain, as far as possible, the exact condition of the health of the live stock in said counties, and to seek to have such counties as shall be found to be free from contagious or infectious diseases exempted from existing or future quarantine regulations of other States or Territories, and the local boards of health in the several counties shall investigate all reported cases of contagious or infectious diseases of live stock in their respective counties, and if found to be contagious or infectious, shall report the same at once to the said State live-stock sanitary board.

SEC. 3. *And be it enacted*, That each member of said board shall be paid the sum of five dollars per day and necessary expenses for time actually spent in the discharge of his duties.

SEC. 4. *And be it enacted*, That the sum of three thousand dollars per year be, and the same is hereby, appropriated, or so much thereof as may be necessary to meet the necessary expenses of said board, including rent, printing, etc.

SEC. 5. *And be it enacted*, That it shall be the duty of all persons practicing veterinary medicine in this State. to report immediately to said board all cases of infectious or contagious diseases among live-stock which may come to their knowledge, and a failure so to do for forty-eight hours after he or they shall come into such knowledge shall be deemed a misdemeanor, and on conviction thereof shall be fined a sum not exceeding fifty dollars for each offence.

SEC. 9. *And be it enacted*, That it shall be unlawful for any person to inoculate any animal in this State with the virus of any infectious or contagious disease incident to animals without the consent of said live-stock sanitary board, and that any persons convicted of this offence shall be fined a sum not less than one hundred nor more than five hundred dollars, in the discretion of the court.

SEC. 7. *And be it enacted*, That for the performances of the duties imposed on them by the act of which this is supplemental, all constables, sheriffs, or deputy sheriffs or other State officers shall be paid as for the performance of similar duties under existing laws.

SEC. 8. *And be it enacted*, That it shall be the duty of all State's attorneys to prosecute all persons accused of violating this act, or the act to which this is a supplement.

SEC. 9. *And be it enacted*, That all rules and regulations formulated and issued by said board in pursuance of the powers hereby conferred on them shall have the force of law, and all violations thereof shall be punished as provided in the original act of eighteen hundred and eighty-four, chapter one hundred and fifty-seven, and all appraisements of animals to be slaughtered, or of buildings to be destroyed, shall be approved by the said board before such animals are slaughtered or such buildings destroyed, and said board shall have the discretion to have such appraised animals destroyed or quarantined.

SEC. 10. *And be it enacted*, That so much of section eight of the act of eighteen hundred and eighty-four, chapter one hundred and fifty-seven, as limits the amount to be used in any two years for the payment of animals slaughtered, be and the same is hereby repealed, and that all acts or parts of acts inconsistent with this act be, and the same are hereby, repealed.

SEC. 11. *And be it enacted*, That this act shall take effect from the date of its passage.

Approved April 1, 1886.

MASSACHUSETTS.

AN ACT to aid in the suppression of contagious diseases among domestic animals.

SECTION 1. *Be it enacted, etc., as follows:* Whoever has knowledge of the existence of a contagious disease among any species of domestic animals in this State, whether such knowledge is obtained by examination or otherwise, shall forthwith give notice thereof to the board of aldermen of the city or the selectmen of the town where such diseased animals are kept, and for failure so to do, shall be punished by a fine not exceeding five hundred dollars, or by imprisonment in jail not exceeding one year.

SEC. 2. The board of aldermen of a city or the selectmen of a town having received notice of a contagious disease among domestic animals in their city or town, shall forthwith inform the board of cattle commissioners of the existence of such contagious disease.

SEC. 3. Section three of chapter ninety of the public statutes is hereby amended so as to read as follows: They may cause all such animals, except those infected with glanders or farcy, to be appraised by three competent and disinterested men, under oath, at the value thereof at the time of the appraisement, and the amount of the appraisement shall be paid as provided in section one; and they shall cause all animals infected with glanders or farcy to be killed without appraisement; but may pay the owner an equitable sum for his services in the killing, and for any reasonable expense incurred by the burial thereof.

SEC. 4. The cattle commissioners, in the necessary discharge of their duties, may administer oaths.

SEC. 5. This act, except for the enforcement of the penalty prescribed in section one, shall take effect upon its passage.

Approved April 9, 1885.

AN ACT in relation to the appointment and tenure of office of the cattle commissioners.

Be it enacted, etc., as follows: The governor, with the advice and consent of the council, shall appoint a board of cattle commissioners of not more than three members, whose term of office shall commence on the first day of October, eighteen hundred and eighty-five, and who shall hold office as follows: One of said members for the term of three years, one for the term of two years, one for the term of one year, and thereafter one of said members shall be appointed annually for the term of three years. The compensation of such commissioners shall not exceed five dollars per day for actual service, in addition to their traveling expenses necessarily incurred. Any member of the board may be removed by the governor and council, and they may terminate the commissions of the entire board when in their judgment the public safety may permit. Vacancies in the board by the expirations of the terms of service or otherwise shall from time to time be filled by appointment by the governor with the consent of the council. The board of cattle commissioners as now constituted shall cease to exist on the thirtieth day of September, eighteen hundred and eighty-five, and the duties now devolving by law upon said board shall thereafter be performed by the board authorized by this act.

Approved June 19, 1885.

AN ACT for the suppression of contagious diseases among domestic animals.

SECTION 1. *Be it enacted by the senate and house of representatives in general court assembled, and by the authority of the same, as follows:* The boards of health of cities and towns, in cases of the existence in this Commonwealth of the disease called pleuro-pneumonia among cattle, or farcy or glanders among horses, or any other contagious or infectious disease among domestic animals, shall cause the animals which are infected or which have been exposed to infection in their respective cities and towns to be secured or collected in some suitable place or places within their cities or towns, and kept isolated; and when taken from the premises or possession of their owners, the expense of their maintenance shall be paid by the city or town wherein the animal is kept, and four-fifths of such payment, when certified by the treasurer of such city or town, shall be refunded by the Commonwealth; such isolation to continue as long as the existence of such disease or other circumstances may render it necessary.

SEC. 2. They may, within their respective cities and towns, prohibit the departure of animals from any enclosure or exclude animals therefrom, and may appoint agents who shall have power to enforce the prohibitions and regulations for which provision is made in sections three and four of this act.

SEC. 3. They may make regulations in writing to regulate or prohibit the passage from, to or through their respective cities or towns, or from place to place within the same, of any cattle or other domestic animals, and may arrest and detain, at the cost of the owners thereof, all animals found passing in violation of such regulations; and may take all other necessary measures for the enforcement of such prohibition, and also for preventing the spread of any disease among the animals of their respective cities and towns and the immediate vicinity thereof.

SEC. 4. Such regulations shall be recorded upon the records of their cities and towns, respectively, and shall be published in such cities and towns in such manner as may be provided in such regulations.

SEC. 5. Any person disobeying the orders of the boards of health, made in conformity with section three, or driving or transporting any animals contrary to the regulations made, published, and recorded as aforesaid, shall be punished by a fine not exceeding five hundred dollars, or by imprisonment not exceeding one year.

SEC. 6. Whoever has knowledge of, or has good reason to suspect the existence of, a contagious disease among any species of domestic animals in this State, whether such knowledge is obtained by a personal examination or otherwise, shall forthwith give notice thereof to the board of health of the city or of the town where such diseased animals are kept; and for failure so to do shall be punished by a fine not exceeding five hundred dollars, or by imprisonment in jail not exceeding one year.

SEC. 7. The board of health of a city or of a town, having received notice of a suspected case of contagious disease among any of the domestic animals in their city or town, shall forthwith make an examination thereof personally, or by a competent person appointed by them for that purpose, and if satisfied there are good reasons for believing that contagion is present, shall immediately inform the cattle commissioners.

SEC. 8. A city or town whose officers refuse or neglect to carry into effect the provisions of the first four and the seventh sections of this act, shall forfeit a sum not exceeding five hundred dollars for each day's neglect.

SEC. 9. The board of health of cities and towns, when in their judgment it is necessary to carry into effect the provisions of this chapter, may within their respective cities and towns take and hold, for a term not exceeding one year, any land without buildings other than barns thereon, upon which to enclose and isolate any animals; and they shall cause the damage sustained by the owner in consequence of such taking and holding to be appraised by the assessors of the city or town wherein the lands so taken are situated; and they shall further cause a description of such land, setting forth the boundaries thereof, and the area as nearly as may be estimated, together with the said appraisal, to be entered on the records of the city or town. The amount of said appraisement shall be paid as provided in section one, in such sums and at such times as the board of health may order. If the owner of land so taken is dissatisfied with said appraisement he may by action of contract recover of the city or town wherein the lands lie a fair compensation for the damages sustained by him, but no costs shall be taxed, unless the damages recovered in such action, exclusive of interest, exceed said appraisement. And the Commonwealth shall re-imburse to the city or town four-fifths of any sum recovered of it in any such action.

SEC. 10. When a board of cattle commissioners, appointed in accordance with the provisions of chapter three hundred and seventy-eight of the acts of eighteen hundred and eighty five, is in existence, and makes and publishes any regulations concerning the extirpation, cure, or treatment of animals infected with or which have been exposed to any contagious disease, such regulations shall supersede those made by boards of health, and boards of health shall carry out and enforce all orders and directions of said commissioners to them directed.

SEC. 11. Said commissioners shall have all the power and authority herein conferred upon boards of health, and in addition may establish hospitals or quarantines, with proper accommodations, wherein, under prescribed regulations, animals by them selected may be confined and treated, for the purpose of determining the varying characteristics of and the methods by which a specific contagion may be disseminated or destroyed; and they may direct boards of health to enforce and carry into effect all such regulations as may, from time to time, be made for that end. And any such officer who refuses or neglects to carry out any such regulation of the commissioners shall be punished by a fine not exceeding five hundred dollars for every such offence.

SEC. 12. The commissioners, when in their judgment the circumstances of the case and the public good require it, may cause to be killed and buried any domestic animals which are infected with or have been exposed to contagious disease; and except as is provided in the following section shall cause such animals to be appraised by three competent, disinterested men, under oath at the fair value thereof in their condition at the time of appraisement, and the amount of the appraisement and necessary expense of the same shall be paid as provided in section one.

SEC. 13. When the commissioners, by an examination of a case of contagious disease among domestic animals, become satisfied that it has been contracted by intention or negligence on the part of the owner or of a person in his employ, or by his consent, or by the use of food material liable to the germs of contagion, they shall cause such animals to be securely isolated at the expense of the owner, or they shall cause them to be killed without appraisal or payment; and in all cases of farcy or glanders, the commissioners having condemned the animal infected therewith, shall cause such animal to be killed without an appraisal, but may pay the owner or any other person an equitable sum for the killing and burial thereof.

SEC. 14. A person who fails to comply with a regulation made or an order given by the commissioners in the discharge of their duty, shall be punished by a fine not exceeding five hundred dollars or by imprisonment not exceeding one year.

SEC. 15. Prosecutions under the preceding section may be maintained in any county.

SEC. 16. All appraisements under this chapter shall be in writing, and signed by the appraisers and certified by the board of health or commissioners, respectively, to the treasurers of the cities and towns where the animals are kept, and forwarded to the auditor of the Commonwealth.

SEC. 17. The commissioners may examine under oath all persons believed to possess knowledge of material facts concerning the existence or dissemination or danger of dissemination of contagious disease among domestic animals; and for this purpose shall have all the powers vested in justices of the peace to take depositions, and to compel witnesses to attend and testify, by chapter one hundred and sixty-nine of the public statutes. All costs and expenses incurred in procuring the attendance of such witnesses shall be allowed and paid to the commissioners from the treasury of the Commonwealth upon being certified to and approved by the State auditor.

SEC. 18. When animals exposed to contagious diseases are killed by order of the commissioners, their carcasses may be inspected by the commissioners or a competent, discreet person appointed by them, and if they are found entirely free of disease and in a wholesome condition for food, they may be sold by them or by their order, and the proceeds of the sales shall be applied in payment of the appraised value of said animals.

SEC. 19. Cattle commissioners now or hereafter appointed shall keep a full record of their doings and report the same to the legislature on or before the tenth day of January in each year, unless sooner required by the governor; and an abstract of the same shall be printed in the annual report of the state board of agriculture.

SEC. 20. When animals are transported within this State from infected localities beyond its boundary lines, such animals may be seized and quarantined by the commissioners, at the expense of the owners thereof, so long as the public safety may require; and if, in their judgment, it is necessary to secure that safety, they may cause such animals to be killed without appraisal or payment for the same.

SEC. 21. No Texan, Mexican, Cherokee, Indian, or other cattle which the cattle commissioners decide spread contagious disease shall be driven on the streets of any city, town, or village, or on any road in this Commonwealth; nor shall they be driven outside the stock-yards connected with any railway in this Commonwealth, between the first day of March and the first day of November.

SEC. 22. In all stock-yards within this Commonwealth said Texan, Mexican, Cherokee, Indian, or other cattle which the cattle commissioners decide may spread contagious disease shall be kept in different pens from those in which other cattle are kept, from the first day of March until the first day of November.

SEC. 23. Any person or persons violating any provisions of the two preceding sections shall be punished by a fine of not less than twenty nor more than one hundred dollars.

SEC. 24. Chapter ninety of the public statutes and chapter one hundred and forty-eight of the acts of the year eighteen hundred and eighty-five are hereby repealed.

Approved, April, 1887.

AN ACT for the suppression of contagious diseases among domestic animals.

SECTION 1. *Be it enacted by the senate and house of representatives in general court assembled, and by the authority of the same*, The boards of health of cities and towns, in case of the existence in this Commonwealth of the disease called pleuro-pneumonia among cattle, or farcy or glanders among horses, or any other contagious or infectious disease among domestic animals, shall cause the animals which are infected, or which have been exposed to infection in their respective cities and towns, to be secured or collected in some suitable place or places within their cities or towns and kept isolated; and, when taken from the premises or possession of their owners, the expense of their maintenance shall be paid by the city or town wherein the animal is kept, and four-fifths of such payment, when certified by the treasurer of such city or town, shall be refunded by the Commonwealth; such isolation to continue as long as the existence of such disease or other circumstances may render it necessary.

SEC. 2. They may, within their respective cities and towns, prohibit the departure of animals from any enclosure or exclude animals therefrom, and may appoint agents who shall have power to enforce the prohibitions and regulations for which provision is made in sections three and four of this act.

SEC. 3. They may make regulations in writing to regulate or prohibit the passage from, to, or through their respective cities or towns, or from place to place within the same, of any cattle or other domestic animals, and may arrest and detain, at the cost of the owners thereof, all animals found passing in violation of such regulations; and may take all other necessary measures for the enforcement of such prohibition, and also for preventing the spread of any disease among the animals of their respective cities or towns and the immediate vicinity thereof.

SEC. 4. Such regulations shall be recorded upon the records of their cities and towns, respectively, and shall be published in such cities and towns in such manner as may be provided in such regulations.

SEC. 5. Any person disobeying the orders of the boards of health, made in conformity with section three, or driving or transporting any animals contrary to the regulations made, published, and recorded as aforesaid, shall be punished by a fine not exceeding five hundred dollars, or by imprisonment not exceeding one year.

SEC. 6. Whoever has knowledge of, or has good reason to suspect, the existence of a contagious disease among any species of domestic animals in this State, whether such knowledge is obtained by personal examination or otherwise, shall forthwith give notice thereof to the board of health of the city or of the town where such diseased animals are kept; and for failure so to do shall be punished by a fine not exceeding five hundred dollars, or by imprisonment in jail not exceeding one year.

SEC. 7. The board of health of a city or of a town, having received notice of a suspected case of contagious disease among any of the domestic animals in their city or town, shall forthwith make an examination thereof personally, or by a competent person appointed by them for that purpose, and if satisfied there are good reasons for believing that contagion is present, shall immediately inform the cattle commissioners.

SEC. 8. A city or town whose officers refuse or neglect to carry into effect the provisions of the first four and the seventh sections of this act shall forfeit a sum not exceeding five hundred dollars for each day's neglect.

SEC. 9. The board of health of cities and towns, when in their judgment it is necessary to carry into effect the provisions of this chapter, may within their respective cities and towns take and hold, for a term not exceeding one year, any land, without buildings other than barns thereon, upon which to enclose and isolate any animals; and they shall cause the damage sustained by the owner in consequence of such taking and holding to be appraised by the assessors of the city or town wherein the lands so taken are situated; and they shall further cause a description of such land, setting forth the boundaries thereof, and the area as nearly as may be estimated, together with the said appraisal, to be entered on the records of the city or town. The amount of said appraisement shall be paid as provided in section one, in such sums and at such times as the board of health may order. If the owner of land so taken is dissatisfied with said appraisement he may by action of contract recover of the city or town wherein the lands lie a fair compensation for the damages sustained by him, but no costs shall be taxed, unless the damages recovered in such action, exclusive of interest, exceed said appraisement. And the Commonwealth shall reimburse to the city or town four-fifths of any sum recovered of it in any such action.

SEC. 10. When a board of cattle commissioners, appointed in accordance with the provisions of chapter three hundred and seventy-eight of the acts of eighteen hundred and eighty-five, is in existence and makes and publishes any regulations concerning the extirpation, cure, or treatment of animals infected with or which have been exposed to any contagious disease, such regulations shall supersede those made by boards of health, and boards of health shall carry out and enforce all orders and directions of said commissioners to them directed.

SEC. 11. Said commissioners shall have all the power and authority herein conferred upon boards of health, and in addition may establish hospitals or quarantines, with proper accommodations, wherein, under prescribed regulations, animals by them selected may be confined and treated, for the purpose of determining the varying characteristics of and the methods by which a specific contagion may be disseminated or destroyed; and they may direct boards of health to enforce and carry into effect all such regulations as may, from time to time, be made for that end. Any such officer who refuses or neglects to carry out any such regulations of the commissioners shall be punished by a fine not exceeding five hundred dollars for every such offense.

SEC. 12. The commissioners, when in their judgment the circumstances of the case and the public good require it, may cause to be killed and buried any domestic animals which are infected with or have been exposed to contagious disease; and, except as is provided in the following section, shall cause such animals to be appraised by three competent, disinterested men, under oath, at the fair value thereof in their condition at the time of appraisement, and the amount of the appraisement and necessary expense of the same shall be paid as provided in section one.

SEC. 13. When the commissioners, by an examination of a case of contagious disease among domestic animals, become satisfied that it has been contracted by intention or negligence on the part of the owner, or of a person in his employ, or by his consent, or by the use of food material liable to the germs of contagion, they shall cause such animals to be securely isolated at the expense of the owner, or they shall cause them to be killed without appraisal or payment; and in all cases of farcy or glanders, the commissioners having condemned the animals infected therewith, shall cause such animals to be killed without an appraisal, but may pay the owner or any other person an equitable sum for the killing and burial thereof.

SEC. 14. A person who fails to comply with a regulation made or an order given by the commissioners in the discharge of their duty, shall be punished by a fine not exceeding five hundred dollars, or by imprisonment not exceeding one year.

SEC. 15. Prosecutions under the preceding section may be maintained in any county.

SEC. 16. All appraisements under this chapter shall be in writing, and signed by the appraisers, and certified by the board of health or commissioners, respectively, to the treasurers of the cities and towns where the animals are kept, and forwarded to the auditor of the Commonwealth.

SEC. 17. The commissioners may examine under oath all persons believed to possess knowledge of material facts concerning the existence, or dissemination, or danger of dissemination of contagious disease among domestic animals; and for this purpose shall have all the powers vested in justices of the peace to take depositions and to compel witnesses to attend and testify, by chapter one hundred and sixty-nine of the public statutes. All costs and expenses incurred in procuring the attendance of such witnesses shall be allowed and paid to the commissioners from the treasury of the Commonwealth upon being certified to and approved by the State auditor.

SEC. 18. When animals exposed to contagious diseases are killed by order of the commissioners, their carcasses may be inspected by the commissioners, or a competent, discreet person appointed by them, and if they are found entirely free of disease and in a wholesome condition for food, they may be sold by them or by their order, and the proceeds of the sale shall be applied in payment of the appraised value of said animals.

SEC. 19. Cattle commissioners now or hereafter appointed shall keep a full record of their doings and report the same to the legislature on or before the tenth day of January in each year, unless sooner required by the governor; and an abstract of the same shall be printed in the annual report of the State board of agriculture.

SEC. 20. When animals are transported within this State from infected localities beyond its boundary lines, such animals may be seized and quarantined by the commissioners, at the expense of the owners thereof, so long as the public safety may require; and if, in their judgment, it is necessary to secure that safety they may cause such animals to be killed without appraisal or payment for the same.

SEC. 21. No Texan, Mexican, Cherokee, Indian, or other cattle which the cattle commissioners decide may spread contagious disease shall be driven on the streets of any city, town, or village, or on any road in this Commonwealth, nor shall they be driven outside the stock-yards connected with any railway in this Commonwealth, between the first day of March and the first day of November.

SEC. 22. In all stock-yards within this Commonwealth said Texan, Mexican, Cherokee, Indian, or other cattle which the cattle commissioners decide may spread contagious disease shall be kept in different pens from those in which other cattle are kept, from the first day of March until the first day of November.

SEC. 23. Any person or persons violating any provision of the two preceding sections shall be punished by a fine of not less than twenty nor more than one hundred dollars.

SEC. 24. Chapter ninety of the public statutes and chapter one hundred and [illegible] of the acts of the year eighteen hundred and eighty-five are hereby repealed.

Approved, May 7, 1887.

MONTANA.

AN ACT to suppress and prevent the dissemination of contagious diseases among domestic animals and Texas cattle.

SECTION 1. *Be it enacted by the legislative assembly of the Territory of Montana*, That the governor of the Territory is hereby authorized to nominate, and by and with the advice and consent of the council, appoint a competent veterinary surgeon, who shall be known as the "Territorial veterinary surgeon," and, on entering on his duties, shall take an oath to well and truly perform his duties as provided by law.

SEC. 2. The duties of said Territorial veterinary surgeon shall be as follows:

(1) To investigate any and all cases of contagious or infectious diseases among cattle, horses, mules, and asses in this Territory, of which he may have a knowledge, or which may be brought to his notice by any resident in the locality where such disease exists; and it shall be his duty, in the absence of specific information, to make visits of inspection to any locality where he may have reason to suspect that there is contagious or infectious diseases.

(2) To inspect, under the regulations of this act, all cattle, horses, mules, and asses which may be brought into this Territory, in any manner whatever, from or through such State, Territory, or foreign country as the governor shall declare by proclamation upon the recommendation of the board of stock commissioners, or otherwise be held in quarantine for purposes of inspection for contagious or infectious diseases. And after the making of such proclamation it shall be the duty of the owner or person in charge of any cattle, horses, mules, or asses arriving in this Territory from or through any State, Territory, or foreign country against which quarantine has been declared, to notify the Territorial veterinary surgeon without delay, and not to allow such animals, or any of them, to leave the place of arrival until they shall have been examined by said surgeon, and his certificate obtained that all are free from disease; and no animal pronounced unsound from disease by the Territorial veterinary surgeon shall be turned loose, or allowed to run at large, or removed or permitted to escape, but shall be held subject to the order of the Territorial veterinary surgeon. Any person failing to comply with this provision shall be deemed guilty of a misdemeanor; and, upon conviction, shall be fined not less than fifty nor more than five hundred dollars for each offense, and shall be liable for any damage and loss that may be sustained by any person or persons by reason of the failure of such owner or agent to comply with the provisions of this section: *Provided*, That the owner of horses, mules, or asses ridden under the saddle or driven in harness into this Territory, or the owner of oxen driven into this Territory under the yoke, and any person coming into this Territory with his own team or teams, shall not be required to notify the Territorial veterinary surgeon, or await the inspection of such work-oxen, team, or teams, but he shall be liable for all loss or damage to any person or persons from or by reason of any contagious or infectious disease brought into the Territory by his animals; and no cattle, horses, mules, or asses shall be held in quarantine in this Territory for a longer period than ninety (90) days, unless contagious or infectious disease shall be found to exist among them.

SEC. 3. In all cases of contagious or infectious disease among domestic animals or Texas cattle in this Territory, the Territorial veterinary surgeon shall have authority to order the quarantine of the infected premises, and in case such disease shall become epidemic in any locality in this Territory, the Territorial veterinary surgeon shall immediately notify the governor of the Territory, who shall thereupon issue his proclamation forbidding any animal of the kind among which said epidemic exists to be transferred from said locality without a certificate from the Territorial veterinary surgeon showing such animal to be healthy. The expenses of holding, feeding, and taking care of all animals quarantined under the provisions of this act, shall be paid by the owner, agent, or person in charge of said stock.

SEC. 4. In case of any epidemic disease where premises have been previously quarantined by the Territorial veterinary surgeon as before provided, he is further authorized and empowered, when in his judgment necessary, to order the slaughter of any or all diseased animals upon said premises and of all animals that have been exposed to contagion or infection under the following restrictions: Said order shall be a written one, and shall be made in duplicate, and there shall be a distinct order and duplicate for each owner of the animals condemned, the original of each order to be filed by the Territorial veterinary surgeon with the secretary of the Territory and the duplicate given to said owner. And further, before slaughtering any animal or animals that have been exposed only, and do not show disease, the Territorial veterinary surgeon shall call in consultation with him two respectable practicing veterinarians or physicians, residents of the Territory; or, if this is impossible, then two reputable and well-known stock-owners, residents of the Territory, and shall have written endorsements upon his order of at least one of said consulting physicians or stock-owners, stating that said action is necessary, before such animal or animals shall be slaughtered.

SEC. 5. Whenever, as herein provided, the Territorial veterinary surgeon shall order the slaughter of one or more animals he shall, at the time of making such order, notify in writing the nearest available justice of the peace, who shall thereupon summon three disinterested citizens who shall be stock-owners of the neighborhood to act as appraisers of the value of such animals. Such appraisers, before entering upon the discharge of their duties, shall be sworn to make a true and faithful appraisement, without prejudice or favor. They shall, after making their appraisement, return certified copies of their valuation, a separate one being made for each owner, together with an accurate description of each animal slaughtered (giving all brands, ear-marks, wattles, age, sex, and class, as to whether American, half-breed, or Texan), to the justice of the peace by whom they were summoned, who shall, after entering the same upon his record and making an endorsement upon each showing it to have been properly recorded, return it, together with the duplicate order of the Territorial veterinary surgeon, to the person or persons owning the animals slaughtered; and it shall be the duty of the Territorial veterinary surgeon to superintend the slaughter of such animals as may be condemned, and also the destruction of the carcasses, which latter shall be by burning to ashes or burying in the earth to a depth of not less than six feet, and shall include every part of the animal and hide, and also excrement, as far as possible. In case the owner of any animal found diseased by the Territorial veterinary surgeon shall kill the same or consent to its being killed by the Territorial veterinary surgeon, without appraisement, then the veterinary surgeon shall cause the same to be burned or buried as cheaply as practicable, as in the case of appraisement.

SEC. 6. The Territorial veterinary surgeon shall make a report at the end of every year to the Territorial board of stock commissioners of all matters connected with his work, and they shall make the same a part of their annual report to the governor, and they shall also transmit to the several boards of commissioners such parts of said reports as they may deem to be of general interest to the breeders of live stock. They shall also give information in writing as soon as they obtain it, to the governor and to the various boards of county commissioners, of each cause of suspicion or fresh conception of disease in each locality, the cause, if known, and the measure adopted to check it.

SEC. 7. Whenever the governor of the Territory shall have good reason to believe that any disease covered by this act has become epidemic in certain localities in another State or Territory, or that conditions exist which render domestic animals and Texas cattle liable to convey disease, he shall thereupon, by proclamation, schedule such localities, and prohibit the importation from them of any live stock of the kind diseased into this Territory, except under such restrictions as he, after consultation with the Territorial veterinary surgeon, may deem proper. Any corporation or any person or persons who, after the publication of such proclamations, shall knowingly receive in charge any such animal or animals from any one of said prohibited districts, and transport or convey the same within the limits of this Territory, shall be deemed guilty of a misdemeanor; and, upon conviction, be fined not less than one thousand dollars and not more than ten thousand dollars for each and every offense, and shall further become liable for any and all damages and loss that may be sustained by any person or persons by reason of the importation or transportation of such prohibited animals.

SEC. 8. It shall be the duty of any person or persons who shall have or suspect that there is upon his or their premises, or upon the public domain, any case of contagious or infectious disease among horses, mules, cattle, or asses, to immediately report the same to the Territorial veterinary surgeon, and a failure to do so, or any attempt to conceal the existence of such disease, or to willfully or maliciously obstruct or resist the said Territorial veterinary surgeon in the discharge of his duty as hereinbefore set forth, shall be deemed a misdemeanor, and any person or persons who shall be convicted of any one of the above acts or omissions shall be fined not less than fifty dollars, nor more than five hundred dollars, for each and every such offense, and shall forfeit all claims to indemity for loss from the Territory; and, upon conviction a second time, shall, in addition to the above-named fine, be imprisoned in the county jail for a term not less than thirty days nor more than six months.

SEC. 9. The following regulations shall be observed in cases of disease covered by this act:

disease; and in case of any animal that may be known to have been affected with or exposed to any such disease, within one year prior to such disposal, due notice of the fact shall be given in writing to the party receiving the animal.

(2) It shall be unlawful to kill for butcher purposes any such animal, to sell, give away, or use any part of it, or its milk, or to remove any part of the skin. A failure to observe these provisions shall be deemed a misdemeanor; and, on conviction, shall be punished by a fine not less than one hundred dollars nor exceeding five hundred dollars. It shall be the duty of the owner or person having in charge any animal affected with, or suspected of being affected with, any contagious or infectious disease, to immediately confine the same in a safe place, isolated from other animals, and with all necessary restrictions to prevent dissemination of the disease until the arrival of the Territorial veterinary surgeon. The above regulations shall apply as well to animals in transit through the Territory as to those resident therein; and the Territorial veterinary surgeon, or his duly authorized agent, shall have full authority to examine, whether in car, or yards, or pastures, or stables, or upon the public domain, all animals passing through the Territory or any part of it, and on detection or suspicion of disease to take possession of and treat and dispose of said animals in the said manner as is prescribed for animals resident in the Territory.

SEC. 10. All claims against the Territory arising from the slaughter of animals under the provisions of this act shall, together with the order of the Territorial veterinary surgeon, and the valuation of the appraisers in each case, be submitted to the Territorial auditor, who shall examine them without unnecessary delay, and for each one that he finds to be equitable and entitled to indemnity under this act, shall issue his warrant on the stock indemnity fund in the hands of the Territorial treasurer for the sum named in the appraiser's report to the person so entitled thereto. In auditing any claim under this act it shall be the duty of the auditor to satisfy himself that it does not come under any class of which indemnity is refused by this act, and he shall require the affidavit of the claimant to this fact, or if the claimant be not cognizant thereof, then some reputable person who is cognizant thereof; and also the certificate of the Territorial veterinary surgeon, whose duty it shall be to inform himself fully of the fact that in his opinion the claim is legal and just, and the auditor may, at his discretion, require further proof. The indemnity to be granted shall be two-thirds of the value of the animals, as determined by the appraisers, with reference to its diminished value because of its being diseased or having been exposed to disease.

It shall be paid to the owner upon his application and the presentation of the proofs prescribed herein, and it shall be the duty of said owner to make such application within six months after the slaughter of the animal for which payment is claimed, failing which, such claim shall be barred by limitation. These payments shall be made by the Territorial treasurer, as already provided, and from the fund provided by this act. The right to indemnity under this act is limited to animals destroyed by reason of the existence, or suspected existence, of some epizootic disease, generally fatal or incurable, such as rinderpest, hoof and mouth disease, pleuro-pneumonia, anthrax, or Texas fever among bovines, and glanders among horses, mules, and asses.

For the ordinary contagious diseases, not in their nature fatal, such as epizootic, influenza in horses, no indemnity shall be paid.

The right to indemnify does not exist, and the payment of such shall not be made in the following cases:

(1) For animals belonging to the United States.

(2) For animals that are brought into the Territory contrary to the provisions of this act.

(3) For animals that are found to be diseased, or that are destroyed because they have been exposed to disease, before or at the time of their arrival in the Territory.

(4) When an animal was previously affected by any other disease, which from its nature and development was incurable and necessarily fatal.

(5) When an owner or person in charge shall have knowingly or negligently omitted to comply with the provisions of sections 8 and 9 of this act.

(6) When an owner or claimant at the time of coming into possession of the animal knew it be diseased, or received the notice specified in the first clause of section 9 of this act.

(7) When the animal or animals have been brought into the Territory within ninety days immediately preceding the outbreak of disease among or upon them.

SEC. 11. The Territorial veterinary surgeon shall receive for his services the sum of three thousand dollars per annum, together with his actual and necessary traveling expenses when in the performance of his duty, and the actual cost of office rent and stationery. These payments shall be made from the funds in the Territorial treasury, upon vouchers signed and sworn to by him and submitted to the

Territorial auditor, who shall draw warrants upon the Territorial treasurer for the amounts found correct, separate vouchers being made for salary and expenses. No person shall be competent under this act to receive the appointment of Territorial veterinary surgeon who is not, at the date of his appointment, a graduate in good standing of a recognized college of veterinary surgeons, either in the United States, Canada, or Europe. He shall hold his office for two years. He may be removed for cause by the governor, who shall also have power to fill the vacancy, as hereinafter provided. The appraisers herein provided for shall each receive three dollars for each day or a part of a day they may be actually employed as such, which shall be paid from the Territorial treasury out of the stock indemnity fund hereinafter provided, upon vouchers which bear the certificate of the justice who summoned them. The justice shall receive his ordinary fee for issuing a summons, to be paid out of the county fund. The members of the board of health, veterinarians, physicians, or stock-owners, called in consultation by the Territorial veterinary surgeon, shall each receive three dollars for each day or part of a day they may be actually employed, and ten cents per mile mileage for distances actually traveled, which sum shall be paid from the Territorial treasury out of the stock indemnity fund hereinafter provided for, upon vouchers certified to by the Territorial veterinary surgeon, and other incidental expenses connected with this work and made his duty by this act, such as causing animals to be slaughtered and their carcasses to be burned and disinfecting infected premises, shall be paid from the Territorial treasury out of the stock-indemnity fund, hereinafter provided for, upon vouchers certified to by him. Before entering upon the discharge of his duties he shall give good and sufficient surety in the sum of five thousand dollars for the proper management of the same. No constructive mileage shall be paid under this act, nor shall the Territorial veterinary surgeon receive any mileage.

SEC. 12. The liability of the Territory for indemnity for animals destroyed, and for fees, costs, and expenses incurred, under the provisions of this act in any year, is limited by, and shall in no case exceed, the amount especially designated for that purpose and for that period, by the terms of this act; nor shall the veterinary surgeon or any one else incur any liability on [the] part of the Territory, under the provisions of this act, in excess of the surplus in the stock indemnity fund hereinafter provided; nor shall any act be performed or property taken under the provisions of this act that will become a charge against the Territory of Montana, further than to the extent provided by said stock indemnity fund.

SEC. 13. Hereafter it shall be the duty each year of the county commissioners of all the counties of the Territory, at the time of making the annual assessment, to levy a special tax not exceeding one-half (½) of one (1) mill on the dollar upon the assessed value of all cattle, horses, mules, and asses in the Territory to be known as the "stock indemnity fund;" said tax shall be levied and collected by the several counties and paid to the Territorial treasurer, in the manner provided by law for the levying, collection, and payment of other Territorial taxes; said fund shall constitute the indemnity fund specified by this act to be used in paying for animals destroyed, and for fees, costs, and expenses provided under the provisions therefor. It shall be used exclusively for that purpose and shall be paid out by the Territorial treasurer as herein provided for.

SEC. 14. The Territorial veterinary surgeon shall select the place or places where the stock shall be quarantined.

SEC. 15. All fines collected under the provisions of this act shall be paid into the stock indemnity fund of the Territory.

SEC. 16. It shall be the duty of the county commissioners of all the counties in the Territory, at their next regular meeting after the passage of this act, to levy the special tax for the year eighteen hundred and eighty-five (1885) of one-half mill, as hereinbefore provided, which shall be collected and paid into the Territorial treasury in the same manner as other Territorial taxes: *Provided*, Where any person owns not exceeding five hundred dollars in value of horses, cattle, or mules, the same shall be exempt from taxation under the provisions of this act.

SEC. 17. Section 13 of the fifth division of the revised statutes of Montana, and all other acts and parts of acts, in conflict with the provisions of this act, be, and the same are hereby, repealed.

SEC. 18. The Territorial veterinary surgeon shall have the power to appoint, from time to time, deputies, not exceeding four in number, at any time he can not personally attend to all the duties required by his office, at a salary not to exceed five dollars per day for each day actually employed, to be paid out of said stock indemnity fund, and shall designate the county or counties for which each deputy is to act. All acts performed by such deputies shall have the same effect as if done by the Territorial veterinary surgeon.

lic highway, or upon the ranges of any other sheep, or within two miles of any sheep corral occupied by any other sheep; and any person failing to comply with the provisions of this act shall be deemed guilty of a misdemeanor, and upon conviction shall be fined not less than fifty dollars for each offense and shall be liable for any damage or loss that may be sustained by reason of the failure to comply with the provisions of this section.

SEC. 2. Hereafter it shall be the duty each year of the county commissioners of the several counties of this Territory to levy a special tax, not exceeding one-half a mill on the dollar, or so much thereof as may be necessary on the assessed valuation of all the sheep in their counties, to be known as a sheep inspector and indemnity fund. Said tax shall be levied and collected by the several counties and paid to the Territorial treasurer in the same manner as is provided by law for the levy and collection of other taxes. Such fund shall constitute the sheep inspector and indemnity fund to be used in the payment of the salaries and expenses of such skilled assistants as the veterinary surgeon may employ, as provided for in section nine of this act, and all other expenditures arising from the provisions of this act, except the pay of the veterinary surgeon.

SEC. 3. Upon receipt of information in writing over the signature of the president or secretary and not less than two members of the executive committee of any regularly organized Territorial, district, or county wool growers' association that any sheep are infected with scab or infectious diseases, such notice shall be prima facie evidence that such disease exists, and the Territorial veterinary surgeon or his deputy shall immediately cause the diseased sheep and all sheep running in the same flock with them to be examined, and if found so diseased to be quarantined and held within a certain limit or place to be defined by him, and such sheep shall be held in quarantine until the owner or person in charge shall have eradicated such scab or infectious diseases effectually. The expense of feeding, holding, clipping, and taking care of all sheep quarantined under the provisions of this act shall be paid by the owner, agent, or person in charge of said sheep.

SEC. 4. It shall be the duty of the veterinary surgeon or his deputy to inspect all sheep of which he may receive notice as provided in section three of this act, and in case the same be not diseased he shall make a certificate stating such fact. But if the sheep are diseased the regulations for their quarantine and keeping shall at once be made.

SEC. 5. In no case shall any sheep held in quarantine be moved or transferred, until the disease shall have been thoroughly eradicated, and a certificate made by the veterinary surgeon stating that he has examined said sheep and that the same are free from scab or infectious diseases: *Provided*, Such sheep may be transferred and removed with the written consent of all sheep owners or managers along the route and in the vicinity of the proposed location; any person violating the provisions of this section shall be deemed guilty of a misdemeanor, and, upon conviction, shall be fined not less than two hundred dollars, nor more than five hundred dollars for each and every offense.

SEC. 6. Whenever the governor of the Territory shall have good reason to believe that any disease covered by this act has become epidemic in certain localities in any other State or Territory, or that conditions exist which render sheep liable to convey disease, he shall thereupon, by proclamation, schedule such localities and prohibit the importation from them of any sheep into this Territory, except under such restrictions as he, after consultation with the Territorial veterinary surgeon, may deem proper. Any corporation, person, or persons, who, after the publication of such proclamation, shall knowingly receive in charge any such sheep from any one of the said prohibited districts and transport or convey the same within the limits of this Territory, shall be deemed guilty of a misdemeanor, and, upon conviction, be fined not less than five hundred dollars and not more than ten thousand dollars for each and every offense, and shall further become liable for any and all damages and loss that may be sustained by any person or persons by reason of the importation or transportation of such prohibited sheep.

SEC. 7. It shall be the duty of any person or persons who shall have or suspect that there is, upon his or their premises, or upon the public domain in their vicinity, any cases of scab, contagious or infectious diseases among sheep, to immediately report the same to the Territorial veterinary surgeon, and any failure to do so or any attempt to conceal the existence of such scab or infectious disease, or wilfully or maliciously obstruct or resist the veterinary surgeon in the discharge of his duty, as hereinbefore set forth, shall be deemed guilty of a misdemeanor, and any person or persons who shall be convicted of so obstructing or resisting said veterinarian shall be fined not less than twenty-five dollars nor more than five hundred dollars for each offense.

case is alleged to exist and make a careful examination of the animals believed to be affected with any such disease, and ascertain, if possible, what, if any, disease exists among the live stock reported to be affected and whether the same is contagious or infectious or not; and if such disease is found to be of a malignant, contagious, or infectious character, he shall direct the temporary quarantine and sanitary regulations necessary to prevent the spread of any such disease and report his finding and actions to the live-stock agents.

SEC. 6. Upon the receipt by any one of the report of the veterinarian provided for in section one (1) of this act, if said agent shall be of the opinion that the exigencies of the case require, he shall immediately convene the three live stock agents together with the veterinarian at such place as he may designate, and if, upon consideration of the report of the veterinarian, the agents shall be satisfied that any contagious or infectious disease exists of a malignant character which seriously threatens the health of domestic animals, they shall proceed at once to the infected district, ascertain and determine the premises or grounds infected, and establish the quarantine, sanitary, and police regulations necessary to circumscribe and exterminate such disease; also to list and describe the domestic animals affected with such disease, and those which have been exposed thereto, and included within the infected district or premises so defined and quarantined with such reasonable certainty as would lead to their identification, and for that purpose the said agents may, in their discretion, cause the live stock so included within the quarantine lines established to be marked or branded in such manner as they may designate; and no domestic animals liable to become infected with the disease or capable of communicating the same, shall be permitted to enter or leave the district, premises, or grounds so quarantined, except by authority of the live-stock agents. The said agents shall also from time to time give and enforce such directions and prescribe such rules and regulations as to separating, mode of handling, treating, feeding, and caring for such diseased and exposed animals as it shall deem necessary to prevent the two classes of animals from coming in contact with each other, and perfectly isolate them from any other domestic animals which have not been exposed thereto and which are susceptible of becoming infected with the disease. And the said agents or any of the members thereof and said veterinarian are hereby authorized, and empowered to enter upon any grounds or premises to carry out the provisions of this act.

SEC. 7. When, in the opinion of the live-stock agents, it shall be necessary to prevent the further spread of any contagious or infectious disease among the live stock of the State, to destroy animals affected with or which have been exposed to any such disease, it shall determine what animal shall be killed, and appraise the same as hereinafter provided, and cause the same to be killed and the carcasses disposed of as, in its judgment, will best protect the health of the domestic animals of the locality.

SEC. 8. Whenever, as in the seventh section of this act provided, the live-stock agents shall direct the killing of any domestic animal or animals, it shall be the duty of the agents to make a fair and faithful appraisement of said animal or animals, and in making the appraisement the contagious disease with which the animal is affected, or to which they have been exposed, shall not be taken into consideration. The amount of the appraisement shall in no case exceed seventy-five dollars ($75) per head for horses and mules, and twenty dollars ($20) per head for cattle: *Provided*, That no animal or animals shall be appraised except those affected with contagious or infectious diseases of a malignant character or such as have been exposed thereto.

SEC. 9. When the agents shall have determined the quarantine and other regulations necessary to prevent the spread among domestic animals of any malignant, contagious, or infectious disease found to exist among the live stock of the State, and given its orders as hereinafter provided, prescribing quarantine and other regulations, they shall notify the governor thereof, who shall issue his proclamation proclaiming the boundary of such quarantine, and the orders, rules, regulations prescribed by the live-stock agents, which proclamation may be published in [illegible] or printed hand bills, posted within the boundaries or on the lines of the district, premises, places, or grounds quarantined: *Provided*, That if the agents decide that it is not necessary by reason of the limited extent of the district in which the disease exists that a proclamation should be issued, then none shall be issued, but the agents shall give such notice as may to them seem best to make the [illegible] established by them effective.

SEC. 10. The agents provided for in this act shall have power to employ, at the expense of the State, such persons and purchase such supplies and material as may be necessary to carry into effect all orders by them given as hereinbefore provided, [illegible] whatsoever shall be employed, nor labor, material, or expense [illegible]

a misdemeanor, and upon conviction thereof shall be fined in any sum not less than one hundred dollars ($100.00) nor more than five hundred dollars ($500.00).

Sec. 17. Any person who shall have in his possession any domestic animal affected with any contagious or infectious disease, knowing such animal to be so affected, or after having received notice that such animal is so affected, who shall permit such animal to run at large, or who shall keep such animal where other domestic animals not affected by or previously exposed to such disease may be exposed to its contagion or infection, or who shall sell, ship, drive, trade, or give away such diseased animal or animals which have been exposed to such infection or contagion, or who shall move or drive away any domestic animal in violation of any direction, rule, regulation, or order establishing and regulating quarantine, shall be deemed guilty of a misdemeanor, and upon conviction thereof shall be fined in any sum not less than one hundred dollars ($100.00) nor more than five hundred dollars ($500.00) for each of such diseased or exposed domestic animals which he shall permit to run at large, or keep or sell, drive, trade or give away, in violation of the provisions of this act: *Provided*, That any owner of any domestic animal which has been affected with or exposed to any contagious or infectious disease may dispose of the same, after having obtained from the veterinarian a bill of health for such animal.

Sec. 18. When any live stock shall be appraised and killed by order of the live-stock agents they shall issue to the owner of the live stock so killed a certificate showing the number and kind and general description of animals killed, and the amount to which holder is entitled, and report the same to the auditor of state, and upon presentation of such certificate to the auditor he shall draw his warrant on the treasurer for the amount therein stated, payable out of any money appropriated for the live-stock indemnity fund.

Sec. 19. Whenever the governor of the State shall have good reason to believe that any dangerous, contagious, or infectious disease has become epizootic in certain localities in other States or Territories or counties, or that there are conditions which render such domestic animals from such infested districts liable to convey such disease, he shall, by proclamation, prohibit the transportation of any live stock of the kind diseased into the State, except under such rules and regulations as may from time to time be prescribed by the live-stock agents. And all such animals arriving in this State shall be examined without delay by the veterinary surgeon or the live-stock agents.

Sec. 20. The owners of any public stock-yards doing business in this State, when requested by the live-stock agents, shall appoint, and keep constantly in their employ, at their expense, a competent inspector of live stock, whose duty it shall be to daily inspect with care all animals brought into the stock-yards in whose employ any such inspector may be; under such rules and regulations as may from time to time be prescribed by the live-stock agents, and upon discharge by such inspector, in such yards, of any animals affected with any malignant, contagious, or infectious disease, he shall direct the manner in which any such diseased animals shall be disposed of so as to prevent the spread of any such contagious or infectious disease, and for this purpose may cause any such diseased animals to be killed and the carcasses to be disposed of at the expense of the owner thereof; but in no event shall any such diseased stock be permitted to be driven or shipped out of any such stock-yards except to some rendering establishment or other suitable place for killing or disposing of such diseased animal, as hereinbefore provided for, and then under such regulations and restrictions as may be necessary to prevent the spread of the disease on account of which any such animals have been condemned: *Provided*, That the owner of any animal or animals, ordered to be destroyed by any inspector, shall have the right to appeal from any decision of such inspector to the veterinarian or live-stock agents, and during the pendency of such appeal the condemned animal shall be kept in strict quarantine unless the veterinarian shall decide such stock is not so diseased, then said expense shall be paid by the owner of such stock-yards: *And provided further*, That no compensation shall be made by the State to the owners of diseased live stock found in public stock-yards and destroyed as herein provided. The inspector of live stock in any public stock-yards in this State shall, on demand of the owner of any live stock passing through any such stock-yards, furnish to said owner a bill of health for any live stock by him inspected, as hereinbefore required, and found to be healthy.

Sec. 21. The live-stock agents or veterinarian shall have the power to call upon any sheriff, under sheriff, deputy sheriff, or constable, to execute their orders, and such officers shall obey the orders of said agents or veterinarian, and the officers performing such duties as provided for by this act shall receive compensation therefor, prescribed by law for like services, to be paid as other expenses of said commission as hereinbefore provided, and any officer may arrest without a warrant, and take before any magistrate of the county, any person found violati[ng the pro]visions of this act, and such officers shall immediately notify the [county attorney] of such arrest, and he shall prosecute the person so offending according[ly].

SEC. 22. Except as otherwise provided in this act, any person who [shall violate,] disregard, or evade, or attempt to violate, disregard, or evade any of the [provisions] of this act, or who shall violate, disregard, or evade any of the rules, r[egulations,] orders, directions of the live-stock agents establishing and governing [quarantine,] shall be deemed guilty of a misdemeanor, and, upon conviction thereof, [shall be] fined in any sum not less than one hundred nor more than five thousand [dollars].

SEC. 23. There shall be levied and assessed upon the assessed value of [all] property in the State in each year one-fourth (¼) of one (1) mill on each dollar thereof, to be known as the live-stock indemnity fund tax. Said [tax shall be] assessed and collected in the same manner and at the same time as is [or may] be, prescribed by law for the assessment and collection of State revenue.

SEC. 24. It shall be the duty of the county treasurers of the several [counties to] preserve the fund thus provided for as a separate fund, and to transmit [the same,] as is now required by law, to the State treasurer, who shall keep the sam[e as a fund] to be known as the live-stock indemnity fund.

SEC. 25. For the purpose of this act, each one of the live-stock agent[s and the State] veterinarian is hereby authorized and empowered to administer oaths a[nd affirma]tions.

SEC. 26. That the live-stock agents be authorized and directed to co-op[erate with] the Commissioner of Agriculture of the United States, or any officer o[r agent] of the General Government, in the suppression and extirpation of any a[nd all con]tagious diseases among domestic animals, and in the enforcement and e[xecution of] any and all acts of Congress to prevent the importation or exportation [of diseased] cattle and the spread of infectious or contagious diseases among domesti[c animals].

SEC. 27. The liability of the State for carrying out the provisions of [this act for] any two years is limited by, and shall in no case exceed, the amount ap[pro]propriated for that purpose and that period.

SEC. 28. All acts and parts of acts inconsistent with this act are hereby [repealed].

SEC. 29. Whereas an emergency exists, this act shall take effect and [be in force] from and after its passage.

NEVADA.

AN ACT to prevent the importation or selling of any domestic animal or animals affec[ted with any] infectious or contagious disease.

SECTION 1. *The people of the State of Nevada, represented in senate and [assembly,] do enact as follows:* It shall not be lawful for the owner or owners of an[y domestic] animal or animals, or any person having them in charge, to knowingly [import or] drive into this State, or into any county within this State, any animal [or animals] having any infectious or contagious disease, and any person or persons so [offending] shall be deemed guilty of a misdemeanor, and on conviction thereof sha[ll be pun]ished by a fine of not less than five dollars nor more than fifty dollars, [or by im]prisonment in the county jail not less than ten days nor more than [fifty] days, or by both such fine and imprisonment, for each and every suc[h diseased] animal so imported or driven into this State, or into any county within [this State].

SEC. 2. Any person who shall sell or dispose of any domestic animal [knowing] the same to be affected with any infectious or contagious disease, withou[t dis]closing the fact to the purchaser, shall be deemed guilty of a misdemean[or, and on] conviction thereof shall be punished by a fine of not less than twenty d[ollars nor] more than one hundred dollars, or by imprisonment in the county jail no[t less than] ten days nor more than fifty days, or by both such fine and imprisonmen[t].

SEC. 3. Any person or persons violating any of the provisions of this [act, in ad]dition to the penalties herein provided, shall be liable for all damages [that may] accrue to the party damaged by reason of said diseased animal or animal[s driven] or imported by said person or persons into this State, or into any cou[nty of the] same, imparting to any domestic animal or animals therein any such [contagious] or infectious disease.

Approved, ——, 1887.

AN ACT to protect the live stock of this State from disease, and providing a penalty f[or] allowing diseased stock to run at large upon the public lands.

SECTION 1. *The people of the State of Nevada, represented in senate and [assembly,] do enact as follows:* It shall be unlawful to drive any horse infected wit[h glanders] or pink-eye; any sheep infected with scab or foot-rot; any neat cattle inf[ected]

Spanish, Texas, or splenic fever, or with pleuro-pneumonia; any hog infected with cholera or trichina, or any of said animals that are infected with, or that have been exposed to, any of the above diseases whatever, along any highway or traveled road in this State.

SEC. 2. The owner of any animal or animals so infected or diseased, as mentioned in section one of this act, or that have been exposed to any contagious disease, and the person or persons in charge thereof, shall keep such animal or animals safely enclosed or securely herded upon lands owned by or held in actual possession by them under the laws of this State by the owner or person in charge of such animal or animals.

SEC. 3. Every person who may violate either of the preceding sections of this act shall be deemed guilty of a misdemeanor, and upon conviction thereof, shall be punished therefor by a fine not less than thirty nor exceeding five hundred dollars, or by imprisonment in the county jail for a term not exceeding six months, or by both such fine and imprisonment, in the discretion of the court, and the owner or owners of any animal or animals injured or damaged by any act or omission, in violation of the provisions of this act, shall be entitled to recover treble the amount of damages sustained from the owner or owners of the diseased live stock from which the contagion came.

Approved, ———, 1887.

NEW JERSEY.

AN ACT concerning contagious and infectious diseases among animals, and to repeal certain acts relating thereto.

1. *Be it enacted by the senate and general assembly of the State of New Jersey*, That in case any contagious or infectious disease shall appear or be suspected to exist in any locality in this State, it shall be the duty of all persons owning or having any interest in animals infected or supposed to be infected, and of any person having knowledge or suspicion thereof, at once to notify the State board of health, or some officer or member of said board, of the facts, and it shall be the duty of the said board, upon receiving such information, or any information in regard thereto, to investigate the same, or cause the same to be investigated, and if any such disease is found to exist, or likely to break out, to quarantine such animal or animals, and to take such precautionary measures with relation to other animals exposed to such disease as shall be deemed necessary, and to enforce such regulations in relation to such diseases as the said board may adopt.

2. *And be it enacted*, That whenever, in the judgment of the said board, its agents or appointees, it shall appear that such disease is not likely to yield to remedial treatment, or that the expense of such treatment will be greater than the value of the animal or animals infected; and when in any case such disease is likely, in the judgment of said board, its agents or appointees, to be communicated to other animals, they shall cause the animals infected to be immediately slaughtered, their remains to be buried at least four feet beneath the surface of the ground, and all places in which the same have been kept to be thoroughly cleansed and disinfected.

3. *And be it enacted*, That when any animal or animals shall be slaughtered as directed in the preceding section, the value of the same may, at the request of said board or any person interested, be ascertained and appraised by three disinterested freeholders resident in this State, who shall make and sign a certificate thereof, in the presence of a witness who shall attest the same; such appraisement shall be made on the basis of the market value of the animal or animals slaughtered, just prior to the time when they became so diseased, and shall be limited to the sum of one hundred dollars for registered animals, and to forty dollars for all others; one-half of the valuation so ascertained shall be paid by the State on the presentation of such certificate, with the approval of the said board indorsed thereon, to the owner or owners.

4. *And be it enacted*, That when any herd or portion thereof has been or is so exposed to any contagious or infectious disease, and the State board of health deem the disease likely to spread to that portion of the herd still unaffected, although isolated or quarantined, said herd may, with the consent of the owner or owners, and with the restrictions agreed upon between them and the executive officer of the State board of health, cause or allow said herd or herds to be inoculated for the prevention of such diseases as can be thus mitigated; but any loss resulting from such inoculations shall not constitute any claim against the State or the board of health: *Provided*, That inoculation for pleuro-pneumonia shall in no case be allowed without the consent and approval of the State board of health, and shall be made under its direction.

5. *And be it enacted*, That when any city, township, or district shall be threatened with any contagious or infectious disease among animals to such an extent as

SEC. 2. A sanitary board, consisting of three practical cattle raisers and owners, one to be appointed in and for each judicial district of the Territory of New Mexico, according to the territorial limits of each as now constituted, hereby is created, to be known as the cattle sanitary board of New Mexico.

The term of office of each member of said board shall be two years from and after his appointment and until his successor shall have been appointed and qualified.

Each member of said board shall be nominated by the governor of the Territory, and appointed by and with the advice and consent of the legislative council.

In case of any vacancy in the membership of said board, from death, resignation, or otherwise, the governor shall fill such vacancy by appointment, and the appointee shall hold such office only during the unexpired term of the office so becoming vacant.

SEC. 3. A majority of the members of said sanitary board shall constitute a quorum, authorized to transact all business properly coming before them under the provisions of this act.

SEC. 4. Said sanitary board is hereby authorized and required to adopt and publish such quarantine rules and regulations as may be necessary to carry into effect the provisions of this act relating thereto and not inconsistent therewith, for the purpose of preventing the introduction into said Territory or the spreading therein of Texas fever, contagious pleuro-pneumonia, or any other contagious or infectious disease affecting cattle.

SEC. 5. It shall be the duty of said board, and they are hereby authorized, to employ some competent veterinary surgeon, who shall be a graduate in good standing in some recognized college of veterinary surgery and science, and when necessary, to bring him to their aid for the inspection of live cattle having, or suspected of having some infectious or contagious disease, or for the examination of any cattle that shall have died, or shall be suspected of having died, of some such disease, as well as for consultation as to the most practical and effective method of stamping out or preventing the spread of any such disease among cattle within said Territory, and for the performance of any other service within the line of their duties, or of his profession, as said board shall determine, and when and where they shall direct.

The said board shall fix the compensation to be paid to said veterinary surgeon at a salary not to exceed the rate of two thousand five hundred dollars per annum, and his actual and necessary traveling expenses in the performance of his duties. Such compensation shall be paid by said board out of the fund hereinafter provided for and at such time as shall be specified in their contract therefor with said veterinary surgeon.

SEC. 6. It shall be the duty of said board to provide suitable books in which they shall cause to be entered true and itemized accounts of all receipts and expenditures of money by them or under their direction, and specifying what for; also an entry therein of the number of all cattle (if any) imported into the Territory, in violation of any of the provisions of this act, so far as the same shall come under their supervision or to their knowledge. And to this end, said board may require said veterinarian to act as its secretary and make the proper entries in said books and to write out the reports, required as hereinafter provided. Said books and all entries therein shall constitute a public record, and at all reasonable times shall be open for examination by any and all parties interested.

SEC. 7. It is and shall be unlawful for any person, persons, company, or corporation, to drive, convey, transport, or aid therein, or to cause or procure to be driven conveyed or transported into the Territory of New Mexico, any cattle from any part of the State of Texas, south and east of a line commencing at the northwest corner of the county of Wichita; thence running due south along the western lines of Wichita and Archer Counties to the northeastern corner of Throckmorton County; thence due west to the northwest corner of said county; thence due south to the southwest corner of Throckmorton County; thence due west to the northwest corner of Shackelford County; thence due south to the southwest corner of said county; thence due west to the northwest corner of Taylor County, thence along the north lines of Nolan and Mitchell Counties to the northwest corner of said Mitchell County; thence due south to the southwest corner of said Mitchell County; thence due west along the south lines of counties ...

State of Texas, and all the counties east and south of the counties hereinbefore mentioned, and situated in the aforesaid State of Texas, during any time in each year between the first day of March and the first day of November.

This section is designed to operate only as a quarantine regulation against the introduction of Texas fever, and shall not be operative against any railroad company or corporation in transporting cattle from the aforesaid prohibited district in the State of Texas, entirely through and beyond the limits of this Territory by rail: *Provided*, Such cattle are not unloaded while in transit through the Territory, except into secure quarantine stock-yards provided by such company or corporation, and used exclusively for that purpose: *And provided further*, That during such transit through the Territory, while such prohibition is in force, such cattle shall be so securely confined that none of them shall get loose, either from the cars or from any such quarantine stock-yards, and go upon the ground outside thereof.

SEC. 8. Whenever it shall come to the knowledge of the said board, or of said veterinarian, that any contagious or infectious disease, other than Texas fever, covered by this act, and the nature of which is known to be fatal to cattle, has become epidemic, or exists in any locality or localities, in any State or Territory beyond the limits of this Territory, they, or either of them, shall immediately communicate the fact to the governor of the Territory, in writing, and thereupon, or when the governor shall otherwise have good reason to believe that any such fatal disease, other than Texas fever, so exists or has become epidemic, it shall be his duty immediately to issue and cause to be published his proclamation, specifying such localities, and thereby prohibit the importation therefrom into this Territory of any cattle, except under such restrictions and safeguards as he may deem proper and shall specify for the protection of cattle in this Territory.

Any person, persons, company, or corporation, who, after the publication of such proclamation, shall knowingly receive in charge any cattle the importation of which into this Territory shall have been so prohibited, or shall drive, transport, or in any manner convey the same to and within the limits of this Territory, or shall knowingly cause or procure the same to be driven, transported, or conveyed into such Territory, in violation of such proclamation, or shall violate any of the provisions of section seven of this act by driving, conveying, or transporting, or aiding therein, or causing or procuring to be driven, conveyed, or transported into this Territory, any cattle which is hereby declared to be unlawful, shall be deemed guilty of a misdemeanor, and upon conviction shall be fined not less than one hundred dollars nor more than five thousand dollars for each and every offense, and shall also become liable in a civil action for any and all damages and loss sustained by any person, persons, company, or corporation, by reason of such importation of such cattle.

SEC. 9. After the issuing and publication of such proclamation by the governor, as provided by this act, and while such proclamation shall continue in force, or while the prohibition against the importation of cattle from certain parts of Texas, as specified in section seven of this act, shall be in force, or either of them, it is and shall be unlawful for any person, persons, company, or corporation to drive or transport, or cause or procure to be driven or transported into this Territory any cattle that by any direct or circuitous route might have come from any place or district covered by such prohibitions, or either of them, without first having obtained a certificate of health from said veterinarian or a permit in writing from said board through any of its employés, under such rules and regulations as such board shall prescribe and publish for the information of the public. Any person failing to comply with this provision, after due notice, shall be deemed guilty of a misdemeanor, and upon conviction shall be fined not less than one hundred dollars nor more than five hundred dollars, and shall also be personally liable for all loss and damages sustained by any person or persons by reason of the introduction of any contagious or infectious disease from the cattle so unlawfully imported into this Territory.

SEC. 10. To aid in the enforcement of the quarantine provisions of this act for the necessary protection of cattle in this Territory, and in ferreting out and detecting any violations thereof, it shall be the duty of said board, and they are hereby authorized to employ for that service, in addition to said veterinarian, as many other competent and discreet persons from time to time as emergencies may arise, as in their judgment they shall deem necessary for the purpose; and shall fix their compensation, which shall not exceed three dollars per day each, while in actual service, and their actual and necessary expenses while in the performance of their duties, as may be agreed upon, and to direct them as to what duties they are to perform, as well as to when, where, and how such duties shall be performed. All such persons respectively so employed shall make true reports in writing to said board of their doings under such directions.

to seem to require more general precautions, the State board of health, the local board of health, and, with the advice and consent of the board of health, may for a time prohibit the bringing of any cattle into such city or district without inspection and a written permission, and may prohibit the running at large of animals in any township, if not already prohibited, for such time as the township board of health shall advise, and the State board of health may call upon local boards of health to discover and report contagious disease and aid in measures for its abatement and prevention.

6. *And be it enacted*, That when any animal or herd of animals is held in quarantine under authority given by the laws of this State to the State board, it shall not be lawful for the owner or keeper thereof to add any animal to said herd, by purchase or otherwise, without the written consent of said board, under penalty of being adjudged guilty of a misdemeanor and fined therefor in a sum not exceeding one hundred dollars.

7. *And be it enacted*, That any person or persons refusing or neglecting to notify said board of health, or any of them, of the existence of pleuro-pneumonia, rinderpest, or any other contagious or infectious disease among animals, shall be deemed and adjudged guilty of a misdemeanor, and upon conviction shall be punished by a fine of not more than two hundred dollars or by imprisonment not exceeding one year, or both, at the discretion of the court, and that if any person or persons shall knowingly buy or sell, or cause to be bought or sold, any animal or animals affected with the pleuro-pneumonia, rinderpest, or any other contagious or infectious disease, or that has been exposed to a contagious or infectious disease, or is a part of any herd or stock held in quarantine, all such person or persons shall be deemed and adjudged guilty of a misdemeanor, and upon conviction thereof shall be punished by a fine not exceeding two hundred dollars, or imprisonment not exceeding one year, or both, at the discretion of the court.

8. *And be it enacted*, That when, by reason of the locality of an infected animal or herd within a city, or by reason of frozen ground or extreme heat, in the judgment of the State board of health, or those acting under its authority, it is inexpedient or impossible to bury any such dead or slaughtered animals on the premises, the board may authorize the veterinarian acting for said board to slash or cut the flesh of the same, and, either under his direct oversight or that of the board of health or contractor for the disposal of dead carcasses, to give the same to the use of a bone-boiling or glue or other establishment for the disposal of dead animals, but in no case shall the same or any part thereof be disposed of as food, and any such disposal of the same shall make the party or parties guilty of a misdemeanor and punishable by a fine not to exceed one hundred dollars, or imprisonment in the county jail for a period not exceeding six months.

9. *And be it enacted*, That if, between the first day of October and the first day of May of any year a veterinarian, who has been regularly graduated in veterinary medicine, desires to make a post-mortem examination of any animal he has attended, or at the request of the owner of any animal that has died within the city limits, he may do so, if such examination is made within twenty hours of the death or slaughter of said animal; in every such case he shall notify the city scavenger or remover of carcasses of animals, of the hour of his examination, and such scavenger shall arrange to remove the carcass in not more than three hours from the beginning of said examination.

10. *And be it enacted*, That it shall be the duty of the State board of health to keep a full and complete record of all the proceedings under this act and report the same annually to the State board of agriculture, and such report shall be printed and form a part of the annual report of said board of agriculture.

11. *And be it enacted*, That the sum of two thousand dollars is hereby appropriated to the State board of health to defray the expenses of the board in the duties imposed by this act, and that the governor, secretary of state, and comptroller be and they are hereby authorized to determine what sum shall be allowed to said board or any member thereof for services in the performance and execution of the duties hereby imposed, but the amount allowed shall not exceed the sum of five hundred dollars in any one year.

12. *And be it enacted*, That if, on account of the prevalence of any contagious disease of animals, or the necessary guarding against the same, any greater expenditure shall seem to be required, the State board of health shall present the matter to the governor, the secretary of state, and the comptroller, who shall authorize such additional amount as they may think necessary, but in no case shall the whole amount thus authorized to be expended exceed five thousand dollars.

13. *And be it enacted*, That all bills for money expended under this act shall be audited by the comptroller of this State, and then submitted to the governor for approval, and after being thus audited and approved by the governor, shall be paid *by the State* treasurer upon warrant of the comptroller.

14. *And be it enacted*, That the following acts, to-wit: (1) A supplement to an act entitled "An act to establish a State board of health," approved March ninth, one thousand eight hundred and seventy-seven, which act was approved on the twelfth day of March, one thousand eight hundred and eighty; (2) A further supplement to an act entitled "A supplement to an act entitled 'An act to establish a State board of health,'" approved March ninth, one thousand eight hundred and seventy-seven, which supplement was approved March twelfth, one thousand eight hundred and eighty, which further supplement was approved on the twenty-third day of March, one thousand eight hundred and eighty-one; (3) A supplement to an act entitled "An act to establish a State board of health," approved March ninth, one thousand eight hundred and seventy-seven, which supplement was approved March twelfth, one thousand eight hundred and eighty, and also a supplement to the further supplement to said act, approved March twenty-third, one thousand eight hundred and eighty-one, which supplement was approved March seventeenth, one thousand eight hundred and eighty-two; (4) Supplement to an act entitled "An act to establish a board of health," approved March ninth, one thousand eight hundred and seventy-seven, and to supplements thereto relating to the contagious diseases of animals, which supplement was approved on March twenty-second, one thousand eight hundred and eighty-three; and all other acts and parts of acts, inconsistent with the provisions hereof, be, and the same are repealed, but any rights acquired under the said acts, or either of them, and any suits pending under the same shall not be affected by the repeal.

15. *And be it enacted*, That this act shall take effect immediately.

Approved May 4, 1886.

NEW MEXICO.

AN ACT to prevent the introduction of diseased cattle into the Territory of New Mexico and to prevent the dissemination of disease therein, and to repeal an act entitled "An act to prevent the introduction of diseased cattle into the Territory of New Mexico," approved March 19, 1884.

Whereas the fact has become well established that cattle imported into the Territory of New Mexico from ranges in any part of the State of Texas south and east of a line commencing at the northwest corner of the county of Wichita; thence running due south along the western line of Wichita and Archer Counties to the northeastern corner of Throckmorton County; thence due west to the northwest corner of said county; thence due south to the southwest corner of Throckmorton County; thence due west to the northwest corner of Shackelford County; thence due south to the southwest corner of said county; thence due west to the northwest corner of Taylor County; thence along the north line of Nolan and Mitchell Counties to the northwest corner of said Mitchell County, thence due south to the southwest corner of said Mitchell County; thence due west along the south lines of the counties of Howard, Martin, and Andrews to a point where the southeast corner of the Territory of New Mexico and the southwest corner of the county of Andrews, in the State of Texas, meet; thence due west along the south boundary line of the Territory of New Mexico to a point where the monuments marking the boundaries between the State of Texas, the Territory of New Mexico, and the State of Chihuahua, in the Republic of Mexico, and erected by the United States Boundary Commission, stand, and are in place, at the date of the enactment of this law; and more particularly the counties of El Paso, Presidio, Pecos, Tom Green, Crockett, Mitchell, Shackelford, Throckmorton, Archer, and Wichita, in the State of Texas, and all the counties east and south of the counties hereinbefore mentioned, and situated in the aforesaid State of Texas, at any time from the first day of March to the first day of November of each year, will communicate to and infect cattle then grazing or living on ranges in said Territory upon or through which such imported cattle shall then stray or be driven, with a certain fatal disease, commonly called and known as Texas fever;

And whereas the fact has also become well established that such imported cattle, while aforesaid communicating such Texas fever, never show any symptoms of the disease from which the same may be determined by an inspection thereof;

And whereas certain other contagious and infectious diseases, and particularly contagious pleuro-pneumonia, have been and are existing and epidemic among cattle in certain localities within the United States and beyond the limits of said territory: Therefore, for sanitary purposes only:

Be it enacted by the legislative assembly of the Territory of New Mexico: The word "cattle" used in the preamble of this act, and whenever used in any of the sections or provisions of such act, shall be understood and construed as bovine animals only, and shall not relate to nor include any other kind of domestic animals.

SEC. 2. A sanitary board, consisting of three practical cattle raisers, one to be appointed in and for each judicial district of the Territory of New according to the territorial limits of each as now constituted, hereby is cr be known as the cattle sanitary board of New Mexico.

The term of office of each member of said board shall be two years from his appointment and until his successor shall have been appointed and qu

Each member of said board shall be nominated by the governor of the and appointed by and with the advice and consent of the legislative coun

In case of any vacancy in the membership of said board, from death, res or otherwise, the governor shall fill such vacancy by appointment, and the shall hold such office only during the unexpired term of the office so vacant.

SEC. 3. A majority of the members of said sanitary board shall constitute authorized to transact all business properly coming before them under the p of this act.

SEC. 4. Said sanitary board is hereby authorized and required to adopt lish such quarantine rules and regulations as may be necessary to carry the provisions of this act relating thereto and not inconsistent therewith, purpose of preventing the introduction into said Territory or the spreading of Texas fever, contagious pleuro-pneumonia, or any other contagious or disease affecting cattle.

SEC. 5. It shall be the duty of said board, and they are hereby authorized, some competent veterinary surgeon, who shall be a graduate in good some recognized college of veterinary surgery and science, and when nece bring him to their aid for the inspection of live cattle having, or suspected o some infectious or contagious disease, or for the examination of any cattle have died, or shall be suspected of having died, of some such disease, as w consultation as to the most practical and effective method of stamping o venting the spread of any such disease among cattle within said Territory, the performance of any other service within the line of their duties, or o fession, as said board shall determine, and when and where they shall direc

The said board shall fix the compensation to be paid to said veterinary a salary not to exceed the rate of two thousand five hundred dollars pe and his actual and necessary traveling expenses in the performance of his

Such compensation shall be paid by said board out of the fund herein vided for and at such time as shall be specified in their contract therefor veterinary surgeon.

SEC. 6. It shall be the duty of said board to provide suitable books in w shall cause to be entered true and itemized accounts of all receipts and exp of money by them or under their direction, and specifying what for; also therein of the number of all cattle (if any) imported into the Territory, in vi any of the provisions of this act, so far as the same shall come under their or to their knowledge. And to this end, said board may require said veter act as its secretary and make the proper entries in said books and to wr reports, required as hereinafter provided. Said books and all entries the constitute a public record, and at all reasonable times shall be open for exa by any and all parties interested.

SEC. 7. It is and shall be unlawful for any person, persons, company, or tion, to drive, convey, transport, or aid therein, or to cause or procure to b conveyed or transported into the Territory of New Mexico, any cattle from of the State of Texas, south and east of a line commencing at the northw of the county of Wichita; thence running due south along the western Wichita and Archer Counties to the northeastern corner of Throckmorton thence due west to the northwest corner of said county; thence due sou southwest corner of Throckmorton County; thence due west to the northwe of Shackelford County; thence due south to the southwest corner of said thence due west to the northwest corner of Taylor County, thence along t lines of Nolan and Mitchell Counties to the northwest corner of said Mitchell thence due south to the southwest corner of said Mitchell County; thence along the south lines of counties of Howard, Martin, and Andrews to a poi the southeast corner of the Territory of New Mexico and the southwest c Andrews County, in the State of Texas, meet; thence due west along t boundary line of the Territory of New Mexico to a point where the mo marking the boundaries between the State of Texas, the State of Chihuahu Republic of Mexico, and the Territory of New Mexico, and erected by th States Boundary Commission, stand, and are in place at the date of the p of this law, and more particularly, the counties of El Paso, Presidio, Pe Green, Crockett, Mitchell, Shackelford, Throckmorton, Archer, and Wichi

State of Texas, and all the counties east and south of the counties hereinbefore mentioned, and situated in the aforesaid State of Texas, during any time in each year between the first day of March and the first day of November.

This section is designed to operate only as a quarantine regulation against the introduction of Texas fever, and shall not be operative against any railroad company or corporation in transporting cattle from the aforesaid prohibited district in the State of Texas, entirely through and beyond the limits of this Territory by rail: *Provided*, Such cattle are not unloaded while in transit through the Territory, except into secure quarantine stock-yards provided by such company or corporation, and used exclusively for that purpose: *And provided further*, That during such transit through the Territory, while such prohibition is in force, such cattle shall be so securely confined that none of them shall get loose, either from the cars or from any such quarantine stock-yards, and go upon the ground outside thereof.

SEC. 8. Whenever it shall come to the knowledge of the said board, or of said veterinarian, that any contagious or infectious disease, other than Texas fever, covered by this act, and the nature of which is known to be fatal to cattle, has become epidemic, or exists in any locality or localities, in any State or Territory beyond the limits of this Territory, they, or either of them, shall immediately communicate the fact to the governor of the Territory, in writing, and thereupon, or when the governor shall otherwise have good reason to believe that any such fatal disease, other than Texas fever, so exists or has become epidemic, it shall be his duty immediately to issue and cause to be published his proclamation, specifying such localities, and thereby prohibit the importation therefrom into this Territory of any cattle, except under such restrictions and safeguards as he may deem proper and shall specify for the protection of cattle in this Territory.

Any person, persons, company, or corporation, who, after the publication of such proclamation, shall knowingly receive in charge any cattle the importation of which into this Territory shall have been so prohibited, or shall drive, transport, or in any manner convey the same to and within the limits of this Territory, or shall knowingly cause or procure the same to be driven, transported, or conveyed into such Territory, in violation of such proclamation, or shall violate any of the provisions of section seven of this act by driving, conveying, or transporting, or aiding therein, or causing or procuring to be driven, conveyed, or transported into this Territory, any cattle which is hereby declared to be unlawful, shall be deemed guilty of a misdemeanor, and upon conviction shall be fined not less than one hundred dollars nor more than five thousand dollars for each and every offense, and shall also become liable in a civil action for any and all damages and loss sustained by any person, persons, company, or corporation, by reason of such importation of such cattle.

SEC. 9. After the issuing and publication of such proclamation by the governor, as provided by this act, and while such proclamation shall continue in force, or while the prohibition against the importation of cattle from certain parts of Texas, as specified in section seven of this act, shall be in force, or either of them, it is and shall be unlawful for any person, persons, company, or corporation to drive or transport, or cause or procure to be driven or transported into this Territory any cattle that by any direct or circuitous route might have come from any place or district covered by such prohibitions, or either of them, without first having obtained a certificate of health from said veterinarian or a permit in writing from said board through any of its employés, under such rules and regulations as such board shall prescribe and publish for the information of the public. Any person failing to comply with this provision, after due notice, shall be deemed guilty of a misdemeanor, and upon conviction shall be fined not less than one hundred dollars nor more than five hundred dollars, and shall also be personally liable for all loss and damages sustained by any person or persons by reason of the introduction of any contagious or infectious disease from the cattle so unlawfully imported into this Territory.

SEC. 10. To aid in the enforcement of the quarantine provisions of this act for the sanitary protection of cattle in this Territory, and in ferreting out and detecting any violations thereof, it shall be the duty of said board, and they are hereby authorized to employ for that service, in addition to said veterinarian, as many other competent and discreet persons from time to time as emergencies may arise, as in their judgment they shall deem necessary for the purpose; and shall fix their compensation, which shall not exceed three dollars per day each, while in actual service, and their actual and necessary expenses while in the performance of their duties, as may be agreed upon, and to direct them as to what duties they are to perform, as well as to when, where, and how such duties shall be performed. All such persons respectively so employed shall make true reports in writing to said board of their doings under such directions.

SEC. 11. Whenever said board, during the continuance in force of any against the importation into this Territory of cattle under any of the this act shall have good reasons to believe or suspect that any such cattle, importation of which such prohibition then exists, have been or, are driven, conveyed, or transported into this Territory, in violation of any tion then existing and in force, it shall be the duty of such board, either members or through said veterinarian, or through one or more of such in their employ, as provided by this act, or through any or either of cumstances shall seem to require, to thoroughly investigate the same, may examine under oath or affirmation any person or persons in charge cattle, or any other person or persons cognizant of any facts or circumstances rial to such investigation, as to any and all facts connected with the transportation of such cattle, including the place or places from which or any of them have been driven or transported; the places or districts which they or any of them have been driven or transported, the length where they or any of them have remained, fed, or grazed, at any designated district; to what contagious or infectious disease of cattle, if any, they them, have been exposed, and when and where; and as to any other facts stances material to such investigation, and reduce such testimony to w cases where the certificate of health or the permit in writing herein shall be refused. To this end the members of said board, said veterinarian other persons as aforesaid, so in the employ of said board, through whom investigation shall be made, hereby are, and each of them is, authorized ter all oaths and affirmations required in any such investigation. If such tion is made by such veterinarian and thereupon he is satisfied that such free from all contagious and infectious diseases specified in this act and w municate any such disease to any cattle in this Territory, he shall deliver son in charge of such cattle a certificate of health to the effect that such healthy and entitled to pass into the Territory, otherwise he shall refuse and if such investigation shall be made by any other person or persons as herein specified to make the same, and thereupon he or they shall be such cattle will not transmit to cattle in this Territory any cattle disease this act, and that the facts and circumstances attending their transport rant the presumption that such cattle are not from that part of the State the importation of cattle from which shall be then prohibited under the he or they shall give to the person in charge of such cattle a written permit the same into the Territory, otherwise such permit shall be refused.

SEC. 12. It shall be the duty of said board to make all useful rules and respecting examinations and investigations for the granting or refusing cates of health and permits, provided for in the next succeeding section and give ample publicity thereto, so that all persons, companies, and co who may desire to drive or transport any cattle into the Territory m veniently advised of what will be required to obtain any such certificate during the existence of any prohibition to the importation of cattle into tory under this act, and of when, where, and to whom applications there made.

SEC. 13. Every person, company, corporation, or their or either of their employés, having in charge cattle destined for introduction into this Ter ing the existence of any prohibition against such importation, under cattle, may make application for said certificate of health or permit to person designated at the place nearest to the proposed point of entrance Territory, specifying in such application the time and place—where and cattle will be ready for inspection and the circumstances of their impo vestigated, which place shall be beyond the boundary lines of the Territory application shall be made at least ten days before the time specified spection. Any person, company, or corporation, or their or either of having cattle in charge to be driven or transported into this Territory from in another State or Territory, may have such inspection and examination place before starting with such cattle if he shall so elect: *Provided*, He s expenses of such inspection and investigation, including per diem and tr penses of the person or officer making the same and designated for that said board.

SEC. 14. Whenever any cattle shall be driven or transported into the without obtaining a certificate of health or permit by the person in charge in any case where such certificate or permit is required by the provisions act, and if such cattle shall have been inspected and an investigation tion thereto and such certificate or permit refused as required by this act cattle may be seized and securely held in quarantine, under such reaso and regulations as shall be prescribed therefor by said board, and as said veterinarian may deem necessary to guard against other cattle becoming affected with any cattle disease covered by this act; and they shall be held in quarantine for such length of time as such veterinarian shall, in his opinion, deem necessary for the sanitary protection of cattle in this Territory. And if such cattle shall not have been so inspected and an investigation had, then the same shall take place wherever the cattle may be found, and they may be seized and held for that purpose and a certificate of health or permit granted or refused as the case may require; and if refused, the cattle may, in like manner, be held in quarantine. All the necessary expenses of quarantine and inspection under the provisions of this section shall be paid by the owner or owners of such cattle.

SEC. 15. All expenses incurred in and by the inspection and quarantine of cattle under the next preceding section (section 14) of this act shall be a lien on such cattle to secure the payment thereof in favor of said boards as an indemnity for expenses so incurred; and all loss and damages incurred and suffered by any person, company, or corporation, by reason of any cattle disease covered by this act, disseminated among or communicated to cattle in this Territory by cattle driven or transported into such Territory in violation of any of the provisions of this act, shall be a lien on the cattle so unlawfully imported in favor of the person, company, or corporation so incurring or suffering such loss or damages thereby. All liens covered by this section shall take precedence and priority over any other lien or incumbrance on any such cattle existing at the time of their unlawful importation as aforesaid, or at any time subsequent thereto. All such liens shall subsist and become effective as security for ultimate payment without any other act or proceeding whatever, and after judgment any such lien may be foreclosed by sale of the cattle on execution.

SEC. 16. In all cases of infectious or contagious disease among cattle in this Territory said board shall have authority to quarantine the infected premises if such disease shall become epidemic on such premises or is of such a nature as to be disseminated among cattle or become epidemic: *Provided*, Said veterinarian shall be of the opinion that such quarantine is necessary for the sanitary protection of other cattle liable to be exposed. Such quarantine shall be conducted in such manner as said veterinarian shall advise, and may include the preventing of any cattle among which such epidemic exists or from which such disease may be disseminated from being transferred from such premises without a certificate of health from such veterinarian to the effect that such cattle are healthy and will not disseminate such disease.

SEC. 17. In all cases of contagious or infectious disease covered by this act other than Texas fever, existing or becoming epidemic on premises previously quarantined as provided by this act, said board is authorized and empowered to cause the slaughter of cattle upon such premises which are known to be so diseased or have been exposed to such disease, when said veterinarian shall decide that the same is necessary for the sanitary protection of other cattle and shall so advise such board, and said board shall be of the same opinion and shall order such slaughter to be done: *Provided however*, That no such cattle shall be slaughtered that have no disease nor have been exposed to any disease except Texas fever. Such slaughter of cattle shall be done under the superintendence of said veterinarian, who, prior thereto, shall notify the nearest justice of the peace and deliver to him the order therefor. Such justice shall thereupon select and summon before him three cattle men of the neighborhood, who shall have no interest in the cattle to be slaughtered, to act as appraisers of the value of such cattle, and administer to each of them an oath to make a true, faithful, and impartial appraisement of the value of the cattle to be slaughtered, without prejudice against, or favor to, any one. Thereupon said appraisers shall inspect such cattle and make such appraisement thereof. They shall also return to each justice certificates of their valuation of each animal so appraised, containing an accurate description thereof, with brands, ear marks, wattles, age, sex, color, and class, as near as may be, one of such certificates to be filed with the justice, one to be delivered to the owner of the cattle to be slaughtered, and one to be transmitted to said board by said justice. The fees of justices of the peace for services as herein provided shall be the same as for similar services as fixed by law, and said appraisers and all the necessary employés for the slaughter of animals and destruction of their carcasses, as provided by this act, shall receive three dollars per day and their necessary expenses while engaged therein, all of which shall be paid by said board or upon their order. Such veterinary surgeon shall also superintend the destruction of the carcasses of each animal and every part thereof, which shall be by burning the same to ashes.

SEC. 18. In making such appraisement said appraisers shall consider the effect of the disease on the value of each animal, and the certificate of such veterinarian as

to the probable fatality of the same. All claims for indemnity to owners of cat
slaughtered as provided by this act shall be presented to said board and passed up
by said board, and allowed and paid upon its order to the extent of the apprais
value of the animals slaughtered, as herein provided, and owned by such claiman
Provided, Such animals are such as the slaughtering of which an indemnity is
lowed under this act and the proceedings in regard to such slaughter and apprai
ment have been regular. Such application shall be accompanied with the certi
cate of appraisement delivered to such owner.

SEC. 19. Owners of cattle appraised and slaughtered as herein provided shall
entitled to indemnity therefor to the extent of such appraised value, except in
following cases:

(1) For animals belonging to the United States.

(2) For cattle brought into the Territory in violation of any of the provisions
this act.

(3) For cattle that had the disease for which they were slaughtered or had
destroyed by reason of exposure to the disease at the time of their arrival into
Territory.

(4) For cattle which the owner or claimant knew to be diseased or had not
thereof at the time they came into his possession.

SEC. 20. The compensation of said veterinary surgeon and all other employés
or under said board, and, in the first instance, all other expenses incurred by
under said board, as provided by this act, shall be paid by said board or upon
order out of the funds hereinafter provided for, such board taking or causing
be taken proper vouchers for all moneys so expended by them.

SEC. 21. In the aggregate amount of money to be expended by said board in
one year they are hereby limited to the amount actually provided for that y
under this act, and at no time shall they incur expenses of any kind, except up
their own responsibility, unless they have sufficient funds on hand to fully pay
same and provided for the purpose under this act.

SEC. 22. Hereafter each year it shall be the duty of the county commissioners
each county in the Territory, at their first meeting after the return of the assessm
of property for taxation by the county assessors, respectively, to levy a special
of one-half (½) of one (1) mill on each dollar of the appraised value of all cattle
their county, to be known as the cattle-indemnity fund. Such special tax shall
collected in the several counties and paid to the Territorial treasurer in the man
provided by law for the collection and payment to such treasurer of other Terri
rial taxes. Such funds shall be kept separate by such treasurer, and shall be u
exclusively for the payment of indemnity claims for cattle that shall be slaughter
and of fees, salaries, wages, costs, and expenses, provided under the provisions
this act, and shall be paid out by such treasurer on the order of said board.
levying such special tax, however, all cattle of any owner, the appraised value
which does not exceed three hundred dollars, shall be exempt from such special t

SEC. 23. Said veterinary surgeon before entering upon the discharge of his du
shall make and subscribe an oath, before some officer authorized to administer oa
to well and impartially perform all professional duties assigned him; and each me
ber of said board before entering upon the discharge of his duties shall take
subscribe an oath to faithfully and impartially discharge his duties to the best of
ability, and execute a bond in the penal sum of five thousand dollars to the Te
tory of New Mexico, with two or more sufficient sureties, conditioned for the fa
ful and impartial performance of his duties as a member of said board. Such b
shall be approved by the governor, and each of said oaths and bonds shall be f
with the Territorial auditor.

SEC. 24. The members of said board shall receive no compensation, except
their actual and necessary expenses while in the performance of their duties,
for such expenses they may be re-imbursed out of said indemnity fund.

SEC. 25. It shall be the duty of such board, and they are hereby required, du
the first week in December of each year, to transmit to the governor a report
their doings under this act, containing a detailed account of all receipts and expe
tures of money by them, together with such other facts within the line of their du
as may be of public interest. And such report shall be transmitted by the gover
to the next succeeding legislative assembly.

SEC. 26. The act of the legislative assembly of the Territory of New Mexico
titled "An act to prevent the introduction of diseased cattle into the Territory
New Mexico," approved March 19, 1884, and all other laws and parts of laws in
flict with this act are hereby repealed.

SEC. 27. This act shall be in force and take effect from and after its passage.

NEW YORK.

AN ACT to co-operate with the United States in the suppression and extirpation of pleuro-pneumonia.

SECTION 1. *The people of the State of New York, represented in senate and assembly, do enact as follows:* The governor is hereby authorized to accept, on behalf of the State, the rules and regulations prepared by the Commissioner of Agriculture, under and in pursuance of section three of an act of Congress approved May twenty-nine, eighteen hundred and eighty-four, entitled "An act for the establishment of a Bureau of Animal Industry to prevent the exportation of diseased cattle and to provide means for the suppression and extirpation of pleuro-pneumonia and other contagious diseases among domestic animals," and to co-operate with the authorities of the United States in the enforcement of the provisions of said act.

SEC. 2. The Inspectors of the Bureau of Animal Industry of the United States shall have the right of inspection, quarantine, and condemnation of animals affected with any contagious, infectious, or communicable disease, or suspected to be so affected, or that have been exposed to any such disease, and for these purposes are hereby authorized and empowered to enter upon any grounds or premises. Said Inspectors shall have the power to call on sheriffs, constables, and peace officers to assist them in the discharge of their duties in carrying out the provisions of the act of Congress approved May twenty-nine, eighteen hundred and eighty-four, establishing the Bureau of Animal Industry; and it is hereby made the duty of sheriffs, constables, and peace officers to assist said Inspectors when so requested, and said Inspectors shall have the same powers and protection as peace officers while engaged in the discharge of their duties.

SEC. 3. All expenses of quarantine, condemnation of animals exposed to disease, and the expenses of any and all measures that may be used to suppress and extirpate pleuro-pneumonia shall be paid by the United States, and in no case shall this State be liable for any damages or expenses of any kind under the provisions of this act.

SEC. 4. This act shall take effect immediately.

Approved April 14, 1887.

OHIO.

AN ACT to amend section 4 of an act to suppress and prevent dissemination of epizootic and communicable diseases of animals in the State of Ohio, passed April 29, 1885.

SECTION 1. *Be it enacted by the general assembly of the State of Ohio,* That section 4 of the above-recited act be amended so as to read as follows:

SEC. 4. That any person having in his possession or under his care any animal which he knows, or has reason to believe, is affected with a dangerously contagious or infectious disease, and does not, without unnecessary delay, make known the same to said board or to some member thereof, or to the sheriff or constable of the proper county, to be by him communicated to said board; or any person or corporation who shall bring into this State, or sell or dispose of any animal, knowing the same to be affected as aforesaid, or any animal having been exposed to such contagion, within three months of such exposure, or shall move the animal so diseased or exposed from the quarantine to which it was ordered by the board of commissioners, or shall move any animal to or from any district in this State declared to be infected with such contagious disease, or shall bring into this State any animal of the kind diseased from any district outside of the State that may at any time be legally declared to be affected with such disease, without the consent of said board, except under such conditions as are or may be prescribed by said board, shall, upon conviction of either of the aforesaid offenses, be fined in any sum not exceeding five hundred dollars. And all proper expense incurred in the quarantining of animals under the provisions of this act shall be paid by the owners thereof, and if the same is refused, after demand made by order of the commissioners, an action may be brought to recover the same with costs of suit, which action may be in the name of the State of Ohio, for the use of the board of live-stock commissioners. It shall be the duty of all sheriffs and constables to execute within their several counties all lawful orders of the said commissioners.

SEC. 2. Original section 4 of the original act is hereby repealed: *Provided*, Such repeal shall not affect any proceedings had or now pending thereunder.

SEC. 3. This act shall take effect and be in force from and after its passage.

Passed March 16, 1887.

OREGON.

THE STOCK-INSPECTOR LAW.

SECTION 1. There shall be appointed by the county court sitting as county commissioners an inspector of stock for each of the counties of the State of Oregon, who shall reside in the counties for which they are appointed, respectively. Each of such inspectors, before entering upon the duties of his office, shall make his oath of office and give an undertaking to the county court, with two or more sufficient sureties, to be approved by the county judge, conditioned for the faithful performance of the duties of his office. It shall be the duty of the inspector to administer oaths and to personally examine all sheep and bands of sheep in their county every spring, between the first day of March and the first day of June, and every fall between the twentieth day of September and the twentieth day of December; and also to examine, free of charge, any other kind of live stock in his county at any time that he may be called upon to do so by a request, in writing, of at least ten persons owning or controlling stock of the class he is by such persons called upon to examine, said persons making a written statement that said stock is affected or infected with some infectious or contagious disease; and if, upon examination, said stock are found to be affected or infected with any infectious or contagious disease, and that there is imminent and immediate danger of the spreading of such disease and that it will cause great and irreparable injury to other stock-owners in the vicinity of said infected or affected stock, the said inspector shall forthwith issue his order quarantining said stock; and he shall engage a sufficient number of persons to hold said stock secure from other stock, and shall, if there be a State officer having charge of such diseases, immediately notify him of the quarantining of such stock, and if there be no such officer, then to the governor. Each inspector shall have power to appoint deputies, not exceeding one for each precinct, for whose acts he shall be responsible, and by any of whom he may perform any act required of him by this act, except the semiannual inspections, which shall be made by the inspector himself in person; and it shall be the duty of the inspector to advertise in at least one local paper, if there be one in his county, at his own expense, the names and post-office address and precinct of any and all of his deputies. Any indebtedness incurred under the provisions of this act, except for which the inspector should pay, may be recovered by such inspector in his official capacity by an action in any court having jurisdiction of the amount.

SEC. 2. Any person, company, corporation, or association intending to bring, or cause to be brought, from any other State or Territory into any of the counties of the State of Oregon any sheep must first obtain from an inspector of stock, duly appointed under this act, a certificate that said sheep are sound and free from all infectious and contagious diseases before crossing the boundary line of said county; and it shall be the duty of every inspector, at the request of any person, company, association, or corporation owning or controlling any sheep in his county or within twenty miles of the line of such county, upon being tendered the amount of his compensation for other special examinations, as herein provided, with all convenient speed to examine any sheep he shall be requested so to examine, and if such sheep be sound and free from all infectious and contagious diseases and are perfectly sound, to give his written certificate to said applicant, over his official signature, setting forth the soundness and freedom from disease of such sheep, and permit and authorize such applicants to move such sheep to such place as may be designated in such permit. Any person violating the provisions of this section shall be deemed guilty of a misdemeanor, and upon conviction thereof shall be punished by a fine of not less than twenty-five nor more than two hundred and fifty dollars.

SEC. 3. Any person, company, corporation, or association desiring to move his or their sheep, which are not sound or are infected or affected with scab or any infectious or contagious disease, shall obtain from the inspector a traveling permit; but such permit shall only be granted for the purpose of moving said sheep to some place where they may be treated for said disease, and by such route as the inspector may designate. Any person, company, or corporation violating the provisions of this section shall be deemed guilty of a misdemeanor, and upon conviction thereof shall be punished by a fine of not less than fifty nor more than five hundred dollars, and any party injured or damaged by reason of the moving of said sheep shall be entitled to recover off of said persons, company, or corporation by a civil action three times the amount of damages, direct and consequential, that said party has actually sustained by reason thereof.

SEC. 4. Whenever on examination of any bands or herds of sheep kept or herded in any county of the State of Oregon the stock inspector shall find such sheep, or any portion of them, affected with scab or scabies, or any infectious or contagious disease, he shall forthwith notify the owner or person in charge of such sheep, in writing, to treat said sheep for said disease within a period of fifteen days from such notice, and also during such period to keep said sheep from contact with other sheep by such means as he may specify; and if, upon examination at the end of fifteen days from such notice, the inspector shall find that said sheep have not been treated for said disease, or have not been kept from contact with other sheep that are sound, the owner or owners, or person or persons controlling said sheep, shall be deemed guilty of a misdemeanor, and, upon conviction thereof, shall be punished by a fine of not less than one hundred nor more than two hundred and fifty dollars; and in case said sheep have not been treated for said disease, the inspector shall immediately take possession of said sheep and treat them for said disease, and all expenses incurred in so doing, including a compensation of three dollars per day for every day or part of a day in which the inspector may be engaged in treating said sheep, shall become a lien upon said sheep, and the inspector shall hold the sheep until the same is paid; or if it be not paid within ten days after such treatment is completed, he shall collect the same, together with the costs and expenses of collection, by advertising and selling said sheep, or so many thereof as may be necessary, in the manner provided by law for sale of personal property upon execution. If, however, upon examination at the end of thirty days from such notice, as before mentioned, the inspector shall find that said sheep have been treated for said disease, but are still infected with the same, then he shall instruct the owner or controller of said sheep to dip said sheep once or more as soon as possible, but with an interval between the dippings of not less than nine nor more than seventeen days; and if upon examination at the end of thirty days further, the inspector finds that said sheep have been treated for said disease, but are still infected, then he shall at once take possession of said sheep and treat them for said disease as above specified. If, however, upon examination he finds said sheep have not been treated for said disease, he shall seize said sheep and treat them for said disease as above specified, and the owner or owners shall be guilty of a misdemeanor, and upon conviction thereof shall be punished by a fine of not less than one hundred nor more than two hundred and fifty dollars: *Provided*, No person, company, or corporation shall be required to dip or treat a band of ewes, or any part of them, in which there are ewes with lambs, at any time from the first of March to the first of May of any year.

SEC. 5. The stock inspector(s) of the several counties of this State shall receive the following annual salaries for their services, to be paid quarterly by their respective counties, to wit:

The stock inspector of Baker County, five hundred dollars; of Benton County, twenty-five dollars; of Clackamas County, twenty-five dollars: of Clatsop County, twenty-five dollars; of Columbia County, twenty-five dollars; of Coos County, twenty-five dollars; of Crook County, eight hundred dollars; of Curry County, twenty-five dollars; of Douglas County, one hundred dollars; of Gilliam County, eight hundred dollars; of Grant County, eight hundred dollars; of Jackson County, one hundred dollars; of Josephine County, twenty-five dollars; of Klamath County, one hundred dollars; of Lake County, three hundred dollars; of Lane County, twenty-five dollars; of Linn County, twenty-five dollars; of Marion County, twenty-five dollars; of Morrow County, eight hundred dollars; of Multnomah County, one hundred dollars; of Polk County, twenty-five dollars; of Tillamook County, twenty-five dollars; of Umatilla County, eight hundred dollars; of Union County, five hundred dollars; of Wasco County, eight hundred dollars; of Washington County, twenty-five dollars; of Yamhill County, twenty-five dollars. The inspector shall also be allowed to collect a fee of $3 per day for every day or part of day in which he shall be engaged inspecting sheep for the purpose of granting traveling permits or certificates of soundness, together with ten cents per mile for the distance necessarily traveled by him in making such inspection, except at semi-annual inspections. Any inspector at any time granting a permit to allow any stock to travel without having at the time first examined said stock shall be deemed guilty of a misdemeanor, and upon conviction thereof shall be punished by a fine of not less than $100 nor more than $250.

SEC. 6. Any person or persons owning or having under their control sheep or bands of sheep which have become infected with scab or other contagious disease for a period of fifteen days, without reporting the same to the inspector in writing, shall be deemed guilty of a misdemeanor, and shall upon conviction thereof be punished by a fine of not less than $25 nor more than $250. Upon receiving such notice the inspector shall proceed as provided in section 4. Any person, company, or corporation violating any of the provisions of this act shall be liable in civil action for all damages sustained by any other person, company, or corporation in consequence of such violation.

SEC. 7. On any actions or proceedings, civil or criminal, arising under this act, all persons having an interest in stock concerning which such action or proceeding is had shall be deemed the owners of such stock, and such owners shall be liable severally and jointly for violations of this act. Any herder, shepherd, or other person in charge of sheep, who shall wilfully refuse to give an inspector information as to the condition of sheep in his charge shall be guilty of a misdemeanor, and upon conviction thereof shall be punished by a fine of not less than $25 nor more than $250. In criminal actions against corporations under this act no arrest shall be necessary, but a summons containing notice of the time and place of trial, together with a copy of the complaint filed before a justice of the peace, or in the court in which the action is commenced, shall be served in the same manner and for the same time as in civil actions.

SEC. 8. Courts of justices of the peace shall have concurrent jurisdiction with the circuit court of all misdemeanors defined in this act except section 3, and of all criminal prosecutions for such misdemeanors. The provisions of this act requiring the stock inspectors to prosecute for violation of its provisions shall not be so construed as to prevent such prosecutions from being commenced and prosecuted by other persons as other criminal actions are commenced and prosecuted.

SEC. 9. It shall be the duty of each inspector of stock in this State to keep record books, in which he shall keep as nearly complete as practicable a description of the marks and brands with which each person in his county marks or brands his horses, cattle, sheep, or hogs; and he shall keep in such records a memoranda of all stray live stock of which he shall be informed or can learn in his county, with as full a description as he can procure thereof, and of their location, and at all reasonable times furnish as full information to all stock-owners inquiring of him concerning the same as with due diligence and care he can in reply to both letters and personal inquiries. Such records shall be fully indexed for convenient reference to the contents thereof, be public records, and subject to inspection by all persons at all reasonable times, and shall be delivered by the inspector at the end of his term of office either to the county court of his county or to his successor in office. If there be no inspector appointed the county clerk shall keep such records.

SEC. 10. Upon the sale, alienation, or transfer of any horse, mare, mule, gelding, colt, jack, jennet, cow, heifer, calf, ox, steer, sheep, or bull the actual delivery of such animal or animals shall be accompanied by a written transfer from the vendor or party selling to the purchaser, giving the number, marks, and brands of each animal sold and delivered; and the purchaser thereof shall immediately deliver to the stock inspector a memorandum thereof under oath, stating the number and marks and brand of each animal so purchased, and from whom and when; and upon the trial of the right of property of any animal the possession without the written transfer herein specified shall be deemed prima facie illegal: *Provided, however*, That this section shall not apply to counties west of the Cascade Mountains.

SEC. 11. Before any person who has purchased or had transferred to him any animal or animals specified in section 10 of this act shall undertake to drive any such animals out of any county of this State he shall make out a memorandum under oath, giving the number of animals and marks and brands of each animal, and whether he raised them or whether he purchased them, and, if so, when and from whom, and immediately deliver said memorandum to the stock inspector or his deputy of said county. Any person violating the provisions of this section shall be deemed guilty of a misdemeanor, and upon conviction thereof shall be fined not less than fifty dollars and not more than two hundred and fifty dollars: *Provided*, That this section shall not apply to any county west of the Cascade Mountains.

SEC. 12. Any person, company, corporation, or association shall, before moving his or their sheep, or any part thereof, from one county to another in this State first obtain from an inspector a traveling permit, and any violation of this section shall be deemed a misdemeanor; and any person, persons, company, or corporation violating the provisions of this section shall be punished by a fine of not less than one hundred dollars nor more than two hundred and fifty dollars.

SEC. 13. It shall be unlawful for any person, company, corporation, or association owning, controlling, or managing any ferry-boat, toll bridge, car, steam-boat, or other thing used for transportation, to allow any sheep to be carried thereon unless the party in charge of said sheep shall first produce a certificate from an inspector appointed under this act, or of an act amendatory to this, that said sheep are free from scab, scabies, and infectious and contagious diseases, and any violation of this section shall be deemed a misdemeanor, and any person or persons, company or corporation, violating the provisions of this section shall be fined not less than one hundred dollars nor more than two hundred and fifty dollars.

SEC. 14. If any person makes a complaint against another of the violation of any [illegible] of this act, and said information proves false, the person so in-

ing shall pay all costs, damages, expenses, and disbursements incurred by rea- of such information.

:c. 15. If any person or persons, company or corporation, in driving or herding sheep should get into their herd any stray sheep, they shall immediately notify owner thereof, or if the owner is unknown, he shall forthwith notify the in- tor of stock thereof, giving the number of said sheep and the brands of each, and person or persons, company or corporation, violating the provisions of this sec- 1 shall be deemed guilty of a misdemeanor, and upon conviction thereof shall be d not less than twenty-five dollars nor more than two hundred and fifty dollars.

EC. 16. That an act entitled "An act to prevent the spreading of contagious or ctious diseases among sheep," approved October 25, 1880, and all acts and parts acts in conflict herewith, are hereby repealed.

EC. 17. In consequence of the rapid spread among stock of contagious and in- tious diseases and irregular transfers of stock, and inasmuch as there is no equate law for the protection of stock-growers, this act shall immediately take ct and become a law from and after its approval by the governor.

Approved February 28, 1887.

SOUTH CAROLINA.

AN ACT to create a department of agriculture, etc.

SECTION 9. The board shall have power, in cases of contagious diseases among y kind of stock or animals, to quarantine or have the same killed and burned.

Approved Dec. 23, 1879.

VIRGINIA.

ACT to co-operate with the United States in the suppression and extirpation of pleuro-pneumonia.

. *Be it enacted by the general assembly of Virginia*, That the governor is hereby horized to accept, on behalf of the State, the rules and regulations prepared by Commissioner of Agriculture under and in pursuance of section 3 of an act of gress approved May 29, 1884, entitled "An act for the establishment of a Bureau Animal Industry, to prevent the exportation of diseased cattle, and to provide ans for the suppression and extirpation of pleuro-pneumonia and other con- ious diseases among domestic animals," and to co-operate with the authorities of United States in the enforcement of the provisions of said act.

. The inspectors of the Bureau of Animal Industry of the United States shall e the right of inspection, quarantine, and condemnation of animals affected h any contagious, infectious, or communicable disease, or suspected to be so af- ted, or that have been exposed to any such disease, and for these purposes are eby authorized and empowered to enter upon any grounds or premises. Said pectors shall have the power to call on sheriffs, constables, and peace officers to ist them in the discharge of their duties in carrying out the provisions of the act Congress approved May 29, 1884, establishing the Bureau of Animal Industry; l it is hereby made the duty of sheriffs, constables, and peace officers to assist l inspectors when so requested; and said inspectors shall have the same powers protection as peace officers while engaged in the discharge of their duties.

. All expenses of quarantine, condemnation of animals exposed to disease, and expenses of any and all measures that may be used to suppress and extirpate uro-pneumonia shall be paid by the United States, and in no case shall this State liable for any damages or expenses of any kind under the provisions of this act.

. This act shall be in force from its passage.

Approved ——— ———, 1887.

WISCONSIN.

ACT to amend chapter 467, laws of 1885, entitled "An act to suppress and prevent the spread of fectious and contagious diseases among domestic animals, and to provide for the appointment of a ate veterinarian."

ECTION 1. *The people of the State of Wisconsin, represented in senate and as- bly, do enact as follows:* Section 2 of chapter 467, laws of 1885, is hereby amended s to read as follows: Section 2. It shall be the duty of the State veterinarian to press and prevent the introduction or spread of contagious diseases among do- stic animals; to co-operate with the State board of health in the management of h diseases as are common to man and animals, or any condition of the lower mals likely to affect the general health of mankind. He shall make scientific dy and such investigations and experiments as he shall deem necessary, and be shall gather and diffuse information relative to the contagious and infectious diseases of animals.

SEC. 2. Section 3 of chapter 467, laws of 1885, is hereby amended so as to read as follows: Section 3. It is hereby made the duty of the various town, village, and city boards of health to take cognizance of contagious and infectious diseases among animals, and to report all cases coming under their observation to the State veterinarian. It is also made their duty to prevent the spread of such diseases, and to co-operate with the State veterinarian, and the local boards of health, or the health officer, are authorized to order quarantine of any animal affected with contagious or infectious disease, or any animal suspected of being affected with or which has been exposed to such disease, and to forbid the removal of such animals from any premises where they may be kept. And in cases where they are unable to determine the nature of any disease the said local boards may request the State veterinarian to make such investigation as may be necessary. Any person who shall remove or allow to be removed any domestic animal so quarantined by the local boards of health or health officers without permission from competent authority shall be guilty of a misdemeanor, and be punished therefor by a fine of not less than twenty dollars and not more than two hundred dollars, or by imprisonment at hard labor of not less than thirty days nor more than one year, and shall forfeit all right to indemnity as herein provided, and be liable to all persons injured thereby for damages by them sustained. The State veterinarian is hereby authorized, if he deem it necessary, to order quarantine of any premises upon which domestic animals are that are afflicted with contagious or infectious disease, or that are suspected to be affected with such disease, or have been exposed to contagious or infectious disease, and to forbid the removal therefrom of any animals susceptible to such disease, said order of quarantine to be in writing and served upon the owner or occupant of the premises upon which said diseased animals are, and notice thereof posted at the usual entrance to said premises; and in case said contagious or infectious disease shall become epidemic in any locality, the State veterinarian shall immediately notify the governor, who shall thereupon, if he deem it necessary, issue a proclamation quarantining said locality, and forbidding the removal therefrom of any animal of the kind diseased, or any kind susceptible to such disease, without permission of the State veterinarian. Any person who shall remove or allow to be removed any domestic animal of the kind diseased, or susceptible to such disease, from any premises so quarantined by the State veterinarian, or locality quarantined by the proclamation of the governor, without permission of the State veterinarian, shall be guilty of a misdemeanor, and punished therefor by a fine of not less than twenty dollars nor more than two hundred dollars, or by imprisonment at hard labor not less than thirty days nor more than one year, and shall forfeit all right to indemnity as herein provided, and be liable to all persons injured thereby for damages by them sustained.

SEC. 3. Section 5 of chapter 467 of the laws of 1885 is hereby amended so as to read as follows: Section 5. Whenever, as herein provided, the State veterinarian shall deem the slaughter of any animal or animals necessary, he shall notify in writing a justice of the peace of the county in which said diseased animals are, describing in said notice the diseased animals with reasonable certainty, stating the name of the owner when known. The said justice of the peace shall, after entering the same upon his docket, summon three disinterested citizens, who shall not be residents of the immediate neighborhood in which the animals are owned or kept. The said appraisers shall, before entering upon the discharge of their duties, be sworn to make a true and faithful appraisement of the value of said animals, without prejudice or favor, and said appraisers shall certify in their return that they have seen said animals destroyed, and in making the appraisement the value put upon the animals shall be what they are worth at the time of the appraisal. If any animal be diseased at the time of the appraisement that fact shall be taken into consideration, and the value put upon it shall be what it shall be worth in its diseased condition. In the case of horses afflicted with glanders the appraised value shall in no case exceed fifty dollars. It shall be the duty of the local health officer or the chairman of the board of health to superintend the slaughter of said animals, and to provide for the disposal of the carcasses and disinfection of the premises. The justice of the peace, when satisfied of the fact, shall issue to the owner a certificate of slaughter, and shall state therein whether or not, in his judgment, the owner is entitled to indemnity.

SEC. 4. Section 7 of chapter 467, laws of 1885, is hereby amended by inserting between the words "disease" and "or," in the tenth line of said section, the following: "Or to permit any animal affected with contagious or infectious disease to run at large or to associate with other animals susceptible to such disease; also by omitting the words "State veterinarian or of some member of the State, or of some," in line six and seven of said section, so that said section when so amended shall read as follows: Section 7. It shall be the duty of any person or the agent of any corporation who shall have reason to suspect that there is upon their premises any animal or animals affected with contagious or infectious disease to immediately report the same to the local board of health, whose duty it shall be to report the same to the State veterinarian, and failure to so report, or any attempt to conceal the existence of such disease, or to permit any animal affected with contagious or infectious disease to run at large or associate with other animals susceptible to such disease, or to obstruct or resist the State veterinarian in the performance of his duty as herein set forth, or to sell, offer for sale, give away, or in any manner part with any animal affected with, or suspected to be affected with, or that has been exposed to any contagious or infectious disease, and any person convicted of any of the above acts or omissions, shall be fined not less than twenty and not more than two hundred dollars, or be imprisoned at hard labor not less than thirty days or more than one year for each offense, and shall forfeit all right to indemnity as herein provided, and be liable to all persons injured thereby for damages by them sustained. The provisions of this act shall apply to all animals in this State, whether resident or in transit, and the State veterinarian is hereby authorized to enter any premises where he has reason to suspect diseased animals are confined, and he may call to his aid, when necessary, the sheriff or any constable of the county in which the diseased or infected animals are; and it is hereby made the duty of such officers to assist the State veterinarian to enforce the provisions of this act when called upon so to do.

SEC. 5. Section 8 of chapter 467, laws of 1885, is hereby amended so as to read as follows: Section 8. All claims against the State arising from the slaughter of animals, as herein provided, shall be made by filing with the secretary of state a copy of the State veterinarian's notice to the justice of the peace and return of the appraisers, which notice and return shall be certified to by the justice of the peace on whose docket they are recorded. The secretary of state shall examine the same, and if satisfied that the amount awarded is just and the owner entitled to indemnity, he shall issue a warrant on the State treasurer for two-thirds the sum named in the appraisers' return; but if he shall have reason to believe that the appraised value is greater than the real value of the animals, he shall be authorized to settle with the owner for such less sum as he shall deem just.

SEC. 6. Section 9 of chapter 467, laws of 1885, is hereby amended by adding at the end thereof the following: Fifth. Or when the owner shall have been guilty of negligence or willfully exposing his animals to the influence of infectious or contagious diseases.

SEC. 7. Section 10 of chapter 467 of the laws of 1885 is hereby amended so as to read as follows: Section 10. The State veterinarian shall receive for his services the sum of two thousand dollars per annum, and there shall be allowed for experimental purposes a sum not to exceed five hundred dollars annually and a sum sufficient to cover his actual and necessary traveling expenses, said sum for experimental purposes and traveling expenses to be approved by the governor. He shall also be entitled to receive the necessary postage, stationery, and usual supplies for the use of his office. He shall, from time to time, issue such bulletins of information as he shall deem advisable, which, together with his report to the governor, shall be printed in such numbers as may be necessary, by the State printer. He may deliver lectures upon veterinary science in the agricultural department of the university, when the same shall not interfere with his other duties. The veterinary surgeons called in consultation shall receive the sum of seven dollars per day for each day actually employed, and their necessary expenses while performing their duties. They shall be paid upon itemized vouchers certified by the State veterinarian and approved by the governor. And no person shall be considered a veterinary surgeon, within the meaning of this act, who is not a regular graduate in good standing of some recognized veterinary college in the United States, Canada, or Europe. The appraisers herein provided shall receive the sum of two dollars for each day actually employed as such, to be paid out of the county funds upon certificate of the justice of the peace by whom they were summoned. The justice of the peace, sheriff, and constable shall receive their fees from their respective counties, as provided by law in criminal cases.

SEC. 8. Section 12 of the act to which this is amendatory is hereby declared to be made applicable to the provisions of this act.

SEC. 9. All acts or parts of acts inconsistent with the provisions of this act are hereby repealed.

SEC. 10. This act shall take effect and be in force from and after its passage and publication.

Approved March 21, 1887.

WYOMING.

AN ACT to suppress and prevent the dissemination of contagious and infectious diseases among domestic animals.

SECTION 1. *Be it enacted by the council and house of representatives of the Territory of Wyoming,* That the governor of the Territory is hereby authorized to nominate, which nomination may be made upon the recommendation of the Stock Growers' Association of the Territory, and by and with the advice and consent of the council appoint (without unnecessary delay after the passage of this act) a competent veterinary surgeon, who shall be known as the Territorial veterinarian, and in entering on his duties shall take an oath to well and truly perform his duties as provided by law.

SEC. 2. The duties of said veterinarian shall be as follows: To investigate any and all cases of contagious or infectious disease among domestic animals in the Territory of which he may have knowledge, or which may be brought to his notice by any resident in the locality where such disease exists. And it shall also be his duty in the absence of specific information to make visits of inspection to any locality where he may have reason to suspect that there is contagious or infectious disease; and to inspect under the regulations of this act all domestic animals that may arrive at any railroad station in this Territory, when these animals are such as to warrant the presumption that they are intended to remain in the Territory, and are to be, or may be, used for breeding purposes therein. And it shall be the duty of the owner, or, in his absence, of the person in charge of such animals so arriving, to notify the Territorial veterinarian without delay, and not to allow said animals, or any of them, to leave the place of arrival until they shall have been examined by the veterinarian and his certificate obtained that all are free from disease. And no animal pronounced unsound by the veterinarian shall be turned loose, removed, or permitted to escape, but shall be held subject to the order of the veterinarian. Any person failing to comply with this provision shall be deemed guilty of a misdemeanor, and, upon conviction, shall be fined not less than fifty nor more than five hundred dollars for each offense.

SEC. 3. In all cases of contagious or infectious disease among domestic animals in this Territory the veterinarian shall have authority to order the quarantine of the infected premises, and in case such disease shall become epidemic in any locality in this Territory the veterinarian shall immediately notify the governor of the Territory, who shall thereupon issue his proclamation forbidding any animal of the kind among which said epidemic exists to be transferred from said locality without a certificate from the veterinarian, showing such animal to be healthy.

SEC. 4. In any case of epidemic disease where premises have been previously quarantined by the Territorial veterinarian, as before provided, he is further authorized and empowered, when in his judgment necessary, to order the slaughter of any or of all diseased animals upon said premises, and of all animals that have been exposed to contagion or infection under the following restrictions: Said order shall be a written one, and shall be made in duplicate, and there shall be a distinct order and duplicate for each owner of the animals condemned, the original of each order to be filed by the veterinarian with the governor, and the duplicate given to said owner. And, further, before slaughtering any animal or animals that has been exposed only and does not show disease the veterinarian shall call in consultation with him two respectable practicing veterinarians or physicians, residents of the Territory, or, if this is impossible, then two reputable and well-known stock owners, residents of the Territory, and shall have the written endorsement upon his order of at least one of said consulting physicians or stock owners, stating that said action is necessary, and the consent of the owner or person in charge, before such animal or animals shall be slaughtered.

SEC. 5. Whenever, as herein provided, the Territorial veterinarian shall order the slaughter of one or more animals he shall, at the time of making such order, notify in writing the nearest justice of the peace, who shall thereupon summon three disinterested citizens (who shall be stock owners) of the neighborhood to act as appraisers of the value of such animals. Such appraisers, before entering upon the discharge of their duties, shall be sworn to make a true and faithful appraisement without prejudice or favor. They shall, after making their appraisement, return certified copies of their valuation, a separate one being made for each owner, together with an accurate description of each animal slaughtered (giving all brands, ear-marks, wattles, age and sex, and class, as to whether American, half-breed, or Texan), to the justice of the peace by whom they were summoned, who shall, after entering the same upon his record and making an endorsement upon each, showing [illegible] to have been properly recorded, return it, together with the duplicate order of the veterinarian, to the person or persons owning the animal slaughtered; and it shall be the duty of the Territorial veterinarian to superintend the slaughter of such animals as may be condemned, and also the destruction of the carcass, which latter shall be by burning to ashes, and shall include every part of the animal and hide, and also excrement as far as possible. He shall cause the said slaughter and burning to be done as cheaply as practicable, and shall pay the expense from the contingent fund hereinafter provided, taking proper vouchers for the same.

SEC. 6. The Territorial veterinarian shall make a report at the end of every year to the governor of all matters connected with his work, and the governor shall transmit to the several boards of county commissioners such parts of said report as may be of general interest to the breeders of live stock. The governor shall also give information in writing, as rapidly as he obtains it, to the various boards of county commissioners, of each cause of suspicion or first eruption of disease in each locality, its course, and the measures adopted to check it.

SEC. 7. Whenever the governor of the Territory shall have good reason to believe that any disease covered by this act has become epidemic in certain localities in another State or Territory, or that conditions exist which render domestic animals liable to convey disease, he shall thereupon by proclamation schedule such localities and prohibit the importation from them of any live stock of the kind diseased into this Territory, except under such restrictions as he may deem proper. Any corporation, or any person or persons, who, after the publishing of said proclamation, shall knowingly receive in charge any such animal or animals from any one of said prohibited districts, and transport or convey the same within the limits of this Territory, shall be deemed guilty of a misdemeanor, and, upon a conviction, fined not less than one thousand dollars nor more than ten thousand dollars for each and every offense, and shall further become liable for any and all damages and loss that may be sustained by any person or persons by reason of the importation or transportation of such prohibited animals.

SEC. 8. It shall be the duty of any person or persons who shall have or suspect that there is upon his or their premises any case of contagious or infectious disease among domestic animals, to immediately report the same to the Territorial veterinarian; and a failure so to do, or any attempt to conceal the existence of such disease, or to willfully or maliciously obstruct or resist the said veterinarian in the discharge of his duty as hereinbefore set forth, shall be deemed a misdemeanor, and any person or persons who shall be convicted of any one of the above acts or omissions shall be fined not less than fifty dollars nor more than five hundred dollars for each and every such offense, shall forfeit all claims for indemnity for loss from the Territory, and, upon conviction a second time shall, in addition to the above-named fine, be imprisoned for a term not less than thirty days nor more than six months.

SEC. 9. The following regulations shall be observed in all cases of disease covered by this act: (1) It shall be unlawful to sell, give away, or in any manner part with any animal affected with or suspected of contagious or infectious disease; and in the case of any animal that may be known to have been affected with or exposed to any such disease within one year prior to such disposal, due notice of the fact shall be given in writing to the party receiving the animal. (2) It shall be unlawful to kill for butcher purposes any such animal, to sell, give away, or use any part of it, or its milk, or to remove any part of the skin. A failure to observe these provisions shall be deemed a misdemeanor, and, on conviction, shall be punished by a fine not less than one hundred dollars nor exceeding five hundred dollars. It shall be the duty of the owner or person having in charge any animal affected with or suspected of any contagious or infectious disease, to immediately confine the same in a safe place, isolated from other animals, and with all necessary restrictions to prevent dissemination of the disease, until the arrival of the Territorial veterinarian.

The above regulations shall apply as well to animals in transit through the Territory as to those resident therein, and the Territorial veterinarian, or his duly authorized agent, shall have full authority to examine, whether in car, or yards, or stables, all animals passing through the Territory, or any part of it, and on detection or suspicion of disease to take possession of and treat and dispose of said animals in the same manner as is prescribed for animals resident in the Territory.

SEC. 10. All claims against the Territory arising from the slaughter of animals under the provisions of this act shall, together with the order of the veterinarian and the valuation of the appraisers, in each case be submitted to the Territorial auditor, who shall examine them without unnecessary delay, and for each one that he finds to be equitable and entitled to indemnity under this act, shall issue his warrant on the Territorial treasurer for the sum named in the appraisers' report.

In auditing any claim under this act it shall be the duty of the auditor to satisfy himself that it does not come under any class for which indemnity is refused by this act, and he shall require the affidavit of the claimant to this fact, or if the claimant be not cognizant thereof, then of some reputable person who is cognizant thereof, and also the certificate of the veterinarian (whose duty it shall be to inform himself fully of the facts) that in his opinion the claim is legal and just, and the auditor may at his discretion require further proof. The indemnity to be granted shall be two-thirds of the ordinary value of the animal, as determined by the appraisers, without reference to its diminished value because of being diseased. It shall be paid to the owner upon his application and the presentation of the proofs prescribed herein; and it shall be the duty of said owner to make such application within six months of the slaughter of the animal for which payment is claimed, failing which such claim shall be barred by limitation.

These payments shall be made by the Territorial treasurer, as before provided, and from the fund provided by this act.

The right to indemnity under this act is limited to animals destroyed by reason of the existence or suspected existence of some epizootic disease, generally fatal and incurable, such as rinderpest, hoof-and-mouth disease, pleuro-pneumonia, anthrax or Texas fever among bovines, glanders among horses, and anthrax among sheep. For the ordinary contagious diseases, not in their nature fatal, such as scab or hoof-rot in sheep, and epizootic influenza in horses, no indemnity shall be paid.

The right to indemnity shall not exist and payment of such shall not be made in the following cases: (1) For animals belonging to the United States; (2) for animals that are brought into the Territory contrary to the provisions of this act; (3) for animals that are found to be diseased or that are destroyed because they have been exposed to disease before or at the time of their arrival in the Territory; (4) when an animal was previously affected by any other disease which, from its nature and development, was incurable and necessarily fatal; (5) when the owner or person in charge shall have knowingly or negligently omitted to comply with the provisions of sections eight and nine of this act; (6) when the owner or claimant at the time of coming in possession of the animal knew it to be diseased or received the notice specified in the first clause of section nine of this act.

SEC. 11. The Territorial veterinarian shall receive for his services the sum of twenty-five hundred dollars per annum, together with his actual necessary traveling expenses when in performance of his duty. These payments shall be made from the funds provided by this act, the salary from the appropriation for salary, and the traveling expenses from the contingent fund, upon vouchers signed and sworn to by him and approved by the governor, separate vouchers being made for salary and expenses. No person shall be competent under this act to receive the appointment of Territorial veterinarian who is not at the date of his appointment a graduate in good standing of a recognized college of veterinary surgery, either in the United States, Canada, or Europe. He shall hold his office for two years, but may be removed for cause by the governor, who shall also have power to fill a vacancy. The veterinarian is hereby authorized, in his discretion, to appoint a deputy, for the performance of whose duties the veterinarian shall be responsible, and who shall exercise such powers as may be deputed to him by the Territorial veterinarian. Such deputy shall receive not exceeding four dollars per day for the time actually employed. The appraisers herein provided for shall each receive five dollars for each day or part of a day they may be actually employed as such, which shall be paid from their county fund upon the certificate of the justice who summoned them. The justice shall receive his ordinary fee for issuing a summons, to be paid out of the county fund. The members of the board of health, veterinarians, physicians, or stock owners, called in consultation by the veterinarian, shall each receive five dollars for each day or part of day they may be actually so employed, and ten (10) cents per mile mileage for distance actually traveled, which sums shall be paid from the veterinarian's contingent fund hereafter provided. For this and other incidental expenses connected with his work and made his duty by this act, such as his traveling expenses, causing animals to be slaughtered and their carcasses burned, and disinfecting infected premises, the veterinarian shall have at his disposal the sum of five thousand dollars, which shall be known as the veterinarian contingent fund.

Before entering upon the discharge of his duties he shall give good and sufficient surety in the sum of five thousand dollars for the proper management of the same. He shall make a sworn statement semi-annually to the governor, supported by full vouchers of the amount disbursed; any part of the five thousand dollars not used shall be covered into the Territorial treasury. No constructive mileage shall be paid under this act.

SEC. 12. The liability of the Territory for indemnity for animals destroyed under the provisions of this act in any two years is limited by, and shall in no case exceed, the amount especially appropriated for that purpose and for that period.

SEC. 13. Hereafter it shall be the duty each year of the Territorial board of equalization at the time of making the annual assessment to levy a special tax, not exceeding one mill on the dollar upon the assessed value of all cattle, sheep, horses, and mules in the Territory, to be known as the stock indemnity fund. Said tax shall be levied and collected by the several counties and paid to the Territorial treasurer in the manner provided by law for the levying, collection, and payment of other Territorial taxes. Said fund shall constitute the indemnity fund specified by this act to be used in paying for animals destroyed under the provisions thereof. It shall be used exclusively for that purpose, and shall be paid out by the Territorial treasurer as hereinbefore provided for.

SEC. 14. This act shall take effect from and after i's passage.

Approved March 8, 1882. Amended March 12, 1886.

QUARANTINE PROCLAMATIONS.

ARIZONA.

TERRITORY OF ARIZONA, EXECUTIVE DEPARTMENT.

Whereas the live-stock sanitary commission of the Territory of Arizona have directed my attention to the fact, that reliable information has reached them that contagious pleuro-pneumonia has made its appearance in a large number of animals within the States of New York, Vermont, Pennsylvania, New Jersey, Delaware, Virginia, Illinois, and the District of Columbia, and is liable to make its appearance in the State of Missouri; that the cattle interests of the Territory are greatly endangered by the prevalence of this plague in the said States owing to importation of cattle therefrom; and

Whereas the immense cattle interests of Arizona are thus menaced, and a heavy loss upon this, one of the most important of our industries, is liable to occur unless precautionary measures are adopted:

Now, therefore, I, C. Meyer Zulick, governor of the Territory of Arizona, by virtue of the authority of law in me vested, do hereby order, establish, and declare a quarantine, to take effect on the first day of June, 1887, against all the said Territory, heretofore mentioned, embracing also England, Scotland, and the Dominion of Canada, on all bovine cattle from said localities coming into the Territory of Arizona, unless they are quarantined at the point of entry prescribed by the rules and regulations of the live-stock sanitary commission of Arizona for a period of sixty days, and retained there until they shall receive a certificate of health signed by the veterinary surgeon of the Territory of Arizona, or some duly authorized deputy under him.

In testimony whereof, I have hereunto set my hand and caused the great seal of the Territory to be hereto affixed.

Done at Prescott, the capital, this twenty-sixth day of May, A. D. 1887.

C. MEYER ZULICK.

By the governor:
WM. C. FOSTER,
Acting Secretary of Territory.

COLORADO.

In accordance with the resolutions of the Colorado State veterinary sanitary board, I, Alva Adams, governor of the State of Colorado, by virtue of the authority in me vested by law, do hereby forbid the importation into this State of any sheep, except rams, shipped by rail from points east of the Mississippi River, unless accompanied by a certificate of health given by the Colorado State veterinary sanitary board.

Also, by this proclamation I forbid the shipment and importation into this State of all cattle coming from the States of Illinois, Missouri, Arkansas, Kentucky, Pennsylvania, West Virginia, Virginia, Maryland, Delaware, New Jersey, New York, Connecticut, Rhode Island, Massachusetts, Vermont, District of Columbia, and the Dominion of Canada, except under such rules, restrictions, and regulations as may be ordered by the Colorado State veterinary sanitary board.

All other proclamations relating to cattle and sheep are hereby withdrawn and annulled.

In testimony whereof, I have set my hand and affixed the great seal of the State of Colorado, this nineteenth day of April, 1887.

ALVA ADAMS,
Governor.

JAMES RICE,
Secretary of State.

DAKOTA.

Whereas by virtue of and pursuant to an act of the legislative assembly of the Territory of Dakota, entitled "An act to suppress and prevent the spread of contagious and infectious diseases among domestic animals," approved March 11, A. D. 1887, it is my duty, when I shall have reason to believe that any contagious or infectious disease has become epidemic in certain localities, by proclamation, to schedule such localities and prohibit the importation from them of any live stock into this Territory, except under such restrictions as I, after consultation with the Territorial veterinary surgeon, may deem proper; and

Whereas I have reason to believe, upon the representation of the Territorial veterinary surgeon, that conditions exist which render domestic animals and Texas cattle in any and all of the counties in the following named States and Territories, viz: Illinois, Pennsylvania, New York, New Jersey, Maryland, Delaware, District of Columbia, Virginia, Vermont, Texas, and the Dominion of Canada, liable to convey disease:

Now, therefore, I, Louis K. Church, governor of the Territory of Dakota, by virtue of the authority conferred upon me by said statute and pursuant to the terms thereof, do hereby schedule the localities hereinbefore named, and I do hereby strictly forbid the importation into the Territory of Dakota of any cattle whatsoever which have been brought from any portion of said scheduled localities, or any of them, except upon certificate of the Territorial veterinary surgeon that such cattle have been subject to a quarantine of ninety days, and except Texas cattle that have been driven overland all the way from Texas, and which are accompanied by a veterinarian's certificate of health.

And I do hereby further forbid the importation into this Territory of any and all cattle driven or shipped from any other State, Territory, or country, unless the same shall be accompanied by a certificate of health, given by the veterinary surgeon of said State, Territory, or country, or his regularly appointed and authorized deputy, who shall have carefully examined all such cattle immediately prior to the giving of such certificate. And when considered necessary, the Territorial veterinary surgeon shall have power to re-inspect, wherever found, all animals covered by this act, and if found diseased or suspected of being diseased, to subject the same to such detention and quarantine as may be deemed expedient in the premises.

And I do hereby further order all persons, corporations, or companies to give due and proper notice to said Territorial veterinary surgeon preceding the arrival at the boundary line of all such live stock as properly comes within the province of this proclamation. All live stock shall be examined or quarantined at such station or stations as shall be designated by the Territorial veterinary surgeon.

And I do also further warn all persons, corporations, or companies whomsoever not in any manner to violate or attempt to violate the prohibition herein contained or contained in said act.

And I do hereby direct all sheriffs, constables, deputies, and other peace officers within this Territory to keep strict watch and to be vigilant and see to it that all the commands of this, my proclamation, are obeyed and respected, and to arrest any and all persons violating the same. And I further direct all such officers to report to me, without delay, all such violations of this, my proclamation.

In testimony whereof, I have hereunto set my hand and caused the seal of the Territory of Dakota to be attached, at the city of Bismarck, the capital of said Territory, this fourth day of June, A. D. 1887.

By the governor.

LOUIS K. CHURCH,
Governor.

M. L. MCCORMACK,
Secretary of Dakota.

ILLINOIS.

PROCLAMATION.

Whereas in pursuance of an act of the general assembly of Illinois, entitled "An act to amend an act entitled 'An act to revise the law in relation to the suppression and prevention of the spread of contagious and infectious diseases among domestic animals,'" approved June 27 1885, in force July 1, 1885: approved and in force April 20, 1887, as amended by an act approved June 15, 1887, in force July 1, 1887, the board of live-stock commissioners of Illinois have reported to me, under date of July 6, 1887, that the disease known as contagious pleuro-pneumonia among cattle now exists throughout the following described geographical district in the State of Illinois, bounded by the following lines, to wit: Commencing at a point on the west shore of Lake Michigan where the south side of Twenty-second street in the city of Chicago, in Cook County, touches said lake; thence west along the south side of said Twenty-second street and on a line extended west to the Desplaines River; thence northwardly along the east shore of said river to the south line of the town of Leyden; thence east to the southwest corner of the town of Jefferson; thence north along the west line of the said town of Jefferson to the northwest corner thereof; thence east along the northern line of the towns of Jefferson and Lake View to Lake Michigan, and thence southerly along the west shore of Lake Michigan to the place of beginning; and

Whereas said board of live-stock commissioners have, in pursuance of said act, reported to me that in their judgment it is necessary to schedule and quarantine such geographical district in order to prevent the spread of said disease in said district and into contiguous territory, and have recommended that I schedule and quarantine said district in accordance with the provisions of sec. 5 of said act: Therefore,

I, Richard J. Oglesby, governor of the State of Illinois, as provided by section 5 of said above entitled act, do hereby make proclamation of the foregoing facts and schedule the above designated geographical district and prohibit all domestic animals of the bovine species within said district from being moved from one premises to another, or over any public highway or any unfenced lot or piece of ground, or from being brought into or taken from said district, except upon obtaining a special permit, signed by the board of live-stock commissioners, or member thereof, or agent or officer of the board duly authorized by it to issue such permits.

This proclamation to go into effect from and after its publication.

In testimony whereof, I hereto set my hand and cause the great seal of State to be affixed. Done at the city of Springfield the day and year first above written.

R. J. OGLESBY.

By the governor:
H. D. DEMENT,
Secretary of State.

RULES GOVERNING THE MOVEMENT OF CATTLE THROUGH THE DISTRICT.

1. No restrictions are placed upon the movement of bovine animals by rail when passing through the district.
2. Any bovine animal brought into said district in violation of quarantine regulations prescribed in the governor's proclamation shall be treated as an infected animal, and liable to condemnation and slaughter under the provisions of law, and the owner and the person in charge thereof will be subject to the penalties provided by law.

JOHN M. PEARSON,
H. McCHESNEY,
E. S. WILSON,
Board of Live-Stock Commissioners.

Approved:
R. J. OGLESBY.

STATE OF ILLINOIS, EXECUTIVE DEPARTMENT,
Springfield, Ill., May 6, 1886.

Whereas, in pursuance of an act of the general assembly of Illinois, entitled "An act to revise the law in relation to the suppression and prevention of the spread of contagious and infectious diseases among domestic animals," approved June 27, 1885, in force July 1, 1885, the board of live-stock commissioners of Illinois reported to me, under date of April 29, 1886, that the condition of cattle south of the thirty-sixth parallel of latitude west of the Mississippi River, and south of the thirty-fifth parallel of latitude east of the Mississippi River, is now such as to render them liable to convey splenic or Texas fever to the cattle of this State if imported into this State between the periods of spring and autumn frosts, as expressed in the following communication:

STATE OF ILLINOIS,
STATE BOARD OF LIVE-STOCK COMMISSIONERS,
Springfield, April 28, 1886.

To Hon. R. J. OGLESBY, *Governor of Illinois:*

In view of the great loss and damage which in past years has been sustained by citizens of this State by reason of splenic or Texas fever, which, according to the best information obtainable, is transmitted to our native cattle only by cattle coming from the country south of the 36th parallel of latitude west of the Mississippi River and south of the 35th parallel of latitude east of the Mississippi River, between the periods of spring and autumn frosts; and whereas, after due examination and investigation, we find that such cattle, if introduced into this State during the period named, will communicate disease to the domestic cattle of this State:

We therefore report to you that the condition of cattle south of the 36th parallel of latitude west of the Mississippi River and south of the 35th parallel of latitude east of the Mississippi River is now such as to render them liable to convey splenic or Texas fever to the cattle of this State if imported into this State during the period designated, which fever is an infectious and extremely fatal disease; and we respectfully recommend that you issue your proclamation scheduling the above-described localities, and prohibit the importation into this State of cattle from the localities scheduled, from the 1st day of April to the 1st day of November of each year, subject to the exceptions and regulations that have been prescribed by this board and approved by you, and which are herewith submitted as a part of this report and recommendation.

J. M. PEARSON,
D. W. SMITH,
H. MCCHESNEY,
Board of Live-Stock Commissioners.

And whereas the said live-stock commissioners have recommended that I issue proclamation according to the terms of the above-entitled act, scheduling such localities, and prohibiting the importation of cattle from such localities into the State of Illinois from the 1st day of April to the 1st day of November of each year, except in accordance with the regulations adopted by said board of live-stock commissioners and approved by the governor, which regulations are herewith submitted and made a part of this proclamation.

Now, therefore, I, Richard J. Oglesby, governor of the State of Illinois, as provided by section 4 of said above entitled act, do hereby make proclamation of the foregoing facts and schedule the above designated localities, being the country south of the thirty-sixth parallel of latitude west of the Mississippi River, and south of the thirty-fifth parallel of latitude east of the Mississippi River, and prohibit the importation of any cattle from the above-mentioned localities into the State of Illinois from the first day of April to the first day of November of each year, except under the regulations hereto attached that have been prescribed by the said board of live-stock commissioners and approved by the governor as follows:

EXCEPTIONS AND REGULATIONS

prescribed by the board of live-stock commissioners, governing the importation of cattle into this State from localities scheduled in the governor's proclamation with reference to splenic or Texas fever:

(1) Cattle from the scheduled localities may, while in transit through this State, be unloaded for the necessary time required in feeding and watering, in regular railroad shipping-pens or feed-yards.

(2) Cattle may be imported from the scheduled localities where they are destined for immediate slaughter in this State, in which case such cattle shall not be driven over public highways or commons where cattle are permitted to range at large.

(3) In case persons are desirous of purchasing any of the above prohibited cattle for purposes of feeding and grazing within this State, such persons shall make application to the State veterinarian, or to this board, for permission to do so, when such cattle shall be placed in quarantine for a period of ninety days, at the owner's expense, under such rules and regulations as shall be prescribed by the board.

This proclamation to go into effect Saturday the fifteenth day of May, eighteen hundred and eighty-six.

In testimony whereof I hereto set my hand and cause the great seal of state to be affixed. Done at the city of Springfield the day and year first above written.

RICHARD J. OGLESBY.

By the governor:
HENRY D. DEMENT,
Secretary of State.

INDIANA.

Whereas information has reached me that pleuro-pneumonia exists in Cook County, in the State of Illinois, and other localities, to an alarming extent; and

Whereas on the 10th day of November, 1885, I issued a proclamation prohibiting the importation of cattle from said State of Illinois, and other scheduled localities, except under the conditions and under the restrictions therein named:

Now, therefore, I, Isaac P. Gray, governor of the State of Indiana, do hereby issue this proclamation, hereby notifying any and all persons that said first-named proclamation is still in full effect, and will be strictly enforced.

In witness whereof I have hereunto set my hand and caused the seal of the State to be affixed at the city of Indianapolis this 11th day of October, 1886.

ISAAC P. GRAY.

By the governor:
W. R. MYERS,
Secretary of State.

IOWA.

Whereas many of the prominent farmers and stock-growers of the State, more and more realizing the extreme danger of pleuro-pneumonia, request that additional restrictions be placed upon the importation of cattle from the State of Illinois:

Therefore, I, William Larrabee, governor of the State of Iowa, do now forbid the importation into this State, from Illinois, of any cattle, except in such special cases as may be approved by the veterinary surgeon of this State and upon compliance with such regulations as he may prescribe.

And I again appeal to all the citizens of the State, and especially to all State, county, and municipal officers, to aid to the best of their abilities to ward off from our State the calamity of an invasion of that dreadful plague.

In testimony whereof I have hereunto set my hand and caused to be affixed the great seal of the State of Iowa. Done at Des Moines, this fifteenth day of February, A. D. eighteen hundred and eighty-seven.

WM. LARRABEE.

By the governor:
FRANK D. JACKSON,
Secretary of State.

KANSAS.

Whereas reliable information has reached the live-stock sanitary commission of the State of Kansas that contagious pleuro-pneumonia of cattle has made its appearance in a large number of animals within the States of Illinois and Ohio, and the Dominion of Canada; and

Whereas the cattle interests of the State of Kansas are greatly endangered by the prevalence of this plague at points situated on the principal avenues of the live-stock traffic of the country, thereby making it possible for the disease to become wide-spread; and

Whereas an outbreak of this disease within the State of Kansas would seriously depreciate the value of our cattle and close the markets of the world against our beef:

Now, therefore, I, John A. Martin, governor of Kansas, do hereby, by virtue of the authority vested in me by law, and in accordance with the recommendation of the live-stock sanitary commission, declare and establish a quarantine against the introduction into this State of all animals of the bovine species coming from the States of Ohio and Illinois, and from the Dominion of Canada, unless all such cattle are quarantined at the point of entry for a period of ninety days, and retained there until they shall receive a certificate of health, signed by the State veterinarian.

In testimony whereof, I have hereunto subscribed my name, and caused to be affixed the great seal of the State. Done at the city of Topeka, on the day and year first above written.

JOHN A. MARTIN.

By the governor:
E. B. ALLEN,
Secretary of State.

MICHIGAN.

EXECUTIVE OFFICE,
Lansing, Michigan, November 28, 1886.

Whereas pleuro-pneumonia, a contagious disease, is now prevailing amongst cattle in the county of Cook, in the State of Illinois;

And whereas large numbers of cattle are being brought into this State from said county of Cook, and there is danger that said disease will be communicated to, and become prevalent amongst, cattle in this State:

Now, therefore, to guard against such danger, and in accordance with the provisions of act No. 182 of the Session Laws of 1885, of this State, being "An act to provide for the appointment of a State live-stock sanitary commission and a State veterinarian, and to prescribe their powers and duties, and to prevent and suppress contagious and infectious diseases among the live stock of the State," it is hereby ordered that no cattle shall be brought from said county of Cook, State of Illinois, into this State to be kept for feeding, or to be slaughtered therein, which have such disease, or have been exposed to the same.

On and after the 1st day of December, 1886, one or more of said commisssioners, or a competent veterinarian appointed by them, will remain in the city of Chicago for the purpose of inspecting all shipments of cattle consigned from said county of Cook to local points in this State, and no cattle shall be shipped into this State as aforesaid from said points without a written certificate and permit from one of said commissioners or veterinarian so appointed.

RUSSELL A. ALGER.

By the governor:
H. A. CONANT,
Secretary of State.

EXECUTIVE OFFICE,
Lansing, Michigan, December 8, 1886.

Whereas reports show that contagious pleuro-pneumonia has been found to exist amongst the cattle of Cook County, Illinois, to a much greater extent and covering a much larger territory than had heretofore been supposed, as shown by the fact that large numbers of cattle are being killed, including not only those which are known to be affected by the disease, but that are supposed to have been exposed to the same within said county of Cook; and

Whereas it is of the utmost importance to the cattle interests of the State of Michigan that every precaution possible should be taken to exclude such disease from this State; and

Whereas in the judgment of the live-stock sanitary commission of this State, established by act No. 182 of the Session Laws of 1885, the precautionary measures hereinafter named ought to be adopted:

It is hereby ordered, in accordance with the act heretofore referred to, that hereafter and until this order is countermanded, no live stock shall be shipped to any place in this State from said county of Cook, in the State of Illinois, either for feeding, [illegible], or other purposes, and that all cattle shipped through the State shall not be unloaded and fed within the State, except at such points as will not expose other cattle.

RUSSELL A. ALGER.

By the governor:
H. A. CONANT,
Secretary of State.

MONTANA.

[illegible] of and pursuant to an act of the legislative assembly of the [illegible], entitled "An act to suppress and prevent the dissemination [illegible] infectious diseases among domestic animals and Texas cattle," approved March 10, A. D., 1885, it is my duty, when I shall have reason to believe that any contagious or infectious disease has become epidemic in certain localities, by proclamation, to schedule such localities and prohibit the importation from them of any live stock into this Territory, except under such restrictions as I, after consultation with the Territorial veterinary surgeon, may deem proper; and

Whereas I have reason to believe, upon the representation of the board of stock commissioners and the Territorial veterinary surgeon, that conditions exist which render domestic animals and Texas cattle in any and all the counties of the following States and Territories, viz., Illinois, Pennsylvania, New York, New Jersey, Maryland, Delaware, District of Columbia, Virginia, Vermont, and Texas, liable to convey disease:

Now, therefore, I, P. H. Leslie, governor of the Territory of Montana, by virtue of the authority conferred upon me by said statute, and pursuant to the terms thereof, do hereby schedule the localities hereinbefore named, and I do hereby strictly forbid the importation into the Territory of any cattle whatsover, which have been brought from any portion of said scheduled localities, or any of them, except upon certificate of the Territorial veterinary surgeon that such cattle have been subject to a quarantine of ninety days, and except Texas cattle that have been driven overland all the way from Texas, and which are accompanied by a veterinarian's certificate of health.

And I do hereby further forbid the importation into this Territory of any and all cattle driven or shipped from any other State, Territory, or country, unless the same shall be accompanied by a certificate of health given by the veterinary surgeon of said State, Territory, or country, or his regularly appointed and authorized deputy, who shall have carefully examined all such cattle immediately prior to the giving of such certificate. And all such cattle shall be examined at such station or stations as shall be designated by the Territorial veterinary surgeon.

And I do hereby warn all persons, corporations, and companies whomsoever, not in any manner to violate, or attempt to violate, the prohibition herein contained, or contained in said act.

And I do hereby direct all sheriffs, constables, stock inspectors, and other peace officers within this Territory to keep strict watch, and to be vigilant, and see to it that all the commands of this, my proclamation, are obeyed and respected, and to arrest any and all persons violating the same. And I further direct all such officers to report to me, without delay, all such violations of this, my proclamation.

In testimony whereof, I have hereunto set my hand and caused the seal of the Territory of Montana to be attached, at the city of Helena, the capital of said Territory, this 26th day of April, A. D. 1887.

P. H. LESLIE.

By the governor:
WM. B. WEBB,
Secretary of Montana.

Whereas, by virtue of and pursuant to an act of the legislative assembly of the Territory of Montana, entitled "An act to suppress and prevent the dissemination of contagious and infectious diseases among domestic animals and Texas cattle," approved March 10, A. D. 1885, it is my duty, when I shall have reason to believe that any contagious or infectious disease has become epidemic in certain localities, by proclamation, to schedule such localities, and prohibit the importation from them of any live stock into this Territory, except under such restrictions as I, after consultation with the Territorial veterinary surgeon, may deem proper; and

Whereas I have reason to believe, upon the representation of the board of stock commissioners and the Territorial veterinary surgeon, that conditions exist which render domestic animals and Texas cattle in any and all of the counties of the following-named States and Territories, viz., Illinois, New York, New Jersey, Pennsylvania, Maryland, Delaware, District of Columbia, Virginia, Texas, and Vermont, liable to convey disease:

Now, therefore, I, P. H. Leslie, governor of the Territory of Montana, by virtue of the authority conferred upon me by said statute, and pursuant to the terms thereof, do hereby schedule the localities hereinbefore named, and I do hereby strictly forbid the importation into the Territory of any cattle whatsoever which have been brought from any portion of said scheduled localities, or any one of them, except upon certificate of the Territorial veterinary surgeon that such cattle have been subject to a quarantine of ninety days, and except Texas cattle that have been driven overland all the way from Texas, and which are accompanied by a veterinarian's certificate of health.

And I do hereby further forbid the importation into this Territory of any and all cattle driven or shipped from any other State, Territory, or country, unless the same shall be accompanied by a certificate of health given by the veterinary surgeon of said State, Territory, or country, or his regularly appointed and authorized deputy, who shall have carefully examined all such cattle immediately prior to the giving of such certificate; and all such cattle shall be examined at such station or stations as shall be designated by the Territorial veterinary surgeon.

And I do hereby warn all persons, corporations, and companies whomsoever, not in any manner to violate or attempt to violate the prohibition herein contained, or contained in said act.

And I do hereby direct all sheriffs, constables, stock inspectors, and other peace officers within this Territory to keep strict watch and to be vigilant, and see to it that all the commands of this, my proclamation, are obeyed and respected, and to arrest any and all persons violating the same: and I further direct all such officers to report to me, without delay, all such violations of this proclamation.

In testimony whereof, I have hereunto set my hand, and caused the seal of the Territory of Montana to be attached, at the city of Helena, the capital of said Territory, this 28th day of April, A. D. 1887.

P. H. LESLIE.

By the governor:
WM. B. WEBB,
Secretary of Montana.

Whereas under the provisions of an act of the legislative assembly of the Territory of Montana, entitled "An act to suppress and prevent dissemination of scab and infectious diseases among sheep," and approved March ten, eighteen hundred and eighty-seven, it is made my duty, upon the recommendation of the president or secretary and two members of the executive committee of any district or county wool-growers' association, to schedule such localities and prohibit the introduction from them of any sheep into this Territory except under such restrictions as I may deem proper; and whereas the recommendations prescribed in said act as the basis of executive action have been filed in this office, which, with the accompanying facts therein set forth, manifestly show that the sheep in any and all States and Territories, to wit: Oregon, Nevada, and California, Washington Territory, Idaho, and Utah, if brought into this Territory are liable to bring with them the disease called scab and other loathsome contagious disorders.

Now, therefore, I, Preston H. Leslie, governor of the Territory of Montana, in obedience to the duty imposed upon me by said statute and the terms thereof, do hereby schedule the locality hereinbefore named, and I do hereby forbid the importation into the Territory of Montana of any sheep whatsoever which have been brought from any portion of said localities, or any of them, except upon the certificate of the Territorial veterinary surgeon that such sheep have been inspected by him or his deputy and found to be clear of said scab and of any infectious disease; and I do hereby warn all corporations, persons, and companies to give due and full notice to the veterinary surgeon of Montana preceding the arrival at the boundary line of all such sheep as come within the provisions of this proclamation; and I enjoin upon all sheriffs, constables, and other peace officers within this Territory to keep strict watch and be vigilant, and see to it that the commands of this proclamation are obeyed and respected, and to arrest all persons who may violate the same.

In witness whereof I have hereto set my hand and caused the seal of the Territory of Montana to be affixed at the city of Helena, the capital of said Territory, this second day of July, eighteen hundred and eighty-seven.

P. H. LESLIE,
Governor.

By the governor:
WM. B. WEBB,
Secretary of Montana.

NEBRASKA.

Whereas the disease known as Texas or splenic fever is common among the cattle of various Southern States; and

Whereas danger to the live-stock interests of Nebraska is apprehended from the introduction of cattle affected with said disease; and

Whereas the live-stock sanitary commission of the State of Nebraska, at a meeting of said commission, held at Lincoln on the second day of March, eighteen hundred and eighty-six, adopted the following resolution:

"*Resolved*, That the governor be requested to prohibit by proclamation the entering into the State of Nebraska of all cattle that have been shipped all or any part of the way from the States of Texas, Arkansas, Louisiana, Alabama, Mississippi, Florida, Georgia, Tennessee, North Carolina, and South Carolina during the months of April, May, June, July, August, September, and October."

Now, therefore, I, James W. Dawes, governor of the State of Nebraska, under the direction of the foregoing resolution, and by virtue of the authority vested in me, do hereby issue my proclamation declaring and establishing quarantine and prohibiting the entry into the State of all cattle that have been shipped all or any part of the way from all or either of the above-named places, except under such rules and regulations as may be prescribed from time to time by the live-stock sanitary commission of this State.

The quarantine so declared and established will be enforced by the live-stock sanitary commission and State veterinarian.

In testimony whereof I have hereunto set my hand and caused to be affixed the great seal of the State of Nebraska.

Done at Lincoln this eighteenth day of March, A. D. eighteen hundred and eighty-six.

JAMES W. DAWES.

By the governor:
E. P. ROGGEN,
Secretary of State.

NEW MEXICO.

It having been communicated to me in writing by the cattle sanitary board of New Mexico that a certain fatal, contagious, and infectious disease, commonly known as pleuro-pneumonia, exists and has become epidemic among bovine cattle in the States of New York, New Jersey, and Illinois, and in the foreign countries of Scotland, England, and the Dominion of Canada, and that such conditions exist as to render such disease liable to be communicated to cattle in the Territory of New Mexico through the importation of cattle from such States and foreign countries, and particularly through the general stock-yards located in the city of Chicago, in the State of Illinois, and in the city of Kansas City, in the State of Missouri; also that cattle have been known to have been exposed to said contagious disease and infected therewith without exhibiting any symptoms thereof for a period of six months from and after such exposure; therefore I, Edmund G. Ross, governor of the Territory of New Mexico, under and by virtue of the power and authority vested in me by law, do hereby forbid the shipment and importation into said Territory, in any manner whatever, of all bovine cattle from either of the above-named States and foreign countries, or through the aforesaid cities of Chicago and Kansas City, or either of them, except upon the conditions and restrictions as follows, to wit:

(1) All bovine cattle coming from either of the above-named States and foreign countries, or through either of the aforesaid cities of Chicago and Kansas City, before being permitted to enter said Territory must be accompanied by reliable documentary evidence under oath to the inspector inspecting the same that they and each and all of them have been outside of each of the above-named States and foreign countries, and have not been unloaded or been in either of the stock-yards in either of the aforesaid cities of Chicago and Kansas City at any time within six months immediately preceding their arrival at the boundary line of the Territory, and that during all that time they or any of them have shown no symptoms of such disease; and, in addition thereto, the inspector inspecting the same must be satisfied from actual inspection that none of them at the time of inspection show any symptoms of such disease.

(2) For the present and until otherwise provided, all bovine cattle coming from either of the above-mentioned States and foreign countries, or that have been in either of the aforesaid cities of Chicago and Kansas City, will be permitted to enter said Territory after inspection only by way of Raton, in said Territory.

(3) All bovine cattle which by any route, direct or indirect, could have been within either of the stock-yards in the aforesaid cities of Chicago and Kansas City within six months prior to inspection shall be inspected before being admitted into said Territory by such inspector as shall be appointed for that purpose by said cattle sanitary board.

(4) If upon such inspection and proofs it shall be ascertained that any of the cattle so inspected can be driven or imported into said Territory without violating any of the terms and conditions of this proclamation or any of the provisions of the law of said Territory applicable thereto, then the same may be admitted into said Territory; otherwise such admission is hereby prohibited.

(5) In addition to the foregoing conditions the inspectors of any cattle under the proclamation may require the importer to furnish satisfactory documentary evi-

dence, under oath, showing each and all the places where the cattle have been during the six months preceding the inspection; and if the inspector shall have good reason to believe or suspect that any of the material proofs offered by the importer are unreliable or insufficient, he may refuse a permit for the entry of the cattle until such reasonable time as may be necessary for him to ascertain the truth.

(6) When the inspector grants a permit for the entry of cattle under this proclamation the same shall be in writing and accompany the cattle to their destination; and while the cattle are in transit into or through the Territory the owner or person in charge shall produce such permit on demand to any other inspector or to any other person whose interests may be affected by the importation of diseased cattle: provided, there shall be no detention of the cattle in transit after producing the proper permit. Any refusal or neglect to so produce a permit shall render the cattle liable to inspection, or to be again inspected at the cost of the owner.

(7) For all inspections of cattle under this proclamation a charge of twenty cents per head of the cattle inspected may be made and collected by the inspector from the owner or person in charge of the cattle.

(8) This proclamation shall take effect and be in force from and after the first day of June, A. D. eighteen hundred and eighty-seven.

In testimony whereof I have hereunto set my official hand and caused to be affixed the great seal of the Territory of New Mexico, the twenty-first day of May, eighteen hundred and eighty-seven.

EDMUND G. ROSS,
Governor.

It having been communicated to me in writing by the cattle sanitary board of New Mexico and from the United States Bureau of Animal Industry that a certain fatal, contagious, and infectious disease, commonly known as pleuro-pneumonia, exists and has become epidemic among bovine cattle in the States of New York, New Jersey, Maryland, the District of Columbia, Virginia, Pennsylvania, and Illinois, and in the foreign countries of England, Scotland, and the Dominion of Canada, and that such conditions exist as to render such disease liable to be communicated to the cattle in the Territory of New Mexico through the importation of the same from such States and foreign countries, and particularly through the general stock-yards located in the city of Chicago, in the State of Illinois, and the city of Kansas City, in the State of Missouri; also that cattle have been known to have been exposed to said contagious disease and infected therewith without exhibiting any symptoms thereof for a period of six months from and after such exposure:

Therefore, I, Edmund G. Ross, governor of the Territory of New Mexico, under and by virtue of the power and authority vested in me by law, do hereby forbid the shipment and the importation into said Territory in any manner whatever of all bovine cattle from either of the above-named States and foreign countries, or through the aforesaid stock-yards or either of them except upon the conditions and restrictions as follows to-wit:

(1) All bovine cattle coming from either of the above-named States and foreign countries, or through either of the aforesaid stock-yards, before being permitted to enter said Territory must be accompanied by reliable documentary evidence under oath, to the satisfaction of the inspector inspecting the same, that they and each and all of them have been outside of each of the above-named States and foreign countries, and have not been unloaded or been in either of the stock-yards aforesaid at any time within six months immediately preceding their arrival at the boundary line of said Territory, and that during all that time they or any of them have shown no symptoms of such disease; and, in addition thereto, the inspector inspecting the same must be satisfied from actual inspection that none of them at the time of inspection show any sign of such disease.

(2) For the present, and until otherwise provided, all bovine cattle coming from either of the above-mentioned States and foreign countries, or that have been in either of the aforesaid stock-yards, will be permitted to enter said Territory after inspection and permit granted only by way of Raton, in said Territory, or via El Paso, Texas.

(3) All bovine cattle hereafter destined for transportation into or through New Mexico, and to cross the north or east boundary line thereof, are subject to inspection as hereinafter provided for the purpose of determining whether they, or any of them are, or are not, from either of the said States or foreign countries, or have, or have not, been in either of the aforesaid stock-yards within six months prior to such inspection, as well as to determine whether any other of the conditions and terms of this proclamation have been violated, or attempted to be violated. Such inspection to be made by such inspectors as the cattle sanitary board shall appoint for that pur-

pose, and to be made under such rules and regulations, not inconsistent with this proclamation, as such board shall prescribe.

(4) If upon such inspection and proof it shall be ascertained that any of the cattle so inspected can be driven and imported into said Territory without violating any of the terms and conditions of this proclamation, or any of the provisions of the law of said Territory applicable thereto, then the same may be admitted into said Territory; otherwise said admission is hereby prohibited.

(5) In addition to the foregoing conditions, the inspectors of any cattle under this proclamation may require the importer to furnish satisfactory documentary evidence, under oath, showing each and all the places where the cattle have been during the six months preceding the inspection; and if the inspector shall have good reasons to believe or suspect that any of the material proofs offered by the importer are unreliable or insufficient, he may refuse a permit for the entry of the cattle until such reasonable time as may be necessary for him to ascertain the truth.

(6) When the inspector grants a permit for the entry of cattle under this proclamation, the same shall be in writing and accompany the cattle to their destination. And while the cattle are in transit into or through the Territory, the owner or person in charge shall produce such permit, on demand, to any other inspector or to any other person whose interest may be affected by the importation of diseased cattle: *Provided*, There shall be no detention of the cattle in transit after producing the proper permit. Any refusal or neglect to so produce a permit on demand, shall render the cattle liable to inspection or to be again inspected at the cost of the owner.

(7) In all cases where the importer gives notice to the inspector to have his cattle inspected under this proclamation, before crossing the boundary line of the Territory, or voluntarily submits to such inspection before crossing such line, and does not violate any of the terms and conditions of this proclamation, there will be no charge for inspection. But in the case of the transportation of cattle into the Territory in violation of this proclamation, or any of the conditions thereof, then the costs of inspection, also of seizure and quarantine of the cattle, will be borne by the importer under the provisions of the quarantine law of the Territory; also his liabilities for damages and penalties, as well as liens on the cattle under that law will attach.

(8) All quarantine proclamations heretofore issued by me are hereby abrogated.

(9) This proclamation shall take effect and be in force immediately.

In testimony whereof I have hereunto set my official hand and caused to be affixed the great seal of the Territory of New Mexico the sixteenth day of August, 1887.

EDMUND G. ROSS,
Governor of New Mexico.

WYOMING TERRITORY.

Whereas by virtue of and pursuant to the act of the legislative assembly of the Territory of Wyoming entitled "An act to suppress and prevent the dissemination of contagious and infectious diseases among domestic animals," approved March 8th, 1882, it is my duty, when I shall have good reason to believe that any contagious or infectious disease has become epidemic in certain localities, or that conditions exist which render domestic animals liable to convey disease, by proclamation to schedule such localities, and to prohibit the importation from them of any live stock into this Territory, except under such restrictions as I may deem proper; and

Whereas a certain contagious or infectious disease called pleuro-pneumonia has become epidemic in certain localities, to-wit, in the counties of Putnam, Westchester, New York, Kings, Richmond, and Queens, in the State of New York; in the counties of Bucks, Montgomery, Philadelphia, Delaware, Chester, and Lancaster, in the State of Pennsylvania; in the counties of Bergen, Hudson, Morris, Essex, Union, Somerset, Hunterdon, Middlesex, Mercer, Monmouth, Ocean, Burlington, Camden, Gloucester, Passaic, and Atlantic, in the State of New Jersey; in the county of Newcastle, in the State of Delaware; and in the counties of Cecil, Harford, Baltimore, Howard, and Carroll, in the State of Maryland; in the District of Columbia; in the county of Fairfax, in the State of Virginia; in the counties of Calloway, Boone, Cole, Audrain, Montgomery, and Osage, in the State of Missouri; and in the county of Travis, in the State of Texas; and

Whereas it is a well-established fact that cattle from the following States, viz., Florida, Alabama, Mississippi, Louisiana, and from portions of Texas, Indian Territory, Tennessee, Arkansas, and South Carolina have the capacity to infect cattle of the States and Territories lying to the northward of them with a fatal disease known as Texas or splenic fever, especially when cattle from such localities have been brought to the States and Territories with such speed as to prevent their losing the power to communicate said disease; and

Whereas owners of cattle from said infectious districts are in the habit of driving such cattle a portion of the way and then shipping them to Wyoming Territory, to the danger and detriment of Wyoming Territory:

Now, therefore, by virtue of the premises aforesaid, and pursuant to said statute, I, Francis E. Warren, governor of the Territory of Wyoming, do hereby schedule the localities first hereinbefore specified, that is to say, said counties in the States of New York, Pennsylvania, New Jersey, Delaware, Maryland, Missouri, Virginia, Texas, and the District of Columbia; and I do hereby proclaim that in said localities and each thereof a certain contagious and infectious disease, to-wit, pleuro-pneumonia, exists in an epidemic form, and I do hereby strictly forbid, as by said statute it is made my duty to do, the importation into this Territory of any neat cattle that have been brought from or through any portion of said scheduled localities, or any one of them.

And by virtue of the premises aforesaid I do hereby forbid, as by said statute it is made my duty to do, the importation into this Territory, prior to November 1st, 1886, of any neat cattle that have been or may be brought in whole or in part by *rail* from the States and Territories hereinbefore specified, unless the owner or owners shall satisfy the Territorial veterinarian that said cattle are from non-infected districts, or have been long enough away from said infected localities to have lost the power of infecting range cattle; and

Whereas neat cattle from said infected districts have been, at divers times since the discovery of the existence of said disease therein, sold and transported to other sections without any regard paid to said disease or the exposure of such cattle thereto, very many of which are now held and owned by persons whose intention it is to transport the same into or through this Territory, and by reason of such unrestricted traffic it is impossible to determine with the certainty the gravity of the situation demands, without the aid of such owners or persons in charge, whether the said cattle thus intended for Wyoming or for transportation through said Territory came from or through any of said scheduled localities or not, or whether they, or any of them, have been exposed to said disease or not, either in said localities or in others not herein specified: and

Whereas neat cattle may have been exposed to said disease and may have the same in its incipient stages, and no diagnosis thereof will answer with certainty whether the animal is thus afflicted or not, and in all cases at least ninety days must elapse before a veterinarian can certify intelligently to the healthfulness of said animal; and

Whereas if any such neat cattle thus diseased, or that have been exposed thereto, should be permitted to enter this Territory, and should thereby come into contact with the cattle of this Territory, the property of the citizens of this Territory would be greatly endangered; and

Whereas very many of said cattle that have or may have been exposed have been and are now being taken to the various shipping stations lying east of the Missouri River, and which have rail connection with this Territory, with the intent of transporting the same into or through this Territory, and inasmuch as it is practically impossible to guard our Territorial lines from being crossed by any or all of such cattle if they be driven:

Now, therefore, by virtue of the premises aforesaid, and pursuant to said statute, I, Francis E. Warren, governor of the Territory of Wyoming, do hereby forbid the importation into or transportation through this Territory of any neat cattle that have been brought from any place lying east of the one hundred and fourth degree of west longitude, which is the east boundary of Wyoming Territory, except only on the conditions and under the restrictions following; that is to say:

(1) That said cattle shall only be brought by rail, and shall first be examined by the Territorial veterinarian or his deputy at Cheyenne or such place as he may designate, and if found on inspection to be free from any symptoms of any contagious or infectious disease, then, and in that case, it shall be the duty of the owner or person in charge of said cattle to reasonably establish the following facts in relation thereto, viz:

That said cattle did not come from or through any of said scheduled localities; that none of said cattle have been exposed to said disease within four months next preceding their shipment.

(2) Upon the truth of each of the foregoing being made manifest to said veterinarian, he shall give to said cattle a certificate reciting the facts thus proven, and also of his examination thereof, together with a careful description of said cattle; whereupon said cattle shall have the freedom of this Territory, and not before; and until such certificates shall be given them they shall be held in said quarantine

yards until such time as the veterinarian shall be satisfied by lapse of time of their freedom from disease, such period of detention to be not longer than ninety days next ensuing their arrival, and if after the expiration of such time they shall not show any symptoms of any infectious or contagious disease, they shall then be allowed the freedom of the Territory.

(3) During the time cattle shall remain in said yards they shall be subject to the rules and regulations then in force concerning cattle held in quarantine, and shall be properly attended to at the expense of the owner thereof.

And I hereby warn all persons and corporations whomsoever not to in any way violate or attempt to violate in any way the prohibitions herein contained, else they shall incur the severe penalties and punishments in said act provided therefor; and to that end, and that this proclamation shall be in all things strictly enforced, I hereby call upon all sheriffs and other officers of this Territory to give to this proclamation and to its rigid enforcement their active and zealous aid; and, further, I respectfully request all persons to report to me any cattle that are now or that may hereafter be on their way to this Territory, and in all other ways in their power to aid in the enforcement of the injunction and commands herein contained.

All former proclamations of quarantine are hereby revoked.

In testimony whereof I have hereunto set my hand and caused the great seal of said Territory to be hereunto affixed.

Done at Cheyenne this eighth day of July, A. D. eighteen hundred and eighty-six.

FRANCIS E. WARREN.

By the governor:

E. S. N. MORGAN,

Secretary of the Territory.

Whereas John L. Marmaduke, governor of the State of Missouri, has furnished me reliable and official information that the disease known as pleuro-pneumonia has not existed during the year last past and does not now exist within the borders of said State;

Now, therefore, I, Francis E. Warren, governor of the Territory of Wyoming, do, by the authority vested in me as governor, hereby proclaim that such portion of my proclamation under date of July 8th, 1886, as schedules for quarantine certain counties within the State of Missouri is hereby revoked.

The State of Missouri will be subject, however, to such conditions and restrictions as said proclamation of July 8, 1886, imposes upon all States, Territories, and districts lying east of the one hundred and fourth degree of west longitude, which is the east boundary of Wyoming Territory.

In testimony whereof, I have hereunto set my hand and caused the great seal of the Territory to be hereunto affixed.

Done at Cheyenne this twenty-seventh day of July, A. D. eighteen hundred and eighty-six.

FRANCIS E. WARREN.

By the governor:

E. S. N. MORGAN,

Secretary of Territory.

Whereas the Territorial veterinarian of Wyoming was dispatched from this Territory to Chicago, Illinois, to ascertain the facts regarding the reported prevalence of contagious pleuro-pneumonia at that point; and

Whereas a communication has been received from the Territorial veterinarian informing me that contagious pleuro-pneumonia exists among the cattle at Chicago, Illinois, to an extent that may endanger the cattle of Wyoming Territory:

Now, therefore, I, Francis E. Warren, governor of the Territory of Wyoming, by virtue of the authority vested in me by law, do hereby forbid the importation into this Territory, from the State of Illinois, of all cattle, except when accompanied by a satisfactory certificate of health issued by the State veterinarian of Illinois, or an inspector of the United States Bureau of Animal Industry, and under such other regulations as may be prescribed by the Territorial veterinarian of Wyoming.

In testimony whereof, I have hereunto set my hand and caused the great seal of this Territory to be hereunto affixed.

Done at Cheyenne this fifth day of October, A. D. eighteen hundred and eighty-six.

FRANCIS E. WARREN.

By the governor:

E. S. N. MORGAN,

Secretary of Territory.

Whereas, by virtue of and pursuant to section 4965 of the Revised Statutes of Wyoming, it is my duty, when I shall have good reason to believe that any contagious or infectious disease has become epidemic in certain localities, or that conditions exist which render domestic animals liable to convey disease, by proclamation to schedule such localities and to prohibit the importation from them of any live stock into this Territory, except under such restrictions as I may deem proper; and

Whereas it has been represented to me by the executive committee of the Stock Growers' Association of the Territory that a certain contagious or infectious disease called pleuro-pneumonia has become epidemic in certain localities, to wit, in the counties of Putnam, West Chester, New York, Kings, Richmond, Queens, and Suffolk, in the State of New York; in the counties of Bucks, Montgomery, Philadelphia, Delaware, Chester, and Lancaster, in the State of Pennsylvania; in the counties of Bergen, Hudson, Morris, Essex, Union, Somerset, Hunterdon, Middlesex, Mercer, Monmouth, Oceau, Burlington, Camden, Gloucester, Passaic, and Atlantic, in the State of New Jersey; in the county of Newcastle, in the State of Delaware; in the counties of Cecil, Harford, Baltimore, Howard, Carroll, and Prince George, in the State of Maryland; in the counties of Cook, Lake, McHenry, Kane, DuPage, and Will, in the State of Illinois; in the county of Fairfax, in the State of Virginia, and in the District of Columbia; and

Whereas in the States of Missouri, Iowa, and Kansas conditions exist which render domestic animals liable to convey disease; and

Whereas it is a well established fact that cattle from the following States, viz: Florida, Alabama, Mississippi, Louisiana, and from portions of Texas, Indian Territory, Tennessee, Arkansas, and South Carolina, have the capacity to infect cattle of the States and Territories lying to the northward of them with a fatal disease known as Texas or splenic fever, especially when cattle from such localities have been brought to the States and Territories with such speed as to prevent their losing the power to communicate said disease; and

Whereas owners of cattle from said infectious districts are in the habit of driving such cattle a portion of the way and then shipping them to Wyoming Territory, to the danger and detriment of Wyoming Territory:

Now, therefore, by virtue of the premises aforesaid, and pursuant to said statute, I, Thomas Moonlight, governor of the Territory of Wyoming, do hereby schedule the localities first hereinbefore specified, that is to say, said counties in the States of New York, Pennsylvania, New Jersey, Delaware, Maryland, Illinois, Virginia, and the District of Columbia; I do hereby proclaim, that in said localities, and each thereof, pleuro-pneumonia exists in an epidemic form, and that in the States of Missouri, Iowa, and Kansas a condition exists which renders domestic animals liable to convey contagious disease, and I do hereby strictly forbid, as by said statute it is made my duty to do, the importation into this Territory of any neat cattle that have been brought from or through any portion of said scheduled localities, or any one of them.

And by virtue of the premises aforesaid, I do hereby forbid, as by said statute it is made my duty to do, the importation into this Territory, prior to November 1, 1887, of any neat cattle that have been or may be brought in whole or in part *by rail* from the States and Territories hereinbefore specified, unless the owner or owners shall satisfy the Territorial veterinarian that said cattle are from non-infected districts, or have been long enough away from said districts to have lost the power of infecting range cattle; and

Whereas neat cattle from said infected districts have been at divers times since the discovery of the existence of said disease therein sold and transported to other sections, without any regard paid to said disease or the exposure of such cattle thereto, very many of which are now held and owned by persons whose intention it is to transport the same into or through this Territory, and by reason of such unrestricted traffic it is impossible to determine with the certainty the gravity of the situation demands, without the aid of such owners or persons in charge, whether the said cattle thus intended for Wyoming, or for transportation through said Territory, came from or through any of said scheduled localities or not, or whether they or any of them, have been exposed to said disease or not, either in said localities or in others not herein specified; and

Whereas neat cattle may have been exposed to said disease and may have the same in its incipient stages, and no diagnosis of the same will answer with certainty whether the animal is thus afflicted or not, and in all cases at least ninety days must elapse before a veterinarian can certify intelligently to the healthfulness of said animal; and

Whereas if any such neat cattle thus diseased, or that have been exposed thereto, should be permitted to enter this Territory, and should thereby come into contact

attle of this Territory, the property of the citizens of this Territory would endangered; and

...very many of said neat cattle that have, or may have been exposed, and are now being taken to the various shipping stations lying east of the river, and which have rail connection with this Territory, with the intent bring the same into or through this Territory, and inasmuch as it is impossible to guard our Territorial lines from being crossed by any or all attle if they be driven:

...erefore, by virtue of the premises aforesaid, and pursuant to said statute, Moonlight, governor of the Territory of Wyoming, do hereby forbid the ...e into or transportation through this Territory of any neat cattle that brought from any place lying east of the one hundred and fourth degree ...ngitude, which is the east boundary of Wyoming Territory, except only ...itions and under the restrictions following; that is to say:

...said cattle shall only be brought by rail, and shall first be examined by ...rial veterinarian, or his deputy, at Cheyenne or such place as he may ...and if found on inspection to be free from any symptoms of any contagious ...fectious disease, then, and in that case, it shall be the duty of the owner ...n charge of said cattle to reasonably establish the following facts in rela...o, viz:

...l cattle did not come from or through any of said scheduled localities; ...one of said cattle have been exposed to said disease within four months ...ding their shipment.

...the truth of each of the foregoing being made manifest to said veteri...shall give to said cattle a certificate reciting the facts thus proven, and ...examination thereof, together with a careful description of said cattle; ...said cattle shall have the freedom of this Territory, and not before; and ...certificates shall be given them they shall be held in said quarantine ...such time as the veterinarian shall be satisfied by lapse of time of their ...m disease, such period of detention to be not longer than ninety days ...g their arrival, and if, after the expiration of such time, they shall not ...ymptoms of any contagious or infectious disease, they shall be allowed ...n of the Territory.

...g the time cattle shall remain in said yards they shall be subject to the ...egulations then in force concerning cattle held in quarantine, and shall ...attended to at the expense of the owner thereof.

...reby warn all persons and corporations whomsoever not to in any way ...ttempt to violate in any way the prohibitions herein contained, else they ...the severe penalties and punishments in said act provided therefor; and ...l, and that this proclamation shall be in all things strictly enforced, I ...upon all sheriffs and other officers of this Territory to give to this procla...l to its rigid enforcement their active and zealous aid; and further, I re...equest all persons to report to me any cattle that are now or that may ...e on their way to this Territory, and in all other ways in their power to ...nforcement of the injunction and commands herein contained.

...r proclamations of quarantine are hereby revoked.

...ony whereof I have hereunto set my hand and caused the great seal of ...ry to be hereunto affixed.

...Cheyenne this sixteenth day of June, A. D. eighteen hundred and ...n.

THOMAS MOONLIGHT.

...overnor:

...SHANNON,

...ecretary of the Territory.

..., by virtue of and pursuant to section 4205 of the revised statutes of ...it is my duty, when I shall have good reason to believe that any conta...fectious disease has become epidemic in certain localities, or that condi...which render domestic animals liable to convey disease, by proclama...dule such localities, and to prohibit the importation from them of any ...nto this Territory, except under such restrictions as I may deem proper;

...it has been represented to me by the executive committee of the Stock...sociation of the Territory, that a certain contagious or infectious dis...pleuro-pneumonia has become epidemic in certain localities, to-wit: ...ties of Putnam, West Chester, New York, Kings, Richmond, Queens, ..., in the State of New York; in the counties of Bucks, Montgomery, ...a, Delaware, Chester, and Lancaster, in the State of Pennsylvania; in the counties of Bergen, Hudson, Morris, Essex, Union, Somerset, Hunterdon, Middlesex, Mercer, Monmouth, Ocean, Burlington, Camden, Gloucester, Passaic, and Atlantic, in the State of New Jersey; in the county of Newcastle, in the State of Delaware; in the counties of Cecil, Harford, Baltimore, Howard, Carroll, and Prince George's, in the State of Maryland; in the counties of Cook, Lake, McHenry, Kane, Du Page, and Will, in the State of Illinois; in the county of Fairfax, in the State of Virginia, and in the District of Columbia; and

Whereas in the States of Missouri, Iowa, and Kansas conditions exist which render domestic animals liable to convey disease; and

Whereas it is a well-established fact that cattle from the following States, viz, Florida, Alabama, Mississippi, Louisiana, and from portions of Texas, Indian Territory, Tennessee, Arkansas, and South Carolina, have the capacity to infect cattle of the States and Territories lying to the northward of them with a fatal disease known as Texas or splenic fever, especially when cattle from such localities have been brought to the States and Territories with such speed as to prevent their losing the power to communicate said disease; and

Whereas owners of cattle from said infectious districts are in the habit of driving such cattle a portion of the way and then shipping them to Wyoming Territory, to the danger and detriment of Wyoming Territory:

Now, therefore, by virtue of the premises aforesaid, and pursuant to said statute, I, Thomas Moonlight, governor of the Territory of Wyoming, do hereby schedule the localities first hereinbefore specified, that is to say, said counties in the States of New York, Pennsylvania, New Jersey, Delaware, Maryland, Illinois, Virginia, and the District of Columbia; I do hereby proclaim that in said localities and each thereof pleuro-pneumonia exists in an epidemic form, and that in the States of Missouri, Iowa, and Kansas a condition exists which renders domestic animals liable to convey contagious disease, and I do hereby strictly forbid, as by said statute it is my duty to do, the importation into this Territory of any neat cattle that have been brought from or through any portion of said scheduled localities, or any one of them.

And by virtue of the premises aforesaid I do hereby forbid, as by said statute it is made my duty to do, the importation into this Territory, prior to November 1, 1887, of any neat cattle that have been or may be brought in whole or in part by rail from the States and Territories hereinbefore specified, unless the owner or owners shall satisfy the Territorial veterinarian that said cattle are from non-infected districts, or have been long enough away from said districts to have lost the power of infecting range cattle; and

Whereas neat cattle from said infected districts have been at divers times since the discovery of the existence of said disease therein sold and transported to other sections, without any regard paid to said disease, or the exposure of such cattle thereto, very many of which are now held and owned by persons whose intention it is to transport the same into or through this Territory, and by reason of such unrestricted traffic it is impossible to determine, with the certainty the gravity of the situation demands, without the aid of such owners or persons in charge, whether the said cattle thus intended for Wyoming, or for transportation through said Territory, came from or through any of said scheduled localities or not, or whether they or any of them have been exposed to said disease or not, either in said localities or in others not herein specified; and

Whereas neat cattle may have been exposed to said disease and may have the same in its incipient stages, and no diagnosis of the same will answer with certainty whether the animal is thus afflicted or not, and in all cases at least ninety days must elapse before a veterinarian can certify intelligently to the healthfulness of said animal; and

Whereas if any such neat cattle thus diseased, or that have been exposed thereto, should be permitted to enter this Territory, and should thereby come into contact with the cattle of this Territory, the property of the citizens of this Territory would be greatly endangered; and

Whereas very many of said neat cattle that have or may have been exposed have been and are now being taken to the various shipping stations lying east of the Missouri River, and which have rail connection with this Territory, with the intent of transporting the same into or through this Territory, and inasmuch as it is practically impossible to guard our Territorial lines from being crossed by any or all of such cattle if they be driven:

Now, therefore, by virtue of the premises aforesaid, and pursuant to said statute, I, Thomas Moonlight, governor of the Territory of Wyoming, do hereby forbid the importation into or transportation through this Territory of any neat cattle that have been brought from any place lying east of the one hundred and fourth degree of west longitude, which is the east boundary of Wyoming Territory, except only on the conditions and under the restrictions following; that is to say:

(1) That said cattle shall only be brought by rail, and shall first be examined by the Territorial veterinarian or his deputy at Cheyenne, or such place as he may designate, and if found on inspection to be free from any symptoms of any contagious or infectious disease, then, and in that case, it shall be the duty of the owner or person in charge of said cattle to reasonably establish the following facts in relation thereto, viz:

That said cattle did not come from or through any of said scheduled localities, and that none of said cattle have been exposed to said disease within four months next preceding their shipment.

(2) Upon the truth of each of the foregoing being made manifest to said veterinarian, he shall give to said cattle a certificate, reciting the facts thus proven, and also of his examination thereof, together with a careful description of said cattle; whereupon said cattle shall have the freedom of this Territory, and not before; and until such certificate shall be given them they shall be held in said quarantine yards until such time as the veterinarian shall be satisfied by lapse of time of their freedom from disease, such period of detention to be not longer than ninety days next ensuing their arrival, and if after the expiration of such time they shall not show any symptoms of any contagious or infectious disease, they shall then be allowed the freedom of the Territory.

(3) During the time cattle shall remain in said yards they shall be subject to the rules and regulations then in force concerning cattle held in quarantine, and shall be properly attended to at the expense of the owner thereof.

And I hereby warn all persons and corporations whomsoever not to in any way violate or to attempt to violate in any way the prohibitions herein contained, else they shall incur the severe penalties and punishments in said act provided therefor, and to that end, and that this proclamation shall be in all things strictly enforced, I hereby call sheriffs and other officers of this Territory to give to this proclamation and to its rigid enforcement their active and zealous aid; and, further, I respectfully request all persons to report to me any cattle that are now or that may hereafter be on their way to this Territory, and in all other ways in their power to aid in the enforcement of the injunction and commands herein contained.

All former proclamations of quarantine are hereby revoked.

In testimony whereof I have hereunto set my hand and caused the great seal of said Territory to be hereto affixed.

Done at Cheyenne this sixteenth day of June, A. D. eighteen hundred and eighty-seven.

THOMAS MOONLIGHT.

By the governor.

S. D. SHANNON,
Secretary of the Territory.

APPENDIX.

INVESTIGATION OF CONTAGIOUS PLEURO-PNEUMONIA.

Inspection of stables, etc., in New Jersey.

Day of month.	Name of owner or person in charge and location of stable.	No. of cattle.	No. with lung-plague.	Condition of stables and animals.
	Inspections by H. W. Rowland, V. S.			
1886.				
Jan. 5	E. Shea, near Bound Brook, Somerset County	5	....	Animals, fair.
5	Barry Farmer, near Bound Brook, Somerset Co	18	1	Fair.
27	M. Torpey, Hoboken, Hudson County	10	....	Animals, fair.
27	Mrs. Torpey, Hoboken, Hudson County	9	....	Fair.
Feb. 12	F. E. Eultz, Jersey City, Hudson County	18	....	Good.
15	J. Williams, near Weehawken, Hudson County	3	1	Animals, fair.
24	Herwitz & Lavential, near Weehawkeen, Hudson County.	86	....	Stables, filthy; animals, fair.
26	Mrs. McGuire, near Jersey City, Hudson County	9	....	Do.
26	Fred. Simmerson, near Jersey City Heights, Hudson County.	11	1	Stables, filthy; animals, not good.
Apr. 2	Cook & Hearney, near Centerville, Essex County.		1	
	Inspections by J. W. Hawk, V. S.			
21	B. Sern, Newark, Essex County	45	....	Animals, fair.
21	Depot, Newark, Essex County	30	....	
26	John Wolst, Elizabeth, Union County	8	....	Good.
26	H. McCandless, Elizabeth, Union County	24	....	Do.
26	T. McCandless, Elizabeth, Union County	25	....	Do.
30	James B. Bardow, Mercertown, Mercer County	23	....	
May 1	G. S. Mitchell, Orange, Essex County	60	....	
3	P. Manley, Belleville, Essex County	16	....	Do.
3	J. Travers, Belleville, Essex County	9	....	Do.
4	W. Marcell, Waverly, Essex County	35	....	Do.
4	W. Pilkington, Waverly, Essex County	4	....	Do.
5	H. Krouse, near Elizabeth, Union County	30	....	Do.
5	A. Neweek, Elizabeth, Union County	30	....	Do.
6	Morris and Essex Depot, Newark, Essex County	88	....	Do.
6	M. Mulligan, Newark, Essex County	28	....	Do.
7	Flanigan & Thompson, South Orange, Essex County.	22	....	Do.
7	H. Hanfield, Newark, Essex County	20	....	Do.
	Inspections by H. W. Rowland, V. S.			
Apr. 5	Warrington, Hoboken, Hudson County	10	....	Animals, good.
21	Marion Neen, Desbrosses street, Hudson County	18	....	Animals, indifferent.
23	Joe Warrington, Hoboken, Hudson County	11	....	Animals, good.
23	Mrs I. Tarper, Hoboken, Hudson County	7	....	Fair
24	S. Kolowsky, near Secaucus, Hudson County	4	....	Good.
24	Commons, near North Bergen, Hudson County	30	....	Animals, indifferent.
26	John Lynch, near Marion, Hudson County	18	C. 1	Stables, filthy; animals, fair.
27	Commons, Weehawken Hudson County	35	....	Animals, good.
28	Commons, Jersey City Heights, Hudson County	10	....	Do.
30	Mrs. McGuire, Hudson County	8	....	Fair.
	Inspections by J. W. Hawk, V. S.			
May 10	Mr Parker, Newark, Essex County	15	....	Good.
11	John Mutler, Irvington, Essex County	25	....	Do.
12	D. Littlefield, Irvington, Essex County	28	....	Stables, filthy; animals, poor.
13	F. Rann, Irvington, Essex County	30	....	Good.
13	G. Reed, East Orange, Essex County	28	....	Stables, filthy; animals, fair.
14	M. Mallory, Roselle, Union County	15	....	Do.

Inspection of stables, etc., in New Jersey—Continued.

Day of month.	Name of owner or person in charge and location of stable.	No. of cattle.	No. with lung-plague.	Condition of stables and animals.
	Inspections by W. B. E. Miller—Continued.			
1896.				
June 3	Edward Ferry, near Farmingdale, Monmouth County.	10	....	Stables, good; animals fair.
3	James H. Butcher, near Farmingdale, Monmouth County.	5	....	Do.
3	Charles H. Butcher, near Farmingdale, Monmouth County.	3	....	Good.
3	John Reed, near Farmingdale, Monmouth Co...	3	....	Do.
3	John E. Stellwell, near Farmingdale, Monmouth County.	10	....	Fair.
3	Joseph Donahue's estate, near Farmingdale, Monmouth County.	6	....	Good.
4	Allen Miller, Bennett's Mills, Ocean County......	10	....	Poor.
4	Edward Miller, Bennett's Mills, Ocean County..	3	....	
4	Charles Applegate, Bennett's Mills, Ocean Co...	3	....	Good.
4	Mrs. J. Vorhees, Prospect, Monmouth County....	1	....	Do.
4	Alfred Vorhees, Prospect, Monmouth County.....	3	....	Do.
4	Joseph Vorhees, Prospect, Monmouth County....	4	....	Do.
4	Conover Vorhees, Prospect, Monmouth County..	6	....	Do.
4	Peter Stellwell, Coontown, Monmouth County..	4	....	Fair.
4	John Hiris, near Prospect, Monmouth County...	5	....	Do.
4	B. S. Montgomery, Coontown, Monmouth Co...	5	....	Do.
4	George Burdge, near Farmingdale, Monmouth County.	3	....	Good.
4	James Burdge, near Farmingdale, Monmouth	5	....	Fair.
4	Samuel Butcher, near Farmingdale, Monmouth County.	8	....	Good.
4	William Bennett, near Farmingdale, Monmouth County.	13	....	Do.
5	Charles Errickson, near Jerseyville, Monmouth County.	4	....	Do.
5	Perrine Donahue, near Jerseyville, Monmouth County.	13	....	Do.
5	James Donahue, near Jerseyville, Monmouth County.	10	....	Do.
5	Joseph Errickson, near Jerseyville, Monmouth County.	4	....	Do.
5	James W. Clayton, near Jerseyville, Monmouth County.	5	....	Do.
5	Charles H. Clayton, near Jerseyville, Monmouth County.	4	....	Do.
5	Joseph Davidson, near Jerseyville, Monmouth County.	2	....	Do.
5	James Schench, near Jerseyville, Monmouth County.	2	....	Do.
5	Joseph Clayton, near Jerseyville, Monmouth County.	9	....	Do.
5	John Schench, near Jerseyville, Monmouth County.	6	....	Do.
5	Perrine Davidson, near Jerseyville, Monmouth County.	12	....	Do.
5	William Pettenger, near Jerseyville, Monmouth County.	8	....	Do.
5	Edward Lewis, near Jerseyville, Monmouth County.	2	....	Do.
5	John Lewis, near Jerseyville, Monmouth County..	6	....	Do.
	Inspections by J. W. Hawk, V. S.			
3	J. Cornell, near Somerville, Somerset County.....	15	....	Good.
4	C. G. Foster, Morristown, Morris County...........	100	....	Do.
4	C. Moody, Morristown, Morris County	30	....	Do.
7	S. E. Garretson, Somerville, Somerset County.....	45	....	Do.
7	A. D. Thompson, Finderne, Somerset County	59	....	Stables, good; animals fair.
8	J. J. Mitchell, near Troy, Morris County.............	38	....	Good.
8	R. Smith, Troy, Morris County	50	....	Do.
8	S. H. Condit, Troy, Morris County	35	....	Do.
8	G. Smith, Troy, Morris County............................	10	....	Do.
9	Morris Freight Depot Newark, Essex County...	38	....	Fair.
	Inspections by W. B. E. Miller, V. S.			
7	Frank Anderson, Hamilton Square, Mercer County.	4	....	Excellent.

Inspection of stables, etc., in New Jersey—Continued.

Day of month.	Name of owner or person in charge and location of stable.	No. of cattle.	No. with lung-plague.	Condition of stables and animals.
	Inspections by W. B. E. Miller—Continued.			
1886.				
June 7	James C. Robbins, near Hamilton Square, Mercer County.	7	....	Good.
7	Hutchinson Anderson, near Hamilton Square, Mercer County.	13	....	Do.
7	Mr. Cubberly, near Hamilton Square, Mercer County.	8	....	Do.
7	Joel Taylor, near Newtown, Mercer County	10	....	Fair.
7	Joseph S. Mount, near Newtown, Mercer County	8	....	Good.
7	John McCabe, near Newtown, Mercer County	9	....	Excellent.
7	James Gorden, near Newtown, Mercer County	7	....	Fair.
8	Isaac W. Nicholson, near Ellisburgh, Camden County.	90	....	Very good.
8	Charles T. Shreeve, near Ellisburgh, Camden County.	7	....	Fair.
8	William C. Wood, near Wrightsville, Camden County.	10	....	Very poor.
8	Richard S. Shivers, near Wrightsville, Camden County.	30	....	Good.
8	Isaac Hinchman, near Wrightsville, Camden County.	10	....	Very good.
8	Silas Beitz & Son, near Wrightsville, Camden County.	40	....	Excellent.
9	Asa Gaewood, near Haddonfield, Camden Co	15	....	Fair.
9	George W. Hopkins, near Haddonfield, Camden County.	8	....	Do.
9	Samuel Wood, near Haddonfield, Camden Co	18	....	Very good.
9	John Storey, Rowandtown, Camden County	6	....	Do.
9	John T. Glover, road to Haddonfield, Camden County.	20	....	Do.
9	Henry C. Cuthbert, road to Haddonfield, Camden County.	18	....	Do.
9	John D. Glover, near Collingswood, Camden County.	14	....	Do.
9	Edward C. Knight, Collingswood, Camden Co	26	....	Excellent.
9	Samuel French, near Camden, Camden County	5	....	Very good.
9	Charles D. E. Costa's estate, near Camden, Camden County.	13	....	Fair.
10	Charles Hendrickson, near Freehold, Monmouth County.	6	....	Poor.
10	Henry Strickland, near Freehold, Monmouth County.	16	....	Good.
10	Cortenius Schench, near Freehold, Monmouth County.	9	....	Stables, good; animals, fair.
10	William Clayton, near Freehold, Monmouth County.	4	....	Fair.
10	Ruliff S. Hendrickson, near Freehold, Monmouth County.	8	....	Do.
[illegible]	David Errickson, near Freehold, Monmouth County.	8	....	Do.
10	David Tamberson, near Freehold, Monmouth County.	14	....	Do.
10	Craig Conover, near Freehold, Monmouth Co	14	....	Poor.
10	William Butcher, near Freehold, Monmouth County.	13	....	Fair.
10	Abijah C. Fisher, near Freehold, Monmouth County.	9	....	Good.
11	Alfred Conover, jr., near Colt's Neck, Monmouth County.	18	....	Fair.
11	Charles Haight, near Colt's Neck, Monmouth County.	20	....	Good.
11	Mr. Scobey, near Colt's Neck, Monmouth Co	6	....	Do.
11	John Giberoon, near Colt's Neck, Monmouth County.	16	....	Do.
11	Forman P. Taylor, near Colt's Neck, Monmouth County.	12	....	Fair.
11	Funis Denise, near Freehold, Monmouth Co	16	....	Do.
11	John Buck, near Freehold, Monmouth County	14	....	Good.
11	William Forman, near Freehold, Monmouth County.	16	....	Do.
12	Sundry parties, near Freehold, Monmouth Co	26	....	Do.
12	Holmes Earl, near Freehold, Monmouth County	8	....	Do.
12	John Vandervere, near Freehold, Monmouth County.	12	....	Do.
12	D. Bowen, Marlborough, Monmouth County	11	....	Do.
12	Mr. Shunn, near Marlborough, Monmouth Co	1	....	Do.

Inspection of stables, etc., in New Jersey—Continued.

Day of month.	Name of owner or person in charge and location of stable.	No. of cattle.	No. with lung-plague.	Condition of stables an animals.
	Inspections by W. B. E. Miller—Continued.			
1886. June 12	John V. N. Willis, near Marlborough, Monmouth County.	18	....	Very good.
12	Robert Schenck, near Marlborough, Monmouth County.	12	....	Good.
12	Albert Fielder, near Marlborough, Monmouth County.	5	....	Do.
12	Charles Conover, near Marlborough, Monmouth County.	13	....	Very good.
12	Mrs. D. Carson, near Marlborough, Monmouth County.	5	....	Good.
14	J. Cuthbert, jr., near Ellisburgh, Monmouth County.	7	....	Do.
14	James L. Morrison, near Marlton, Burlington County.	14	....	Do.
14	Benjamin Cooper, near Marlton, Burlington County.	12	....	Do.
14	Zebidee Wills, jr., near Marlton, Burlington Co..	20	....	Do.
14	E. Tomlinson, near Marlton, Burlington County..	20	....	Do.
14	Samuel Griscomb, near Marlton, Burlington County.	10	....	Do.
14	S. Lippincott, near Marlton, Burlington County..	10	....	Do.
14	William Graff, near Ellisburgh, Burlington Co..	15	....	Do.
14	A. Cuthbert, near Ellisburgh, Burlington County.	13	....	Do.
15	J. T. Wiley, near Ellisburgh, Burlington County.	10	....	Do.
15	Elwood Rockhill, near Ellisburgh, Camden Co..	13	....	Do.
15	Joseph K. Lippincott, Ellisburgh, Camden Co...	25	....	Do.
15	Edward B. Davis, Ellisburgh, Camden County...	13	....	Do.
15	Alfred Bates, Ellisburgh, Camden County..........	15	....	Do.
15	Clark Grigg, Ellisburgh, Camden County..........	6	....	Do.
15	Elwood Evans, Ellisburgh, Camden County........	45	....	Do.
15	S. Redman, Ellisburgh, Camden County	6	....	Do.
15	Jesse Anderson, Ellisburgh, Camden County.......	16	....	Fair.
15	Joseph Fowler, Ellisburgh, Camden County.......	9	....	Good.
16	Samuel T. Cole, Colestown, Camden County.....	12	....	Fair.
16	J. H. and Isaac W. Cole, Colestown, Camden County.	45	....	Good.
16	Charles Cole, Colestown, Camden County..........	10	....	Do.
16	William D. Cole, Colestown, Camden County.	16	....	Do.
16	Thomas Matchett, Colestown, Camden County..	15	....	Poor.
16	Samuel Hewlings, Colestown, Camden County..	12	....	Good.
16	David L. Burroughs, Colestown, Camden Co......	15	....	Do.
16	Amos Kaighn, Colestown, Camden County........	20	....	Do.
17	Mrs. Hendrickson, Middletown, Camden Co	5	....	Do.
17	Edward Burroughs, near Merchantville, Camden County.	5	....	Do.
17	Samuel L. Burroughs, near Merchantville, Camden County.	18	....	Do.
17	Joseph Fisher, near Merchantville, Camden Co..	6	....	Do.
17	Harrison Robbins, near Merchantville, Camden County.	3	....	Very good.
17	Hon. Thomas H. Dudley, near Merchantville, Camden County.	8	....	Do.
18	Joseph T. Field, Middletown, Monmouth County.	13	....	Do.
18	E. W. Conover, Middletown, Monmouth County..	8	....	Good.
18	Charles Condert, Middletown, Monmouth Co....	20	....	Do.
18	Harris Conover, Middletown, Monmouth Co	8	....	Do.
19	George Sherman, Leonardville, Monmouth Co.	8	....	Very good.
19	William Sherman, Leonardville, Monmouth Co..	13	....	Good.
	Inspections by J. W Hawk, V. S.			
14	J. Draker, East Orange, Essex County..............	15	....	Good.
15	J. Becker, Hilton, Essex County.................. . ..	15	....	Do.
16	R. R. Taylor, near Somerville, Somerset County..	10	....	Stables, fair; animals poor.
17	F. Housmer, Middleville, Essex County	22	....	Good.
18	P. Evans, near Morristown, Morris County..	19	....	Stables, filthy; animals fair.
18	S. H. Young, near Morristown, Morris County..	30	....	Good.
18	D. Burnet, Munrow, Morris County..................	18	....	Do.
18	S. Turis, Munrow, Morris County..........	19	....	Stables, filthy; animals poor.
21	J. Frasey, South Somerville, Somerset County...	16	....	Good.

Inspection of stables, etc., in New Jersey—Continued.

Day of month.	Name of owner or person in charge and location of stable.	No. of cattle.	No. with lung-plague.	Condition of stables and animals.
	Inspections by W. B. E. Miller, V. S.			
1886.				
June 21	Wm. Campbell, Plainfield, Middlesex County	5	....	Good.
21	Charles W. Ayers, near Plainfield, Middlesex County.	10	....	Do.
21	Jos. W. Johnson, near Plainfield, Middlesex County.	45	....	Do.
21	Manning Stelle, near Plainfield, Middlesex County.	6	....	Do.
22	Nathan Robbins, Metuchen, Middlesex County	20	....	Excellent.
22	Lewis Ayers, Metuchen, Middlesex County	10	....	Good.
22	Wesley Bennett, Metuchen, Middlesex County	12	....	Do.
23	John J. Holly, near Plainfield, Middlesex County.	75	....	Stables, excellent; animals, very good.
23	John R. Potter, near Plainfield, Middlesex County.	7	....	Good.
23	A. C. Potter, near Plainfield, Middlesex County.	10	....	Do.
23	Richard Potter, near Plainfield, Middlesex County.	10	....	Do.
23	Wm. H. Potter, near Plainfield, Middlesex County.	12	....	Do.
25	Wm. C. Callahan, Roadstown, Cumberland County.	12	....	Do.
25	Lewis Mount, near Roadstown, Cumberland County.	1	....	Do.
26	Mrs. Porch, near Roadstown, Cumberland County.	18	....	Do.
26	George Ware, near Roadstown, Cumberland County.	7	....	Do.
26	David Hins, near Roadstown, Cumberland County.	7	....	Do.
26	Berry Porch, near Roadstown, Cumberland County.	5	....	Do.
26	Charles Ware, near Roadstown, Cumberland County.	1	....	Do.
29	T. G. Williams, road to Wilson Station, Burlington County.	24	....	Very good.
29	Mrs. P. Gallagher, Camden, Camden County	6	1	Stables, fair; animals, good.
30	James L. Hewitt, near Paulsborough, Gloucester County.	15	....	Fair.
30	C. N. Shuster, near Paulsborough, Gloucester County.	15	....	Good.
30	Isaac Thompson, near Paulsborough, Gloucester County.	20	....	Do.
30	Wilson Fitzgerald, near Paulsborough, Gloucester County.	17	....	Do.
July 1	Isaac T. Allen, Paulsborough, Gloucester County	18	....	Do.
1	Dan. Packer, road to Gloucester County	5	....	Do.
1	Wm. Lloyd, road to Gloucester County	26	....	Do.
1	John W. Hannold, road to Gloucester County	25	....	Do.
2	Capt. John Edward, Dennisville, Cape May County.	13	....	Do.
2	Capt. Charles Carroll, Dennisville, Cape May County.	5	....	Do.
2	Sundry parties, Dennisville, Cape May County	25	....	Poor.
2	J. W. Crandal, jr., Dennisvile, Cape May County	4	....	Fair.
2	J. W. Crandal, sr., Dennisville, Cape May County	11	....	Do.
3	Squire Baymore, Goshen, Cape May County	4	....	Good.
3	Sundry owners, Goshen, Cape May County	32	....	Fair.
3	W. D. Tomlin, Goshen, Cape May County	2	....	Good.
3	James Chester, Goshen, Cape May County	7	....	Do.
3	Andrew Tomlin, Goshen, Cape May County	18	....	Do.
	Inspections by J. W. Hawk, V. S.			
June 23	M. Bergen, Bloomfield, Essex County	15	....	Good.
23	S. Pierson, East Orange, Essex County	25	....	Do.
26	F. Frelinghuysen, Somerville, Somerset County	26	....	Do.
26	C. Hulick, near Somerville, Somerset County	25	....	Do.
26	D. Dilly, Somerville, Somerset County	40	....	Do.
29	T. Shepherd, near Bound Brook, Somerset County.	18	....	Do.

Inspection of stables, etc., in New Jersey—Continued.

Day of month.	Name of owner or person in charge and location of stable.	No. of cattle.	No. with lung-plague.	Condition of stables and animals.
	Inspections by W. B. E. Miller, V. S.			
1886.				
July 8	Sundry owners, near Moorestown, Burlington County.	22	....	Good.
9	Hugh Hatch, near Bellair, Camden County	9	....	Do.
10	Joseph Coleman, Dutch Neck, Mercer County	7	....	Do.
10	Wm. P. Walton, Dutch Neck, Mercer County	1	....	Do.
	Inspections by H. W. Rowland, V. S.			
June 1	M. Teel, Hoboken, Hudson County	18	....	Not good.
1	W. Muller, Hoboken, Hudson County	14	....	Fair.
2	Miss Johannah, Marion, Hudson County	19	....	Do.
4	P. Dickle, Weehawken, Hudson County	18	....	Do.
4	E. Buks, Weehawken, Hudson County	12	....	Animals, good.
6	Dan Haller, Greenville, Hudson County	25	....	Do.
6	Dennis Hogan, Greenville, Hudson County	22	....	Stables, fair; animals, good.
7	M. Torpey, Hoboken, Hudson County	8	....	Fair.
8	L. Stortenbocker, Hoboken, Hudson County	17	....	Do.
12	P. Coyle, Jersey City Heights, Hudson County	25	....	Stables, good; animals, fair.
12	Mrs. Tate, Jersey City Heights, Hudson County	15	....	Fair.
12	N. Hoglen, Jersey City Heights, Hudson County	12	....	Do.
15	C. W. Curney, Englewood, Bergen County	18	....	Good.
15	Fred Miller, Englewood, Bergen County	7	....	Stables, fair; animals, good.
16	John S. Edsal, Englewood, Bergen County	10	....	Fair.
16	Captain and Mayor Moore, Englewood, Bergen County.	15	....	Good.
16	J. B. Balmlieu, Englewood, Hudson County	11	....	Fair.
18	Mrs. Kates, near West Hoboken, Hudson County	11	....	Stables, fair; animals, good.
18	W. Smeeders, West Hoboken, Hudson County	18	....	Do.
18	George Katlin, West Hoboken, Hudson County	18	....	Stables, filthy; animals, fair.
19	John Lynch, Jersey City Heights, Hudson County.	20	....	Do.
21	John Mahoney, Greenville, Hudson County	10	....	Fair.
21	M. Curry, Greenville, Hudson County	20	....	Stables, fair; animals, good.
22	H. Sterms, Fairview, Bergen County	16	....	Fair.
22	W. J. Dowd, Fairview, Bergen County	10	....	Stables, fair; animals, good.
23	John Brick, near Marion, Hudson County	8	....	Good.
26	L. Mannis, Union, Hudson County	14	....	Do.
26	Theo. Eaglin, Union, Hudson County	13	....	Fair.
26	Peter Brease, Union, Hudson County	20	....	Stables, fair; animals, good.
28	M. Nugesson, Union, Hudson County	24	....	Fair.
28	S. Meeks, Wehawken, Hudson County	17	....	Stables, fair: animals, good.
28	Fliurily, near West New York, Hudson County	16	....	Fair.
29	P. Marks, near Guttenburgh, Hudson County	30	....	Animals fair.
30	Pat Mally, Jersey City Heights, Hudson County	15	....	Stables, good; animals, fair.
30	N. Fenning, Jersey City Heights, Hudson County.	16	....	
	Inspections by J. W. Hawk, V. S.			
July 6	J. Tease, Union, Union County	25	....	Good.
6	M. McMan, Union, Union County	6	....	Do.
6	M. C. Craig, Union, Union County	20	....	Stables, good; animals, fair.
6	A. Burnet, near Union, Union County	12	....	Good.
7	W. Linsey, near Union, Union County	30	....	Do.
7	L. Wenz, near Union, Union County	15	....	Do.
7	J. Wade, near Union, Union County	20	....	Do.
8	W. Clayton, near Elizabeth, Union County	20	....	Stables, fair; animals, poor.
8	J. Sunison, near Elizabeth, Union County	12	....	Good.
10	F. Force, Northfield, Essex County	40	....	Stables, good; animals, fair.
12	Mrs. Lathrop, near Madison, Morris County	40	....	Good.
13	W. P. Ely, near Madison, Morris County	85	....	Do.
13	Mr. Wolf, Hanover Neck, Morris County	20	....	Do.

Inspection of stables, etc., in New Jersey—Continued.

Day of month.	Name of owner or person in charge and location of stable.	No. of cattle.	No. with lung-plague.	Condition of stables and animals.
	Inspections by J. W. Hawk—Continued.			
1886.				
July 22	Mr. Dodd, Bellville, Hunterdon County	30	....	Good.
23	Mr. Somers, Newark, Hunterdon County	10	....	Do.
23	Commons, West Newark, Hunterdon County	26	....	Animals, fair.
24	J. B. Rall, Plainfield road, Union County	12	....	Good.
24	D. Fink, Branch Mills, Union County	35	....	Do.
24	M. J. High, near Cranford, Union County	15	....	Stables, fair; animals, good.
24	H. Miller, Plainfield road, Union County	16	....	Stables, fair; animals, poor.
28	G. Granzell, Westfield road, Union County	10	....	Stables, good; animals, poor.
28	J. Skuder, Cranford Station, Union County	16	....	Do.
28	B. Pierson, Westfield road, Union County	10	....	Do.
28	O. Pierson, Westfield road, Union County	18	....	Do.
29	M. Hand, Lyons Farms, Essex County	18	....	Do.
31	Mr. Martin, Rosell, Union County	12	....	Do.
31	J. Conner, near Elizabeth, Union County	10	....	Fair.
31	Mrs. Moyse, near Elizabeth, Union County	16	....	Stables, good; animals, fair.
31	D. Mulford, Rosell, Union County	16	....	Good.
31	J. Deraisnier, near Elizabeth, Union County	80	....	Stables, fair; animals, good.
	Inspections by W. B. E. Miller, V. S.			
26	B. Harker, near Wrightstown, Burlington Co	18	....	Very good.
26	Thomas Harker, Wrightstown, Burlington Co	14	....	Good.
27	J. B. Pugh, Wrightstown, Burlington County	24	....	Do.
27	John Evans, near Jobstown, Burlington County	33	....	Do.
28	George ——, near Gloucester, Camden County	8	....	Do.
29	Sundry owners, near Pennsville, Salem County	100	....	Do.
31	W. P. Taylor, near Yardville, Mercer County	13	....	Do.
31	Charles Taylor, near Yardville, Mercer County	6	....	Stables, good; animals, fair.
Oct. 11	George B. Pease, Verona, Essex County	4	1	Good.
12	Jacob Kirby, Harrisonville, Gloucester County	21	1	Do.
12	J. Moore, Harrisonville, Gloucester County	18	....	Do.
13	Edward Kirby, Harrisonville, Gloucester Co	10	....	Do.
13	George Hornor, Harrisonville, Gloucester Co	26	....	Do.
14	George H. Kirby, Harrisonville, Gloucester Co	11	1	Do.
14	Chalkley Kirby, Harrisonville, Gloucester Co	12	....	Do.
16	Joseph M. Borton, near Woodstown, Salem Co	11	....	Do.
16	Isaac Kaudle, near Woodstown, Salem County	1	....	Do.
16	Smith & Hewitt, near Woodstown, Salem County	18	....	Do.
18	A. G. Richiell, road to Elmer, Salem County	12	....	Do.
18	Samuel Flitcraft, road to Elmer, Salem County	12	....	Do.
19	John S. Redstroke, Sharpstown, Salem County	9	....	Do.
20	James S. Hartshorne, near Vincentown, Burlington County.	40	2	Do.
21	Edward Bozartle, Pemberton, Burlington Co	11	....	Do.
22	James Cliver, Pointville, Burlington County	12	....	Stables, good; animals, fair.
23	Barney Gordon, Allowaystown, Salem County	11	....	Good.
25	Edward Ridgway, Plattsburg, Burlington Co	20	....	Very good.
25	John Collins, near Wrightstown, Burlington County.	21	....	Do.
26	James E. Stiles, Vincentown, Burlington County	1	....	Do.
27	Andrew Griscomb, near Salem, Salem County	15	....	Do.
28	Jacob Kirby, Hawsonville, Gloucester County	23	1	Do.
28	Frank Pancoast, Hawsonville, Gloucester Co	15	....	Do.
29	Samuel Moore, near Swedesborough, Gloucester County.	20	1 sus.	Do.
30	Geo. W. Coles, Camden, Camden County	....	1	Stables, good; animals, poor.
Nov. 1	C. H. Richman, road to Woodstown, Salem County.	20	....	Good.
1	Alfred Remsen, Yorktown, Salem County	12	....	Do.
1	Isaac Sickler, Yorktown, Salem County	18	....	Do.
11	Elmer Duill, near Woodstown, Salem County	26	4	Do.
12	Phillip Lippincott, near Mount Holly, Salem County.	10	....	Do.
18	E. W. Coffin, road to Glendale, Camden County	35	....	Do.
19	James Lukins, road to Woodbury, Gloucester County.	9	....	Do.
19	Andrew Blake, road to Woodbury, Gloucester County.	20	....	Do.

Inspection of stables, etc., in New Jersey—Continued.

Day of month.	Name of owner or person in charge and location of stable.	No. of cattle.	No. with lung-plague.	Condition of stables and animals.
	Inspections by W. B. E. Miller—Continued.			
1886.				
Nov. 20	Edward Comp, public road, Gloucester County.	20	....	Good.
22	Reeves Filteraft, road to Yorktown, Salem County.	20	....	Stables, very good; animals, good.
22	Henry A. Richman, road to Woodstown, Salem County.	31	....	Do.
23	Alice Hargrove, road to Pines, Burlington County.	11	....	Fair.
23	Wm. Clivers, road to Swarthville Burlington County.	30	....	Stables, very good; animals, bad.
24	B. Deacon Haines, public road, Burlington County.	8	....	Stables, very good; animals, fair.
24	Jos. A. Jones, road to Medford, Burlington County.	7	....	Good.
25	W. H. Evans & Brother, road to Medford, Burlington County.	12	....	Stables, good; animals, bad.
26	Samuel Evans, near Mount Laurel, Burlington County.	18	....	Do.
26	Job Garwood, near Mount Laurel, Burlington County.	8	....	Do.
27	John Craig, Milford, Burlington County...........	85	....	Good.
30	Leander Clemiger, road to Medford, Burlington County.	10	....	Do.
30	Winfield Haines, road to Medford, Burlington County.	12	....	Stables, good; animals, fair.
30	Charles Taylor, road to Gloucester, Burlington County.	9	....	Do.
30	Arthur Haines, road to Vincentown, Burlington County.	11	....	Do.
Dec. 1	Henry A. Richman, near Richmanville, Burlington County.	31	....	Good.
2	Hewitt & Smith, road to Sharpsburgh, Burlington County.	12	....	Do.
2	J. K. Lippencott, road to Sharpsburgh, Burlington County.	43	....	Do.
7	Stacy B. Taylor, road to Plattsburgh, Burlington County.	25	4	Stables, very good; animals, good.
10	J. Craigy, road to Haddonfield, Burlington County.	85	....	Good.
11	Samuel Evans, road to Marlton, Burlington County.	18	....	Stables, good; animals, fair.
13	Newkirk Van Meter, near Elmer, Salem Co......	16	....	Good.
14	Thomas E. Morris, road to Freehold, Monmouth County.	12	....	Very good.
15	Joel T. Haines, road to Jobstown, Burlington County.	38	....	Do.
17	A. H. Stratton, road to Haddonfield, Camden County.	20	....	Good.
17	Ray & Dobbs, road to Ashland, Camden County..	24	....	Do.
21	Burlington County Almshouse, near Pemberton, Burlington County.	40	....	Do.

Inspection of abattoirs and ferries in New Jersey.

Day of month.	Name of owner or person in charge and location of stable.	No. of cattle.	No. with lung-plague.	Condition of stables and animals.
	Inspections by H. W. Rowland, V. S.			
1886.				
Jan. 2	Abattoir, Jersey City stock-yards, Hudson Co....	....	....	Animals, fair.
4	........do....................................	....	....	
6	........do....................................	....	....	Do.
8	........do....................................	....	....	Do.
11	........do....................................	3	....	Do.
13	........do....................................	....	....	Animals, indifferent.
16	Hoboken Ferries, Jersey City stock-yards, Hudson County.	....	....	Do.
18	Hoboken Street Ferry, Jersey City stock-yards, Hudson County.	3	....	Do.
20	Abattoir, Jersey City stock-yards, Hudson Co.....	....	....	Do.
22	Pavonia Ferries, Jersey City stock-yards, Hudson County.	....	1	Animals, fair.
25	Desbrosses Ferry, Jersey City stock-yards, Hudson County.	....	....	Animals, good.

Inspection of abattoirs and ferries in New Jersey—Continued.

Day of month.	Name of owner or person in charge and location of stable.	No. of cattle.	No. with lung-plague.	Condition of stables and animals.
	Inspections by H. W. Rowland—Continued.			
1886.				
Jan. 26	Pavonia Ferry, Jersey City stock-yards, Hudson County.			Animals, indifferent.
27	Hoboken Ferry, Jersey City stock-yards, Hudson County.			Animals, fair.
29	Desbrosses Street Ferry, Jersey City stock-yards, Hudson County.			Animals, indifferent.
Feb. 1	Hoboken Ferry, Hoboken, Hudson County			Animals, good.
1	Stock-yards, near Jersey City, Hudson County		2	Animals, indifferent.
3	Hoboken Ferries, Hoboken, Hudson County			Animals, good.
3	Abattoirs, Jersey City, Hudson County			Do.
5	Stock Yards, Jersey City, Hudson County			Do.
8	Hoboken Ferries, Piers 34 and 35, Hudson Co.			Do.
8	Abattoirs, near Jersey City, Hudson County		2	Animals, indifferent.
10	Pavonia Ferry, Piers 34 and 35, Hudson County			Animals, good.
10	Abattoirs, Jersey City, Hudson County			Animals, indifferent.
12	do			Do.
15	Stock-yards, Jersey City, Hudson County			Animals, good.
17	Abattoirs, Jersey City, Hudson County			Do.
19	do			Do.
19	Hoboken Ferries, Jersey City, Hudson County.			Do.
24	Pavonia Ferry, Jersey City, Hudson County			Animals, fair.
24	Abattoir, Jersey City, Hudson County			Animals, indifferent.
26	Hoboken Ferry, near Hoboken, Hudson County.			Animals, good.
26	Stock-yards, Jersey City, Hudson County		3	Animals, indifferent.
26	Pavonia Ferry, Jersey City, Hudson County			Animals, good.
Mar. 1	Pavonia Ferries, Jersey City, Hudson County			Do.
1	Stock-yards, Jersey City, Hudson County			Do.
3	Stock-yards, Jersey City, Hudson County		1	Do.
3	Hoboken Ferry, Jersey City, Hudson County			Do.
5	Stock-yards, Jersey City, Hudson County			Do.
5	Pavonia and Central Ferries, Jersey City, Hudson County.			Do.
8	Pavonia Ferry, Jersey City, Hudson County			Animals, indifferent.
10	Desbrosses Street Ferry, Jersey City, Hudson County.	2		Animals, poor.
10	Stock-yards, Jersey City, Hudson County.			Animals, good.
16	Cortlandt Street Ferry, Jersey City, Hudson County.			Animals, fair.
16	Hoboken Ferry, Jersey City, Hudson County			Animals, good.
16	Stock-yards, Jersey City, Hudson County			Do.
19	Stock-yards, Jersey City, Hudson County		2	Do.
19	Pavonia Ferry, Jersey City, Hudson County			Do.
24	Pavonia Ferry, Jersey City, Hudson County			Animals, indifferent.
24	Stock-yards, Jersey City, Hudson County		1	Animals, good.
26	Hoboken Ferry, Jersey City, Hudson County			Do.
26	Stock-yards, Jersey City, Hudson County		4	Animals, indifferent.
29	Hoboken and Pavonia Ferries, Jersey City, Hudson County.			Do.
29	Stock-yards, Jersey City, Hudson County			Do.
31	Stock-yards, Jersey City, Hudson County.		3	Do.
31	Pavonia Ferry, Jersey City, Hudson County			Animals, fair.
Apr. 1	Jersey City Stock-yards and Ferries, Jersey City, Hudson County.			Do.
2	Hoboken Ferry, Jersey City, Hudson County			
5	Ferries, Jersey City, Hudson County			Animals, good.
7	Pavonia Ferry, Jersey City, Hudson County			Do.
9	Jersey City Stock-yards and Abattoir, Jersey City, Hudson County.		2	Do.
9	Ferries, Jersey City, Hudson County			Do.
10	Hoboken Ferry, Jersey City, Hudson County		3c.	Animals, indifferent.
12	Abattoir, Jersey City, Hudson County.			Animals, good.
26	Ferries, Jersey City, Hudson County			Do.
27	Pavonia Ferry, Jersey City, Hudson County			
28	Stock-yards, Jersey City Heights, Hudson Co.			Good.
29	Hoboken Ferry, Jersey City, Hudson County		2c.	Animals, indifferent.
30	Ferry, Jersey City, Hudson County	10		Animals, fair.
May 1	Hoboken Ferries, Hoboken, Hudson County			Good.
1	Ferries, Jersey City, Hudson County			Do.
3	Stock-yards, Jersey City, Hudson County.			Do.
3	Pavonia Ferries, Jersey City, Hudson County.			Do.
3	Abattoirs, Jersey City, Hudson County			Do.
4	Central Ferries, Jersey City, Hudson County			Do.
5	Hoboken Ferries, Hoboken, Hudson County			Do.
5	Pavonia Ferries, Jersey City, Hudson County			Do.

Inspection of abattoirs and ferries in New Jersey—Continued.

Day of month.	Name of owner or person in charge and location of stable.	No of cattle.	No. with lung-plague.	Condition of stables and animals.
	Inspections by H. W. Rowland—Continued.			
1886.				
ay 7	Abattoir, Jersey City, Hudson County		2	Good.
7	Hoboken Ferries, Hoboken, Hudson County			Do.
7	Weehawken Ferry, Weehawken, Hudson Co			Do.
10	Stock-yards, Jersey City, Hudson County			Do.
10	Hoboken Ferries, Hoboken, Hudson County			Do.
10	Pavonia Ferries, Jersey City, Hudson County			Do.
10	Ferry, Weehawken, Hudson County			Do.
11	Ferry, Jersey City, Hudson County			
12	Hoboken Ferries, Hoboken, Hudson County			Do.
12	Stock-yards, Jersey City, Hudson County		2c.	Do.
12	Central Ferry, Jersey City, Hudson County			Do.
14	Hoboken Ferry, Hoboken, Hudson County			Do.
14	Stock-yards, Jersey City			Do.
17	......do			Do.
17	Pavonia Ferry, Jersey City			Do.
18	Hoboken Ferries, Hoboken			Do.
18	Cortlandt Street Ferry, Jersey City			Do.
21	Stock-yards, Jersey City		6c.	Do.
21	Hoboken Ferries, Hoboken			Do.
21	Pavonia Ferries, Jersey City			Do.
22	Central Ferries, Jersey City			Do.
24	Stock-yards, Jersey City		1c.	Do.
24	Hoboken Ferries, Jersey City			Do.
26	Ferries, Hoboken			Do.
25	Stock-yards, Jersey City		2c.	Do.
25	Pavonia Ferry, Jersey City			Do.
31	Central Ferry, Jersey City			Do.
31	Hoboken Ferries, Hoboken			Do.
31	Pavonia Ferry, Jersey City			Do.
31	Stock-yards, Jersey City		2c.	Do.
ly 1	Abattoir, Jersey City			Do.
1	Pavonia Ferry, Hoboken			Do.
1	Hoboken Ferries			Do.
2	Abattoir, Jersey City			Do.
2	Pavonia Ferry		1	Do.
2	Central Ferries, Jersey City			Do.
2	Pavonia Ferries, Hoboken			Do.
4	Abattoir, Jersey City			Do.
6	Abattoir, Hoboken		3	Do.
7	Abattoir, Jersey City			Do.
7	Hoboken Ferries, Hoboken, Hudson County			Do.
7	Pavonia Ferries, Jersey City, Hudson County			Do.
8	Hoboken Ferries			Do.
9	Pavonia Ferries, Jersey City, Hudson County			Do.
9	Hoboken Ferries, Hoboken, Hudson County		2c.	Do.
9	Abattoirs, Jersey City, Hudson County			Do.
9	Hoboken Ferries, Hoboken, Hudson County			Do.
9	Abattoirs, Jersey City, Hudson County			Do.
10	Cortlandt Street Ferry, near Hoboken, Hudson County.			Do.
10	Pavonia Ferry, Jersey City, Hudson County			Do.
12	......do		1c.	Do.
14	Stock-yards, Jersey City, Hudson County			Do.
14	Hoboken Ferries, Hoboken			Do.

Reinspections in New Jersey.

Day of month.	Name of owner or person in charge and location of stable.	No of cattle.	No. with lung-plague.	Condition of stables and animals.
	Inspections by H. W. Rowland, V. S.			
1886.				
pr. 7	M. Torpher, near Hoboken, Hudson County	12		Fair.
7	F. E. Eulitz, near Marion, Hudson County	18		Good.
9	Hurwitz & Laventhial, Jersey City and Hoboken, Hudson County.	89		Fair.
22	Hurwitz & Laventhial, near Weehawken, Hudson County.	87		Do.
23	M. Torpher, near Hoboken, Hudson County	8		Do.
27	Hurwitz & Laventhial, Weehawken, Hudson County.	86		Do.
30	F. E. Eulitz, near Jersey City, Hudson County	18		Good.
ay 4	Patrick Coyle, West Hoboken, Hudson County	15		Fair.
4	David Van Vose, West Hoboken, Hudson Co	29		Very clean.

Reinspection in New Jersey—Continued.

Day of month.	Name of owner or person in charge and location of stable.	No. of cattle.	No. with lung-plague.	Condition of stables and animals.
	Inspections by H. W. Rowland—Continued.			
1886. May 5	M. Feinberger, near Secaucus, Hudson County	110	1c.	Stables, filthy; animals fair.
6	A. Gutgar, near Secaucus, Hudson County	8		
6	M. Brochwell, West Hoboken, Hudson County	8		Stables, fair; animals good.
6	J. Block, near Hoboken, Hudson County	27		Good.
11	Hurwetz & Laventhial, near Weehawken, Hudson County.	60		Stables, filthy; animals, fair.
22	M. Stockfish, near Bergen, Hudson County	24		Stables, good; animals, fair.
24	Mrs. Plogg, near Jersey City Rocks, Hudson County.	6		Stables, not good; animals fair.
26	C. Astfelix, near Guttenburgh, Hudson County	8	2c.	Stables, filthy; animals, fair.
28	A. Sterm, Fairview, Bergen, Hudson County	20		Fair.
28	M. Sherman, near Tenafly, Hudson County	6		Good.
	Inspections by J. W. Hawk, V. S.			
18	Mr. Culberson, East Orange, Essex County	35		Stables, fair; animals, good.
19	E. Condit, Centreville, Hunterdon County	16		Good.
19	B. Harkey, Centreville, Hunterdon County	20		Stables, filthy; animals, fair.
21	F. Blankie, Linden, Union County	70		Stables, good; animals, fair.
25	J. C. Higgins, Three Bridges, Hunterdon County	16		Good.
26	C. Castro, Waverly, Essex County	18		Do.
	Inspections by W. B. E. Miller, V. S.			
	John Dawson, near Salem, Salem County	21		Good.
	Charles Hewitt, near Woodstown	13	1c.	Do.
25	Robt. Smith, Wrightsville, Camden County	16	2c.	Do.
28	Martin Cloran, Gloucester, Camden County	2	2c.	Poor.
	Inspections by J. W. Hawk, V. S.			
June 3	E. G. Brown, near Somerville, Somerset County	41	2	Stables, filthy.
9	M. Noll, East Orange, Essex County	41		Good.
9	J. F. Pierson, East Orange, Essex County	32		Fair.
	Inspections by W. B. E. Miller, V. S.			
17	Robert Smith, Wrightsville, Camden County	15	2	Fair.
18	George A. Brown, Middletown, Monmouth Co	6	1	Good.
	Inspections by J. W. Hawk, V. S.			
10	M. Molty, near South Orange, Essex County	45		Good.
14	Mr. Harrison, Newark, Essex County	22		Do.
14	Mr. Wetzel, East Orange, Essex County	14		Do.
15	J. Conelly, near Springfield, Essex County.	12		Do.
15	T. Burnett, Middleville, Essex County	16		Do.
16	H. Burnett & Bro., near Middleville, Essex Co	22		Do.
17	E. G. Brown, near Somerville, Somerset County	27		Stables, filthy; animals, fair.
21	W. Hawkins, near Middleville, Essex County	25		Good.
21	W. Hamilton, Somerville, Somerset County	35		Do.
21	E. G. Brown, near Somerville, Somerset County	27		Stables, filthy; animals, fair.
21	M. Gilderstin, near Finderne, Somerset County	16		Good.
	Inspections by W. B. E. Miller, V. S.			
24	Newkirk Vanmetre, near Elmer, Salem County	18		Good.
21	Joseph E. Mayhew, near Elmer, Salem County	12		Do.
21	Charles Hewitt, near Woodstown, Salem County	13	1	Do.
25	Lewis Mount, near Roadstown, Cumberland County.	11		Do.
28	Martin Cloran, Gloucester City, Camden County	6	1	Fair.
28	Robert Smith, Wrightsville, Camden County	15	1	Good.
23	J. Maxfield, Bloomfield, Essex County	65		Do.
26	F. B. Stout, near Somerville, Somerset County	20		Do.

Inspections in New Jersey—Continued.

Day of month.	Name of owner or person in charge and location of stable.	No. of cattle.	No. with lung-plague.	Condition of stables and animals.
	Inspections by W. B. E. Miller—Continued.			
1886.				
[J]une 28	J. W. Wilson, Newark, Essex County	18	....	Good.
28	J. Martin, Newark, Essex County	21	....	Stables, filthy; animals, fair.
29	B. Farmer, Bound Brook, Somerset County	41	....	Do.
29	B. Tucker, East Bound Brook, Somerset County	15	....	Good.
	Inspections by H. W. Rowland, V. S.			
	William Blacher, Marion, Hudson County	9	....	Animals, good.
	C. Asfelix, Guttenburgh, Hudson County	6	....	Stables, dirty; animals, not good.
23	John O'Conner, Jersey City Heights, Hudson County.	12	....	Animals, good.
30	Patrick Brady, Jersey City Heights, Hudson County.	28	....	Stables, fair; animals, good.
	Inspections by W. B. E. Miller, V. S.			
[Ju]ly 6	L. M. Rocass, near Plainfield, Middlesex County	13	....	Good.
6	Bernard Farmer, near Bound Brook, Somerset County.	17	....	Do.
7	Newkirk Van Meter, near Elmer, Salem County	18	....	Do.
9	Mrs. P. Gallagher, Camden, Camden County	5	....	Fair.
	Inspections by J. W. Hawk, V. S.			
8	P. Ball, near Middleville, Essex County	20	....	Good.
8	H. Ball, near Middleville, Essex County	25	....	Do.
3	A. B. Brown, near Middleville, Essex County	45	....	Do.
6	W. C. Headly, near Union, Union County	18	....	Do.
12	H. W. V. Meyers, near Madison, Morris County	83	....	Do.
	Inspections by W. B. E. Miller, V. S.			
14	Samuel N. Rhoades, near Mount Ephraim, Camden County.	42	....	Very good.
	Hugh Hatch, near Bellair, Camden County	9	1	Do.
16	Robert Smith, Wrightsville, Camden County	15	1	Do.
23	Mrs. Gallagher, Camden, Camden County	5	....	Fair.
	Inspections by H. W. Rowland, V. S.			
23	H. Hatch, Bellair, Camden County	1	....	Good.
13	S. Greenleaf, New Durham, Hudson County	18	....	
22	John Hannan, Pamapo, Hudson County	11	....	Stables, fair; animals, good.
22	Frank Mullican, Pamapo, Hudson County	17	....	Animals, good.
26	W. Harrison, Bayonne, Hudson County	15	....	Do.
	Inspections by J. W. Hawk, V. S.			
15	M. Wynans, near Linden, Union County	23	....	Fair.
15	J. Wynans, Trimley Point, Union County	20	....	Good.
16	J. Miller, Easton Turnpike, Hunterdon County	30	....	Do.
21	T. H. Decker, Franklin, Essex County	30	....	Do.
	F. Underhill, Lyon's Farm, Essex County	20	....	Do.
	Day Bros., Lyon's Farm, Essex County	28	....	Do.
	Morris and Essex depot, Newark, Essex County	35	....	Do.
	B. Haywood, East Orange, Essex County	12	....	Do.
	H. Frick, East Orange, Essex County	25	....	Do.
22	Morris and Essex depot, Newark, Essex County	40	....	Do.
23	J. Marcell, Lyon's Farms, Essex County	40	....	Do.
	Inspections by W. B. E. Miller, V. S.			
	Martin Clornn, Gloucester, Camden County	6	1	
	Newkirk Van Meter, near Elmer, Salem County	18	....	Good.
	Charles Hewitt, near Woodstown, Salem County	13	1a.	Do.
[N]ov.	Ely Joyce, near Vincentown, Burlington County	10	1	Do.
28	Jas. S. Hartshorn, Vincentown, Burlington Co.	38	1	Do.
30	Josephus N. Sooy, road to Vincentown, Burlington County.	9	2	Do.
4	J. Moore, road to Woodstown, Gloucester County.	10	....	Do.
4	Jacob Kirby, road to Woodstown, Gloucester County.	23	1	Do.

Inspections in New Jersey—Continued.

Day of month.	Name of owner or person in charge and location of stable.	No. of cattle.	No. with lung-plague.	Condition of stables and animals.
	Inspections by W. B. E. Miller—Continued.			
1886. Nov. 4	George Horner, road to Woodstown, Gloucester County.	26	....	Good.
4	Edward Krily, near Harrisonville, Gloucester County.	10	....	Do.
5	John S. Redstrake, Sharptown, Salem County...	9	....	Do.
6	Robert Smith, Wrightsville, Camden County......	13	....	Fair.
6	Hugh Hatch, Bellair, Camden County	8	....	Good.
8	W. H. Evans, Lumberton, Burlington County ...	16	2 sus.	Do.
8	Edwin Dudley, Medford, Burlington County	6	....	Do.
8	Clayton Stackhouse, Medford, Burlington Co	23	....	Do.
9	Samuel Moore, near Swedesborough, Gloucester County.	20	....	Do.
10	George H. Kirby, near Avis Mills, Gloucester County.	11	1c.	Do.
10	Frederick Van Meter, near Elmer, Salem County	16	....	Do.
11	Charles Hewitt, near Woodstown, Salem County	16	....	Do.
	Inspection by W. H. Wray, V. S.			
5	T. M. Richardson, Belair Road, Baltimore Co......	16	15	Stables, good; animals, very good.
	Inspections by W. B. E. Miller, V. S.			
20	S. N. Rhoades, Mount Ephraim, Camden County	25	....	Do.
23	J. N. Tooy, road to Vincentown, Burlington County.	7	1	Stables, good; animals, bad.
23	James T. Hartshorn, road to Mount Holly, Burlington County.	35	....	Do.
24	Ely Joyce, road to Medford, Burlington County..	9	....	Do.
24	Edwin Dudley, road to Medford, Burlington County.	8	....	Do.
25	W. H. Evans, road to Medford, Burlington County.	14	....	Do.
26	Clayton Stackhouse, near Medford, Burlington County.	22	1	Do.
29	........do..	22	1	Do.
29	W. H. Evans & Bro., near Lumberton, Burlington County.	26	....	Stables, good; animals, fair.
Dec. 1	Elmer Duell, near Woodstown, Burlington County.	25	4	Good.
3	James Hartshorne, road to Mount Holly, Burlington County.	34	....	Stables, good; animals, bad.
3	William Cliver, road to Smithville, Burlington County.	21	....	Good.
4	William Powell, Camden, Camden County.........	7	....	Poor.
6	W. H. Evans, road to Medford, Burlington County.	26	....	Do.
6	W. H. Evans & Bro., near Lumberton, Burlington County.	12	....	Do.
8	Stacy B. Taylor, road to Plattsburgh, Burlington County.	24	8	Stables, very good; animals, good.
11	Job Ganwood, near Mount Laurel, Burlington County.	8	....	Good.
15	Stacy B. Taylor, road to Plattsburgh, Burlington County.	17	4	Stables, very good; animals good.
16	James Hartshorne, road to Mount Holly, Burlington County.	35	....	Stables, good; animals, fair.
16	William Cliver, road to Smithville, Burlington County.	29	....	Stables, very good; animals, fair.
17	E. W. Coffin, road to Glendale, Burlington County.	35	....	Good.
20	Stacy B. Taylor, road to Plattsburgh, Burlington County.	18	4	Do.
22	Newkirk Van Meter, near Elmer, Burlington County.	18	....	Do.
23	W. H. Evans, road to Medford, Burlington County.	26	....	Do.
23	Clayton Stackhouse, near Medford, Burlington County.	21	1	Do.
24	William Cliver, near Vincentown, Burlington County.	29	....	Stables, good; animals, fair.
24	James S. Hartshorne, road to Mount Holly, Burlington County.	53	....	Do.
28	Stacy B. Taylor, Wrightstown, Burlington County.	17	4	Good.

Inspections in New Jersey—Continued.

Day of month.	Name of owner or person in charge and location of stable.	No. of cattle.	No. with lung-plague.	Condition of stables and animals.
	Inspections by W. B. E. Miller—Continued.			
1886.				
Dec. 29	Elmer Duell, near Woodstown, Burlington County.	25	....	Good.
29	George H. Kirby, near Avis Mills, Burlington County.	11	1	Do.
30	Newkirk Van Meter, near Elmer, Salem County	18	....	Do.

Inspections in Maryland.

Day of month.	Name of owner or person in charge and location of stable.	No. of cattle.	No. with lung-plague.	Condition of stables and animals.
	Inspections by W. H. Rose, V. S.			
1886.				
Jan. 7	Mr. Bartholow, east of Highlandtown, Baltimore County.	62	5c.	Stables, foul; animals, fair.
7	Mr. B. Miller, east of Highlandtown, Baltimore County.	64	3c.	Poor.
8	David Wolf, 1 mile northeast of Baltimore, Baltimore County.	25	2c.	Fair.
8	Daniel Shane, 1½ miles northeast of Baltimore, Baltimore County.	18	2c.	Stables, foul; animals, poor.
8	C. C. A. Roelkey, 2 miles northeast of Baltimore, Baltimore County.	13	....	Poor.
8	Mrs. Reilly, 1 mile northeast of Baltimore, Baltimore County.	16	4c.	Stables, foul; animals, poor.
8	Mrs. Sachs, 1½ miles northeast of Baltimore, Baltimore County.	28	5c.	Stables, poor; animals, fair.
12	Mr. Register, near Belair road, Baltimore County	20	4c.	Stables, foul; animals, poor.
13	Mr. Lord, Monktown, Baltimore County...........	10	....	Fair.
14	Mr. Davidson, Belair, Harford County..........	....	....	
15	Slaughter-houses, East Baltimore, Baltimore County.	60	....	
16	Mr. Kraemer, Sharp street, Baltimore, Baltimore County.	22	3c.	Stables, foul; animals, poor.
16	Geo. Sachs, Hanover street, South Baltimore, Baltimore County.	20	3c.	Poor.
16	Ed. Sachs, Hanover street, South Baltimore, Baltimore County.	13	1c.	Stables, foul; animals, poor.
16	Mr. Vogal, Washington road, Baltimore County..	24	2c.	Stables, fair; animals, fat.
21	Mr. Merling, Highlandtown, Baltimore County..	16	....	
21	Christian Avert, Highlandtown, Baltimore Co ..	16	2c.	Fair.
21	A. Winderling, Highlandtown, Baltimore County	17	....	
21	Mrs. Clay & Sons, Highlandtown, Baltimore County.	53	....	Stables, poor; animals, fair.
22	Wm. Brindall, Highlandtown, Baltimore County	16	4c.	Stables, foul; animals, poor.
22	Mr. Schmeiser, Highlandtown, Baltimore County	7	....	Fair.
22	David Markell, Highlandtown, Baltimore County	13	....	
22	Mr. Weimbeck, Highlandtown, Baltimore County	14	....	
22	L. Kiefer, Canton, Baltimore County	30	4c.	Do.
22	John Zorn, Canton, Baltimore County...............	13	1c.	Stables, foul; animals, poor.
23	John Dickman, Hanover street, Baltimore, Baltimore County.	20	....	Fair.
23	Captain Weaver, Hanover street, Baltimore, Baltimore County.	9	1c.	
23	John Hiller, Hanover street, Baltimore, Baltimore County.	16	1c.	Stables, poor; animals, fair.
23	Mr. Walter, Hanover street, Baltimore, Baltimore County.	7	1c.	Stables, foul; animals, fair.
23	Mrs. Hamberger, South Baltimore, Baltimore County.	12	....	Fair.
23	Milchler Jordan, South Baltimore, Baltimore County.	24	....	Stables, fair; animals, fat.
25	Calverton Stock-Yards, Baltimore, Baltimore County.	312	....	Poor.
26	Jacob Weddle, Wilkins avenue, Baltimore County.	10	1c.	Do.
26	Christian Heisler, near Clairmont, Baltimore County.	40	5c.	Do.

Inspections in Maryland—Continued.

Day of month.	Name of owner or person in charge and location of stable.	No. of cattle.	No. with lung-plague.	Condition of stables and animals.
	Inspections by W. H. Rose—Continued.			
1886.				
Jan. 27	Gerard Watts, Wilkins avenue, Baltimore County.	60	4c.	Stables, clean; animals, fair.
27	Long Green and Dulaney Valley, Baltimore County.	......	8c.	
18	Mr. German, Harford road, Baltimore County..	10	....	Poor.
18	Mr. Ward, Harford road, Baltimore County......	9	....	
19	Mr. Joekel, Herring Run, Baltimore County......	....	....	
19	Mr. Bernham, 1½ miles east of Baltimore, Baltimore County.	....	....	
29	C. S. Beebe, 3 miles north of Baltimore, Baltimore County.	8	....	
	Inspections by T. W. Spranklin, V. S.			
June 29	J. W. Garrett, Baltimore County....................	13	....	Stables, perfect; animals, good.
29	J. W. Garrett, Baltimore County.........	5	....	Do.
29	T. Heinecker, Govanstown, Baltimore County...	8	....	Stables, indifferent; animals, good.
29	W. H. Laneham, Govanstown, Baltimore County.	2	....	Stables, good; animals, indifferent.
	D. Wolf, Baltimore County	30	....	Good.
29	E. F. Raphel, Upper Falls, Baltimore County......	11	....	Do.
30	J. Hammond, Upper Falls, Baltimore County......	3	....	Do.
30	F. B. Gorsuch, Long Green, Baltimore County...	18	....	Stables, good; animals, perfect.
30	A. Miller, Upper Falls, Baltimore County	12	....	Good.
30	E. A. Gorsuch, Long Green, Baltimore County...	13	....	Do.
30	T. Armstrong, Glen Arm, Baltimore County......	20	....	Perfect.
30	J. H. Gorsuch, Kingsville, Baltimore County.....	8	....	Stables, indifferent; animals, good.
30	H. Kennard, Upper Falls, Baltimore County......	15	....	Good.
30	F. Cardwell, Upper Falls, Baltimore County......	6	....	Do.
July 3	H. Gerken, Wetheredville, Baltimore County....	70	....	Stables, indifferent; animals, good.
3	E. Malloee, Baltimore County............................	32	....	Good.
3	G. E. French, Arlington, Baltimore County	21	....	Do.
3	J. E. Dorsey & Co., Arlington, Baltimore County..	60	....	Do.
3	D. Lutz, Arlington, Baltimore County..........	27	....	Stables, bad; animals, indifferent.
3	C. E. Goldsborough, Wetheredville, Baltimore County.	27	....	Stables, perfect; animals, good.
3	A. Chapman, Arlington, Baltimore County.........	5	....	Stables, indifferent; animals, good.
	Mr. Stalzenpuch, Baltimore County....................	4	....	Indifferent.
	J. Dickman, Baltimore County..........................	22	....	Good.
	C. Weaver, Baltimore County...........................	7	....	Indifferent.
	J. Heller, Baltimore County...	15	....	Animals, indifferent.
	G. Sachs, Baltimore County..............................	25	....	Do.
	E. Sachs, Baltimore County..............................	13	....	Do.
	M. Jordan, Baltimore County............................	22	....	Animals, good.
	J. Creamer, Baltimore County..........................	15	....	Do.
	C. Vogal, Baltimore County..............................	15	....	Indifferent.
3	C. Kuhn, Baltimore County..............................	10	....	Do.
5	Mrs. Betz, Baltimore County............................	2	....	Stables, indifferent; animals, good.
5	G. Dittman, Baltimore County..........................	7	....	Do.
5	F. Miller, Baltimore County	18	....	Do.
5	Mrs. Kacser, Baltimore County	13	....	Stables, perfect; animals, good.
	Mrs. Hartman, Baltimore County........................	2	....	Good.
5	L. Kieffer, Baltimore County............................	25	....	Do.
5	J. Dorn, Baltimore County................................	12	....	Indifferent.
7	Kunklo, Baltimore County.................................	12	....	Do.
7	Mrs. Riley, Baltimore County............................	12	....	Stables, good; animals, indifferent.
7	Mr. Sachs, Baltimore County............................	15	....	Good.
7	Mrs. M. Zinkand, Baltimore County...................	28	....	Stables, indifferent; animals, good.
7	M. N. Register, Baltimore County.....................	18	....	Stables, bad; animals, indifferent.
7	J. Nuth, Baltimore County................................	31	....	Good.
7	W. Douglas, Baltimore County..........................	40	....	Stables, bad; animals, indifferent.
7	G. Bartholew, Fairview, Baltimore County.........	55	....	Good.

Inspections in Maryland—Continued.

Day of month.	Name of owner or person in charge and location of stable.	No. of cattle.	No. with lung-plague.	Condition of stables and animals.
	Inspections by T. W. Spranklin—Continued.			
1886. July 7	M. Roeder, Baltimore County	10	....	Indifferent.
9	S. Hare, Baltimore County	31	....	Good.
9	E. J. Green, Baltimore County	5	....	Stables, indifferent; animals, good.
9	D. Stevens, Woodberry, Baltimore County	40	6	Stables, very bad; animals, indifferent.
9	W. Wyman, Charles Street avenue, Baltimore County.	7	....	Good.
9	C. H. Baker, Melvale, Baltimore County	21	....	Stables, indifferent; animals, good.
9	C. Engleheart, Huntington avenue, Baltimore County.	15	....	Stables, bad; animals, indifferent.
10	F. N. Peets, Highlandtown, Baltimore County	14	....	Good.
10	Mr. Ehrich, Highlandtown, Baltimore County	10	....	Do.
10	J. Weinbeck, Highlandtown, Baltimore County	15	....	Stables, indifferent; animals, good.
10	B. Wolf, Highlandtown, Baltimore County	11	....	Good.
10	G. Wolf, Highlandtown, Baltimore County	13	....	Indifferent.
10	B. B. Noha, Highlandtown, Baltimore County	20	....	Stables, bad; animals, good.
10	J. Geier, Highlandtown, Baltimore County	11	....	Good.
10	J. Schmidt, Highlandtown, Baltimore County	11	....	Stables, indifferent; animals, good.
10	S. Bauernfind, Highlandtown, Baltimore County	11	....	Do.
10	R. Ebert, Highlandtown, Baltimore County	15	....	Good.
10	C. Schmidt, Highlandtown, Baltimore County	23	....	Do.
10	J. Clay, Highlandtown, Baltimore County	28	....	Stables, indifferent; animals, good.
10	F. Young, Highlandtown, Baltimore County	11	....	Good.
10	J. J. Hiller, Highlandtown, Baltimore County	21	....	Do.
10	G. Prell, Highlandtown, Baltimore County	16	....	Stables, bad; animals, good.
10	Clay Bros., Highlandtown, Baltimore County	44	....	Stables, indifferent; animals, good.
10	A. Wenterling, Highlandtown, Baltimore County.	16	....	Good.
14	Blank, Bay View Asylum, Baltimore County	13	....	Do.
14	W. Riddel, Patapsco Neck, Baltimore County	10	....	Indifferent.
14	J. Stevenson, Patapsco Neck, Baltimore County	10	....	Fair.
14	G. R. Richardson, Patapsco Neck, Baltimore County.	6	....	Do.
14	J. Tuchton, Bay View, Baltimore County	31	Sus.	Do.
14	H. Lene, Bay View, Baltimore County	7	....	Do.
14	H. Stahm, jr., Bay View, Baltimore County	14	Sus.	Do.
14	C. Deem, Bay View, Baltimore County	1	....	Do.
14	J. Schorn, Patapsco Neck, Baltimore County	8	....	Good.
14	G. Link, Philadelphia road, Baltimore County	16	Sus.	Fair.
14	J. Campbell, Patapsco Neck, Baltimore County	38	3c.	Stables, bad; animals, fair.
14	J. B. Miller, Highlandtown, Baltimore County	1	1a.	Fair.
17	J. Nichols, Park Heights, Baltimore County	16	Sus.	Stables, good; animals, fair.
17	A. Creaghan, Pikesville, Baltimore County	30	....	Fair.
17	D. C. Gray, Brooklandville, Baltimore County	12	....	Do.
17	Mr. Murphy, Pimlico, Baltimore County	25	....	Stables, fair; animals, good.
17	J. Schluderburger, Highlandtown, Baltimore County.	1	Sus.	Good.
17	W. S. Langemann, Washington street (extended), Baltimore.	75	Sus.	Stables, fair; animals, good.
17	D. Wolf, Homestead, Baltimore	30	Sus.	Good.
17	D. S. Stevens, Green Spring avenue, Baltimore	48	....	Stables, fair; animals, good.
17	W. K. Armstrong, Green Spring avenue, Baltimore.	17	....	Fair.
17	G. W. Adler, Park Heights, Baltimore	6	Sus.	Do.
17	Unknown, Woodberry, Baltimore County	70	....	Animals, good.
17	B. S. Woodston, Mount Washington, Baltimore County.	9	....	Stables, fair; animals, good.
17	Unknown, Hampden, Baltimore County	30	....	Animals, good.
20	G. Rye, Perry Hall, Baltimore County	6	....	Stables, bad; animals, indifferent.
20	H. Winskler, Saint Joseph, Baltimore County	9	....	Fair.
20	Hadline, Saint Joseph, Baltimore County	21	....	Do.
20	G. Soth, Perry Hall, Baltimore County	11	....	Do.

Inspections in Maryland—Continued.

Day of month.	Name of owner or person in charge and location of stable.	No. of cattle.	No. with lung-plague.	Condition of stables and animals.
	Inspections by T. W. Spranklin—Continued.			
1886.				
July 20	Chisler, Perry Hall, Baltimore County	3	....	Fair.
20	Rohmick, Putty Hill, Baltimore County	2	....	Stables, fair; animals, good.
20	J. Kraastel, Putty Hill, Baltimore County	7	2c.	Fair.
20	M. Bessold, Putty Hill, Baltimore County	10	....	Do.
20	H. Burgmeyer, Putty Hill, Baltimore County	5	....	Stables, fair; animals, good.
20	Blackburn, Perry Hall, Baltimore County	14	....	Fair.
20	H. Moore, Perry Hall, Baltimore County	9	....	Do.
20	Hargust, Fullerton, Baltimore County	3	....	Do.
20	J. Kline, Fullerton, Baltimore County	10	....	Stables, fair; animals, good.
20	A. Paul, Saint Joseph, Baltimore County	4	....	Do.
20	Trost, Saint Joseph, Baltimore County	4	....	Fair.
20	G. Closeman, Saint Joseph, Baltimore County	2	....	Do.
20	R. Meyers, Perry Hall, Baltimore County	3	1a.	Do.
21	T. B. Gatch, Raspeburg, Baltimore County	22	....	Do.
21	J. A. Cole, Raspeburg, Baltimore County	23	....	Good.
21	J. G. Carter, Raspeburg, Baltimore County	20	....	Do.
21	G. P. Quick, Gardenville, Baltimore County	8	....	Stables, fair; animals, good.
21	T. Biddesir, Gardenville, Baltimore County	16	....	Good.
21	J. Friskey, Gardenville, Baltimore County	4	....	Fair.
21	J. W. Evans, Belair road, Baltimore County	18	....	Good.
21	T. M. Richardson, Raspeburg, Baltimore County.	19	....	Do.
21	G. Friskey, Georgetown, Baltimore County	7	....	Stables, bad; animals, fair.
21	J. G. Erdman, Gardenville, Baltimore County	8	....	Good.
21	G. Hosstetter, Gardenville, Baltimore County	4	1c.	Stables, fair; animals, good.
21	J. Gutman, Raspeburg, Baltimore County	4	....	Good.
21	H. Berger, Canton, Baltimore County	22	....	Fair.
23	J. Schmidtman, Canton, Baltimore County	4	....	Do.
23	V. Gransea, Orangeville, Baltimore County	51	....	Do.
23	C. Hall, Hall Springs, Baltimore County	23	....	Stables, fair; animals, good.
23	H. Nordroff, Harlan road, Baltimore County	6	....	Fair.
23	P. Lacy, Canton, Baltimore County	6	....	Do.
23	F. Marten, Canton, Baltimore County	30	4c.	Do.
23	F. Mehring, Canton, Baltimore County	6	....	Do.
23	A. Keen, Canton, Baltimore County	2	....	Stables, fair; animals, good.
23	J. Neabelin, Canton, Baltimore County	26	....	Do.
23	G. Deehl, Canton, Baltimore County	10	....	Fair.
23	G. H. Erdman, Hall Springs, Baltimore County	2	....	Stables, fair; animals, good.
27	C. Linsy, Lauraville, Baltimore County	3	2c.	Fair.
27	F. Crowder, Lauraville, Baltimore County	2	....	Good.
27	T. German, Maysville, Baltimore County	18	....	Fair.
27	H. Gebb, Lauraville, Baltimore County	4	....	Good.
27	Knox, Lauraville, Baltimore County	2	....	Stables, fair; animals, good.
27	A. Otto, Lauraville, Baltimore County	3	....	Good.
27	J. Beeder, Lavender Hill, Baltimore County	5	....	Fair.
27	J. Mattox, Lavender Hill, Baltimore County	4	....	Do.
27	R. A. Whiteford, Lavender Hill, Baltimore County	6	....	Do.
27	G. Emmel, Lauraville, Baltimore County	3	....	Do.
27	List & Schulz, Lauraville, Baltimore County	5	....	Do.
27	W. Weitzel, Lauraville, Baltimore County	2	....	Good.
27	Cap. Leckeford, Lauraville, Baltimore County	3	....	Do.
27	D. Standenmeyer, Lauraville, Baltimore County	10	....	Stables, bad; animals, fair.
27	J. Standenmeyer, Lauraville, Baltimore County	6	....	Stables, fair; animals, good.
27	T. Gebb, Lauraville, Baltimore County	15	....	Good.
28	J. Grorner, Hall Springs, Baltimore County	6	....	Fair.
28	E. Richardson, Lauraville, Baltimore County	13	....	Good.
28	M. Mann, Hall Springs, Baltimore County	2	....	Do.
28	R. Erdman, Hall Springs, Baltimore County	3	....	Do.
28	A. Anft, Hall Springs, Baltimore County	35	....	Stables, fair; animals, good.
28	J. Deitz, Hall Springs, Baltimore County	7	....	Good.
28	H. Hausman, Mount Carmel, Baltimore County	7	....	Fair.

Inspections in Maryland—Continued.

Day of month.	Name of owner or person in charge and location of stable.	No of cattle.	No. with lung-plague.	Condition of stables and animals.
	Inspections by T. W. Spranklin—Continued.			
1886. July 28	A. Sapp, Mount Carmel, Baltimore County	5	....	Stables, bad; animals, fair.
28	J. Elliott, Mount Carmel, Baltimore County	2	....	Stables, fair; animals, good.
28	J. Guisring, Patapsco Neck, Baltimore County	2	....	Fair.
28	Jackson, Patapsco Neck, Baltimore County	2	....	Do.
28	Schneider, Canton, Baltimore County	10	....	Do.
28	J. A. Bauer, Baltimore County	10	....	Do.
29	P. Lee, 186 McHenry street, Baltimore, Baltimore County.	3	....	Stables, bad; animals, fair.
29	C. Keefer, 103 Amity street, Baltimare, Baltimore County.	7	....	Fair.
29	A. Griffen, Washington avenue, Baltimore Co	8	....	Do.
29	J. Seina, 6 Washington avenue, Baltimore Co	4	....	Do.
29	A. Hofheing, 10 Washington avenue, Baltimore County.	10	....	Do.
29	M. McKenney, 32 Washington avenue, Baltimore County.	6	....	Do.
29	C. Kroder, 250 Washington avenue, Baltimore County.	6	....	Do.
29	J. Sullivan, Baltimore County	17	....	Do.
29	O. Reed, Cathill, Baltimore County	20	....	Stables, bad; animals, fair.
29	R. Moore, Glenmore, Baltimore County	40	....	Good.
29	J. Ward, Hamilton avenue, Baltimore County	4	....	Stables, fair; animals, good.
29	J. Neidherdt, Hamilton avenue, Baltimore Co	2	....	Fair.
30	C. Heisler, Wilkens, Baltimore County	37	....	Do.
30	J. Wedgle, Wilkens, Baltimore County	12	....	Do.
30	J. Baer, Washington road, Baltimore County	10	....	Do.
30	H. Arnold, Washington road, Baltimore County	4	....	Stables, fair; animals, good.
30	H. Schaeffer, Washington road, Baltimore Co	9	....	Fair.
30	L. Zaiser, Baltimore County	100	....	Do.
30	G. S. Watts, Beveile Farm, Baltimore County	51	....	Good.
31	T. Wagman, Spring street, Baltimore, Baltimore County.	5	....	Stables, bad; animals, fair.
31	J. Barton, Spring street, Baltimore, Baltimore County.	17	....	Fair.
31	P. Kenner, 215 Eden street, Baltimore, Baltimore County.	2	....	Good.
31	J. Grogan, 85 Harford avenue, Baltimore, Baltimore County.	1	....	Do.
31	P. Kenney, 113 Greenmount avenue, Baltimore, Baltimore County.	3	....	Fair.
31	J. Wright, 145 Greenmount avenue, Baltimore Baltimore County.	1	....	Do.
31	T. Grogan, 66 McKim street, Baltimore County.	3	....	Stables, bad; animals, fair.
31	P. Keetly, 319 Greenmount avenue, Baltimore County.	4	....	Stables, bad; animals, good.
31	P. Ganley, Belvidere street	9	....	Stables, fair; animals, good.
	W. H. O'Brien, 188 North Front street	4	....	Fair.
31	P. Casey, 20 Addison street	3	....	Do.
Aug. 32	C. J. Baker, Frederick road, Baltimore County	12	....	Stables, bad; animals, fair.
3	W. Baker, Frederick road, Baltimore County	5	....	Stables, bad; animals, good.
3	House of Refuge, Frederick road, Baltimore County.	5	....	Stables, fair; animals, good.
3	J. Stewart, Milengton, Baltimore County	9	....	Stables, good; animals, fair.
3	H. Yienger, Milengton, Baltimore County	5	....	Do.
3	J. Farrel, Milengton, Baltimore County	9	....	Good.
3	Wilhelm, Milengton, Baltimore County.	5	....	Fair.
3	W. Nelson, Milengton, Baltimore County	16	....	Do.
3	E. Gratz, Frederick road, Baltimore County	2	....	Do.
3	J. Tiepe, Frederick road, Baltimore County	5	....	Stables, fair; animals, good.
4	A. Paul, Belair road, Baltimore County	4	....	Fair.
4	A. Dumer, Belair, Baltimore County	4	....	Stables, fair; animals, good.
4	G. L. Rye, Belair, Baltimore County	6	....	Fair.

Inspections in Maryland—Continued.

Day of month.	Name of owner or person in charge and location of stable.	No. of cattle.	No. with lung-plague.	Condition of stables and animals.
	Inspections by T. W. Spranklin—Continued			
1886.				
Aug. 4	J. Nickel, Park Height, Baltimore County	17		
4	C. O. Kemp, Park Height, Baltimore County	6	1 a.	Fair.
4	G. N. Stubbs, Arlington, Baltimore County	8		Do.
4	E. N. Manolee, Park Height, Baltimore County	30	2 c.	Do.
4	G. W. Alder, Park Height, Baltimore County	6	2 a.	
9	F. O'Neal, Oxford, Baltimore County	6		Good.
9	P. Gapeto, Oxford, Baltimore County	2	1 c.	Do.
9	G. P. Unvergagt, Baltimore County	1		Do.
9	G. O'Neal, Baltimore County	1		Do.
9	P. Dugman, Baltimore County	1		Stables, good; animals, fair.
9	G. Kahler, Baltimore County	2		Good.
9	G. Oliver, Baltimore County	4		Do.
9	Realer, Baltimore County	1		Fair.
9	S. Roeder, Oxford, Baltimore County	1		Good.
9	P. Gass, Baltimore County	3		Stables, fair; animals, good.
9	Matthews, Baltimore County	2		Fair.
9	J. Matler, Baltimore County	1		Do.
9	Mrs. Gibson, Baltimore County	15		Do.
11	W. Patterson, Baltimore Counnty	1		Do.
11	N. Votz, 242 South Broadway, Baltimore County	1	1a.	Stables, good; animals, bad.
11	T. Wilson, Baltimore County	1		Fair.
11	H. Luntz, Bay View, Baltimore County	8	1	Do.
11	D. Burkheart, York road, Baltimore County	2		Stables, good; animals, fair.
11	W. H. Wilson, Baltimore County	2		Fair.
11	G. Clark, Baltimore County	1		Stables, fair; animals, good.
11	J. Maxfield, Baltimore County	1		Do.
11	Mr Smith, Oxford, Baltimore County	1		Do.
12	C. Wolf, Orangeville, Baltimore County	4		Do.
12	Counselman, Orangeville, Baltimore County	3		Fair.
12	D. Steavens, Orangeville, Baltimore County	1		Stables, fair; animals, good.
12	H. Kimmel, Orangeville, Baltimore County	1		Do.
12	Sisters of the Poor, Baltimore City, Baltimore County.	4		Good.
12	M. Lee, Baltimore County	2		Do.
12	Patterson, Baltimore County	1		Stables, fair; animals, good.
12	Gibbett, Baltimore County	1	1c.	Fair.
12	G. W Reaver, Orangeville, Baltimore County	1		Good.
12	W. H. Hein, Orangeville, Baltimore County	1		Stables, bad; animals, fair.
12	W. H. Kline, Orangeville, Baltimore County	1		Good.
12	H. Trabundt, Orangeville, Baltimore County	2		Stables, fair; animals, good.
12	M. Melsher, Orangeville, Baltimore County	2		Do.
12	G. Ogler, Orangeville, Baltimore County	3		Do.
13	J. Orem, Orangeville, Baltimore County	3		Good.
13	O'Neal, Orangeville, Baltimore County	3		Stables, fair.
13	T. F. Kenley, Orangeville, Baltimore County	1		Do.
13	C. Beck, Orangeville, Baltimore County	2		Do.
13	Schmidtman, Orangeville, Baltimore County	2		Do.
13	H. Schmidt, Orangeville, Baltimore County	7		Stables, good.
13	M Heenley, Orangeville, Baltimore County	3		Do.
13	Hosstetter, Rosedale, Baltimore County	2		Do.
13	Mr. Ross, Rosedale, Baltimore County	1		Stables, fair.
13	P. Rheling, Rosedale, Baltimore County	18		Fair.
13	J. Eidman, Rosedale, Baltimore County	4	2c.	Stables, bad; animals, fair.
14	G. M. Wilson, Rosedale, Baltimore County	10		Stables, fair; animals, good.
14	G. Snyder, Belair road, Baltimore County	10		Do.
14	J. Strayling, Belair road, Baltimore County	1		Bad.
14	J. H. Snyder, Belair road, Baltimore County	5		Stables, fair; animals, good.
14	H. Snyder, Belair road, Baltimore County	7		Do.
14	J. W. Evans, Belair road, Baltimore County	16	2a.	Fair.
14	G. Reidel, Rosedale, Baltimore County	3	1c.	Stables, fair; animals, good.

Inspections in Maryland—Continued.

Day of month.	Name of owner or person in charge and location of stable.	No. of cattle.	No. with lung-plague.	Condition of stables and animals.
	Inspections by T. W. Spranklin—Continued.			
1886.				
Aug. 14	Rhudolf, Belair road, Baltimore County	2		Fair.
14	J. S. Rettiger, Rosedale, Baltimore County	6		Stables, fair; animals good.
14	M. F. Kine, Rosedale, Baltimore County	2		Good.
14	G. Frederick, Rosedale, Baltimore County	3		Do.
14	McCormack, Rosedale, Baltimore County	13		Do.
14	T. Lutz, Rosedale, Baltimore County	3		Do.
18	W. Cochran, York road, Baltimore County	6		Do.
18	F. Christ, Georgetown, Baltimore County	8		Do.
18	G. Brehm, Georgetown, Baltimore County	4		Do.
18	M. Bernheart, Georgetown, Baltimore County	2		Do.
18	A. Ford, Georgetown, Baltimore County	4		Animals, good.
18	H. Greensfield, Mount Orange, Baltimore Co	4		Do.
18	G. Baker, Mount Orange, Baltimore County	17		Do.
18	H. Stealpher, Chesterville, Baltimore County	22		Do.
18	B. Wolf, Highlandtown, Baltimore County	10	1a.	Fair.
18	J. F. Heigh, Oakland, Baltimore County	1		
18	B. Hackerman, 68 Harrison street, Baltimore County.	5	1a.	Stables, fair; animals good.
18	C. Fischer, Orangeville, Baltimore County	4		Do.
18	W. Sley, Orangeville, Baltimore County	10		Do.
18	F. Link, Loney's lane, Baltimore County	1		Do.
18	J. Kelly, Chesterville, Baltimore County	1		Do.
18	B. W. Hardesty, Chesterville, Baltimore County	2		Do.
18	N. Kress, Chesterville, Baltimore County	2		Good.
20	H. Vols, Philadelphia road, Baltimore County	12		Stables, bad; animals, fair.
20	Houbert, Baltimore County	1		Do.
20	Botlenfelter, Baltimore County	1		Do.
20	C. Evering, Baltimore County	3		Good.
20	J. Gross, Baltimore County	29	2a.	Stables, bad; animals, good.
20	J. Reltiger, Rosedale, Baltimore County	7	2a.	Stables, bad; animals, fair.
20	J. Eidman, Rosedale, Baltimore County	4	1	Stables, fair; animals, good.
20	W. Peters, Baltimore County	1		Do.
20	E. Taylor, Baltimore County	2		Fair.
20	C. Shultz, Baltimore County	4		Stables, fair; animals, good.
20	J. Betz, Baltimore County	8		Fair.
20	H. Hausman, Patapsco Neck, Baltimore County	7	1a.	Do.
20	J. Schmidt, Highlandtown, Baltimore County	10	1a.	Do.
	Inspections by C. K. Dyer, V. S.			
19	Clayton M. Ellroy, Highlandtown, Baltimore County.	9	2	Stables, good; animals poor.
20	Phillip Lentz, Hookstown road Baltimore Co	6		Good.
20	Dr. Francis W. Patterson, Liberty road, Baltimore County.	11		Do.
20	E. Mallonee, Hookstown road, Baltimore County.	40		Do.
21	Phillip Fix, Hookstown, Baltimore County	2		Do.
21	Richard Disney, Hookstown, Baltimore County.	1		Do.
21	A. H. Schwabelant, Lexington avenue, Baltimore	5		Do.
23	Jacob Levian, road to Baltimore, Baltimore Co.	3		Do.
23	Mitchell Bros., road to Baltimore, Baltimore Co.	16		Do.
23	Henry Lohr, road to Baltimore, Baltimore Co	1		Do.
23	John Gross, road to Baltimore, Baltimore Co	1		Do.
23	Robt. J. Disney, road to Baltimore, Baltimore County.	1		Do.
23	Wm. Hall, road to Baltimore, Baltimore County.	2		Do.
23	J. J. Luby, road to Baltimore, Baltimore County.	1		Do.
23	Chris Heisel, Main street, Catonsville, Baltimore County.	1		Do.
23	Mrs. Leinbock, Main street, Catonsville, Baltimore County.	1		Do.
23	Mr. Erdman, Main street, Catonsville, Baltimore County.	1		Do.
23	Mrs. Muendlein, Main street, Catonsville, Baltimore County.	2		Do.
23	Mrs. Gazelle, road to Franklintown, Baltimore County.	1		Do.
23	Amandora Rich, road to Franklintown, Baltimore County.	11		Do.

Inspections in Maryland—Continued.

Day of month.	Name of owner or person in charge and location of stable.	No. of cattle.	No. with lung-plague.	Condition of stables and animals.
	Inspections by C. K. Dyer—Continued.			
1886. Aug. 23	John Zehner, road to Franklintown, Baltimore County.	1	....	Good.
23	L. Keidel, road to Catonsville, Baltimore Co.	8	....	Do.
23	Wm. Knabe, road to Catonsville, Baltimore Co.	1	....	Do.
23	Dr. Ebeling, road to Catonsville, Baltimore Co.	3	....	Do.
23	Adam Graber, road to Catonsville, Baltimore Co.	1	....	Do.
23	Geo. R. Grangers, road to Catonsville, Baltimore County.	2	....	Do.
23	Chas. E. Hand, road to Catonsville, Baltimore County.	8	....	Do.
23	Wm. Wooltong, road to Catonsville, Baltimore County.	2	....	Do.
23	A. L. Crasby, road to Catonsville, Baltimore County.	9	....	Do.
23	Henry Seick, road to Catonsville, Baltimore County.	4	....	Do.
23	John Eberhart, road to Catonsville, Baltimore County.	1	....	Do.
23	Chas. Bonce, Main street, Franklintown, Baltimore County.	1	....	Do.
23	Chas. Lebro, Main street, Franklintown, Baltimore County.	1	....	Do.
23	Joseph Stinul, Main street, Franklintown, Baltimore County.	1	....	Do.
23	Mrs. Pell	2	....	Do.
23	William Beaumont, road to..........	2	....	Do.
23	Frank Linton, road to	13	....	Stables, filthy; animals fair.
24	John Teacker, Arlington avenue, Waverly, Baltimore County.	8	....	Good.
24	Henry Digman, Arlington avenue, Waverly, Baltimore County.	11	....	Stables, poor; animals fair.
24	Mrs. Austin, York road, Govanstown, Baltimore County.	1	....	Good.
24	William Reiman, York road, Govanstown, Baltimore County.	23	....	Do.
24	Daniel Solan, York road, Govanstown, Baltimore County.	12	....	Do.
24	James Dugan, York road, Govanstown, Baltimore County.	4	....	Do.
24	John O'Brien, York road, Govanstown, Baltimore County.	1	.....?.....	Do.
24	James Melligan, York road, Govanstown, Baltimore County.	7	....	Do.
24	Mr. Richardson, York road, Govanstown, Baltimore County.	1	....	Do.
24	William Henry, York road, Govanstown, Baltimore County.	3	....	Do.
24	Mr. Mills, York road, Govanstown, Baltimore County.	1	....	Do.
24	Mrs. Cross, York road, Govanstown, Baltimore County.	2	....	Do.
24	Fred. Vonkapff, York road, Govanstown, Baltimore County.	19	....	Do.
24	Fisher's estate, York road, Govanstown, Baltimore County.	8	....	Do.
24	John Owens, York road, Govanstown, Baltimore County.	6	....	Do.
24	Fred. Groom, York road, Govanstown, Baltimore County.	20	....	Do.
24	John Emery, road to Cromwell's bridge, Baltimore County.	2	....	Do.
24	Jacob Wisner, road to Cromwell's bridge, Baltimore County.	34	....	Do.
24	D. H. Rice, road to Cromwell's bridge, Baltimore County.	33	....	Do.
24	Arthur W. Shanklin, road to Cromwell's bridge, Baltimore County.	20	....	Do.
24	S. E. Parks, road to Cromwell's bridge, Baltimore County.	17	....	Do.
24	Samuel Chew, road to Cromwell's bridge, Baltimore County.	24	....	Do.
25	Mrs. M. T. Preston, road to Darlington bridge, Baltimore County.	19	2a.	Do.

Inspections in Maryland—Continued.

	Name of owner or person in charge and location of stable.	No. of cattle.	No. with lung-plague.	Condition of stables and animals.
	Inspections by C. K. Dyer—Continued.			
27	Sundry owners, road to Washington bridge, Baltimore County.	32	....	Good.
27	John Smith, road to Washington bridge, Baltimore County.	7	....	Stables, filthy; animals, fair.
27	C. Canary, road to Washington, Baltimore Co....	4	....	Good.
27	Henry Tieman, road to Washington, Baltimore County.	3	....	Do.
27	Jacob Churb, road to Washington, Baltimore County.	2	....	Do.
27	C. Kaline, road to Washington, Baltimore Co...	1	....	Do.
27	George Grab, road to Washington, Baltimore County.	3	....	Do.
27	J. Crab, road to Washington, Baltimore County..	3	....	Do.
27	Henry Shriver, road to Washington, Baltimore County.	5	....	
27	Robert Ford, Remington avenue, Baltimore	1	....	
28	Samuel Hare, Remington avenue, Baltimore......	35	....	Stables, fair; animals, good.
28	J. J. McCann, Remington avenue, Baltimore......	1	1	Good.
28	Mrs. Engelhart, Remington avenue, Baltimore...	16	....	Fair.
28	Patrick Kirby, Remington avenue, Baltimore....	2	....	Good.
28	George Barnes, Remington avenue, Baltimore...	2	....	Do.
28	John Brown, Remington avenue, Baltimore.......	1	....	Do.
28	Charles W. Little, Remington avenue, Baltimore.	3	....	Do.
28	Edward J. Green, Remington avenue, Baltimore.	7	....	Do.
28	Mack Knowles, Remington avenue, Baltimore..	1	....	Do.
28	Mrs. O'Brien, Remington avenue, Baltimore . .	2	....	Do.
28	Mrs. Morris, Remington avenue, Baltimore......	1	....	Do.
28	Mrs. Brick, Remington avenue, Baltimore..........	1	....	Do.
28	Henry Minz, Remington avenue, Baltimore......	1	....	Do.
30	J. W. H. Klein, Belair road, Baltimore County...	8	....	Do.
31	Chris. Schnovel, road to Finksburgh, Carroll County.	3	....	Do.
31	Leonard Rosenberger, road to Finksburgh, Carroll County.	11	8	Stables, good; animals, poor.
31	Edward Ludwig, Pikesville, Baltimore County..	1	....	Good.
31	Wm. Shirley, road to Pimlico, Baltimore County..	2	1	Do.
	Inspections by T. W. Spranklin, V. S.			
24	Mrs. Dames, Homestead, Baltimore County........	1	....	Stables, good; animals, fair.
24	Mr. Cator, Waverly Baltimore County..............	4	....	Good.
24	C. Owens, Waverly, Baltimore County..............	1	....	Do.
24	G. Carter, Waverly, Baltimore County..............	1	....	Stables, fair; animals, good.
24	J. Brown, Waverly, Baltimore County...............	1	....	Stables, fair.
24	P. Roach, Waverly, Baltimore County...............	1	....	Do.
24	Mr. Kilroy, Govanstown, Baltimore County.....	1	....	Stables, good.
24	W. Waters, Waverly, Baltimore County	1	....	Stables, fair.
24	J. A. Price, Waverly, Baltimore County	3	....	Do.
24	F. Davis, Waverly, Baltimore County.	2	....	Stables, good.
24	M. Mulligan, Waverly, Baltimore County..........	1	....	Stables, fair.
24	H. Dickelman, Waverly, Baltimore County.......	11	....	Stables, bad; animals, fair.
24	J. Tickel, Waverly, Baltimore County...............	3	....	Stables, fair; animals, good.
25	J. S. Gitling, Liberty road, Baltimore County....	38	....	Do.
25	Mr. Hall, Liberty road, Baltimore County	2	....	Do.
25	Dr. J. Bull, Highland Park, Baltimore County. ..	2	....	Good.
25	J. Ruhall, 238 Hollins street, Baltimore County...	6	....	Stables, fair.
25	A. E. Groff, Highland Park, Baltimore County...	22	....	Do.
25	Igleberger, Liberty road, Baltimore County.	2	....	Do.
25	Mr. C. Bostle, Liberty road, Baltimore County....	5	....	Do.
25	P. Craine, Liberty road, Baltimore County.	18	....	Do.
25	J. Kapple, Liberty road, Baltimore County...	3	....	Do.
25	J. Wagner, Liberty road, Baltimore County.	2	....	Do.
25	C. Buck, Liberty road, Baltimore County	15	....	Do.
25	Mr. Magee, Fulton place, Baltimore County........	2	....	Do.
25	O. Meyers, Fulton place, Baltimore County.....	15	....	Do.
25	T. Airy, Fayette street, Baltimore County.........	22	....	Do.

Inspections in Maryland—Continued.

Day of month.	Name of owner or person in charge and location of stable.	No. of cattle.	No. with lung-plague.	Condition of stables and animals.
	Inspections by T. W. Spranklin—Continued.			
1886. Aug. 27	T. E. Williams, Mount Washington, Baltimore County.	8	....	Stables, fair; animals, good.
27	Sundry owners, Mount Washington, Baltimore County.	12	....	Do.
27	E. Cowling, Rockland, Baltimore County	17	....	Stables, good; animals, fair.
27	C. Debough, Rockland, Baltimore County	9	....	Stables, fair; animals, good.
27	M. A. Smith, Falls road, Baltimore County	5	....	Do.
27	P. McMahan, Falls road, Baltimore County	3	....	Good.
27	S. Hook, Falls road, Baltimore County	4	....	Do.
27	C. Kaste, Falls road, Baltimore County	2	....	Stables, fair; animals, good.
27	G. Heavel, Falls road, Baltimore County	9	....	Do.
27	P. O'Connell, Mount Washington, Baltimore County	5	....	Do.
27	K. Lehr, Mount Washington, Baltimore County	5	....	Do.
28	A. Busch, Govanstown, Baltimore County	1	....	Good.
28	J. Murray, Govanstown, Baltimore County	3	....	Stables, fair; animals, good.
28	G. Griffith, Govanstown, Baltimore County	2	....	Do.
28	G. McGrevy, Govanstown, Baltimore County	4	....	Do.
28	P. K. Brady, 38 Lancaster street, Baltimore County.	2	....	Fair.
28	Mr. Lynch, 13 Lancaster street, Baltimore County.	2	....	Do.
28	J. Samuel, 309 South Bond street, Baltimore County.	2	....	Do.
28	Mrs. E. Burger, 335 South Bond street, Baltimore.	3	....	Stables, fair; animals, good.
30	A. Paul, Belair road, Baltimore County	4	....	Do.
30	G. Rye, Belair road, Baltimore County	5	....	Stables, bad; animals, fair.
30	H. Repkey, Belair road, Baltimore County	2	....	Fair.
30	J. Dingler, Belair road, Baltimore County	4	....	Stables, bad; animals, good.
30	J. Oster, Perry Hall, Baltimore County	11	....	Do.
30	K. Rhinert, Perry Hall, Baltimore County	9	....	Stables, bad; animals, fair.
30	R. Smith, Belair road, Baltimore County	15	....	Stables, fair; animals, good.
30	L. Tremper, Perry Hall, Baltimore County	6	....	Do.
30	J. Cook, Perry Hall, Baltimore County	13	....	Do.
31	J. H. Goss, Rossville, Baltimore County	24	....	Good.
31	G. F. Walters, Stemmer's Run, Baltimore Co	8	....	Stables, fair; animals, good.
31	J. N. Foss, Eastern avenue road, Baltimore County.	35	....	Good.
31	J. C. Fulchtor, Eastern avenue road, Baltimore County.	31	....	Stables, fair.
	Inspections by W. H. Rose, V. S.			
Sept. [illegible]	John Dorn, Canton, Baltimore County	15	3	
[illegible]	J. E. Dorsey, Arlington, Baltimore County	60	....	
	Inspections by T. W. Spranklin, V. S.			
4	W. Nelson, Millington, Baltimore County	16	....	Good.
4	A. Wilhelm, Millington, Baltimore County	4	....	Stables, fair; animals, good.
4	[illegible] Farrell, Millington, Baltimore County	9	....	Good.
4	H. Wenger, Millington, Baltimore County	5	....	Do.
[illegible]	C. Heisler, Baltimore County	38	....	Do.
[illegible]	[illegible] Stewart, Millington, Baltimore County	10	....	Do.
[illegible]	H. Schaefer, Washington road, Baltimore County	9	1a.	Bad.
[illegible]	J. W. Evans, Gardenville, Baltimore County	....	2a.	Fair.
[illegible]	J. H. Goss, Rossville, Baltimore County	22	2a.	Do.
[illegible]	W. [illegible], Washington road, Baltimore County	89	....	Good.
9	[illegible] Pline, Govanstown, Baltimore County	12	....	Do.
9	[illegible], Govanstown, Baltimore County	4	....	Do.
10	H. Wolf, Highlandtown, Baltimore County	10	....	Do.
10	[illegible], Baltimore County	4	....	Stables, fair; animals, good.

Inspections in Maryland—Continued.

Day of month.	Name of owner or person in charge and location of stable.	No. of cattle.	No. with lung-plague.	Condition of stables and animals.
	Inspections by T. W. Spranklin—Continued.			
1886. pt. 10	W. Strong, Highlandtown, Baltimore County	1	....	Good.
10	J. G. Miller, Highlandtown, Baltimore County	24	....	Do.
10	G. Preil, Highlandtown, Baltimore County	17	2c.	Fair.
10	P. Malkes, Highlandtown, Baltimore County	10	....	Do.
10	L. Clay, Highlandtown, Baltimore County	44	1a.	Stables, fair; animals, good.
10	S. G. Knapp, Gardenville, Baltimore County	3	....	Do.
11	P. Harder, Liberty road, Baltimore County	2	....	Do.
11	F. Gore, Liberty road, Baltimore County	4	1	Do.
11	O. Mephan, Liberty road, Baltimore County	1	....	Do.
11	C. Gore, Liberty road, Baltimore County	7	....	Bad.
11	J. Smith, Liberty road, Baltimore County	16	....	Stables, bad; animals, fair.
11	H, Litmer, Liberty road, Baltimore County	8	....	Stables, fair; animals, good.
11	C. E. Goldsborough, Liberty road, Baltimore County.	25	....	Good.
11	H. Gerken, Liberty road, Baltimore County	72	....	Stables, fair; animals, good.
	Inspections by Trumbower and Dyer.			
8	Henry Shriver, Washington road, Baltimore County.	5	2	Fair.
10	William Prangley, Waverly, Baltimore County	1	....	Stables, good; animals, fair.
10	Mrs. Foote, Waverly, Baltimore County	2	1	
11	William H. Lease, out from Frederick, Frederick County.	1	....	
14	Thomas Fassett, Rising Sun, Cecil County	....	....	
15	J. D. Child, 7 miles from Cockeysville, Baltimore County.	8	....	
16	Fred. Gore, 5 miles from city, Baltimore County	4	1c.	
18	James R. Whiteford, Cambria Station, Harford County.	7	....	
20	Paul Harter, 4 miles from city, Baltimore Co	2	1c.	
20	Charles Gore, 4 miles from city, Baltimore Co	7	2	
20	Mr. Hiller, 750 Hanover street, Baltimore Co	13	2c.	
20	Mrs. A. Deickman, 720 Hanover street, Baltimore County.	19	1c.	
	Inspections by Mr. C. K. Dyer, V. S.			
1	William Shirley, near Pimlico, Baltimore Co	2	....	
2	William Amos, near Baltimore, Baltimore Co	6	....	
2	William Shirley, Baltimore County	2	....	
2	James Nickel, Pimlico, Baltimore County	1	1	
3	Charles Kuhn, Highlandtown, Baltimore Co	6	....	
3	John Doran, Canton, Baltimore County	....	2c.	
3	John Hiller, 750 Hanover street, Baltimore	13	....	
4	John Heins, 506 Light street, Baltimore	1	1	
4	Henry Schriver, Washington Road, Baltimore County.	5	3	
4	Mr. Schafer, Washington Road, Baltimore Co	9	1	
6,7	Nimrod Dorsey, Ellicott City, Howard County	61	29	
8	Mr. Guirmot, Pimlico, Baltimore County	1	....	
8	C. Lyon Rogers, near Pikesville, Baltimore Co	40	....	
8	Hampy Stump, near Pikesville, Baltimore Co	12	....	
8	Norman Stump, near Pikesville, Baltimore Co	8	....	
8	Harrison Stump, near Pikesville, Baltimore Co	25	....	
8	Mrs. C. Stump, near Pikesville, Baltimore Co	12	....	
8	H. C. Winchester, near Pikesville, Baltimore Co	12	....	
10	Mr. Cowling, Rocklandville, Baltimore County	17	....	
10	Mr. Debaugh, Rocklandville, Baltimore County	9	....	
10	Mr. Vaughn, Mount Washington, Baltimore Co	35	....	
11	William Gent, Shawan, Baltimore County	8	....	
13	George Brown, Cockeysville, Baltimore County	12	1	
14	D J Foley, Ellicott City, Howard County	40	....	
15	Ephraim Mallonee, near Pimlico, Baltimore Co	40	3	
15	Mr. Perott, Woodburn, Baltimore County	8	1	
16	Wm. Kempske, Pimlico, Baltimore County	8	....	
17	F. Brosenna, Ellicott City, Howard County	61	....	
18	J. J. Wilson, Govanstown, Baltimore County	1	....	
18	Wm. Lannahan, Govanstown, Baltimore County	4	....	
18	M. J. Kilroy, Govanstown, Baltimore County	1	....	

Inspections in Maryland—Continued.

Day of month.	Name of owner or person in charge and location of stable.	No. of cattle.	No. with lung-plague.	Condition of stables and animals.
	Inspections by C. K. Dyer—Continued.			
1888. Sept. [illegible]	John Dengner, Putty Hill, Baltimore County	3	1	
[illegible]	Mr. Cay, Highlandtown, Baltimore County	46	2	Stables, filthy; animals, fair.
	Inspections by W. H. [illegible], V. S.			
[illegible]	V. [illegible], Pimlico Road, Baltimore County	8	2	
	Inspections by W. H. [illegible], V. S.			
[illegible]	Jas. Brown, [illegible]ville, Baltimore County	....	1	
[illegible]	[illegible] Kean, [illegible] Road, Baltimore County	10	....	Good.
[illegible]	[illegible], [illegible], Baltimore County	8	1	
[illegible]	[illegible], Washington Road, Baltimore County	1	....	
[illegible]	[illegible], Washington Road, Baltimore County	5	2	
	Inspections by E. W. [illegible], V. S.			
[illegible]	[illegible] Bros., Highlandtown, Baltimore County	19	....	Stables, fair.
[illegible]	[illegible], Highlandtown, Baltimore County	12	....	Stables, good; animals, fair.
[illegible]	[illegible], Highlandtown, Baltimore County	18	....	Good.
[illegible]	[illegible], Highlandtown, Baltimore County	1	....	Stables, fair.
[illegible]	[illegible], Highlandtown, Baltimore County	11	....	Stables, bad; animals, fair.
[illegible]	[illegible], Highlandtown, Baltimore County	16	....	Stables, good; animals, fair.
[illegible]	[illegible], Highlandtown, Baltimore County	15	....	Good.
[illegible]	[illegible], Highlandtown, Baltimore County	18	....	Do.
[illegible]	[illegible], Highlandtown, Baltimore County	10	....	Do.
[illegible]	[illegible], Highlandtown, Baltimore County	15	....	Do.
[illegible]	[illegible], Canton, Baltimore County	28	....	Fair.
[illegible]	[illegible], Canton, Baltimore County	16	....	Stables, fair; animals, good.
[illegible]	[illegible], Canton, Baltimore County	2	....	Stables, bad; animals, good.
[illegible]	[illegible], Canton, Baltimore County	7	....	Fair.
[illegible]	[illegible], Canton, Baltimore County	1	....	Stables, good; animals, fair.
[illegible]	[illegible], Canton, Baltimore County	2	....	Good.
[illegible]	[illegible], Canton, Baltimore County	2	....	Stables, good; animals, fair.
[illegible]	[illegible], Canton, Baltimore County	2	....	Fair.
[illegible]	[illegible], Patapsco Neck, Baltimore County	14	....	Do.
[illegible]	[illegible], Patapsco Neck, Baltimore County	7	....	Do.
[illegible]	[illegible], Philadelphia road, Baltimore County	21	....	Do.
[illegible]	[illegible], Canton, Baltimore County	12	....	Good.
[illegible]	[illegible], Canton, Baltimore County	13	....	Do.
[illegible]	[illegible], Canton, Baltimore County	11	....	Stables, good; animals, fair.
[illegible]	[illegible], Canton, Baltimore County	25	....	Good.
[illegible]	[illegible], Canton, Baltimore County	10	....	Do.
[illegible]	[illegible], Harford road, Baltimore County	8	....	Stables, fair; animals, good.
[illegible]	[illegible], Harford road, Baltimore County	21	....	Good.
[illegible]	[illegible], Harford road, Baltimore County	14	1c.	Do.
[illegible]	[illegible], Harford road, Baltimore County	18	....	Do.
[illegible]	[illegible], Baltimore County	4	....	Stables, fair; animals, good.
[illegible]	[illegible], Baltimore County	5	1c.	Stables, bad; animals, fair.
[illegible]	[illegible], Baltimore County	5	1	Animals, fair.
	Inspections by C. K. Dyer, V. S.			
[illegible]	[illegible], corner Hanover and Mc-[illegible], Baltimore	15	....	Good.
[illegible]	[illegible], corner Hanover and Ray [illegible], Baltimore	10	....	Stables, fair; animals, good.

Inspections in Maryland—Continued.

Day of month.	Name of owner or person in charge and location of stables.	No. of cattle.	No. with lung-plague.	Condition of stables and animals.
	Inspection by M. R. Trumbower, V. S.			
1886. Sept. 22	Charles Carroll, College Station	1		
	Inspections by C. K. Dyer, V. S.			
23	Captain Weaver, corner Hanover and Winen streets, Baltimore.	7	....	Good.
23	Henry Killenbery, 787 Charles street, Baltimore	5	....	Do.
23	Cora Reip, 130 West street, Baltimore	5	5c.	Stables, filthy; animals, poor.
23	Charles H. Weaver, 386 Charles street, Baltimore	5	....	Good.
	Inspection by M. R. Trumbower, V. S.			
23	Charles Spitznagle, limits on Philadelphia road	40	10c.	Stables, good; animals, fair.
	Inspection by Trumbower and Dyer, V. S.			
24	Ambrose Winterling, Highlandtown, Baltimore County.	15	2	Good.
	Inspections by M. R. Trumbower, V. S.			
25	B. M. Hangley, 39 Cumberland street, Baltimore	4	1	
27	Catharine Wolf, near Smallwood post-office, Carroll County.	2	....	Fair.
27	William Yeager, Smallwood post-office, Carroll County.	3	....	Bad.
27	John Frick, Smallwood post-office, Carroll County.	1	....	Animals, bad.
27	George Taylor, near Smallwood post-office, Carroll County.	4	1	Animals, fair.
27	Elisha Ogg, near Smallwood post-office, Carroll County.	1	....	Animals, bad.
27	John Leffert, 3½ miles from Westminster, Carroll County.	2	....	Stables, bad; animals, fair.
	Jacob Crist, Smallwood post-office, Carroll County.	1	....	Animals, good.
	Conrad Kress, Smallwood post-office, Carroll County.	2	....	Animals, fair.
	Emery Zeph, Smallwood post-office, Carroll County.	12	....	Animals, good.
	Isaac Green, near Smallwood post-office	5	....	Do.
	Charles Kress, Smallwood post-office	3	....	Do.
	Abdiah Bollinger, near Smallwood post-office	1	1c.	Animals, fair.
	Inspections by T. W. Spranklin, V. S.			
25	Jordon, Cross street, Baltimore	22	....	Stables, fair; animals, good.
	C. Hamberger, Hanover street, Baltimore	13	....	Do.
	W. Walters, Hanover street, Baltimore	10	....	Stables, bad; animals, fair.
	W. Houldse, Cross and Scott streets, Baltimore	3	....	Good.
	J. Bauline, Cross and Scott streets, Baltimore	6	....	Stables, fair; animals, good.
	J. Krops, Chestnut street	2	....	Do.
	J. Vogtmar	2	....	Fair.
	Sheppard Asylum	20	....	Good.
	Mr. Campbell	37	....	Stables, fair; animals, good.
	Mr. Seacone	29	....	Fair.
	Inspections by C. K. Dyer, V. S.			
28	Julius Sachs	6	....	
28	Doenberg & Lohrfenck, 62 Spring st., Baltimore	2	....	Good.
28	John Hood	1	....	Do.
28	M. Crichton, Cal., Hol. and Baltimore streets, Baltimore.	1	....	Do.
28	John M. Curtis, 71 North Calvert st., Baltimore	1	....	Do.
28	P. S. George, 7 Franklin street, Baltimore	1	....	Do.

Inspections in Maryland—Continued.

Day of month.	Name of owner or person in charge and location of stable.	No. of cattle.	No. with lung-plague.	Condition of stables and animals.
	Inspections by C. K. Dyer—Continued.			
1886. Sept. 28	J. J. Turner, sr., 81 Pleasant street, Baltimore	1	....	Good.
28	Michael Cunningham, 444 Holliday street, Baltimore.	1	....	Do.
28	J. J. Turner, jr., 86 Pleasant street, Baltimore	1	....	Do.
27	Mrs. Nagle, 12 Addison street, Baltimore	3	....	Do.
	S. A. Rice, 9 Frederick street, Baltimore	1	....	Do.
	John Sullivan, 8 Swan street, Baltimore	17	....	Do.
	B. Hackeman, 86 Harrison street, Baltimore	4	....	Do.
	John Geigan, Lombard & Front sts., Baltimore	1	....	Do.
	Owen Reynolds, 26 S. Front street, Baltimore	1	....	Do.
	Moses Goldberg, 46 E. Pratt street, Baltimore	2	....	Do.
	L. M. Burningham, Forest and Hillen streets, Baltimore.	1	....	Do.
	Mrs. Casey, 24 Addison street, Baltimore	3	....	Do.
	Thos. Magnest, 74 N. High street, Baltimore	2	....	Do.
	Stephen Lewis, 119 N. High street, Baltimore	4	....	Do.
	Carrol S. Street, Hiller near Market streets, Baltimore.	1	....	Do.
	Moses Moses, 81 Watson street, Baltimore	1	....	Do.
	Hannah O'Brien, 188 N. Front street, Baltimore	4	....	Do.
	George Tourney, 130 N. Front street, Baltimore	1	....	Do.
29	Mrs. Spence, 20 Cornet street, Baltimore	3	....	Do.
	Mr. Franklin, 20 Forest street, Baltimore	5	....	Do.
	John Fox, 24 Cornet street, Baltimore	3	....	Do.
	Mr. Hertzburg, 20 Forest street, Baltimore	1	....	Do.
	George Kuhn, Canton street, Baltimore	2	....	Do.
	Inspections by W. H. Wray, V. S.			
	Theo. Marling, corner First avenue and Bank st.	16	2c.	Good.
29	Sam J. Messersmith, Pennsylvania avenue extended, Baltimore.	1	1	
30	John Kaiss, Annapolis road, Baltimore County	10	10	
Oct. 1	Columbus Isaacs, Ellicott City, Howard County	6		
4	E. Cowling, Brooklandville, Baltimore County	17	8c.	
4	Dr. F. W. Patterson, Hookstown road, Baltimore County.	13	4c.	Stables, good; animals excellent.
5	C. Peppler, Pennsylvania avenue extended, Baltimore.	1	1	
	Inspections by T. W. Spranklin, V. S.			
1	J. Browers, Harford road, Baltimore County	9	....	Stables, fair; animals good.
1	J. Cook, Belair road, Baltimore County	12	....	Fair.
1	H. Law, Belair road, Baltimore County	9	....	Stables fair; animals good.
1	H. Reachert, Belair road, Baltimore County	9	1a.	Good.
1	Mr. Gegner, Highlandtown, Baltimore County	4	1a.	Stables, bad; animals, fai
5	J. Vogtmeyer, Philadelphia road, Baltimore County.	1	1a.	Fair.
5	Mr. Biemiller, Patapsco Neck, Baltimore Co	50		Good.
5	Mr. Deitz, Mount Carmel road, Baltimore County	6	....	Good.
5	F. Murring, Canton, Baltimore County	7	1a.	Stables, bad; animals, fai
	Inspections by C. K. Dyer, V. S.			
5	Lewis Height, rear 118 St. Paul street, Baltimore	1		Good.
5	M. Conovan, 20 Richmond street, Baltimore	2	....	Do.
5	James Pentland, corner Oliver and Greenmount avenue, Baltimore.	1	....	Do.
	Bernard Berger, Belvidere street, Baltimore	1	....	Do.
5	Ichabod Jean, 175 Charles street, Baltimore	1	....	Do.
5	Thomas Coffey, West Eager and Charles streets, Baltimore.	1	....	Do.
5	Patrick Ganley, Belvidere street, Baltimore	9	....	Stables, fair; animal good.

Inspections in Maryland—Continued.

Day of month.	Name of owner or person in charge and location of stable.	No. of cattle.	No. with lung-plague.	Condition of stables and animals.
	Inspections by C. K. Dyer—Continued.			
.886.				
[illegible] 5	John Codovi, 85 Greenmount avenue, Baltimore	1	....	Good.
5	Patrick Kenny, 113 Greenmount avenue, Baltimore.	3	....	Stables, filthy; animals, good.
5	Joseph Grogan, 85 Harford avenue, Baltimore.....	1	....	Stables, fair; animals, poor.
5	Thomas Grogan, 66 McKim street, Baltimore......	3	....	Good.
5	John Wright, 145 Greenmount avenue, Baltimore.	1	....	Do.
5	Thomas Caddin, 157 Greenmount avenue, Baltimore.	1	....	Do.
5	Mrs. Honora Keelty, corner Federal and Greenmount avenues, Baltimore.	4	3c.	Stables, filthy; animals, fair.
6	Powell Harding, 4 miles on Liberty road, Baltimore County.	2	1c.	Stables, filthy; animals, poor.
8	Jacob Kühnle, 440 Fort avenue, Baltimore County.	3	2a.	Stables, poor; animals, good.
8	J. W. Jewens, near Perryman's, Harford Co	11	....	Stables, good; animals, poor.
8	Patrick O'Brien, Falls road, Baltimore County...	9	{*2 †1}	Good.
9	Mrs. N. K. Disney, Owing's Mills, Baltimore County.	29	14	Do.
9	George S. Byerly, Owing's Mills, Baltimore County.	8	{†3 *1}	Do.
	Inspections by T. W. Spranklin, V. S.			
6	P. Gebb, Harford road, Baltimore County	15	....	Good.
6	G. Smith, Fair Oak farm, Baltimore County......	37	....	Do.
6	O. Read, Harford road, Baltimore County..........	23	....	Stables, bad; animals, good.
6	T. German, Harford road, Baltimore County......	18	....	Good.
6	T. M. Richardson, Belair road, Baltimore Co	20	1a.	Do.
	Inspections by C. K. Dyer, V. S.			
12	Lewis Pailhorne, Fall road, Baltimore County...	16	{†1 *1}	Good.
13	Michael Wetzberger, 1036 North Broadway, Baltimore County.	9	....	Do.
13	George Weigel, 22 North Chester street, Baltimore.	8	2c.	Stables, fair; animals, good.
13	Various persons, Hampden, Baltimore County...	90	2c.	Fair.
14	E. Biemiller, Patapsco Neck, Baltimore County..	49	....	Good.
14	Mrs. Zuickahn, Philadelphia road, Baltimore County.	32	....	Do.
15	Charles H. Baker, Falls road, Baltimore County..	22	....	Do.
	Inspections by W. H. Wray, V. S.			
	J. H. Kohnle, 440 Fort avenue, Baltimore..........	3	1	Stables, good; animals, fair.
12 12	Charles Mahring, Sixteenth street, Baltimore.....	7	....	Stables, poor; animals, fair.
15	John F. Dannaker, Hampden, Baltimore County..	2	....	Good.
	Inspections by C. K. Dyer, V. S.			
16	John Schmidt, 415 Eastern avenue, Highlandtown.	12	....	Good.
16	B. Wolf, 907 Third avenue, Highlandtown	9	....	Do.
16	John Selig, Elliott street, Canton...........	1	....	Do.
18	Henry Hausman, Mt. Carmel road, Highlandtown.	6	1a.	Do.
18	Henry Lanz, extension Eastern avenue	8	....	Do.
18	Charles Khun, 415 East street, Canton	12	4c.	Do.
19	Milton Amos, No. 3 Payson street, Baltimore	6	....	Do.
19	John Eidman, Rosedale post-office	3	....	Do.
21	Mr. Kline, Belair road, Baltimore County	10	....	Do.
21	John Dengler, Belair road, Baltimore County...	6	1c.	Do.
21	Joseph Kratle, Belair road, Baltimore County...	7	4c.	
22	John S. Gittings, Hookstown road, Baltimore County.	40	....	

* Acute. † Chronic.

Inspections in Maryland—Continued.

Day of month.	Name of owner or person in charge and location of stable.	No. of cattle.	No. with lung-plague.	Condition of stables and animals.
	Inspections by C. K. Dyer—Continued.			
1886.				
Oct. 22	Peter Jensen, Orleans street, Baltimore County	4	2	Fair.
25	Frank Wagner, 9 Brown's alley, Baltimore	12		Good.
26	Henry Lentz, near Bay View, Baltimore County	8		Fair.
26	Gehart Zenk, Canton street, Baltimore	15	8c.	Do.
26	John Clay, Lombard street, Baltimore	28		Stables, filthy; animals, bad.
	Inspections by W. H. Wray, V. S.			
16	Lewis Pallhorne, Crosskeyes, Baltimore County	17	1	Good.
18	J. Nichols, Hookstown road, Baltimore County	17	13	Fair.
18	C. O. Kemp, Hookstown road, Baltimore County	5		Good.
19	J. A. Gegner, East avenue and First street, Baltimore.	3		Do.
21	John Hiller, 750 Hanover street, Baltimore	13		Animals, good.
25	Mr. Busch, Philadelphia road, Baltimore County	5		Animals, fair.
26	J. Grauer, Harford road, Baltimore County	7	3	Animals, good.
	Inspections by T. W. Spranklin, V. S.			
20	W. Johnson, Rockland, Baltimore County	8		Good.
21	C. Fischer, Loney's Lane, Baltimore County	4		Do.
21	P. Holland, Philadelphia road	11		Stables, fair.
22	J. G. Miller, Highlandtown	27		Stables, good.
25	J. Schreorer	6		Good.
25	M. T. Horner	24		Do.
25	F. Corse, Clairmount	4		Do.
25	G. Quick	8		Do.
25	M. Scheeler, Boley's lane	9		Do.
25	E. Hein, Boley's lane	2		Stables, fair.
25	J. Meyer, Boley's lane	1		Stables, good.
25	H. Rosner	6		Stables, fair.
26	J. Guntrun, Gardensville	7		Stables, good.
26	Keyworth, Arlington, Baltimore County	2		Stables, fair; animals good.
	Inspections by C. K. Dyer, V. S.			
26	Lenhart Trumper, near Perry Hall, Baltimore County.	7	1a.	Animals, fair.
28	Mrs. Mena Duvel, near Uniontown, Baltimore County.	6		
29	Geo. H. Franc, near Uniontown, Baltimore Co	1		Good.
29	C. Millbach, near Uniontown, Baltimore County	26		Do.
29	Mrs. M. Kay, Uniontown, Baltimore County	3		Do.
29	Robert Gable, Uniontown, Baltimore County	1		Do.
29	Mrs. Steinaker, near Uniontown, Baltimore Co	25		Do.
	Inspections by T. W. Spranklin, V. S.			
29	W. Schwarz, Belair road, Baltimore County	5		Good.
29	J. Grist, Belair road, Baltimore County	3		Do.
29	F. Christ, Belair road, Baltimore County	2		Do.
29	M. Bryne, Belair road, Baltimore County	9		Stables, fair; animal good.
29	P. Wagman, Belair road, Baltimore County	9		Stables, bad; animal fair.
30	C. Smith, Hamilton avenue, Baltimore	14		Fair.
30	J. Ellis, Harford road, Baltimore County	12		Good.
Nov. 2	Charles N. Bush, Liberty road	1	1	Fair.
2	Richard Disney, 3½ miles on Hookstown road, Baltimore County.	1	1	Do.
3	A. Kaulitz, 9 miles on Eastern avenue, Baltimore County.	8	1	Good.
3	John Mateling, Rossville post-office, Baltimore County.	2	1	Do.
4	Mrs. C. T. Belt, 518 Rowland avenue, Baltimore	2	2	Stables, good; animal fair.
4	John Loeber, 5 miles on Harford road, Baltimore County.	18	18c.	Good.
	Inspections by Dyer & Martinet, V. S.			
1	Wm. E. Read, Powhatan road, Baltimore Co	43		Animals, good.
1	George Cairnes, Hampden, Baltimore County	2		
2	Theo. German, Harford road, Baltimore County	18	18	Stables, good; animal fair.

Inspections in Maryland—Continued.

Day of month.	Name of owner or person in charge and location of stable.	No. of cattle.	No. with lung-plague.	Condition of stables and animals.
	Inspection by W. H. Wray, V. S.			
1886. Nov. 1	O. J. Martinet, 4 miles on Belair road, Baltimore County.	6	....	Good.
	Inspection by C. K. Dyer, V. S.			
4	Evan P. Green, Easton, Talbot County..............	12	....	Animals, good.
	Inspections by Dyer and Martinet, V. S.			
5	Geo. Smith, near Govanstown, Baltimore Co.....	31	....	Animals, fair.
6	William Chew, near Windsor, Carroll County ...	10	....	Do.
8	Binhas Wagman, Belair road, Baltimore County..	9	....	
9	Joseph Winkler, near Perry Hall, Baltimore County.	12	4c.	Stables, filthy; animals, fair.
	Inspections by W. H. Wray, V. S.			
10	Adam Bucheit, 734 Fort avenue, Baltimore.........	1	1	Poor.
10	Jennie Wisman, near Horner's bone factory, Baltimore.	1	1	Do.
	Inspections by Dyer and Martinet, V. S.			
10	Joseph Kuhn, near Arlington, Baltimore County.	21	21	
10	Chas. T. Cockey, near Pikesville, Baltimore Co...	4	4	
	Inspection by C. K. Dyer, V. S.			
11	Hiram Krinber, Highlandtown, Baltimore Co....	1	....	
	Inspection by W. H. Wray, V. S.			
11	Mrs. Crabson, Hampden, Baltimore County.......	2	1	Good.
	Inspection by C. K. Dyer, V. S.			
11	M. Slade, Highlandtown, Baltimore County	12	....	
	Inspection by W. H. Martinet, V. S.			
11	William Williams, Bird Hill post-office, Carroll County.	4	4a.	
	Inspection by C. K. Dyer, V. S.			
11	Mrs. Louisa Wempey, near Highlandtown, Baltimore County.	5	....	
	Inspections by Dyer and Martinet, V. S.			
12	Conrad Schmidt, corner Eighth and Lombard streets, Baltimore.	18	2c.	Stables, good; animals, fair.
12	Aug. Schmidt, corner Seventh and Lombard streets, Baltimore.	11	10	Do.
13	Mrs. Mary Zinkard, Philadelphia road, Baltimore County.	32	2	Do.
13	Chas. Hall, Philadelphia road, Baltimore Co	32	2	
	Inspections by W. H. Wray, V. S.			
13	Edward Gore, Arlington, Baltimore County.......	1	1	Stables, fair; animals, good.
15	H. Eckert, stock-yards, Baltimore County..........	1	1	Animals, fair.
15	B. Wagman, Belair road, Baltimore County..	8	8	
15	John Hiller, 750 Hanover street, Baltimore.........	13	....	Good.
	Inspections by Dyer and Martinet, V. S.			
15	Sebastian North, Monument street, Baltimore.....	7	4c.	
15	Fred. W. Young, Highlandtown, Baltimore Co .	12	12c.	Animals, very poor.
15	Alois Auft, near Monument street, Baltimore......	40	2c.	Fair.
	Inspections by T. W. Spranklin, V. S.			
15	John Doran, O'Donnell and Boulder streets, Baltimore.	12	12	Stables, fair; animals, good.

Inspections in Maryland—Continued.

Day of month.	Name of owner or person in charge and location of stable.	No. of cattle.	No. with lung-plague.	Condition of stables and animals.
	Inspections by T. W. Spranklin—Continued.			
1886. Nov. 15	G. Erdman, Hall Springs, Baltimore County	1		
15	E. F. Able, Hillen road, Baltimore County	25		Stables, good.
15	W. Thorne, Hillen road, Baltimore County	3		Fair.
15	S. Inawold, Harford road, Baltimore County	13		Stables, fair; animals, good.
15	O. Kohn, Loney's Lane, Baltimore County	15		Bad.
	Inspections by Dyer & Martinet, V. S.			
16	Mrs. Herring, Highlandtown, Baltimore County	3		Fair.
16	Theo. Vondecker, Highlandtown, Baltimore Co.	1		Good.
16	Louis Markel, Highlandtown, Baltimore County	13	2c.	Fair.
16	Lorenz Weinberg, Highlandtown, Baltimore Co.	15	2c.	Good.
16	Louis Kiefer, Clinton street, Canton	21		Bad.
17	Christian Wolf, north of O'Donnell st., Canton	16	15	Do.
17	Charles A. Whitely, Hookstown road, Baltimore County.	1		Stables, bad; animal, fair.
17	William Brandell, Dillon and Third streets, Baltimore.	18	11	
17	Daniel E. Ensor, Hookstown road, Baltimore County.	1		Fair.
18	Matthias Jeorg, Dillon and Third st., Canton	11		Do.
18	Fred Bancer, Highlandtown, Baltimore County	2		Poor.
18	R. McMahon, Falls road, Baltimore County	3		Good.
18	George Evell, Falls road, Baltimore County	9		Do.
19	George Prall, Highlandtown, Baltimore County	18	8	Fair.
19	John N. Betz, Third and O'Donnell st., Canton	16	1c.	Good.
19	John G. Miller, Third and Lombard streets, Highlandtown.	21	10	Do.
20	Henry Buddmeirr, corner Hudson street, Canton	31		Do.
20	John Heinlein, 814 Clinton street, Canton	7		Bad.
20	Johanna Devlin, Chesapeake street, Canton	4	4c.	Stables, bad; animals, fair.
	Inspections by T. W. Spranklin, V. S.			
20	J. Creamer, Sharp street extended, Baltimore	16		Good.
20	J. Griesecker, Washington road, Baltimore Co.	1		Stables, good; animal, fair.
20	C. H. Weaver, Washington road, Baltimore Co.	1		Good.
20	M. Jorden, Cross and Hamburg sts., Baltimore	20		Stables, fair; animals, good.
20	S. Rice & Co., Frederick road, Baltimore County	2		Do.
20	J. H. Miller, Washington road, Baltimore Co.	1		Do.
22	John F. Weisener, Belair avenue, Baltimore	6		Do.
	Inspections by Dyer and Martinet, V. S.			
22	John Bankert, 60 East Biddle street, Baltimore	1		
22	Mary Ennig, 107 Castile street, Baltimore	8		Do.
22	George Baurnschmidt, Belair ave., Baltimore	1		Do.
	Inspection by W. H. Wray, V. S.			
22	John L. Yater, jr., 421 York road, Waverly	1	1	Stables, good; animal, fair.
	Inspections by W. Dimond, V. S.			
22	John E. Deeds, Bird Hill, Carroll County	6	3	Stables, poor; animals, fair.
22	James Slade, Smallwood, Carroll County	9		Good.
22	Mrs. R. Davis, Bird Hill, Carroll County	1		Do.
	Inspections by Dyer & Martinet, V. S.			
23	Mary Baker, Belair avenue, Baltimore	1	1c.	Fair.
23	Joseph Krastle, Putty Hill post-office, Baltimore County.	7	4c.	Good.
23	George C. Krach, Putty Hill post-office, Baltimore County.	1		Stables, fair; animals, good.
23	Mr. Younger, Belair avenue, Baltimore	1	1	Good.
23	Henrietta Trust, Putty Hill, Baltimore	5		Stables, bad; animals, fair.
23	Louis Muth, Belair avenue, Baltimore	3	1	Good.

Inspections in Maryland—Continued.

Day of month.	Name of owner or person in charge and location of stable.	No. of cattle.	No. with lung-plague.	Condition of stables and animals.
	Inspection by W. H. Wray, V. S.			
1886. Nov. 23	J. E. Dorsey & Co., Arlington, Baltimore County..	69	....	Stables, excellent; animals, good.
	Inspection by T. W. Spranklin, V. S.			
23	W. Langermann, Washington road extended, Baltimore County.	80	....	Good.
	Inspections by Dyer & Martinet, V. S.			
24	Mr. Assaver, Vonderhost's lane, Baltimore County.	1	....	Fair.
24	Charles Chalk, Hoffman street, Baltimore..........	21	....	Stables, fair; animals, good.
24	John Wilson, Luzerne, near Oliver street, Baltimore.	2	....	Fair.
24	Mary Langemann, 1718 Belair avenue, Baltimore.	5	....	Good.
24	William Jones, East Preston street extended, Baltimore.	4	4	Stables, bad; animals, fair.
24	John J. Smith, Sunnybrook, Baltimore County...	5	....	
24	Elias Robertson, Luzerne and Oliver streets, Baltimore.	1	1c.	
24	Conrad Roemer, 1867 Belair avenue, Baltimore...	2	....	Stables, fair; animals, good.
	Inspection by W. Dimond, V. S.			
26	J. H. Miller, Clarksville, Howard County..	38	....	Good.
	Inspection by T. W. Spranklin, V. S.			
26	S. Wempe, Corsen lane, Baltimore County.........	5	....	Stables, fair; animals, good.
	Inspections by W. H. Martinet, V. S.			
26	Gertrude Gacken, McElderry and Madeira Hill...	8	....	Stables, bad; animals, fair.
26	Julius Sachs, 279 Orleans street, Baltimore..........	19	1	Stables, good; animals, fair.
26	Christian Matthias, Burke street, south of Monument, Baltimore.	5	3c.	Bad.
26	Nicholas Glos, Burke street, south of Monument, Baltimore.	5	1c.	Stables, bad; animals, fair.
	Inspection by Dyer & Martinet, V. S.			
26	Thomas Grogan, East Hoffman street extended, Baltimore.	1	....	Good.
	Inspection by C. K. Dyer, V. S.			
26	Peter Cask, near Philadelphia road, Baltimore County.	16	....	
	Inspections by Dyer & Martinet, V. S.			
27	Henry Hoeck, 180 Sterling street, Baltimore......	2	....	Good.
27	Saint Joseph's Hospital, Caroline and Hoffman streets, Baltimore.	6	....	Do.
27	Peter McKenny, 215 North Eden street, Baltimore.	2	....	Stables, fair; animals, good.
27	Joseph Barbon, 238 Madison street, Baltimore.....	10	7c.	Bad.
27	Mary Kelly, 1607 Harfordavenue, Baltimore........	6	2c.	Fair.
27	Martin Mayford, 4 Point lane, Baltimore............	2	1c.	Stables, good; animals, fair.
29	Conrad Ritz, 815 Castle street, Baltimore............	2	....	Stables, poor; animals good.
	Inspection by W. Dimond, V. S.			
29	Abram Snallinger, 1638 East Madison street, Baltimore.	1	....	Good.
	Inspections by Dyer & Martinet, V. S.			
29	Hebrew Hospital, East Monument street, Baltimore.	1	1s.	Good.

Inspections in Maryland—Continued.

Day of month.	Name of owner or person in charge and location of stable.	No. of cattle.	No. with lung-plague.	Condition of stables and animals.
	Inspections by Dyer & Martinet—Continued.			
1886. Nov. 29	Michael Lynch, 801 North Ann street, Baltimore.	2	2c.	Stables, bad; animals, fair.
29	Philip Newman, 215 North Central avenue, Baltimore.	4	3c.	Fair.
29	Donberg & Lohefink, 432 North Spring street, Baltimore.	19	5a.	Good.
	Inspections by W. Dimond, V.S.			
29	Anton Valentine, 813 Castle street, Baltimore....	2	....	Stables, fair; animals, good.
29	Patrick Bussell, 901 Broadway, Baltimore.........	1	....	Stables, good; animals, fair.
30	Henry Pinies, 1638 East Broadway, Baltimore....	2	2c.	Stables, fair; animals, poor.
30	Loyd H. Robinson, 7 Aisquith street, Baltimore.	7	....	Good.
	Inspections by Dyer & Martinet, V.S.			
30	George W. Corner, 24 North Broadway, Baltimore.	1	....	Fair.
30	Jacob Haas & Son, 635 North Eden street, Baltimore.	10	....	Good.
30	Michael Wurtzberger, 1036 North Broadway, Baltimore.	14	....	Stables, fair; animals, good.
Dec. 1	T. J. Rusk, jr., 25 North Collington avenue, Baltimore.	1	....	Good.
1	Amelia Greenwald, 2110 Fairmont avenue, Baltimore.	1	....	Fair.
1	John Beivhardt, 900 Aisquith street, Baltimore.	2	....	Stables, good; animals, bad.
1	William Fraser, 1744 Belair avenue, Baltimore...	1	....	Good.
1	Maggie Pohlman, 2224 East Monument street, Baltimore.	1	1c.	Fair.
1	K. Baum, Fayette street, Baltimore......................	2	....	Good.
1	Nicholas Tegges, 168 Fairmount street, Baltimore.	1	1c.	Do.
	Inspections by W. Dimond, V.S.			
1	John Bien, 2228 McElderry street, Baltimore......	1	....	Do.
1	Samuel Fox, 423 North Broadway, Baltimore.....	1	....	Do.
1	Peter Lautenkloe, 2036 Jefferson street, Baltimore.	1	....	Fair.
2	N. Rosenthal, Calverton Stock Yards, Baltimore.	10	....	Good.
2	Calverton Stock-Yards, Baltimore......................	22	....	Do.
2	........do..	....	....	Fair.
	Inspections by Dyer & Martinet, V.S.			
2	James Hughes, 2636 East Fayette street, Baltimore.	1	....	Stables, good; animal, fair.
2	Patrick Sweeny, 2815 East Fayette street, Baltimore.	2	2c.	Fair.
2	Edward Smith, 2915 East Fayette street, Baltimore.	2	2c.	Do.
2	Patrick Murray, 3020 East Fayette street, Baltimore.	2	1c.	Do.
2	Kasmer Vogel, Washington, Baltimore County..	21	2a.	Good.
	Inspection by W. H. Wray, V.S.			
3	J. E. Swift, 3½ miles on Belair road, Baltimore County.	11	1c.	Fair.
	Inspections by W. Dimond, V.S.			
3	Miller A. Brewer, near Calverton Stock-Yards, Baltimore County.	33	....	Stables, excellent; animals, good.
3	Unknown, Calverton Stock-Yards, Baltimore County.	19	....	Fair.

Inspections in Maryland—Continued.

Day of month.	Name of owner or person in charge and location of stable.	No. of cattle.	No. with lung-plague.	Condition of stables and animals.
	Inspections by Dyer & Martinet, V. S.			
1886.				
[illegible]. 3	Alexander Blair, 3000 East McElderry street, Baltimore.	3	1c.	Stables, good; animals, fair.
3	William H. Kline, Loney's lane, Baltimore	1	....	Good.
3	John Dennison, Charles street, south of Chase street, Baltimore.	1	....	Do.
3	Otto Kahn, Loney's lane, Baltimore County	15	4c.	Fair.
3	John Wienkneit, 556 East Fayette street, Baltimore.	1	1c.	Do.
3	Patrick Holland, 1821 East Fayette street, Baltimore.	9	4c.	Stables, fair; animals, good.
4	William Langmann, Broadway near Bound avenue, Baltimore.	7	....	Stables, good; animals, fair.
	Inspections by W. H. Martinet, V. S.			
4	William Langmann, 1740 Washington street, Baltimore.	77	....	Good.
4	William Blotkamp, 1732 East Lombard street, Baltimore.	2	1c.	Do.
4	John Schmidt, 9 South Chappell street, Baltimore.	2	....	Do.
	Inspection by T. W. Spranklin, V. S.			
4	George L. Barkley, 1725 East Lombard street, Baltimore.	1	....	Good.
	Inspection by W. Dimond, V. S.			
4	H. Garrett, Charles street avenue, Baltimore	3	1c.	Animals, fair.
	Inspection by W. H. Wray, V. S.			
4	Unknown, Calverton Stock-Yards, Baltimore	18	....	Fair.
	Inspections by Dyer & Martinet, V. S.			
4	Mrs. M. Pohlman, 2224 East Monument street, Baltimore.	1	....	Fair.
4	Mary Fernheimer, 174-176 South Register street, Baltimore.	4	....	Good.
4	Mrs. E. Burger, 835 South Bond street, Baltimore.	4	....	Do.
4	Thomas R. Brady, 34 Lancaster street, Baltimore.	2	....	Fair.
4	Mary Lynch, 13 Lancaster street, Baltimore	2	....	Good.
4	Jacob Samuel, 809 South Bond street, Baltimore	1	....	Do.
	Inspections by W. H. Martinet, V. S.			
4	A. Rosenthal & Son, 41 South Eden street, Baltimore.	20	....	Good.
	Fred. A. Booth, East Pratt street, Baltimore	1	....	Do.
7	W. H. Thompson, 114 South Washington street, Baltimore.	2	1c.	Stables, good; animals, fair.
7	Nicholas Balzer, 103 South Washington street, Baltimore.	8	2c.	Do.
7	W. J. Wolf, 301 South Central avenue, Baltimore	1	....	Good.
7	Chas. Breebeck, 1750 Eastern avenue, Baltimore	1	....	Do.
13	Henry Calender, 57 Patapsco street, Baltimore	1	....	Fair.
13	Thos. S. Hamlin, 301 East Winder st., Baltimore	1	....	Good.
	Inspections by W. H. Wray, V. S.			
13	Henry Pine, 1638 Baltimore street, Baltimore	2	1	Fair.
13	Jos. Barton, 238 Madison street, Baltimore	16	7	Poor.
	Inspections by W. Dimond, V. S.			
6	Henry Eckart, 20 Lexington street, Baltimore	43	....	Stables, fair; animals, poor.
7	Chas. W. Hartman, 400 Lancaster street, Baltimore.	2	....	Good.

Inspections in Maryland—Continued.

Day of month.	Name of owner or person in charge and location of stable.	No. of cattle.	No. with lung-plague.	Condition of stables and animals.
	Inspections by C. K. Dyer, V. S.			
188[illegible]. Dec. [illegible]	[illegible] Brauninger, 3[illegible] Canton avenue, Baltimore.	1	....	Good.
[illegible]	[illegible] Doyle, 1[illegible] Canton avenue, Baltimore........	2	....	Stables, poor; animals, good.
[illegible]	Caroline Bush, 1[illegible] South Regester street, Baltimore.	2	....	Stables, poor; animals, fair.
[illegible]	Pat. Flynn, [illegible] Eastern avenue, Baltimore........	2	....	Stables, poor; animals, good.
[illegible]	John L[illegible], Frederick road, Baltimore..........	28	....	Stables, good; animals, fair.
	Inspection by W. Dimond, V. S.			
[illegible]	[illegible], Calverton stock-yards, Baltimore....	39	....	Animals, good.
	Inspections by W. H. Martinet, V. S.			
[illegible]	Joseph [illegible], 1[illegible] Cuba street, Baltimore......	6	....	Good.
[illegible]	Joseph W[illegible], [illegible] East Lombard street, Baltimore.	9	2c.	Fair.
[illegible]	[illegible] Fogarty, 1[illegible] Fort avenue, Baltimore...	2	....	Good.
[illegible]	Margaret M[illegible], [illegible] Curley street, Baltimore...	2	....	Do.
[illegible]	[illegible], [illegible] Elliott street, Baltimore....	1	....	Do.
[illegible]	[illegible], 2[illegible] Elliott street, Baltimore......	1	....	Do.
	Inspections by C. K. Dyer, V. S.			
[illegible]	[illegible], [illegible] Patuxent street, Baltimore......	3	....	Do.
[illegible]	[illegible], [illegible] Hudson street, Baltimore...	8	....	Do.
[illegible]	[illegible], [illegible] Bank street, Baltimore..............	1	....	Do.
[illegible]	[illegible] Fitzgerald, 1[illegible] Fort avenue, Baltimore.	4	....	Do.
[illegible]	[illegible], Fort avenue, opposite Hull street, Baltimore.	6	....	Stables, fair; animals, poor.
[illegible]	[illegible] Augustus [illegible], [illegible] Alice Anna street, Baltimore..	1	....	Fair.
	Inspections by W. H. Martinet, V. S.			
[illegible]	[illegible], [illegible] Towson street, Baltimore.....	2	....	Fair.
[illegible]	[illegible], [illegible] Hull street, Baltimore	1	....	Do.
[illegible]	[illegible], [illegible] Haubert street, Baltimore...	1	....	Do.
[illegible]	[illegible], Cor. Marriott and Decatur streets, Baltimore.	2	....	Do.
	Inspections by C. K. Dyer, V. S.			
[illegible]	[illegible], [illegible] Garrett avenue, Baltimore..	4	....	Good.
[illegible]	[illegible], [illegible] Haubert street, Baltimore..	3	2	Fair.
[illegible]	[illegible], [illegible] Burroughs street, Baltimore......	6	....	Good.
[illegible]	[illegible], [illegible] street, Baltimore....	3	....	Stables, fair; animals, poor.
[illegible]	[illegible], [illegible] Hull street, Baltimore......	2	....	Good.
	Inspections by W. Dimond, V. S.			
[illegible]	[illegible], Calverton stock-yards, Baltimore	37	....	Animals, fair.
[illegible]	[illegible], Calverton stock-yards, Baltimore....	8	....	Animals, very good.
[illegible]	[illegible], Calverton stock-yards, Baltimore	7	....	Animals, poor.
[illegible]	[illegible], Calverton stock-yards, Baltimore.	6	....	Animals, fair.
	[illegible], Calverton stock-yards, Baltimore	17	....	Do.
	[illegible], Calverton stock-yards, Baltimore...	6	....	Animals, good.
	[illegible], Calverton stock-yards, Baltimore.	3	....	Animals, fair.
	Inspection by W. M. Wray, V. S.			
	[illegible] Preston street, Baltimore....	4	2	Stables, poor; animals, fair.
	Inspections by C. K. Dyer, V. S.			
[illegible]	[illegible], [illegible] street, Baltimore	1	....	Stables, filthy; animals, poor.
[illegible]	[illegible] street, Baltimore.........	1	....	
[illegible]	[illegible] street, Baltimore... ...	16	....	Good.
[illegible]	[illegible] street, Baltimore	1	....	Do.
[illegible]	[illegible] street, Baltimore..........	2	....	Do.
	[illegible] William street, Baltimore.	3	....	Do.

Inspections in Maryland—Continued.

Day of month.	Name of owner or person in charge and location of stable.	No. of cattle.	No. with lung-plague.	Condition of stables and animals.
	Inspection by W. H. Wray, V. S.			
1886. Dec. 10	D. M. Nesbit, College Station, Prince George's County.	50	8	Good.
	Inspections by W. H. Martinet, V. S.			
10	Mary Minster, 1710 Light street, Baltimore	1		Fair.
10	Wesley Elliet, 1520 Covington street, Baltimore	1	1c.	Do.
10	Henry Osterhaus, 1501 William street, Baltimore	7		Good.
10	John Crocol, 129 East Clement street, Baltimore	2		Fair.
10	Fred. D. Jenkins, 121 Gittings street, Baltimore			Stables, fair; animals, good.
10	J. Fred. Hawkins, 1014 Light street, Baltimore	1		Stables, good; animals, good.
	Inspection by W. Dimond, V. S.			
10	Unknown, Calverton stock-yards, Baltimore	18		Animals, fair.
	Inspections by C. K. Dyer, V. S.			
11	J. C. Weaver, 1960 Hanover street, Baltimore	6		Good.
11	William Walter, Race and McComas streets, Baltimore.	7		Do.
	Inspections by W. H. Martinet, V. S.			
11	John Hiller, 1916 Hanover street, Baltimore	14		Fair.
11	James Galloway, 1958 Hanover street, Baltimore	1		Stables, fair; animals, good.
11	Mrs. Kate Hamburger, 2050 Hanover street, Baltimore.	15		Good.
11	Gottlieb Weaver, 91 West Randall street, Baltimore.	6	2c.	Fair.
	Inspections by W. Dimond, V. S.			
11	Charles Klinger, 16 Wilson street, Baltimore	16		Good.
11	John Leavy, 18 Wilson street, Baltimore	4		Stables, fair; animals, good.
	Inspections by W. H. Martinet, V. S.			
13	Theodore Jones, 2302 Hanover street, Baltimore	1		Fair.
13	John Noland, 1609 Marshall street, Baltimore	1		Good.
13	Charles Hamlin, 1939 Marshall street, Baltimore	1		
13	Edw. Sachs, 2338 South Hanover street, Baltimore.	14		Do.
	Inspections by C. K. Dyer, V. S.			
13	Geo. B. Weiken, 1936 South Charles street, Baltimore.	2		Good.
13	John Wer.·lein, 1900 Light street, Baltimore	1		Do.
13	George Rose, 1418 Light street, Baltimore	2		Do.
	Inspections by W. H. Wray, V. S.			
8	Mr. Proctor, Cambria, Harford County	8		Good.
6	Lewis Muth, 1766 Belair road, Baltimore County	3		Excellent.
	Inspections by W. Dimond, V. S.			
13	Unknown, Calverton, Baltimore County	28		Animals, fair.
14	W. H. Stansburg, Hillen road, Baltimore Co	22		Good.
14	J. S. Fair, Hillen road, Baltimore County	3		Do.
14	T. Taylor, Hillen road, Baltimore County	13		Do.
	Inspections by W. H. Martinet, V. S.			
14	John Kropf, 1115 Chestnut alley, Baltimore	2		Fair.
14	John Hamilton, 45 West West street, Baltimore	1		Stables, fair; animals, good.
14	John A. Rixse, 110 South Eutaw street, Baltimore.	5		Stables, filthy; animals, fair.
14	R. Henschen, 1022 Sharp street, Baltimore	1		Stables, good; animal, fair.
14	Melchoir Jordan, 11 Race street, north of Cross street, Baltimore.	22		Good.

Inspections in Maryland—Continued.

Day of month.	Name of owner or person in charge and location of stable.	No. of cattle.	No. with lung-plague.	Condition of stables and animals.
	Inspections by C. K. Dyer, V. S.			
1886. Dec. 14	Chas. H. Weaver, 1116 South Charles street, Baltimore.	5	....	Good.
14	James Creamer, 1210 South Charles street, Baltimore.	19	....	Do.
14	Geo. W. Della, 1144 Hanover street, Baltimore...	1	....	Do.
14	Barbara Heilman, 117 West Hamburg street, Baltimore.	4	....	Do.
14	Wm. Holdgrefe, 1152 Russell street, Baltimore...	8	....	Do.
	Inspections by W. H. Wray, V. S.			
14	B. M. Houghey, Pennsylvania avenue, Baltimore.	8	1	Good.
14	Charles Mehring, Mount Carmel road, Baltimore.	7	1	Poor.
	Inspections by W. Dimond, V. S.			
14	C. Prostle, Garrison street, Baltimore	8	....	Stables, poor; animals fair.
14	Julius Wolf, 32 Calverton street, Baltimore........	12	....	Stables, good; animals excellent.
14	Unknown, Calverton stock-yards, Baltimore.....	9	....	Animals, good.
	Inspections by W. H. Martinet, V. S.			
15	Wm. Lloyd, 1 West Pratt street, Baltimore........	8	....	Fair.
15	John Bauerlein, 1005 Scott street, Baltimore......	7	....	Do.
15	Ferd. Fenniman, 619 South Fremont street, Baltimore.	1	....	Good.
15	Dr. C. G. Linthicum, 623 Columbia avenue, Baltimore.	1	....	Fair.
15	Henry Middendorf, 1142 Battery avenue, Baltimore.	1	....	Stables, fair; animals good.
15	A. J. Reeder, 544 East Cross street, Baltimore.....	1	....	Good.
	Inspections by C. K. Dyer, V. S.			
15	Mrs. Harrigan, 170 Columbia avenue, Baltimore..	4	....	Good.
15	Chas. Loney, South Paca street, Baltimore.........	2	....	Animals, good.
15	C. G. Kriel, 5 West Henrietta street, Baltimore...	2	....	Do.
15	Henry Sander, 1159 Johnson street, Baltimore.....	21	4c.	Do.
	Inspections by W. Dimond, V. S.			
15	Unknown, Calverton stock-yards, Baltimore	21	....	Animals, good.
15	Mr. Eohart, Lexington street, Baltimore..	6	....	Stables, good; animals fair.
	Inspections by W. H. Martinet, V. S.			
16	John Reilly, 632 Campbell street, Baltimore........	8	....	Good.
16	Jas. Flaherty, 922 Columbia avenue, Baltimore...	8	....	Stables, fair; animals good.
16	Jas. Flaherty, 928 Columbia avenue, Baltimore...	6	....	Good.
16	Mary Harrigan, 412 Scott street, Baltimore.........	3	....	Fair.
16	Patrick Coogan, 318 South Poppleton street, Baltimore.	2	....	Do.
16	Patrick Leahy, 925 McHenry street, Baltimore...	3	1c.	Do.
16	J. R. Deuchter, Ridgley and Bayard streets, Baltimore.	2	....	Good.
	Inspections by C. K. Dyer, V. S.			
16	Edw. Stowman, 1543 Ridgley street, Baltimore...	2	....	Good.
16	J. C. Kriechbaum, 536 Cross street, Baltimore....	3	....	Do.
16	Andrew Ever, 514 Campbell street, Baltimore.....	3	....	Do.
16	Mrs. B. Miller, 880 Columbia avenue, Baltimore..	9	....	Do.
16	George Short, 874 Columbia avenue, Baltimore...	1	....	Do.
16	Peter Monahan, 849 McHenry street, Baltimore..	4	....	Do.
16	Martin Cavanaugh, 853 Ramsey street, Baltimore.	2	....	Do.
	Inspections by W. H. Wray, V. S.			
16	Jacob Haas, stock-yards, Baltimore....................	7	....	Animals, good.
16	Jacob Bousman, stock-yards, Baltimore.............	20	....	Do.

Inspections in Maryland—Continued.

Day of month.	Name of owner or person in charge and location of stable.	No. of cattle.	No. with lung-plague.	Condition of stables and animals.
	Inspections by W. Dimond, V. S.			
1886. Dec. 16	Miller & Brewer, stock-yards, Calverton, Baltimore.	15	....	Animals, good.
16	Hartley & Co., stock-yards, Calverton, Baltimore.	5	....	Animals, poor.
16	Mr. Echart, stock-yards, Calverton, Baltimore...	4	....	Animals, fair.
16	Mr. Goodman, stock-yards, Calverton, Baltimore.	3	....	
16	Unknown, stock-yards, Calverton, Baltimore....	18	....	Do.
	Inspections by W. H. Martinet, V. S.			
17	James Lyons, 1117 Washington road, Baltimore.	6	....	Animals, fair.
17	Joseph Ruholl, 1122 Hollins street, Baltimore.....	7	2c.	Do.
17	Henry Schmidt, 1129 Washington road, Baltimore.	6	....	Stables, fair; animals, good.
17	Annie Hofheintz, 1129 Washington road, Baltimore.	10	....	Fair.
17	Ellen Boyle, 53 Dewberry alley, Baltimore.........	3	....	Stables, fair; animals, good.
17	John Moon, 1134 Sassafras street, Baltimore......	2	....	Fair.
	Inspections by C. K. Dyer, V. S.			
17	Patrick Kavanaugh, 1123 Washington avenue, Baltimore.	10	2c.	Good.
17	Mrs. Mary McKenny, 1151 Washington avenue, Baltimore.	11	....	Do.
17	Anthony Griffen, 1115 Washington avenue, Baltimore.	12	....	Do.
17	John Riordan, 118 Carrolton avenue, Baltimore..	5	....	Do.
17	Mrs. K. Donovan, 110 Dewberry avenue, Baltimore.	2	....	Do.
17	Mrs. O'Keefe, 319 Amity street, Baltimore..........	8	....	Good.
	Inspections by W. Dimond, V. S.			
17	W. E. Miller, Bird Hill, Carroll County...........	3	....	Stables, fair; animals, good.
17	J. H. Hawley, Mechansville, Carroll County	16	....	Good.
17	C. Delmar, Mechansville, Carroll County............	12	....	Stables, fair; animals, good.
	Inspections by Dyer and Martinet, V. S.			
18	Silas H. Stocksdale, Falls road, Baltimore County.	1	1a.	
18	Dr. George H. Cairns, Roland avenue, Baltimore	2	1c.	Stables, good; animals, fair.
	Inspection by W. Dimond, V. S.			
18	Unknown, Calverton stock-yards, Baltimore......	14	....	
	Inspection by T. W. Spranklin, V. S.			
20	G. Gegner, Highlandtown, Baltimore................	3	....	Fair.
	Inspections by W. H. Martinet, V. S.			
20	Julia Shannon, 1120 W. Pratt street, Baltimore...	1	....	Fair.
20	Catharine Delker, 1303 Washington road, Baltimore.	1	1c.	Do.
20	A. Gerber, 402 South Calhoun street, Baltimore...	5	1c.	Do.
20	G. Zipprian, Western Scheutzen Park, Baltimore.	1	....	Good.
20	G. Yaiser, 286 S. Fulton street, Baltimore...........	3	....	Do.
20	Mr. Miller, Washington avenue, Baltimore.........	1	....	Fair.
20	J. Braver, 403 Monroe street, Baltimore.............	1	....	Do.
20	Sisters of Charity, southeast corner Carey and Lexington streets, Baltimore.	3	1c.	Do.
	Inspections by C. K. Dyer, V. S.			
20	J. Griesecker, Washington avenue extended, Baltimore.	1	....	
20	Mr. Weaver, Washington avenue extended, Baltimore.	1	....	

Inspections in Maryland—Continued.

Day of month.	Name of owner or person in charge and location of stable.	No. of cattle.	No. with lung-plague.	Condition of stables and animals.
	Inspections by C. K. Dyer—Continued.			
1886.				
Dec. 20	J. F. Strehlein, 1905 W. Pratt street, Baltimore...	18	....	
20	Clement Krager, 217 Washington avenue, Baltimore.	6	....	Good.
20	Pat Ryan, 1116 West Pratt street, Baltimore..	2	....	Do.
	Inspections by W. H. Wray, V. S.			
20	Silas H. Stockdale, Hampden, Baltimore Co......	1	1	Stables; animal, fair.
20	Dr. George H. Cairns, Hampden, Baltimore Co...	2	1c.	Good.
20	Henry Menz, Washington road, Baltimore Co....	1	....	Do.
	Inspections by W. Dimond, V. S.			
20	Seth A. Holton, Hyattsville, Prince George's County.	4	4	Stables, good; animals fair.
20	C. C. Weston, Laurel, Howard County................	61	....	Fair.
	Inspection by T. W. Spranklin, V. S.			
21	O. Kahn, Loney's Lane, Baltimore County........	11	....	Bad.
	Inspections by W. H. Martinet, V. S.			
21	Sisters of Good Shepherd, Hollins and Mount streets, Baltimore.	3	....	Good.
21	L. Blankner, 1940 West Fayette street, Baltimore.	4	....	Stables, fair; animals good.
21	P. B. Farley, 204 South Carey street, Baltimore..	4	....	Stables, bad; animals fair.
21	J. J. Hiller, Addison alley, Baltimore..................	1	....	Fair.
21	J. H. Shaeffy, 1015 West Pratt street, Baltimore.	1	1c.	Stables, good; animal fair.
	Inspections by C. K. Dyer, V. S.			
21	Mary Vaughn, 412 South Calhoun street, Baltimore.	4	....	Stables, fair; animals good.
21	Mrs. B. Derrenterger, 2104 Lexington street, Baltimore.	1	....	Good.
21	T. B. Silcott, 2037 Lexington street, Baltimore	1	....	Do.
21	A. Nolan, 406 South Calhoun street, Baltimore...	1	....	Do.
21	James H. Airey, Lexington and Monroe streets, Baltimore.	17	4	Fair.
21	C. Rohr, Calverton road, Baltimore County.......	21	....	Animals, good.
	Inspections by W. Dimond, V. S.			
21	Unknown, Calverton stock-yards, Baltimore.. ..	8	....	Animals, good.
22	Charles Winder, 9 miles from Easton, Talbot County.	12	....	Good.
	Inspections by W. H. Martinet, V. S.			
22	J. W. Seemer, 6 miles from Easton, Talbot County.	11	....	Fair.
22	Lewis Myers, 19 North Carey street, Baltimore County.	1	....	Good.
	Inspections by C. K. Dyer, V. S.			
22	C. H. Downes, 234 Gilmore street, Baltimore .. .	2	....	Good.
22	John Mayinschein, 1229 Saratoga street, Baltimore.	2	....	Do.
22	P. Faher, 482 Saratoga street, Baltimore............	1	....	Stables, poor; animals good.
22	Bernard Kroeger, 2015 Frederick avenue, Baltimore.	15	....	Good.
22	A. Rosenthal & Son, 41 South Eden street, Baltimore.	1	....	Do.
22	William Brendel, corner Third and Dillon streets, Baltimore.	17		Stables, poor; animals fair.
	Inspection by W. H. Wray, V. S.			
22	Mrs. Mary Coons, Mount Vernon street, Baltimore.	1	1	Fair.

Inspections in Maryland—Continued.

Day of month.	Name of owner or person in charge and location of stable.	No. of cattle.	No. with lung-plague.	Condition of stables and animals.
	Inspections by W. H. Wray—Continued.			
1886. Dec. 23	Unknown, Calverton stock-yards, Baltimore County.	24	....	Animals, good.
	Inspection by W. Dimond, V. S.			
23	M. O'Neal, Waverly, Baltimore County	6	....	Fair.
	Inspection by T. W. Spranklin, V. S.			
23	Emil Runge, northeast corner Green and Lombard streets, Baltimore.	1	....	Fair.
	Inspections by W. H. Martinet, V. S.			
23	D. Oppenheimer, 219 West German street, Baltimore.	1	....	Fair.
23	Jos. Bergman, 515 West Baltimore street, Baltimore.	1	....	Good.
23	David Little, 2030 Lexington avenue, Baltimore.	1	....	Fair.
23	J. Sternheimer, 117 South Paca street, Baltimore.	2	....	Good.
23	James Kaufman, northwest corner Paca and Pratt streets, Baltimore.	2	....	Do.
	Inspections by C. K. Dyer, V. S.			
23	Patrick Newell, Franklin, west of Franklin street, Baltimore.	2	....	Stables, poor; animals, good.
23	Jacob Reed, West Baltimore street, Baltimore	1	....	Good.
23	Frank Harmison, 2021 West Baltimore street, Baltimore.	1	....	Do.
23	Sisters of Bon Secours, 2000 West Baltimore street, Baltimore.	1	....	Do.
23	Christopher Lipp, 2023 West Baltimore street, Baltimore.	2	....	Do.
	Inspections by W. Dimond, V. S.			
23	F. Pressler, Liberty road, Baltimore.	16	....	Stables, poor; animals, fair.
23	Dornberg & Lauerfink, Calverton stock-yards, Baltimore.	2	....	Animals, fair.
23	C. Emerick, Calverton stock-yards, Baltimore	8	....	Animals, poor.
23	J. Sachs, Calverton stock-yards, Baltimore	8	....	Animals, good.
	Inspections by W. H. Martinet, V. S.			
24	Jos. Goldstein, 632 West German street, Baltimore	3	....	Stables, fair; animals, good.
24	Wm. Schulkagel, 1215 West Saratoga street, Baltimore.	1	....	Fair.
24	J. G. Shwartz, 121 North Schroeder street, Baltimore.	1	....	Stables, good; animals, fair.
24	Moses Ring, 752 West Lexington street, Baltimore.	1	....	Fair.
24	G. M. Hutton, corner Baltimore and Fremont streets, Baltimore.	8	....	Good.
24	S. Adler, 309 West Fayette street, Baltimore	1	....	Fair.
	Inspections by C. K. Dyer, V. S.			
24	Princes Goldstein, 633 West German street, Baltimore.	5	....	Good.
24	Leopold Pfefferborn, 709 West Lombard street, Baltimore.	1	....	Do.
24	Michael Seebold, 764 Saratoga street, Baltimore.	1	....	Do.
24	C. D. Morningstar, 513–515 West Franklin street, Baltimore.	1	....	Do.
24	D. Coblens & Sons, 3 North Paca street, Baltimore.	1	....	Do.
24	Henry Spillman, near Blue Ridge, Baltimore County.	8	....	Stables, filthy; animals, fair.
24	Unknown, Calverton stock-yards, Baltimore	20	....	Animals, fair.
24	Mrs. L. Bauerfiend, Highlandtown, Baltimore County.	11	4	
27	Unknown, Calverton stock-yards, Baltimore	34	....	Animals, good.

Inspections in Maryland—Continued.

Day of month.	Name of owner or person in charge and location of stable.	No. of cattle.	No. with lung-plague.	Condition of stables and animals.
	Inspections by W. H. Martine, V. S.			
1886.				
Dec. 27	Fred'k Bauer, 250 West Biddle street, Baltimore	1	....	Fair.
27	Edw. J. Connelly, North Eutaw street, Baltimore.	1	....	Do.
27	Griffin & Marion, 1011 Eutaw street, Baltimore	1	....	Do.
27	P. Gaierty, 219 West Modison street, Baltimore	1	....	Good.
27	M. O'Neil, 406 Orchard street, Baltimore	1	....	Do.
27	D. P. J. Thorn, 1208 Park avenue, Baltimore	1	....	Do.
27	W. F. Jackson, 218 West Monument street, Baltimore.	1	....	Do.
	Inspections by C. K. Dyer, V. S.			
27	J. L. Crise, 1124 Madison avenue, Baltimore	1	....	Fair.
27	G. W. Crook, 1120 Madison avenue, Baltimore	1	....	Good.
27	Garrett Stack, 245 Dolphin street, Baltimore	1	....	Stables, fair; animals, good.
27	N. Popplein, 1709 Eutaw Place, Baltimore	2	....	Good.
27	F. A. Crook, 1320 Madison avenue, Baltimore	1	....	Fair.
27	William Frush, 1029 Madison avenue, Baltimore	1	....	Do.
27	Dr. F. A. Brewster, 1017 Madison avenue, Baltimore.	1	....	Do.
	Inspection by W. Dimond, V. S.			
28	Unknown, Calverton stock-yards, Baltimore	19	....	Do.
	Inspections by W. H. Martinet, V. S.			
28	John McCormick, 913 Park avenue, Baltimore	10	2c.	Good.
28	James Maguire, 335 Bloom street, Baltimore	2	....	Stables, bad; animals, fair.
28	C. A. Thomas, 2423 Pennsylvania avenue, Baltimore.	2	....	Good.
28	H. Waterman, 1357 Fremont street, Baltimore	8	....	Do.
23	Joseph Dammen, 731 Lauvale street, Baltimore	1	....	Do.
	Inspections by C. K. Dyer, V. S.			
28	William G. Oler, 2107 Madison avenue, Baltimore.	1	....	Good.
28	St. Vincent's Infant Asylum, 1403 Division street, Baltimore.	6	....	Do.
28	Annie Hock, 1426 Pennsylvania avenue, Baltimore.	2	....	Stables, filthy; animals, good.
	Inspection W. H. Wray, V. S.			
28	Seth A. Horton, Hyattsville. Prince George's County.	4	3	Stables, good; animals fair.
	Inspection by W. Dimond, V. S.			
28	William Gutman, Quaker lane, Baltimore County.	1	1	Stables, fair; animals, poor.
	Inspections by T. W. Spranklin, V. S.			
29	C. Gore, Liberty road, Baltimore County	7	....	Stables, fair; animals, good.
29	Paul Harden, Liberty road, Baltimore County	2	....	Stables, bad; animals, fair.
29	P. Arthur, Liberty road, Baltimore County	4	....	Stables, fair; animals, good.
29	F. Gore, Liberty road, Baltimore County	4	....	Do.
29	P. Louis Liberty road, Baltimore County	12	....	Fair.
29	H. Litman, Liberty road, Baltimore County	8	....	Do.
	Inspection by W. Dimond, V. S.			
29	Unknown, Calverton Stock-Yards, Baltimore	28	....	Fair.
	Inspections by W. H. Martinet, V. S.			
29	Mary C. Eidman, 2122 Pennsylvania avenue, Baltimore.	1	....	Animal, fair.
29	Thomas Whelan, 543 Kirby's lane, Baltimore	1	....	Fair.
29	James Magee, 1148 Gilmore street Baltimore	3	2c.	Do.

Inspections in Maryland—Continued.

Day of month.	Name of owner or person in charge and location of stable.	No. of cattle.	No. with lung-plague.	Condition of stables and animals.
	Inspections by W. H. Martinet—Continued.			
1886. Dec. 29	John Mogan, 808 Mount street, Baltimore	1	....	Fair.
29	Franklin Wilson, 1610 Edmonson avenue, Baltimore.	1	....	Good.
29	P. Schwinn, 728 Chappell street, Baltimore	1	....	Stables, bad; animal, fair.
29	Mary Kline, 712 Chappell street, Baltimore	3	....	Good.
	Inspections by C. K. Dyer, V. S.			
29	Saint Catharine's Institute, 701 Arlington avenue, Baltimore.	2	....	Good.
29	Louis Fink, 1814 Edmonson avenue, Baltimore	3	....	Do.
29	John Farrell, Old Cathedral Cemetery, Baltimore.	2	....	Do.
29	Aaron Burr, Lafayette avenue, extended, Baltimore.	2	....	Do.
29	Jacob Hock, Carey and Chappell streets, Baltimore.	5	....	Do.
29	Mr. Scarborough, 1526 North Fremont street, Baltimore.	1	....	Do.
29	Dr. Condon, 326 North Mount street, Baltimore	1	....	Do.
30	Thomas McDonald, 1230 Division st., Baltimore	2	....	Do.
30	John F. Ford, 1536 North Gilmore street, Baltimore.	2	....	Do.
30	E. A. Kaufman, 709 Cumberland street, Baltimore.	1	....	Do.
30	Dr. J. L. Warfield, Liberty road grove, No. 2, Baltimore.	1	....	Do.
30	Alex Brown, 704 Cathedral street, Baltimore	1	....	Do.
	Inspections by W. H. Martinet, V. S.			
30	G. S. Brown, 706 Cathedral street, Baltimore	1	....	Do.
30	L. Campbell, 1718 Calhoun street, Baltimore	2	....	Fair.
30	Dr. L. C. Olds, 1504 North Gilmore street, Baltimore.	1	....	Do.
30	Wm. Haughey, 1605 North Gilmore street, Baltimore.	1	....	Do.
31	Mrs. Melissa Baker, Liberty road grove, No. 2, Baltimore.	1	....	Good.
31	Peter Burns, 532 Townshend street, Baltimore	2	....	Do.
	Inspections by C. K. Dyer, V. S.			
31	J. O'Neil, 1330 North Gilmore street, Baltimore	1	....	Do.
31	O. A. Myers, 1804 Lorman street, Baltimore	18	....	Do.
	Inspections by T. W. Sprankilin, V. S.			
31	C. Hall, Eleventh street, Orangeville, Baltimore County.	32	....	Stables, bad; animals, fair.
31	H. Stern, Bay View, Baltimore County	15	....	Do.
31	H. Lantz, Bay View, Baltimore County	8	....	Fair.
	Inspections by W. H. Martinet, V. S.			
31	M. Carling, 63 Pennsylvania avenue, Baltimore	11	....	Good.

Reinspections in Maryland.

Day of month.	Name of owner or person in charge and location of stable.	No. of cattle.	No. with lung-plague.	Condition of stables and animals.
	Inspections by C. K. Dyer, V. S.			
1886.				
Aug. 19	John Schmidt, Highlandtown, Baltimore Co......	12	1	Good.
19	Blasius Wolf, Highlandtown, Baltimore Co.......	11	....	Fair.
21	J. Register, York road, Baltimore County.........	19	....	Good.
28	Henry Schriver, Washington road, Baltimore County.	5	2	Stables, fair; animals good.
30	Herman Geken, Wetheredville, Baltimore Co.....	72	....	Good.
30	Dorsey & Co., Arlington.............................	54	....	Do.
Sept. 2	William Amos, near Baltimore........................	6	....	
3	Louis Clay, Highlandtown..............................	44	2	
3	Mrs. Anna Dieckman, 720 Hanover street..........	18	2a.	Fair.
16	Ephraim Mallonee, near Pimlico......................	....	....	
21	Mrs. A. Dieckman, 720 Hanover street..............	20	12c.	
	Inspection by W. H. Wray, V. S.			
10	Mrs. A. Dieckman, 720 Hanover street...............	19	3	Fair.
	Inspections by W. H. Rose, V. S.			
15	J. Retiger, Philadelphia road............................	5	2c.	
15	J. Eidman, Philadelphia road..........................	3	3c.	
	Inspections by Rose and Wray, V. S.			
16	H. Shafer, Washington road............................	9	4	Stables, filthy; animals fair.
16	A. Paul, Belair road.......................................	4	2	
	Inspection by Trumbower and Rose, V. S.			
17	John H. Gross, Philadelphia road......................	22	13	Stables, good; animals fair.
	Inspections by W. H. Wray, V. S.			
20	George Brown, Brooklandville...........................	15	1	
[illegible]	John H. Gross, Philadelphia road......................	22	14	
	Inspections by C. K. Dyer, V. S.			
22	John Heing, Light street.................................	2	....	
22	George Sach, 1010 Hanover street.....................	24	....	Good.
22	Ewd. Sach, 1008 Hanover street........................	15	....	Do.
	Inspection by W. H. Wray, V. S.			
22	Mrs. A. Dieckman, 720 Hanover street...............	20	12	Stables, filthy; animals fair.
	Inspection by C. K. Dyer, V. S.			
23	Hiller, Baltimore..	13	....	Fair.
	Inspections by W. H. Wray, V. S.			
23	John Dengler, Belair road, Baltimore County.....	6	1	
[illegible]	Eph. Mallonee, Hookstown road, Baltimore County.	38	3	
	Inspections by Trumbower and Dyer, V. S.			
23	Chas. Spitznagle, Highlandtown, Baltimore Co...	40	12	Fair.
[illegible]	Lewis Clay, Light street, Baltimore..................	44	9	Bad.
	Inspections by M. R. Trumbower, V. S.			
	Ephraim Mallonee, near Smallwood P. O., Carroll County.	....	3	
	Chris. Schnable, near Smallwood P. O., Carroll County.	2	2	Fair.
24	Leonard Rosenberger, 2 miles from Owings's Mills, Baltimore.	7	2c.	Animals, fair.
27	J. T. Stephens, Hookstown road........................	22	9	Stables, very good; animals, fair.
	Inspections by W. H. Wray, V. S.			
28	Ephraim Mallonee, 130 West street, Baltimore...	38	3	
24	Mrs. Cora Reip, Philadelphia road, Baltimore...	5	3	

Reinspections in Maryland—Continued.

Day of month.	Name of owner or person in charge and location of stable.	No. of cattle.	No. with lung-plague.	Condition of stables and animals.
	Inspections by W. H. Wray—Continued.			
1886. Sept. 24	C. Spitznagle, corner Third avenue and Pratt street, Baltimore,	38	12	
28	A. Henterling, 39 Cumberland street, Baltimore..	15	2c.	
28	B. M. Hangley, Hanover street extended, Baltimore.	4	1a.	
	Inspections by T. W. Spranklin, V. S.			
28	E. Sachs, Hanover street extended, Baltimore...	14	....	Fair.
25	G. Sachs, Sharp street, Baltimore	24	....	Stables, bad.
25	J. Kramer, Hanover street, Baltimore....	16	....	Stables, fair; animals, good.
25	A. Deickman, Hanover street, Baltimore	20	1a.	Fair.
25	J. C. Weaver, Philadelphia road, Baltimore County.	7	....	Stables, good; animals, good.
2	J. Eidman, Philadelphia road, Baltimore Co......	3	....	Stables, bad; animals, fair.
27	J. Beltiger, Philadelphia road, Baltimore Co.......	5	....	Stables, fair; animals, good.
	Inspection by C. K. Dyer, V. S.			
29	Charles Huhn, Canton, Baltimore County	10	3	Stables, fair; animals, good.
	Inspections by W. H. Wray, V. S.			
29	C. Spitznagle, Philadelphia road, Baltimore County.	88	....	
30	J. T. Stephens, Owing's Mills, Baltimore County..	22	9	
30	O. H. Disney, Owing's Mills, Baltimore County..	18	1	
Oct. 1	John Kaiss, Annapolis road, Baltimore County..	10	10	
1	C. Spitznagle, Philadelphia road, Baltimore County.	....	....	
2	T. A. Seth, Baltimore County	6	4	Good.
2	John Kaiss, Annapolis road, Baltimore County...	10	10	Stables, good; animals, fair.
5	George B. Brown, Brooklandville, Baltimore County.	15	....	Good.
5	Mrs. A. Dieckman, 720 Hanover street, Baltimore.	....	....	
6	A. Bollinger, Westminster, Carroll County	1	....	
6	C. Sohnable, Westminster, Carroll County	2	2	Stables, good; animals, poor.
	Inspections by T. W. Spranklin, V. S.			
5	Mr. J. H. Gross, Philadelphia road, Baltimore County.	20	1a.	Fair.
5	B. Wolf, Highlandtown, Baltimore County	9	....	Do.
	Inspections by C. K. Dyer, V. S.			
6	Fred. Gore, 4 miles on Liberty road, Baltimore County.	3	2c.	Poor.
6	Chas. Gore, 4 miles on Liberty road, Baltimore County.	8	....	Good.
6	W. Kempski, Baltimore County	8	....	Stables, fair.
7	John Kunkle, Darley Park, Baltimore County..	15	1	Poor.
9	J. T. Stephens, Owing's Mills, Baltimore County.	22	9	Good.
	Inspections by W. H. Wray, V. S.			
7	H. Spitznagle, Philadelphia road, Baltimore Co..	....	5	
7	Ephraim Mallonee, Hookstown, Baltimore Co....	34	1	
8	Patrick O'Brien, Falls road, Baltimore County...	9	2	
8	J. Foghtman, Rosedale P. O., Baltimore County..	1	1	
9	C. Spitznagle, Philadelphia road, Baltimore Co..	....	....	
11	C. Spitznagle, Philadelphia road, Baltimore Co ..	....	5	
12	C. Spitznagle, Philadelphia road, Baltimore Co...	....	5	Stables, good; animals, poor.
12	A. Paul, Belair road, Baltimore County	5	2	Good.
12	John Dengler, Belair road, Baltimore County...	6	....	Stables, good; animals, fair.
12	H. Reichert, Terry Hall, Baltimore County	9	1	Stables, good; animals, fair.
13	Henry Steffy, Hampden, Baltimore County	1	1	
13	O. H. Disney, Owing's Mills, Baltimore County..	18	....	Do.

Reinspections in Maryland—Continued.

Day of month.	Name of owner or person in charge and location of stables.	No. of cattle.	No. with lung disease.	Condition of stables and animals.
	Inspections by T. W. Spranklin—Continued.			
1896. Oct. 26	J. S. Nickel, Park Height, Baltimore County	17	....	Stables, bad; animals, good.
26	C. Kemp, Park Height, Baltimore County	3	....	Good.
	Inspections by W. H. Wray, V. S.			
27	William Kemski, Pimlico road, Baltimore Co	8	1	Good.
28	J. Graner, Harford road, Baltimore County	4	4	Stables, good; animals, fair.
29	A. Busch, Philadelphia road, Baltimore County	4	2	Do.
29	John Clay, Lombard street, Baltimore	28	15	Stables, filthy; animals, fair.
	Inspections by C. K. Dyer, V. S.			
27	John Clay, Lombard street, Baltimore	28	15c.	
27	J. Graner, Harford road, Baltimore County	4	4	
28	T. M. Richardson, Belair road, Baltimore Co	17	....	Good.
28	H. Reichert, near Perry Hall, Baltimore County	7	5	Animals, fair.
29	John Kaiss, near Uniontown, Baltimore County	9	....	
	Inspections by T. W. Spranklin, V. S.			
29	J. G. Erdman, Belair road, Baltimore County	8	....	Good.
29	G. Smith, Fair Oak Farm, Baltimore County	24	....	Do.
29	D. Lutz, Liberty road, Baltimore County	25	....	Stables, bad; animals, good.
30	J. W. Garrett, Harford road, Baltimore County	16	4c.	Good.
30	H. Becker, Canton road, Baltimore County	35	....	Do.
30	Beimiller, Patapsco Neck, Baltimore County	45	....	Do.
30	J. Smith, Canton, Baltimore County	19	....	Fair.
30	A. Sapp, Patapsco Neck, Baltimore County	14	....	Do.
30	D. Shehan, Jenkins lane, Baltimore County	20	....	Do.
	Inspections by W. H. Wray, V. S.			
30	Henry Kelenberg, 798 South Charles street, Baltimore.	6	2	Stables, poor; animals, fair.
30	J. Eidman, 208 South Eutaw street, Baltimore	3	1	Good.
30	J. Kuhule, 440 Fort avenue, Baltimore	2	....	Stables, poor; animals, good.
Nov. 1	T. M. Richardson, 4 miles on Belair road, Baltimore County.	17	1	Good.
1	Lenhart Tramper, 10 miles on Belair road, Baltimore County.	7	1	Do.
3	E. Cowling, Brooklandville road, Baltimore County.	6	2	Do.
4	R. Disney, 3½ miles on Hookstown road, Baltimore County.	1	1	Stables, good; animals, fair.
	Inspections by Dyer and Martinet, V. S.			
Oct. 30	A. Kaulitz, Eastern avenue, Baltimore	9	5	Stables, filthy; animals, poor.
30	John Mateling, near Rossville, Baltimore County	2	1	Animals, fair.
Nov. 1	Chas. T. Belt, 518 Rowland avenue, Baltimore	2	2	Stables, good; animals, fair.
2	T. M. Richardson, Belair road, Baltimore County	16	16	Good.
3	Theo. German, 5 miles on Harford road, Baltimore County.	18	18	Do.
3	Jacob Weddle, Wilkins avenue, Baltimore	9	....	
	Inspections by T. W. Spranklin, V. S.			
5	J. H. Gross, Stemen's Run, Baltimore County	20	3c.	Fair.
5	S. Hair, Hunting avenue, Baltimore County	28	....	Stables, fair; animals, good.
5	M. C. Engelheart, Hunting avenue extended, Baltimore County.	17	....	Fair.
5	J. Rettiger, Rosedale, Baltimore County	5	....	Good.
5	A. Busch, Philadelphia road, Baltimore County	4	....	Fair.
5	P. Holland, Philadelphia road, Baltimore County	10	....	Stables, fair; animals, good.
5	G. Zink, Philadelphia road, Baltimore County	15	2c.	Fair.
5	M. Zinkard, Philadelphia road, Baltimore Co	21	....	Do.

Reinspections in Maryland—Continued.

Day of month.	Name of owner or person in charge and location of stable.	No. of cattle.	No. with lung-plague.	Condition of stables and animals.
	Inspections by T. W. Sprankin—Continued.			
1886.				
Nov. 9	Geo. H. Cairnes, Hampden, Baltimore County	2	1	Good.
6	Joseph White, 2 Burroughs street, Baltimore	4	2	Fair.
8	D. Wolf, Waverly, Baltimore County	33		Good.
8	G. Oliver, Waverly, Baltimore County	8		Stables, bad; animals, fair.
8	J. Geier, Highlandtown, Baltimore County	18		Stables, fair; animals, good.
8	Mrs. Gibson, Waverly, Baltimore County	15		Fair.
8	P. Goss, Waverly, Baltimore County	4		Good.
8	A. Auft, Monument street, extended, Baltimore	46		Stables, bad; animals, fair.
8	J. Schmidt, Eastern avenue, Highlandtown, Baltimore County.	12		Fair.
8	P. Nalkys, Highlandtown, Baltimore County	11		Do.
8	Noha Brothers, Eastern avenue, Canton, Baltimore County.	16		Stables, fair; animals, good.
8	J. Chabson, Hampden, Baltimore	2	1	Stables, good; animals, fair.
	Inspections by W. H. Wray, V. S.			
8	J. Nichols, Hookstown road, Baltimore County	17	13	Poor.
8	B. Hackerman, 68 Harrison street, Baltimore	4	3	Fair.
	Inspections by T. W. Sprankin, V. S.			
10	Bartholow, Pr' psco Neck, Baltimore County	50		Stables, good; animals, good.
10	H. Stohm, Patapsco Neck, Baltimore County	15		Stables, fair; animals, good.
10	H. Linz, Patapsco Neck, Baltimore County	8		Do.
10	J. G. Dietz, Mount Carmel road, Baltimore Co	10		Good.
10	Bay View Asylum, Baltimore	10		Do.
11	James S. Nickel, Hookstown road, Baltimore County.	17	13	Poor.
	Inspections by W. H. Wray, V. S.			
11	Wm. Kemski, Pimlico road, Baltimore County	8	4	Fair.
13	B. Hackerman, 68 Harrison street, Baltimore	4	1	Stables, poor; animals, fair.
	Inspections by Dyer and Martinet, V. S.			
13	Aug. Schmidt, corner Seventh and Lombard streets, Baltimore.	11	10	Stables, good; animals, fair.
13	Conrad Schmidt, corner Eighth and Lombard streets, Baltimore.	18	2c.	Good.
	Inspections by W. H. Wray, V. S.			
15	Joseph Kuhn, 5 miles on Liberty road, Baltimore.	21	2a.	Good.
15	Ben Hackerman, 60 Harrison street, Baltimore		1a.	
	Inspections by T. W. Sprankin, V. S.			
15	Staatsmeyer & Son, Harford road, Baltimore	5		Good.
15	H. Nordhoff, Hall Springs, Baltimore County	7		Fair.
15	D. Staatsmeyer, Hamilton avenue, Baltimore	9		Good.
15	W. H. Kline, Philadelphia road, Baltimore County.	1		Fair.
15	B. Lacy, Harford road, Baltimore County	6		Do.
16	F. Young, Highlandtown, Baltimore County	12	5c.	Stables, fair; animals, bad.
16	J. Kunkle, Harford road, Baltimore County	14		Good.
16	J. R. Wood, Hamilton avenue, Baltimore County	5		Do.
16	J. Sullivan, Swann street, Baltimore County	16		Do.
16	D. Shehan, Loney's lane, Baltimore County	20		Stables, fair; animals, good.
16	M. M. Riley, Harford road, Baltimore County	12		Stables, good; animals, fair.
16	A. Sachs, Harford road, Baltimore County	21		Good.
16	J. Roeder, Harford road, Baltimore County	9		Fair.
	Inspection by W. H. Wray, V. S.			
16	C. T. Cookey, near Pikesville, Baltimore County	4		Good.

Reinspections in Maryland—Continued.

Day of month.	Name of owner or person in charge and location of stable.	No. of cattle.	No. with lung-plague.	Condition of stables and animals.
	Inspection by Dyer and Martinet, V. S.			
1886. Nov. 16	Sebastian Noeth, Monument street, Baltimore	8	4c.	Stables, good; animals, fair.
	Inspections by W. H. Wray, V. S.			
17	John Doran, O'Donnell & Bouldon	12	11	Stables, poor; animals, fair.
17	H. Eckert, stock-yards	1	1	Fair.
18	William Williams, 6 miles from Westminster, Carroll County.	4	4	Stables, good; animals, fair.
19	Theodore Marling, First and Bank streets, Baltimore.	16	6c.	Fair.
19	Lewis Clay, Highlandtown, Baltimore County	46	9	Stables, poor; animals, fair.
20	John H. Gross, Philadelphia road, Baltimore County.	20	20	Stables, good; animals, fair.
	Inspections by T. W. Spranklin, V. S.			
	J. Creamer, Sharp street, extended, Baltimore	16	....	Good.
	C. Heisler, Wilkenson avenue, Baltimore	42	....	Do.
	J. Bair, Washington road, Baltimore	13	....	Stables, good; animals, fair.
	C. Vogal, Washington road, Baltimore	20	....	Stables, fair; animals, good.
	H. Schaffer, Washington road, Baltimore	10	4	Bad.
	Inspections by Dyer & Martinet, V. S.			
	Anton Paul, Putty Hill, Baltimore County	6	5c.	
	Joseph Krastle, Putty Hill, Baltimore County	7	4	Good.
	H. Becker, O'Donnell street, Canton	45	....	Do.
	H. Hausman, Patapsco Neck, Baltimore	6	1c.	Stables, fair; animals, good.
	Biemiller, Patapsco Neck, Baltimore	52	....	Good.
	Inspection by W. Dimond, V. S.			
	John J. Smith, Sunnybrook, Baltimore	5	....	Fair.
	Inspections by T. W. Spranklin, V. S.			
	Mr. Park, Canton, Baltimore County	11	....	Good.
	L. Keifer, Clinton street, Canton	31	....	Stables, fair; animals, good.
	N. Register, Boley's lane, Baltimore County	30	....	Fair.
	B. Wolf, Highlandtown, Baltimore County	10	....	Good.
	Z. Weinbeck, First avenue, Baltimore	18	....	Stables, fair; animals, good.
	F. Miller, 7 Hudson street, Baltimore	21	1c.	Fair.
	T. Biddison, Belair road, Gardenville	20	....	Stables, bad; animals, fair.
	J. Friskey, Belair road, Gardenville	4	....	Stables, fair; animals, good.
	J. G. Carter, Belair road, Raspeburg	25	....	Stables, bad; animals, fair.
	J. Erdman, Belair road	7	....	Good.
	J. H. Cole, Belair road	26	....	Do.
	H. Berger, Belair road, Raspeburg	19	....	Stables, bad; animals, fair.
	H. Raspe, Belair road, Raspeburg	8	....	
	G. Hosstetter, Belair road, Gardenville	5	....	Good.
27	G. Quick, Belair road, Gardenville	8	....	Stables, fair; animals, good.
27	A. R. Quick, Belair road, Gardensville	8	....	Fair.
	Inspection by Dyer and Martinet, V. S.			
30	Geo. Weigel, 113 North Chester street, Baltimore	10	2c.	Fair.
	Inspections by W. H. Wray, V. S.			
30	Domberg & Lohrfink, 432 North Spring street, Baltimore.	20	1	Good.
30	Julius Sachs & Son, 279 Orleans street, Baltimore	19	4	Stables, good; animals, fair.

Reinspections in Maryland—Continued.

Day of month.	Name of owner or person in charge and location of stable.	No. of cattle.	No. with lung-plague.	Condition of stables and animals.
	Inspections by W. H. Wray—Continued.			
1886. Dec. 2	Benj. Hackerman, 68 Harrison street, Baltimore..	8	1	Stables, poor; animals, fair.
2	J. G. Miller, corner Third and Lombard streets, Baltimore.	31	1	Stables, excellent; animals, good.
	Inspection by W. Dimond, V. S.			
2	J. Sachs & Son, Calverton stock-yards...............	7	....	Animals, fair.
	Inspections by W. H. Wray, V. S.			
3	Henry Schafer, Washington road, Baltimore County.	10	1	Stables, filthy; animals, poor.
3	Hebrew Hospital Association, East Monument street, Baltimore.	1	....	Excellent.
3	Nicholas Tegges, 168 Fairmount street, Baltimore.	1	....	Do.
3	Jacob Hass & Son, 635 North Eden street, Baltimore.	19	....	Stables, excellent; animals, good.
	Inspections by T. W. Spranklin, V. S.			
4	E. Biemiller, Patapsco Neck, Baltimore County..	58	....	Good.
4	C. Lanahan, Govanstown, Baltimore County	6	....	Do.
4	W. Lanahan, Govanstown, Baltimore County.....	7	....	Do.
4	H. Becker, Canton, Baltimore County...............	38	....	Do.
	Inspections by W. H. Wray, V. S.			
6	J. Weinkneit, 558 E. Fayette street, Baltimore...	1	....	Stables, good; animals, excellent.
6	C. Matthias, 614 Burke street, Baltimore............	5	....	Good.
6	W. Abbitt, Eastern avenue, Baltimore................	18	....	Fair.
8	P. Malkus, Canton, Baltimore County	11	....	Do.
8	S. Bauerfind, Highlandtown, Baltimore County..	11	Sus.	Stables, fair; animals, good.
8	B. Wolf, Highlandtown, Baltimore County.......	10	....	Fair.
8	J. Schmidt, Highlandtown, Baltimore County...	12	....	Stables, fair; animals good.
8	J. Nuth, Boley's lane, Baltimore County............	38	....	Good.
8	N. Register, Baltimore County...........................	28	....	Stables, fair; animals good.
10	J. Schmidt, Canton, Baltimore County..............	9	....	Fair.
10	P. Wolf, Canton, Baltimore County....................	17	2c.	Stables, fair; animals, bad.
	Inspections by W. H. Martinet, V. S.			
13	George Sachs, 2300 Hanover street, Baltimore...	28	....	Stables, fair; animals very poor.
13	George Weaver, sr., 1301 Light street, Baltimore..	11	....	Good.
	Inspection by C. K. Dyer, V. S.			
13	George Weaver, jr., 1322 Light street, Baltimore..	9	....	Good.
	Inspections by W. H. Wray, V. S.			
13	William Blotkamp, 1732 East Lombard street, Baltimore.	2	....	Good.
13	M. Lynch, 801 North Ann street, Baltimore	2	....	Stables, good; animals fair.
	Inspection by T. W. Spranklin, V. S.			
8	Noha Bros., Eastern avenue, Baltimore.....	22	....	Fair.
	Inspections by W. H. Wray, V. S.			
9	J. Bankert, 60 East Biddle street, Baltimore.......	1	....	Good.
9	Elias Robertson, Luzerne and Oliver streets, Baltimore.	1	....	Do.
9	Mrs. Mary Baker, 1620 Belair street, Baltimore,..	1	....	Do.
9	Kasimere Vogal, Washington road, Baltimore County.	21	....	Stables, good; animals, excellent.
9	G. E. French, Arlington road, Baltimore County..	26	....	Good.

Reinspections in Maryland—Continued.

Day of month.	Name of owner or person in charge and location of stable.	No. of cattle.	No. with lung-plague.	Condition of stables and animals.
	Inspections by T. W. Spranklin, V. S.			
1886. Dec. 9	T. Keyworth, Arlington road, Baltimore County..	2	....	Good.
9	Dorsey & Co., Arlington road, Baltimore County..	67	....	Do.
9	H. Gerken, Arlington road, Baltimore County ...	80	....	Fair.
	Inspection by W. H. Martinet, V. S.			
9	Joseph White, 2 Burroughs street, Baltimore......	2	....	Good.
	Inspections by T. W. Spranklin, V. S.			
10	L. Weinbeck, Canton, Baltimore County...........	18	1a.	Stables, fair; animals, good.
10	J. Beets, Canton, Baltimore County.....................	17	....	Good.
	Inspections by C. K. Dyer, V. S.			
11	Mrs. Anna Dickman, 720 Hanover street, Baltimore.	19	....	Good.
13	Cora Reip, 130 West street, Baltimore.................	5	....	Stables, filthy; animals, poor.
13	John Heints, rear 1440 Light street, Baltimore...	2	2 c.	Do.
	Inspection by T. W. Spranklin, V. S.			
14	R. Moore, Glenmore street, Baltimore.	42	....	Good.
	Inspections by W. H. Wray, V. S.			
14	Lewis Clay, Highlandtown, Baltimore County...	51	3	Stables, filthy; animals, poor.
14	Henry Shriver, Washington road, Baltimore County.	5	2	Good.
14	Lorenz Weinberg, Dillon street, corner Third avenue, Baltimore.	17	2	Fair.
15	Jacob Weddle, Wilkins avenue, Baltimore.........	10	3 c.	Good.
16	Nicholas Baulzer, 103 South Washington street, Baltimore.	3	....	Do.
16	Joseph Weinman, 351 East Lombard street, Baltimore.	9	2	Stables, good; animals, fair.
17	Otto Kahn, Loney's lane, Baltimore County.	16	5	Stables, fair; animals, poor.
17	J. E. Swift, Belair road......................................	9	....	Stables, fair; animals, good.
17	Mr. Deeds, Bird Hill, Carroll County..................	6	......3 c.	Stables, poor; animals, fair.
18	D. M. Nesbit, College Station, Prince George's County.	47	2	Good.
20	H. Nordhoff, Lauraville, Baltimore County.......	8	....	Do.
	Inspections by T. W. Spranklin, V. S.			
20	E. Biemiller, Mt. Carmel road, Baltimore Co	52	....	Good.
20	H. Becker, O'Donnold street, Baltimore.............	45	....	Do.
20	List & Shultz, Lauraville, Baltimore County......	11	....	Do.
20	E. Richards, Harford road, Baltimore County...	10	....	Stables, bad; animals, good.
20	A. Keen, Canton, Baltimore County.....................	2	....	Good.
	Inspections by W. H. Wray, V. S.			
20	H. Shriver, Washington road, Baltimore County..	4	....	Good.
20	Mrs. N. K. Disney, Owing's Mills, Baltimore County.	28	2 c.	Stables, good; animals, fair.
20	J. T. Stephens, Owing's Mills, Baltimore County..	20	2 c.	Good.
	Inspections by T. W. Spranklin, V. S.			
21	A. Sapp, Patapsco Neck, Baltimore County	17	....	Good.
21	M. Deitz, Highlandtown, Baltimore County	9	....	Fair.
21	J. Rost, Patapsco Neck, Baltimore County.........	8	....	Good.
21	F. Marton, Highlandtown, Baltimore County. ..	30	....	Stables, good; animals, fair.
21	A. Auft, Mine Bank lane, Baltimore County......	37	....	Fair.
21	J. Neberline, Fifteenth street and First avenue, Baltimore County.	23	....	Good.
21	S. Bauerfind, Highlandtown, Baltimore County..	11	1a.	Stables, fair; animals, good.

Reinspections in Maryland—Continued.

Day of month.	Name of owner or person in charge and location of stable.	No. of cattle.	No. with lung-plague.	Condition of stables and animals.
	Inspection by W. H. Wray, V. S.			
1886. Dec. 21	C. O. Kemp, Hookstown road, Baltimore County..	4	....	Good.
	Inspections by T. W. Spranklin, V. S.			
22	Noha Bros., Highlandtown, Baltimore County...	23	....	Stables, fair; animals, good.
22	J. Creamer, S. Sharp street extended, Baltimore..	19	....	Fair.
22	H. Schmidt, Hamilton avenue, Baltimore County..	18	....	Good.
22	C. Vogal, Washington road, Baltimore County..	22	....	Do.
22	W. Langsmann, Washington street extended, Baltimore County	85	....	Do.
23	M. Gibson, Homestead, Baltimore County.........	15	....	Stables, fair; animals, good.
23	D. Shehan, Waverly, Baltimore County.............	20	....	Stables, bad; animals, good.
23	D. Wolf, Homestead, Baltimore County..............	32	....	Good.
23	J. Nuth, Corse's farm, Baltimore County............	86	....	Do.
23	Frantz Wagner, 66 Browne's lane, Baltimore County.	14	....	
	Inspection by W. H. Wray, V. S.			
23	Eph. Mallonee, Hooks town road, Baltimore Co..	84	11	Stables, poor; animals, fair.
	Inspections by T. W. Spranklin, V. S.			
24	M. Riley, Harford road, Baltimore County.........	12	....	Stables, good; animals, fair.
24	A. Sachs, Harford road, Baltimore County..........	23	....	Good.
24	J. Roeder, Harford road, Baltimore County.......	10	....	Fair.
24	M. Goss, Homestead, Baltimore County............	4	....	Good.
24	Kunkle, Harford road, Baltimore County	14	....	Do.
22	H. Grusender, Loney's lane, Baltimore County...	4	....	Do.
24	G. Baker, Loney's lane, Baltimore County.........	18	....	Stables, fair; animals, good.
24	N. Regester, Corse's farm, Baltimore County......	28	....	Stables, bad; animals, fair.
24	G. Oliver, Homestead, Baltimore County............	4	....	Stables, bad.
	Inspections by C. K. Dyer, V. S.			
24	Mrs. Cronin, 120 Callender alley, Baltimore.........	6	....	Stables, poor; animals, fair.
28	Chas. Klinger, 548 Wilson street, Baltimore.........	15	....	Good.
28	John Learey, 546 Wilson street, Baltimore..........	4	....	Do.
	Inspection by W. H. Wray, V. S.			
28	D. M. Nesbit, College Station, Prince George's County.	45	2	Stables, good; animals, fair.
	Inspections by T. W. Spranklin, V. S.			
29	Thompson & Love, 308 Castle street, Baltimore...	2	....	Stables, good; animals, fair.
29	J. Kuhn, Liberty road, Baltimore County...........	19	....	Good.
29	C. Smith, Liberty road, Baltimore County...........	18	....	Stables, fair; animals, fair.
	Inspections by W. H. Wray, V. S.			
29	Jas. S. Nickel, Hookstown road, Baltimore County.	17	18	Stables, poor; animals, fair.
29	J. E. Swift, four miles on Belair road, Baltimore	8	8	Poor.
29	Mrs. Bauerfind, Gough and Fifth streets, Baltimore County.	11	1	Do.
29	B. Hackerman, 68 Harrison street, Baltimore, County.	2	1	Do.
30	James Nickel, three miles on Hookstown road, Baltimore County.	17	6	Stables, fair; animals, fair.
30	Susan E. Blucher, Chestnut street, Hampden, Baltimore County.	1	1	Stables, poor; animals, fair.
	Inspections by T. W. Spranklin, V. S.			
31	J. Campbell, Patapsco Neck, Baltimore County...	85	....	Stables, fair; animals, fair.
31	Bay View Asylum, Bay View, Baltimore Co	14	....	Good.
31	G. Bartholow, Bay View, Baltimore County......	50	....	Stables, good; animals, fair.

Inspections in the District of Columbia.

Day of month.	Name of owner or person in charge and location of stable.	No. of cattle.	No. with lung-plague.	Condition of stables and animals.
	Inspections by W. H. Rose, V. S.			
86.				
ne 8	Mrs. Flanagan, near Benning's road	9	....	Poor.
8	Mrs. Gazenbach, near Benning's road	1	....	Fair.
8	Mrs. J. Douglas, near Benning's road	4	....	Do.
8	Dr. Kilbourne, near Benning's road	1	....	Do.
8	Mr. Rupert, northeast of Boundary	1	....	Do.
8	Geo. Dore, northeast of Boundary	1	....	Do.
8	James Foley, northeast of Boundary	6	....	Do.
8	Thos. Hanrahan, northeast of Boundary	11	....	Stables, fair; animals, poor.
8	Wm. Bradley, northeast of Boundary	10	....	Do.
8	Mrs. Bennett, northeast of Boundary	2	....	Fair.
8	John Mason, northeast of Boundary	14	....	Poor.
10	Mr. Thursby, Third street, S. W.	4	2c.	Do.
10	John Whitten, corner 4½ and P streets, S. W.	2	....	Animals, poor.
10	Mr. Spillman, corner 4½ and P streets, S. W.	2	....	Animals, fair.
10	Mr. Long, corner 4½ and P streets, S. W.	2	....	Poor.
10	U. S. Arsenal, foot of 4½ street, S. W.	14	....	Fair.
10	Mrs. Pritchard, near 4½ street, S. W.	1	....	Stables, foul; animals, poor.
12	Jacob Abler, corner 17th and C streets, S. E.	2	....	Animals, fair.
12	Mrs. Hughes, corner 17th and D streets, S. E.	1	....	Do.
12	Mr. Clancy, corner 17th and D streets, S. E.	3	....	Do.
12	Mr. Gill, corner 16th and E streets, S. E.	6	....	Animals, poor.
12	Albert Domdy, Pennsylvania avenue, between Fourteenth and Fifteenth streets, S. E.	10	....	Poor.
12	Pat Conners, Fifteenth street, between D and E streets, N. E.	21	....	Do.
12	John Crawford, 17th and East Cap. street, N. E.	14	....	Stables, fair; animals, poor.
12	Elizabeth Flynn, A street, between Fourteenth and Fifteenth streets, N. E.	3	....	Poor.
12	Richard Horn, A street, S. E., near jail	3	....	Do.
12	Mrs. J. Bensinger, A street, S. E., near jail	1	....	Do.
12	Mrs. Dover, A street, S. E. near jail	1	....	Animals, poor.
16	Michael Tuohy, 418 Third street, S. E.	4	....	Fair.
16	Pat Hallaran, 746 Sixth street, S. E.	5	....	Stables, poor; animals, fair.
16	Bert Dalton, Georgia avenue, S. E.	5	....	Animals, poor.
16	Mr. Suit, Georgia avenue, S. E.	1	....	Do.
16	Mr. Cox, Eleventh street, S. E.	1	....	Do.
16	Mrs. Mahoney, I street, between Twelfth and Thirteenth streets, S. E.	5	....	Do.
16	Samuel Schwartz, Thirteenth and L streets, S. E.	5	....	Animals, fair.
16	James Thomas, 1318 Georgia avenue, S. E.	6	....	Do.
16	Mr. Doonan, Georgia avenue, S. E.	2	....	Do.
16	John Schwartsman, Thirteenth and D sts., S. E.	2	....	Fair.
16	Pat Henry Hurley, corner Fourteenth and H streets, S. E.	11	....	Poor.
16	Mrs. Wilson, 1237 F street, N. E.	4	....	Stables, poor; animals, fair.
17	Miss Kirton, D st., between Eighth and Ninth streets, N. E.	4	....	Animals, poor.
17	James Childs, Sixth between Twelfth and Thirteenth streets, N. E.	1	....	Do.
17	Thomas McIntyre, 1320 B street, N. E.	3	....	Poor.
17	James Grey, 217 Fourteenth street, N. E.	2	....	Do.
17	James Elder, 1233 Maryland avenue, N. E.	2	1sus.	Do.
17	Mary Green, 216 E street, N. E.	1	....	Animals, poor.
17	Mr. Dwyer, Second street near G, N. E.	1	....	Animals, fair.
17	Thomas Welsh, 405 Second street, N. E.	1	....	Poor.
17	Mrs. Merritt, corner C street and Massachusetts avenue, N. E.	2	....	Do.
17	Dennis Harrison, corner Thirteenth and B streets, N. E.	1	....	Do.
17	Richard Bruce, corner Thirteenth and B st., N. E.	1	....	Do.
18	James Lewis, Bladensburgh road, N. E.	11	....	Stables, poor; animals, fair.
18	James Brown, Bladensburgh road, N. E.	4	....	Stables, fair; animals, poor.
	Thomas I. Samuels, Bladensburgh road, N. E.	1	....	Poor.
	Officer Slack, Bladensburgh road, N. E.	10	....	Animals, poor.
18	Thomas Fenwick, near Ivy City, N. E.	2	....	Poor.
18	Mrs. C. M. McCarty, near Mount Olivet Cemetery, N. E.	5	1c.	Stables, poor; animals, fair.
18	Mr. Sewilski, Bladensburgh road, N. E.	8	....	Poor.

Inspections in the District of Columbia—Continued.

Day of month.	Name of owner or person in charge and location of stable.	No. of cattle.	No. with lung-plague.	Condition of stables and animals.
	Inspections by W. H. Rose—Continued.			
1886.				
June [illegible]	William Hoover, Bladensburgh road, N. E	2	....	Poor.
[illegible]	Mr. Firestein, Hickey's lane, N. E	1	....	Fair.
[illegible]	Charles Wayhousen, Hickey's lane, N. E	6	....	Do.
[illegible]	John Boyle, Hickey's lane, N. E	16	....	Stables, poor; animals fair.
[illegible]	Kelly, Crosby & Co., Palmer lane, N. E	18	....	Fair.
[illegible]	Dr. Palmer, Palmer lane, N. E	2	....	Do.
[illegible]	Deaf and Dumb Asylum, Kendall Green, N. E	8	....	Do.
[illegible]	Mrs. Mulcahey, Bladensburgh road, N. E	6	....	Animals, fair.
[illegible]	Little Sisters of the Poor, Bladensburgh road, N. E	3	....	Do.
[illegible]	Cornelius Curtain, Third street, between K and L streets, N. E	8	....	Fair.
[illegible]	Mrs. Johannah [illegible], Fourth street and Boundary, N. E	5	....	Animals, fair.
[illegible]	Conrad [illegible], corner Fifth and L streets, N. E	3	....	Fair.
[illegible]	Thomas [illegible], [illegible] Fifth street, N. E	2	....	Do.
[illegible]	Thomas Donahue, I street, between Sixth and Seventh, N. E	6	....	Poor.
[illegible]	Richard [illegible], [illegible] M street, N. E	4	....	Animals, fair.
[illegible]	Mrs. Dun, F street, near First street, N. W	1	....	Do.
[illegible]	Mrs. Stark, F street, near First street, N. W	1	....	Do.
[illegible]	Mrs. James Lyons, First street, near H, N. E	2	....	Do.
[illegible]	Mr. Murphy, F street, between Third and Fourth streets, N. E	1	....	Do.
[illegible]	Mr. A. [illegible], Jackson alley, N. E	2	....	Do.
[illegible]	Mrs. [illegible], H street, near First street, N. E	2	....	Animals, poor.
[illegible]	[illegible], [illegible] Fourth street, N. E	2	....	Fair.
[illegible]	[illegible] Kane, [illegible] street, between H and I, N. E	1	....	Animals, fair.
[illegible]	[illegible] Stadler, corner [illegible] and H streets, N. E	1	....	Fair.
[illegible]	[illegible], [illegible] H street, N. E	1	....	Animals, fair.
[illegible]	[illegible], G street, between Sixth and Seventh streets, N. E	1	....	Do.
[illegible]	[illegible], [illegible] Tenth street, N. E	2	....	Stables, poor; animals fair.
[illegible]	[illegible], [illegible] Seventh street, N. E	3	....	Animals, fair.
[illegible]	[illegible], corner Jackson alley	4	....	Do.
[illegible]	[illegible], corner [illegible] and Boundary, N. E	1	....	Fair.
[illegible]	[illegible], [illegible] Fourth street, N. E	3	....	Animals fair.
[illegible]	[illegible], corner Delaware avenue and [illegible], N. E	8	....	Fair.
[illegible]	[illegible], [illegible] street, N. E	6	....	Do.
[illegible]	[illegible], corner [illegible] and I streets, N. E	1	1c.	Stables, poor; animals fair.
[illegible]	[illegible], corner [illegible] and Connecticut avenue	1	....	Fair.
[illegible]	[illegible], corner [illegible] and N streets	2	....	Animals, fair.
[illegible]	[illegible], Columbia avenue, near Twenty-[illegible] street	10	....	Stables, poor; animals fair.
[illegible]	[illegible], Philip's alley	1	....	Animals, fair.
[illegible]	[illegible], corner [illegible] and M streets	2	....	Animals, poor.
[illegible]	[illegible], corner [illegible] and M streets	2	....	Do.
[illegible]	[illegible], [illegible] between Twenty-fourth and [illegible] streets	2	....	Poor.
[illegible]	[illegible], corner Connecticut avenue and S street	2	....	Animals, fair.
[illegible]	[illegible] Woods	5	....	Fair.
[illegible]	[illegible] Nineteenth street	2	....	Poor.
[illegible]	[illegible] Woods	8	1c.	Do.
[illegible]	[illegible] and Boundary	10	....	Animals, poor.
[illegible]	[illegible] S street	6	1c.	Do.
[illegible]	[illegible] street	9	....	Fair.
[illegible]	[illegible] street	2	....	Do.
[illegible]	[illegible] Nineteenth street	2	....	Stables, poor; animals fair.
[illegible]	[illegible] Nineteenth street	3	....	Do.
[illegible]	[illegible], Columbia avenue	3	....	Fair.
[illegible]	[illegible], Columbia avenue	9	....	Stables, poor; animals fair.
[illegible]	[illegible], Columbia avenue	1	....	Animals, fair.
[illegible]	[illegible], Columbia avenue	2	....	Stables, clean; animals good.
[illegible]	[illegible]	14	....	Stables, clean; animals fair.
	[illegible]	27	....	Stables, fair; animals poor.

Inspections in the District of Columbia—Continued.

Day of month.	Name of owner or person in charge and location of stable.	No. of cattle.	No. with lung-plague.	Condition of stables and animals.
	Inspections by W. H. Rose—Continued.			
1886. June 24	Mr. Deane, Columbia avenue and Boundary	2		Stables, clean; animals, fair.
24	Mrs. McNamnee, P street between Twentieth and Twenty-first streets, N. W.	2		Stable, foul; animals, poor.
24	Mrs. Butler, Columbia avenue and Boundary, N. W.	1		Fair.
25	Mrs. McKeever, Boundary, between Sixteenth and Seventeenth streets, N. W.	8		Stables, poor; animals, fair.
25	Mrs. Lewiston, Champagne avenue, N. W	1		Poor.
25	Mrs. Smith, Champagne avenue, N. W	1		Do.
25	Thos. Cullerton, Champagne avenue, N. W	4		Stables, poor; animals, fair.
25	George Door, Champagne avenue, N. W	7	1c.	Fair.
25	Mrs. M. Conners, Champagne avenue, N. W	24	2c.	Stables, foul; animals, poor.
25	Mr. Casey, 1428 H street, N. W	9		Fair.
25	Thos. Fitz, 1256 Twenty-third street, N. W	4		Poor.
25	Mrs. Flaherty, 24th street, near M street, N. W	2		Stables, poor; animals, fair.
25	Daniel Hoonan, 1252 Twenty-third street, N. W	2	2	Do.
25	Jas. Hollaran, 1254 Twenty-third street, N. W	1		Fair.
25	Columbia Hospital, Pennsylvania avenue between 24th and 25th streets, N. W.	2		Stables, clean; animals, fair.
28	Jeremiah Downey, 621 I street, S. W	6		Animals, poor.
28	Mrs. C. Flynn, 1006 Sixth street, S. W	6	1 sus.	Fair.
28	Jno. Flaherty, 624 K street, S. W	2		Stables, foul; animals, fair.
28	Mrs. Campbell, South Capitol street, S. W	1		Poor.
28	Mrs. Rheagan, Third street, S. W	2	1	Do.
28	Thos. McIrath, 709 Second street, S. W	8		Animals, fair.
28	Mary Connors, 120 F street, S. W	8		Do.
28	Mrs. Mangen, 612 Second street, S. W	1		Do.
28	Mrs. Guynon, 614 Second street, S. W	1		Do.
28	Mrs. M. Maloney, 624 Second street, S. W	2		Do.
28	Pat Donohue, 125 F street, S. W	4		Stables, poor; animals, fair.
28	Jno. Downey, Limerick avenue and Third street, S. W.	8		Do.
28	Mr. Brown, E and South Capitol streets, S. W	1		Stables, fair; animals, poor.
28	Fred. Springman, corner D and South Capitol streets, S. W.	1		Fair.
30	Calvin Shoomaker, 2088 Seventh street N. W	2		Animals, poor.
30	Mrs. Reice, 2040 Seventh street, N. W	2		Animals, fair.
30	John Green, 2219 Seventh street, N. W	1		Stables, poor; animals, fair.
30	Mrs. Federline, Seventh street, N. W	2		Do.
30	Mrs. Pon Dexter, Seventh street, N. W	1		Do.
30	Mrs. B. Meyers, Seventh street, N. W	8		Stables, fair; animals, poor.
30	James A. McCauley, corner Summer avenue and Seventh street.	2		Fair.
30	Dennis Murphy, Ninth street, north of Boundary	10		Do.
30	Bridget White, Seventh street.	5		Poor.
30	Mary Morrissey, Seventh street, near Boundary	13		Do.
30	Robert Barrett, corner Whitney avenue and Seventh street.	8		Stables, poor; animals, fair.
July 7	Mrs. Pernor, corner Whitney avenue and Seventh street.	1		Animals, fair.
7	Mrs. May, Whitney avenue and Seventh street	1		Do.
7	Mr. O'Shea, Ninth street, near Commons	23		Animals, very poor.
7	H. Gaskin	1		Stables, clean; animals, poor.
7	Soldiers' Home, Ninth street, near Commons	75		Animals, poor.
7	Mr. Shultz, Seventh street.	1		Animals, fair.
7	Mr. Widmeyer, Seventh street	1		Do.
7	Scheutzen Park, Ninth street, near Whitney	2		Stables, fair; animals, fair.
7	Mrs. C. Chinn, Ninth street, Whitney	9		Animals, very poor.
7	Mrs. W. Harrison, corner Seventh street and Soldiers' Home.	2		Fair.
8	A. G. Mount, Ninth street, N. W	36		Do.
8	Thomas Smallwood, 14th street (extended)	2		Animals, poor.
8	Mr. Davis, north of Boundary	3		Animals, fair.
8	Mrs. Pickston, near Scheutzen Park	1		Animal, very poor.

Inspections in the District of Columbia—Continued.

Day of month.	Name of owner or person in charge and location of stable.	No. of cattle.	No. with lung-plague.	Condition of stables and animals.
	Inspections by W. H. Rose—Continued.			
1886. July 8	Mr. Sticklein, opposite Scheutzen Park	1		Animals, very poor.
8	E. O. Scagg, opposite Scheutzen Park	1		Animal, fair.
8	Mrs. Connors, opposite Scheutzen Park	1		Do.
8	F. Westermeyer, opposite Scheutzen Park	1		Do.
8	Mr. Berry, near Whitney avenue	6		Do.
8	William McKay, Ninth street, N. W	11		Animals, fair.
8	Mrs. B. Keefe, Ninth street, N. W	6		Poor.
8	Leo. Shmeltze, Ninth street, N. W	4		Fair.
8	Mrs. Thompson, Ninth street, N. W	2		Poor.
8	Mrs. Tobin Conners, Ninth street, N. W	1		Do.
8	Nicholas Beck, Ninth street, N. W.	4		Stables, poor; animals, fair.
8	John Driscoll, Ninth street, N. W	2		Do.
8	Mr. Rupert, Ninth street, N. W	5		Stables, poor; animals, poor.
8	John Lynch, Grant avenue, N. W	4		Stables, poor; animals, fair.
8	Mrs. Sullivan, Grant avenue, N. W	2	1a.	Poor.
8	Thomas Dunnegan, Grant avenue, N. W	8	2c.	Stables, fair; animals, poor.
10	H. Daley, northwest of Boundary	4		Poor.
10	John Howard, northwest of Boundary	5		Animals, fair.
10	Mrs. Shea, northwest of Boundary	8		Do.
10	Michael Shugrue, northwest of Boundary	20		Poor.
10	Thomas Gerry, northwest of Boundary	3		Animals, fair.
10	James Allman, northwest of Boundary	23		Animals, poor.
10	Little Soloman, northwest of Boundary	6		Do.
10	Curtis I. Gilbert, northwest of Boundary	10		Stables, poor; animals, fair.
10	Mr. Pfifering, northwest of Boundary	5		Animals, fair.
10	Big Soloman, northwest of Boundary	17		Do.
10	William Chord, northwest of Boundary	11		Fair.
10	John Connell, northwest of Boundary	10		Stables, poor; animals, fair.
10	James Carr, northwest of Boundary	2		Do.
10	Michael Burke, northwest of Boundary	8		Poor.
10	Wm. Dudley, Morris lane	1		Animals, fair.
10	Mr. Seinor, Morris lane	1		Do.
10	John Moore, Morris lane	2		Do.
10	Martha Tibbs, northwest of Boundary	1		Stables, poor; animals, fair.
10	Wm. Butler, northwest of Boundary	1		Poor.
10	Wm. Addison, northwest of Boundary	2		Stables, poor; animals, fair.
10	Mrs. Kate Lucas, northwest of Boundary	8		Poor.
10	Louis Davis, northwest of Boundary	8		Do.
10	Mr. Banks, northwest of Boundary	1		Do.
12	Mr. White, Old Bladensburgh Road	2		Animals, fair.
12	Mrs. Mary Bresnahan, Glenwood road	1		Do.
12	Mrs. Emma Beale, Glenwood road	1		Fair.
12	Daniel Allman, Glenwood road	22		Do.
12	H. Hartung, Glenwood road	17		Fair.
12	Mrs. Flavin, Glenwood road	3		Poor.
12	Mrs. McCarthy, Glenwood road	2		Animals, fair.
12	John Merritt, Glenwood road	2		Poor.
12	Patrick Cudmore, Glenwood road	12		Animals, poor.
12	Almshouse, northeast of Boundary	10		Fair.
14	Mrs. Roach, Edgewood	13		Do.
14	Moses Maddy, Edgewood	4		Stables, poor; animals, very poor.
14	Mrs. Sprague, Edgewood	2		Fair.
14	Michael O'Connor, Edgewood	10	1c.	Do.
15	Mr. Carmack, Bladensburgh road	6		Stables, fair; animals, poor.
15	Reform School, Bladensburgh road	11		Do.
15	Mr. Carlton, Bladensburgh road	16		Stables, clean; animals, fair.
15	Mr. Bradshaw, Bunker Hill	10		Animals, poor.
15	Mrs. Matthews, Bunker Hill	15		Do.
15	Samuel Cease, Bunker Hill	14		Animals, fair.
15	John Lacey, north of Brentwood road	8		Poor.
15	Mr. Welsh, north of Brentwood road	1		Fair.
15	Isaac Quackenbush, north of Brentwood road	21		Stables, fair; animals, good.

Inspections in the District of Columbia—Continued.

Day of month.	Name of owner or person in charge and location of stable.	No. of cattle.	No. with lung-plague.	Condition of stables and animals.
	Inspections by W. H. Rose—Continued.			
1886.				
July 15	Albert Wall, north of Brentwood road	13	....	Poor.
15	Albert Gutlip, north of Brentwood road	1	....	Fair.
15	John Sardou, north of Brentwood road	1	....	Do.
15	James Dalgleish, north of Brentwood road	1	....	Do.
15	John Small, north of Brentwood road	1	....	Do.
15	Mr. Frank, north of Brentwood road	1	....	Do.
15	Mr. Hillner, north of Brentwood road	1	....	Do.
15	Alfred Heitmuller, north of Brentwood road	11	....	Stables, poor; animals, fair.
15	Moses Stearman, north of Brentwood road	8	....	Do.
15	Mr. Murphy, cor. Twenty-second and D streets	1	....	Poor.
16	Mrs. Mary Fox, near corner 22d and D sts., N. W.	1	....	Stables poor; animals, fair.
16	Miss McLaughlin, 118 G street, N. W	2	....	Fair.
16	Mrs. Elizabeth Chism, 731 23d street, N. W	3	....	Stables, poor; animals, fair.
16	Washington Payton, New York avenue, near Twenty-first street, N. W.	1	....	Stables, foul; animals, poor.
16	Jno. K. Pfiel, B street, near 22d street, N. W	1	....	Fair.
16	Sisters Infant Asylum, corner Twenty-fourth and K streets, N. W.	3	....	Stables, poor; animals, poor.
16	Mrs. Townley, E and 21st streets, N. W	2	....	Do.
16	Mrs. E. Kendall, C, near Twenty-first st., N. W.	2	....	Do.
16	Pat Donohue, Twenty-second and D sts., N. W.	1	....	Do.
16	United States Observatory, 23d and E sts., N. W.	1	....	Stables, clean; animals, fair.
16	John Hughes, 924 Twenty-seventh st., N. W	3	....	Stables, poor; animals, fair.
16	Mrs. Wm. McCullom, Hughes alley, N. W	2	....	Do.
17	Mr. Windon, Hughes alley, N. W	1	....	Do.
17	Mary Hart, corner Second and I streets, S. E	1	....	Animals, fair.
17	Mr. Waters, corner New Jersey avenue and K street, S. E.	1	....	Do.
17	Mrs. Griffin, Third st. and Virginia ave., S. E	2	....	Animals, poor.
17	Henry Henson, corner Fourth and G sts., S. E	1	....	Animals, fair.
17	Benj. Romer, near S. Capitol street, S. E	1	....	Animals, poor.
17	Dennis Bailey, near S. Capitol street, S. E	1	....	Animals, fair.
17	Emmitt Hunt, near First street, S. E	1	....	Do.
17	Mr. Smith, S. Capitol street, between M and N streets, S. E.	1	....	Do.
17	John Brickley, 1000 M street, S. E	2	....	Do.
17	Mr. Bailey, N street, near First street, S. E	1	....	Stables, poor; animals, fair.
17	A. & Wm. Richards, South Capitol street, near First street, S. E.	5	....	Animals, fair.
17	Chas. Sanderson, Seventh street, between L and M streets, S. E.	1	....	Animals, poor.
17	Mr. Sullivan, corner Second and E. sts., S. E	3	....	Fair.
17	Dr. Smith, 4th street, near Virginia ave., S. E	2	1c.	Animals, fair.
17	Mrs. Meade, Virginia ave., near 3d street, S. E	1	....	Do.
17	Philip Boil, Virginia ave., near 4th street, S. E	1	....	Animals, poor.
17	Henry Rogers, H street, near First street, S. E	1	....	Animals, good.
17	A. Richardson, corner Third street and Virginia avenue, S. E.	1	....	Animals, fair.
17	Mr. Farren, 212 N street, S. E	2	....	Stables, poor; animals, fair.
17	United States navy-yard, foot of Eighth st., S. E	5	....	Fair.
19	Mrs. Francis Baylor, 325 Eighth street, N. E	4	....	Poor.
19	Mrs. Edward Bresnahan, 816 C street, N. E	3	1a.	Do.
19	Wm. George, 619 B street, N. E	2	....	Do.
19	Providence Hospital, corner Second and D sts., N. E.	2	....	Stables, clean; animals, fair.
19	Thos. Healy, 617 A street, N. E	2	....	Poor.
19	Thos. Noone, 22 Fifth street, N. E	2	1c.	Do.
19	Mrs. Clancy, 18 Fifth street, N. E	2	....	Do.
19	Thos. O'Brien, 11 D street, N. E	1	....	Do.
19	Mrs. Ellen Flynn, 105 Eleventh street, N. E	3	1c.	Do.
19	Catharine Lynch, 11 Seventh street, N. E	2	Sus.	Stables, poor; animals, fair.
19	Bridget Reilly, Ninth street, between D and E streets, N. E.	4	....	Poor.
19	Pat Kalicher, 810 D street, N. E	6	1c.	Stables, clean; animals, poor.
19	Pat Connell, 1945 Twelfth street, N. E	5	....	Fair.

Inspections in the District of Columbia—Continued.

Day of month.	Name of owner or person in charge and location of stable.	Size of stable.	Size within limits prescribed.	Condition of stable and animals.
	Inspections by W. H. [illegible]—Continued.			
1884.				
Aug. 11	John W. Brown, Soldiers' Home road			Animals fair.
11	Mr. Roberts, Soldiers' Home road			Do.
11	F. [illegible], Soldiers' Home road			Do.
[illegible]	Thomas Dunn, near Ninth street, N. W.			Do.
[illegible]	August Edmunds, near Ninth street, N. W.			Do.
[illegible]	Mr. Cain, near Fourteenth street extended			Animals poor.
[illegible]	Alex Cruickshank, Huron street, Mount Pleasant			Do.
[illegible]	Mr. Sprague, Columbia avenue			Animals fair.
[illegible]	Mr. C. Kain, Mount Pleasant			Do.
[illegible]	Charles King, Mount Pleasant			Animals poor.
[illegible]	Robert Hawton, Mount Pleasant			Do.
[illegible]	John Summers, Mount Pleasant			Do.
[illegible]	[illegible], Fourteenth street extended			Animals fair.
[illegible]	Mr. [illegible], Mount Pleasant			Do.
[illegible]	Mr. Thomas [illegible], Mount Pleasant			Do.
[illegible]	William [illegible] & Son, Mount Pleasant			Do.
[illegible]	Mr. Sullivan, Mount Pleasant			Do.
[illegible]	Mr. Carroll, Mount Pleasant			Do.
[illegible]	Mr. [illegible], north of Boundary			Animals poor.
[illegible]	Mr. Lawler, north of Boundary			Fair.
[illegible]	L. Cullinan, Jackson alley, N. E.			Do.
[illegible]	Mrs. Crane, Jackson alley, N. E.			Stables poor, animals fair.
[illegible]	Mrs. Mary Powell, Jackson alley, N. E.			Poor.
[illegible]	Henry Bandy, E street, N. E.			Do.
[illegible]	Mrs. M. Farrell, [illegible] street, N. E.			Animals fair.
[illegible]	Mrs. M. Mahoney, [illegible] street, N. E.			Poor.
[illegible]	John Liverpool, Uniontown			Animals fair.
[illegible]	Henry Harvey, Uniontown			Do.
[illegible]	Mr. Hoadley, south of Uniontown			Do.
17	Insane Asylum, south of Uniontown	[illegible]		Stables good, animals fair.
17	Frank Walker, south of Uniontown			Fair.
17	I. W. Payne, south of Uniontown			Poor.
17	Joseph Waller, south of Uniontown			Animals poor.
17	Samuel Smith, south of Uniontown			Stables poor, animals fair.
17	Mrs. Downey, Uniontown			Animals fair.
17	Mrs. Joseph Karr, Uniontown			Do.
17	Geo. F. Pyles, Uniontown			Do.
17	Mr. Tasy, Uniontown			Animals poor.
17	Geo. Smallwood, Garfield			Animals fair.
17	Wm. Curran, Garfield			Do.
17	Mrs. Henson, Garfield			Do.
17	Gill Thomas, Uniontown			Fair.
18	Mr. Thomas, Uniontown			Animals fair.
18	Mr. Roary, Uniontown			Do.
18	C. R. Smith, Uniontown			Do.
18	Mrs. Mosser, Uniontown			Do.
18	Marden King, Uniontown			Do.
18	Mrs. Lee, Uniontown			Do.
18	Wm. King, Uniontown			Do.
18	Mr. Hanes, Uniontown			Do.
18	Joseph Fenx, Uniontown			Do.
18	Mr. Bevins, Uniontown			Do.
18	Mr. Humphrey, Uniontown			Fair.
19	Mr. Allen, Uniontown			Animals fair.
19	Henry Anderson, Uniontown			Do.
19	John H. Anderson, Uniontown			Do.
19	T. J. Anderson, Uniontown			Do.
19	Allen Anderson, Uniontown			Do.
19	Mr. Beck, Uniontown			Do.
19	Mr. Pitcher, Uniontown			Animals fair.
18	Fred. Douglas, Uniontown			Do.
19	Dr. Green, Uniontown			Do.
19	Mrs. Clements, Uniontown			Stables fair.
19	Mr. Pitts, Uniontown			Animals fair.
19	William Fastnaught, Uniontown			Do.
18	Mr. Grimes, Uniontown			Poor.
18	Mr. Bo[illegible], S. E. of Uniontown			Animals fair.
18	J. Harrington, S. E. of Uniontown			Do.
				Stables poor, animals [illegible].
18	Mr. Nevall, S. E. of Uniontown			Do.
				Stables fair, animals [illegible].
18	German Orphans' Asylum, S. E. of Uniontown			Do.

Inspections in the District of Columbia—Continued.

Day of month.	Name of owner or person in charge and location of stable.	No. of cattle.	No. with lung-plague.	Condition of stables and animals.
	Inspections by W. H. Rose—Continued.			
1886.				
Aug. 18	Phil. Simpson, Marlborough road	9	....	Animals, poor.
18	Schure & Simpson, Marlborough road	1	....	Animals, fair.
18	Mr. Frye, Marlborough road	25	....	Fair.
18	Mr. Golden, Good Hope Hill	1	....	Animals, fair.
[illegible]	Mr. C. Smith, near Loftborough road	26	....	
[illegible]	Joseph Davis, near Loftborough road	29	....	Animals, poor.
[illegible]	Mr. Rosenbush, near Loftborough road	8	....	
[illegible]	L. P. Hasel, near Loftborough road	6	....	
[illegible]	Godfrey Goebel, near Loftborough road	8	....	
[illegible]	Sec. Whitney, near Tenallytown	2	....	
[illegible]	William Woodie, Chain Bridge road	8	....	Animals, poor.
[illegible]	Mr. Freeman, Conduit road	5	....	Animals, fair.
[illegible]	John Holland, Chain Bridge road	8	....	Do.
[illegible]	Charles Weaver, Chain Bridge road	16	....	Do.
[illegible]	Michael Shugrue, Conduit road	11	....	Fair.
[illegible]	Charles McCarty, Conduit road	8	....	Animals, fair.
[illegible]	Pat. Kelly, Warren street, Georgetown	1	....	Animals, poor.
[illegible]	John Donohue, Lofborough road	18	....	Fair.
[illegible]	Jerry Collins, Thirty-sixth street, Georgetown	2	....	Animals, fair.
[illegible]	Mrs. Canon, Congress street, Georgetown	1	....	Do.
[illegible]	Georgetown College, Fayette street, Georgetown.	13	....	Do.
[illegible]	Academy of the Visitation, Fayette street, Georgetown.	12	....	Do.
[illegible]	Daniel O'Connor, near Third street, Georgetown.	6	....	Stables, fair; animals poor.
[illegible]	John Brislaham, High street, Georgetown	8	....	Animals, poor.
[illegible]	Mrs. Mahal, O street, Georgetown	3	....	Animals, fair.
[illegible]	Pat Connors, O street, Georgetown	1	....	Do.
[illegible]	Mrs. Anna Bateman, corner Third street, Georgetown	3	....	Do.
[illegible]	John May, Dunbarton avenue, Georgetown	3	....	Stables, poor; animals fair.
[illegible]	Mrs. Annie Selox, Dunbarton avenue, Georgetown	4	....	Animals, fair.
[illegible]	Mrs. Baker, High street, Georgetown	1	....	Do.
[illegible]	Mrs. Kleman, Creek lane, Georgetown	2	....	Do.
[illegible]	Mr. Folke, Creek lane, Georgetown	1	....	Do.
[illegible]	John Callahan, Market lane, Georgetown	10	....	Do.
[illegible]	Dr. Richards, Georgetown	1	....	Do.
[illegible]	Mrs. Mankins, Thirty-fifth street, Georgetown	1	....	Do.
[illegible]	Mrs. Holden, Fifth street, Georgetown	2	....	Do.
[illegible]	Mrs. Lee, Thirty-fifth street, Georgetown	4	....	Do.
[illegible]	Benj. Johnson, Warren street, Georgetown	8	....	Do.
[illegible]	Mrs. Devine, Georgetown	1	....	Do.
[illegible]	Charles Knight, Prospect street, Georgetown	1	....	Do.
[illegible]	Richard Hamil, Bridge street, Georgetown	1	....	Do.
[illegible]	Mr. Wagner, corner Market and O streets, Georgetown.	1	....	Do.
[illegible]	Mrs. Catharine Hurley, O street, Georgetown.	3	....	Animals, poor.
[illegible]	Mrs. Daly, Second street, Georgetown	1	....	Animal, fair.
[illegible]	John Harrigan, Thirty-sixth street, Georgetown.	6	....	Animals, poor.
[illegible]	Daniel Garner, Lincoln street, Georgetown	3	....	Animals, fair.
[illegible]	Peter Donohue, Warren street, Georgetown	2	....	Do.
[illegible]	Mrs. Reves, Road street, Georgetown	1	....	Do.
[illegible]	Mr. Hogan, Warren street, Georgetown	1	....	Do.
[illegible]	Mrs. Driscoll, Warren street, Georgetown	1	....	
[illegible]	Louis Alexander, Foxhall road	8	....	
[illegible]	John Quinn, Foxhall road	2	....	
[illegible]	Capt. W. A. Maddox, Foxhall road	11	....	
[illegible]	Mr. E. Andrews, Tennallytown	21	....	
[illegible]	Mrs. Thomas Hume, Tennallytown	8	....	
[illegible]	Fred Bengeiter, Tennallytown	16	....	
[illegible]	Samuel Burrows, River road	20	....	
[illegible]	Mrs. Nune, Tennallytown road	2	....	
[illegible]	Mr. Ryan, Tennallytown road	5	....	
[illegible]	Thomas Frene, Tennallytown road	6	....	
[illegible]	Nicholas Connelly, Tennallytown road	7	....	
[illegible]	Jacob Kenally, Tennallytown road	1	....	
[illegible]	William McLean, Tennallytown road	2	....	
[illegible]	George Kenally, Tennallytown road	3	....	
[illegible]	John Brown, Conduit and Canal road	1	....	
[illegible]	John Beck, Canal road	14	....	Animal, fair.
[illegible]	Mr. Rice, Chain Bridge road	7	....	Poor.
[illegible]	Mr. May, Conduit road	19	....	Animals, fair.
		[illegible]	....	Fair.

Inspections in the District of Columbia—Continued.

Day of month.	Name of owner or person in charge and location of stable.	No. of cattle.	No. with lung-plague.	Condition of stables and animals.
	Inspections by W. H. Rose—Continued.			
1886.				
Aug. 20	Thomas Ready, Conduit	3		Fair.
20	Timothy O'Neal, Conduit	13		Animals, fair.
20	William H. Allder, Conduit	13		Fair.
20	James Shugrue, Conduit	2		Do.
20	Fred. Wetzel, Conduit	12		Animals, fair.
20	Thomas Sullivan, Conduit	12		Animals, poor.

Inspections in Kentucky.

Day of month.	Name of owner or person in charge and location of stable.	No. of cattle.	No. with lung-plague.	Condition of stables and animals.
	Inspections by W. H. Wray, V. S.			
1886.				
Feb. 18	F. Parks, Cynthiana, Harrison County	115		Stables dangerous.
19	Pat Fitzpatrick, Cynthiana, Harrison County	10		
Mar. 17	Wm. T. Handy, Cynthiana, Harrison County	10	4	
17	Mrs. Roberts, Cynthiana, Harrison County	1	1	
18	Irving Cox, Cynthiana, Harrison County	2	2	
19	Est. J. K. Lake, Cynthiana, Harrison County	72	7	
20	F. Sullivan, Cynthiana, Harrison County	2		
20	James Brenan, Cynthiana, Harrison County	1		
20	Mrs. D. Shea, Cynthiana, Harrison County	3		
20	W. E. Slade, Cynthiana, Harrison County	3		
20	T. J. Megibben, Cynthiana, Harrison County	4		
20	James Doyle, Cynthiana, Harrison County	1		
20	F. Reynolds, Cynthiana, Harrison County	2		
20	John Cronin, Cynthiana, Harrison County	1		
20	Mrs. Stewart, Cynthiana, Harrison County	1		
20	A. W. Lydick, Cynthiana, Harrison County	1		
20	M. Bridwell, Cynthiana, Harrison County	4		
20	J. T. Martin, Cynthiana, Harrison County	1		
May 3	Frank Craig, Berry Station, Harrison County	1	1	
4	Patrick Fitzpatrick, Cynthiana, Harrison County	10		

Inspections in Illinois.

Day of month.	Name of owner or person in charge and location of stable.	No. of cattle.	No. with lung-plague.	Condition of stables and animals.
	Inspections by Murray & Rose, V. S.			
1886.				
Sept. 30	P. H. Rice, near Western avenue, Chicago, Cook County.	207	2a.	Stable, poor; animals, fat.
Oct. 1	Michael Kalb, Whisky Point road, Cook County.	25		Animals, poor.
1	Mr. Peterson, Whisky Point road, Cook County.	44	1c.	Do.
2	Elston road, Cook County	45		Do.
2	Daniel Beckam, Elston road, Cook County	75	1a.	Do.
4	John Brennock & Co., Globe Station, Indiana			
	Inspections by Trumbower & Rose, V. S.			
1	Riverdale Distillery Co., Riverdale Station, Cook County.	1013		Good.
2	Mr. Kern, Villa Ridge, Cook County	2	1c.	
2	William Zemay, Villa Ridge, Cook County	3	1c.	
2	Elvey Brothers, Villa Ridge, Cook County	1		Animal, good.
2	Louis Webb, Villa Ridge, Cook County	1	1c.	Animal, fair.
2	Silas Palmer, Villa Ridge, Cook County	9	2c.	Do.
2	Ira L. Harvey, Villa Ridge, Cook County	5		Good.
2	J. Quinn, Villa Ridge, Cook County	50	3	Animals, fair.
	Inspections by H. W. Rowland, V. S.			
Sept. 29	Phœnix Distilleries, Chicago, Cook County	2		
29	Shoefeltz Distilleries, Chicago, Cook County			
	Inspections by Rowland & Hawk, V. S.			
2	On Commons, Chicago, Cook County		1	Animal, fair.
2	On Commons, Chicago, Cook County	40		Do.
2	W. Wolf, Lake avenue, near Chicago	10		Do.
2	M. Foster, near Chicago	4		Do.

Inspections in Illinois—Continued.

Day of month.	Name of owner or person in charge and location of stable.	No. of cattle.	No. with lung-plague.	Condition of stables and animals.
	Inspections by Rowland and Hawk—Continued.			
1886.				
Sept. 2	Mike Calk, Chicago avenue	34	....	
2	On the Commons, near Chicago	70	....	Animals, fair.
2	T. J. Sprague, Kidsey avenue, near Chicago	17	....	Do.
2	Miss Titman, near Chicago	6	....	Do.
2	M. Hults, California, Chicago	12	....	Do.
4	M. Noebe, Wepple street, Chicago	5	....	Do.
4	Mrs. Burns, Park avenue and Stanton street	4	....	Do.
4	M. Raleigh, Hoen and Washington streets	1	....	Do.
4	Mrs. Sherman, Hoen and Washington streets	1	....	Do.
Oct. 4	M. Chale, Lincoln and Western streets, Chicago	1	....	Fair.
4	M. Sherwood, near Chicago, Chicago	1	....	Animal, fair.
4	Dr. Newman, corner Ashland and Monroe streets, Chicago.	1	....	Fair.
4	Geo. Wolf, Wilcox avenue, Chicago	1	....	Do.
4	D. Marrett, corner Lincoln and Monroe streets, Chicago.	1	....	Do.
4	M. Pinkerton, Ashton street, Chicago	1	....	Do.
4	M. Jones, Madison avenue, Chicago	1	....	Do.
4	Dr. Davis, Lincoln and Adams streets, Chicago	1	....	Do.
4	M. Bullex, Warren avenue, Chicago	1	....	Do.
4	Mrs. Richard, Lincoln and Western streets, Chicago.	1	....	Do.
4	Mr. Carpenter, West street, Chicago	1	....	Do.
4	Mr. Chamberlain, 515 Adams street, Chicago	1	....	Do.
4	Mr. Windern, Irving avenue, Chicago	1	....	Do.
4	M. Holden, Clina street, Chicago	1	....	Do.
4	M. Gardner, Lincoln and Western streets, Chicago.	1	....	Do.
4	D. S. Waldon, near Chicago, Chicago	18	....	Do.
4	D. Aber, Irving avenue, Chicago	35	....	Do.
4	Unknown, Chicago and California streets, Chicago.	13	....	Do.
4	M. Foot, 1159 Madison auenue, Chicago	1	....	Do.
4	Mrs. Chamberlain, Park avenue and Stanton street, Chicago.	6	....	Do.
4	Unknown, 737 Adams street, Chicago	1	....	Do.
4	M. Parker, Jackson street, Chicago	29	....	Do.
4	J. Durant, Wood street, Chicago	1	....	Do.
4	McCleashe, Adams and Clina streets, Chicago	1	....	Do.
5	Unknown, Chicago	75	....	Do.
5	John Reily, 104 Fairfield avenue, Chicago	6	....	Do.
5	M. Hannan, Park avenue, near Washington street, Chicago.	3	....	Do.
5	Pat. Burns, Washington avenue, Chicago.	6	....	Do.
5	I. Miller, Artesian and Fulton streets, Chicago	8	....	Do.
5	Dan Mullen, Chicago	1	....	Animal, poor.
6	On Prairies, California avenue, Chicago	70	....	Animals, fair.
	Inspections by Drs. Murray and Rose.			
5	Union Stock-Yards, South Thirty-ninth street, Chicago, Ill.	....	....	
5	Union Stock-Yards, Chicago	....	....	
6	Mr. Huhn, 3920 Butterfield street, Chicago	10	3c.	
6	Mr. Millen, west end of city, Chicago	1	1a.	
7	Mr. Scheineman, 3919 Butterfield street, Chicago	6	2c.	Stables, foul; animals poor.
8	John Muller, Fiftieth and School streets, Chicago.	19	1a.	
9	Phœnix Distillery	....	....	
	Inspections by W. H. Rose, V. S.			
11	Henry Bear, Hyde Park, Cook County	26	1c.	Fair.
11	Various persons, Sixty-ninth and State streets, Chicago.	110	....	
	Inspections by Herr & Rose, V. S.			
12	Messrs. Fink & Wagner, Jefferson, Cook County	6	1	Animals, poor.
12	John S. Burkle, near Jefferson, Cook County	27	2	Poor.
12	Morris Ryan, Jefferson, Cook County	66	3	Animals, poor.
15	Chrs. Mulson, 4011 Butterfield street, Lake	10	1	Stables, fair; animals poor.
15	Frederick Scheineman, 3919 Butterfield street, Lake.	6	2c.	Poor.

Inspections in Illinois—Continued.

Day of month.	Name of owner or person in charge and location of stable.	No. of cattle.	No. with lung-plague.	Condition of stables and animals.
	Inspections by Herr and Ross—Continued.			
1886.				
Oct. 15	Charles Hohn, 3920 Butterfield street, Lake	10	2c.	Poor.
15	Frank Ott, 4420 Wentworth avenue, Lake	7	1c.	Stables, poor; animals, fair.
15	William Zerba, 4432 Wentworth avenue, Lake	11	2c.	Do.
15	Frederick Stralon, 4445 School street, Lake	11	2c.	Do.
15	Frederick Shodobba, 4323 Tracy avenue, Lake	8	1c.	Do.
15	Fritz Bergman, 4315 Tracy avenue, Lake	10	1c.	Fair.
15	F. Weimaster, 3933 Butterfield street, Lake	2	1c.	Do.
15	Mr. Biefuchs, 3947 Butterfield street, Lake	2	1c.	Do.
16	Charles Smith, 353 Bristol street, Lake	5		Stables, poor; animals, fair.
16	James Close, 355 Forty-fifth street, Lake	6		Do.
16	John Miller, corner School and Bristol streets	19	2c.	Stables, foul; animals, fair.
16	Martin Leonard, 4540 School street, Lake	2		Fair.
16	Chris. Minke, 4455 Shytliff avenue, Lake	1		
	Inspection by W. H. Ross, V. S.			
16	Robert McCullough, 4439 Atlantic street, Town of Lake.	2		Animals, fair.
	Inspections by Herr and Ross, V. S.			
16	William Washer and M. Miller, corner Tracey avenue, Town of Lake.	2		Fair.
16	Mrs. Lizzie Reed, 4430 Wentworth avenue, Town of Lake.	1		
16	Thomas Dolan, 4441 Atlantic street, Town of Lake.	1		
16	James Bateson, 339 43d street, Town of Lake	1		
	Inspections by Thomas J. Herr, V. S.			
6	Schufeld's Distillery, Chicago	982		Fair.
9	Miller, Lake View	2		Good.
9	J. D. Le Moyne, Lake View	9	5	Do.
11	Max Herf, 171 Clybourn Place, Chicago	7		Stables, good; animals, fair.
11	Phœnix Distillery, Clybourn place, Chicago	1.000	9	Poor.
	Inspections by Trumbower and Herr, V. S.			
4	John Warren, Blackberry, Kane County	57		Good.
5	Hon. John Stewart, Blackberry, Kane County	160		Do.
	Inspections by Rowland and Hawk, V. S.			
7	Mr. Bartlich, Hinman and Plesia streets, Chicago			Fair.
7	Mr. Grofle, 25th street, near Railroad, Chicago	1		Do.
7	Mr. Shooks, Palmer street, Chicago	3		Do.
7	W. Mullen, Forty-fourth street, Chicago	20		Do.
7	E. Jeskey, Forty-fourth street, Chicago	21		Do.
7	Mr. Bross, Twentieth street, Chicago	4	1	Do.
7	Mr. Nickle, Twentieth street, Chicago	8		Do.
7	M. Lass, Nineteenth street, Chicago	1		Do.
7	M. Martin, Twenty-first street, Chicago	5		Do.
7	M. Hofferman, Twenty-second street, Chicago	5		Do.
7	M. Wooch, Plesia street, Chicago	7		Do.
7	M. Cableauch, Nineteenth street, Chicago	1		Do.
7	Mr. Flinch, Twenty-first street, Chicago	2		Do.
7	Mr. Benze, Nineteenth street, Chicago	5		Do.
7	P. Feely, Twenty-first street, Chicago	14	5c.	Do.
7	Mr. Gorman, Twenty-second street, Chicago			Do.
7	Unknown, Twenty-second street, Chicago	2		Do.
7	M. Peeper, Twenty-third street, Chicago	3		Do.
7	Mr. Washer, Twentieth street, Chicago	1		Do.
7	M. Gentz, Twenty-fourth street, Chicago	1		Do.
7	Mr. Notch, Hinman street, Chicago	2		Do.
7	Mr. Fredox, Twenty-first street, Chicago	3		Do.
7	Mr. Boomem, Twentieth street, Chicago	1		Do.
7	Mr. Hennings, Twentieth street, Chicago	140		Do.
7	Mr. Sholtz, Hinman street, Chicago	4		Do.
7	Jewlis Henry, Thirty-fifth street, Chicago	7		Do.

Inspections in Illinois—Continued.

Day of month.	Name of owner or person in charge and location of stable.	No. of cattle.	No. with lung-plague.	Condition of stables and animals.
	Inspections by Rowland and Hawk—Continued.			
1886. Oct. 7	William Suffirnee, Thirty-fifth street, Chicago	10		Fair.
7	Mr. Rilew, along Canal street, Chicago	2		Do.
7	Mr. Clonk, Thirty-third street, Chicago	1		Do.
7	Mr. Shope, Thirty-third street, Chicago	1		Do.
7	Mr. Keller, Thirty-third street, Chicago	2		Do.
7	Mr. Nogruss, Thirty-third street, Chicago	2		Do.
7	On prairie, Thirty-third street, Chicago	28		Do.
7	On prairie, Weston avenue, Chicago	13	1e.	Do.
7	Henry Wolfe, Weston avenue, Chicago	35		Do.
7	On prairie, Thirty-eighth street, Chicago	10		Do.
7	On prairie, Thirty-ninth street, Chicago	130		Do.
7	On prairie, Thirty-ninth street, Chicago	11		Do.
7	Mr. Haycar, Stone avenue, Chicago	1		Do.
7	J. Bones, Bishop street, Chicago	1		Do.
7	T. Shea, Stone avenue, Chicago	2		Do.
7	F. Caulkey, Dryo street, Chicago	9		Do.
7	M. Bishop, Ashland avenue, Chicago	1		Do.
7	C. Bones, Forty-seventh street, Chicago	1		Do.
7	T. Burneis, Ashland avenue, Chicago	1		Do.
7	Mr. Hausenfaunt, Forty-seventh street, Chicago	2		Do.
7	J. Crunbast, Ashland avenue, Chicago	3		Do.
11	Mr. Johnston, Jestine street, Chicago	3		Do.
11	I. Smith, Ashland avenue, Chicago	2		Do.
11	Mr. Hill, Jestine street, Chicago	5		Do.
11	J. McCalester, Jestine street, Chicago	2		Do.
11	Mr. Smith, Forty-ninth street, Chicago	2		Do.
11	M. Bombes, Jestine street, Chicago	4		Do.
11	Theo. Miller, Page, Chicago	6		Do.
11	On prairie, near California avenue, Chicago	13		Do.
11	George Foltwell, California avenue, Chicago	6		Do.
11	Mr. Hooper, Laughlin street, Chicago	10		Do.
11	Mr. Wagner, Forty-seventh street, Chicago	2		Do.
11	C. Crump, Forty-seventh street, Chicago	1		Do.
11	H. Potts, Laughlin street, Chicago	2		Do.
11	Mrs. Goph, Forty-fourth street, Chicago	2		Do.
11	Mr. McCurdy, Forty-fourth street, Chicago	2		Do.
12	On prairie, near Chicago	10		Do.
12	M. Geiber, Archer avenue, Chicago	1		Do.
12	M. Dickman, Archer avenue, Chicago	1		Do.
12	W Slaker, Thirty-seventh street, Chicago	1		Do.
12	J. Baker, Fifty-second street, Chicago	38		Do.
12	N. Garrete, Fiftieth street, Chicago	1		Do.
12	Mr. McCormack, Fiftieth street, Chicago	1		Do.
12	Mr. Beam, Fifty-first street, near Chicago	1		Do.
12	Mr. Johnston, Fifty-first street, near Chicago	9		Do.
12	E. Freds, Fifty-first street, near Chicago	6		Do.
12	Mr O'Brien, Morrisfield avenue, near Chicago	3		Do.
12	J. Shannon, Morrisfield avenue, Chicago	2		Do.
12	Mr. Hanley, Morrisfield avenue, Chicago	1		Do.
12	G. Gantz, Morrisfield avenue, Chicago	1		Do.
12	T. Elkins, 33 Court street, near Chicago	2		Do.
12	T. Leonard, Thirty-third street, near Chicago	2		Do.
12	Mr. Hogan, Thirty-third street, near Chicago	2		Do.
13	A. J. Snell, Saint John's Place, near Chicago	1		Do.
13	S. Mortimer, Saint John's Place, near Chicago	5		Do.
13	On prairie, Garfield Park, near Chicago	75		Do.
13	P. Wall, Semore street, near Chicago	9		Do.
	Inspections by M. R. Trumbower, V. S.			
8	J. H. Wadsworth, Geneva, Kane County	3		Animals, good.
8	Frank Lennartz, Geneva, Kane County	2		Do.
8	Patrick McCoy, Geneva, Kane County	1		Animals, poor.
8	D. B. Moore, Saint Charles, Kane County	1		Animals, good.
11	F. B. Bowron, Geneva, Kane County	38		Good.
11	Shields Brothers, one-half mile south of Bartlett Station, Du Page County	17		Animals, good.
11	Charles Foote, 2 miles south of Wayne Station, Du Page County.	60		Good.
11	John Smith, 7 miles northeast of Wayne Station, Du Page County.	6		Animals, good.
11	Julius Vogt, 4 miles northeast of Wayne Station, Du Page County.			Do.
12	John Landers, Geneva, Kane County	1		Do.

Inspections in Illinois—Continued.

Day of month.	Name of owner or person in charge and location of stable.	No. of cattle.	No. with lung-plague.	Condition of stables and animals.
	Inspections by M. R. Trumbower—Continued.			
1886.				
Oct. 12	Jas. Marshall, Geneva, Kane County	1	....	Animals, good.
12	H. O. Lawson, Geneva, Kane County	1	....	Do.
12	J. M. Kendall, Geneva, Kane County	1	....	Do.
12	Michael Naviens, Geneva, Kane County	1	....	Do.
12	John Van Vort, Geneva, Kane County	1	....	Do.
12	A. B. Baker, Geneva, Kane County	1	....	Do.
12	James Quinn, Geneva, Kane County	1	....	Do.
12	L. Gooley, Geneva, Kane County	1	....	Do.
12	Ed. Stockton, Geneva, Kane County	1	....	Do.
12	Lyman German, Geneva, Kane County	1	....	Do.
12	Andrew Hausen, Geneva, Kane County	2	....	Do.
12	Captain Yates, Geneva, Kane County	1	....	Do.
12	Lyman Long, Geneva, Kane County	1	....	Do.
12	B. M. Peterson, Geneva, Kane County	1	....	Do,
12	S. N. Cooper, Geneva, Kane County	1	....	Do.
12	Ed. Masterson, Geneva, Kane County	1	....	Do.
12	Charles Patten, Geneva, Kane County	1	....	Do.
12	Court-house lot, Geneva, Kane County	3	....	Do.
12	William Stroud, Geneva, Kane County	1	....	Do.
12	Thomas Clancey, Geneva, Kane County	2	....	Do.
12	James Herrington, Geneva, Kane County	1	....	Do.
12	Swede, Geneva, Kane County	1	....	Do.
12	Town, Geneva, Kane County	1	....	Do.
12	William Cannon, Geneva, Kane County	1	....	Do.
12	....	1	....	Do.
12	James Long, Geneva, Kane County	1	....	Do.
12	....	1	....	Do.
12	J. H. Wadsworth, Geneva, Kane County	3	....	Do.
12	Oscar Nelson, Geneva, Kane County	2	....	Do.
12	Philip McGreen, jr., Geneva, Kane County	1	....	Do.
12	Mr. Lunn, Geneva, Kane County	1	....	Do.
12	Swede, Geneva, Kane County	1	....	Do.
12	John Bohen, Geneva, Kane County	1	....	Do.
12	Andrew Linds, Geneva, Kane County	1	....	Do.
12	M. Anderson, Geneva, Kane County	1	....	Do.
12	Strum, Geneva, Kane County	1	....	Do.
12	Mrs. Seeburg, Geneva, Kane County	2	....	Do.
12	Solomon Swanson, Geneva, Kane County	1	....	Do.
12	Nelson Nelson, Geneva, Kane County	1	....	Do.
12	Philip McGreen, jr., Geneva, Kane County	1	....	Do.
12	Mrs. Nelson, Geneva, Kane County	1	....	Do.
12	Peter Anderson, Geneva, Kane County	1	....	Do.
12	Daniel Peterson, Geneva, Kane County	1	....	Do.
12	Andrew Ristrum, Geneva, Kane County	1	....	Do.
12	Mrs. Johnson, Geneva, Kane County	1	....	Do.
12	John Myers, Geneva, Kane County	1	....	Do.
12	Andy Kelly, Geneva, Kane County	1	....	Do.
12	H. Matteson, Geneva, Kane County	1	....	Do.
12	Eastman Donaldson, Geneva, Kane County	2	....	Do.
12	John Gooley, Geneva, Kane County	1	....	Do.
12	H. P. Bean, Geneva, Kane County	3	....	Do.
12	C. E. Maun, Geneva, Kane County	3	....	Do.
12	George Lantz, Geneva, Kane County	2	....	Do.
12	Smith, Geneva, Kane County	2	....	Do.
12	George Ripley, Geneva, Kane County	2	....	Do.
12	R. Richards, Geneva, Kane County	2	....	Do.
12	P. D. Turner, Geneva, Kane County	1	....	Do.
12	Peter Jackson, Geneva, Kane County	1	....	Do.
12	James Rathbone, Geneva, Kane County	3	....	Do.
12	J. H. Ticknor, Geneva, Kane County	1	....	Do.
12	Levi Updyke, Geneva, Kane County	1	....	Do.
12	Charles Johnson, Geneva, Kane County	1	....	Do.
12	George Hesty, Geneva, Kane County	1	....	Do.
12	O. F. Shultz, Geneva, Kane County	1	....	Do.
12	Nelson Lufbaum, Geneva, Kane County	1	....	Do.
12	H. Bennett, Geneva, Kane County	2	....	Do.
12	Andy Loudine, Geneva, Kane County	1	....	Do.
12	Mrs. Bachman, Geneva, Kane County	1	....	Do.
12	Elliott Johnson, Geneva, Kane County	1	....	Do.
12	William Carner, Geneva, Kane County	1	....	Do.
12	Pat Carney, Geneva, Kane County	1	....	Do.
12	Mrs. Burr, Geneva, Kane County	2	....	Do.
12	S. B. Miller, Geneva, Kane County	1	....	Do.

Inspections in Illinois—Continued.

Day of month.	Name of owner or person in charge and location of stable.	No. of cattle.	No. with lung-plague.	Condition of stables and animals.
	Inspections by W. H. Rose—Continued.			
1886. Oct. 21	James Barrett, 3750 La Salle street, Town of Lake	3		Poor.
21	Jno. Wilk, 3753 Butterfield street, Town of Lake	3	1c.	Stables, poor; animals, fair.
21	William Baker, 3721 Butterfield street, Town of Lake.	6	3c.	Stables, poor; animals, very poor.
21	Michael Keefe, 3719 Butterfield street, Town of Lake.	1		Fair.
21	Pat. Welsh, 3708 Butterfield street, Town of Lake.	1		Stables, fair; animals, poor.
	Inspections by Thos. J. Herr, V. S.			
19	Union Rendering Company, Stock Yards, Town of Lake.	7	5	
20	......do	1		
20	......do	3	3	
20	......do	2	2	
21	......do	1		
21	......do	2	2	
21	......do	1	1	
22	......do	1		
22	......do	3	3	
22	......do	1	1	
23	......do	6	6	
23	......do	2	1	
23	......do	1	1	
23	......do	1	1	
	Inspections by H. W. Rowland, V. S.			
15	A. Lannert, on prairie, near Chicago	1		Animals, fair.
15	Mr. Dean, Indiana street, Chicago	1		Animals, good.
15	Erman Clany, 331 Ohio street, Chicago	2		Do.
15	John Keeley, on prairie, near Chicago	6		Animals, fair.
15	John Campbell, on prairie, near Chicago	6		Do.
15	P. Hicks, on prairie, near Chicago	1		Do.
16	Mr. Weyman, 625 Carol avenue, Chicago	3		Do.
16	W. Patterson, 18 Sheddon street, Chicago	1		Do.
16	Unknown, on prairie, Chicago	15		Do.
16	Martin McCue, 105 Fairfield avenue, Chicago	1		Do.
16	C. Wolfe, 1515 West Lake street, Chicago	12		Do.
16	Christian Goleb, 130 California avenue, Chicago	10		Do.
16	Mrs. C. Griffin, Seamore street, Chicago	4		Do.
16	Dan. Corrigan, 81 Seamore street, Chicago	7		Do.
18	Silas Palmer, Warren avenue, Chicago	3		Do.
18	Augustus Eaton, 1372 Carol avenue, Chicago	1		Do.
18	Garret Trimmer, 90 Fairfield avenue, Chicago	2		Do.
18	Pat. Burnes, 1198 Fulton street, Chicago	6		Do.
18	L. Barkley, 1248 Fulton street, Chicago	1		Do.
18	Peter Boman, 142 California avenue, Chicago	1		Do.
18	P. Curman, 558 Fulton street, Chicago	4		Do.
18	T. P. Hicks, 910 West Lake street, Chicago	1		Do.
18	John Keef, 89 Washington avenue, Chicago	6		Do.
18	A. Martin, 37 Western avenue, Chicago	1		Do.
18	James McAndrews, 890 Washington street, Chicago.	1		Do.
18	M. Kinmare, 1381 West Lake street, Chicago	1		Do.
18	M. Kelly, 101 Fairfield avenue, Chicago	6		Do.
18	W. R. Mumford, 293 West Lake street, Chicago	1		Do.
18	J. H. Trunkey, 366 Walnut street, Chicago	1		Do.
18	J. G. Stevens, 1501 West Lake street, Chicago	3		Do.
18	F. Nerenger, 1314 West Lake street, Chicago	2		Do.
18	F. B. Ogden, 682 Park avenue, Chicago	2		Do.
19	C. K. G. Billings, 470 Washington street, Chicago.	1		Do.
19	A. Bartlett, 475 Randolph street, Chicago	1		Do.
19	John Burnes, 9 Stanton street, Chicago	6		Do.
19	James Connelly, 1155 Madison street, Chicago	1		Do.
19	John Campbell, 471 Park avenue, Chicago	6		Do.
19	Michael Fitzgerald, 368 Carol avenue, Chicago	7		Do.
19	A. J. Foote, 1159 Madison street, Chicago	1		Do.
19	A. H. Goble, 554 Fulton street, Chicago	1		Do.
19	P. Haag, 1113 Madison street, Chicago	1		Do.
19	M. Jordon, 1146 Madison street, Chicago	1		Do.

Inspections in Illinois—Continued.

Day of month.	Name of owner or person in charge and location of stable.	No. of cattle.	No. with lung-plague.	Condition of stables and animals.
	Inspections by H. W. Rowland—Continued.			
1886. Oct. 19	Eliza Jones, 1121 Madison street, Chicago	1		Animals, fair.
19	Mrs. S. Kelly, 1017 Madison street, Chicago	1		Do.
19	M. Lynch, 1148 Madison street, Chicago	2		Do.
19	A. Lamott, 728 Fulton street, Chicago	1		Do.
19	F. Moldenhaur, 80 San Francisco street, Chicago	3		Do.
19	R. P. Peters, 811 Fulton street, Chicago	1		Do.
19	A. J. Snell, 425 Washington street Chicago	1		Do.
19	J. Wiltsie, 1236 Madison street, Chicago	1		Do.
20	M. Q. Atkins, 737 Adams street, Chicago	1		Do.
20	A. M. Billings, 514 West Lake street, Chicago	1		Do.
20	E. K. Butler, 271 Warren street, Chicago	1		Do.
20	Henry Curtis, 735 Monroe street, Chicago	1		Do.
20	J. W. Litchfield, 783 Monroe street, Chicago	1		Do.
20	E. D. Morse, 806 West Madison street, Chicago	1		Do.
20	M. Stanwood, Walnut st., near Kinzie, Chicago	1		Do.
20	Marie Sherman, 702 Washington B., Chicago	1		Do.
20	M. Voorhees, 172 Albany avenue, Chicago	1		Do.
20	C. R. Williams, 51 Seely avenue, Chicago	1		Do.
20	W. O. Carpenter, 517 Adams street, Chicago	1		Do.
21	William Chapman, 515 Adams street, Chicago	1		Do.
21	John Watson, on prairie, near Chicago	2		Do.
21	Mr. Shock, on prairie, near Chicago	1		Do.
21	Asa Don, 516 Adams street, Chicago	1		Do.
21	Mr. Smith, Monroe and Madison sts., Chicago	3		Do.
21	Dr. Newman, on prairie, near Chicago	1		Do.
21	M. William Durant, on prairie, near Chicago	1		Do.
21	George Sherwood, on prairie, near Chicago	1		Do.
21	Mr. Webb, on prairie, near Chicago	1		Do.
21	Dr. Margrett, on prairie, near Chicago	1		Do.
21	William Winderson, on prairie, near Chicago	1		Do.
21	Henry Towne, on prairie, near Chicago	1		Do.
21	Mrs. G. W. Bokow, 886 Monroe street, Chicago	2		Do.
22	C. J. Cooper, 153 South Levitt street, Chicago	1		Do.
22	Albert B. Cole, 1025 Wilcox avenue, Chicago	1		Do.
22	M. Doby, 525 Adams street, Chicago	1		Do.
22	William H. Durant, 626 Monroe street, Chicago	1		Do.
22	M. Everick, Ashland and Monroe sts., Chicago	1		Do.
22	J. L. Higgie, 625 Adams street, Chicago	1		Do.
22	E. H. Holden, 631 Adams street, Chicago	1		Do.
22	Daniel Kennedy, 1006 Monroe street, Chicago	1		Do.
22	Mr. Eugene Margrette, 708 West Monroe street, Chicago.	1		Do.
22	Andrew McClay, 627 Adams street, Chicago	1		Do.
22	Dr. Newman, 554 West Monroe street, Chicago	1		Do.
22	John Smith, 113 Hoyne avenue, Chicago	1		Do.
22	Lewis S. Sass, 847 Monroe street, Chicago	1		Do.
22	George Sherwood, 513 Adams street, Chicago	1	1c.	Do.
22	Edward Teale, 522 Adams street, Chicago	2		Do.
22	Mrs. P. P. Wears, 653 Adams street, Chicago	1		Do.
22	William Winterson, 166 Irving Place, Chicago	1		Do.
22	Mr. Webb, 998 Monroe street, Chicago	1		Do.
22	William Chaplin, 515 Adams street, Chicago	1		Do.
23	Mr. M. Kelley, Fairfield avenue, Chicago	6		Do.
23	Conrod Knoch, 16 Whipple street, Chicago	6		Do.
23	Charles Cosman, corner Lake and Leamore streets, Chicago.	1		Do.
23	Unknown, on prairie, near Chicago	17		Do.
23	Mr. C. Holet, 136 California avenue, Chicago	10		Do.
23	James McGuire, Kidzie and Madison streets, Chicago.	1		Do.
23	John Madindorpt, Wilcox avenue, Chicago	6		Do.
23	Henry Parker, Kidzie and Jackson streets, Chicago.	32		Do.
25	Mrs. O'Brien, Belknap avenue, Chicago	1		Do.
25	Mrs. McCurdy, Belknap avenue, Chicago	4		Do.
25	William Hand, Taylor street, Chicago	3		Do.
25	Mrs. Ray, 12th and Taylor streets, Chicago	3		Do.
25	Mrs. G. Briant, 12th and Loomis streets, Chicago	1		Do.
25	C. Campbell, 13th Place and Loomis streets, Chicago.	1		Do.
25	Mrs. Ryan, 13th Place and Laflin street, Chicago	2		Do.
25	John Cosgrove, Laflin street, Chicago	1		Do.
25	J. Belcher, Ashland avenue, Chicago	2		Do.
25	T. Cottrell, Palina street and Ashland avenue, Chicago.	1		Do.

Inspections in Illinois—Continued.

Day of month.	Name of owner or person in charge and location of stable.	No. of cattle.	No. with lung-plague.	Condition of stables and animals.
	Inspections by H. W. Rowland—Continued.			
1886. Oct. 25	Thomas Canon, Harbard street, Chicago	14		Animals, fair.
25	Dr. McNeal, 148 Warren avenue, Chicago	2		Do.
25	Mrs. McGraw, Hoyne avenue, Chicago	3		Do.
25	William Smith, 160 Augustus street, Chicago	1		Do.
85	Mrs. Brennan, Belknap avenue, Chicago	3		Do.
25	Mr. Moore, 13th Place and 13th street, Chicago	3		Do.
25	Mr. H. Echer, 161 Augustus street, Chicago			
25	Mrs. Kent, Thirteenth Place, Chicago	4		Animals, fair.
26	Mr. Rocklow, Dudley and Augustus streets, Chicago.	2		
26	T. Faloey, 666 West Ohio street, Chicago	2		
26	P. Rely, 27 Brown street, Chicago	7		
26	Mr. Lancraff, Dudley and Augusta streets, Chicago.	3		
26	Thomas Nash, 240 Ashland avenue, Chicago	1	1a.	
26	John Keys, 177 Kenzie street, Chicago	1	1a	
26	Mr. Fitzgerald, Hoyne street, near Chicago avenue, Chicago.	2		
26	Mr. Hassett, on Prairie, Chicago	3		Animals, fair.
26	Mr. Sheridan, corner Ohio and Noble streets, Chicago.	5	3c.	
	Inspections by W. H. Ross, V. S.			
26	John Webber, Geneva, Kane County	42		Fair.
27	Frederick Buenger, 4033 Dearborn street, Town of Lake.	10	1c.	Stables, foul; animals, poor.
27	Michael Gerry, 4075 Dearborn street, Town of Lake.	2		Animals, poor.
27	Edward Moll, 4000 State street, Town of Lake	1		Animals, fair.
27	Henry Graper, 3959 Dearborn street, Town of Lake.	1		Do.
27	Mrs. H. Bellfress, 3928 Dearborn street, Town of Lake.	1		Do.
27	Geo. Webb, 4010 Dearborn street, Town of Lake	1		Do.
27	James Cole, 3820 Dearborn street, Town of Lake	1		Do.
27	Charles Polzin, 3818 State street, Town of Lake	1		Do.
28	W. O. Goodman, 1722 Michigan street, Town of Lake.	1		Do.
28	T. C. Dobbins, 1825 Michigan avenue, Chicago	1		Do.
28	Chas. H. Schawb, 1709 Michigan av., Chicago	1		Do.
28	Mr. T. Booth, 1737 Wabash avenue, Chicago	1		Do.
28	Mr. A. Booth, 1638 Michigan avenue, Chicago	1	1	Animal, poor.
28	Jacob Rosenberg, 1620 Michigan av., Chicago	1		Animals, fair.
29	Dr. Wm. Byford, 1832 Indiana avenue, Chicago	1		Do.
29	Geo. F. Bissell, 2008 Prairie avenue, Chicago	1		Do.
29	Levi Rosenfield, 2026 Prairie avenue, Chicago	1		Do.
29	Chas. Mohns, 1839 Indiana avenue, Chicago	1		Do.
29	Mr. E. G. Keith, 1900 Prairie avenue, Chicago	1		Do.
29	Edson Keith, 1906 Prairie avenue, Chicago	1		Do.
29	Samuel Allerton, 1936 Prairie avenue, Chicago	1		Do.
29	Geo. P. Gore, 1926 Indiana avenue, Chicago	2		Do.
29	Jno. M. Clarke, 2000 Prairie avenue, Chicago	1		Do.
29	C. D. Peacock, 1713 Indiana avenue, Chicago	1		Do.
29	B. P. Moulton, 1912 Prairie avenue, Chicago	2		Do.
29	Wm. Greg, 2010 Prairie avenue, Chicago	1		Do.
29	C. R. Cummings, 1641 Indiana avenue, Chicago	1		Do.
29	W. C. Grant, 1610 Indiana avenue, Chicago	1		Do.
30	Frank Hanson, 1720 Michigan avenue, Chicago	1		Do.
30	E. McHenry, 1815 Indiana avenue, Chicago	1		Do.
30	Mrs. Geo. Armour, 1945 Prairie avenue, Chicago	1	1	Animal, poor.
30	W. B. Walker, 2027 Prairie avenue, Chicago	1		Animal, fair.
30	Jno. B. Carson, 2035 Prairie avenue, Chicago	1		Animal, poor.
30	S. A. Talmon, 2031 Prairie avenue, Chicago	1		Do.
30	B. Adams, 2021 Prairie avenue, Chicago	1		Animal, fair.
30	Geo. A. Armour, 1932 Calumet avenue, Chicago	1		Do.
30	Wm. Armour, 2017 Calumet avenue, Chicago	1		Do.
30	P. C. Hanford, 2008 Calumet avenue, Chicago	1		Do.
30	W. H. Mitchell, 2004 Calumet avenue, Chicago	1		Do.
30	John Sears, 2016 Calumet avenue, Chicago	1		Do.
Nov. 1	A. B. Adams, 2249 Calumet avenue, Chicago	1		Fair.
1	Moses Adams, 2227 Calumet avenue, Chicago	1		Do.
1	Henry Berg, 2218 Calumet avenue, Chicago	1		Do.
1	Moses Bensinger, 2217 Calumet avenue, Chicago	1		Do.

Inspections in Illinois—Continued.

	Name of owner or person in charge and location of stable.	No. of cattle.	No. with lung-plague.	Condition of stables and animals.
	Inspections by W. H. Rose—Continued.			
1	James Rosenbalm, 2229 Calumet avenue, Chicago.	1	....	Fair.
1	Mr. McDermot, 2247 Calumet avenue, Chicago...	1	....	Do.
1	C. L. Raymond, 2239 Calumet avenue, Chicago...	1	....	Stables, clean; animals, fair.
1	H. H. Cohn, 2240 Calumet avenue, Chicago,........	1	....	Fair.
1	D. W. Irwin, 35 Twenty-second street, Chicago...	1	....	Stables, clean; animals, fair.
1	M. Rothchild, 2112 Prairie avenue, Chicago........	1	....	Do.
1	A. Price, 2219 Prairie avenue, Chicago..................	1	....	Animals, fair.
2	Esau Harlock, 2528 Calumet avenue, Chicago.....	1	....	Animals, poor.
2	John Flanders, 2708 South Park avenue, Chicago.	1	....	Animals, fair.
2	W. S. Henderson, 2438 Indiana avenue, Chicago..	1	....	Do.
2	Dr. D. T. Nelson, 2400 Indiana avenue, Chicago..	1	....	Do.
2	E. Buckingham, 2036 Prairie avenue, Chicago.....	1	....	Do.
2	Dr. B. M. Tucker, 2317 Wabash avenue, Chicago..	1	....	Animals, poor.
2	Martin Maylaw, 2216 Indiana avenue, Chicago...	1	....	Animals, fair.
2	Ferdinand Peck, 2259 Wabash avenue, Chicago..	1	....	Stables, clean; animals, fair.
3	Michael Cuddy, 3138 Michigan avenue, Chicago..	1	....	Do.
3	Gilbert Shaw, 2708 South Park avenue, Chicago..	1	....	Do.
3	C. Briggs, 3226 Wabash avenue, Chicago............	1	....	Do.
3	J. Knowles, 3123 Forest avenue, Chicago...........	1	....	Stables, fair; animals, fair.
3	Frank Logan, 2919 Prairie avenue, Chicago........	1	....	Stables, clean; animals, good.
3	W. Miller, 3118 Calumet avenue, Chicago,..........	1	....	Stables, clean; animals, fair.
3	Mr. Jacobs, 164 Thirtieth street, Chicago	1	....	Fair.
3	Louisa Haddock, 2976 Michigan avenue, Chicago.	1	....	Do.
3	Wm. S. Everett, 2947 Prairie avenue, Chicago	1	....	Stables, poor; animals, fair.
3	Jno. H. Whitman, 3330 Wabash avenue, Chicago..	1	....	Fair.
3	C. D. Hancock, 3232 Wabash avenue, Chicago.....	1	....	Do.
3	O. Robertson, 3150 Wabash avenue, Chicago........	1	....	Do.
3	H. E. Malloy, 3135 Prairie avenue, Chicago.........	1	1c.	Stables, poor; animals, fair.
4	Mrs. Chaffee, 2714 Wabash avenue, Chicago.........	1	....	Fair.
4	Henry Cooley, 3117 Michigan avenue, Chicago ...	1	....	Do.
4	E. E. Maxwell, 2804 Prairie avenue, Chicago	1	....	Do.
4	S. H. Sweet, 2940 Prairie avenue, Chicago..........	1	....	Stables, clean; animals, fair.
4	Chas. W. Briggs, 2816 Michigan avenue, Chicago..	1	....	Do.
4	Jno. W. Loomis, 2939 Wabash avenue, Chicago...	2	....	Poor.
4	C. J. Singer, 2926 Michigan avenue, Chicago........	1	....	Fair.
4	Pat. O'Neill, 20 Ray street, Chicago.....................	2	....	Stables, poor; animals, fair.
5	Daniel Wren, 2536 Wabash avenue, Chicago.........	1	....	Fair.
5	Max. Weiman, 2544 Michigan avenue, Chicago ...	1	....	Stables, clean; animals, fair.
5	Jno. H. McAvoy, 2321 Calumet avenue, Chicago..	1	....	Fair.
5	Dr. A. Brooke, 2548 Indiana avenue, Chicago......	1	....	Do.
5	Sisters of Mercy, 2834 Wabash avenue, Chicago...	3	....	Do.
5	W. H. Pering, 2447 State street, Chicago.............	2	....	Stables, poor; animals, fair.
5	Henry Cherrie, 2541 Wabash avenue, Chicago	2	....	Stables, fair; animals, poor.
22	John Ellis, Geneva, Kane County.........................	19	....	Stables, good; animals, fair.
	Inspections by M. R. Trumbower, V. S.			
22	Samuel Fritz, 2 miles west of Geneva, Kane County.	20	....	In field; animals, fair.
23	Ed. Biglow, Geneva, Kane County.......................	3	....	Animals, good.
25	John B. Moore, 1 mile east of Geneva, Kane County.	35	....	Stable, good.
26	Crawford, Saint Charles, Kane County..............	18	....	Stable, good; animals, fair.
26	Peter Swanson, 3 miles north of Geneva, Kane County.	18	....	Animals, good.
26	Mr. Lockhart, Saint Charles, Kane County.........	1	....	Animals, fair.
26	Bronsett, Saint Charles, Kane County.................	2	....	Animals, good.
26	Mr. Selmon, Saint Charles, Kane County...........	1	....	Do.

Inspections in Illinois—Continued.

Day of month.	Name of owner or person in charge and location of stable.	No. of cattle.	No. with lung-plague.	Condition of stables and animals.
	Inspections by M. R. Trumbower—Continued.			
1886. Oct. 27	Aug. England, Saint Charles, Kane County	1	.....	Animals, good.
27	Jno. England, Saint Charles, Kane County	1	.....	Do.
27	B. F. Hunt, Saint Charles, Kane County	2	.....	Do.
27	Mr. Pease, Saint Charles, Kane County	1	.....	Do.
29	Theo. Kahler, 208 Hickory avenue, Chicago	4	2c.	Fair.
Nov. 1	James Roney, 196 Michigan avenue, Chicago	4	.....	Animals, good.
	Inspections by Thos. J. Herr, V. S.			
Oct. 25	Union Rendering Company, stock-yards, Town of Lake.	1	.....	
25	Union Rendering Company, stock-yards, Town of Lake.	1	.....	
26	Union Rendering Company, stock-yards, Town of Lake.	1	1	
26	Michael O'Brien, 4056 Atlantic street, Town of Lake.	1	.....	Good.
27	Union Rendering Company, stock-yards, Town of Lake.	6	6	
27	Union Rendering Company, stock-yards, Town of Lake.	1	1	
28	Union Rendering Company, stock-yards, Town of Lake.	1	1	
29	Union Rendering Company, stock-yards, Town of Lake.	1	1	
30	Union Rendering Company, stock-yards, Town of Lake.	2	.....	
30	Union Rendering Company, stock-yards, Town of Lake.	1	.....	
30	Union Rendering Company, stock-yards, Town of Lake.	3	3	
Nov. 1	Union Rendering Company, stock-yards, Town of Lake.	1	.....	
2	Union Rendering Company, stock-yards, Town of Lake.	3	.....	
2	Union Rendering Company, stock-yards, Town of Lake.	4	.....	
3	Union Rendering Company, stock-yards, Town of Lake.	1	1	
	Inspections by W. H. Rose, V. S.			
6	B. Ganzel, Hyde Park, Cook County	66	.....	Poor.
6	Dr. J. G. Berry, 3659 Halsted street, Chicago	1	.....	
10	S. H. Sweet, Hyde Park, Cook County	1	.....	Stables, poor; animals, good.
	Inspections by Trumbower and Rose, V. S.			
19	Jno. Hopkins, 848 47th street, Town of Lake	1	.....	Stables, fair.
19	Thos. Brown and Geo. Walton, 4625 Halsted street, Town of Lake.	2	.....	Stables, poor; animals, fair.
19	Michael Quinn, 717 Dexter street, Town of Lake.	4	.....	Fair.
19	Aug. Stuhlmacher, 631 Forty-sixth street, Town of Lake.	11	.....	Stables, poor; animals, fair.
19	Chas. Moore, 636 Forty-sixth street, Town of Lake.	2	.....	Stables, fair; animals, good.
19	John Prentiss, 748 Forty-seventh street, Town of Lake.	1	.....	Stables, good; animal, fair.
19	Mrs. Mary Powers, 734 Forty-seventh street, Town of Lake.	1	.....	Good.
19	Merritt Kelly, 744 Forty-seventh street, Town of Lake.	1	.....	Fair,
19	Charles Baker, 802 Forty-seventh street, Town of Lake.	1	.....	Stables, good; animal, poor.
19	William Schneider, 138 Forty-seventh street, Town of Lake.	14	.....	Poor.
19	Richard Powers, 730 Forty-seventh street, Town of Lake.	1	.....	Stables, poor; animal, fair,
19	Charles Walters, 703 Forty-seventh street, Town of Lake.	1	.....	Poor.
19	William Murray, 710 Dexter street, Town of Lake.	1	.....	Stables, poor; animal, fair.
19	Patrick O'Neal, 706 Dexter street, Town of Lake	1	.....	Fair.
19	George Winkelmann, 606 Forty-sixth street	1	.....	Good.

Inspections in Illinois—Continued.

Day of month.	Name of owner or person in charge and location of stable.	No. of cattle.	No. with lung-plague.	Condition of stables and animals.
	Inspections by Trumbower and Rose—Continued.			
1886. Nov. 19	John W. Dymock, 601 Forty-sixth street	2	....	Stables, good; animals, fair.
19	Charles Kalhorn, 628 Forty-sixth street	2	....	Stables, poor; animals, fair.
	Charles Ba'lrig, 4525 Halsted street	1	....	Stables, clean; animal, good.
	Richard Ryan, 4239 Winter street	7	....	Stables, foul; animals, poor.
	J. Y. Thompson, 4449 Halsted street	1	....	Fair.
	Timothy Kelleher, 4523 Halsted street	1	....	Do.
	C. R. Hastings, 803 Forty-third street	1	....	Stables, fair; animal, good.
	Joseph Forest, 4530 Sherman street	1	....	Stables, fair.
	Richard Barry, 4218 Winter street	6	....	Stables, foul; animals, fair.
20	William White, 4228 Emerald avenue	1	....	Fair.
20	David Lowbenstein, 4454 Emerald avenue	1	....	Stables, fair; animal, good.
	Inspections by W. H. Rose, V. S.			
23	Thomas Nolan, 737 Thirty-sixth street, Chicago	1	....	Stables, fair; animals, poor.
23	Michael O'Connell, 3457 Wallace street, Chicago	2	....	Fair.
23	Michael McGuinness, 3427 Wallace street, Chicago.	2	....	Stables, clean; animals, poor.
23	James J. Reilly, 3528 Fifth avenue, Chicago	8	....	Stables, poor; animals, good.
23	James Mahoney, 3510 Fifth avenue, Chicago	1	....	Fair.
23	William Overhue, 3114-3116 Portland avenue Chicago.	8	....	Stables, fair; animals, poor.
	John Smith, 3120 Portland avenue, Chicago	6	....	Poor.
	Thomas Kenny, 3233 La Salle street, Chicago	3	....	Do.
23	John H. Nichols, 3213 La Salle street, Chicago	2	....	Fair.
23	Peter Segessenman, 3201 La Salle street, Chicago.	7	....	Stables, fair; animals, poor.
	John Ertinger, 3257 Wentworth avenue, Chicago.	5	....	Fair.
	James Maloney, 3023 La Salle street, Chicago	8	....	Do.
23	John Murphy, 3029 La Salle street, Chicago	1	....	Do.
23	Conrad Schlegel, 3546 Parnell avenue, Chicago	1	....	Stables, poor; animal, fair.
23	Charles Shannon, 548 33d street, Chicago	8	....	Stables, foul; animals, fair.
23	R. Brown, Eagle Heart place, Chicago	2	....	Do.
	Inspection by Ross & Trumbower, V. S.			
23	Joseph Emory, Geneva, Kane County	28	....	Stables, good; animals, fair.
	Inspections by W. H. Rose, V. S.			
	Timothy O'Donnell, 744 37th street, Chicago	8	....	Stables, poor.
24	Charles Guinee, 748 38th street, Chicago	8	....	Fair.
24	Peter Cooney, corner Butler and Thirty-ninth streets, Chicago.	4	....	Stables, poor; animals, fair.
24	Eli Carroll, 742 Thirty-seventh street, Chicago	3	....	Poor.
24	James Sullivan, 3750 Butler street, Chicago	2	....	Stables, poor.
24	Mrs. M. Fitzpatrick, near corner Thirty-fifth and Parnell streets, Chicago.	1	....	Fair.
24	Jerry McNamara, 3730 Butler street, Chicago	1	....	Stables, poor.
24	John Powers, 3621 Dashiel street, Chicago	8	....	Fair.
24	Fred. Walter, 3613 Dashiel street, Chicago	2	....	Do.
24	Michael O'Brian, 3545 Dashiel street, Chicago	2	....	Stables, fair.
24	James Sheridan, 3543 Dashiel street, Chicago	5	....	Stables, poor; animals, fair.
24	James McCormick, 3535 Dashiel street, Chicago	3	....	Poor.
24	William Smith, 3519 Dashiel street, Chicago	15	....	Stables, poor; animals, fair.
24	Patrick O'Hern, 3603 Lowe avenue, Chicago	6	....	Stables, fair; animals, poor.
24	John London, 3610 Lowe avenue, Chicago	7	....	Fair.
24	David Ray, 139 Lytle street, Chicago	4	....	Do.
24	John Heinold, 3611 Lowe avenue, Chicago	2	....	Do.
24	Dennis Sullivan, 3614 Wallace street, Town of Lake.	7	....	Do.

Inspections in Illinois—Continued.

Day of month.	Name of owner or person in charge and location of stable.	No. of cattle.	No. with lung-plague.	Condition of stables and animals.
	Inspections by W. H. Rose—Continued.			
1886. Nov. 24	Patrick Casey, 3936 Wallace street, Town of Lake.	3	....	Stables, poor; animals, fair.
24	Thomas Sullivan, 3918 Wallace street, Town of Lake.	1	....	Stables, fair.
24	Mrs. Elizabeth Markham, 759 Thirty-ninth street, Town of Lake.	2	....	Stables, poor; animals, fair.
24	Michael Kenny, 3912 Dashiel street, Town of Lake.	1	....	Do.
4	Union Rendering Company, stock-yards, Town of Lake.	....	....	
5	........do	2	2	
6	........do	6	6	
8	........do	2	1	
9	........do	1	1	
10	R. Brown, Halsted street, Town of Lake	3	....	
10	Union Rendering Company, stock-yards, Town of Lake.	1	....	
11	........do	1	1	
12	........do	2	2	
13	........do	....	....	
15	........do	1	1	
16	........do	1	1	
17	........do	1	1	
18	........do	1	1	
18	........do	3	3	
19	........do	1	....	
20	........do	....	....	
22	........do	21	....	
22	........do	....	....	
23	........do	....	....	
24	........do	1	1	
25	........do	1	1	
26	........do	1	....	
27	........do	3	2	
27	........do	1	....	
	Inspections by M. R. Trumbower, V. S.			
26	John Brannock, 29 McAllister place, Chicago	2	....	Fair.
26	August Mahlman, 1087 W. Lake street, Chicago	1	....	Good.
26	William Hannon, 310 Congress street, Chicago	4	....	Stables, bad; animals, fair.
26	Michael Palm, 21 Millen street, Chicago	1	....	Fair.
26	Mrs. Thomas Finn, 84 Millen street, Chicago	5	....	Do.
26	William Brown, 14 Millen street, Chicago	1	....	Do.
26	Mrs. Ellen McCarty, Belknap street, Chicago	4	....	Stables, bad; animals, poor.
26	Timothy Murphy, 13 Belknap street, Chicago	1	....	Stables, bad; animals, fair.
26	John Brennan, 15 Belknap street, Chicago	3	....	Poor.
26	Andrew O'Brien, 12 Belknap street, Chicago	3	....	Do.
26	Lawrence Moran, 30 Walter street, Chicago	3	....	Stables, poor; animals, good.
26	Fred Bay, 543 Twelfth street, Chicago	1	....	Good.
26	John Merkel, 545 Twelfth street, Chicago	1	....	Do.
26	Owen Sheehan, 7 Eleventh street, Chicago	6	....	Stables, good; animals, fair.
26	James Finn, 27 Eleventh street, Chicago	7	....	Do.
26	Mrs. Mary Kelly, 29 West Eleventh street, Chicago.	4	....	Stables, fair; animals, fair.
26	Thomas Sheehan, 314 Throop street, Chicago	1	....	Good.
26	James Gillen, 466 Harrison street, Chicago	1	....	Stables, fair; animals, good.
27	John Drehan, 232 Thirteenth place, Chicago	1	....	Good.
27	John Thompson, 229 Thirteenth place, Chicago	9	....	Fair.
27	Louis Pallace, 219 Thirteenth place, Chicago	2	....	Do.
27	C. Campbell, 166 Thirteenth place, Chicago	1	....	Do.
27	John Hough, 431 Harrison street, Chicago	3	....	Good.
	Inspections by W. H. Rose, V. S.			
27	Henry Libben, 541 Hoyne street, Town of Lake	3	....	Fair.
27	Henry Kreuger, 535 Hoyne street, Town of Lake	2	....	Stables, poor; animals, fair.

Inspections in Illinois—Continued.

Day of month.	Name of owner or person in charge and location of stable.	No. of cattle.	No. with lung-plague.	Condition of stables and animals.
	Inspections by W. H. Rose—Continued.			
1886. Nov. 27	Louis Hoeft, George street, Town of Lake	1		Stables, fair; animals, good.
27	F. Weichman & Bro., corner of Roby and Diversy streets, Town of Lake.	79		Poor.
27	M. V. Platt, 1175 Claybourne avenue, Town of Lake.	2		Stables, poor; animals, fair.
27	Henry Hier, Diversy street, Town of Lake	3		Stables, fair; animals, good.
30	James Kincade, St. Louis avenue, Chicago	2		Fair.
	Inspections by T. J. Herr, V. S.			
29	Union Rendering Company, stock-yards, Town of Lake.	1		
29	Do.	2	2	
Dec. 1	Do.	1		
20	Do.			
24	I. L. Harvey, 3 miles from Turner Junction, Du Page County.	21		Stables, good; animals, poor.
	Inspections by Herr & Melvin, V. S.			
27	Henry Prince, corner Sheridan street and Pierson avenue, town of Jefferson.	1		Stables, fair; animal, good.
27	James Inman, 89 Heine street, town of Jefferson	2		Stables, good; animals, fair.
27	Jacob Bruysacher, 29 Humboldt street, town of Jefferson.	2		Do.
27	William Baragivanath, corner Humboldt street and North avenue, town of Jefferson.	1		Do.
27	Bernard Lavin, 80 Humboldt street, town of Jefferson.	1		Stables, good; animal, good.
27	Frank Leidecke, Meadt street, town of Jefferson	1		Stables, good; animals fair.
27	Henry Peters, 116 California avenue, town of Jefferson.	2		Do.
27	Mrs. M. Segner, North avenue and Sheridan streets, town of Jefferson.	8		Do.
27	Mrs. Roberts, 17 Mozart street, town of Jefferson	1		Do.
27	J. R. Austin, 100 Humboldt street, town of Jefferson.	1		Good.
27	Louis Hanson, corner Wabansie and Meadt streets, town of Jefferson.	1		Stables, good; animal, fair.
27	Gotlieb Waterful, 10 Sheridan street, town of Jefferson.	3		Do.
27	Gustav Duske, corner Wabansie and Simons avenues, town of Jefferson.	1		Do.
	Inspections by M. R. Trumbower, V. S.			
27	W. F. Murdock, Dickens avenue, town of Jefferson.	1		Stables, fair; animal, good.
27	August Moertzscky, 2 Ballow street, town of Jefferson.	2		Fair.
27	Gaden Bros., Kimbel avenue, town of Jefferson	14		Do.
27	Frank Benson, Kimbel avenue, town of Jefferson.	10		Stables, good; animals, fair.
27	Richard Evans, Kimbel avenue, town of Jefferson.	4		Good.
27	Edward Simons, Kimbel avenue, town of Jefferson.	4		Do.
	Inspections by Herr & Melvin, V. S.			
	Charles Kraft, 685 Maplewood street, town of Jefferson.	1		Do.
	Henry Pauly, near Bloomingdale street, town of Jefferson.	14		Fair.
	John D. Freese, Courtland and Seymore streets, town of Jefferson.	1		Good.
28	Albert Low, 17 Homer street, town of Jefferson	1		Stables, fair; animal, good.
28	E. Hellickson, Seymore and Bloomingdale streets, town of Jefferson.	5		Good.

Inspections in Illinois—Continued.

Day of month.	Name of owner or person in charge and location of stable.	No. of cattle.	No. with lung-plague.	Condition of stables and animals.
	Inspections by Herr & Melvin—Continued.			
1886. Dec. 28	Herman Netz, 44 Moffett street, town of Jefferson.	1	....	Good.
28	John Wilson, 725 Bloomingdale road, town of Jefferson.	6	....	Stable, fair; animals, good.
28	Henry Hartwig, Moffat street and Western avenue, town of Jefferson.	8	....	Fair.
28	John Errart, 47 Courtland street, town of Jefferson.	4	....	Stables, fair; animals, good.
28	W. A. Weyland, 1594 Milwaukee avenue, town of Jefferson.	1	....	Good.
28	P. W. Bender, 1596 Milwaukee avenue, town of Jefferson.	1	....	Do.
28	S. Edmason, corner Seymour street, town of Jefferson.	1	....	Do.
28	Fred. Lanoch, 108 Washtenaw avenue, town of Jefferson.	1	....	Fair.
28	Lawrence Techer, corner Rockwell and Homer streets, town of Jefferson.	1	....	Good.
28	C. Hilden, Fairfield avenue, near Bloomingdale road, town of Jefferson.	10	....	Stables, bad; animals, fair.
28	Chrs. Smith, 103 Grose avenue, town of Jefferson.	8	....	Good.
28	Fred. Otto, 116 Washtenaw avenue, town of Jefferson.	1	....	Do.
28	Nick Bailer, corner Fairfield avenue and Bloomingdale road, town of Jefferson.	1	....	Stables, good; animal, fair.
28	Henry Jacobs, 110 Washtenaw avenue, town of Jefferson.	4	....	Stables, bad; animals, fair.
28	Peter Hanson, Rockwell street, town of Jefferson.	2	....	Stables, fair; animals, poor.
	Inspection by T. J. Herr, V. S.			
29	Union Rendering Company, stock-yard, town of Lake.		....	
	Inspections by Trumbower & Melvin, V. S.			
30	Gotlieb Koch, 903 North Western avenue, town of Jefferson.	5	....	Bad.
30	Henry Sweet, corner Milwaukee street and Powell avenue, town of Jefferson.	2	....	Good.
30	Daniel Simmerlin, 945 North Weston avenue, town of Jefferson.	1	....	Stables, bad; animal, fair.
30	Deitrich Freise, Berlin street and Medley avenue, town of Jefferson.	2	....	Stables, good; animals, fair.
30	Arne Anderson, corner Maplewood street and Wabansie avenue, town of Jefferson.	1	....	Do.
30	J. E. Frederich, corner Ellis place and Wabensie avenue, town of Jefferson.	1	....	Do.
30	William Schuth, 1281 North Western avenue, town of Jefferson.	1	....	Do.
30	Henry Raphs, corner Powell street and Clara place, town of Jefferson.	1	....	Good.
30	A. Steinham, corner Powell street and Clara place, town of Jefferson.	1	....	Do.
30	George N. Grumley, 111 Perry avenue, town of Jefferson.	2	....	Stables, fair; animals, good.
30	Fred. Protrartz, Ellis place, town of Jefferson.	1	....	Fair.
30	George Klein, 57 Perry avenue, town of Jefferson.	1	....	Stables, fair; animal, good.
30	August Watchsmith, 63 Perry avenue, town of Jefferson.	1	....	Fair.
30	Herman Papsein, 1691 Milwaukee avenue, town of Jefferson.	1	....	Fair.
30	Charles Fesgora, Hoffman avenue, town of Jefferson.	4	....	Do.
30	John Kruger, 52 Hoffman avenue, town of Jefferson.	1	....	Good.
30	Henry Rodiak, 6 Hoffman avenue, town of Jefferson.	1	....	Do.
30	August Schnabel, Berlin street, town of Jefferson.	1	....	Do.
30	Frank Ditlaff, 951 Weston avenue, town of Jefferson.	3	....	Stables, good; animals, very good.

INDEX.

O

Page